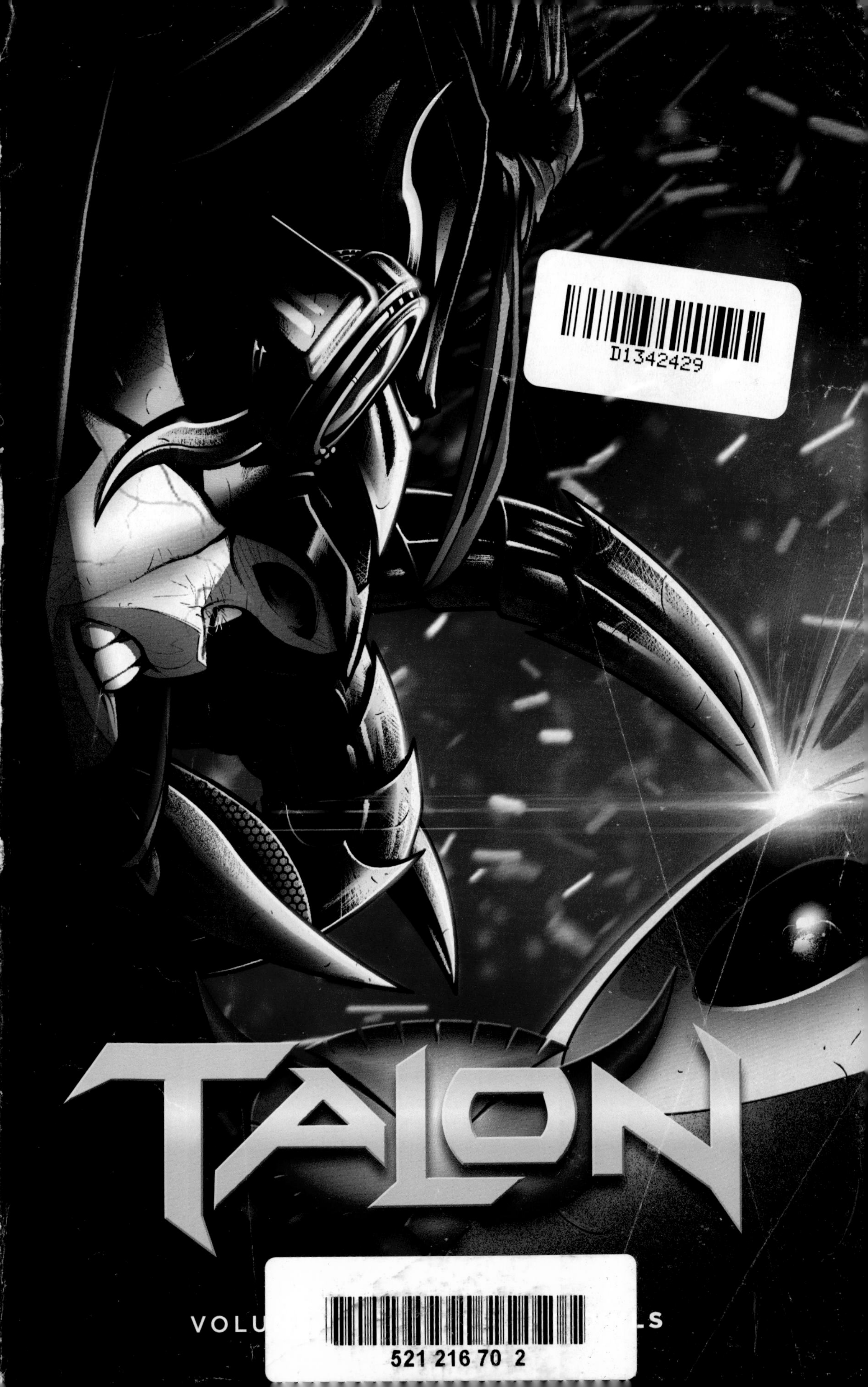
TALON
VOLU
LS

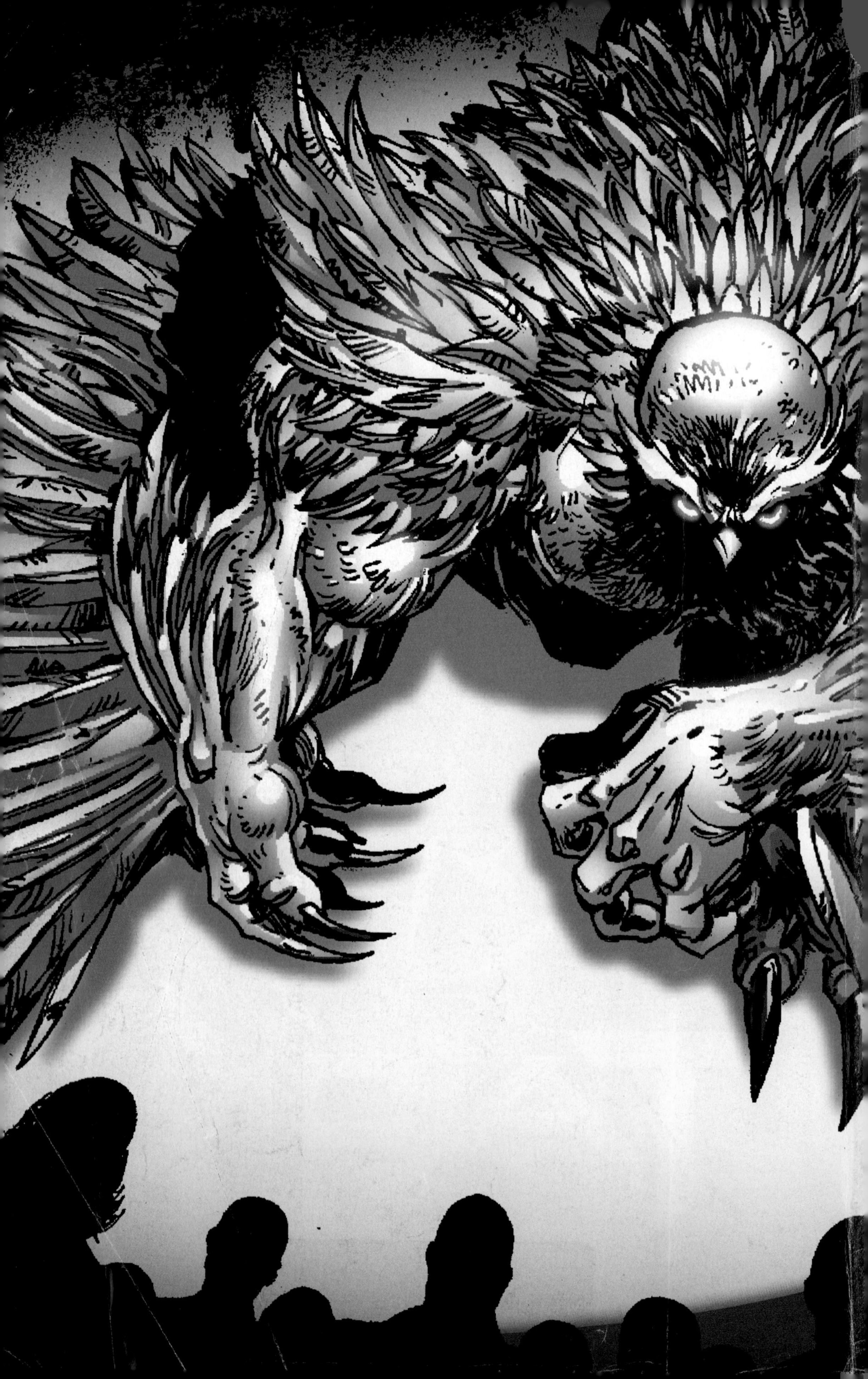

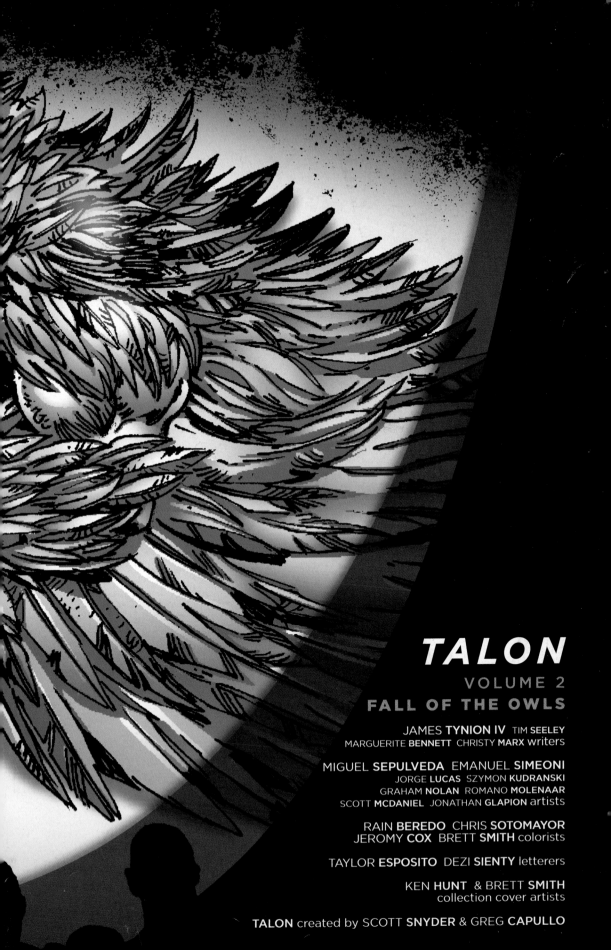

TALON
VOLUME 2
FALL OF THE OWLS

JAMES **TYNION IV** TIM **SEELEY**
MARGUERITE **BENNETT** CHRISTY **MARX** writers

MIGUEL **SEPULVEDA** EMANUEL **SIMEONI**
JORGE **LUCAS** SZYMON **KUDRANSKI**
GRAHAM **NOLAN** ROMANO **MOLENAAR**
SCOTT **MCDANIEL** JONATHAN **GLAPION** artists

RAIN **BEREDO** CHRIS **SOTOMAYOR**
JEROMY **COX** BRETT **SMITH** colorists

TAYLOR **ESPOSITO** DEZI **SIENTY** letterers

KEN **HUNT** & BRETT **SMITH**
collection cover artists

TALON created by SCOTT **SNYDER** & GREG **CAPULLO**

KATIE KUBERT RACHEL GLUCKSTERN Editors – Original Series DARREN SHAN Assistant Editor – Original Series
ROWENA YOW Editor ROBBIN BROSTERMAN Design Director – Books ROBBIE BIEDERMAN Publication Design

BOB HARRAS Senior VP – Editor-in-Chief, DC Comics

DIANE NELSON President DAN DIDIO and JIM LEE Co-Publishers
GEOFF JOHNS Chief Creative Officer
JOHN ROOD Executive VP – Sales, Marketing and Business Development
AMY GENKINS Senior VP – Business and Legal Affairs NAIRI GARDINER Senior VP – Finance
JEFF BOISON VP – Publishing Planning MARK CHIARELLO VP – Art Direction and Design
JOHN CUNNINGHAM VP – Marketing TERRI CUNNINGHAM VP – Editorial Administration
ALISON GILL Senior VP – Manufacturing and Operations HANK KANALZ Senior VP – Vertigo and Integrated Publishing
JAY KOGAN VP – Business and Legal Affairs, Publishing JACK MAHAN VP – Business Affairs, Talent
NICK NAPOLITANO VP – Manufacturing Administration SUE POHJA VP – Book Sales
COURTNEY SIMMONS Senior VP – Publicity BOB WAYNE Senior VP – Sales

TALON VOLUME 2: FALL OF THE OWLS

DC Comics, 1700 Broadway, New York, NY 10019
A Warner Bros. Entertainment Company.
Printed by RR Donnelley, Salem, VA, USA. 5/29/14. First Printing.

ISBN: 978-1-4012-4625-9

Certified Chain of Custody
20% Certified Forest Content,
80% Certified Sourcing
www.sfiprogram.org
SFI-01042
APPLIES TO TEXT STOCK ONLY

Library of Congress Cataloging-in-Publication Data

Tynion, James, IV, author.
Talon. Volume 2, The Fall of the Owls / James Tynion IV ; [illustrated by] Miguel Sepulveda.
pages cm. — (The New 52!)
ISBN 978-1-4012-4625-9 (paperback)
1. Graphic novels. I. Sepulveda, Miguel Angel, illustrator. II. Title. III. Title: Fall of the Owls.
PN6727.T96T35 2014
741.5'973—dc23
2013049634

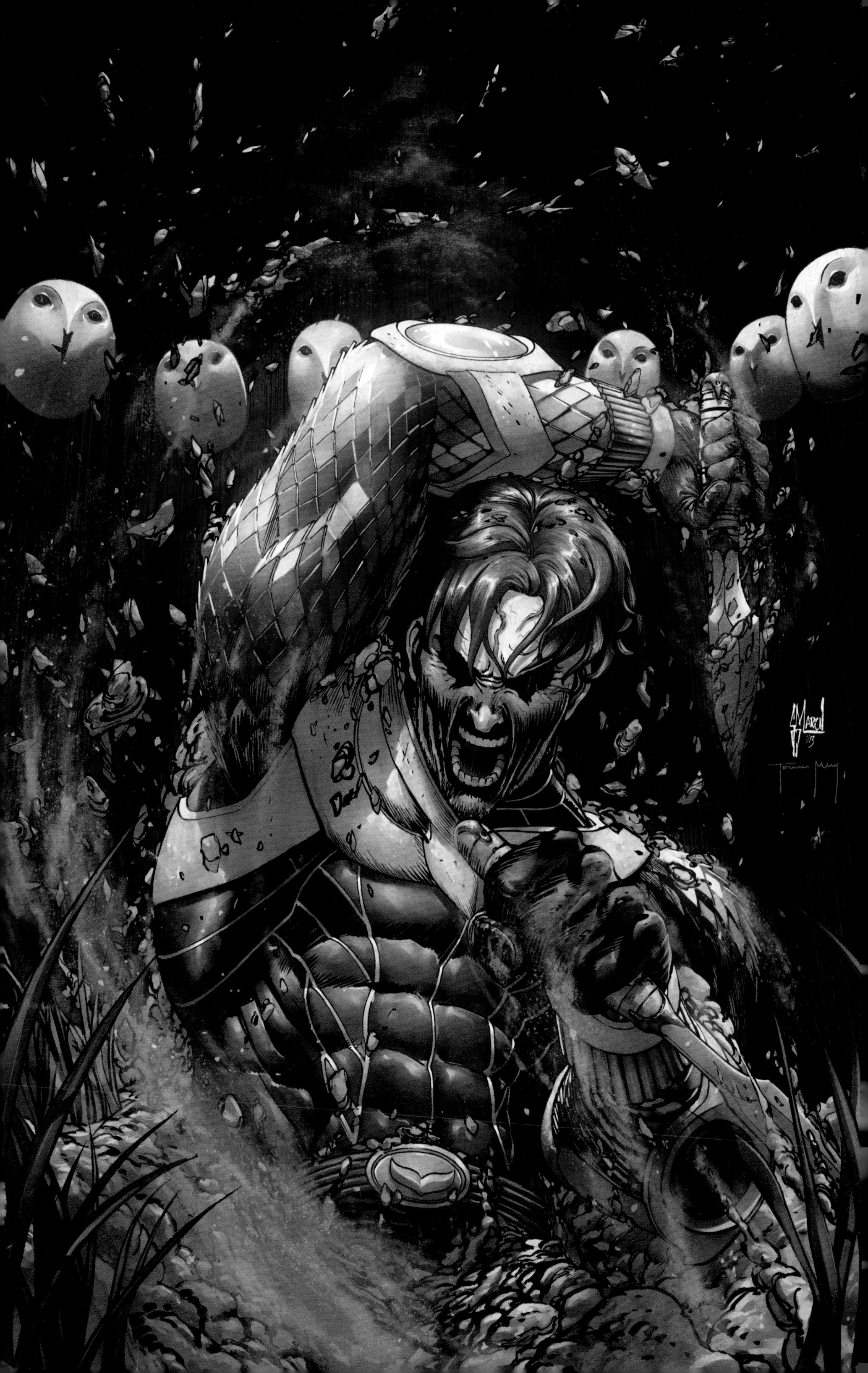

DON'T BE AFRAID OF THE DARK

JAMES TYNION IV writer MIGUEL SEPULVEDA artist cover art by GUILLEM MARCH & TOMEU MOREY

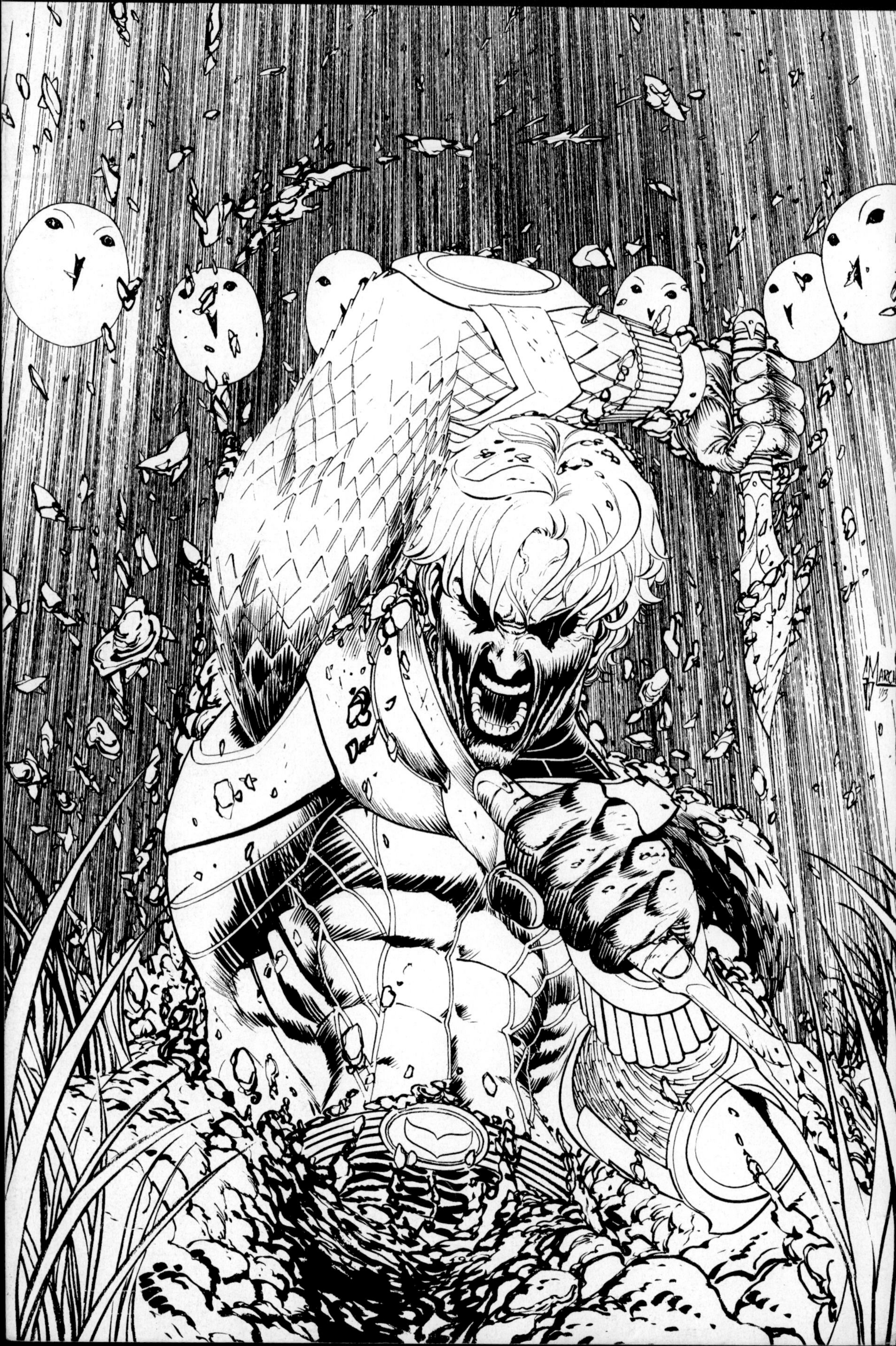

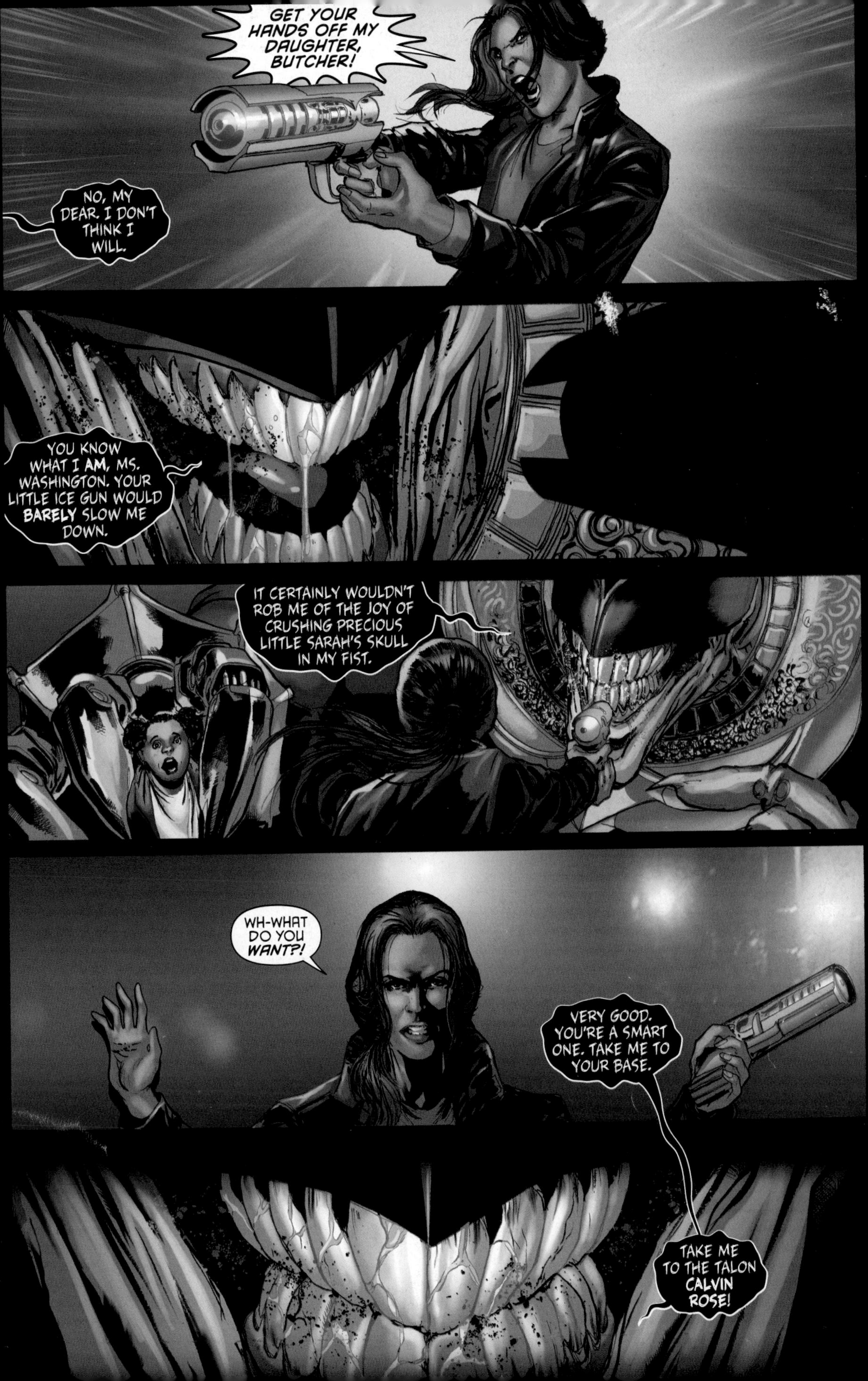
GET YOUR HANDS OFF MY DAUGHTER, BUTCHER!
NO, MY DEAR. I DON'T THINK I WILL.
YOU KNOW WHAT I AM, MS. WASHINGTON. YOUR LITTLE ICE GUN WOULD BARELY SLOW ME DOWN.
IT CERTAINLY WOULDN'T ROB ME OF THE JOY OF CRUSHING PRECIOUS LITTLE SARAH'S SKULL IN MY FIST.
WH-WHAT DO YOU WANT?!
VERY GOOD. YOU'RE A SMART ONE. TAKE ME TO YOUR BASE.
TAKE ME TO THE TALON CALVIN ROSE!

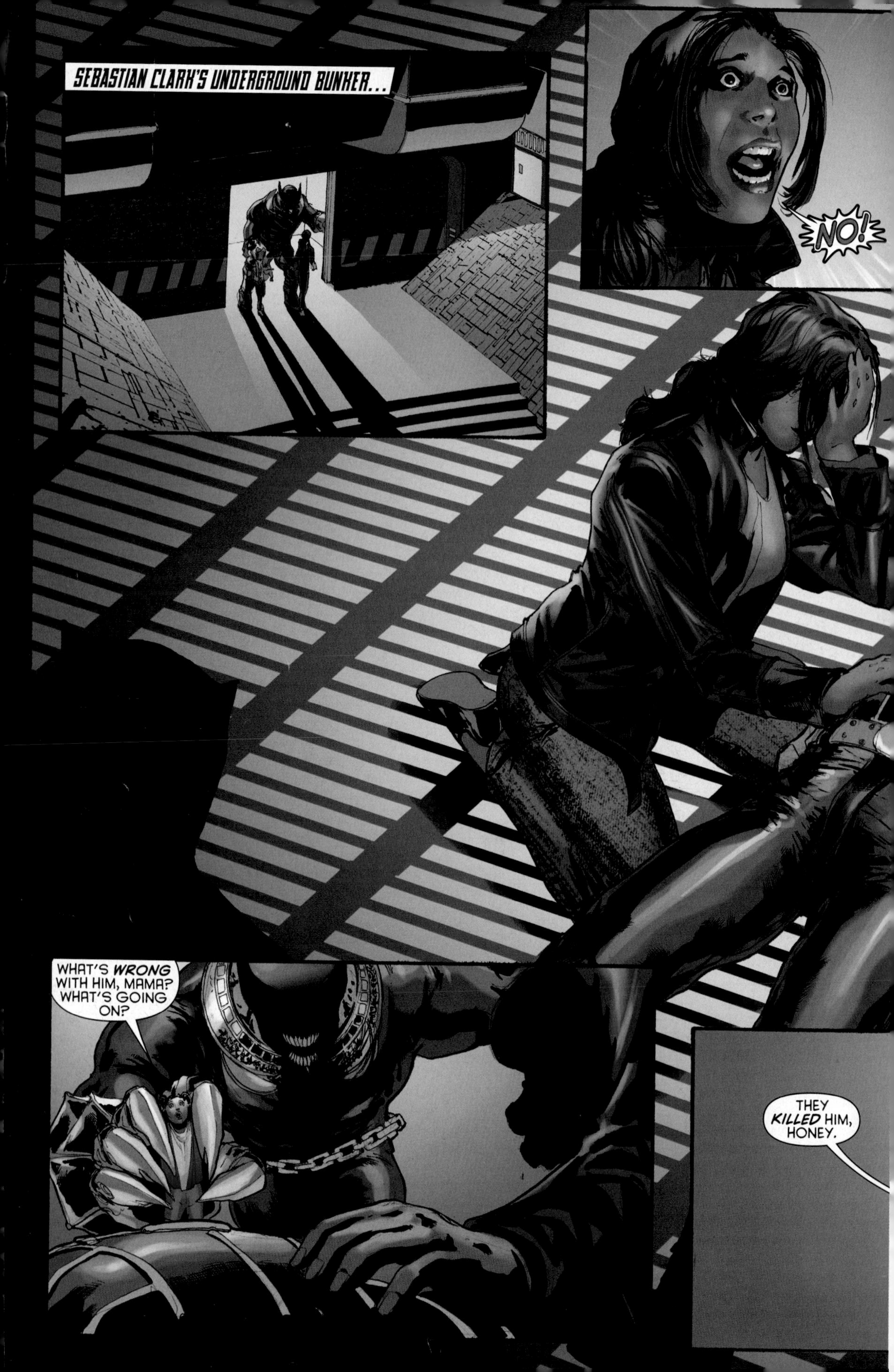

SEBASTIAN CLARK'S UNDERGROUND BUNKER...
NO!
WHAT'S WRONG WITH HIM, MAMA? WHAT'S GOING ON?
THEY KILLED HIM, HONEY.

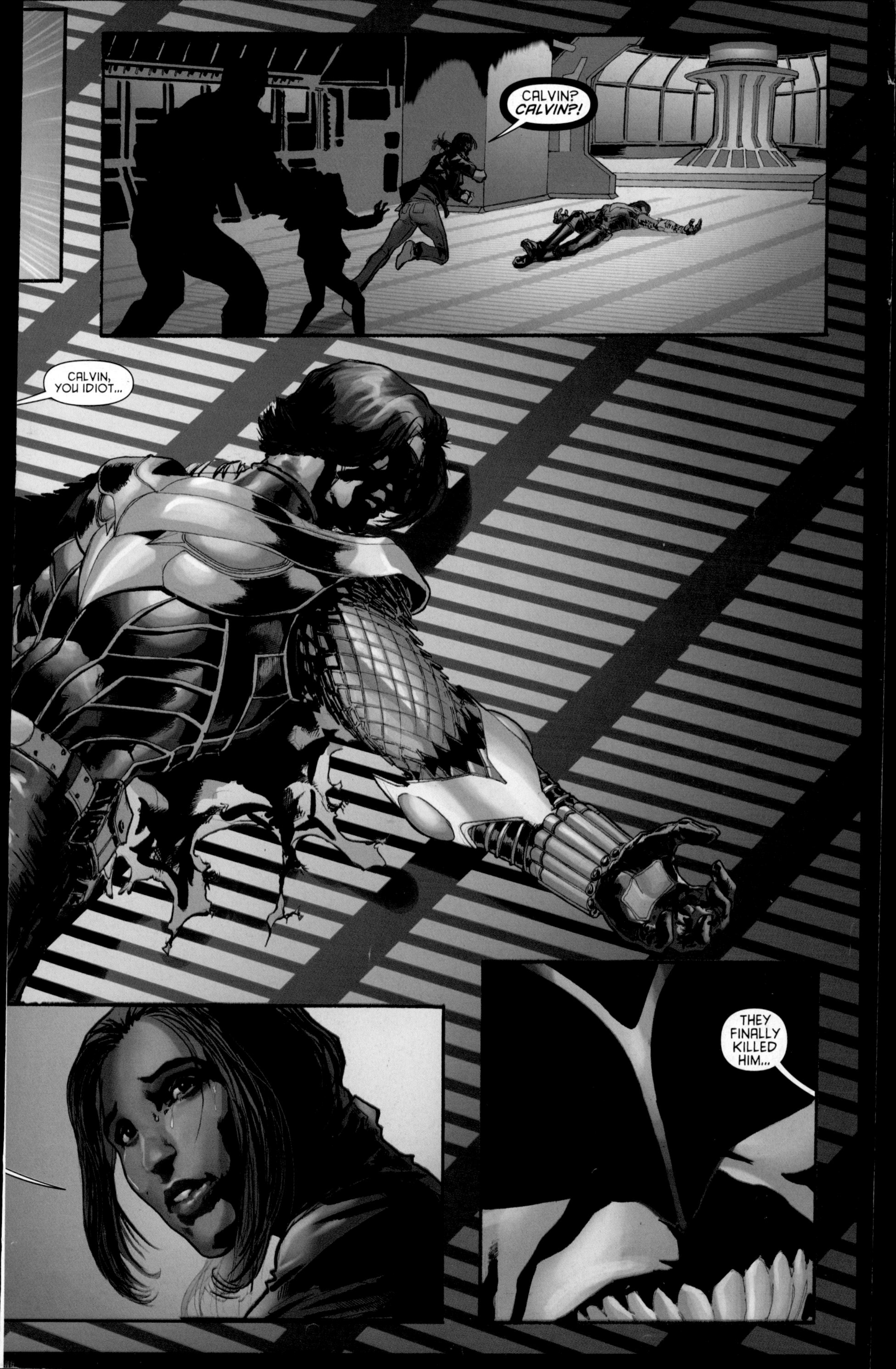
CALVIN? CALVIN?!
CALVIN, YOU IDIOT...
THEY FINALLY KILLED HIM...

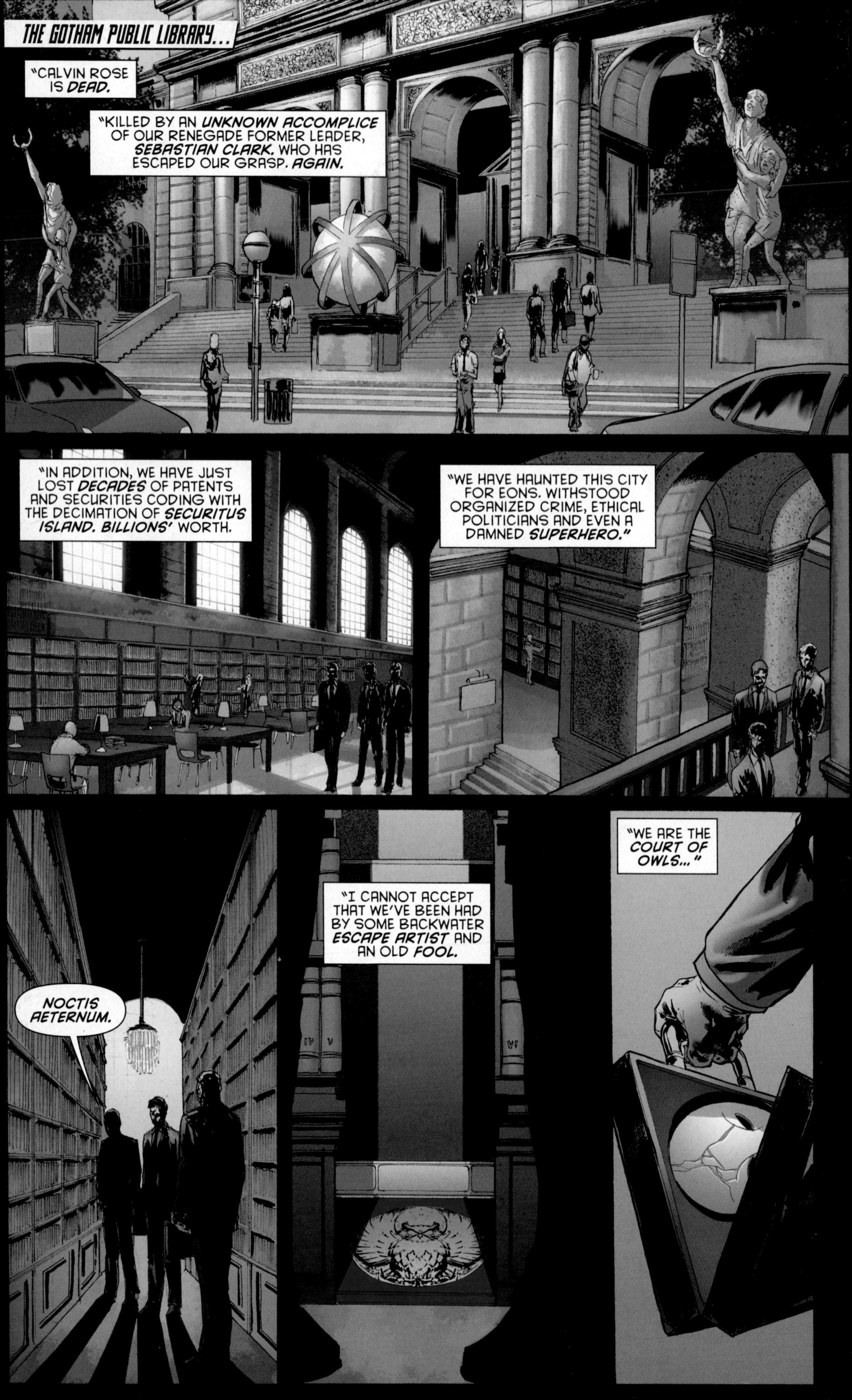
THE GOTHAM PUBLIC LIBRARY...
"CALVIN ROSE IS DEAD.
"KILLED BY AN UNKNOWN ACCOMPLICE OF OUR RENEGADE FORMER LEADER, SEBASTIAN CLARK. WHO HAS ESCAPED OUR GRASP. AGAIN.
"IN ADDITION, WE HAVE JUST LOST DECADES OF PATENTS AND SECURITIES CODING WITH THE DECIMATION OF SECURITUS ISLAND. BILLIONS' WORTH.
"WE HAVE HAUNTED THIS CITY FOR EONS. WITHSTOOD ORGANIZED CRIME, ETHICAL POLITICIANS AND EVEN A DAMNED SUPERHERO."
NOCTIS AETERNUM.
"I CANNOT ACCEPT THAT WE'VE BEEN HAD BY SOME BACKWATER ESCAPE ARTIST AND AN OLD FOOL.
"WE ARE THE COURT OF OWLS..."

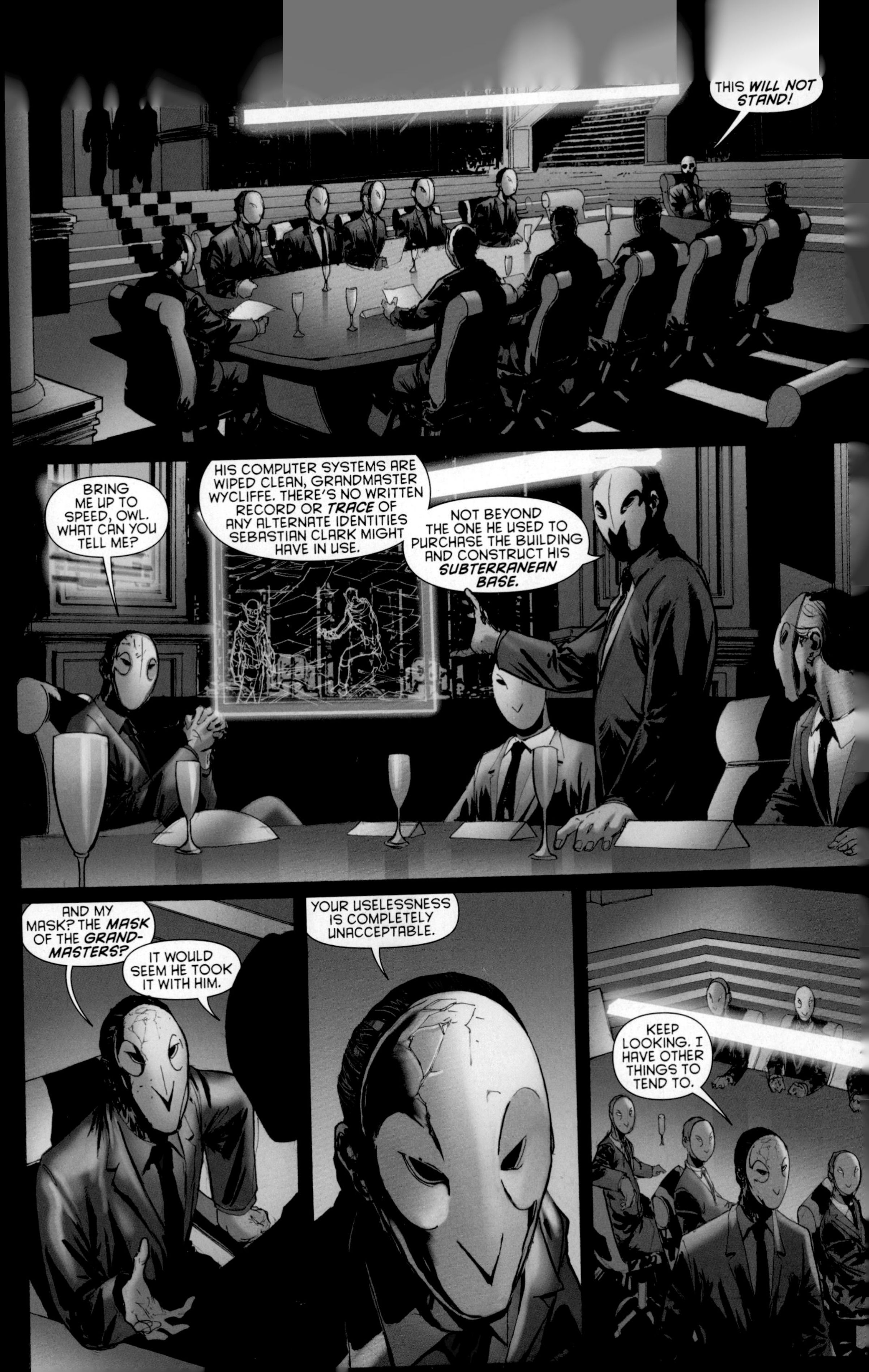
THIS WILL NOT STAND!
BRING ME UP TO SPEED, OWL. WHAT CAN YOU TELL ME?
HIS COMPUTER SYSTEMS ARE WIPED CLEAN, GRANDMASTER WYCLIFFE. THERE'S NO WRITTEN RECORD OR TRACE OF ANY ALTERNATE IDENTITIES SEBASTIAN CLARK MIGHT HAVE IN USE.
NOT BEYOND THE ONE HE USED TO PURCHASE THE BUILDING AND CONSTRUCT HIS SUBTERRANEAN BASE.
AND MY MASK? THE MASK OF THE GRAND-MASTERS?
IT WOULD SEEM HE TOOK IT WITH HIM.
YOUR USELESSNESS IS COMPLETELY UNACCEPTABLE.
KEEP LOOKING. I HAVE OTHER THINGS TO TEND TO.

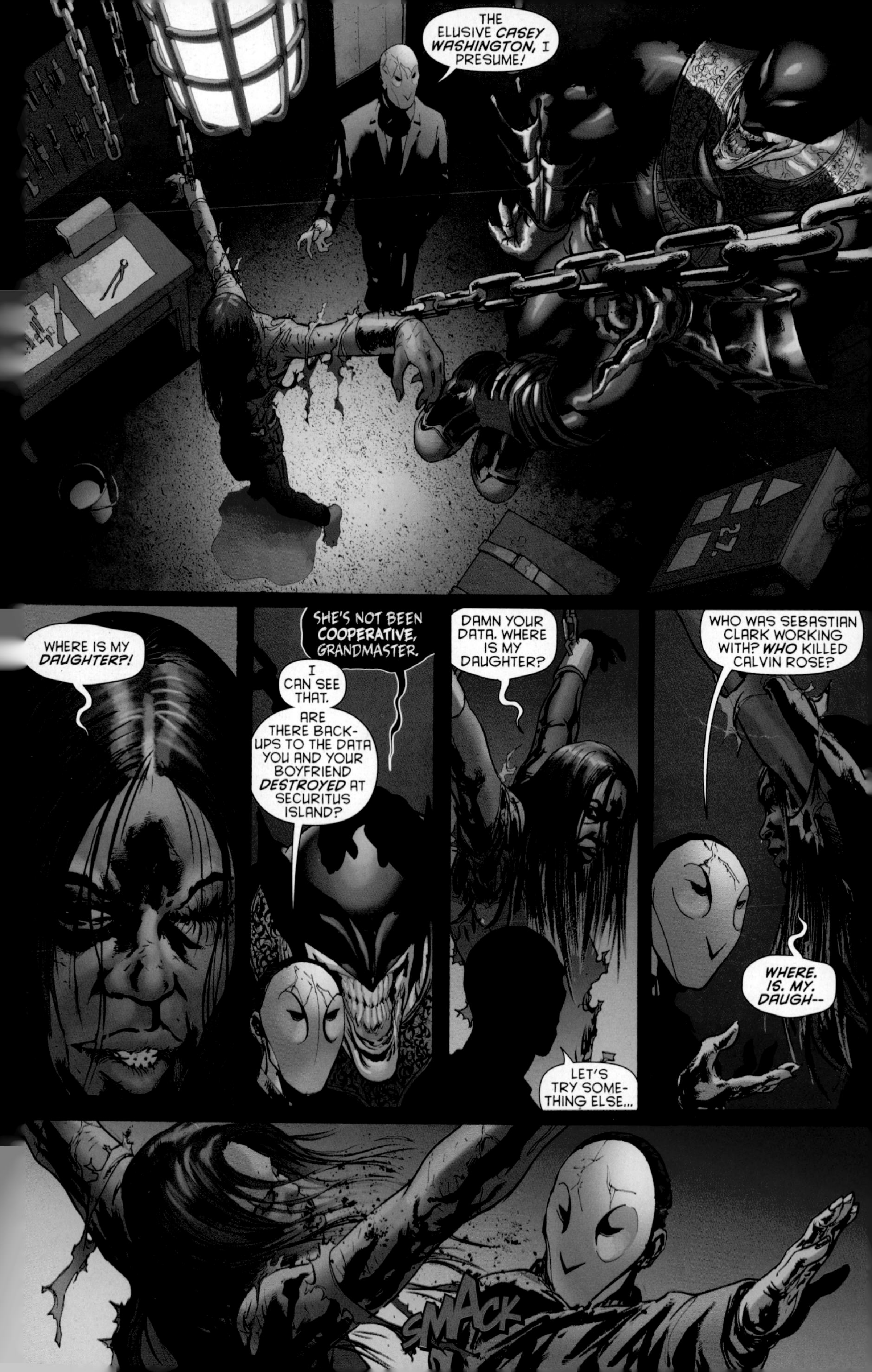
THE ELUSIVE CASEY WASHINGTON, I PRESUME!
WHERE IS MY DAUGHTER?!
SHE'S NOT BEEN COOPERATIVE, GRANDMASTER.
I CAN SEE THAT.
ARE THERE BACK-UPS TO THE DATA YOU AND YOUR BOYFRIEND DESTROYED AT SECURITUS ISLAND?
DAMN YOUR DATA. WHERE IS MY DAUGHTER?
LET'S TRY SOME-THING ELSE...
WHO WAS SEBASTIAN CLARK WORKING WITH? WHO KILLED CALVIN ROSE?
WHERE. IS. MY. DAUGH--
SMACK

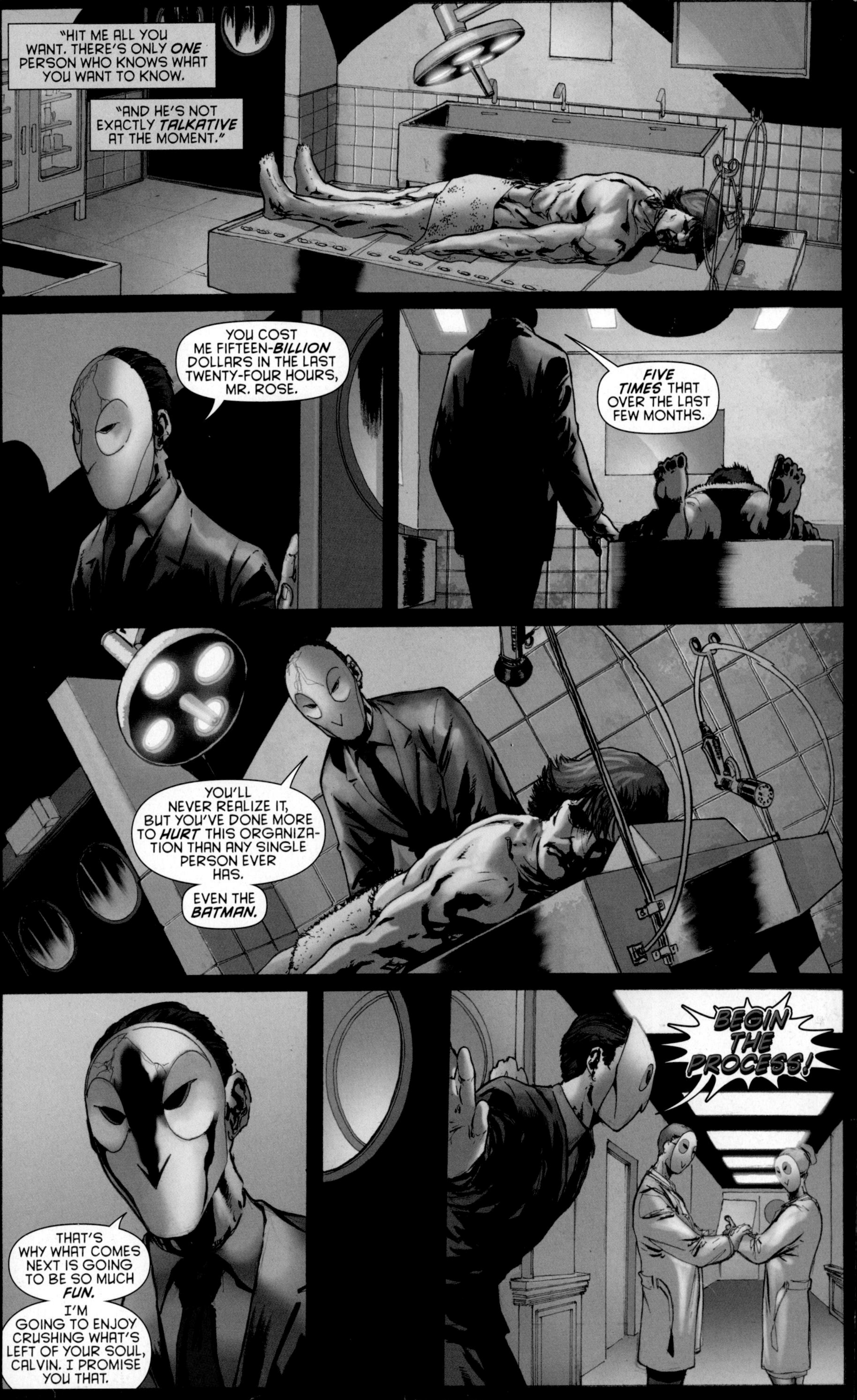
"HIT ME ALL YOU WANT. THERE'S ONLY ONE PERSON WHO KNOWS WHAT YOU WANT TO KNOW.
"AND HE'S NOT EXACTLY TALKATIVE AT THE MOMENT."
YOU COST ME FIFTEEN-BILLION DOLLARS IN THE LAST TWENTY-FOUR HOURS, MR. ROSE.
FIVE TIMES THAT OVER THE LAST FEW MONTHS.
YOU'LL NEVER REALIZE IT, BUT YOU'VE DONE MORE TO HURT THIS ORGANIZATION THAN ANY SINGLE PERSON EVER HAS.
EVEN THE BATMAN.
THAT'S WHY WHAT COMES NEXT IS GOING TO BE SO MUCH FUN.
I'M GOING TO ENJOY CRUSHING WHAT'S LEFT OF YOUR SOUL, CALVIN. I PROMISE YOU THAT.
BEGIN THE PROCESS!

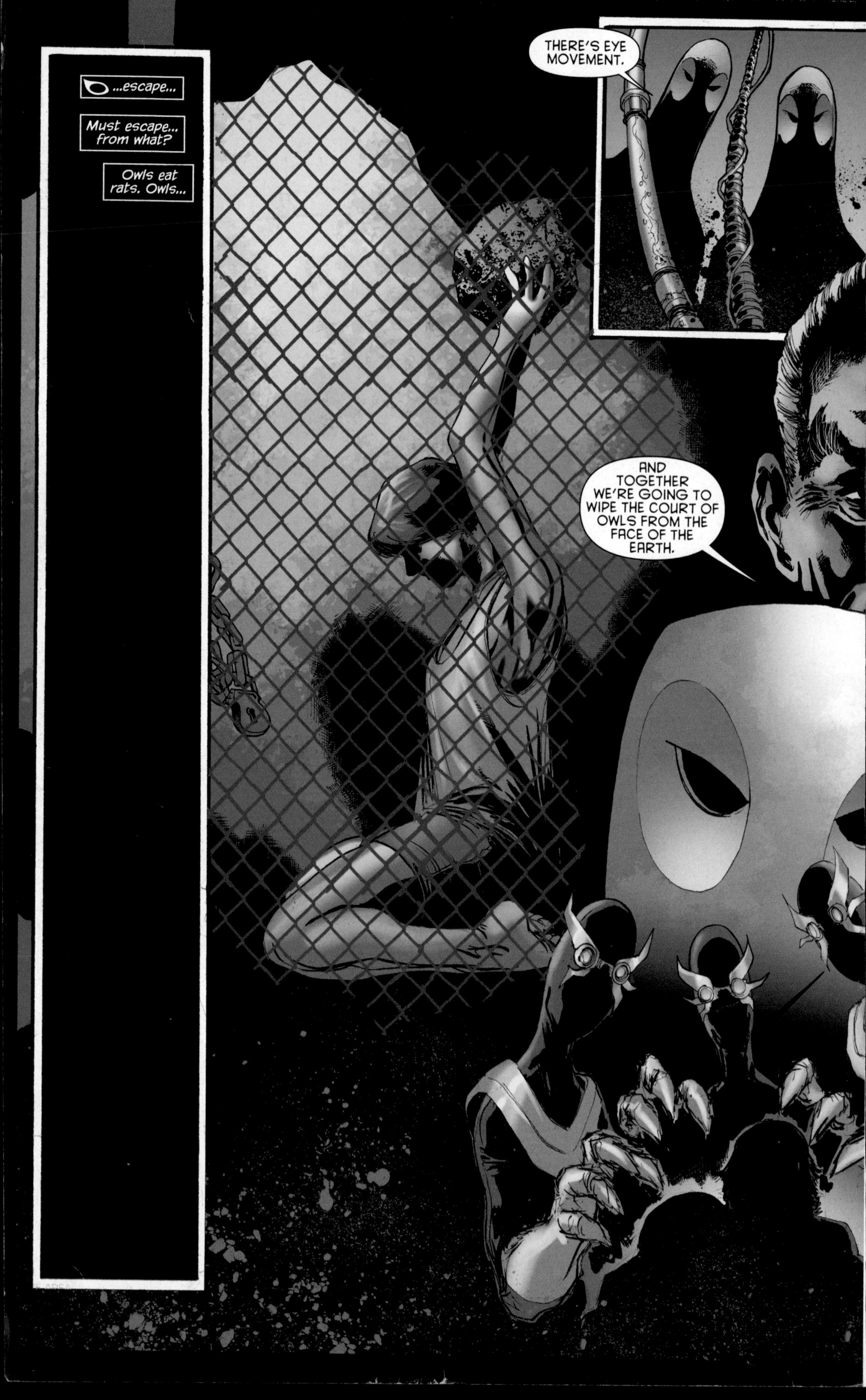
...escape...
Must escape... from what?
Owls eat rats. Owls...
THERE'S EYE MOVEMENT.
AND TOGETHER WE'RE GOING TO WIPE THE COURT OF OWLS FROM THE FACE OF THE EARTH.

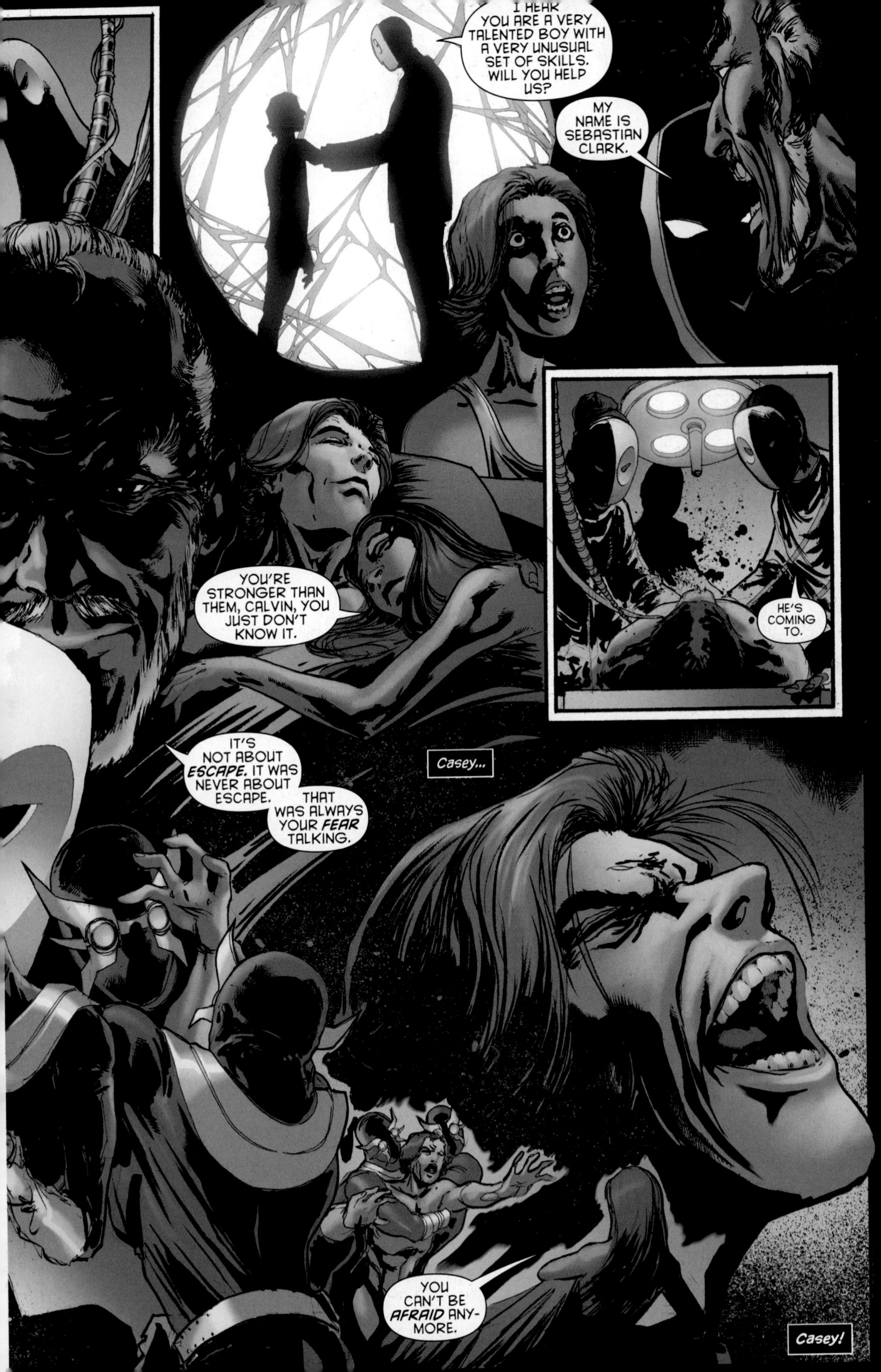
I HEAR YOU ARE A VERY TALENTED BOY WITH A VERY UNUSUAL SET OF SKILLS. WILL YOU HELP US?
MY NAME IS SEBASTIAN CLARK.
YOU'RE STRONGER THAN THEM, CALVIN, YOU JUST DON'T KNOW IT.
HE'S COMING TO.
IT'S NOT ABOUT ESCAPE. IT WAS NEVER ABOUT ESCAPE.
THAT WAS ALWAYS YOUR FEAR TALKING.
Casey...
YOU CAN'T BE AFRAID ANY-MORE.
Casey!

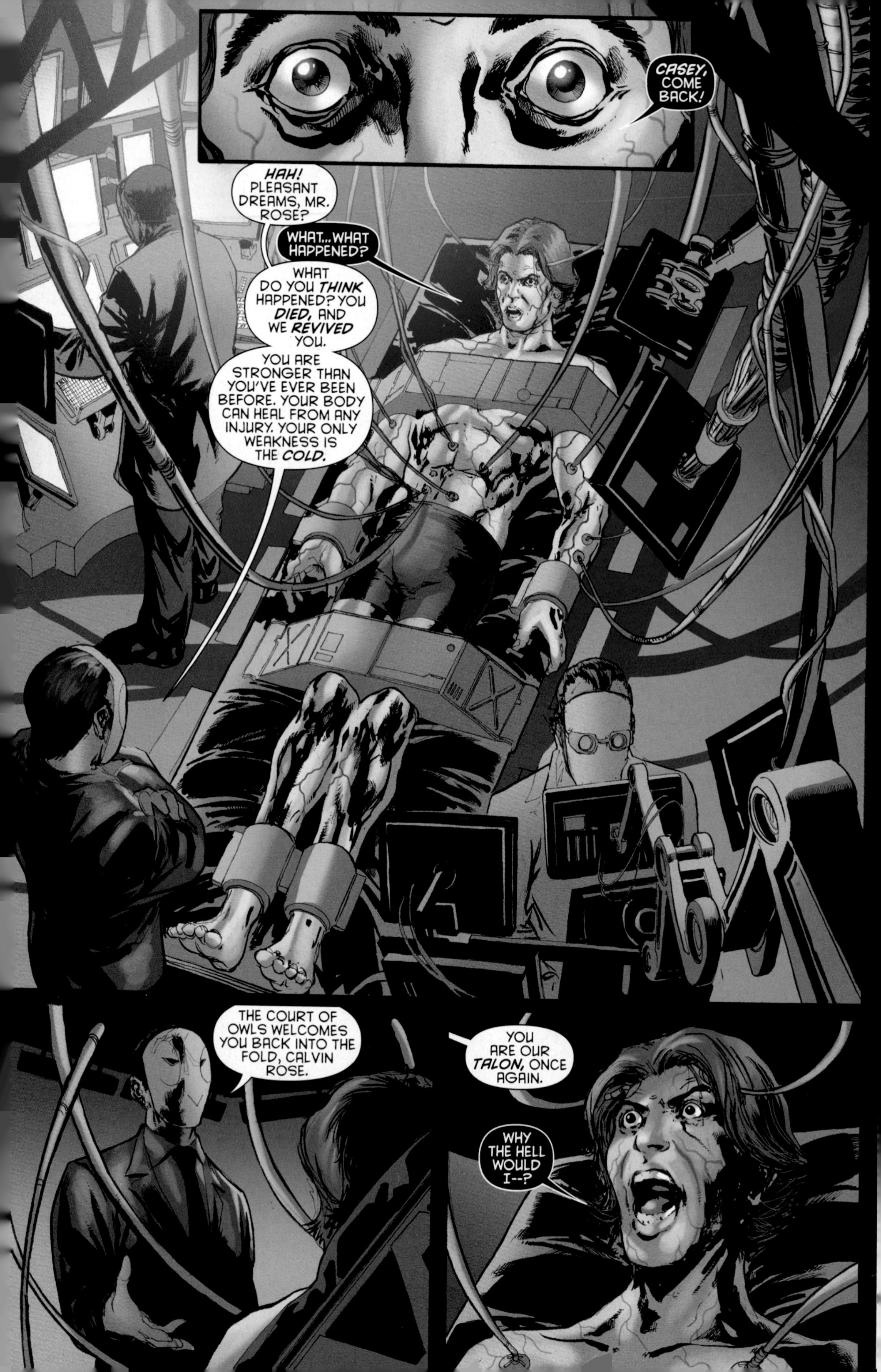
CASEY, COME BACK!
HAH! PLEASANT DREAMS, MR. ROSE?
WHAT...WHAT HAPPENED?
WHAT DO YOU THINK HAPPENED? YOU DIED, AND WE REVIVED YOU.
YOU ARE STRONGER THAN YOU'VE EVER BEEN BEFORE. YOUR BODY CAN HEAL FROM ANY INJURY. YOUR ONLY WEAKNESS IS THE COLD.
THE COURT OF OWLS WELCOMES YOU BACK INTO THE FOLD, CALVIN ROSE.
YOU ARE OUR TALON, ONCE AGAIN.
WHY THE HELL WOULD I--?

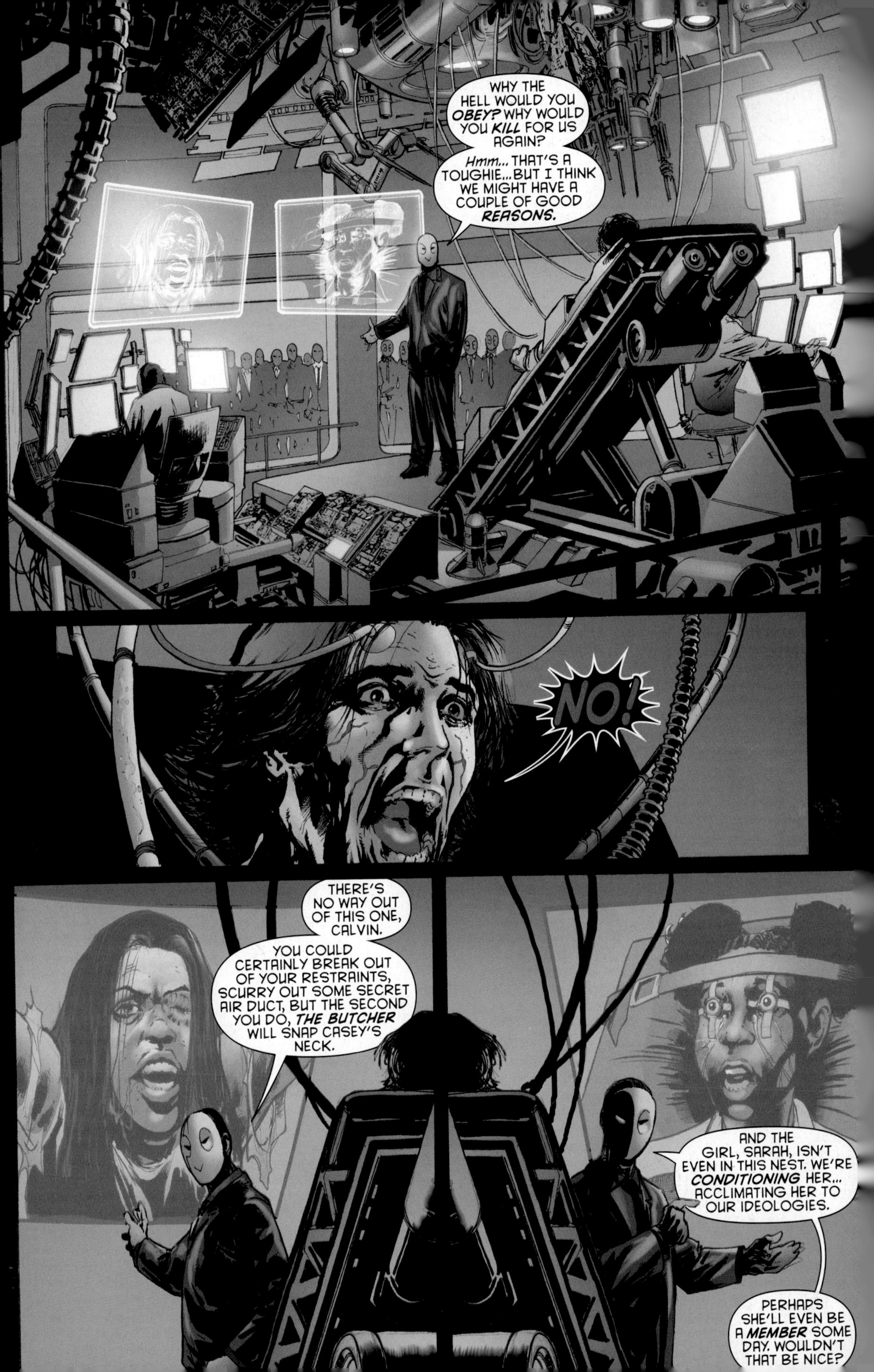
WHY THE HELL WOULD YOU OBEY? WHY WOULD YOU KILL FOR US AGAIN?
Hmm... THAT'S A TOUGHIE...BUT I THINK WE MIGHT HAVE A COUPLE OF GOOD REASONS.
NO!
THERE'S NO WAY OUT OF THIS ONE, CALVIN.
YOU COULD CERTAINLY BREAK OUT OF YOUR RESTRAINTS, SCURRY OUT SOME SECRET AIR DUCT, BUT THE SECOND YOU DO, THE BUTCHER WILL SNAP CASEY'S NECK.
AND THE GIRL, SARAH, ISN'T EVEN IN THIS NEST. WE'RE CONDITIONING HER... ACCLIMATING HER TO OUR IDEOLOGIES.
PERHAPS SHE'LL EVEN BE A MEMBER SOME DAY. WOULDN'T THAT BE NICE?

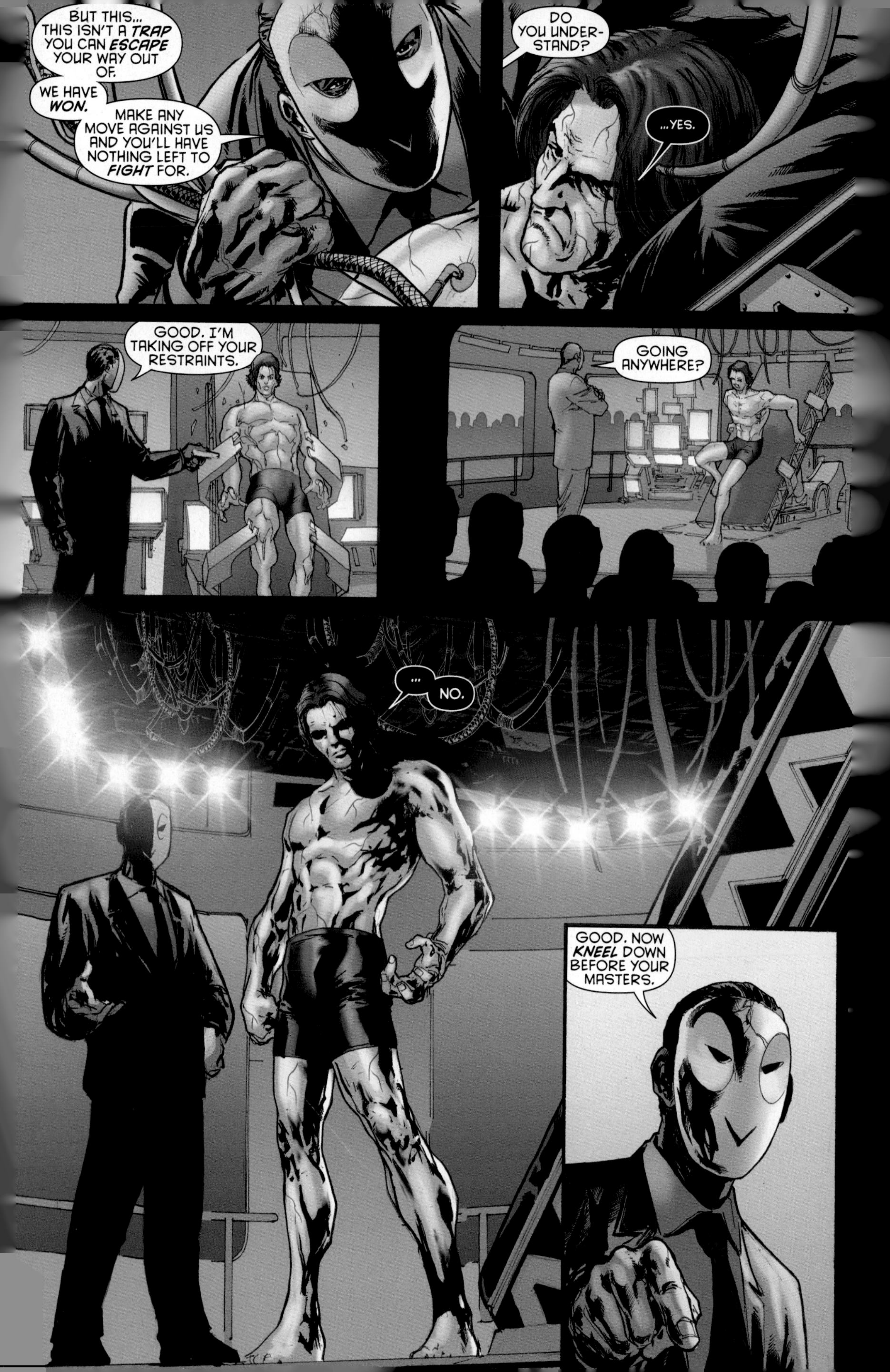
BUT THIS... THIS ISN'T A TRAP YOU CAN ESCAPE YOUR WAY OUT OF.
WE HAVE WON.
MAKE ANY MOVE AGAINST US AND YOU'LL HAVE NOTHING LEFT TO FIGHT FOR.
DO YOU UNDER-STAND?
...YES.
GOOD. I'M TAKING OFF YOUR RESTRAINTS.
GOING ANYWHERE?
...
NO.
GOOD. NOW KNEEL DOWN BEFORE YOUR MASTERS.

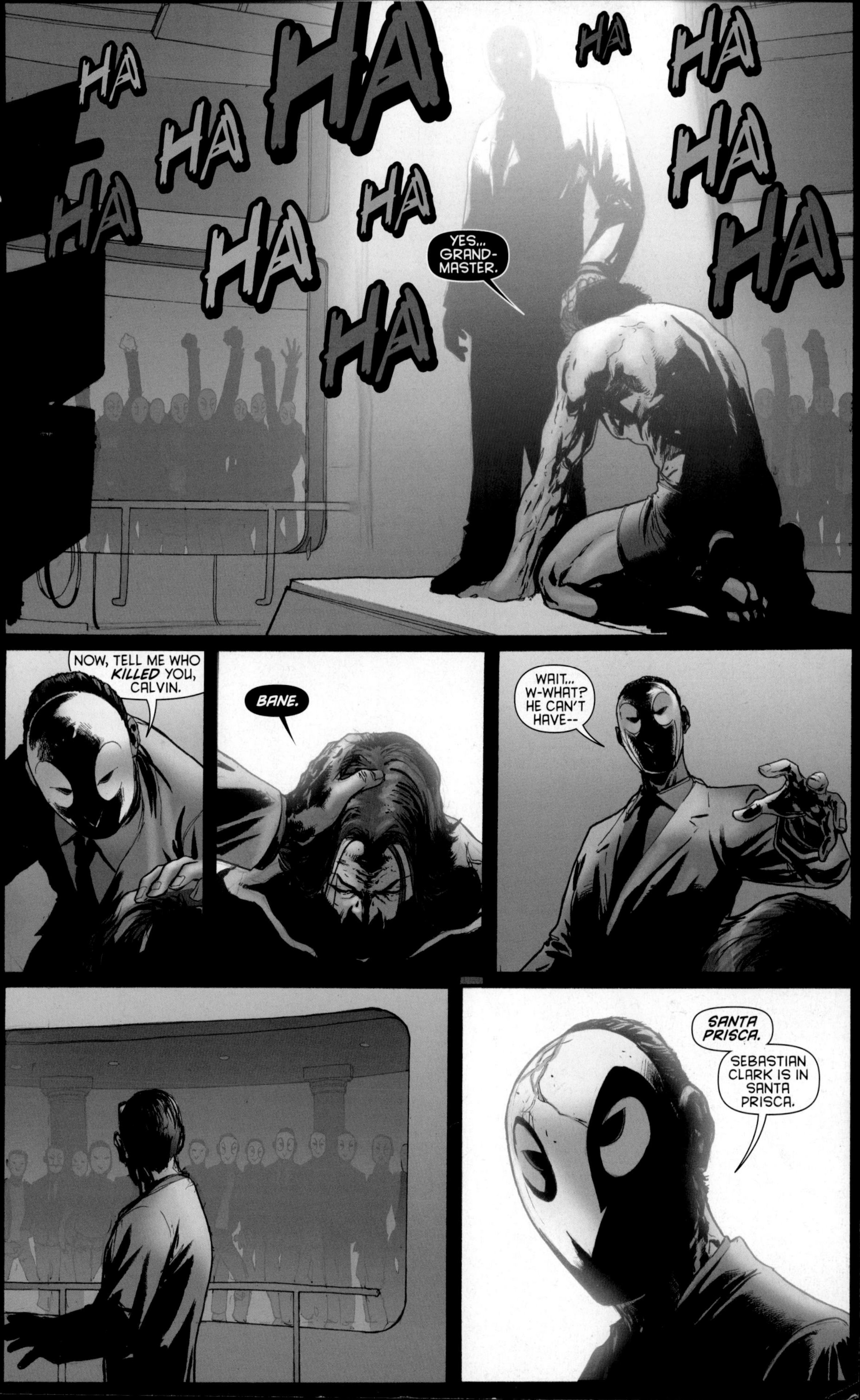
HA HA HA HA HA HA HA HA HA HA HA HA HA
YES... GRAND-MASTER.
NOW, TELL ME WHO *KILLED* YOU, CALVIN.
BANE.
WAIT... W-WHAT? HE CAN'T HAVE--
SANTA PRISCA.
SEBASTIAN CLARK IS IN SANTA PRISCA.

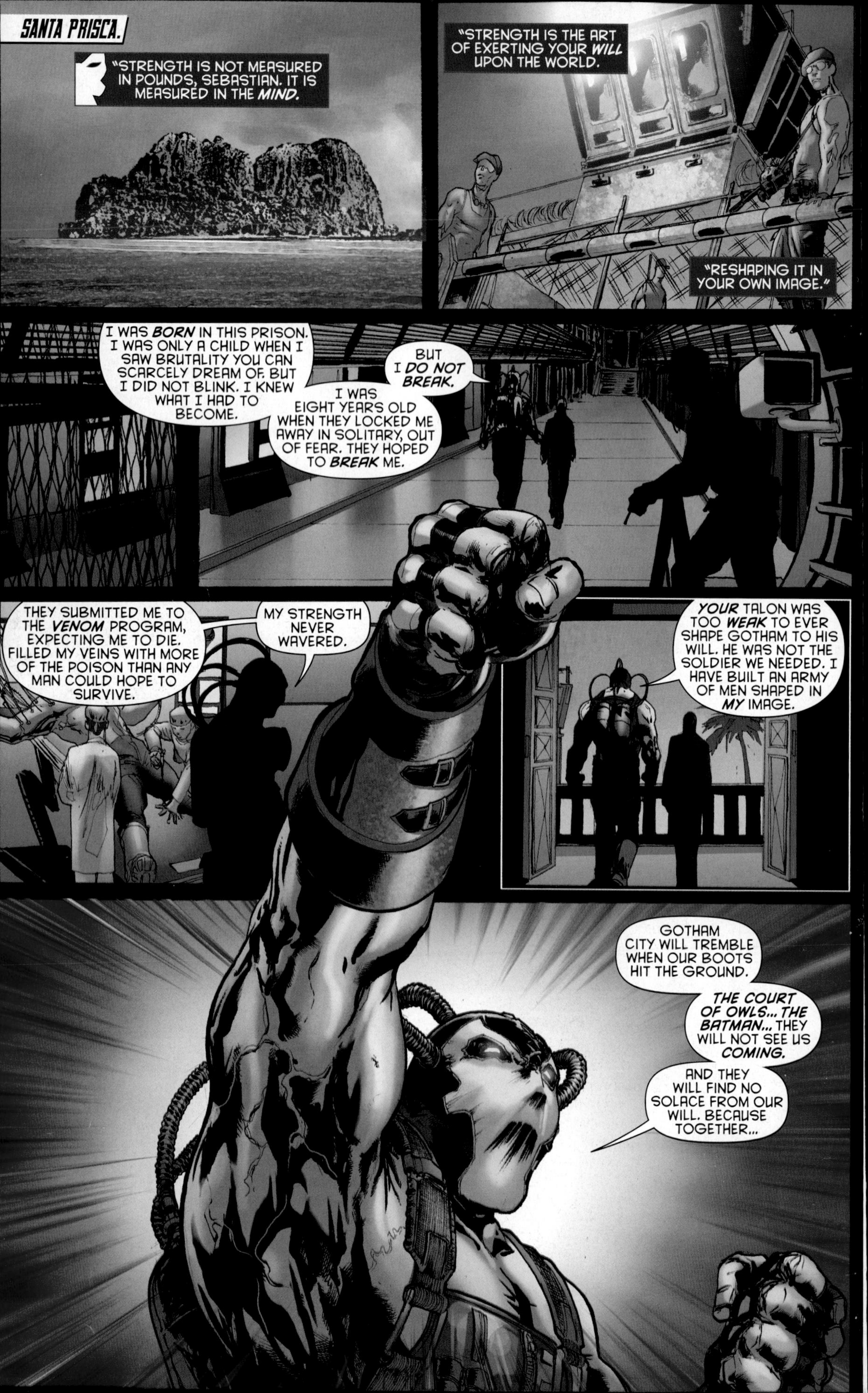
SANTA PRISCA.
"STRENGTH IS NOT MEASURED IN POUNDS, SEBASTIAN. IT IS MEASURED IN THE MIND.
"STRENGTH IS THE ART OF EXERTING YOUR WILL UPON THE WORLD.
"RESHAPING IT IN YOUR OWN IMAGE."
I WAS BORN IN THIS PRISON. I WAS ONLY A CHILD WHEN I SAW BRUTALITY YOU CAN SCARCELY DREAM OF. BUT I DID NOT BLINK. I KNEW WHAT I HAD TO BECOME.
I WAS EIGHT YEARS OLD WHEN THEY LOCKED ME AWAY IN SOLITARY, OUT OF FEAR. THEY HOPED TO BREAK ME.
BUT I DO NOT BREAK.
THEY SUBMITTED ME TO THE VENOM PROGRAM, EXPECTING ME TO DIE. FILLED MY VEINS WITH MORE OF THE POISON THAN ANY MAN COULD HOPE TO SURVIVE.
MY STRENGTH NEVER WAVERED.
YOUR TALON WAS TOO WEAK TO EVER SHAPE GOTHAM TO HIS WILL. HE WAS NOT THE SOLDIER WE NEEDED. I HAVE BUILT AN ARMY OF MEN SHAPED IN MY IMAGE.
GOTHAM CITY WILL TREMBLE WHEN OUR BOOTS HIT THE GROUND.
THE COURT OF OWLS... THE BATMAN... THEY WILL NOT SEE US COMING.
AND THEY WILL FIND NO SOLACE FROM OUR WILL. BECAUSE TOGETHER...

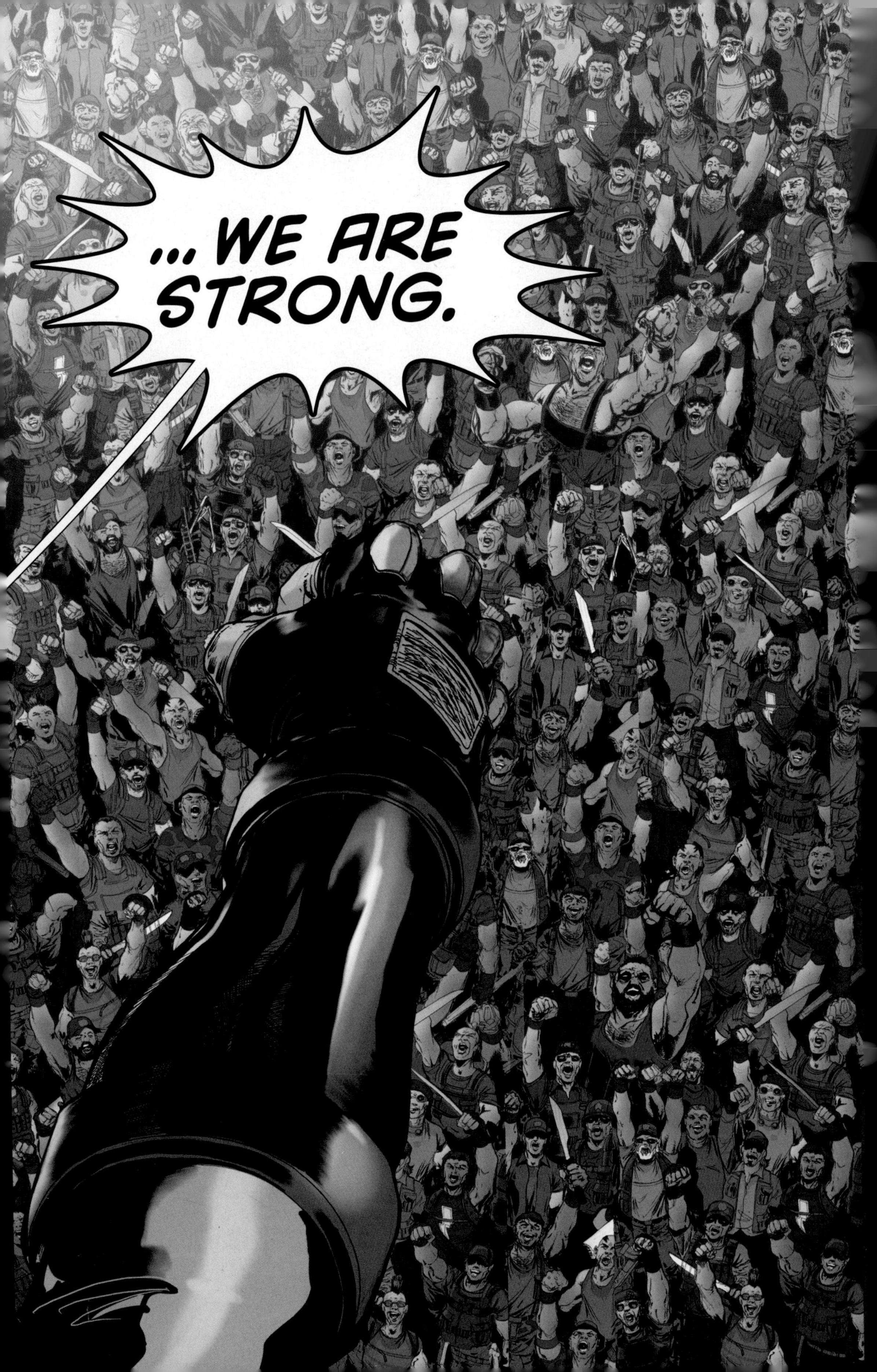
...WE ARE STRONG.

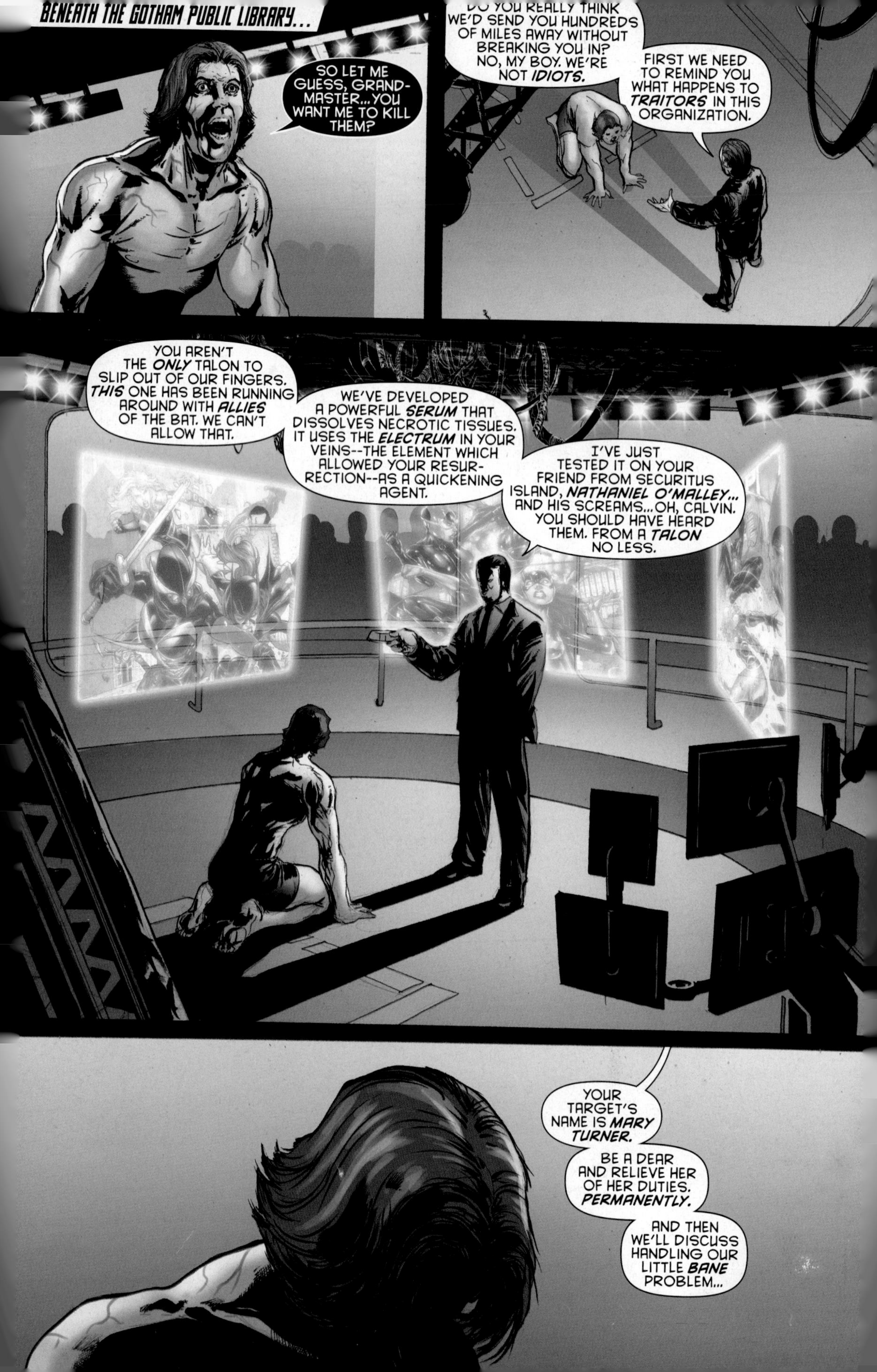

BENEATH THE GOTHAM PUBLIC LIBRARY...
SO LET ME GUESS, GRAND-MASTER...YOU WANT ME TO KILL THEM?
DO YOU REALLY THINK WE'D SEND YOU HUNDREDS OF MILES AWAY WITHOUT BREAKING YOU IN? NO, MY BOY. WE'RE NOT IDIOTS.
FIRST WE NEED TO REMIND YOU WHAT HAPPENS TO TRAITORS IN THIS ORGANIZATION.
YOU AREN'T THE ONLY TALON TO SLIP OUT OF OUR FINGERS. THIS ONE HAS BEEN RUNNING AROUND WITH ALLIES OF THE BAT. WE CAN'T ALLOW THAT.
WE'VE DEVELOPED A POWERFUL SERUM THAT DISSOLVES NECROTIC TISSUES. IT USES THE ELECTRUM IN YOUR VEINS--THE ELEMENT WHICH ALLOWED YOUR RESUR-RECTION--AS A QUICKENING AGENT.
I'VE JUST TESTED IT ON YOUR FRIEND FROM SECURITUS ISLAND, NATHANIEL O'MALLEY... AND HIS SCREAMS...OH, CALVIN. YOU SHOULD HAVE HEARD THEM. FROM A TALON NO LESS.
YOUR TARGET'S NAME IS MARY TURNER.
BE A DEAR AND RELIEVE HER OF HER DUTIES. PERMANENTLY.
AND THEN WE'LL DISCUSS HANDLING OUR LITTLE BANE PROBLEM...

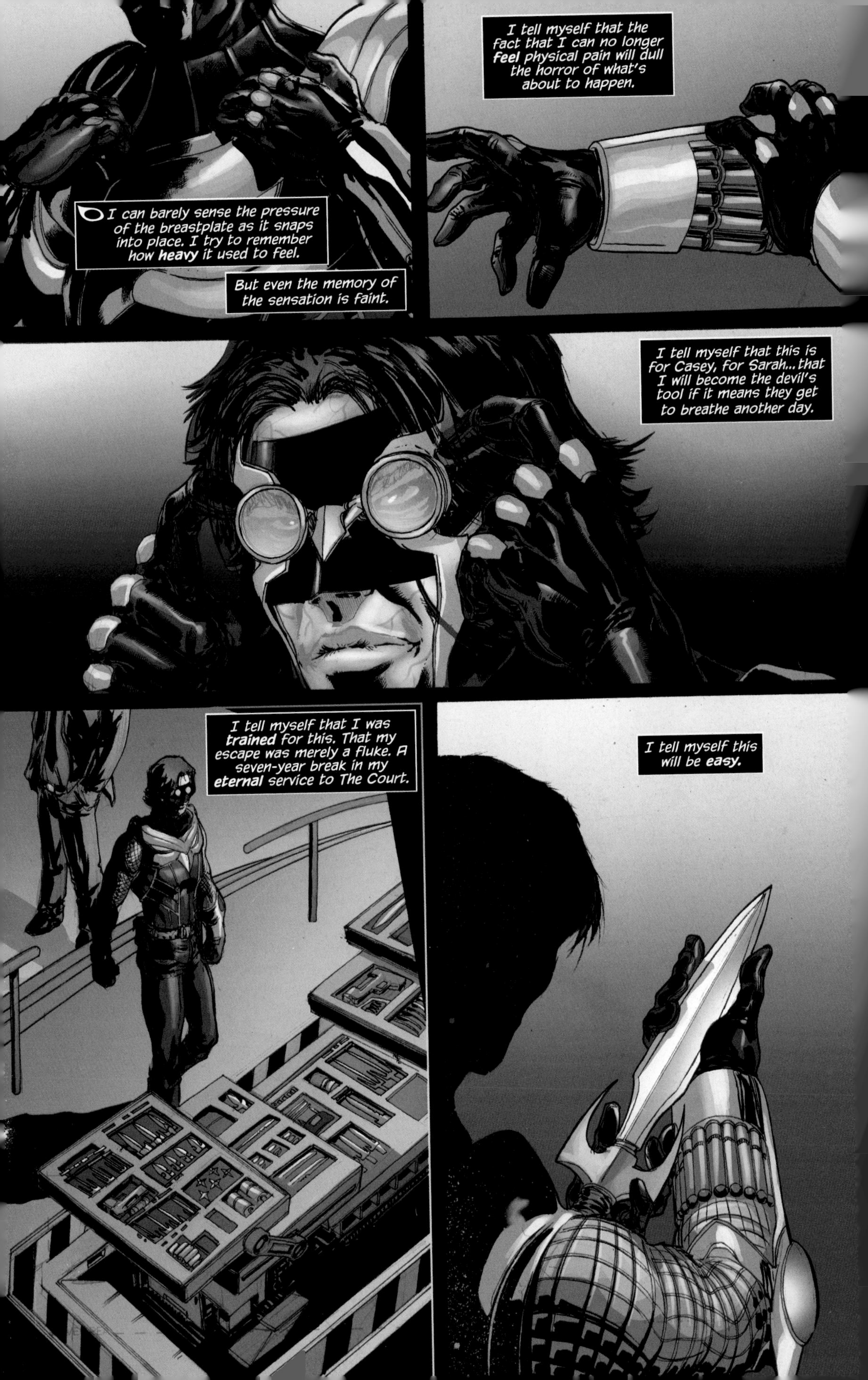
I can barely sense the pressure of the breastplate as it snaps into place. I try to remember how **heavy** it used to feel.
But even the memory of the sensation is faint.
I tell myself that the fact that I can no longer **feel** physical pain will dull the horror of what's about to happen.
I tell myself that this is for Casey, for Sarah... that I will become the devil's tool if it means they get to breathe another day.
I tell myself that I was **trained** for this. That my escape was merely a fluke. A seven-year break in my **eternal** service to The Court.
I tell myself this will be **easy.**

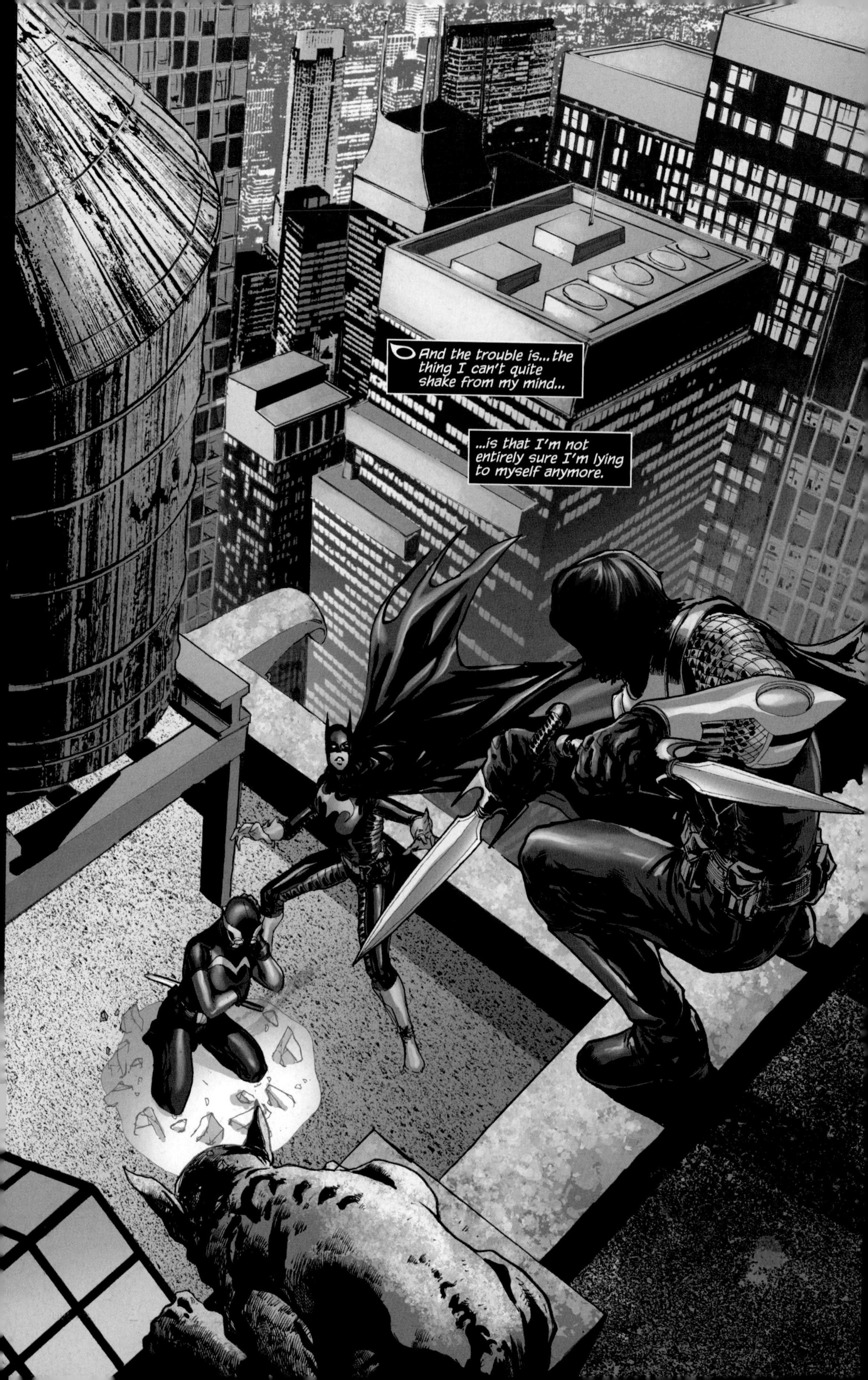
And the trouble is...the thing I can't quite shake from my mind...
...is that I'm not entirely sure I'm lying to myself anymore.

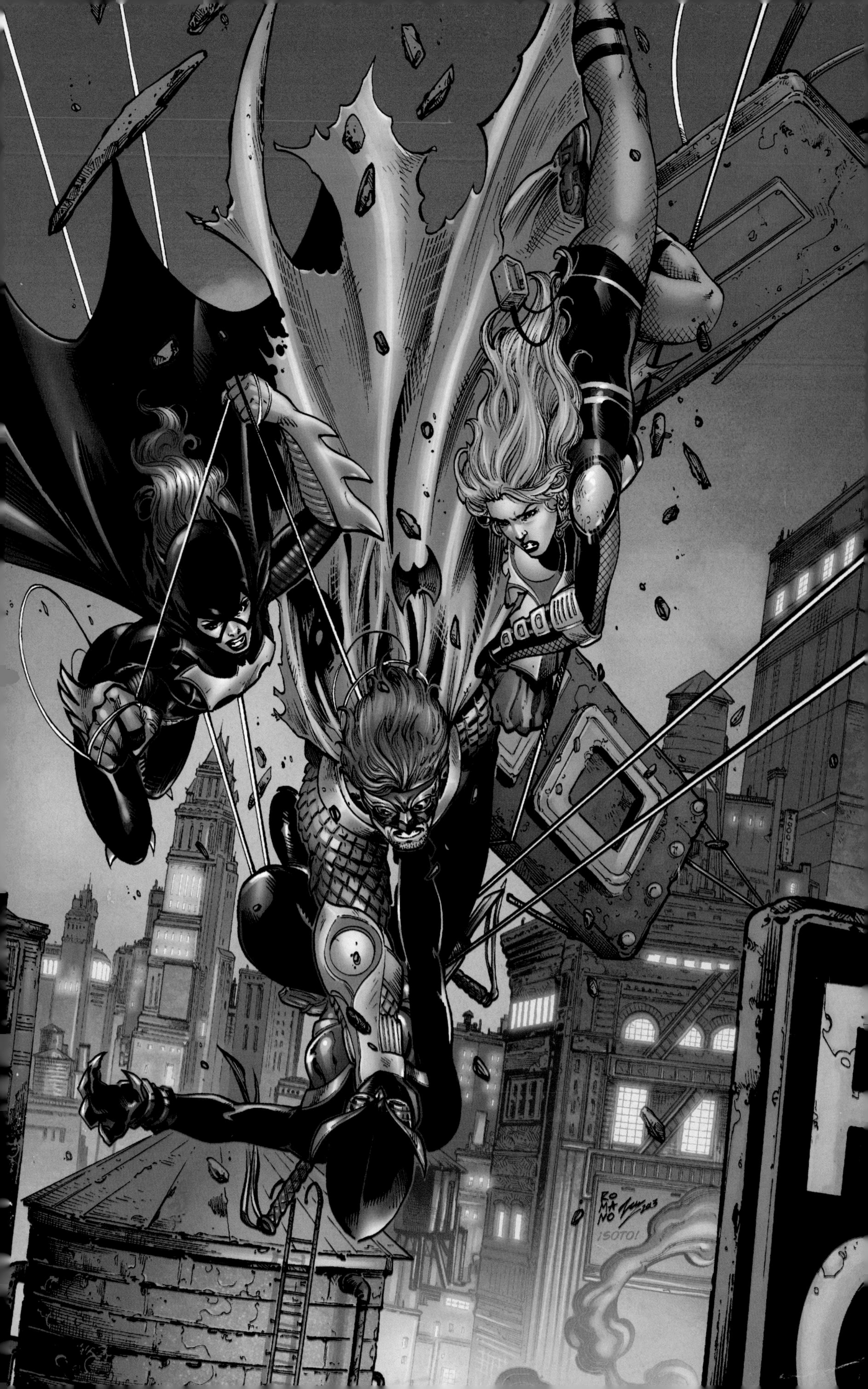
RO
MA
NO
¡SOTO!

TALON VS. TALON

CHRISTY MARX writer ROMANO MOLENAAR penciller SCOTT MCDANIEL breakdowns JONATHAN GLAPION inker
cover art by ROMANO MOLENAAR, VICENTE CIFUENTES & CHRIS SOTOMAYOR

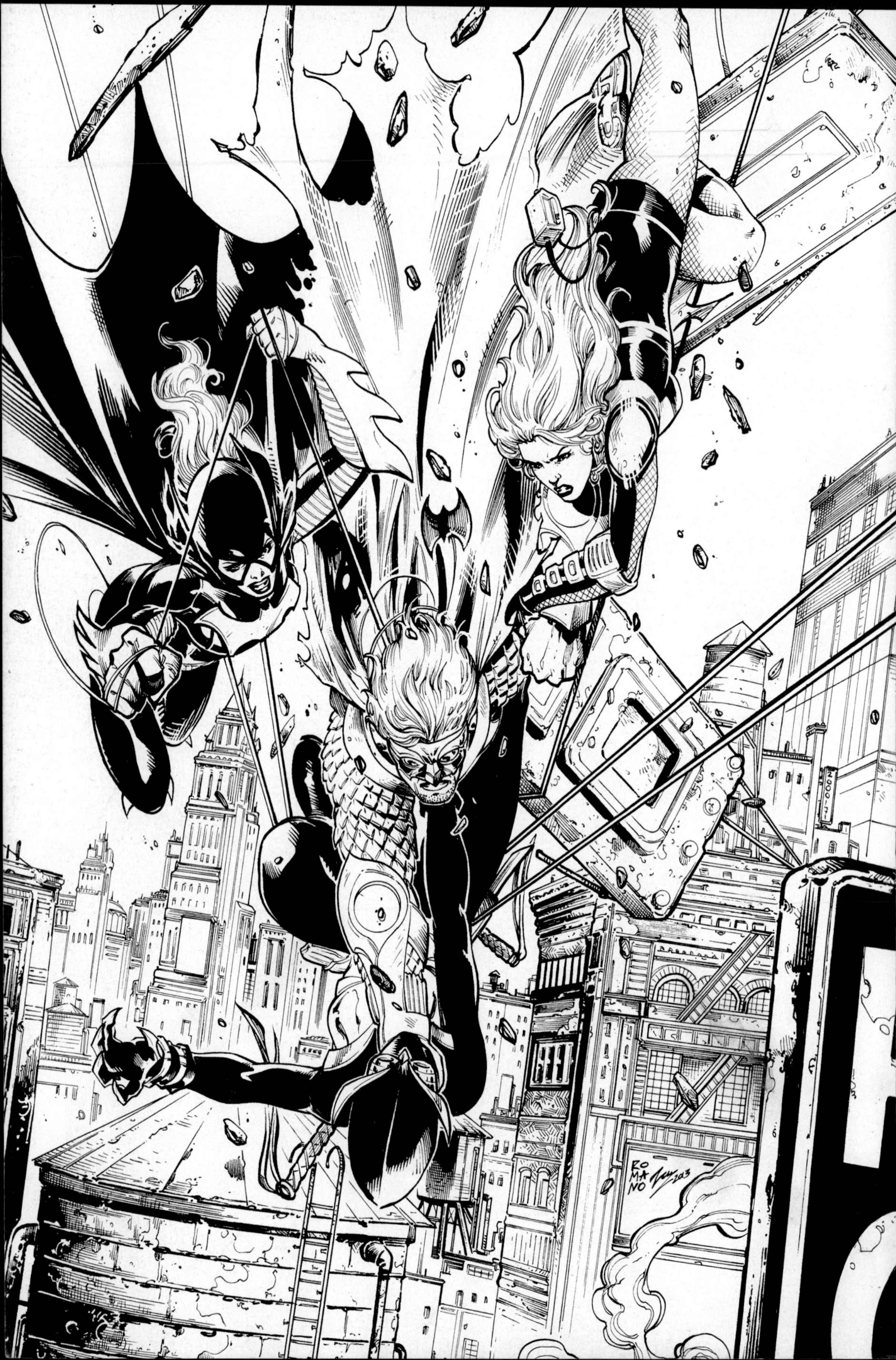

ROMANO 2013

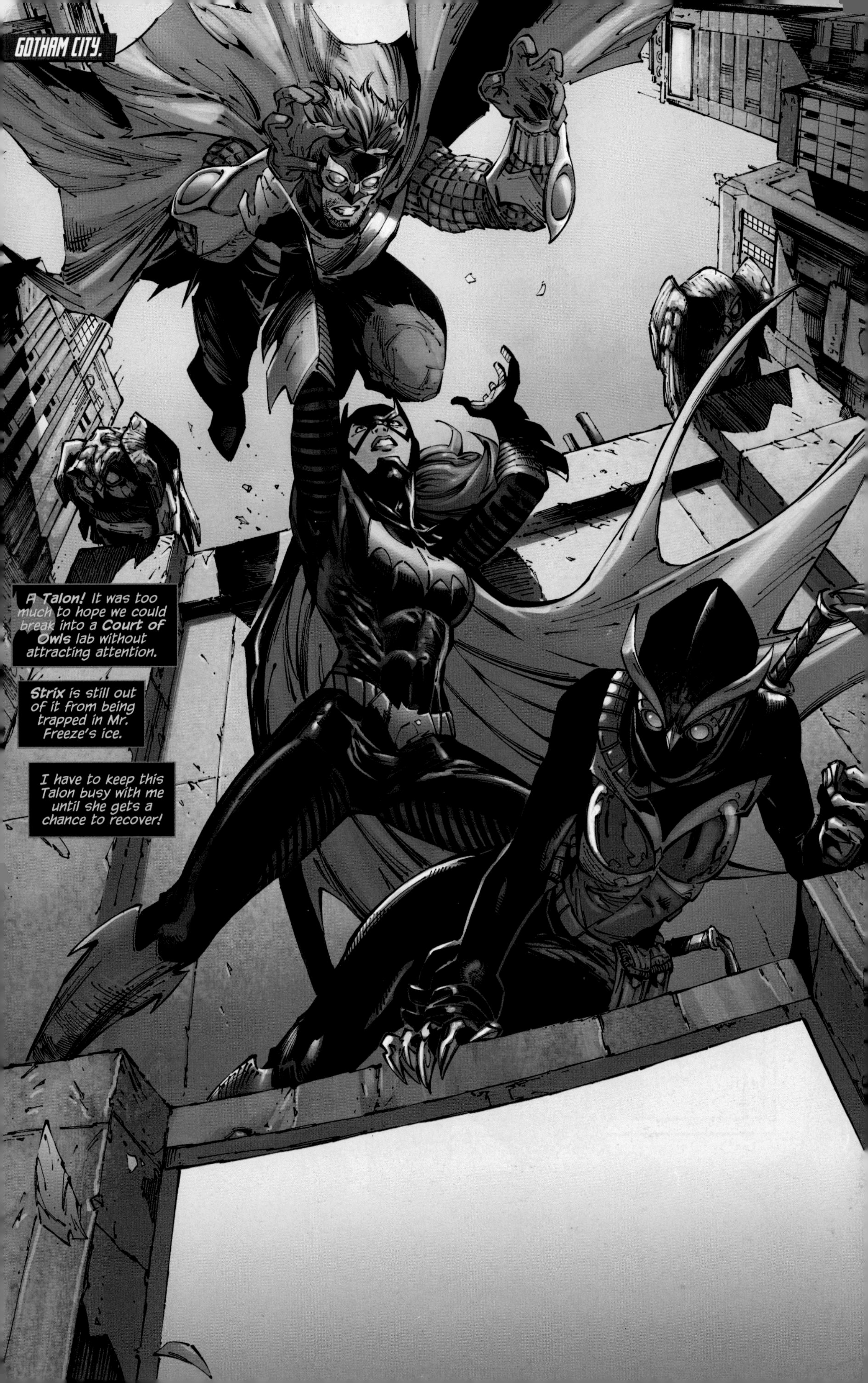
GOTHAM CITY.
A Talon! It was too much to hope we could break into a Court of Owls lab without attracting attention.
Strix is still out of it from being trapped in Mr. Freeze's ice.
I have to keep this Talon busy with me until she gets a chance to recover!

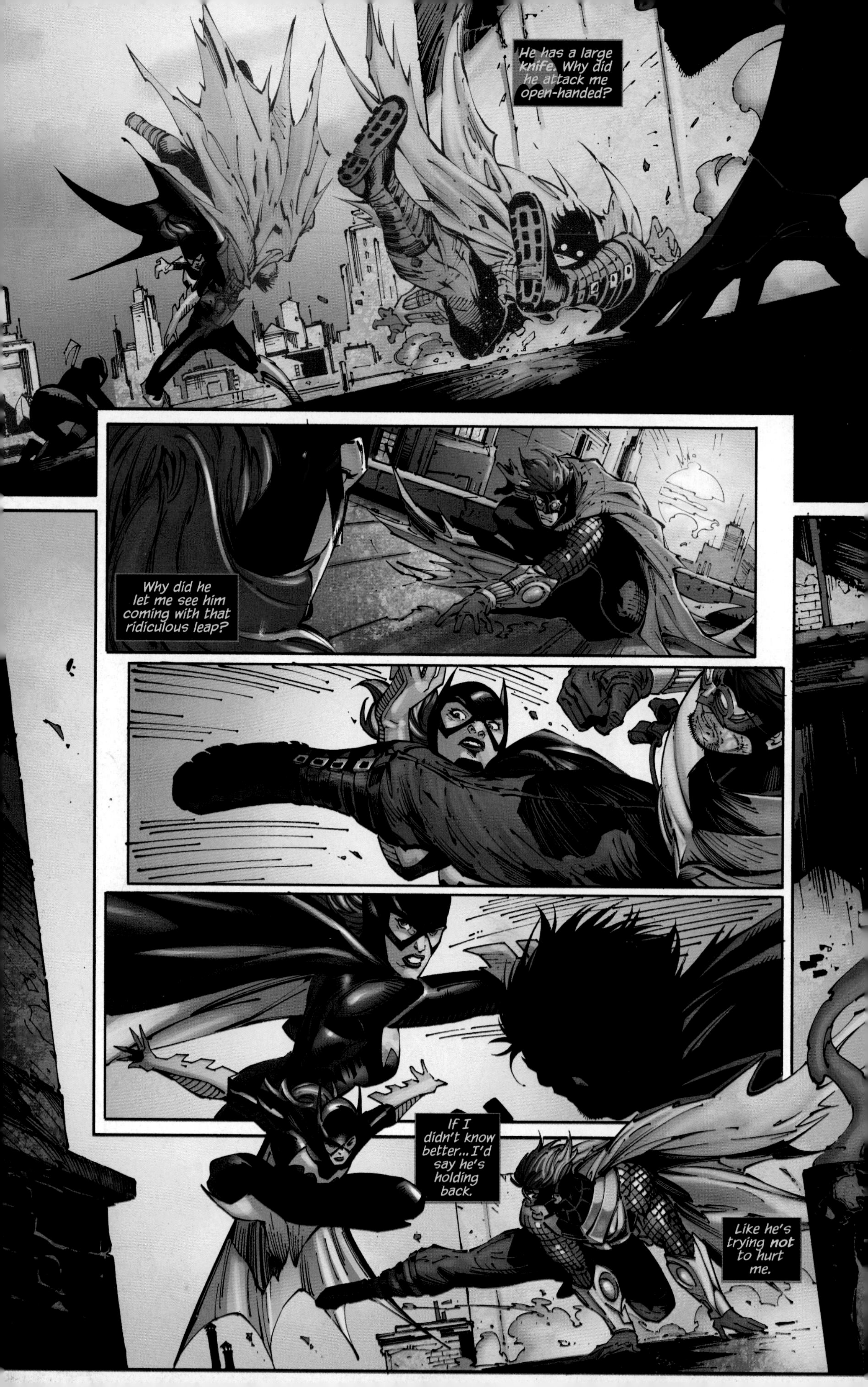
He has a large knife. Why did he attack me open-handed?
Why did he let me see him coming with that ridiculous leap?
If I didn't know better... I'd say he's holding back.
Like he's trying **not** to hurt me.

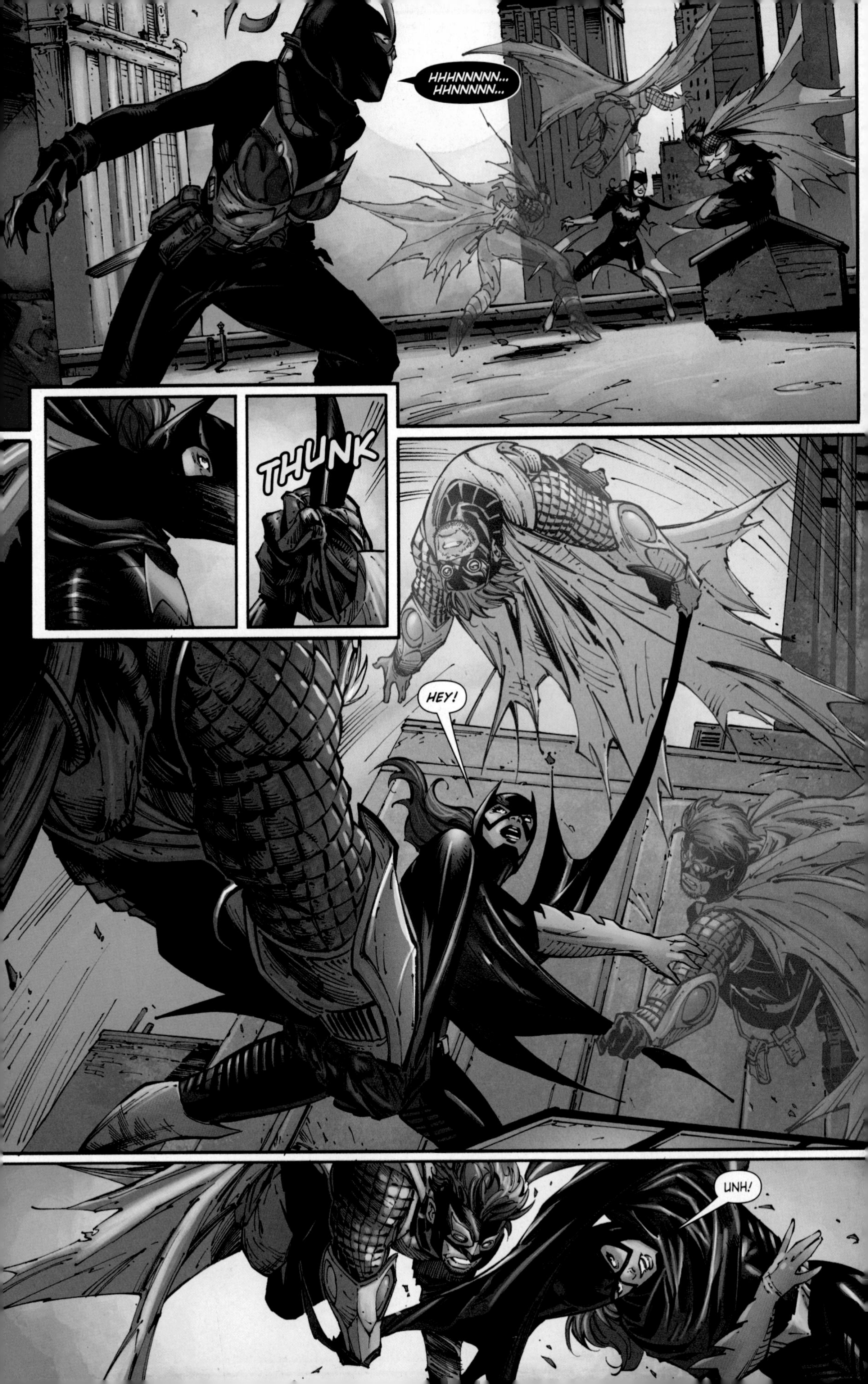
HHHNNNNN...
HHNNNNN...
THUNK
HEY!
UNH!

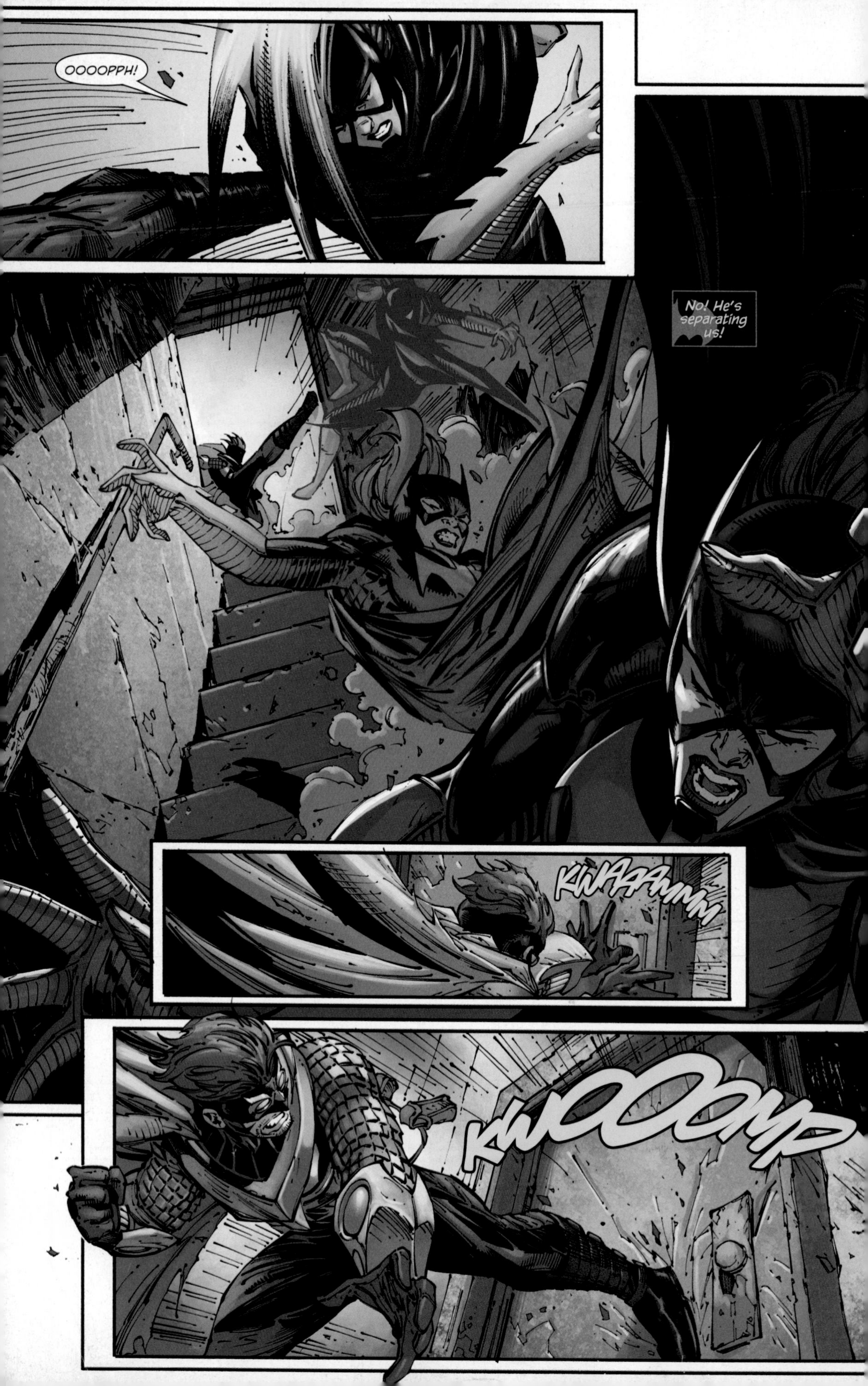
OOOOPPH!
No! He's separating us!
KWAAAMMM
KWOOOMP

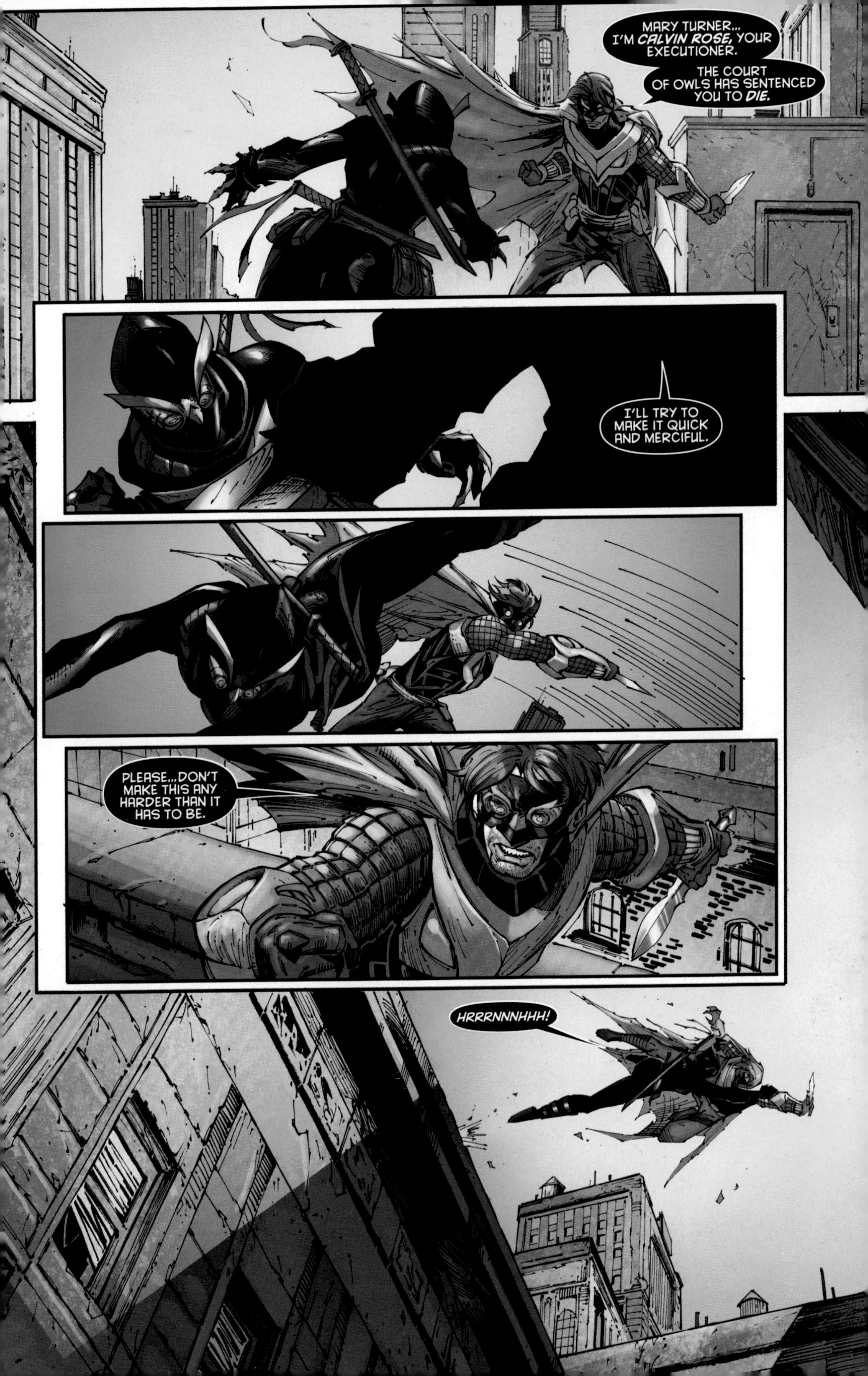
MARY TURNER... I'M CALVIN ROSE, YOUR EXECUTIONER.
THE COURT OF OWLS HAS SENTENCED YOU TO DIE.
I'LL TRY TO MAKE IT QUICK AND MERCIFUL.
PLEASE...DON'T MAKE THIS ANY HARDER THAN IT HAS TO BE.
HRRRNNNHHH!

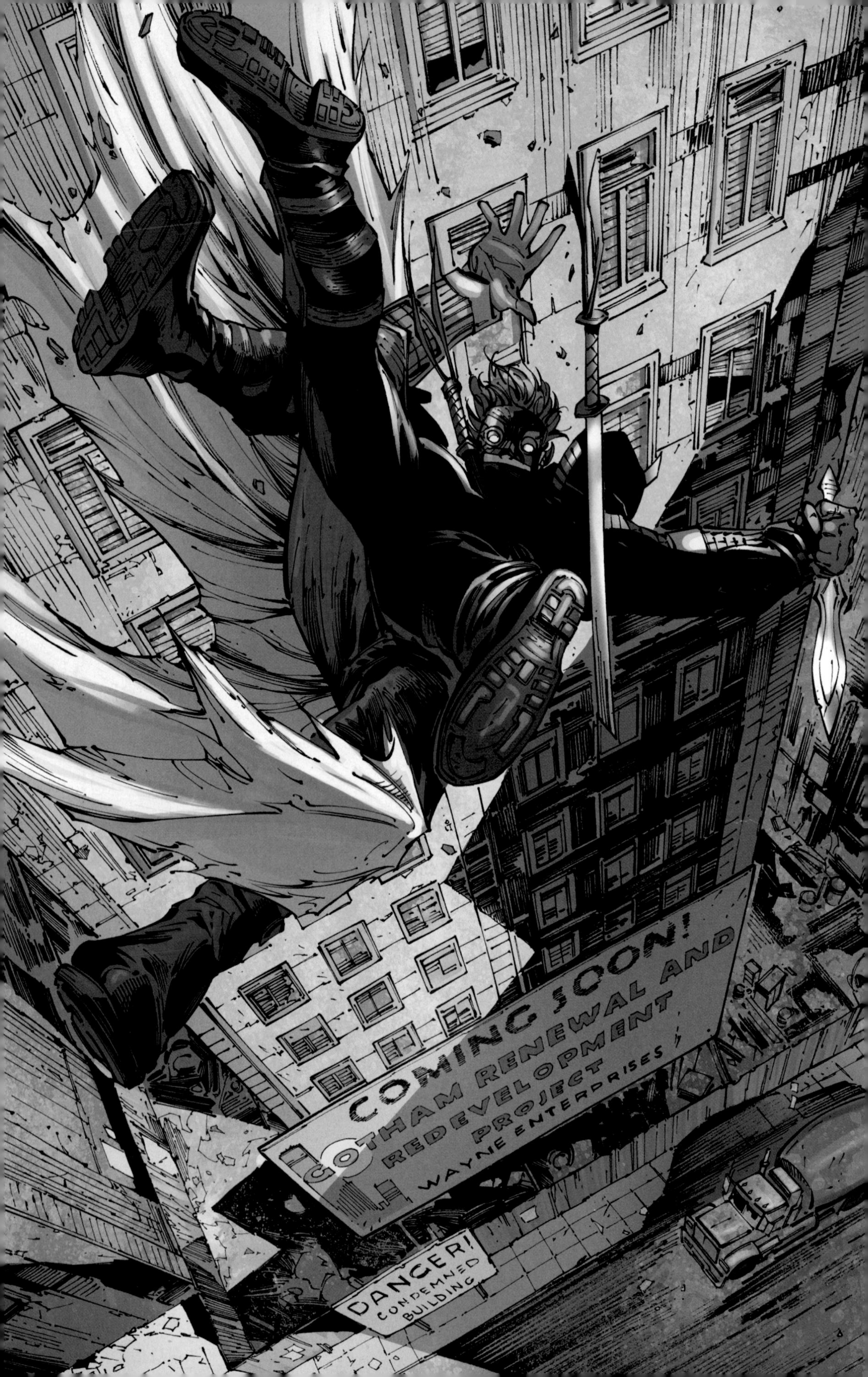
COMING SOON!
GOTHAM RENEWAL AND REDEVELOPMENT PROJECT
WAYNE ENTERPRISES
DANGER! CONDEMNED BUILDING

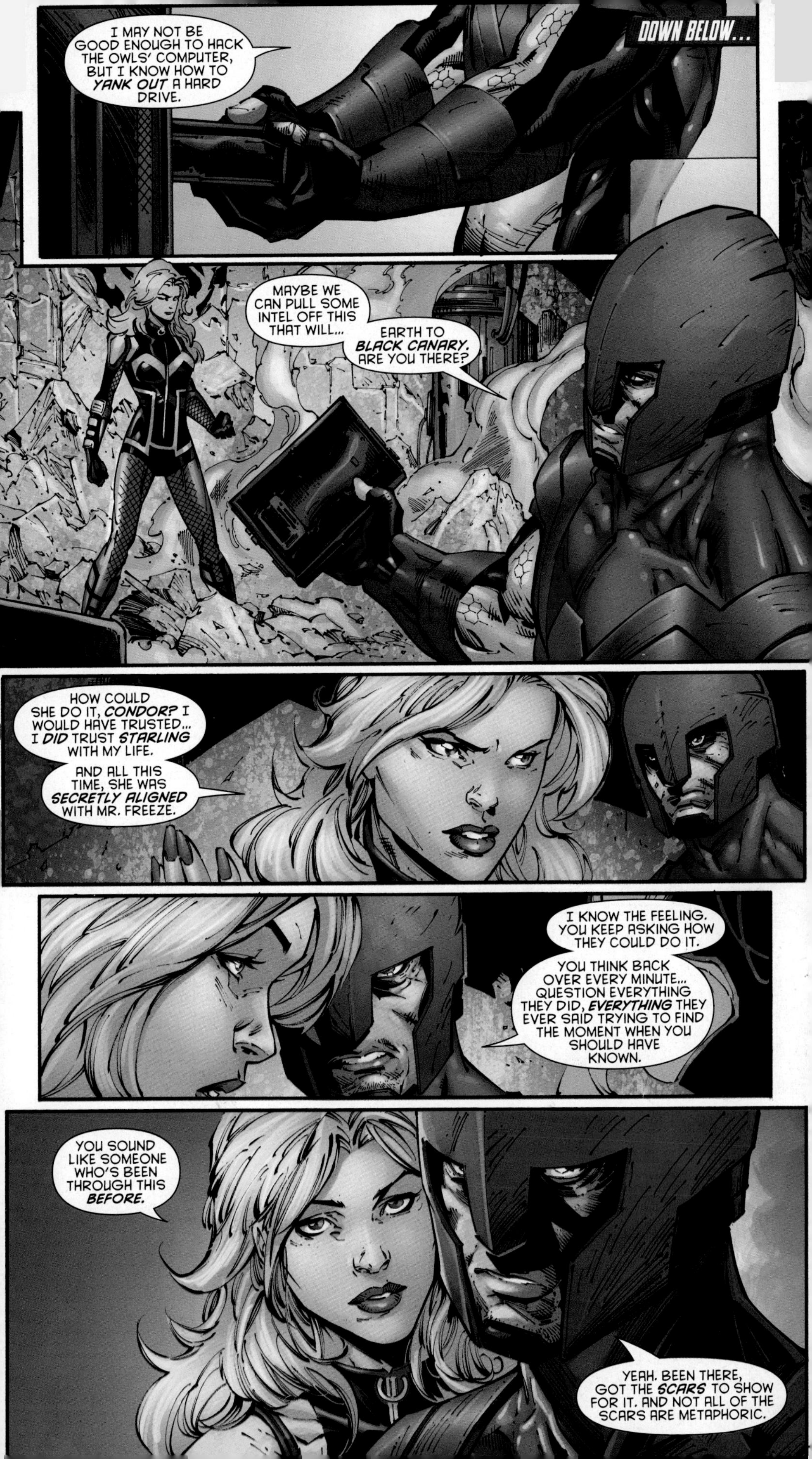
DOWN BELOW...
I MAY NOT BE GOOD ENOUGH TO HACK THE OWLS' COMPUTER, BUT I KNOW HOW TO YANK OUT A HARD DRIVE.
MAYBE WE CAN PULL SOME INTEL OFF THIS THAT WILL...
EARTH TO BLACK CANARY. ARE YOU THERE?
HOW COULD SHE DO IT, CONDOR? I WOULD HAVE TRUSTED... I DID TRUST STARLING WITH MY LIFE.
AND ALL THIS TIME, SHE WAS SECRETLY ALIGNED WITH MR. FREEZE.
I KNOW THE FEELING. YOU KEEP ASKING HOW THEY COULD DO IT.
YOU THINK BACK OVER EVERY MINUTE... QUESTION EVERYTHING THEY DID, EVERYTHING THEY EVER SAID TRYING TO FIND THE MOMENT WHEN YOU SHOULD HAVE KNOWN.
YOU SOUND LIKE SOMEONE WHO'S BEEN THROUGH THIS BEFORE.
YEAH. BEEN THERE, GOT THE SCARS TO SHOW FOR IT. AND NOT ALL OF THE SCARS ARE METAPHORIC.

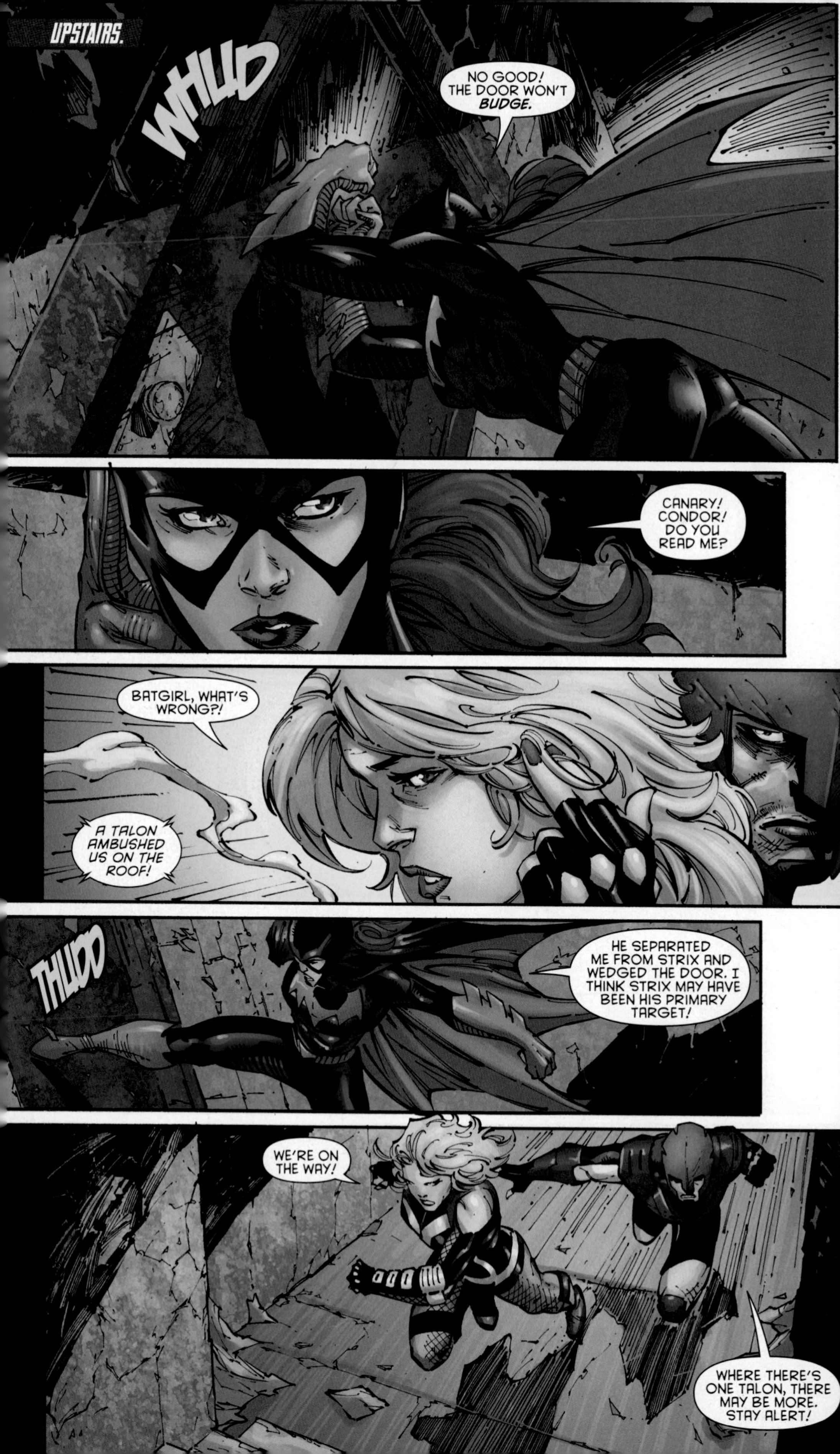
UPSTAIRS.
WHUD
NO GOOD! THE DOOR WON'T BUDGE.
CANARY! CONDOR! DO YOU READ ME?
BATGIRL, WHAT'S WRONG?!
A TALON AMBUSHED US ON THE ROOF!
THUDD
HE SEPARATED ME FROM STRIX AND WEDGED THE DOOR. I THINK STRIX MAY HAVE BEEN HIS PRIMARY TARGET!
WE'RE ON THE WAY!
WHERE THERE'S ONE TALON, THERE MAY BE MORE. STAY ALERT!

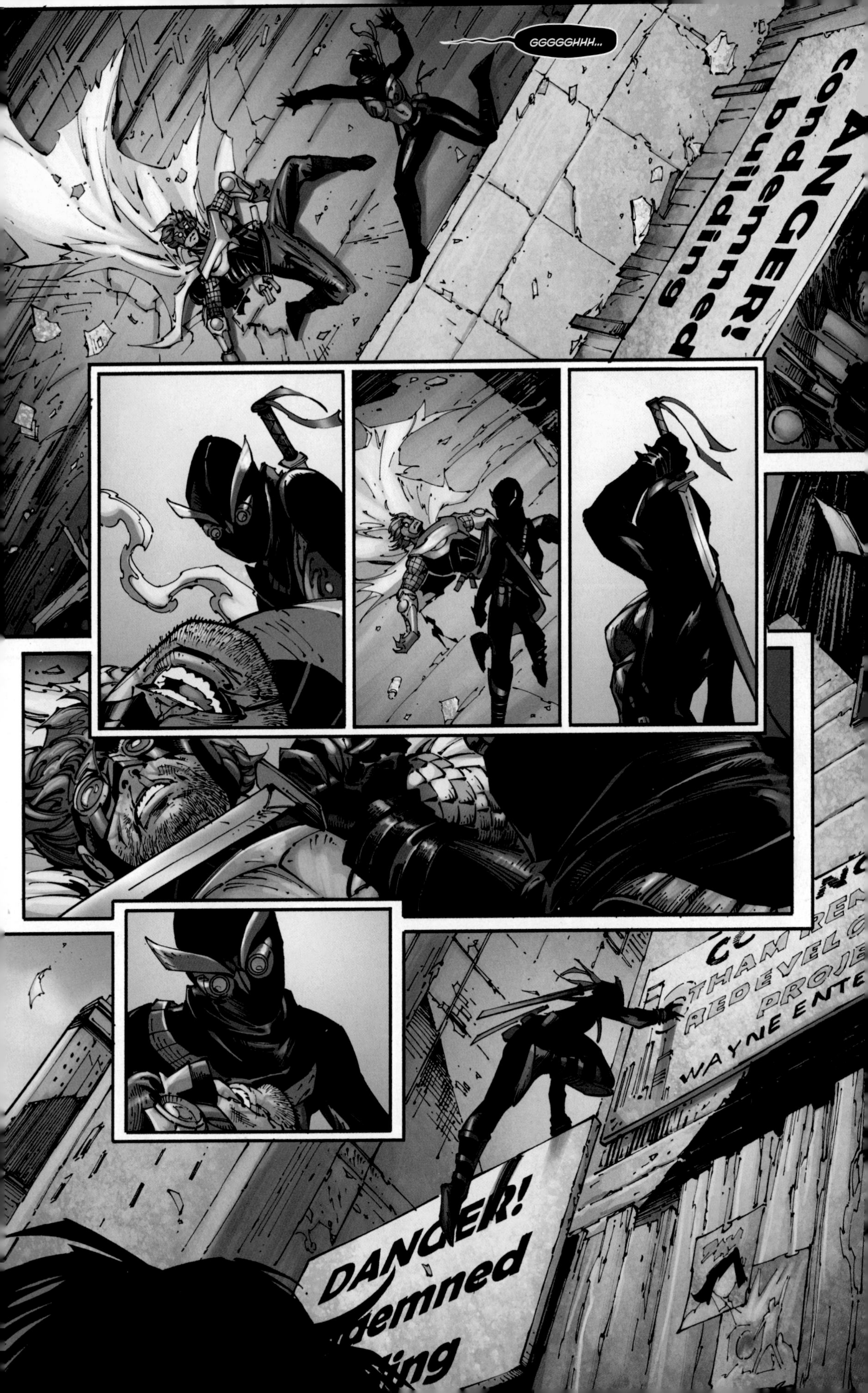
GGGGGHHH...
condemned
building
DANGER!

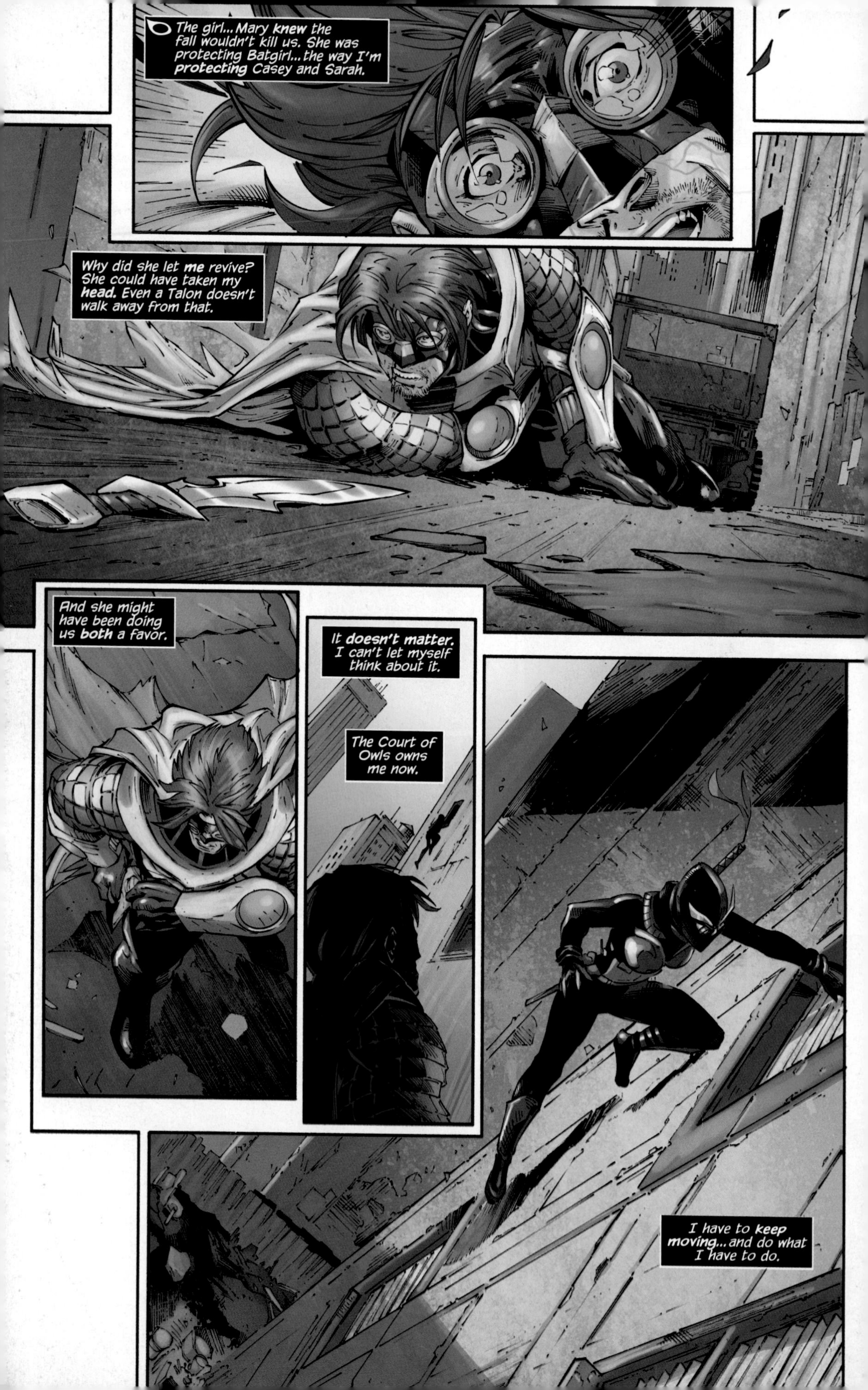
The girl... Mary **knew** the fall wouldn't kill us. She was protecting Batgirl... the way I'm **protecting** Casey and Sarah.
Why did she let **me** revive? She could have taken my **head.** Even a Talon doesn't walk away from that.
And she might have been doing us **both** a favor.
It **doesn't matter.** I can't let myself think about it.
The Court of Owls owns me now.
I have to **keep moving**... and do what I have to do.

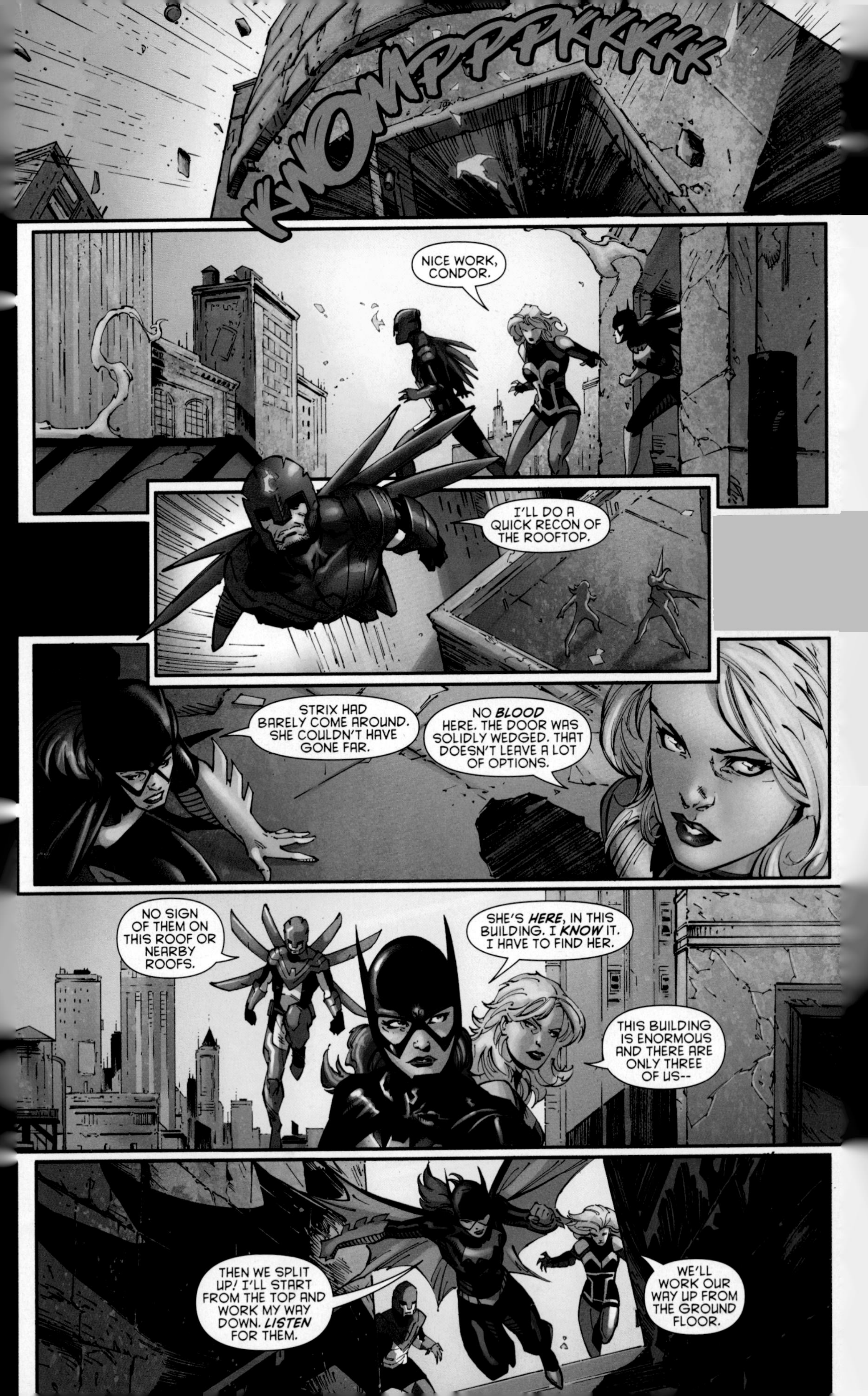

KWOMPPPKKKK
NICE WORK, CONDOR.
I'LL DO A QUICK RECON OF THE ROOFTOP.
STRIX HAD BARELY COME AROUND. SHE COULDN'T HAVE GONE FAR.
NO BLOOD HERE. THE DOOR WAS SOLIDLY WEDGED. THAT DOESN'T LEAVE A LOT OF OPTIONS.
NO SIGN OF THEM ON THIS ROOF OR NEARBY ROOFS.
SHE'S HERE, IN THIS BUILDING. I KNOW IT. I HAVE TO FIND HER.
THIS BUILDING IS ENORMOUS AND THERE ARE ONLY THREE OF US--
THEN WE SPLIT UP! I'LL START FROM THE TOP AND WORK MY WAY DOWN. LISTEN FOR THEM.
WE'LL WORK OUR WAY UP FROM THE GROUND FLOOR.

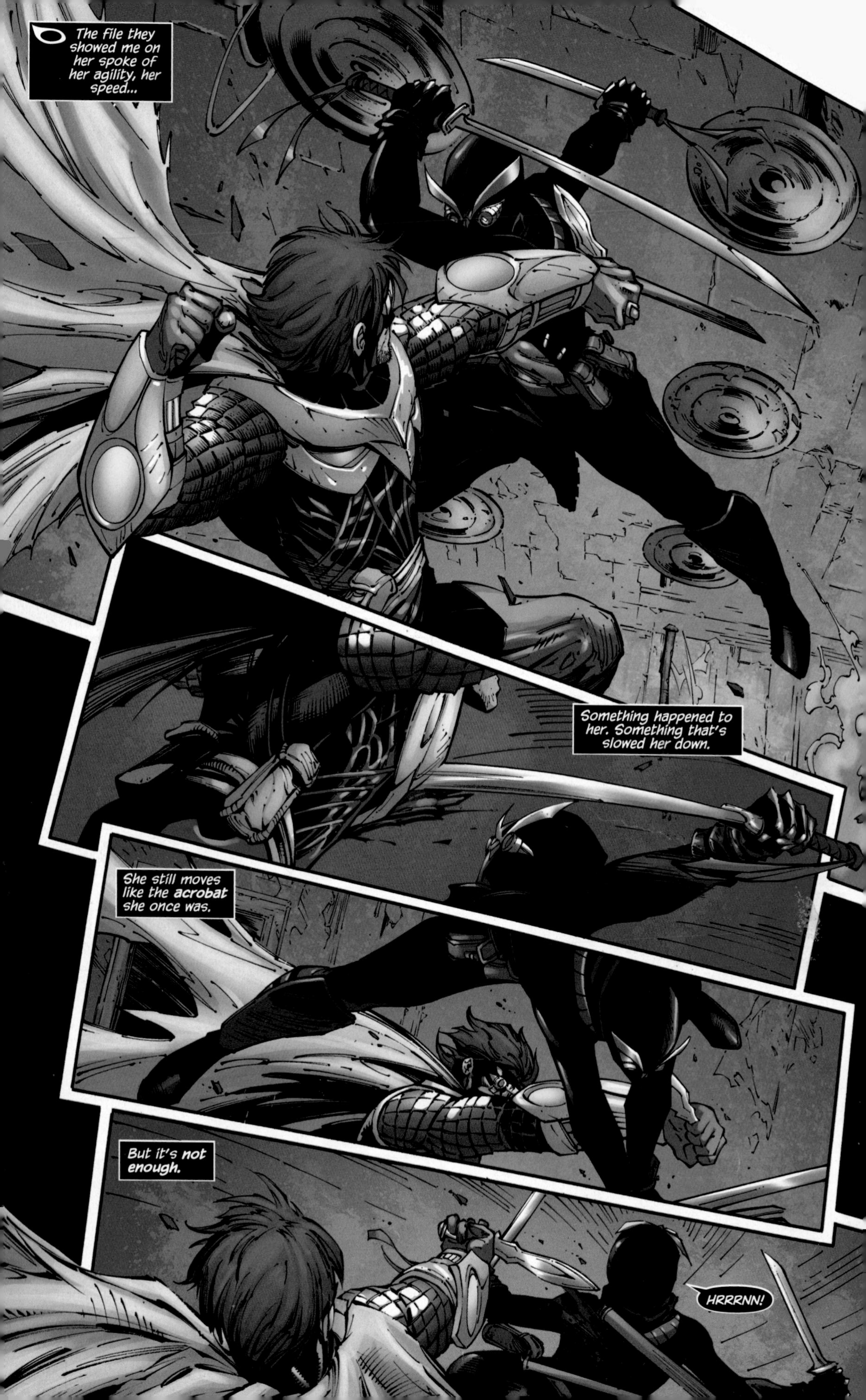

The file they showed me on her spoke of her agility, her speed...
Something happened to her. Something that's slowed her down.
She still moves like the **acrobat** she once was.
But it's **not** enough.
HRRRNN!

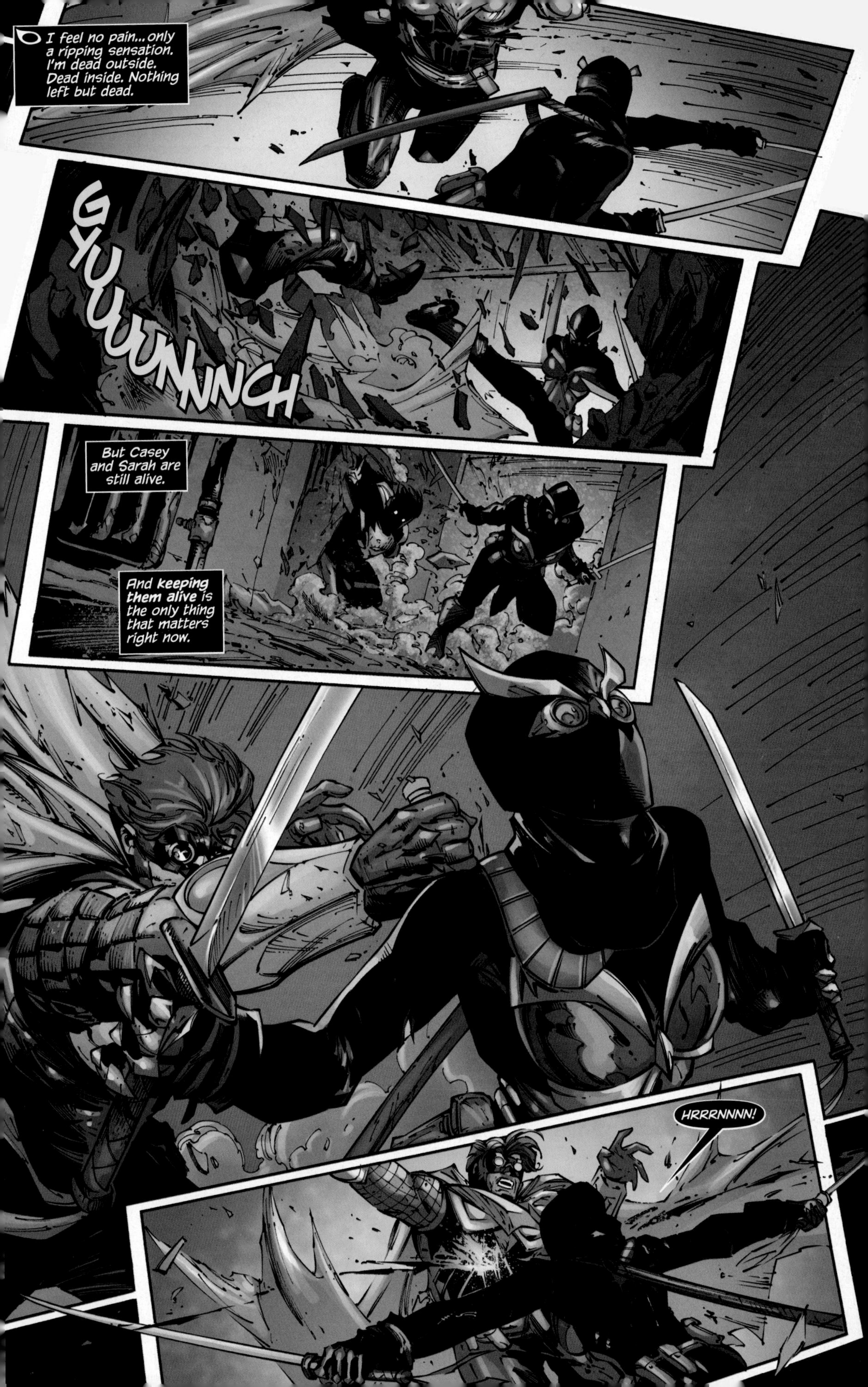
I feel no pain...only a ripping sensation. I'm dead outside. Dead inside. Nothing left but dead.
GYUUUNNNCH
But Casey and Sarah are still alive.
And keeping them alive is the only thing that matters right now.
HRRRNNNN!

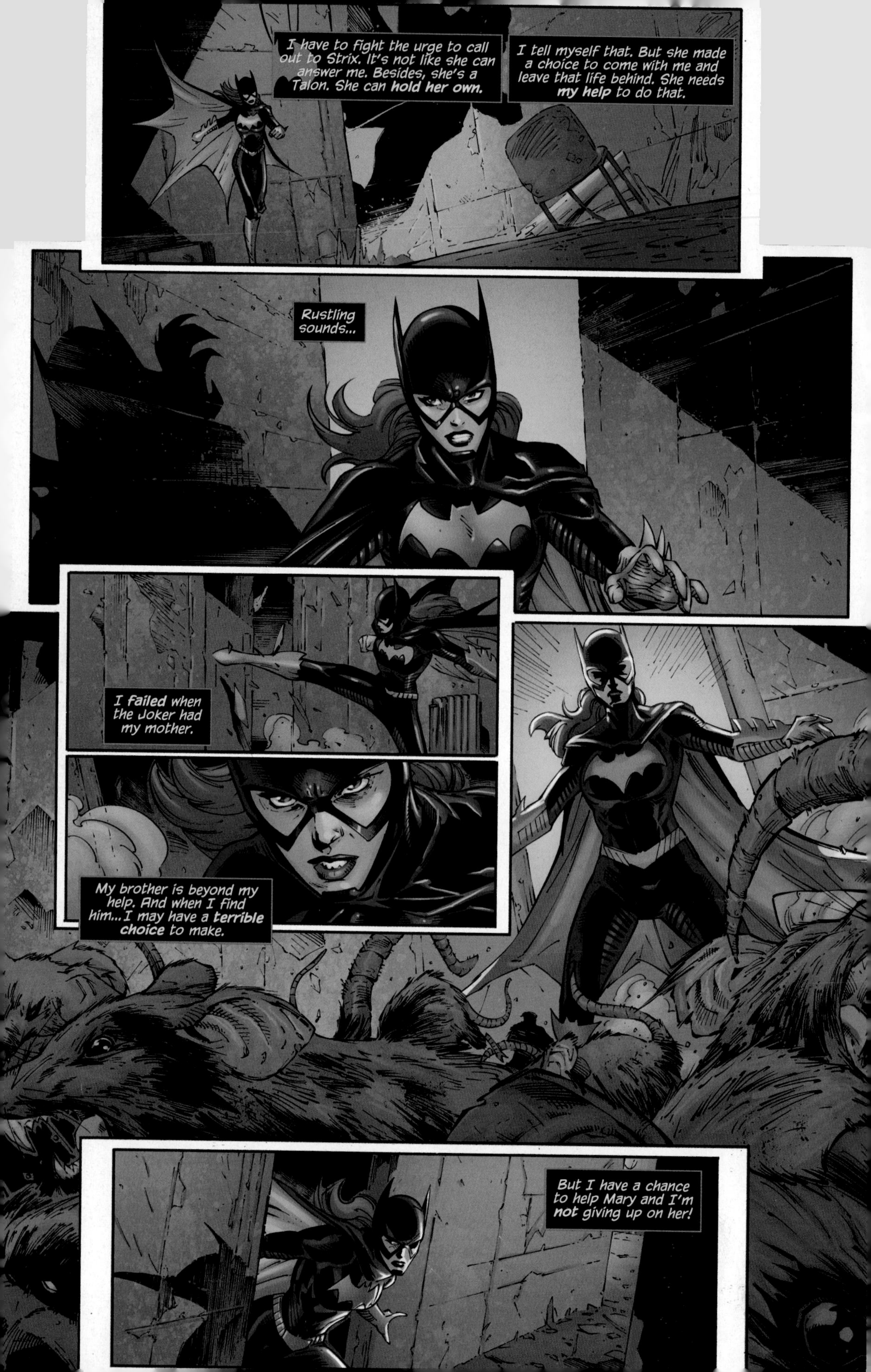
I have to fight the urge to call out to Strix. It's not like she can answer me. Besides, she's a Talon. She can **hold her own.**
I tell myself that. But she made a choice to come with me and leave that life behind. She needs **my help** to do that.
Rustling sounds...
I **failed** when the Joker had my mother.
My brother is beyond my help. And when I find him...I may have a **terrible choice** to make.
But I have a chance to help Mary and I'm **not** giving up on her!

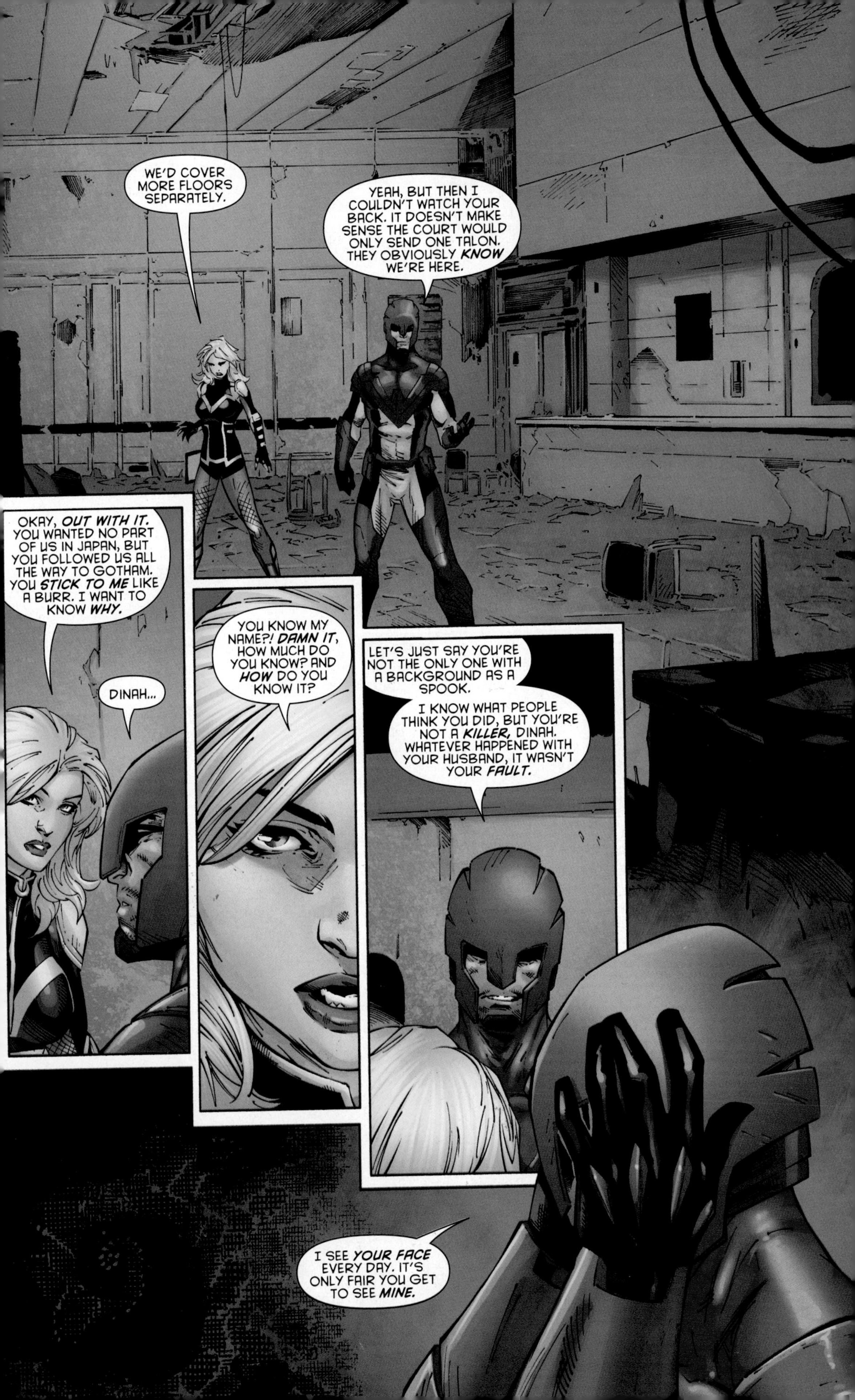

WE'D COVER MORE FLOORS SEPARATELY.
YEAH, BUT THEN I COULDN'T WATCH YOUR BACK. IT DOESN'T MAKE SENSE THE COURT WOULD ONLY SEND ONE TALON. THEY OBVIOUSLY *KNOW* WE'RE HERE.
OKAY, *OUT WITH IT.* YOU WANTED NO PART OF US IN JAPAN, BUT YOU FOLLOWED US ALL THE WAY TO GOTHAM. YOU *STICK TO ME* LIKE A BURR. I WANT TO KNOW *WHY.*
DINAH...
YOU KNOW MY NAME?! *DAMN IT,* HOW MUCH DO YOU KNOW? AND *HOW* DO YOU KNOW IT?
LET'S JUST SAY YOU'RE NOT THE ONLY ONE WITH A BACKGROUND AS A SPOOK.
I KNOW WHAT PEOPLE THINK YOU DID, BUT YOU'RE NOT A *KILLER,* DINAH. WHATEVER HAPPENED WITH YOUR HUSBAND, IT WASN'T YOUR *FAULT.*
I SEE *YOUR FACE* EVERY DAY. IT'S ONLY FAIR YOU GET TO SEE *MINE.*

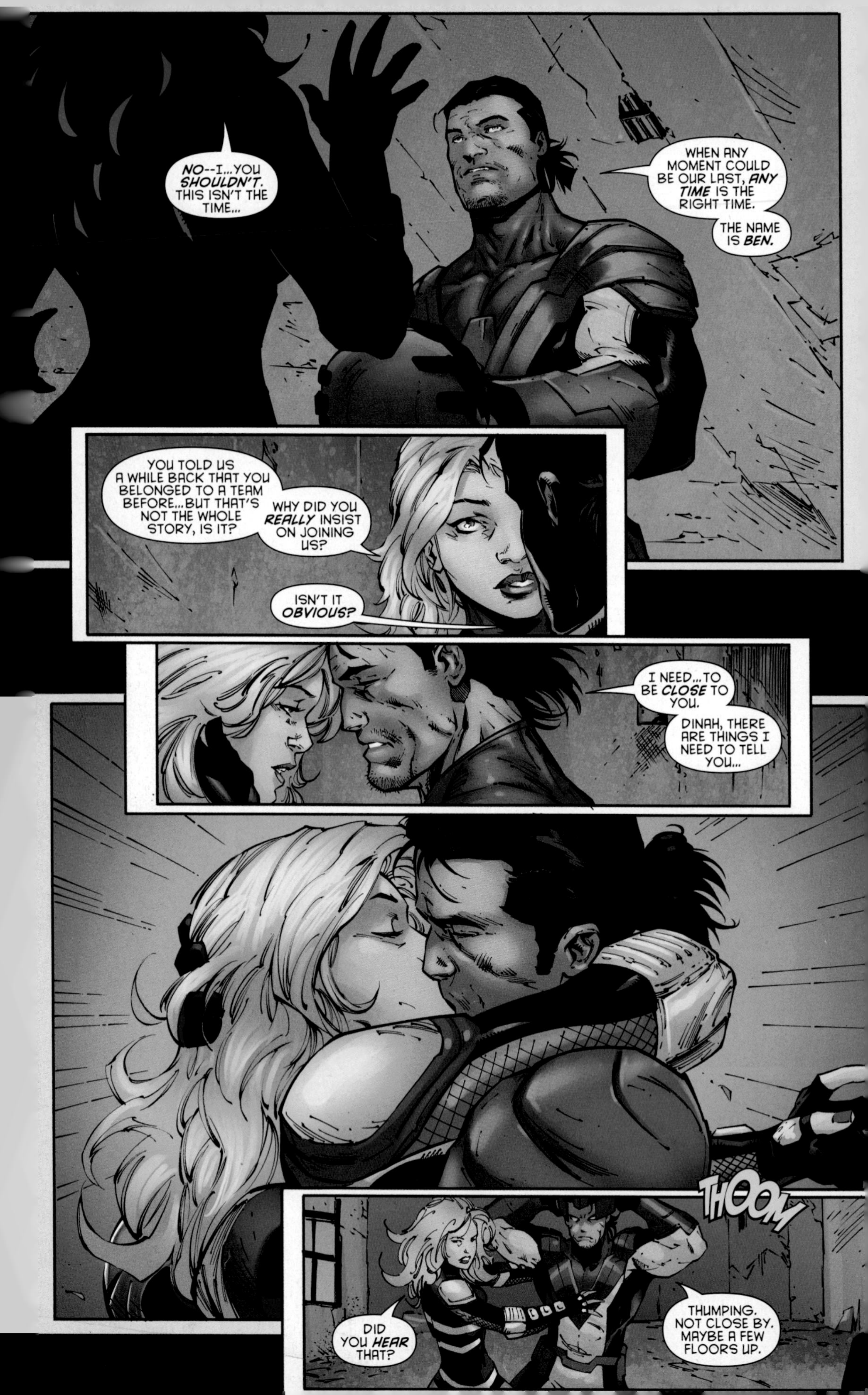

NO--I...YOU SHOULDN'T. THIS ISN'T THE TIME...
WHEN ANY MOMENT COULD BE OUR LAST, ANY TIME IS THE RIGHT TIME.
THE NAME IS BEN.
YOU TOLD US A WHILE BACK THAT YOU BELONGED TO A TEAM BEFORE...BUT THAT'S NOT THE WHOLE STORY, IS IT?
WHY DID YOU REALLY INSIST ON JOINING US?
ISN'T IT OBVIOUS?
I NEED...TO BE CLOSE TO YOU.
DINAH, THERE ARE THINGS I NEED TO TELL YOU...
THOOM
DID YOU HEAR THAT?
THUMPING. NOT CLOSE BY. MAYBE A FEW FLOORS UP.

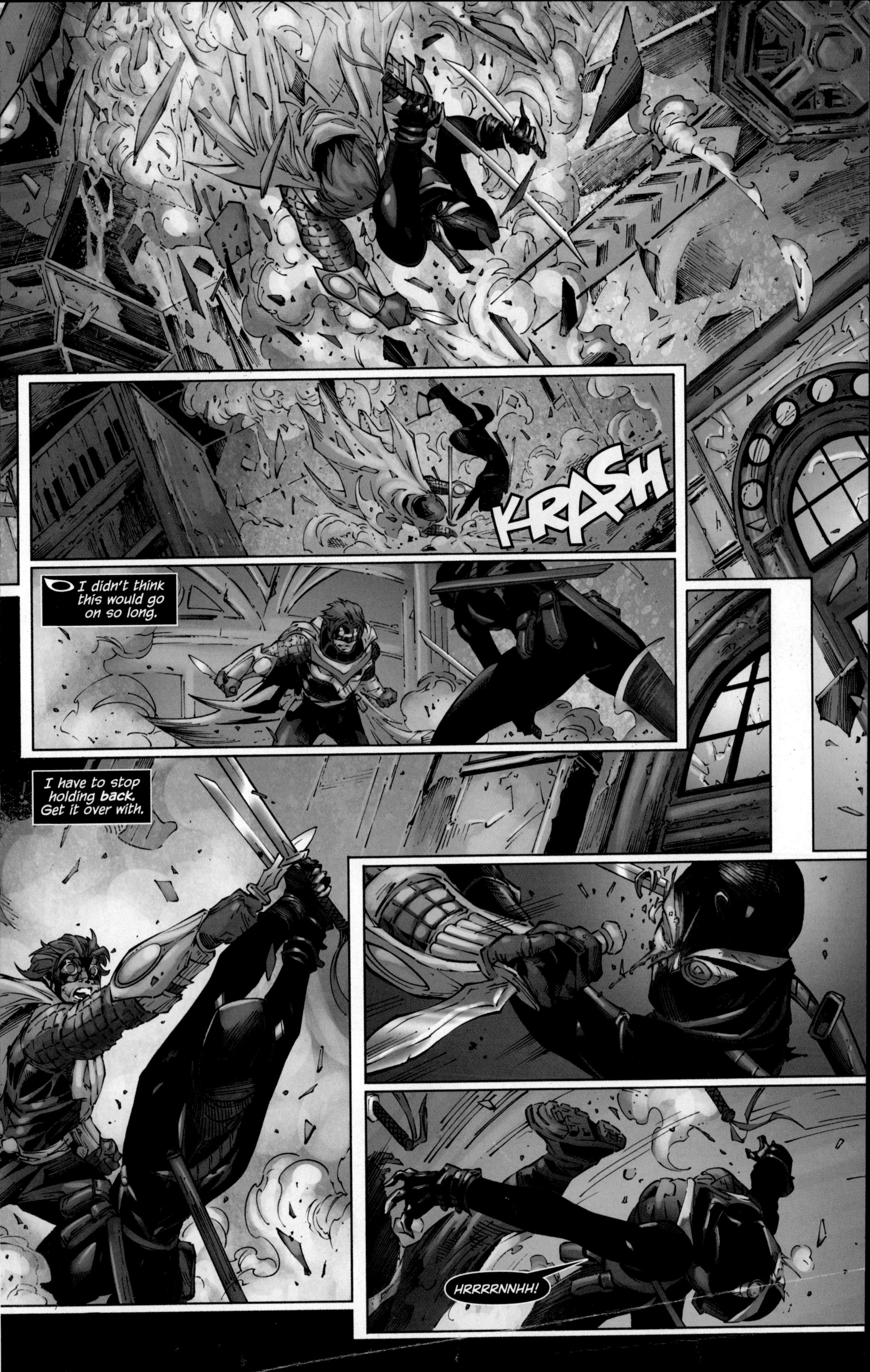
KRASH
I didn't think this would go on so long.
I have to stop holding back. Get it over with.
HRRRRNNHH!

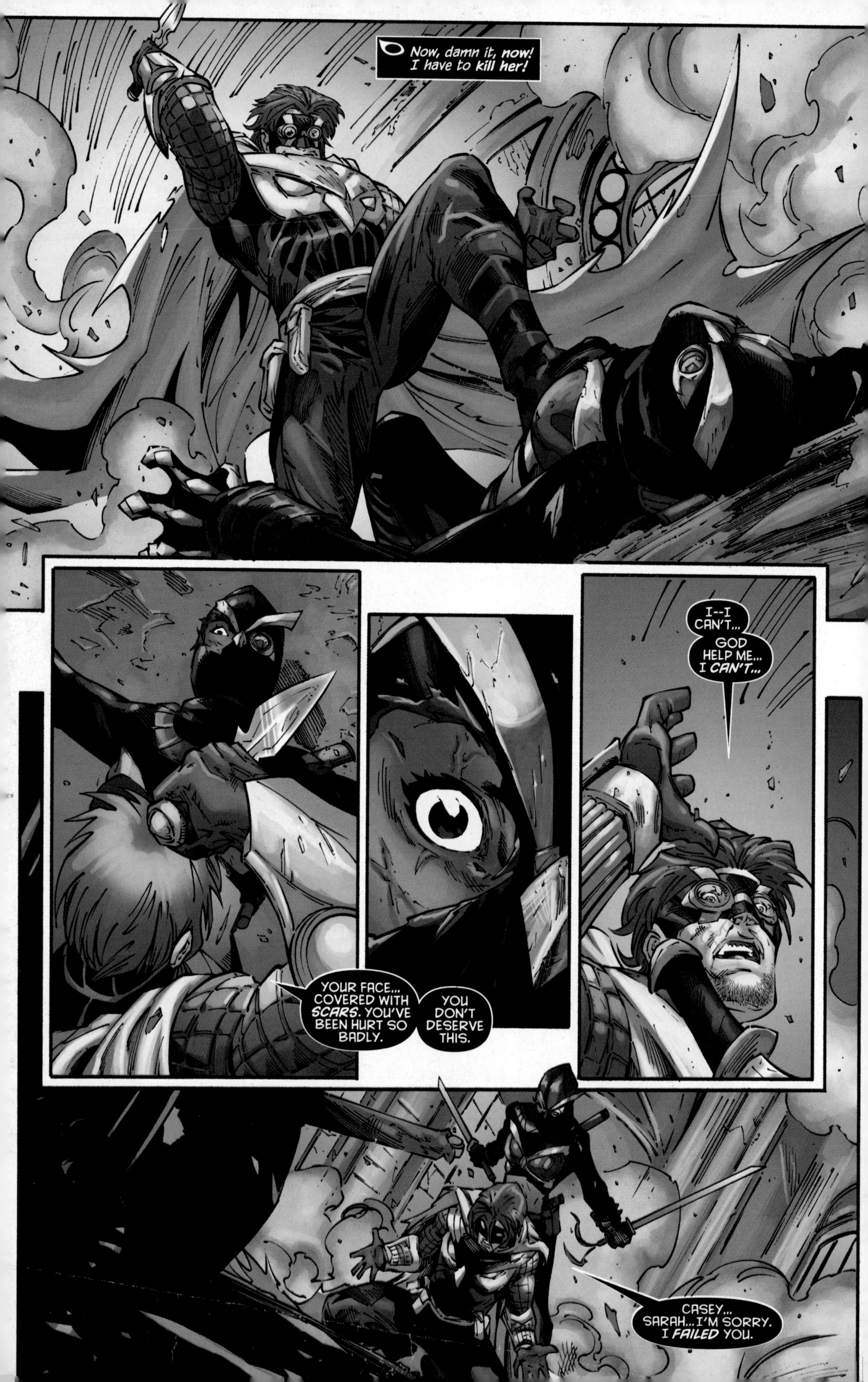
Now, damn it, now! I have to kill her!
YOUR FACE... COVERED WITH SCARS. YOU'VE BEEN HURT SO BADLY.
YOU DON'T DESERVE THIS.
I--I CAN'T...
GOD HELP ME... I CAN'T...
CASEY... SARAH... I'M SORRY. I FAILED YOU.

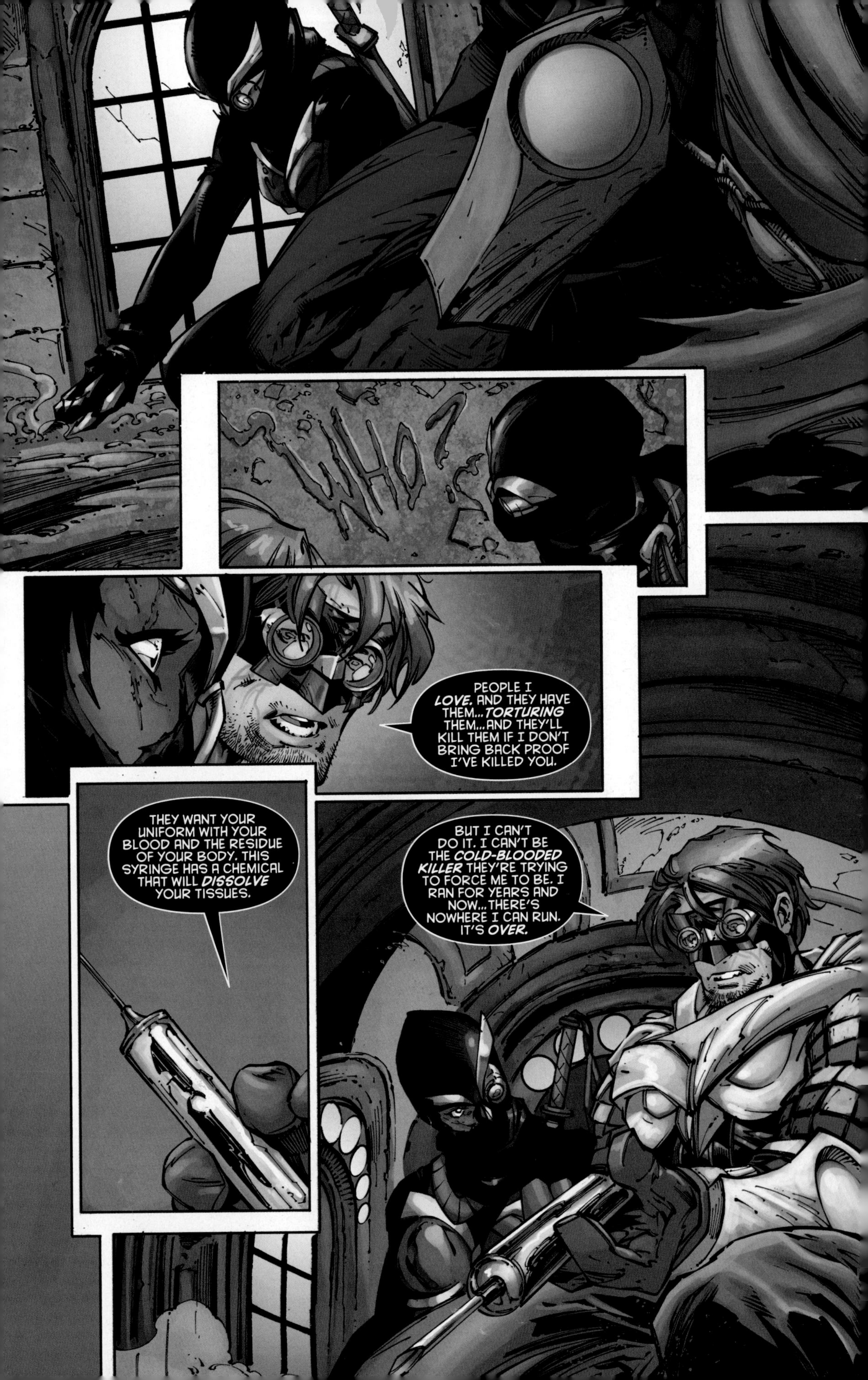
WHO?
PEOPLE I LOVE. AND THEY HAVE THEM...TORTURING THEM...AND THEY'LL KILL THEM IF I DON'T BRING BACK PROOF I'VE KILLED YOU.
THEY WANT YOUR UNIFORM WITH YOUR BLOOD AND THE RESIDUE OF YOUR BODY. THIS SYRINGE HAS A CHEMICAL THAT WILL DISSOLVE YOUR TISSUES.
BUT I CAN'T DO IT. I CAN'T BE THE COLD-BLOODED KILLER THEY'RE TRYING TO FORCE ME TO BE. I RAN FOR YEARS AND NOW...THERE'S NOWHERE I CAN RUN. IT'S OVER.

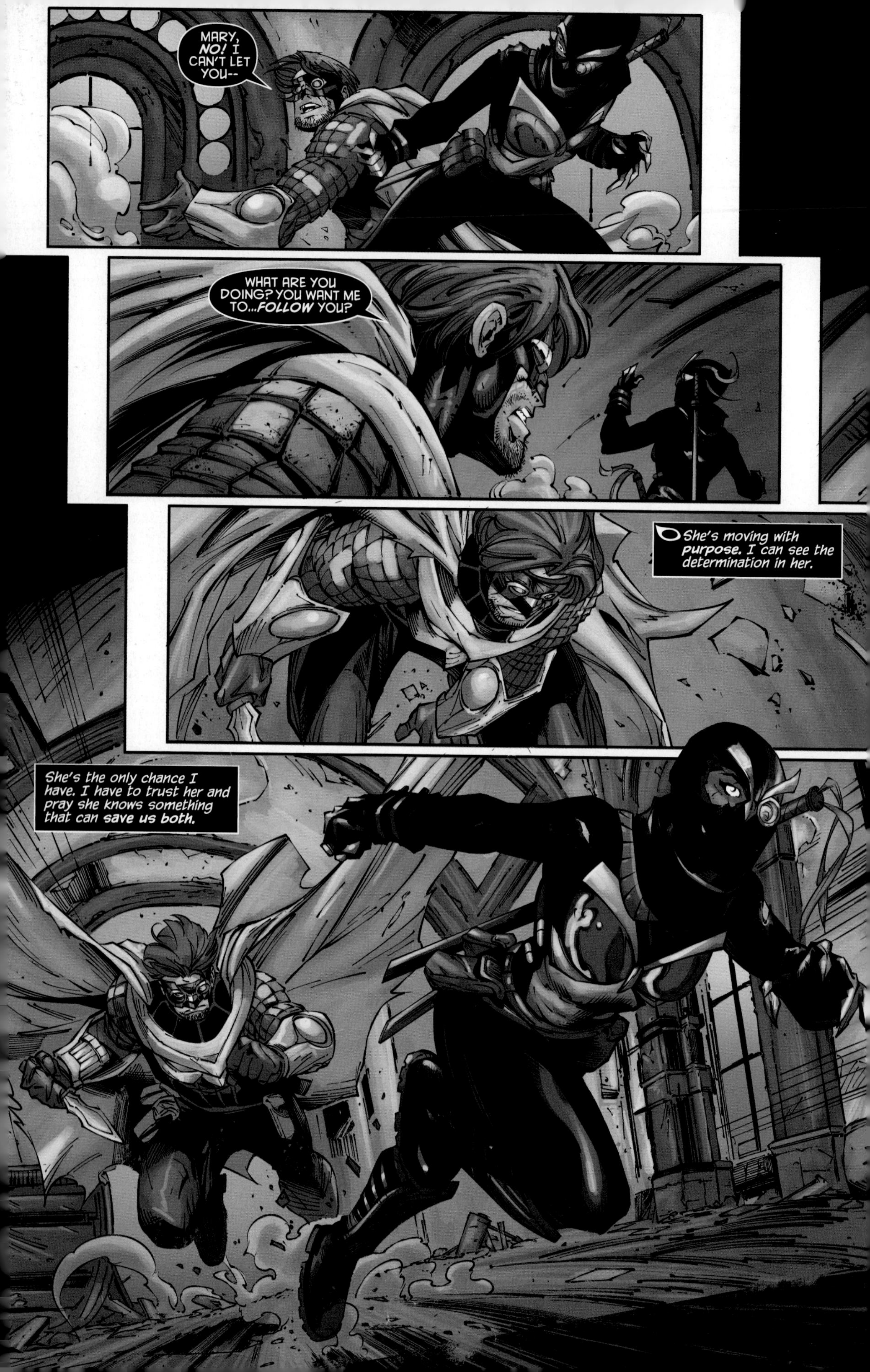
MARY, NO! I CAN'T LET YOU--
WHAT ARE YOU DOING? YOU WANT ME TO...FOLLOW YOU?
She's moving with purpose. I can see the determination in her.
She's the only chance I have. I have to trust her and pray she knows something that can save us both.

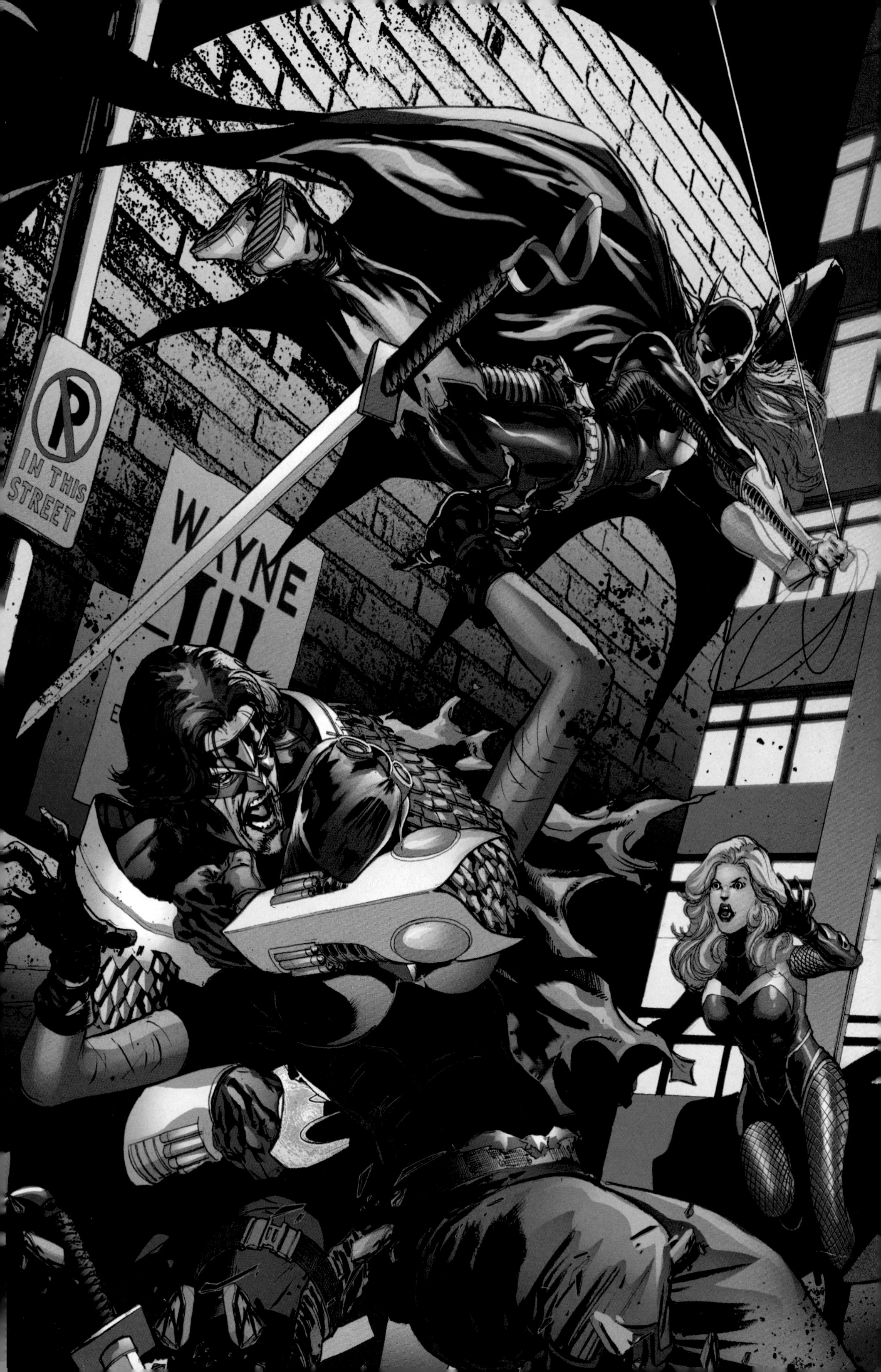
IN THIS STREET

UNEASY

JAMES TYNION IV writer **GRAHAM NOLAN** layouts **MIGUEL SEPULVEDA** finishes cover art by **MIGUEL SEPULVEDA & RAIN BEREDO**

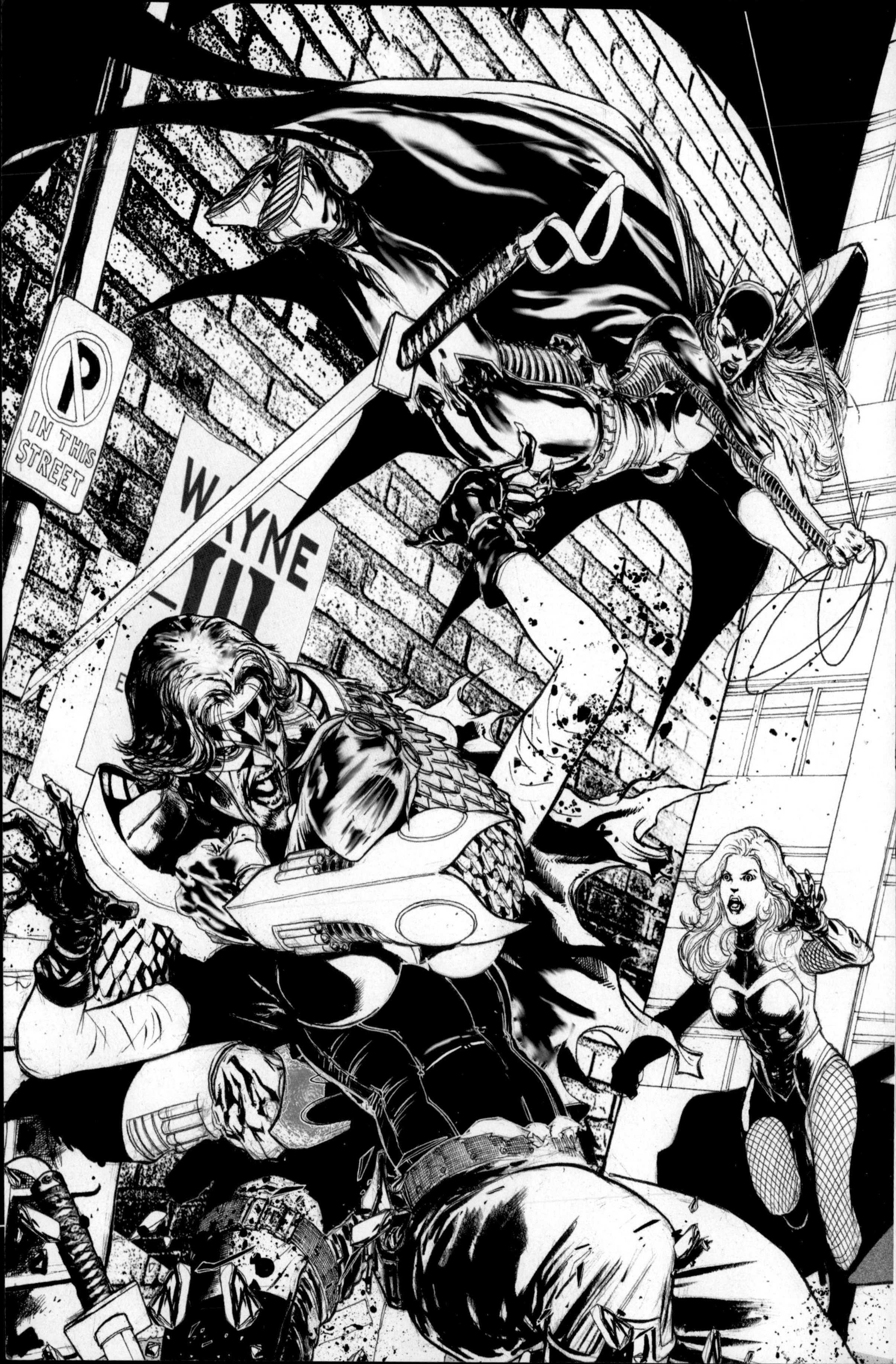
P
IN THIS STREET
WAYNE

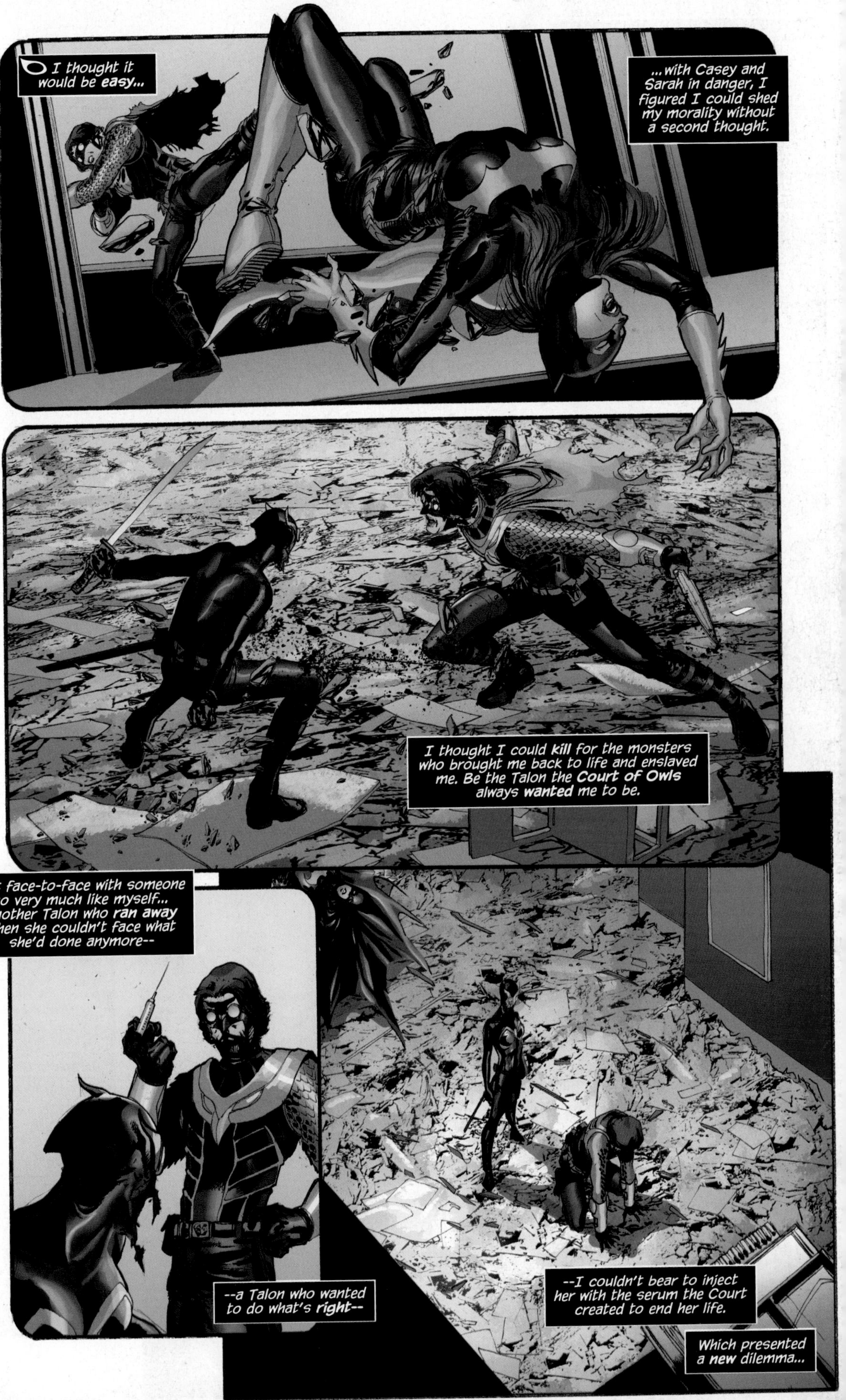
I thought it would be easy...
...with Casey and Sarah in danger, I figured I could shed my morality without a second thought.
I thought I could kill for the monsters who brought me back to life and enslaved me. Be the Talon the Court of Owls always wanted me to be.
But face-to-face with someone so very much like myself... another Talon who ran away when she couldn't face what she'd done anymore--
--a Talon who wanted to do what's right--
--I couldn't bear to inject her with the serum the Court created to end her life.
Which presented a new dilemma...

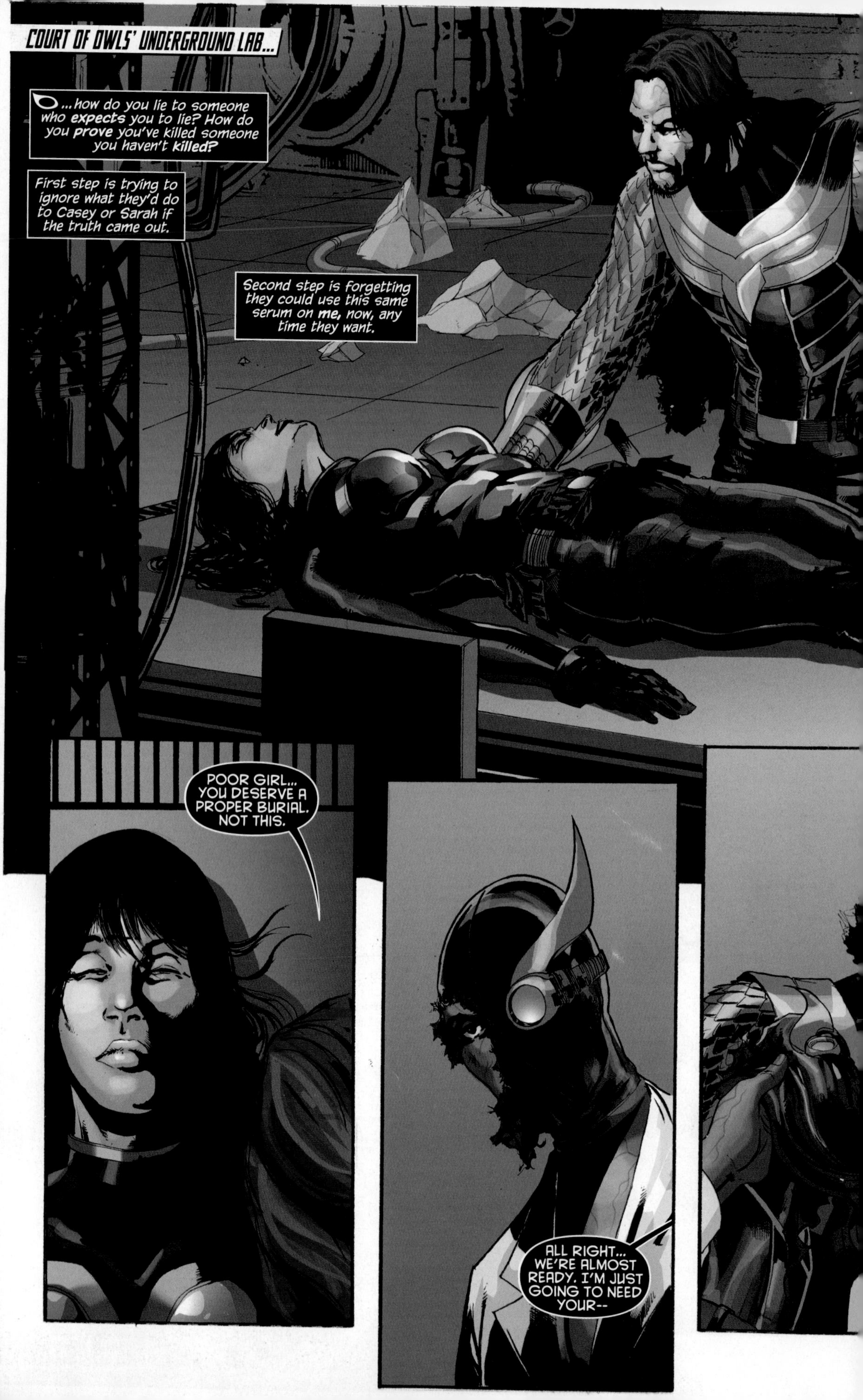
COURT OF OWLS' UNDERGROUND LAB...
...how do you lie to someone who expects you to lie? How do you prove you've killed someone you haven't killed?
First step is trying to ignore what they'd do to Casey or Sarah if the truth came out.
Second step is forgetting they could use this same serum on me, now, any time they want.
POOR GIRL... YOU DESERVE A PROPER BURIAL. NOT THIS.
ALL RIGHT... WE'RE ALMOST READY. I'M JUST GOING TO NEED YOUR--

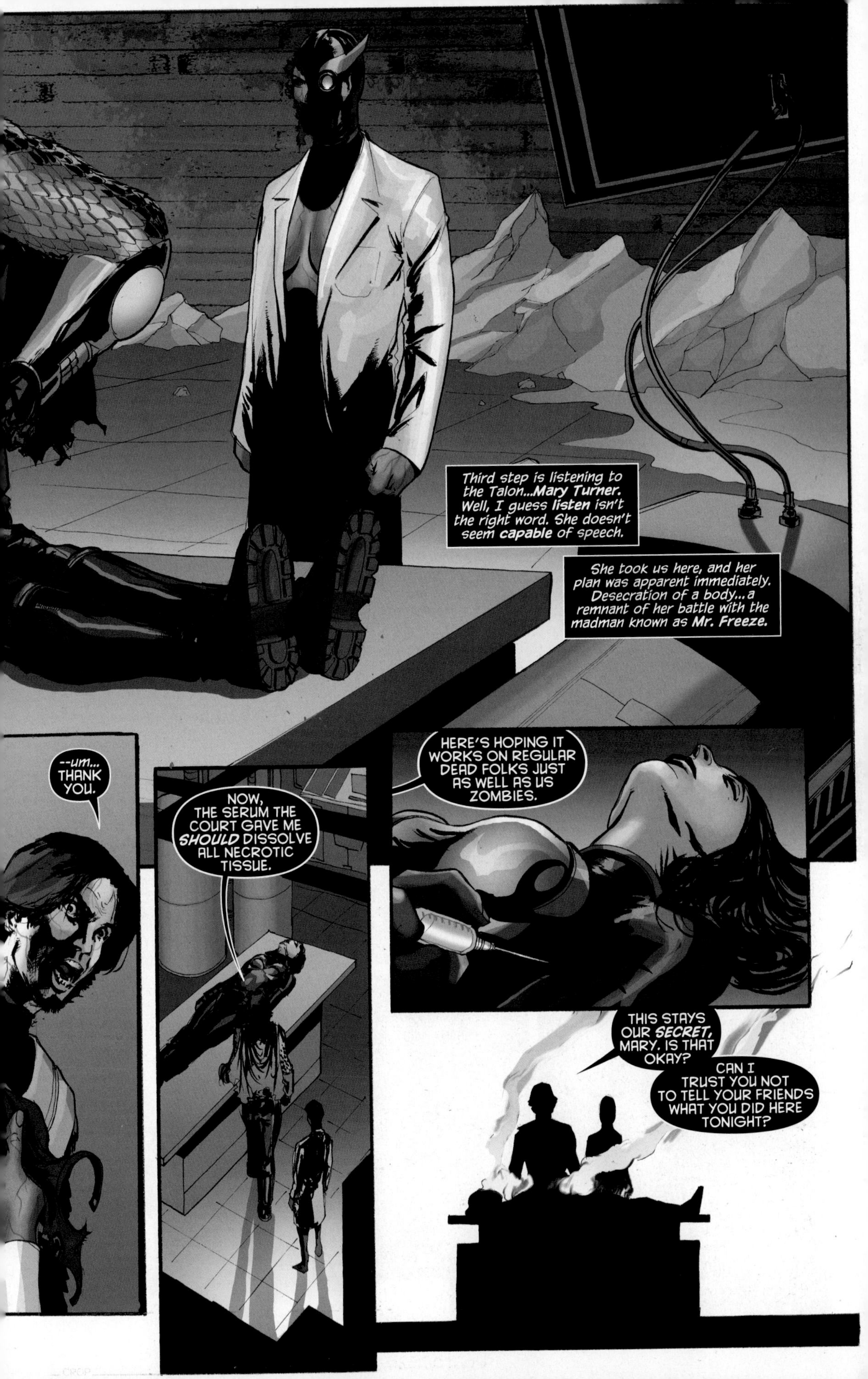

Third step is listening to the Talon...Mary Turner. Well, I guess listen isn't the right word. She doesn't seem capable of speech.
She took us here, and her plan was apparent immediately. Desecration of a body...a remnant of her battle with the madman known as Mr. Freeze.
--um... THANK YOU.
NOW, THE SERUM THE COURT GAVE ME SHOULD DISSOLVE ALL NECROTIC TISSUE.
HERE'S HOPING IT WORKS ON REGULAR DEAD FOLKS JUST AS WELL AS US ZOMBIES.
THIS STAYS OUR SECRET, MARY. IS THAT OKAY?
CAN I TRUST YOU NOT TO TELL YOUR FRIENDS WHAT YOU DID HERE TONIGHT?

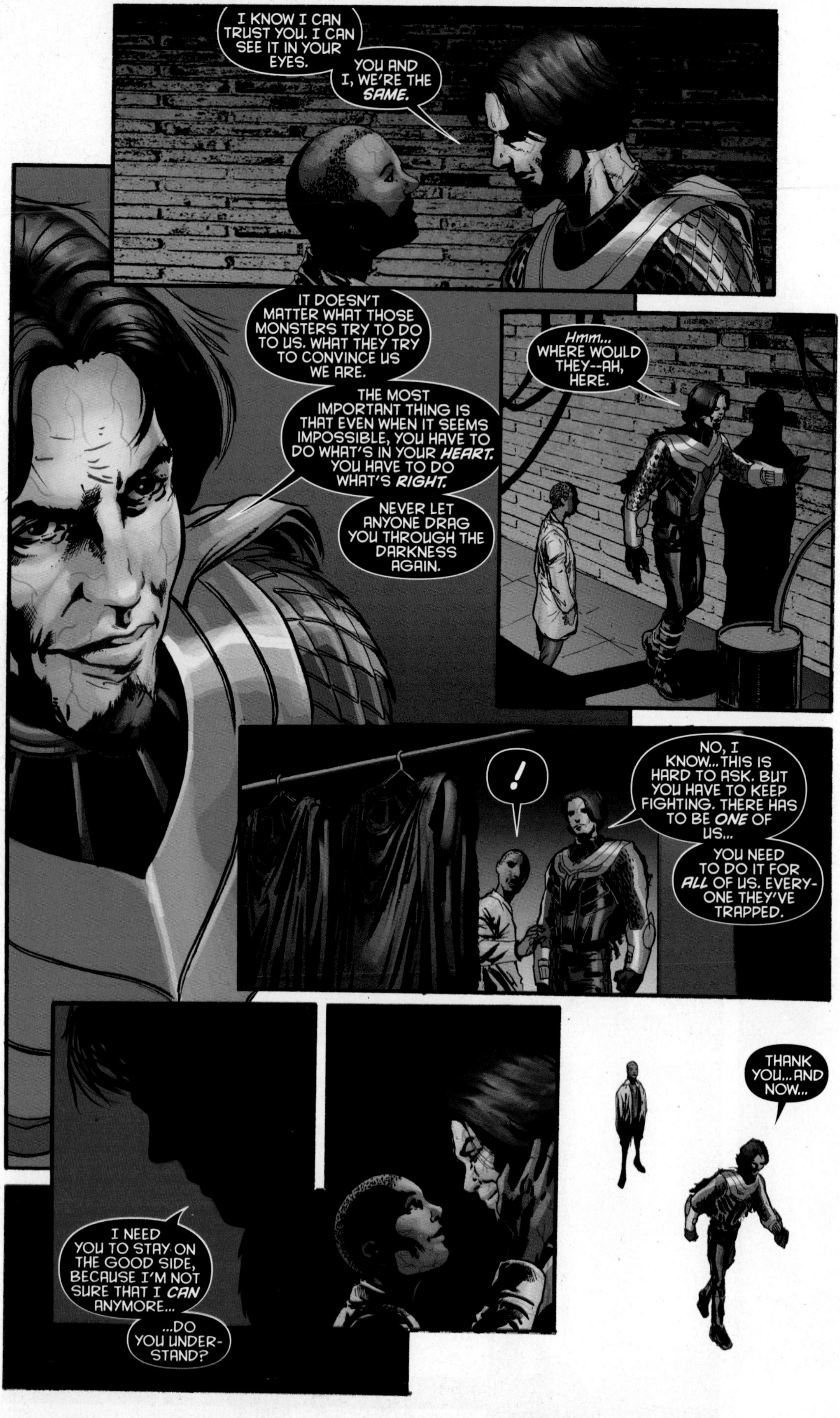
I KNOW I CAN TRUST YOU. I CAN SEE IT IN YOUR EYES.
YOU AND I, WE'RE THE *SAME.*
IT DOESN'T MATTER WHAT THOSE MONSTERS TRY TO DO TO US. WHAT THEY TRY TO CONVINCE US WE ARE.
THE MOST IMPORTANT THING IS THAT EVEN WHEN IT SEEMS IMPOSSIBLE, YOU HAVE TO DO WHAT'S IN YOUR *HEART.* YOU HAVE TO DO WHAT'S *RIGHT.*
NEVER LET ANYONE DRAG YOU THROUGH THE DARKNESS AGAIN.
Hmm... WHERE WOULD THEY--AH, HERE.
!
NO, I KNOW... THIS IS HARD TO ASK. BUT YOU HAVE TO KEEP FIGHTING. THERE HAS TO BE *ONE* OF US...
YOU NEED TO DO IT FOR *ALL* OF US. EVERYONE THEY'VE TRAPPED.
I NEED YOU TO STAY ON THE GOOD SIDE, BECAUSE I'M NOT SURE THAT I *CAN* ANYMORE...
...DO YOU UNDERSTAND?
THANK YOU...AND NOW...

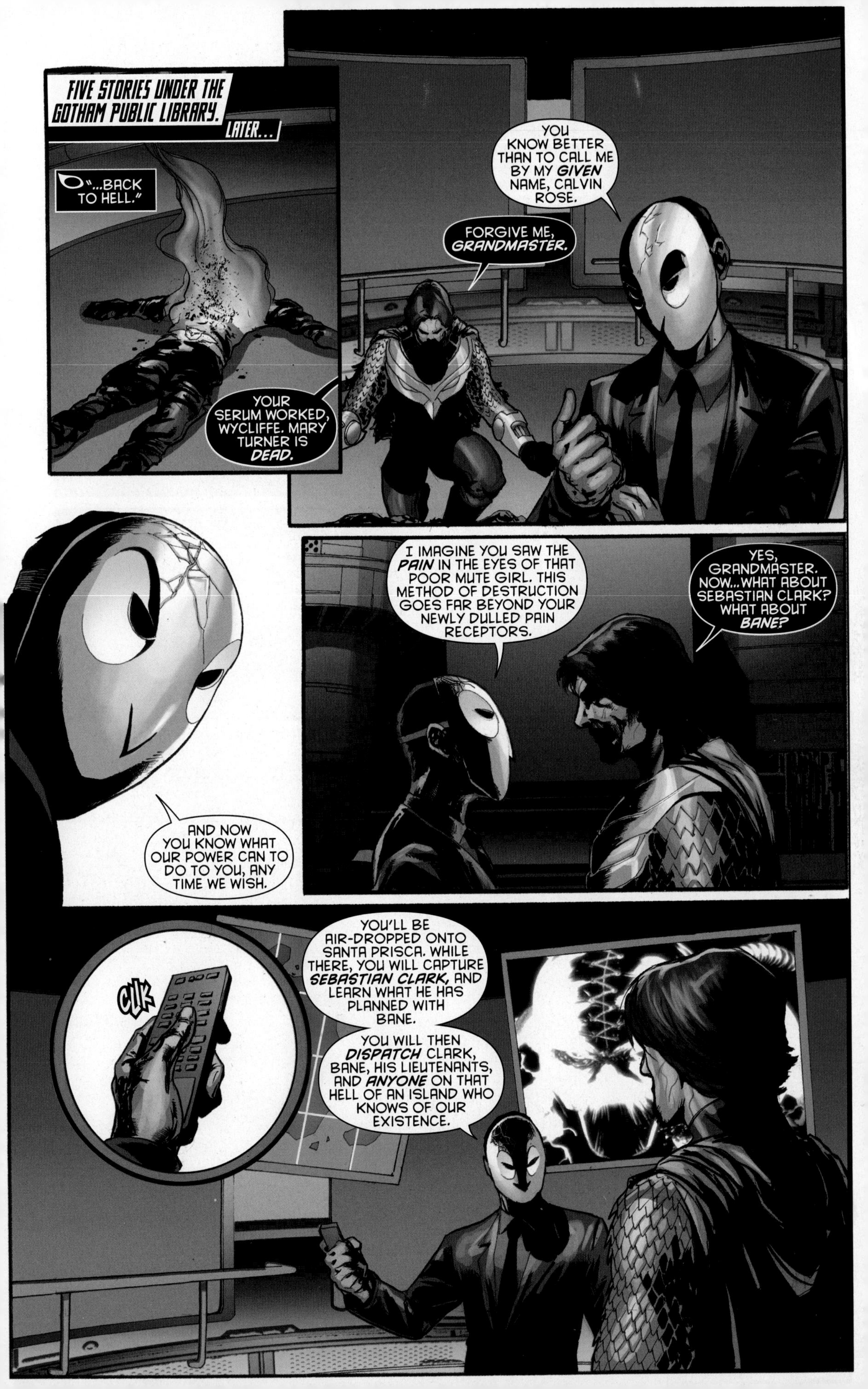
FIVE STORIES UNDER THE GOTHAM PUBLIC LIBRARY.
LATER...
"...BACK TO HELL."
YOUR SERUM WORKED, WYCLIFFE. MARY TURNER IS DEAD.
YOU KNOW BETTER THAN TO CALL ME BY MY GIVEN NAME, CALVIN ROSE.
FORGIVE ME, GRANDMASTER.
AND NOW YOU KNOW WHAT OUR POWER CAN TO DO TO YOU, ANY TIME WE WISH.
I IMAGINE YOU SAW THE PAIN IN THE EYES OF THAT POOR MUTE GIRL. THIS METHOD OF DESTRUCTION GOES FAR BEYOND YOUR NEWLY DULLED PAIN RECEPTORS.
YES, GRANDMASTER. NOW...WHAT ABOUT SEBASTIAN CLARK? WHAT ABOUT BANE?
CLIK
YOU'LL BE AIR-DROPPED ONTO SANTA PRISCA. WHILE THERE, YOU WILL CAPTURE SEBASTIAN CLARK, AND LEARN WHAT HE HAS PLANNED WITH BANE.
YOU WILL THEN DISPATCH CLARK, BANE, HIS LIEUTENANTS, AND ANYONE ON THAT HELL OF AN ISLAND WHO KNOWS OF OUR EXISTENCE.

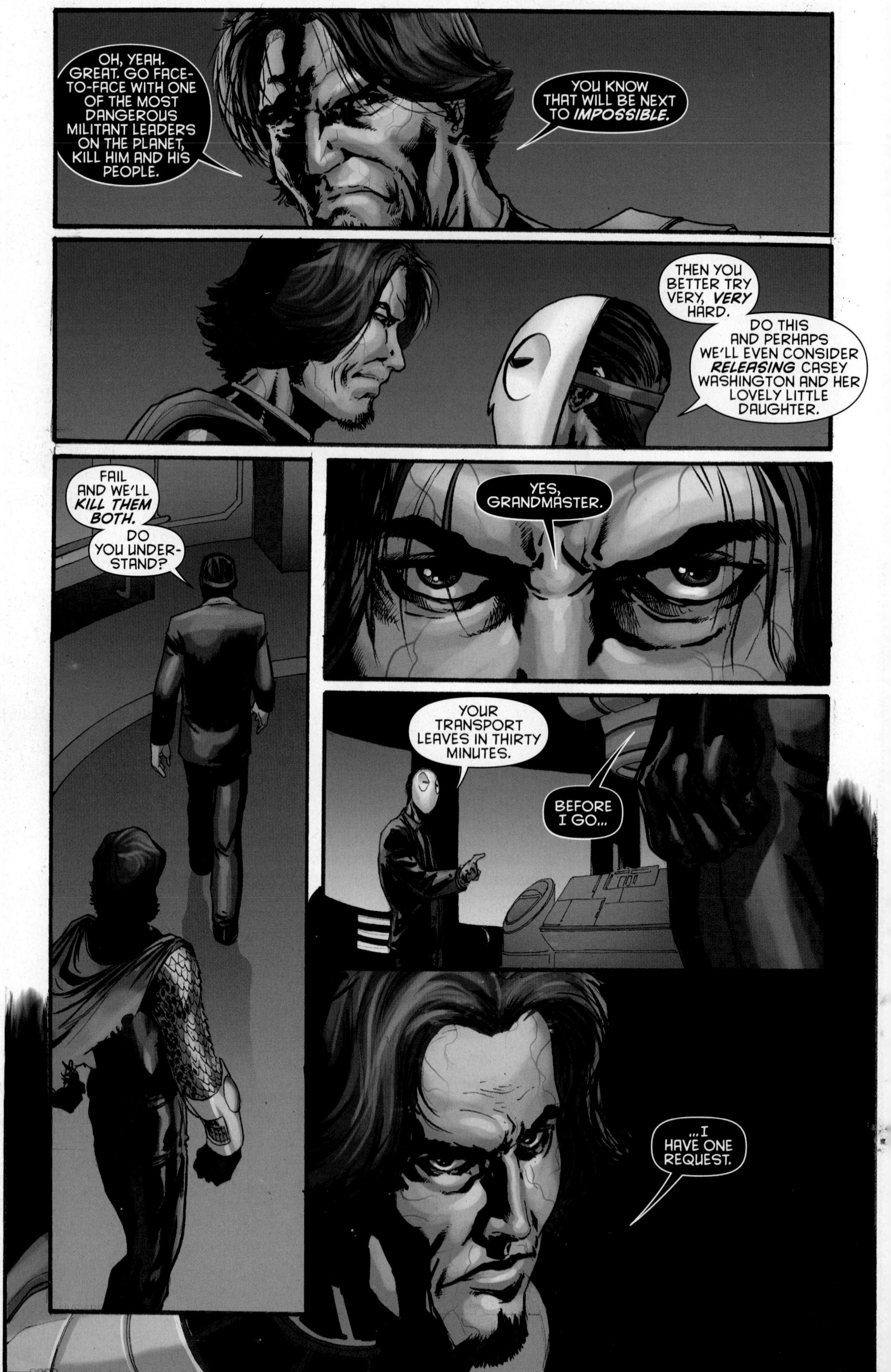
OH, YEAH. GREAT. GO FACE-TO-FACE WITH ONE OF THE MOST DANGEROUS MILITANT LEADERS ON THE PLANET, KILL HIM AND HIS PEOPLE.
YOU KNOW THAT WILL BE NEXT TO *IMPOSSIBLE.*
THEN YOU BETTER TRY VERY, *VERY* HARD.
DO THIS AND PERHAPS WE'LL EVEN CONSIDER *RELEASING* CASEY WASHINGTON AND HER LOVELY LITTLE DAUGHTER.
FAIL AND WE'LL *KILL THEM BOTH.*
DO YOU UNDER-STAND?
YES, GRANDMASTER.
YOUR TRANSPORT LEAVES IN THIRTY MINUTES.
BEFORE I GO...
...I HAVE ONE REQUEST.

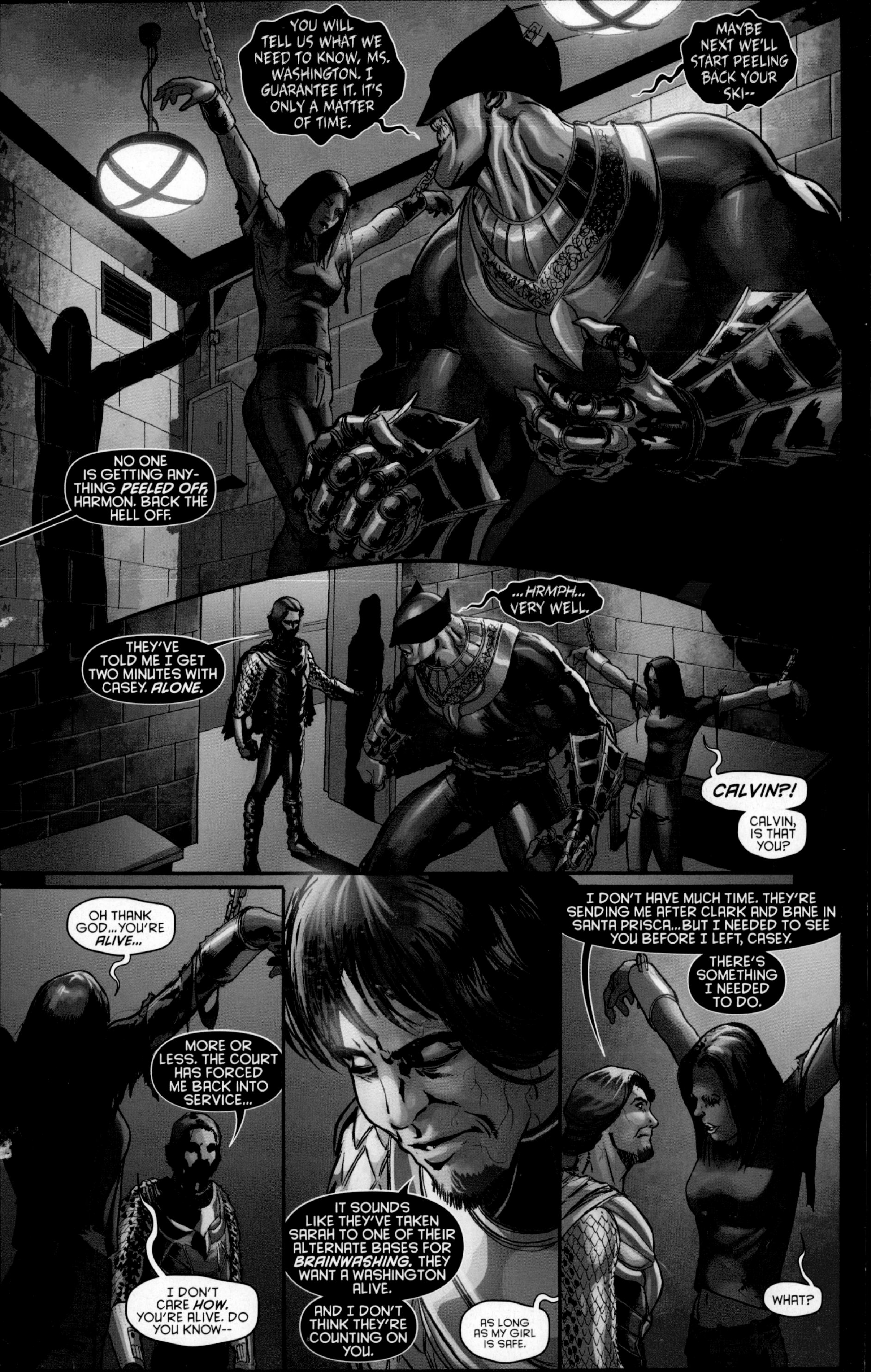
YOU WILL TELL US WHAT WE NEED TO KNOW, MS. WASHINGTON. I GUARANTEE IT. IT'S ONLY A MATTER OF TIME.
MAYBE NEXT WE'LL START PEELING BACK YOUR SKI--
NO ONE IS GETTING ANY-THING PEELED OFF, HARMON. BACK THE HELL OFF.
...HRMPH... VERY WELL.
THEY'VE TOLD ME I GET TWO MINUTES WITH CASEY. ALONE.
CALVIN?!
CALVIN, IS THAT YOU?
OH THANK GOD...YOU'RE ALIVE...
MORE OR LESS. THE COURT HAS FORCED ME BACK INTO SERVICE...
I DON'T CARE HOW. YOU'RE ALIVE. DO YOU KNOW--
IT SOUNDS LIKE THEY'VE TAKEN SARAH TO ONE OF THEIR ALTERNATE BASES FOR BRAINWASHING. THEY WANT A WASHINGTON ALIVE.
AND I DON'T THINK THEY'RE COUNTING ON YOU.
AS LONG AS MY GIRL IS SAFE.
I DON'T HAVE MUCH TIME. THEY'RE SENDING ME AFTER CLARK AND BANE IN SANTA PRISCA...BUT I NEEDED TO SEE YOU BEFORE I LEFT, CASEY.
THERE'S SOMETHING I NEEDED TO DO.
WHAT?

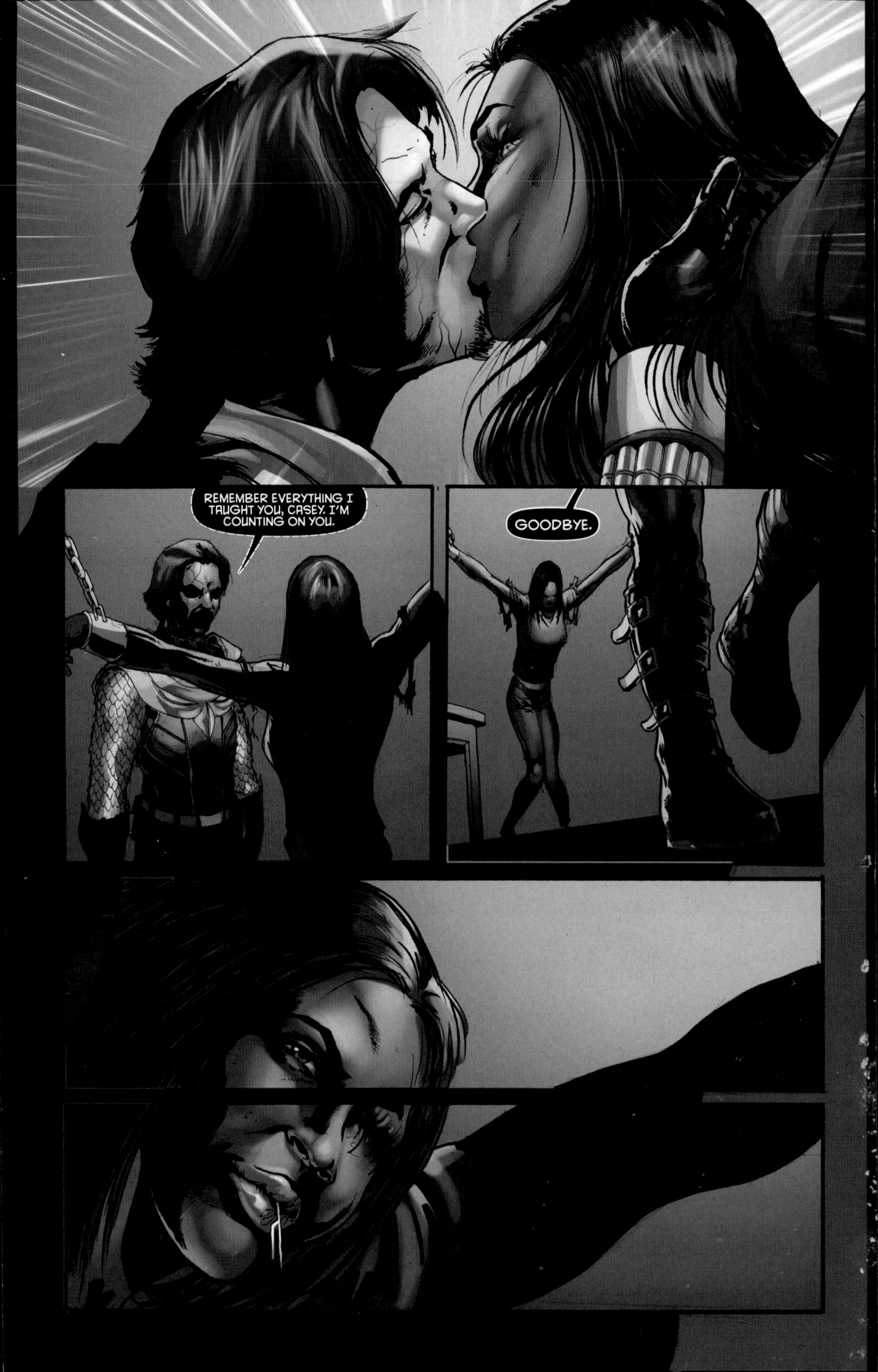
REMEMBER EVERYTHING I TAUGHT YOU, CASEY. I'M COUNTING ON YOU.
GOODBYE.

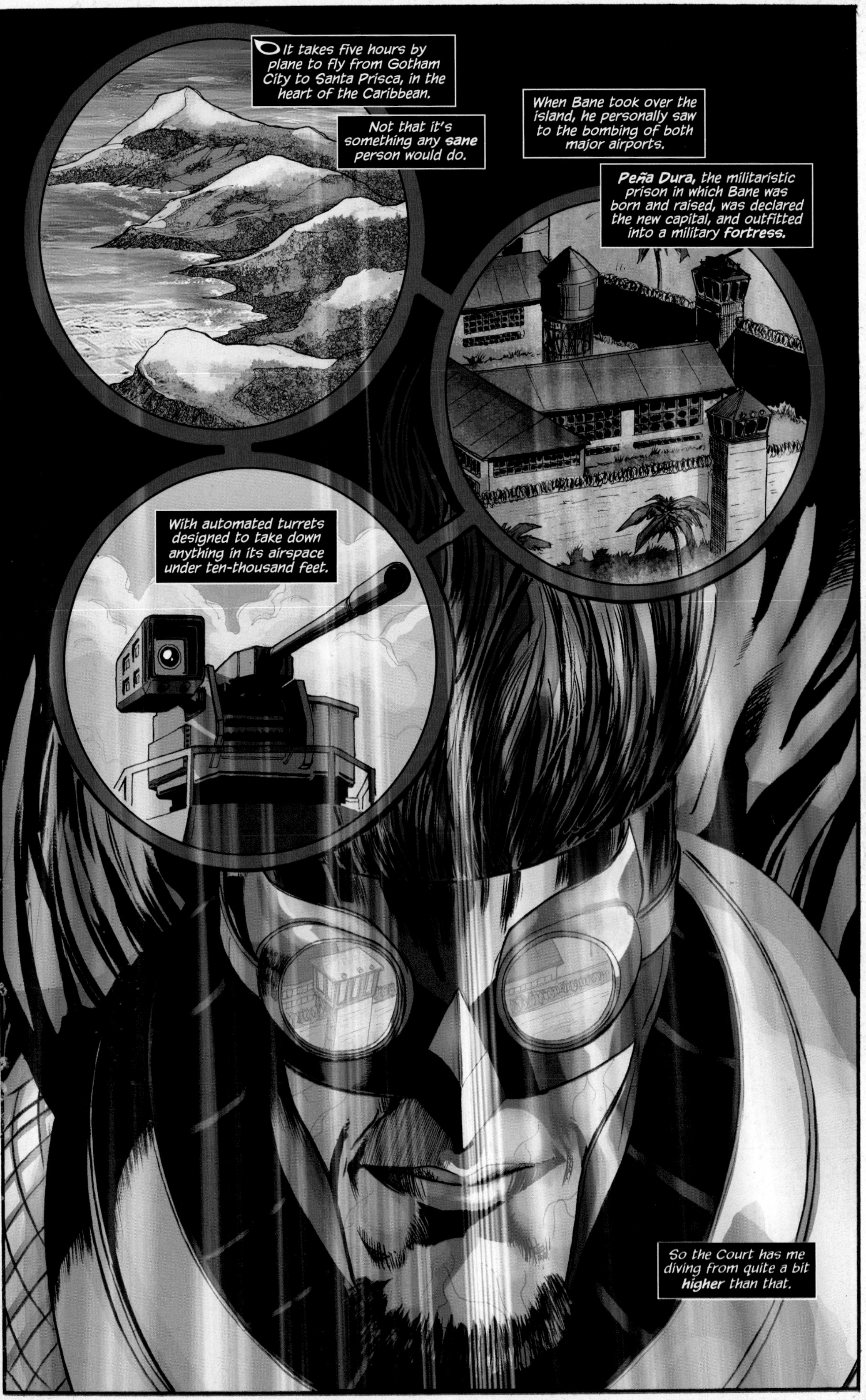
It takes five hours by plane to fly from Gotham City to Santa Prisca, in the heart of the Caribbean.
Not that it's something any **sane** person would do.
When Bane took over the island, he personally saw to the bombing of both major airports.
Peña Dura, the militaristic prison in which Bane was born and raised, was declared the new capital, and outfitted into a military **fortress.**
With automated turrets designed to take down anything in its airspace under ten-thousand feet.
So the Court has me diving from quite a bit **higher** than that.

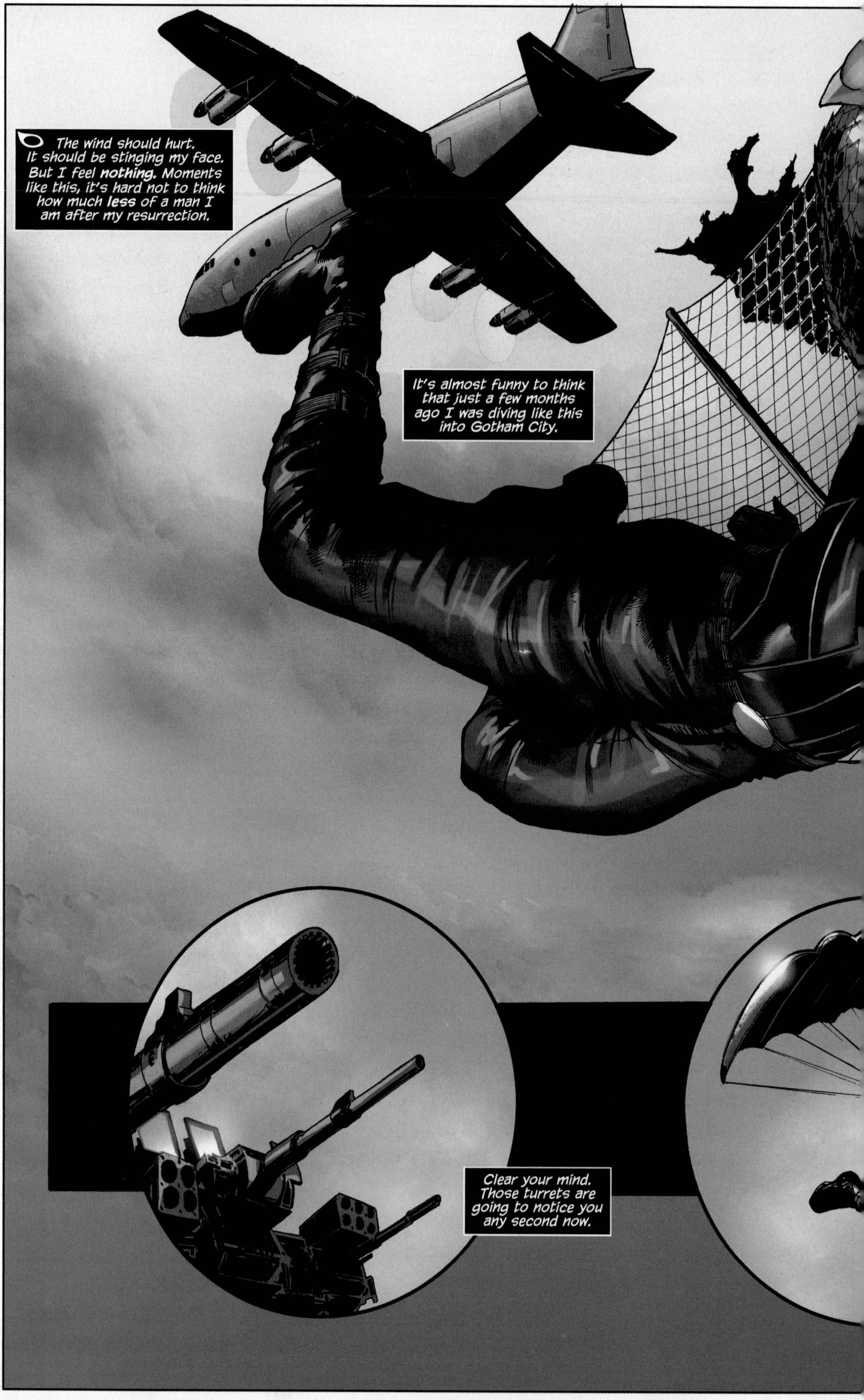
The wind should hurt. It should be stinging my face. But I feel **nothing.** Moments like this, it's hard not to think how much **less** of a man I am after my resurrection.
It's almost funny to think that just a few months ago I was diving like this into Gotham City.
Clear your mind. Those turrets are going to notice you any second now.

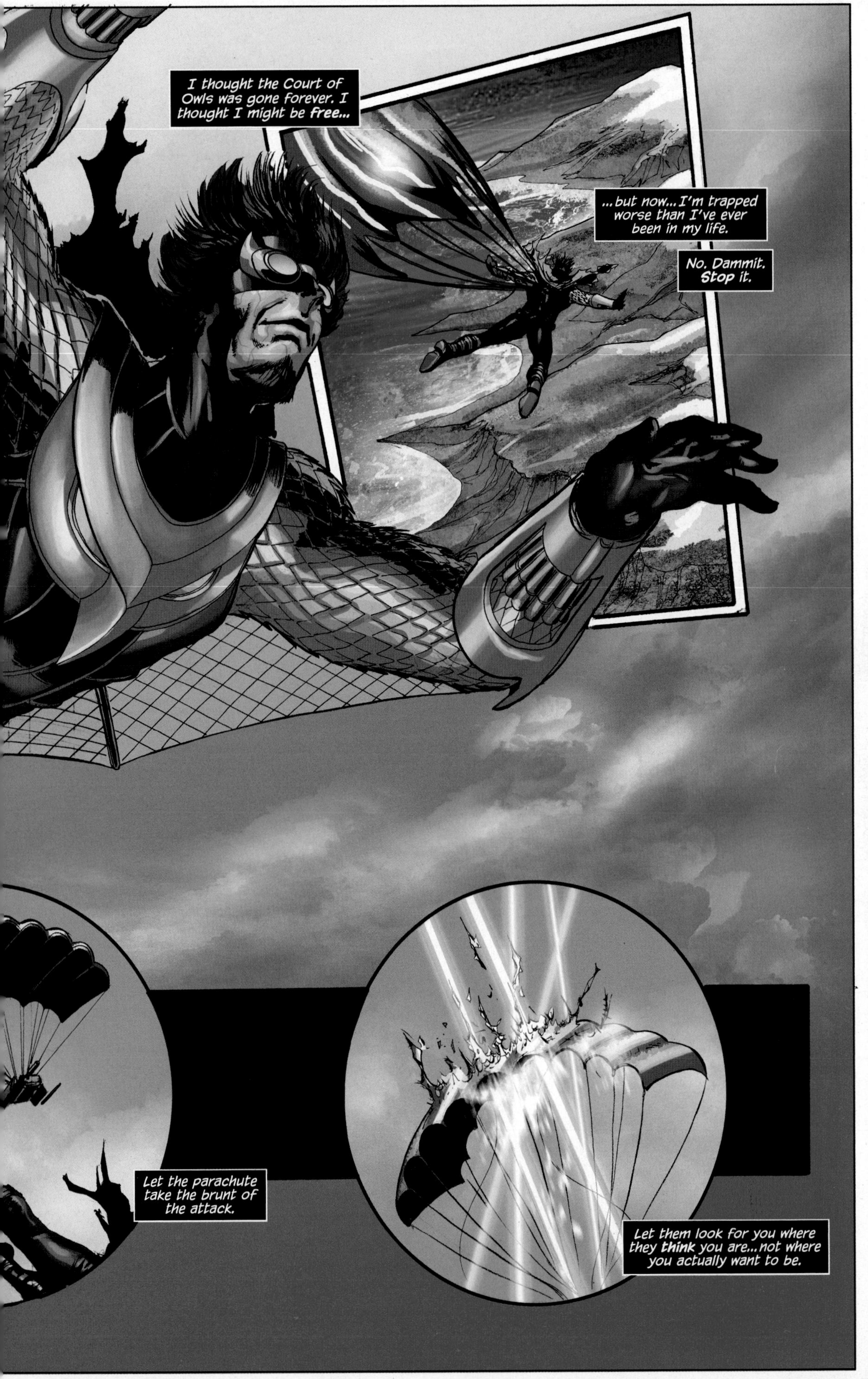

I thought the Court of Owls was gone forever. I thought I might be free...
...but now... I'm trapped worse than I've ever been in my life.
No. Dammit. Stop it.
Let the parachute take the brunt of the attack.
Let them look for you where they think you are... not where you actually want to be.

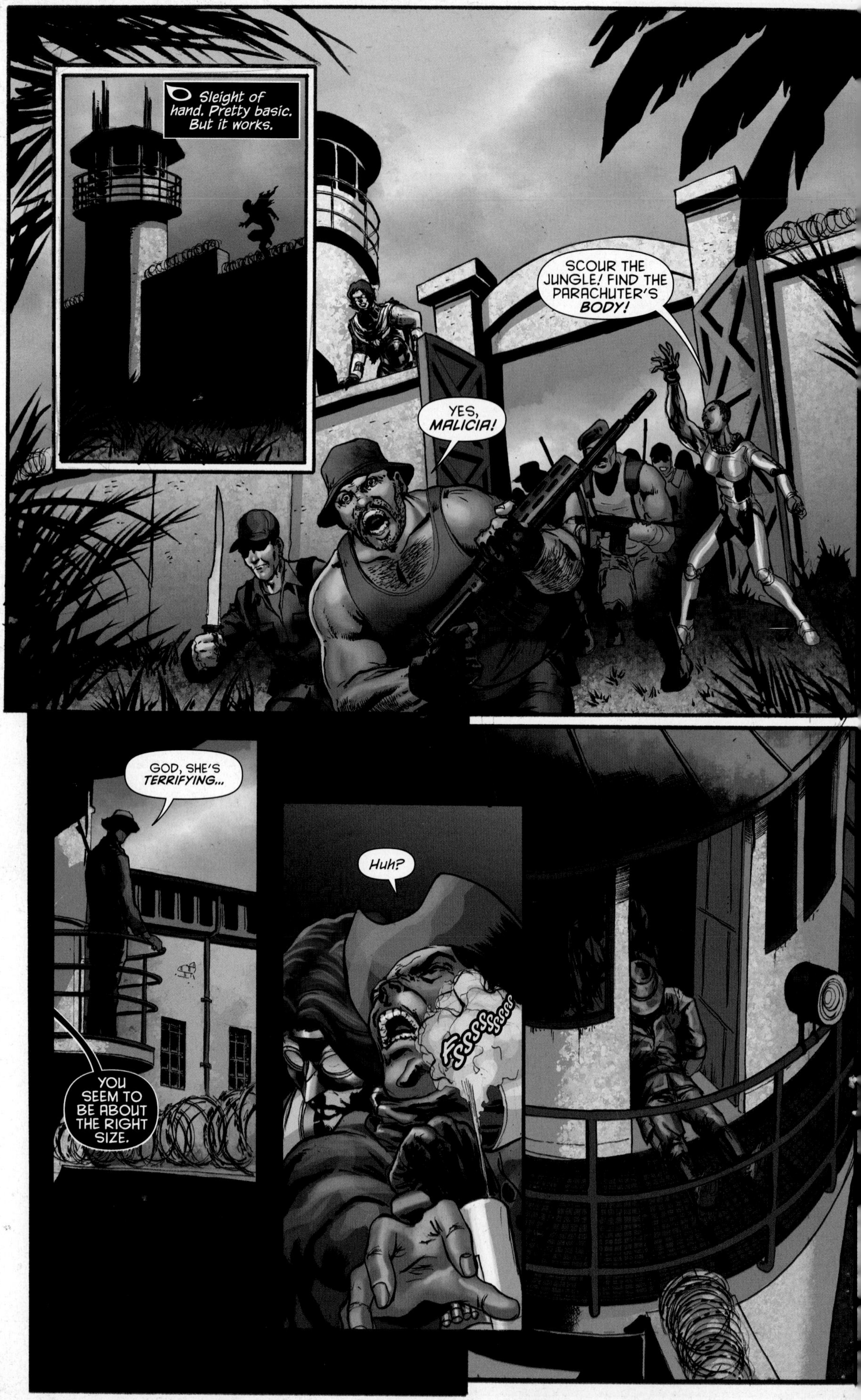
Sleight of hand. Pretty basic. But it works.
SCOUR THE JUNGLE! FIND THE PARACHUTER'S BODY!
YES, MALICIA!
GOD, SHE'S TERRIFYING...
YOU SEEM TO BE ABOUT THE RIGHT SIZE.
Huh?
FSSSSSSSSS

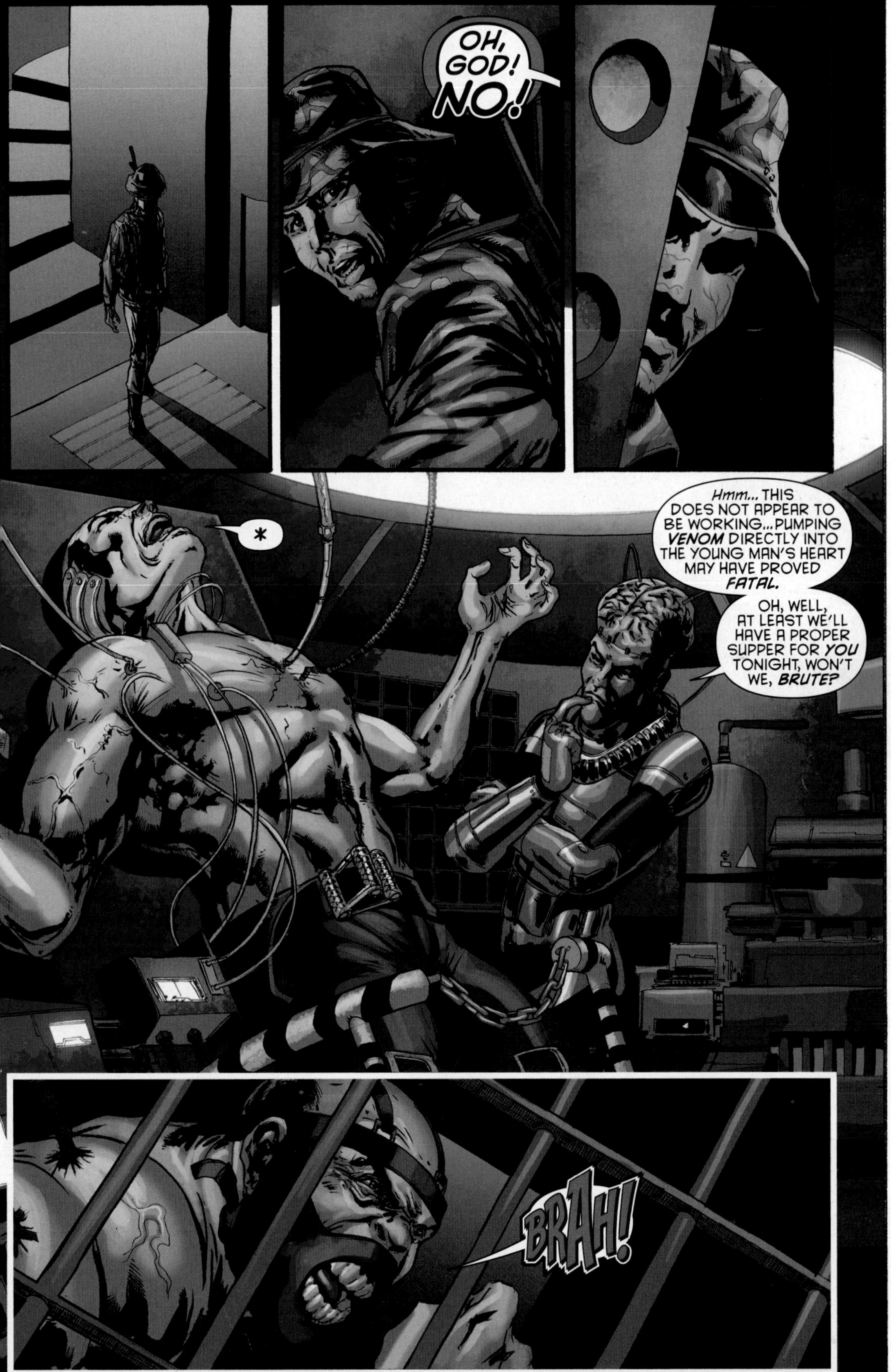
OH, GOD! NO!
*
Hmm... THIS DOES NOT APPEAR TO BE WORKING... PUMPING VENOM DIRECTLY INTO THE YOUNG MAN'S HEART MAY HAVE PROVED FATAL.
OH, WELL, AT LEAST WE'LL HAVE A PROPER SUPPER FOR YOU TONIGHT, WON'T WE, BRUTE?
BRAH!

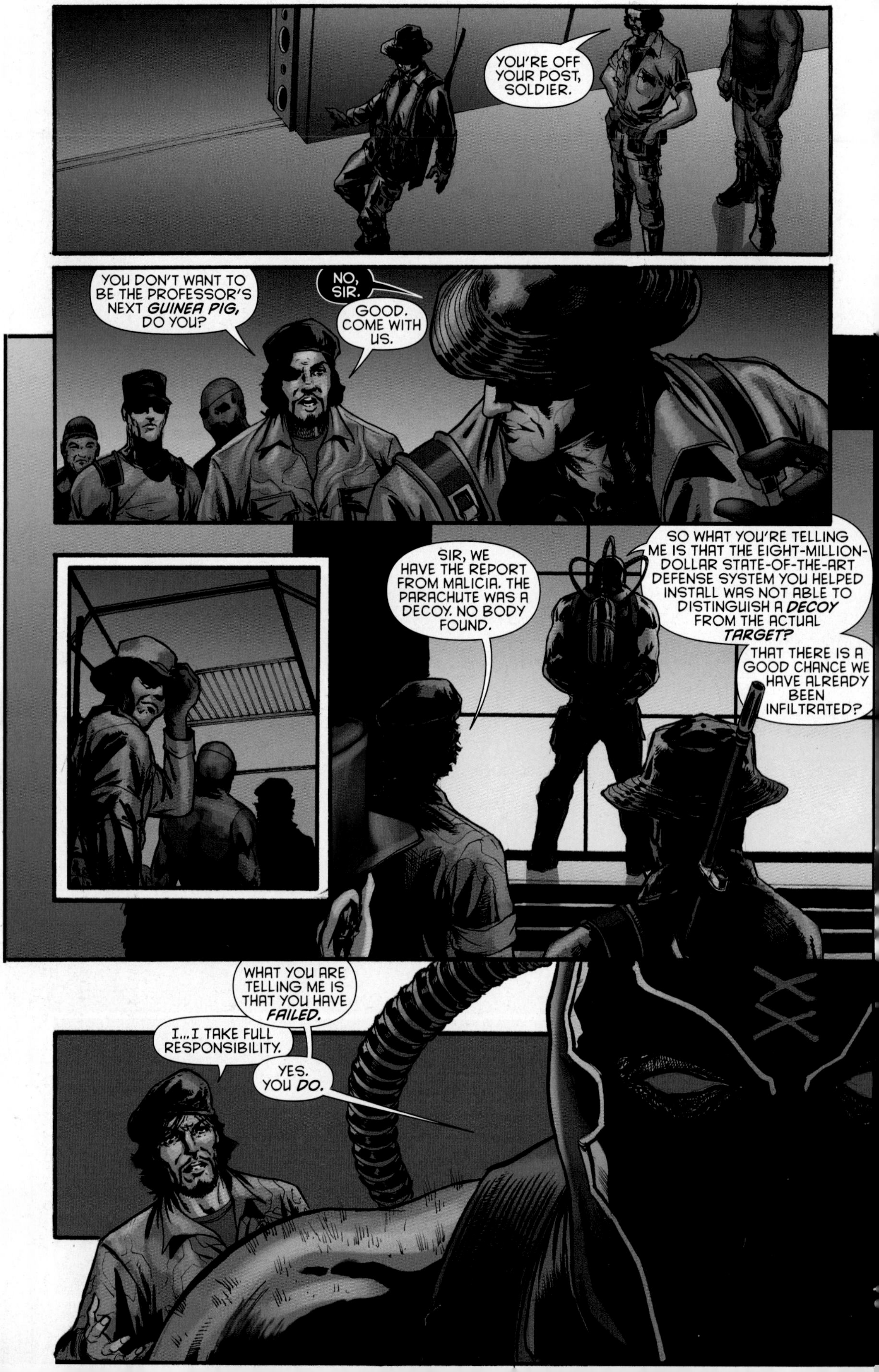
YOU'RE OFF YOUR POST, SOLDIER.
YOU DON'T WANT TO BE THE PROFESSOR'S NEXT *GUINEA PIG,* DO YOU?
NO, SIR.
GOOD. COME WITH US.
SIR, WE HAVE THE REPORT FROM MALICIA. THE PARACHUTE WAS A DECOY. NO BODY FOUND.
SO WHAT YOU'RE TELLING ME IS THAT THE EIGHT-MILLION-DOLLAR STATE-OF-THE-ART DEFENSE SYSTEM YOU HELPED INSTALL WAS NOT ABLE TO DISTINGUISH A *DECOY* FROM THE ACTUAL *TARGET?*
THAT THERE IS A GOOD CHANCE WE HAVE ALREADY BEEN INFILTRATED?
WHAT YOU ARE TELLING ME IS THAT YOU HAVE *FAILED.*
I...I TAKE FULL RESPONSIBILITY.
YES. YOU *DO.*

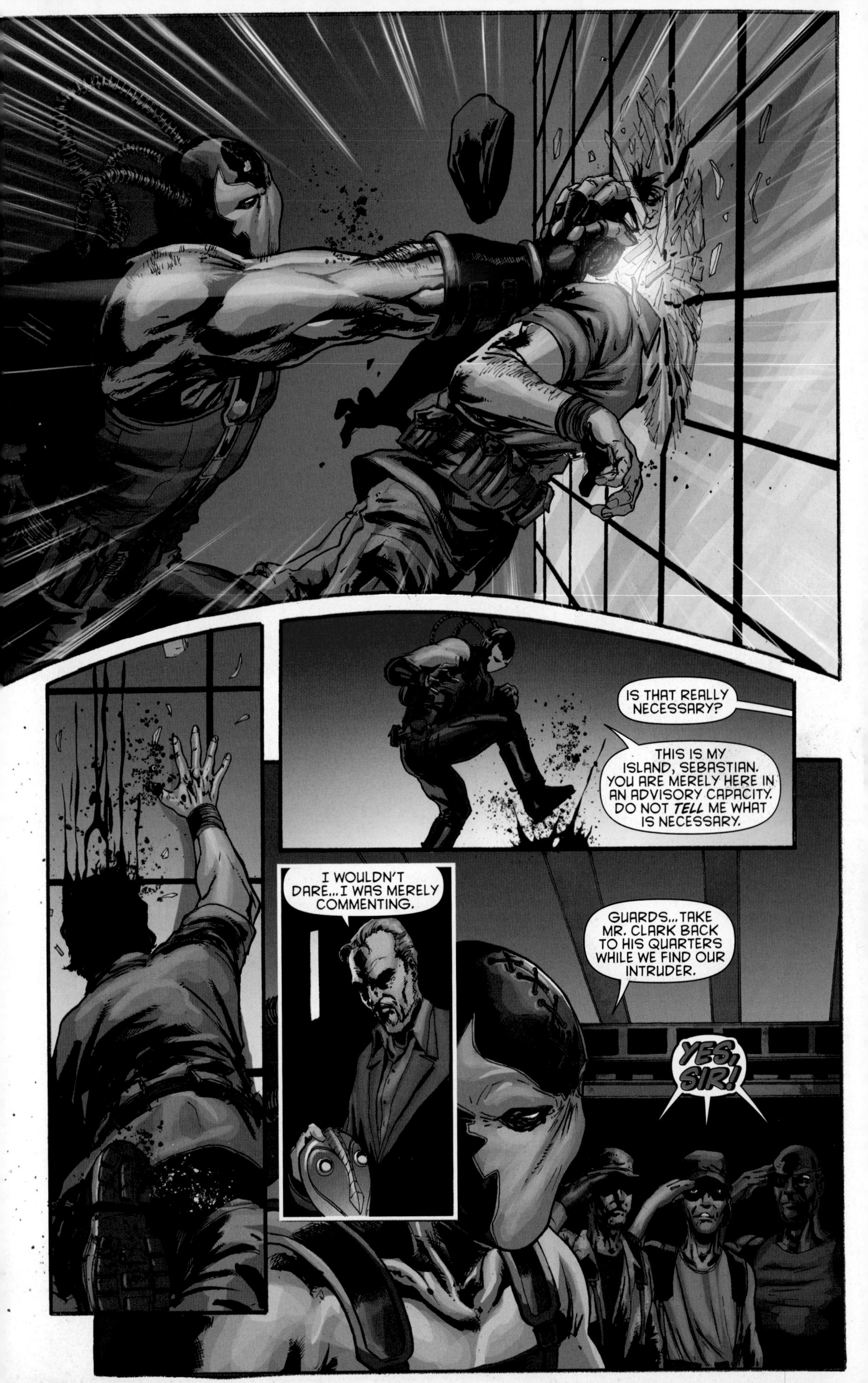
IS THAT REALLY NECESSARY?
THIS IS MY ISLAND, SEBASTIAN. YOU ARE MERELY HERE IN AN ADVISORY CAPACITY. DO NOT *TELL* ME WHAT IS NECESSARY.
I WOULDN'T DARE...I WAS MERELY COMMENTING.
GUARDS...TAKE MR. CLARK BACK TO HIS QUARTERS WHILE WE FIND OUR INTRUDER.
YES, SIR!

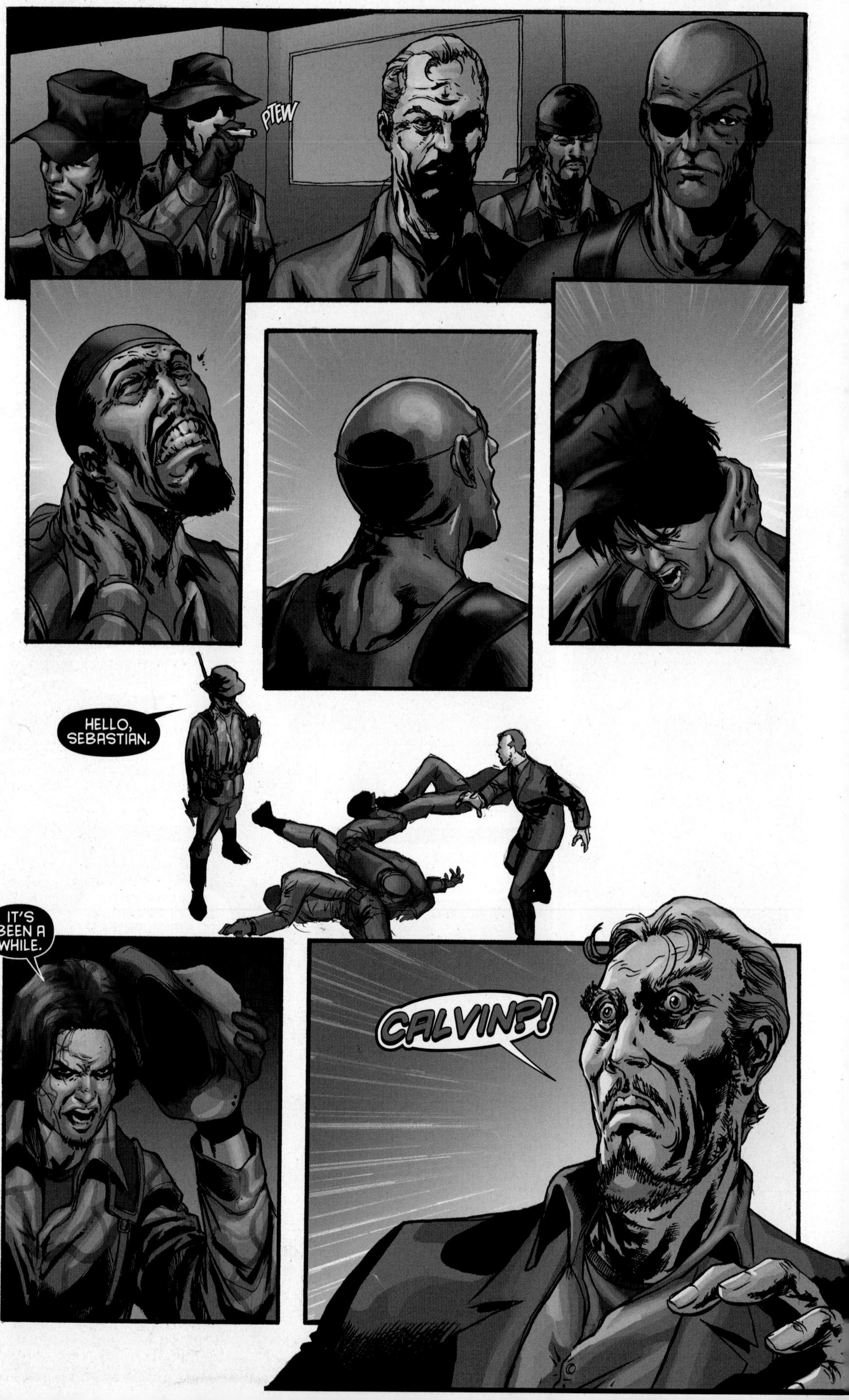
PTEW
HELLO, SEBASTIAN.
IT'S BEEN A WHILE.
CALVIN?!

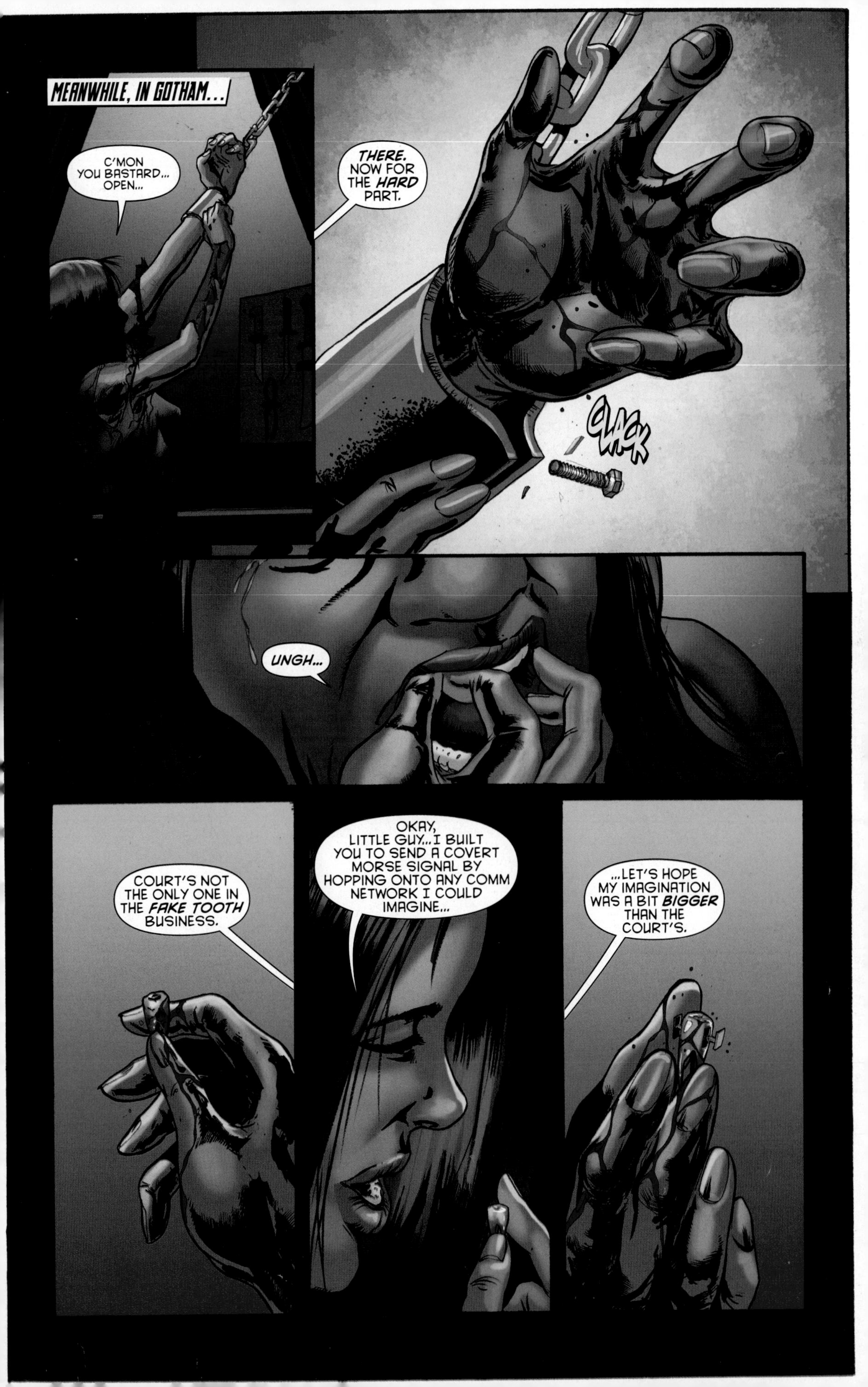
MEANWHILE, IN GOTHAM...
C'MON YOU BASTARD... OPEN...
THERE. NOW FOR THE HARD PART.
CLACK
UNGH...
COURT'S NOT THE ONLY ONE IN THE FAKE TOOTH BUSINESS.
OKAY, LITTLE GUY... I BUILT YOU TO SEND A COVERT MORSE SIGNAL BY HOPPING ONTO ANY COMM NETWORK I COULD IMAGINE...
...LET'S HOPE MY IMAGINATION WAS A BIT BIGGER THAN THE COURT'S.

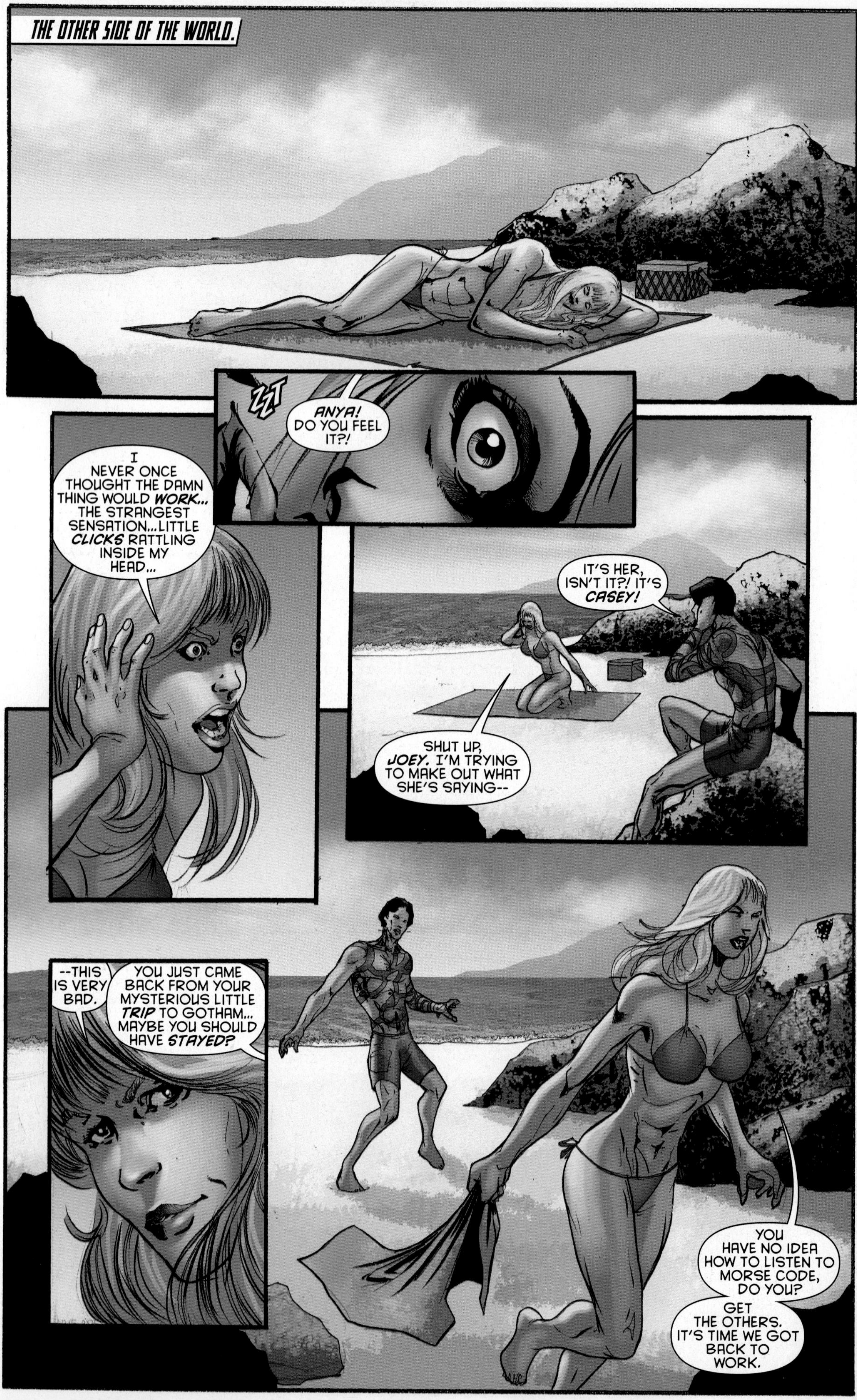
THE OTHER SIDE OF THE WORLD.
ZZZT
ANYA! DO YOU FEEL IT?!
I NEVER ONCE THOUGHT THE DAMN THING WOULD WORK... THE STRANGEST SENSATION... LITTLE CLICKS RATTLING INSIDE MY HEAD...
IT'S HER, ISN'T IT?! IT'S CASEY!
SHUT UP, JOEY. I'M TRYING TO MAKE OUT WHAT SHE'S SAYING--
--THIS IS VERY BAD.
YOU JUST CAME BACK FROM YOUR MYSTERIOUS LITTLE TRIP TO GOTHAM... MAYBE YOU SHOULD HAVE STAYED?
YOU HAVE NO IDEA HOW TO LISTEN TO MORSE CODE, DO YOU?
GET THE OTHERS. IT'S TIME WE GOT BACK TO WORK.

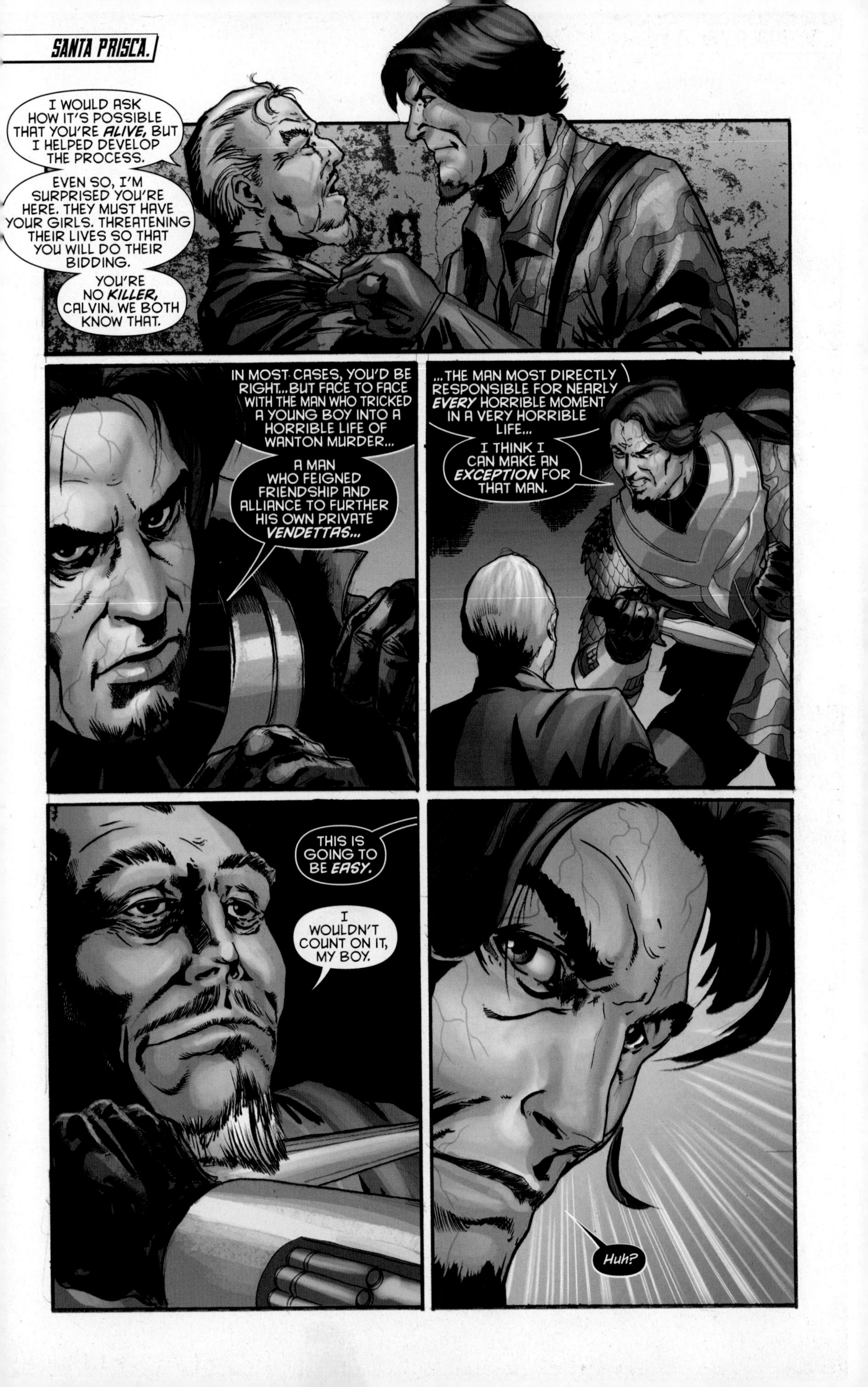
SANTA PRISCA.
I WOULD ASK HOW IT'S POSSIBLE THAT YOU'RE ALIVE, BUT I HELPED DEVELOP THE PROCESS.
EVEN SO, I'M SURPRISED YOU'RE HERE. THEY MUST HAVE YOUR GIRLS. THREATENING THEIR LIVES SO THAT YOU WILL DO THEIR BIDDING.
YOU'RE NO KILLER, CALVIN. WE BOTH KNOW THAT.
IN MOST CASES, YOU'D BE RIGHT...BUT FACE TO FACE WITH THE MAN WHO TRICKED A YOUNG BOY INTO A HORRIBLE LIFE OF WANTON MURDER...
A MAN WHO FEIGNED FRIENDSHIP AND ALLIANCE TO FURTHER HIS OWN PRIVATE VENDETTAS...
...THE MAN MOST DIRECTLY RESPONSIBLE FOR NEARLY EVERY HORRIBLE MOMENT IN A VERY HORRIBLE LIFE...
I THINK I CAN MAKE AN EXCEPTION FOR THAT MAN.
THIS IS GOING TO BE EASY.
I WOULDN'T COUNT ON IT, MY BOY.
Huh?

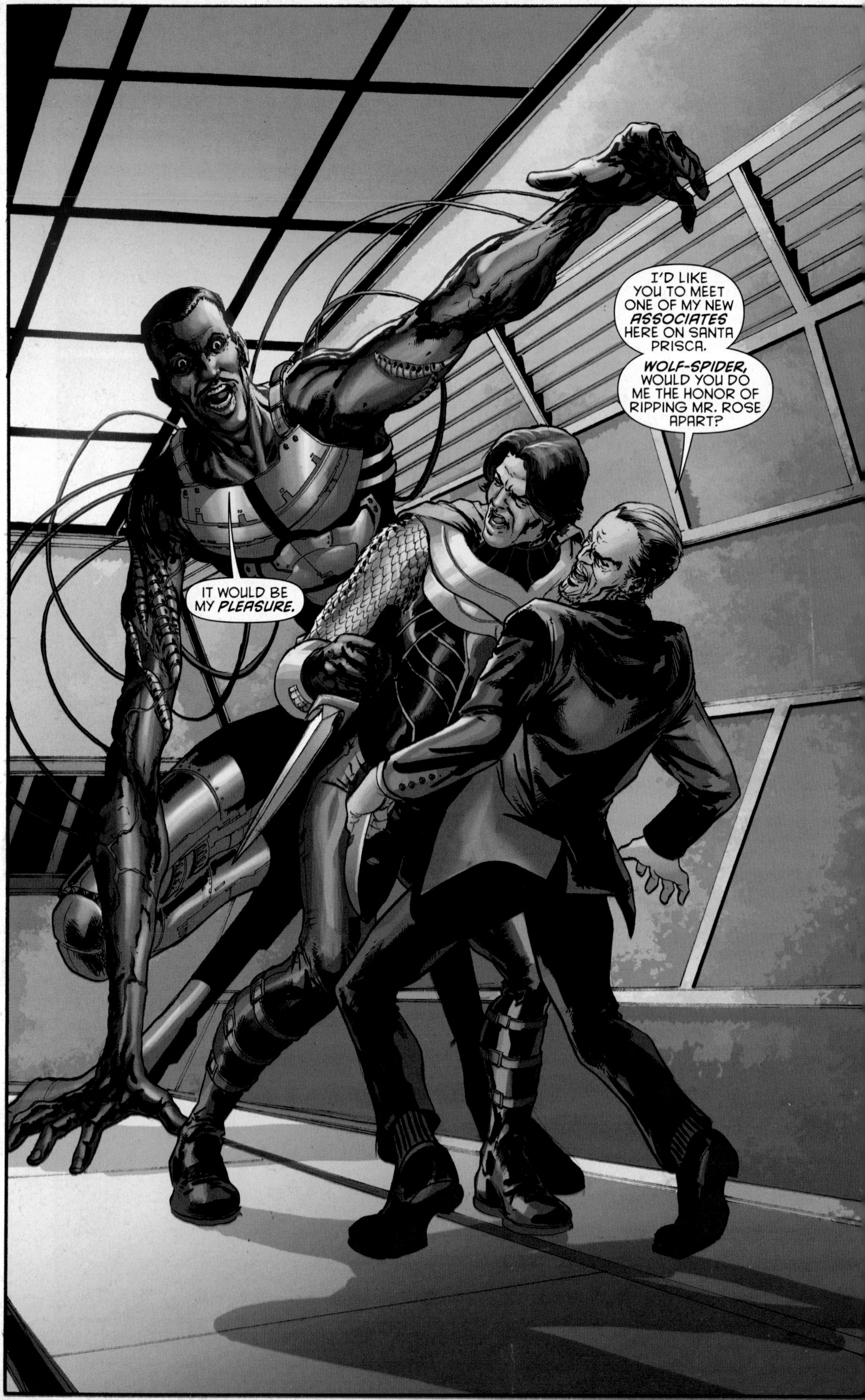
I'D LIKE YOU TO MEET ONE OF MY NEW ASSOCIATES HERE ON SANTA PRISCA.
WOLF-SPIDER, WOULD YOU DO ME THE HONOR OF RIPPING MR. ROSE APART?
IT WOULD BE MY PLEASURE.

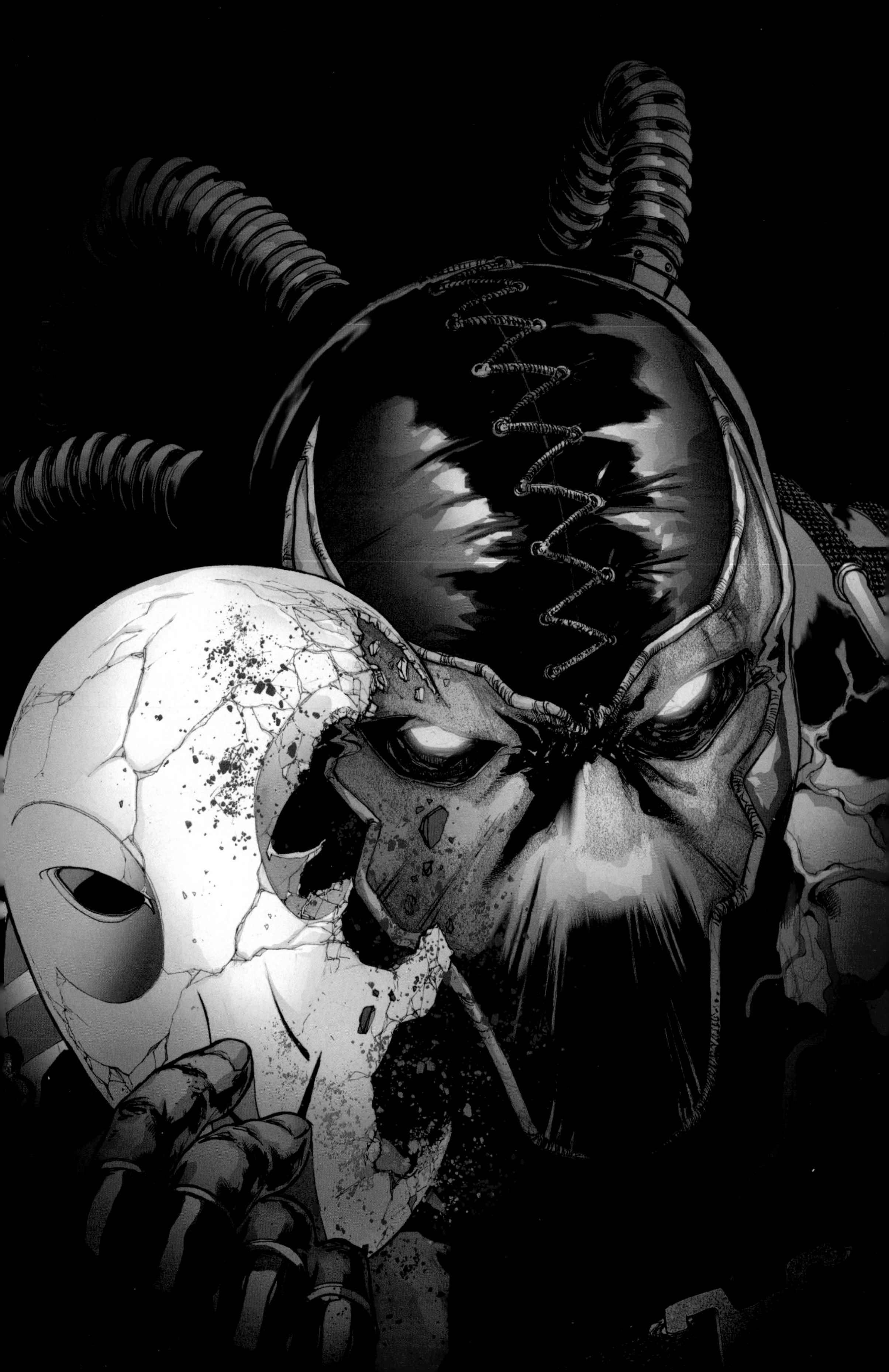

JAMES TYNION IV writer MIGUEL SEPULVEDA & SZYMON KUDRANSKI artists cover art by MIGUEL SEPULVEDA & RAIN BEREDO

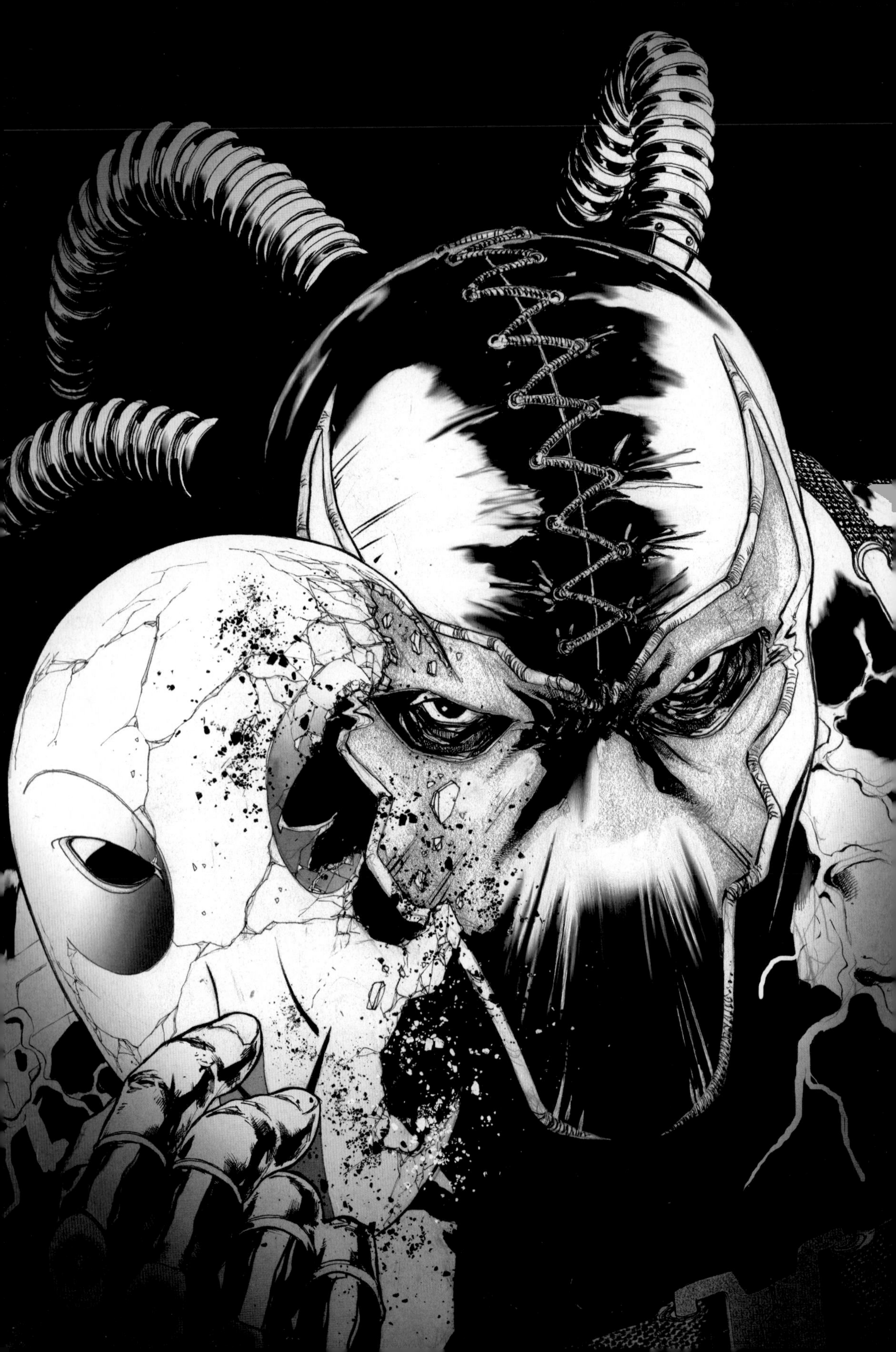

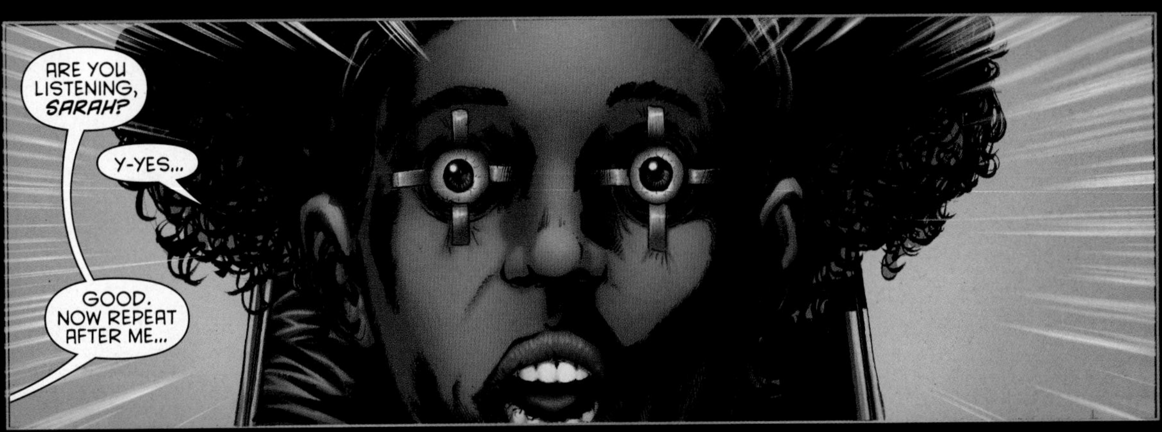
ARE YOU LISTENING, *SARAH?*
Y-YES...
GOOD. NOW REPEAT AFTER ME...
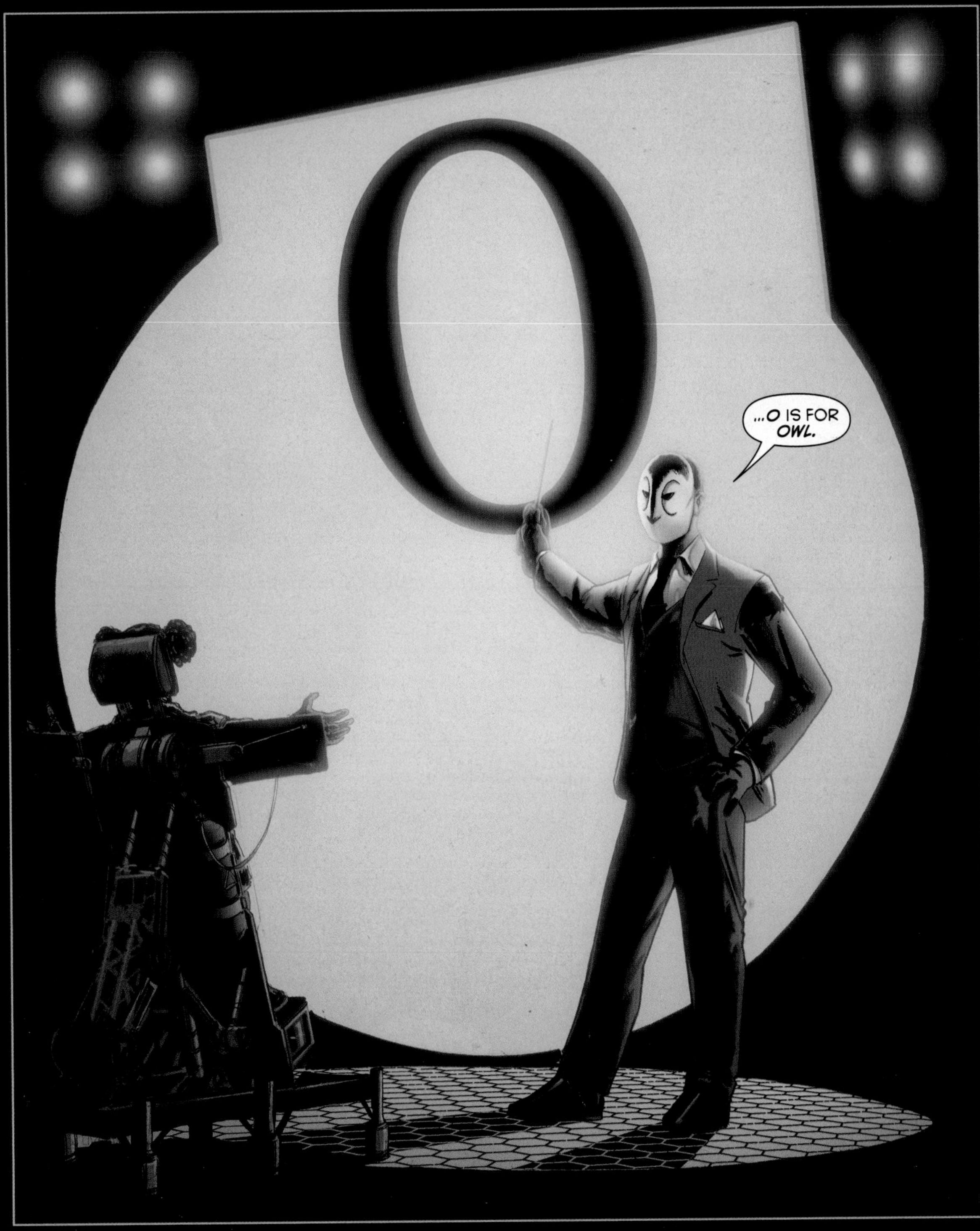
O
...O IS FOR *OWL.*

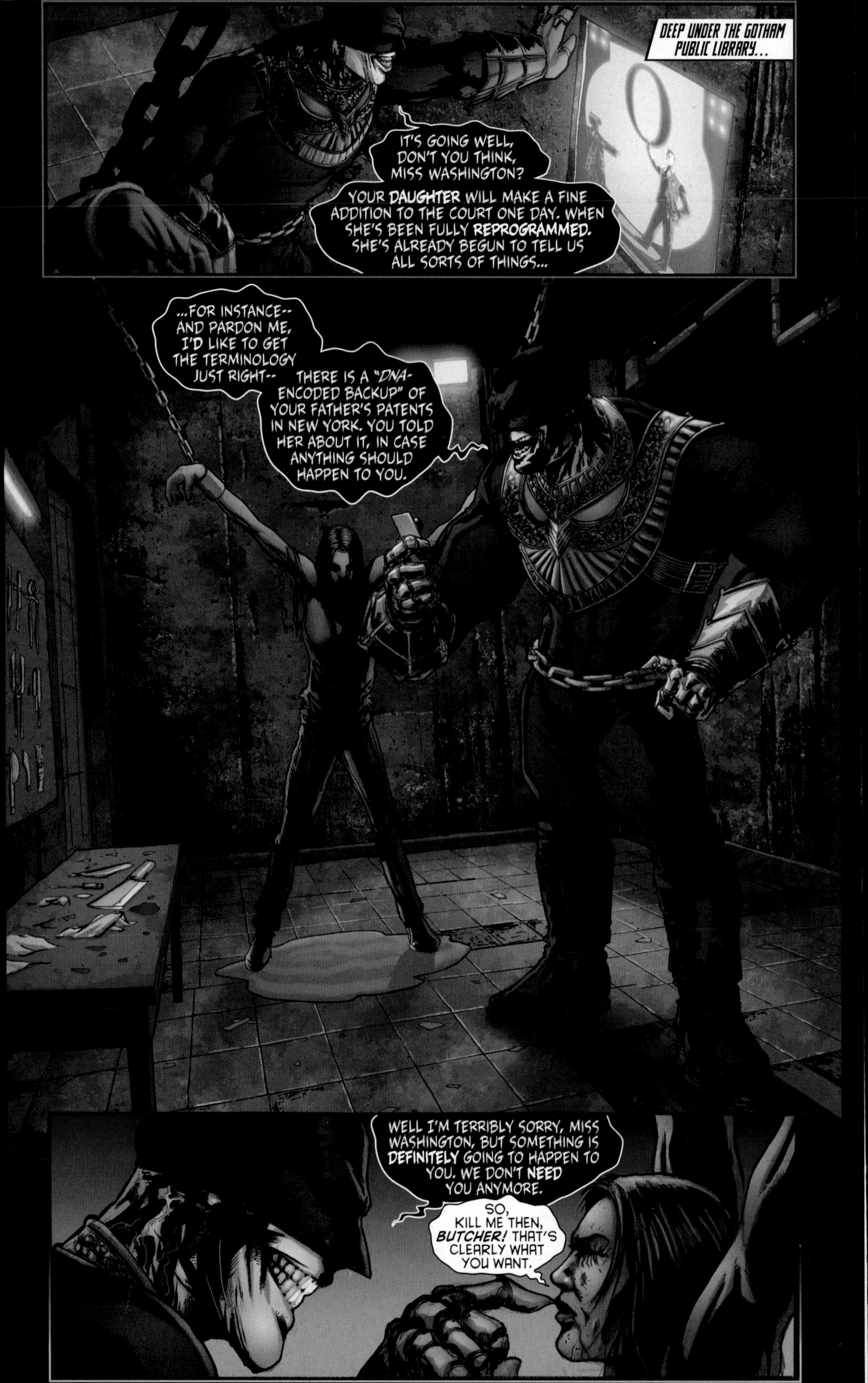
DEEP UNDER THE GOTHAM PUBLIC LIBRARY...
IT'S GOING WELL, DON'T YOU THINK, MISS WASHINGTON?
YOUR DAUGHTER WILL MAKE A FINE ADDITION TO THE COURT ONE DAY. WHEN SHE'S BEEN FULLY REPROGRAMMED. SHE'S ALREADY BEGUN TO TELL US ALL SORTS OF THINGS...
...FOR INSTANCE-- AND PARDON ME, I'D LIKE TO GET THE TERMINOLOGY JUST RIGHT--
THERE IS A "DNA-ENCODED BACKUP" OF YOUR FATHER'S PATENTS IN NEW YORK. YOU TOLD HER ABOUT IT, IN CASE ANYTHING SHOULD HAPPEN TO YOU.
WELL I'M TERRIBLY SORRY, MISS WASHINGTON, BUT SOMETHING IS DEFINITELY GOING TO HAPPEN TO YOU. WE DON'T NEED YOU ANYMORE.
SO, KILL ME THEN, BUTCHER! THAT'S CLEARLY WHAT YOU WANT.

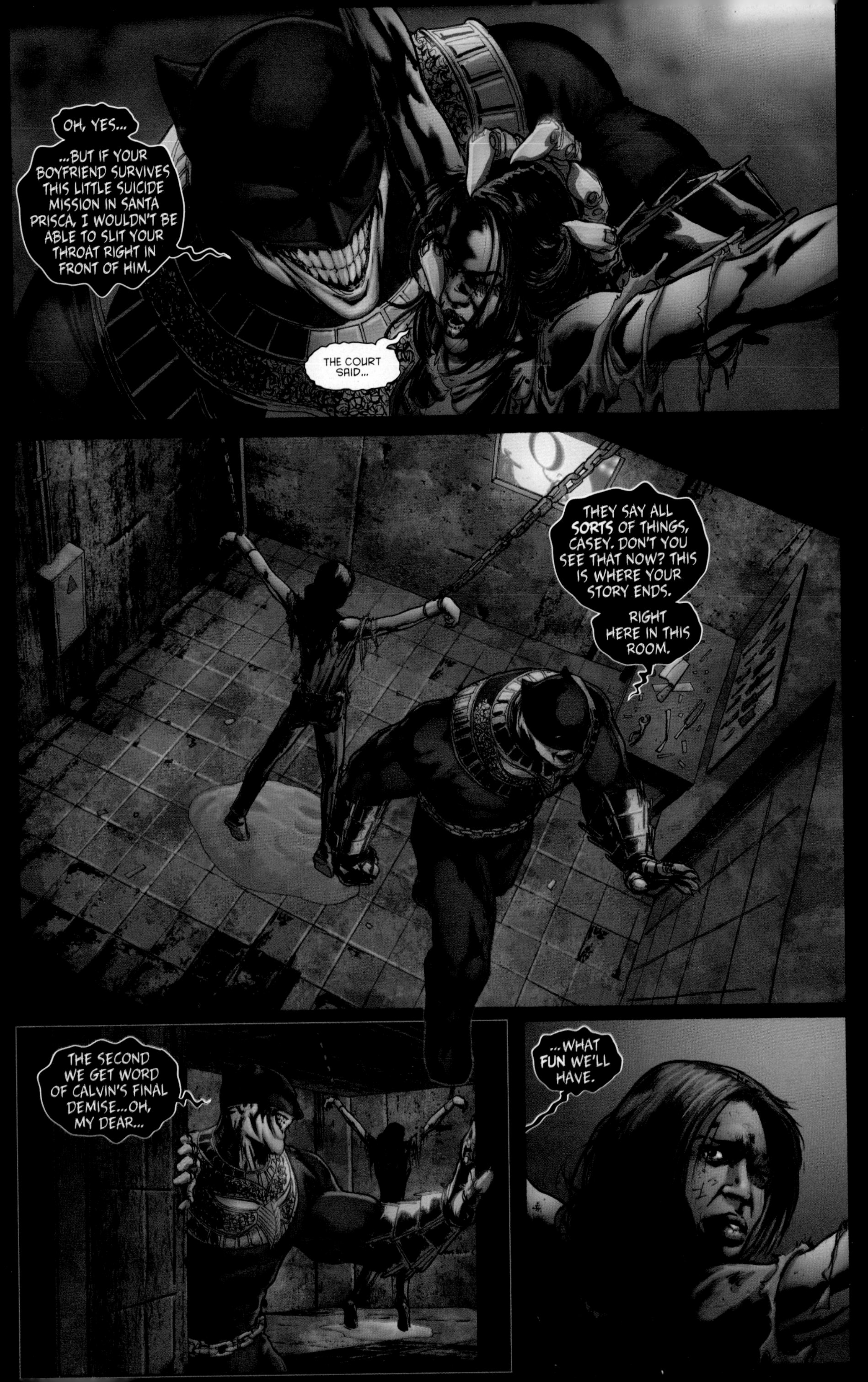
OH, YES...
...BUT IF YOUR BOYFRIEND SURVIVES THIS LITTLE SUICIDE MISSION IN SANTA PRISCA, I WOULDN'T BE ABLE TO SLIT YOUR THROAT RIGHT IN FRONT OF HIM.
THE COURT SAID...
THEY SAY ALL SORTS OF THINGS, CASEY. DON'T YOU SEE THAT NOW? THIS IS WHERE YOUR STORY ENDS.
RIGHT HERE IN THIS ROOM.
THE SECOND WE GET WORD OF CALVIN'S FINAL DEMISE...OH, MY DEAR...
...WHAT FUN WE'LL HAVE.

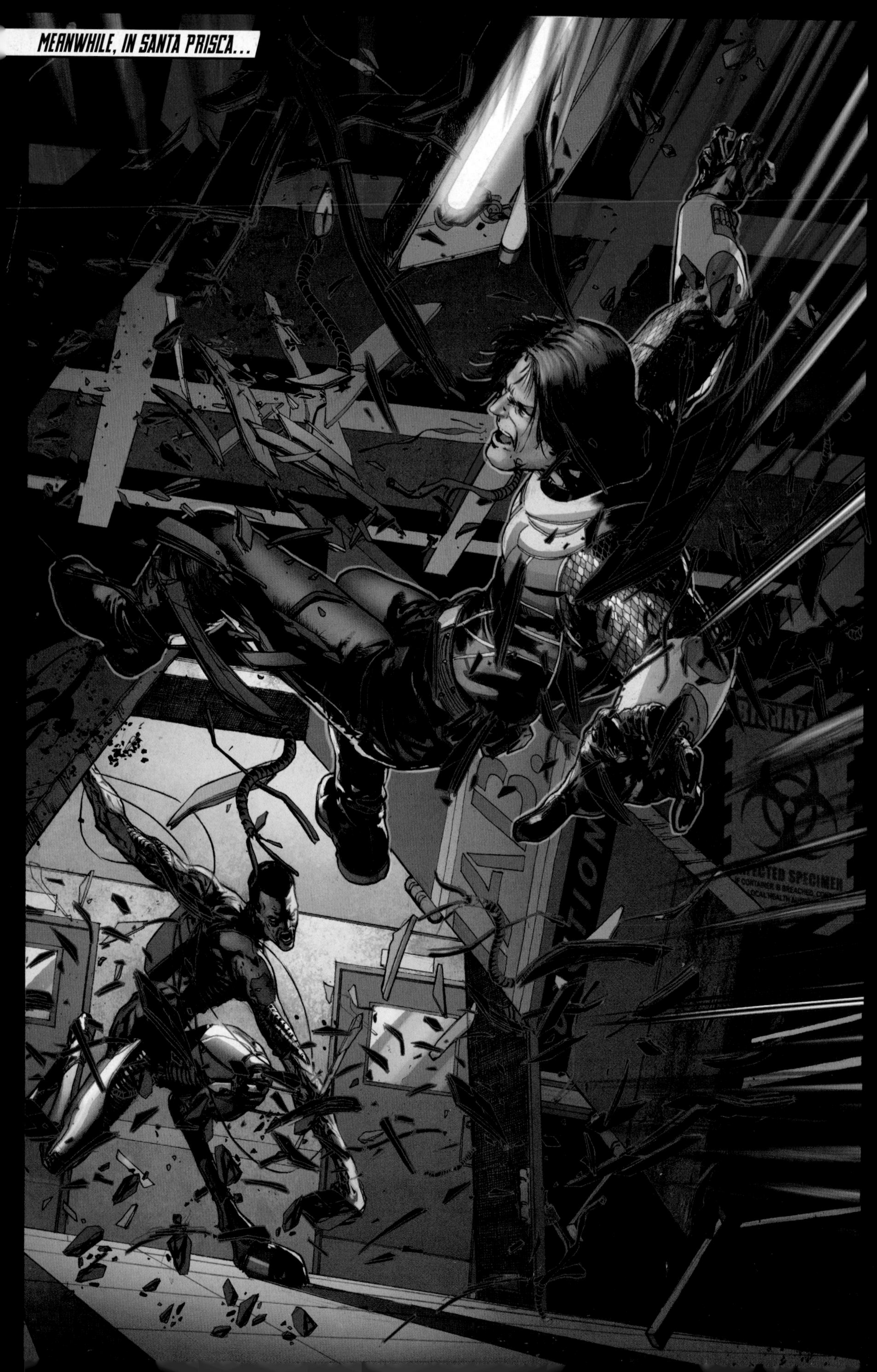
MEANWHILE, IN SANTA PRISCA...

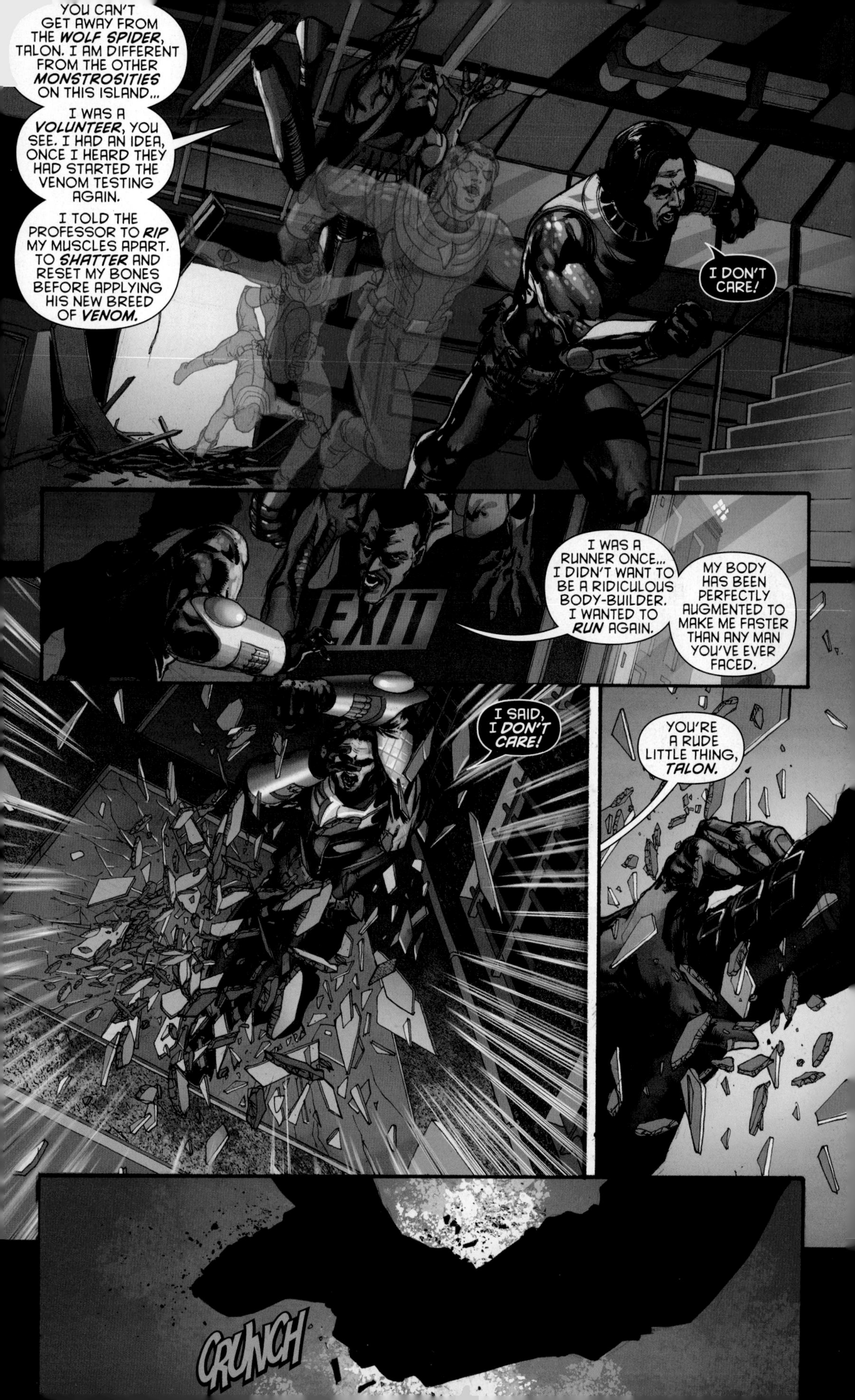
YOU CAN'T GET AWAY FROM THE WOLF SPIDER, TALON. I AM DIFFERENT FROM THE OTHER MONSTROSITIES ON THIS ISLAND...
I WAS A VOLUNTEER, YOU SEE. I HAD AN IDEA, ONCE I HEARD THEY HAD STARTED THE VENOM TESTING AGAIN.
I TOLD THE PROFESSOR TO RIP MY MUSCLES APART. TO SHATTER AND RESET MY BONES BEFORE APPLYING HIS NEW BREED OF VENOM.
I DON'T CARE!
EXIT
I WAS A RUNNER ONCE... I DIDN'T WANT TO BE A RIDICULOUS BODY-BUILDER. I WANTED TO RUN AGAIN.
MY BODY HAS BEEN PERFECTLY AUGMENTED TO MAKE ME FASTER THAN ANY MAN YOU'VE EVER FACED.
I SAID, I DON'T CARE!
YOU'RE A RUDE LITTLE THING, TALON.
CRUNCH

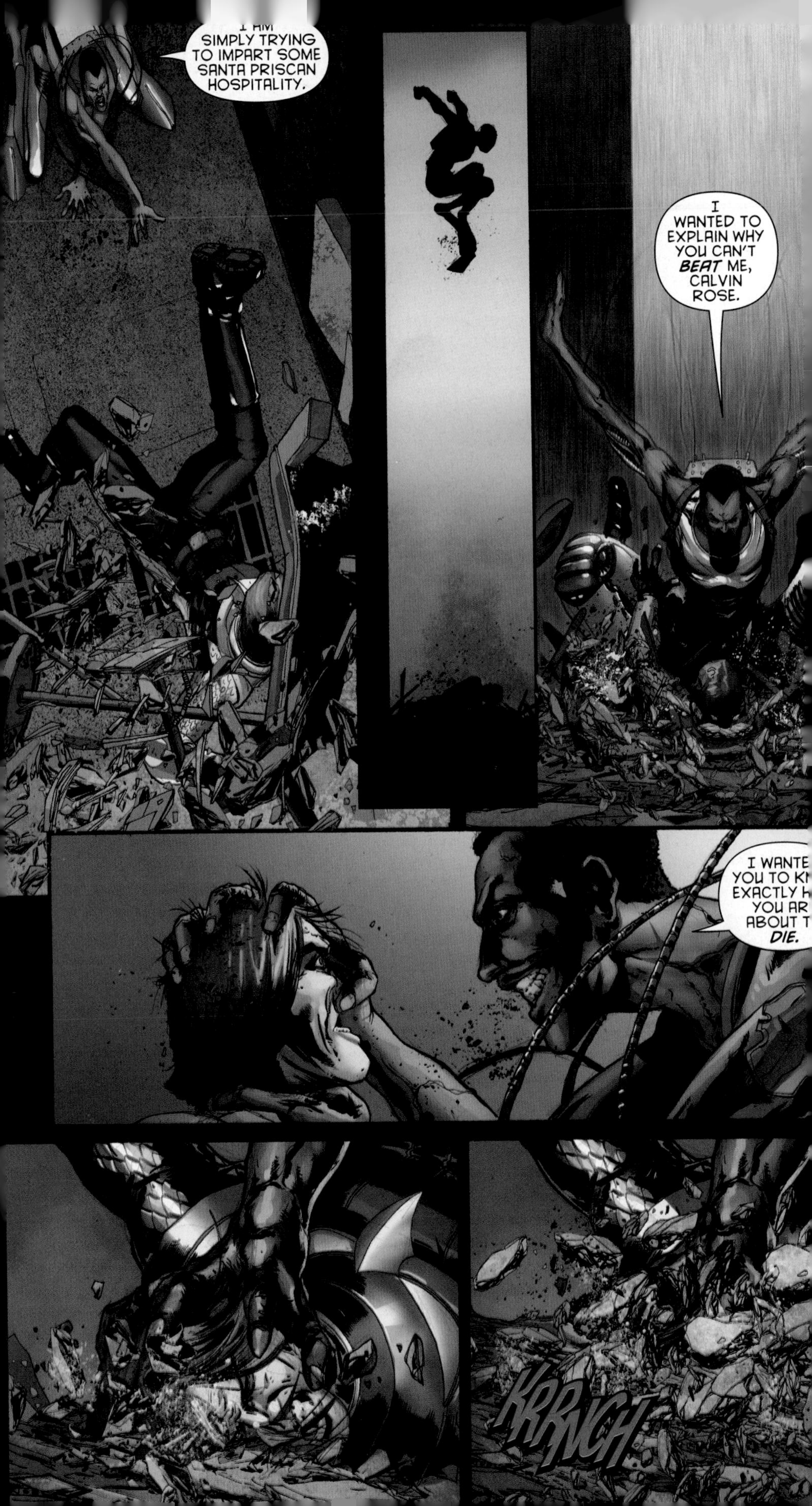
I AM SIMPLY TRYING TO IMPART SOME SANTA PRISCAN HOSPITALITY.
I WANTED TO EXPLAIN WHY YOU CAN'T BEAT ME, CALVIN ROSE.
I WANTE YOU TO KN EXACTLY H YOU AR ABOUT T DIE.
KRRNCH

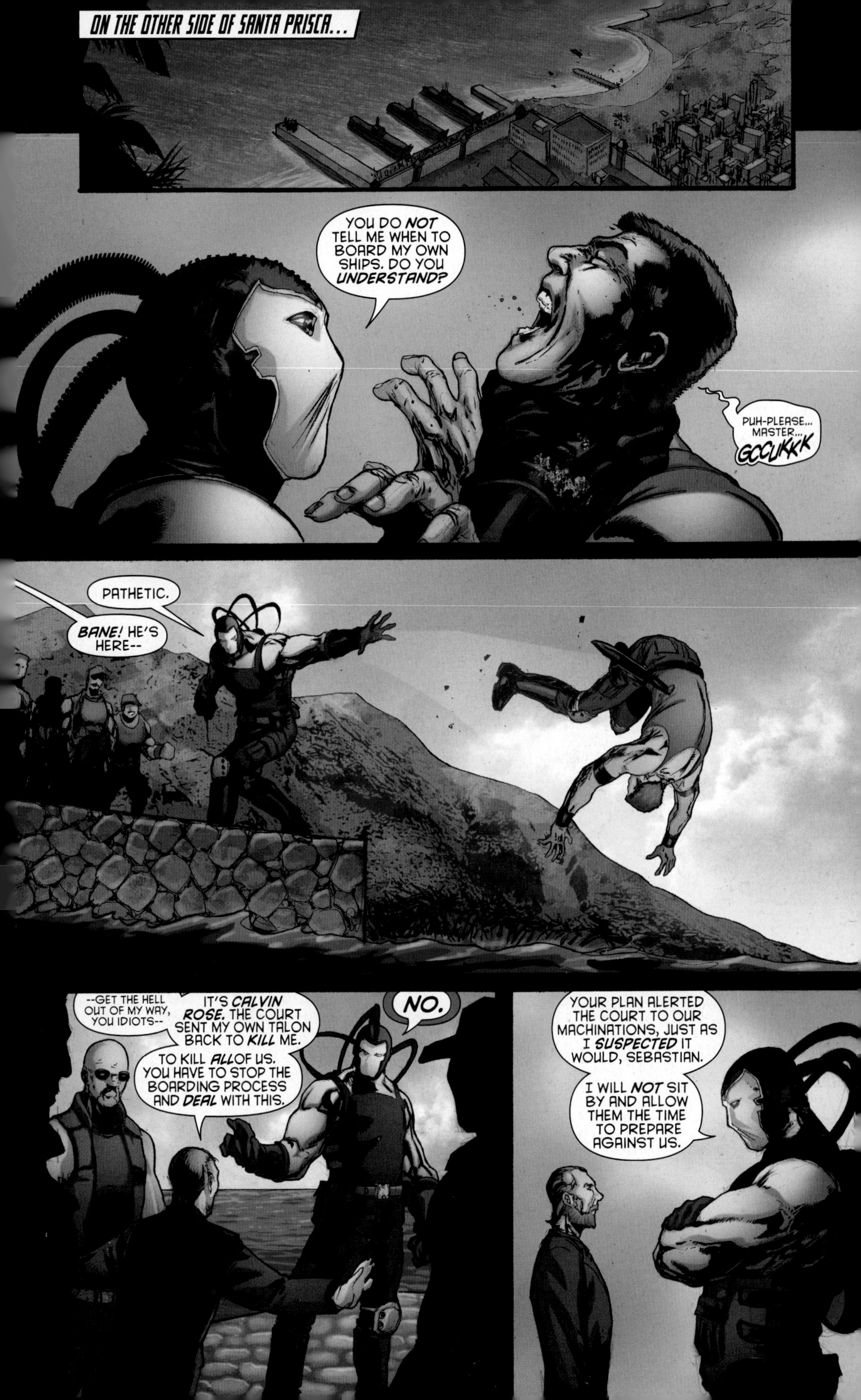
ON THE OTHER SIDE OF SANTA PRISCA...
YOU DO NOT TELL ME WHEN TO BOARD MY OWN SHIPS. DO YOU UNDERSTAND?
PUH-PLEASE... MASTER...
GCCUKKK
PATHETIC.
BANE! HE'S HERE--
--GET THE HELL OUT OF MY WAY, YOU IDIOTS--
IT'S CALVIN ROSE. THE COURT SENT MY OWN TALON BACK TO KILL ME.
TO KILL ALL OF US. YOU HAVE TO STOP THE BOARDING PROCESS AND DEAL WITH THIS.
NO.
YOUR PLAN ALERTED THE COURT TO OUR MACHINATIONS, JUST AS I SUSPECTED IT WOULD, SEBASTIAN.
I WILL NOT SIT BY AND ALLOW THEM THE TIME TO PREPARE AGAINST US.

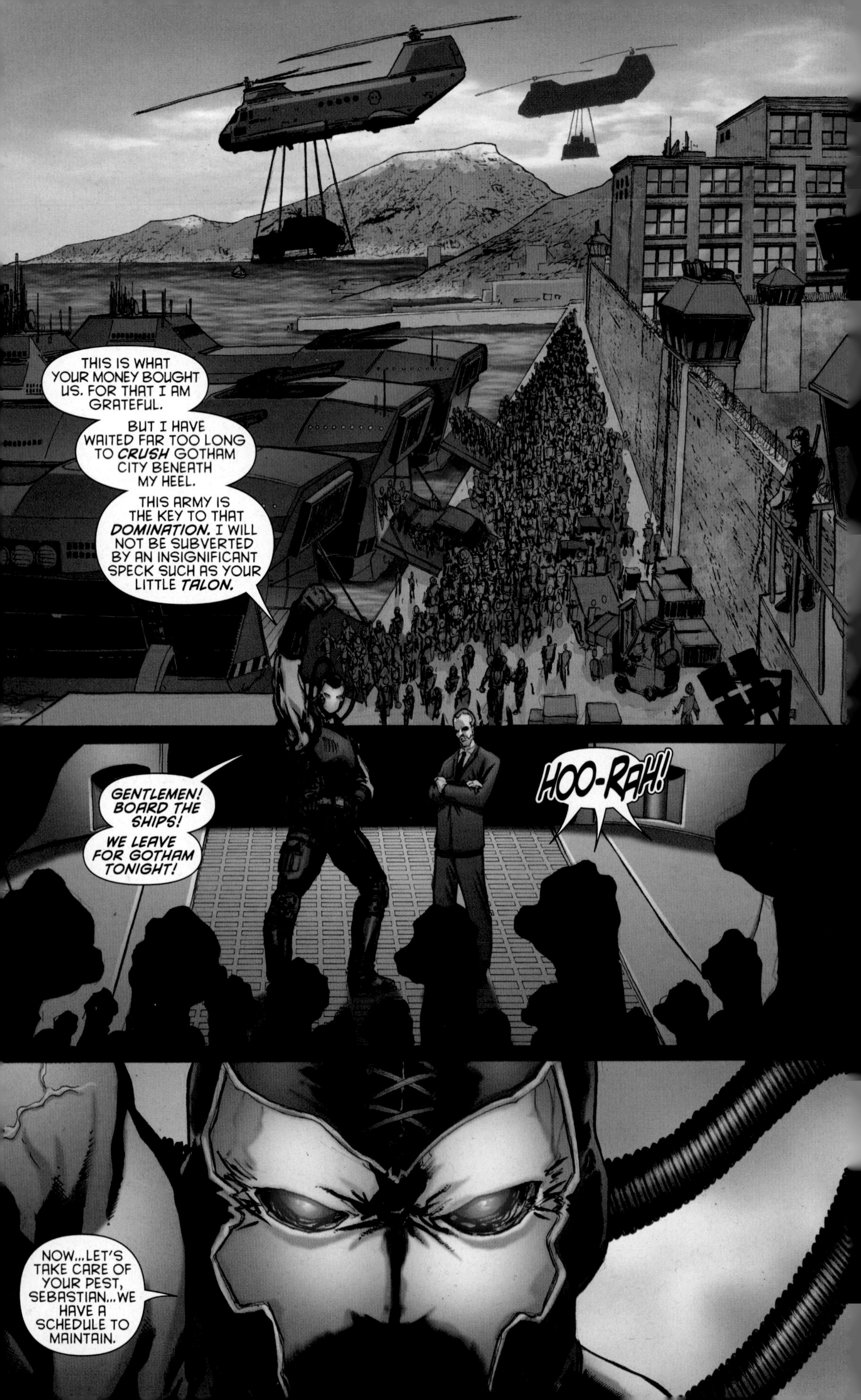
THIS IS WHAT YOUR MONEY BOUGHT US. FOR THAT I AM GRATEFUL.
BUT I HAVE WAITED FAR TOO LONG TO *CRUSH* GOTHAM CITY BENEATH MY HEEL.
THIS ARMY IS THE KEY TO THAT *DOMINATION.* I WILL NOT BE SUBVERTED BY AN INSIGNIFICANT SPECK SUCH AS YOUR LITTLE *TALON.*
GENTLEMEN! BOARD THE SHIPS! WE LEAVE FOR GOTHAM TONIGHT!
HOO-RAH!
NOW...LET'S TAKE CARE OF YOUR PEST, SEBASTIAN...WE HAVE A SCHEDULE TO MAINTAIN.

MALICIA...
THIS IS *WOLF-
SPIDER*. I HAVE
THE INTRUDER...

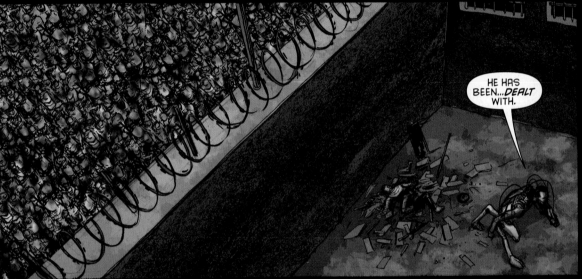

HE HAS
BEEN...*DEALT*
WITH.

YEAH. NOT
SO MUCH.

HAVING
A *HEALING
FACTOR* REALLY
IS A GAME-
CHANGER,
ISN'T IT?

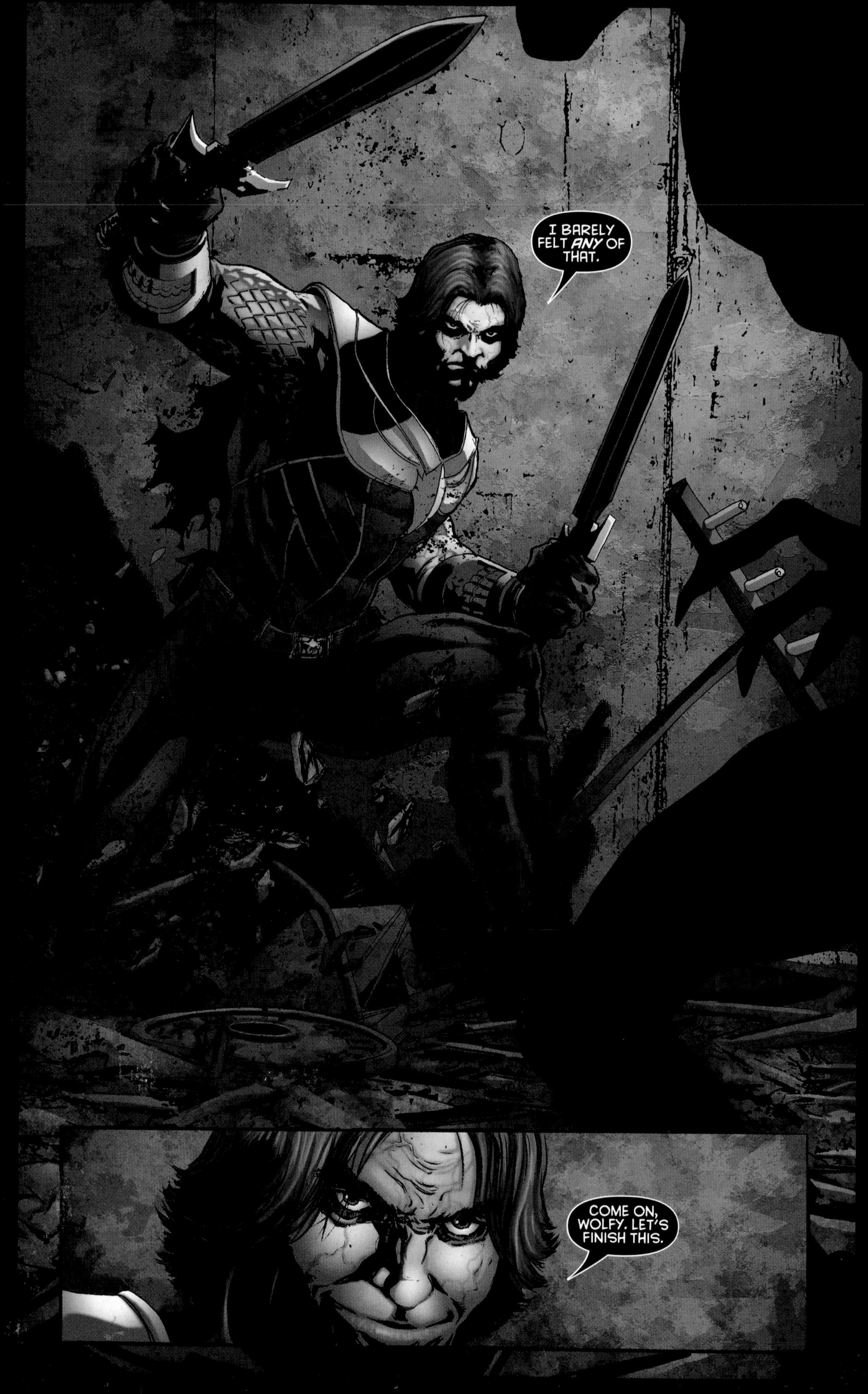
I BARELY FELT ANY OF THAT.
COME ON, WOLFY. LET'S FINISH THIS.

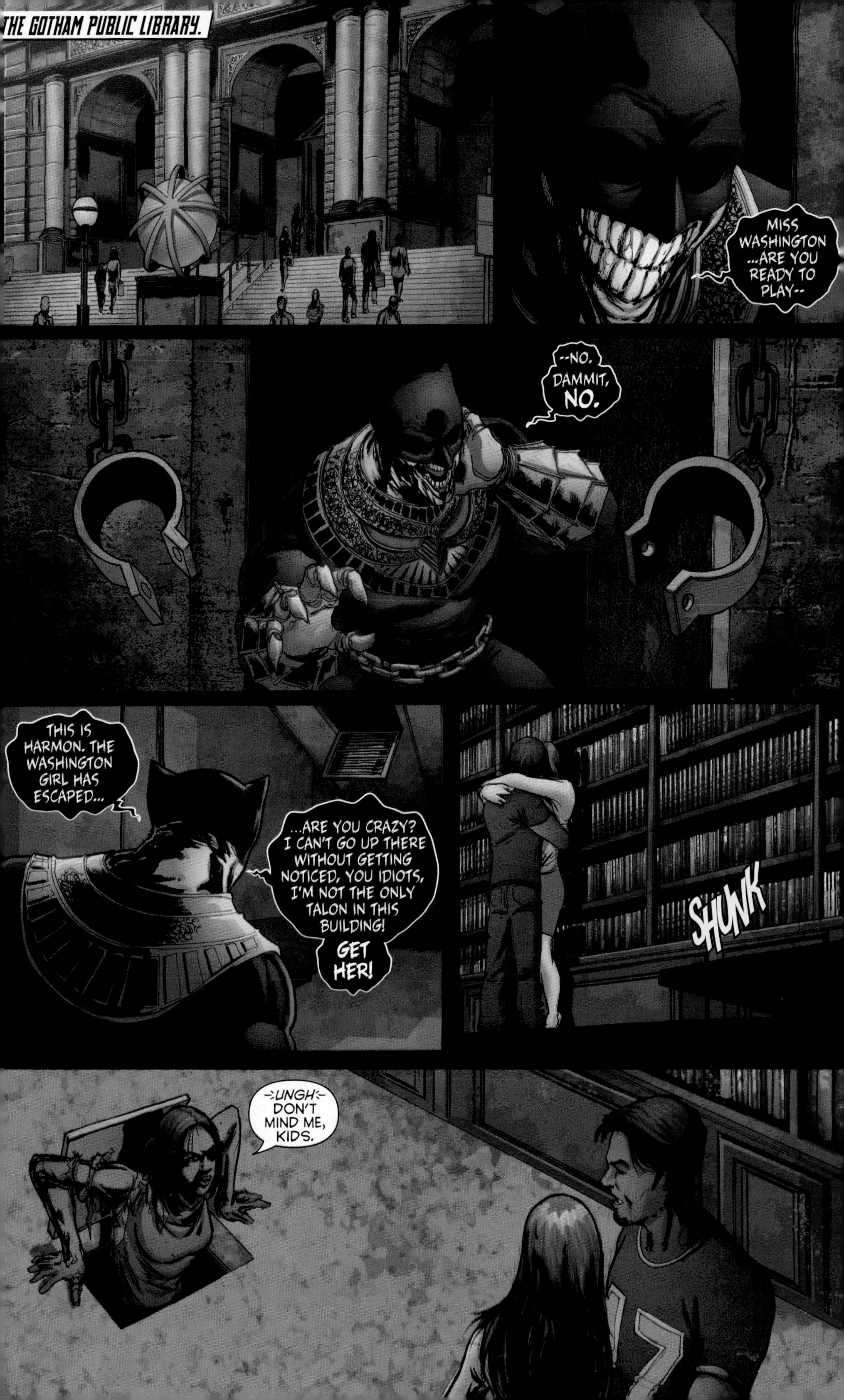
THE GOTHAM PUBLIC LIBRARY.
MISS WASHINGTON ...ARE YOU READY TO PLAY--
--NO. DAMMIT, NO.
THIS IS HARMON. THE WASHINGTON GIRL HAS ESCAPED...
...ARE YOU CRAZY? I CAN'T GO UP THERE WITHOUT GETTING NOTICED, YOU IDIOTS, I'M NOT THE ONLY TALON IN THIS BUILDING! GET HER!
SHUNK
-UNGH- DON'T MIND ME, KIDS.

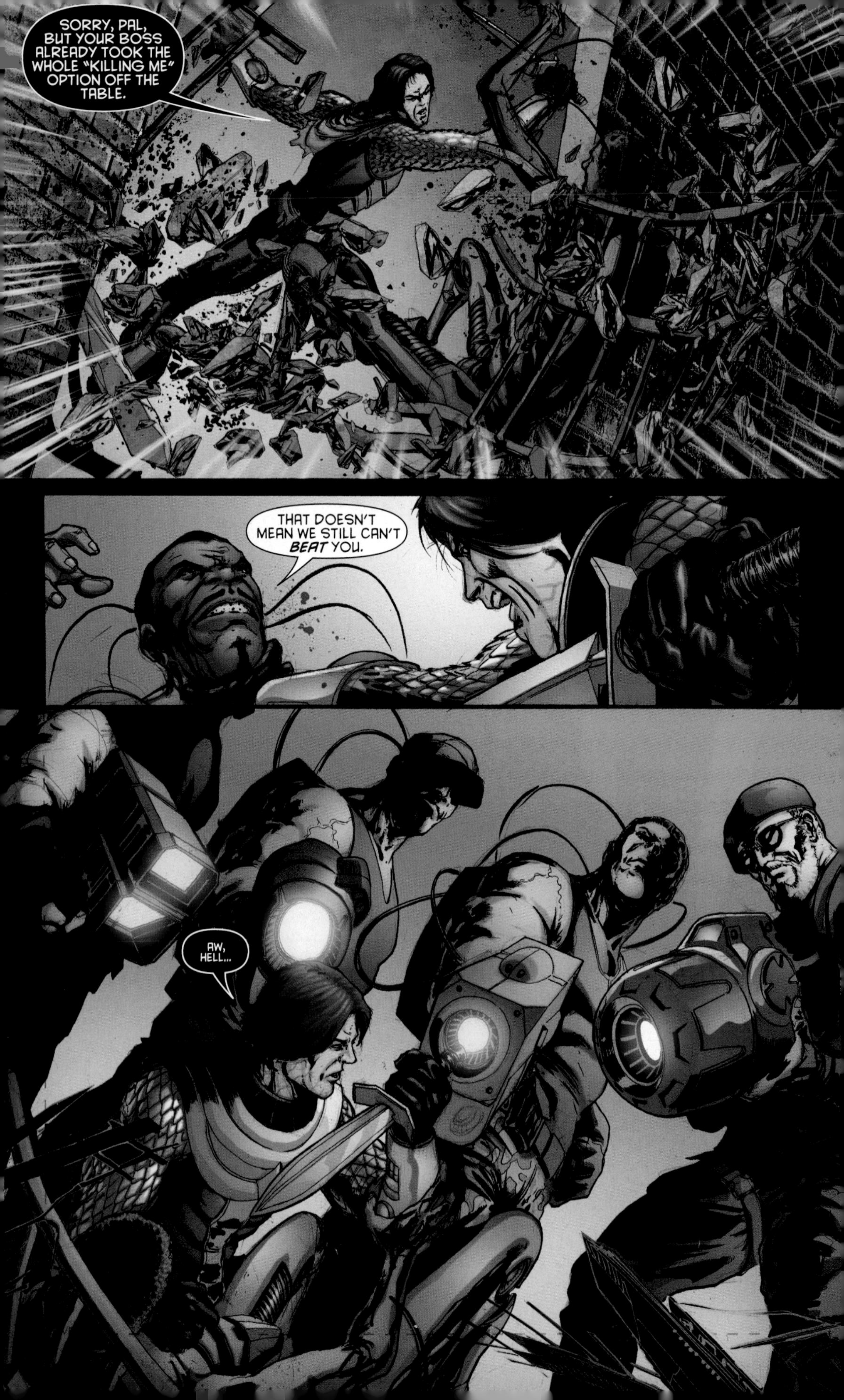
SORRY, PAL, BUT YOUR BOSS ALREADY TOOK THE WHOLE "KILLING ME" OPTION OFF THE TABLE.
THAT DOESN'T MEAN WE STILL CAN'T *BEAT* YOU.
AW, HELL...

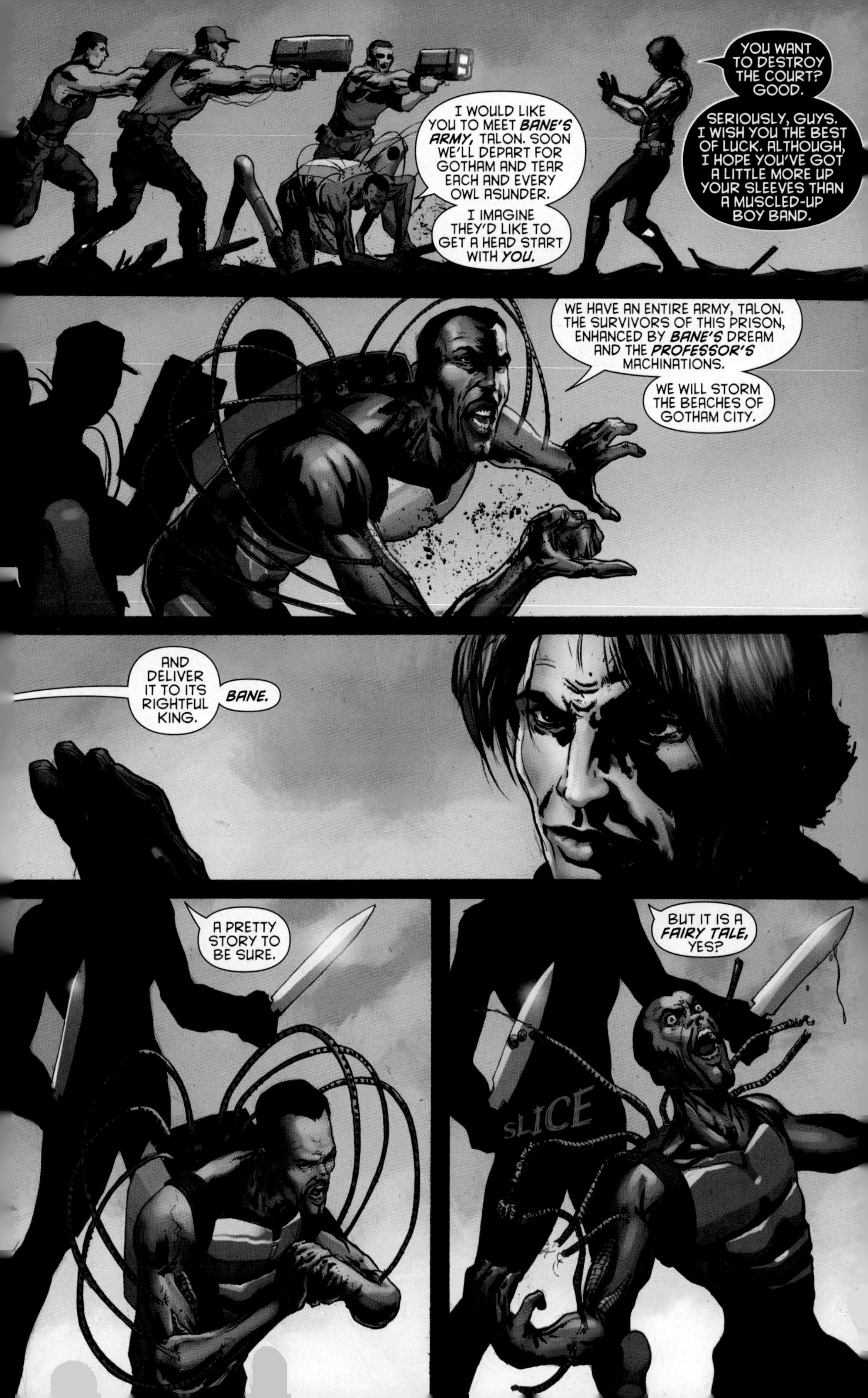
I WOULD LIKE YOU TO MEET BANE'S ARMY, TALON. SOON WE'LL DEPART FOR GOTHAM AND TEAR EACH AND EVERY OWL ASUNDER.
I IMAGINE THEY'D LIKE TO GET A HEAD START WITH YOU.
YOU WANT TO DESTROY THE COURT? GOOD.
SERIOUSLY, GUYS. I WISH YOU THE BEST OF LUCK. ALTHOUGH, I HOPE YOU'VE GOT A LITTLE MORE UP YOUR SLEEVES THAN A MUSCLED-UP BOY BAND.
WE HAVE AN ENTIRE ARMY, TALON. THE SURVIVORS OF THIS PRISON, ENHANCED BY BANE'S DREAM AND THE PROFESSOR'S MACHINATIONS.
WE WILL STORM THE BEACHES OF GOTHAM CITY.
AND DELIVER IT TO ITS RIGHTFUL KING.
BANE.
A PRETTY STORY TO BE SURE.
BUT IT IS A FAIRY TALE, YES?
SLICE

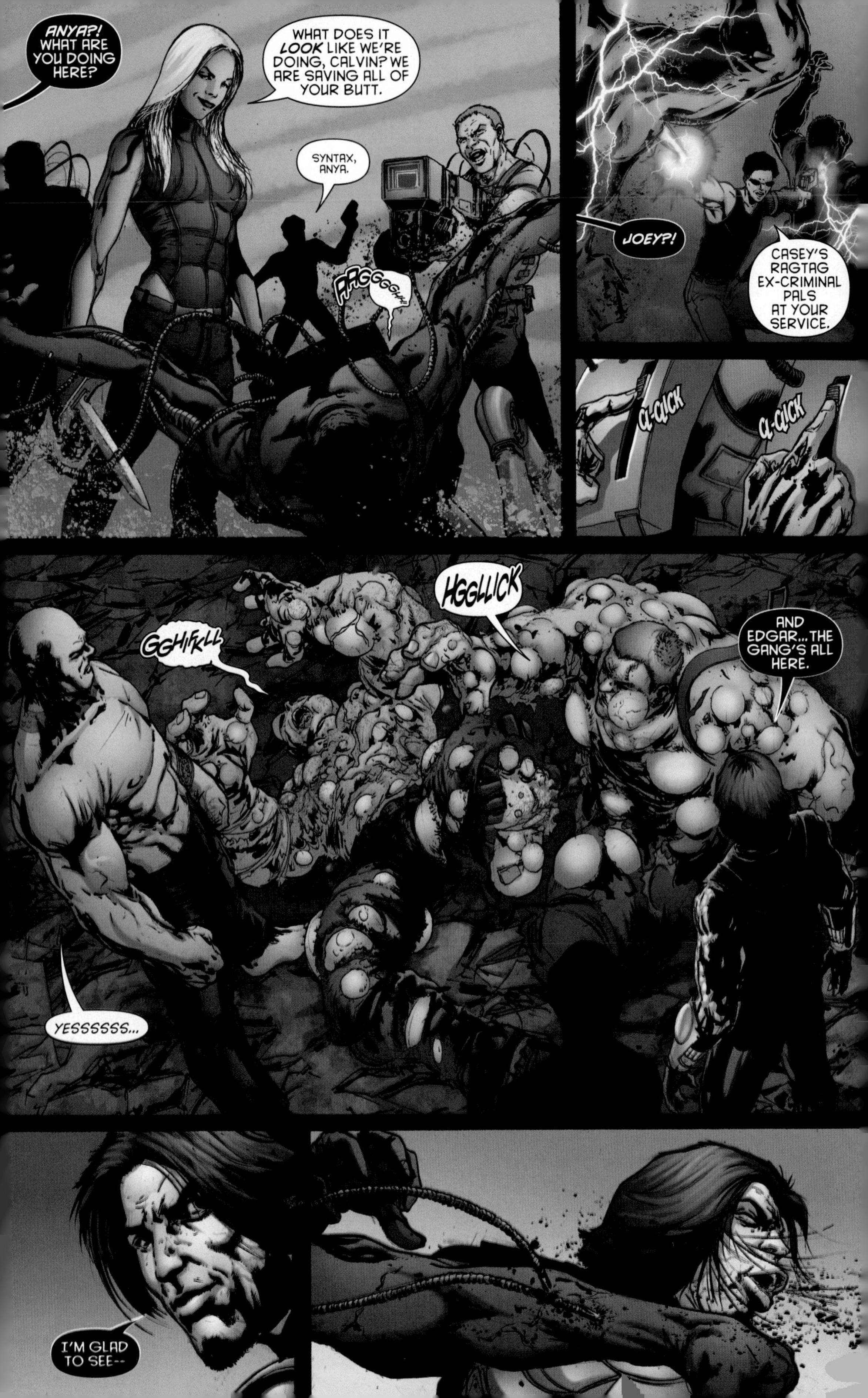
ANYA?! WHAT ARE YOU DOING HERE?
WHAT DOES IT LOOK LIKE WE'RE DOING, CALVIN? WE ARE SAVING ALL OF YOUR BUTT.
SYNTAX, ANYA.
AAGGGGHH!
JOEY?!
CASEY'S RAGTAG EX-CRIMINAL PALS AT YOUR SERVICE.
CL-CLICK
CL-CLICK
GGHFKLL
HGGLLICK
AND EDGAR... THE GANG'S ALL HERE.
YESSSSSS...
I'M GLAD TO SEE--

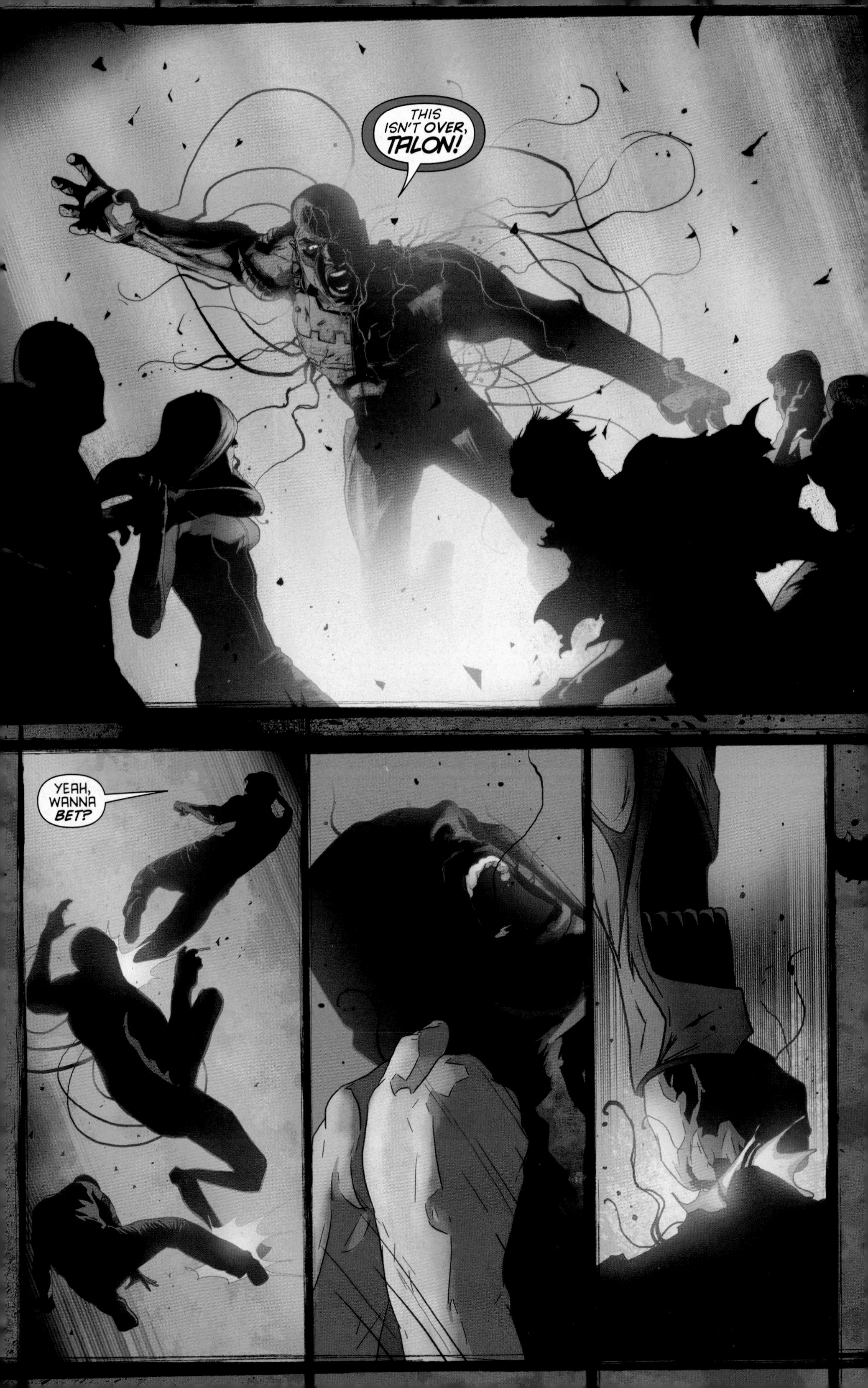
THIS ISN'T OVER, TALON!
YEAH, WANNA BET?

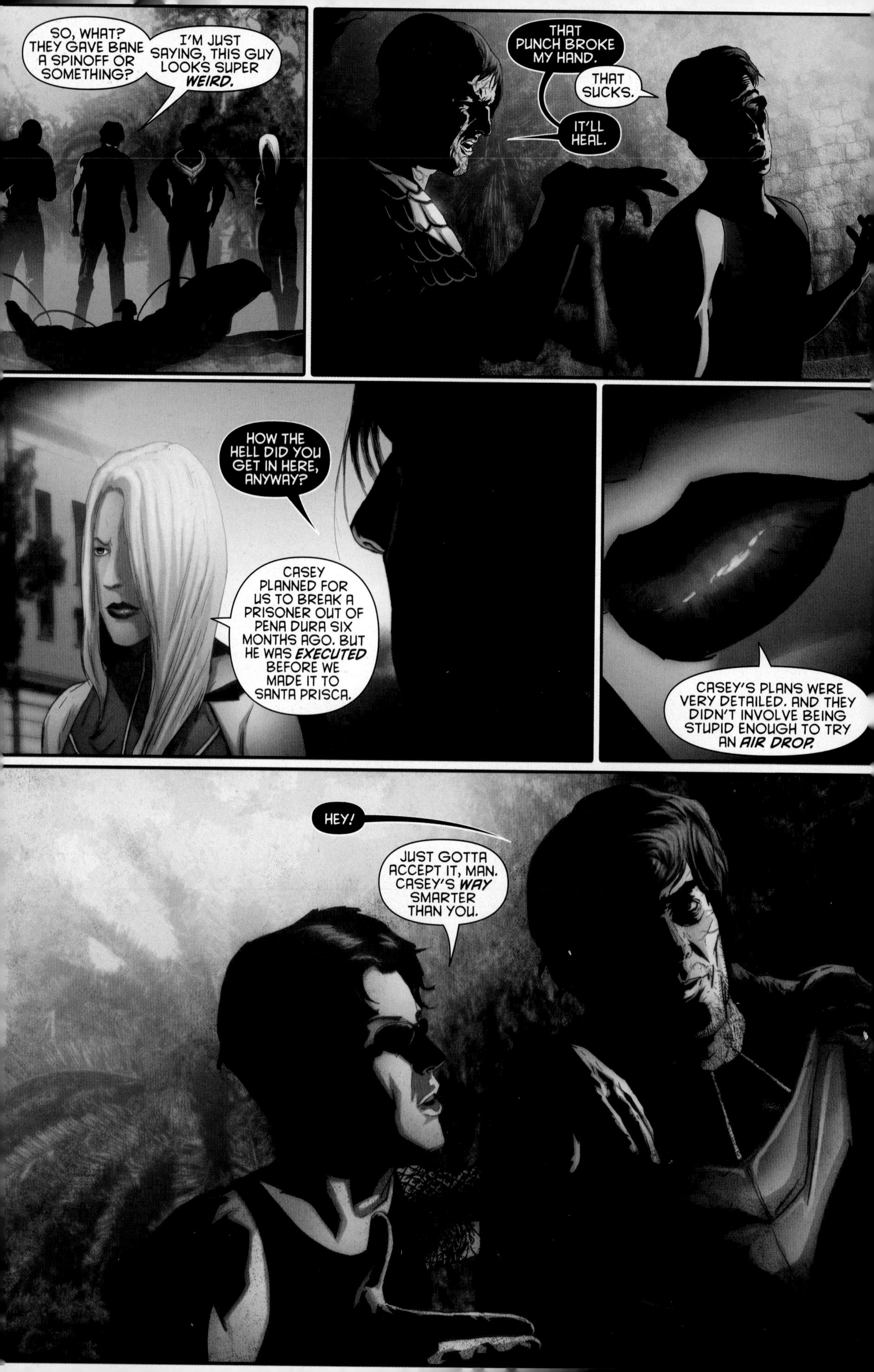
SO, WHAT? THEY GAVE BANE A SPINOFF OR SOMETHING?
I'M JUST SAYING, THIS GUY LOOKS SUPER *WEIRD.*
THAT PUNCH BROKE MY HAND.
THAT SUCKS.
IT'LL HEAL.
HOW THE HELL DID YOU GET IN HERE, ANYWAY?
CASEY PLANNED FOR US TO BREAK A PRISONER OUT OF PENA DURA SIX MONTHS AGO. BUT HE WAS *EXECUTED* BEFORE WE MADE IT TO SANTA PRISCA.
CASEY'S PLANS WERE VERY DETAILED. AND THEY DIDN'T INVOLVE BEING STUPID ENOUGH TO TRY AN *AIR DROP.*
HEY!
JUST GOTTA ACCEPT IT, MAN. CASEY'S *WAY* SMARTER THAN YOU.

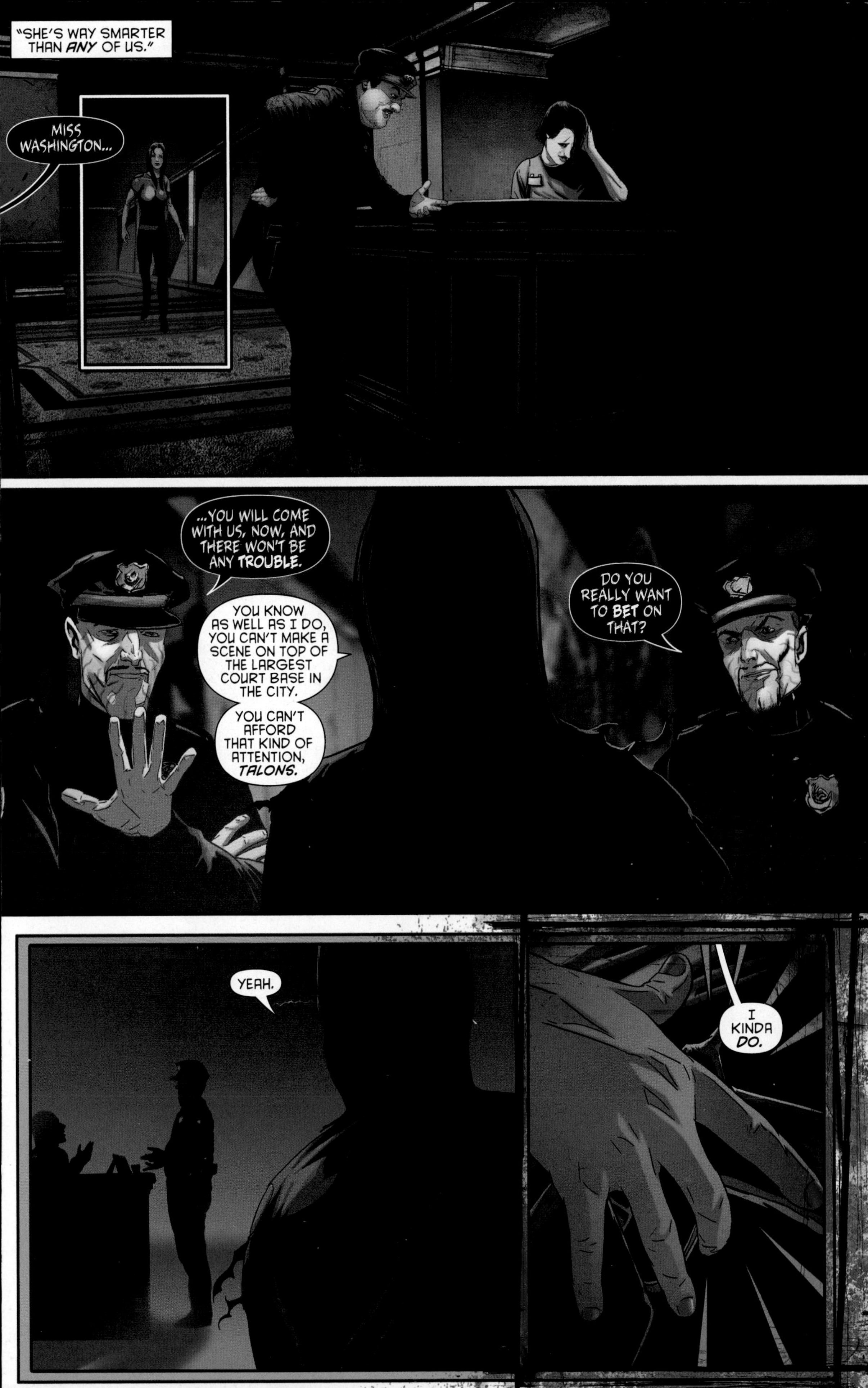
"SHE'S WAY SMARTER THAN *ANY* OF US."
MISS WASHINGTON...
...YOU WILL COME WITH US, NOW, AND THERE WON'T BE ANY **TROUBLE.**
YOU KNOW AS WELL AS I DO, YOU CAN'T MAKE A SCENE ON TOP OF THE LARGEST COURT BASE IN THE CITY.
YOU CAN'T AFFORD THAT KIND OF ATTENTION, ***TALONS.***
DO YOU REALLY WANT TO **BET** ON THAT?
YEAH.
I KINDA *DO.*

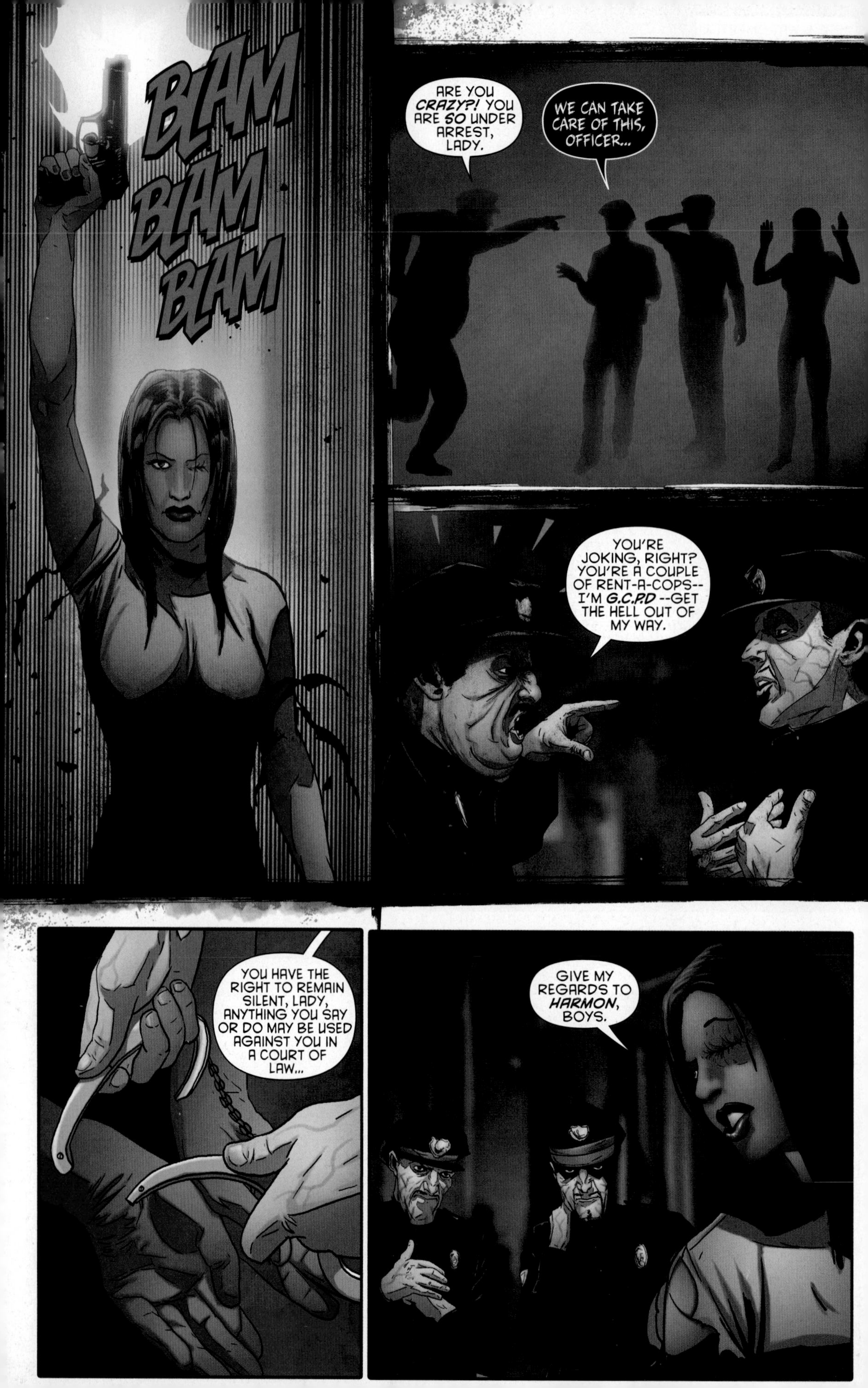
BLAM
BLAM
BLAM
ARE YOU CRAZY?! YOU ARE SO UNDER ARREST, LADY.
WE CAN TAKE CARE OF THIS, OFFICER...
YOU'RE JOKING, RIGHT? YOU'RE A COUPLE OF RENT-A-COPS-- I'M G.C.P.D --GET THE HELL OUT OF MY WAY.
YOU HAVE THE RIGHT TO REMAIN SILENT, LADY, ANYTHING YOU SAY OR DO MAY BE USED AGAINST YOU IN A COURT OF LAW...
GIVE MY REGARDS TO HARMON, BOYS.

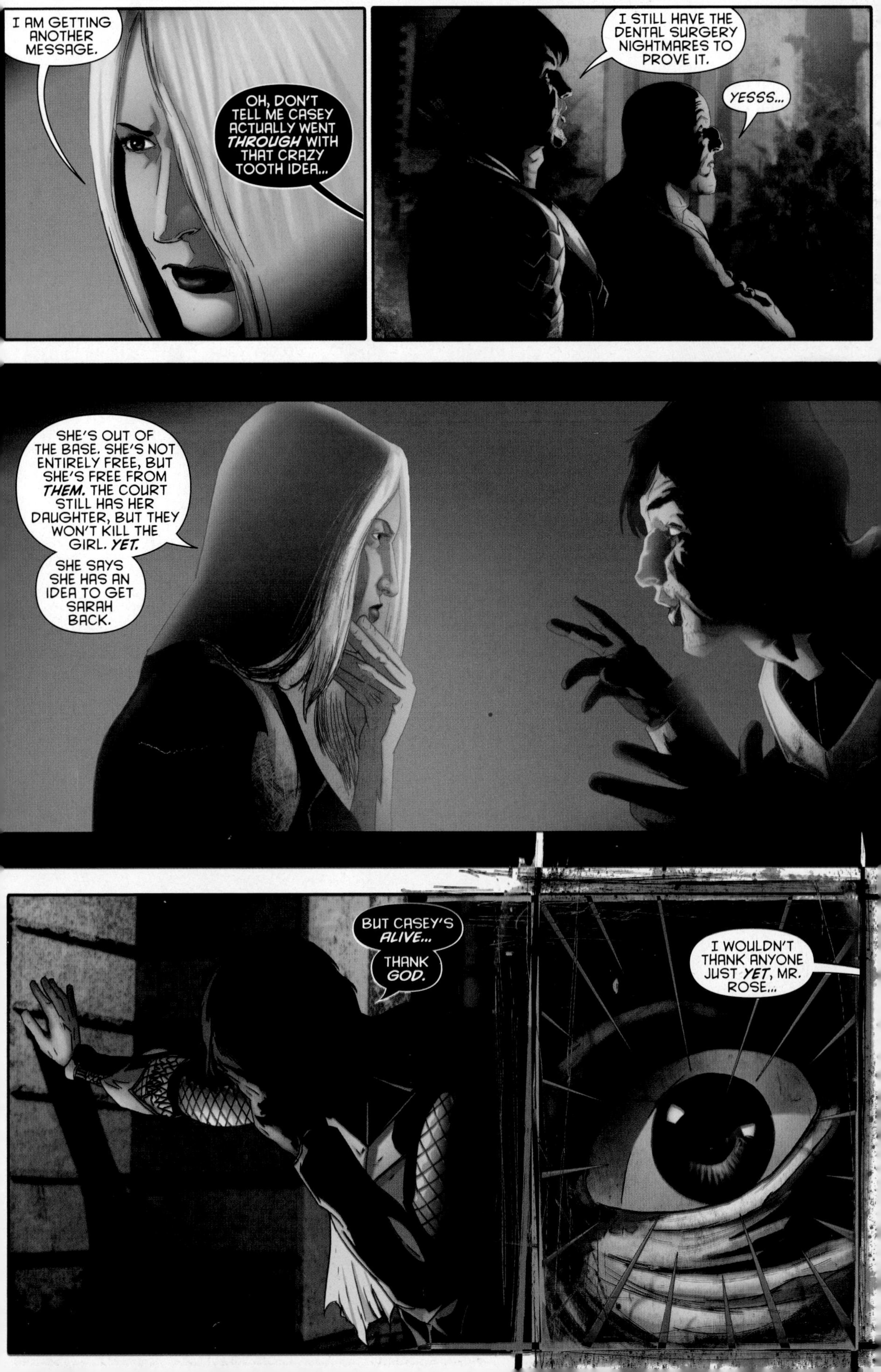
I AM GETTING ANOTHER MESSAGE.
OH, DON'T TELL ME CASEY ACTUALLY WENT *THROUGH* WITH THAT CRAZY TOOTH IDEA...
I STILL HAVE THE DENTAL SURGERY NIGHTMARES TO PROVE IT.
YESSS...
SHE'S OUT OF THE BASE. SHE'S NOT ENTIRELY FREE, BUT SHE'S FREE FROM *THEM.* THE COURT STILL HAS HER DAUGHTER, BUT THEY WON'T KILL THE GIRL. *YET.*
SHE SAYS SHE HAS AN IDEA TO GET SARAH BACK.
BUT CASEY'S *ALIVE*...
THANK *GOD.*
I WOULDN'T THANK ANYONE JUST *YET*, MR. ROSE...

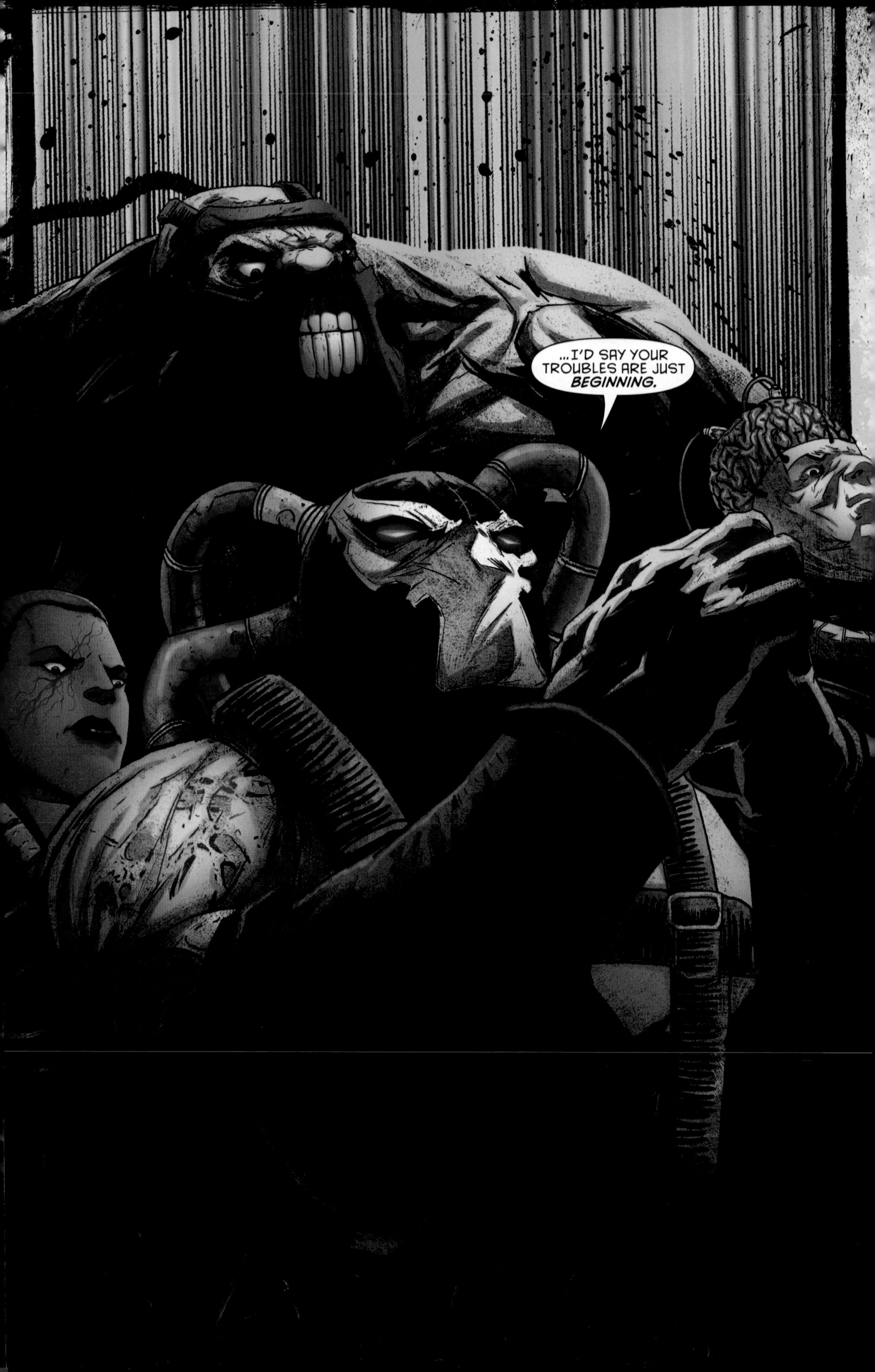
...I'D SAY YOUR TROUBLES ARE JUST *BEGINNING.*

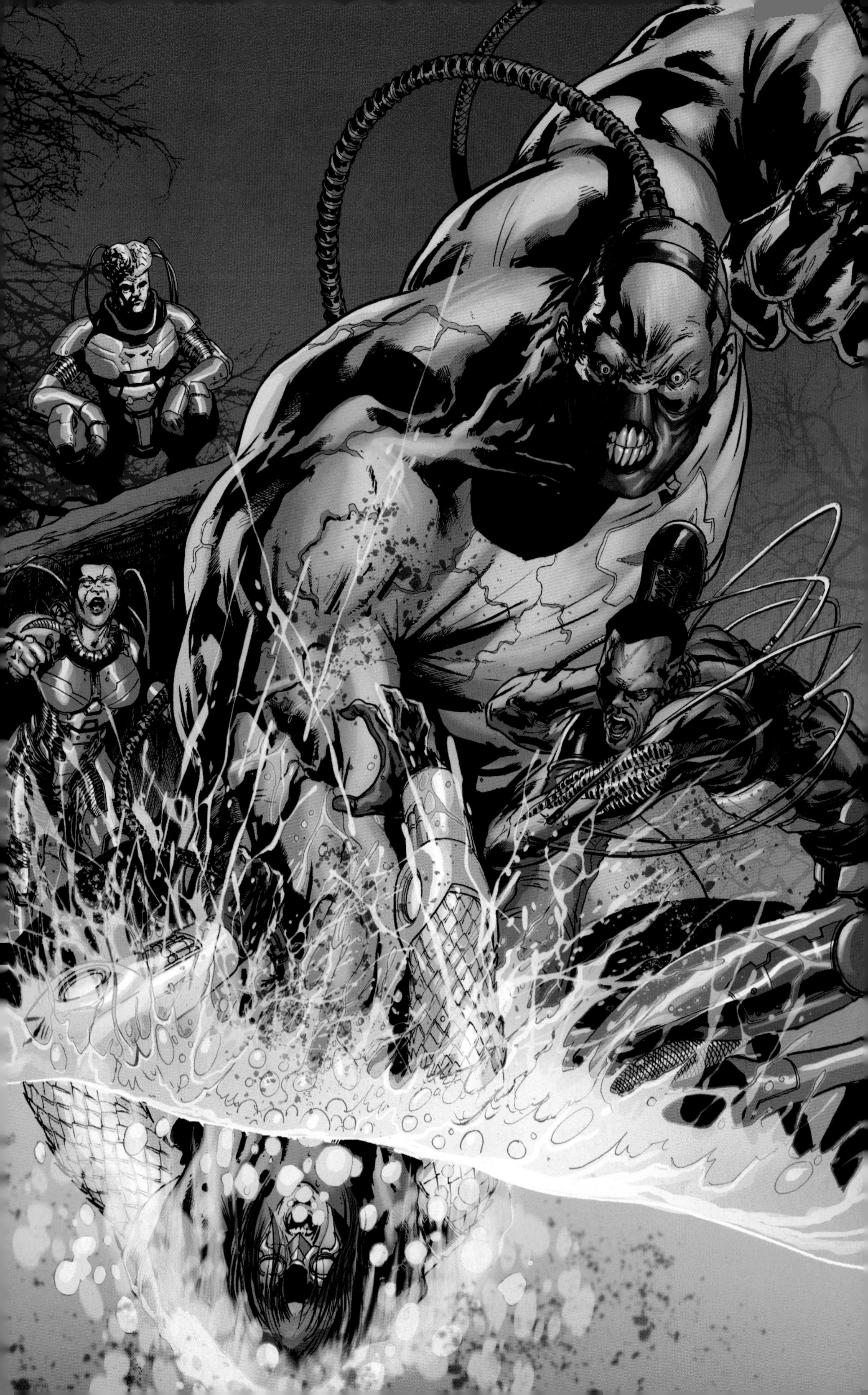

TRUE STRENGTH

JAMES TYNION IV writer SZYMON KUDRANSKI artist cover art by MIGUEL SEPULVEDA & RAIN BEREDO

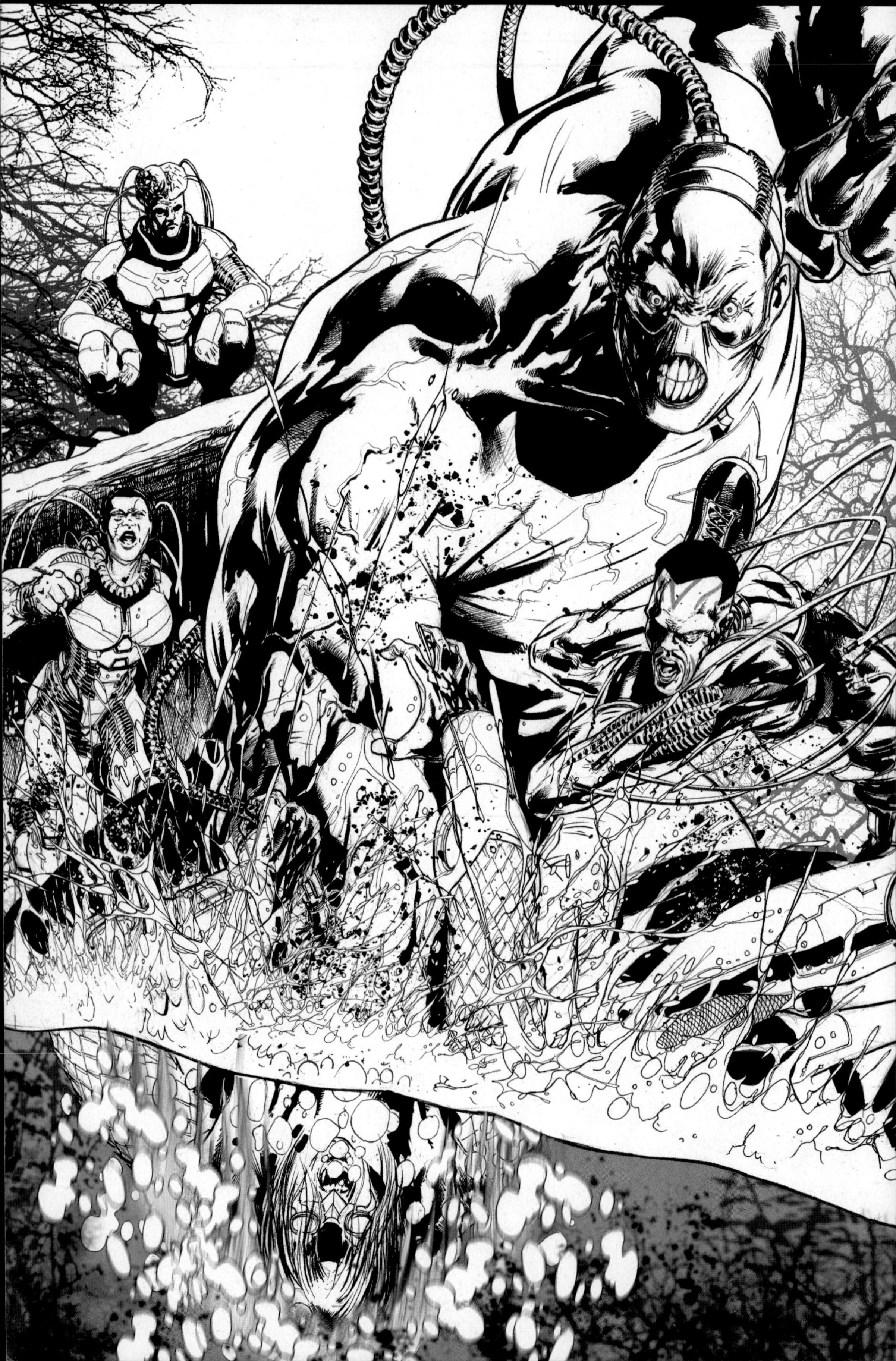

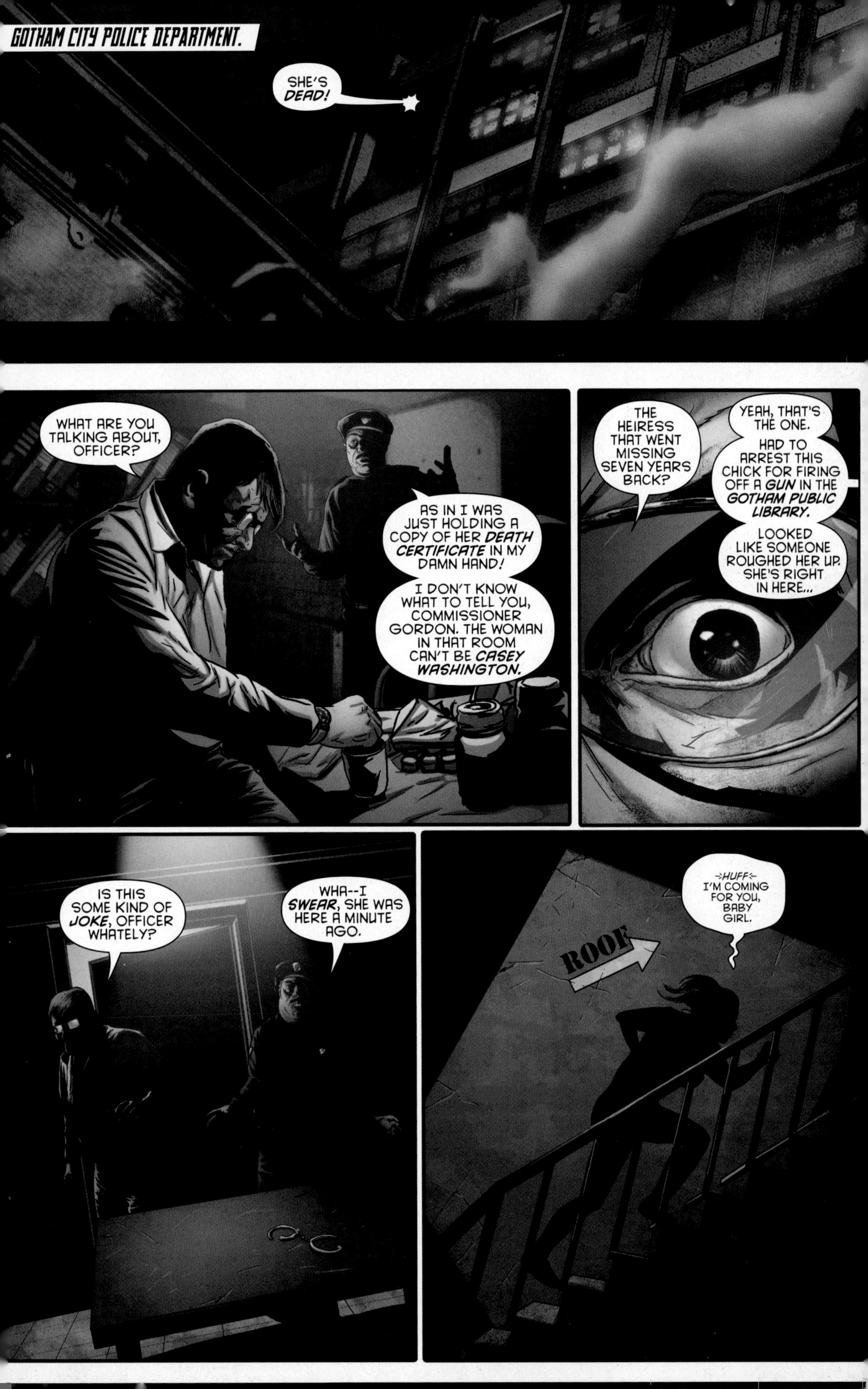
GOTHAM CITY POLICE DEPARTMENT.
SHE'S DEAD!
WHAT ARE YOU TALKING ABOUT, OFFICER?
AS IN I WAS JUST HOLDING A COPY OF HER DEATH CERTIFICATE IN MY DAMN HAND!
I DON'T KNOW WHAT TO TELL YOU, COMMISSIONER GORDON. THE WOMAN IN THAT ROOM CAN'T BE CASEY WASHINGTON.
THE HEIRESS THAT WENT MISSING SEVEN YEARS BACK?
YEAH, THAT'S THE ONE.
HAD TO ARREST THIS CHICK FOR FIRING OFF A GUN IN THE GOTHAM PUBLIC LIBRARY.
LOOKED LIKE SOMEONE ROUGHED HER UP. SHE'S RIGHT IN HERE...
IS THIS SOME KIND OF JOKE, OFFICER WHATELY?
WHA--I SWEAR, SHE WAS HERE A MINUTE AGO.
ROOF
HUFF
I'M COMING FOR YOU, BABY GIRL.

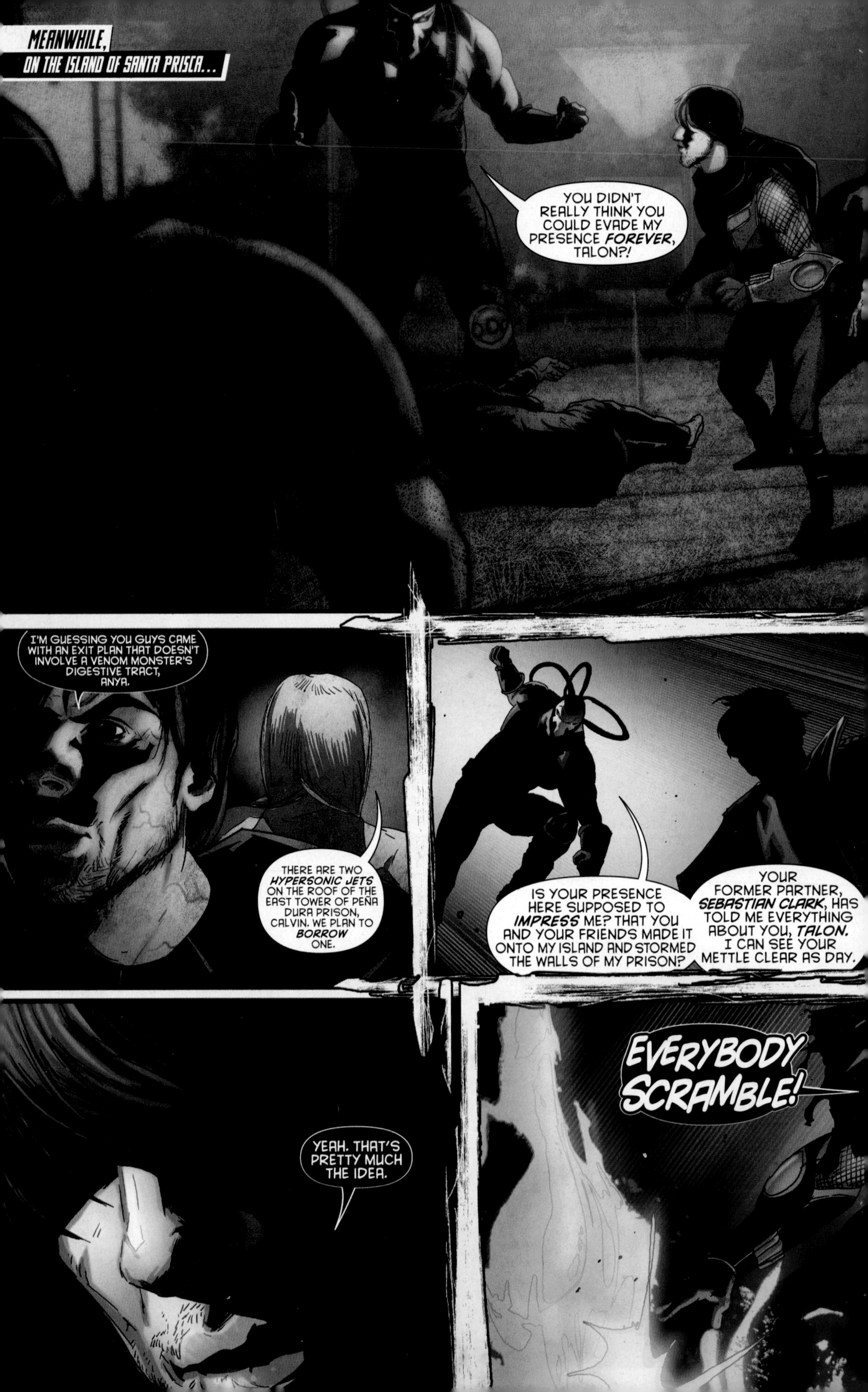
MEANWHILE, ON THE ISLAND OF SANTA PRISCA...
YOU DIDN'T REALLY THINK YOU COULD EVADE MY PRESENCE FOREVER, TALON?!
I'M GUESSING YOU GUYS CAME WITH AN EXIT PLAN THAT DOESN'T INVOLVE A VENOM MONSTER'S DIGESTIVE TRACT, ANYA.
THERE ARE TWO HYPERSONIC JETS ON THE ROOF OF THE EAST TOWER OF PEÑA DURA PRISON, CALVIN. WE PLAN TO BORROW ONE.
IS YOUR PRESENCE HERE SUPPOSED TO IMPRESS ME? THAT YOU AND YOUR FRIENDS MADE IT ONTO MY ISLAND AND STORMED THE WALLS OF MY PRISON?
YOUR FORMER PARTNER, SEBASTIAN CLARK, HAS TOLD ME EVERYTHING ABOUT YOU, TALON. I CAN SEE YOUR METTLE CLEAR AS DAY.
YEAH. THAT'S PRETTY MUCH THE IDEA.
EVERYBODY SCRAMBLE!

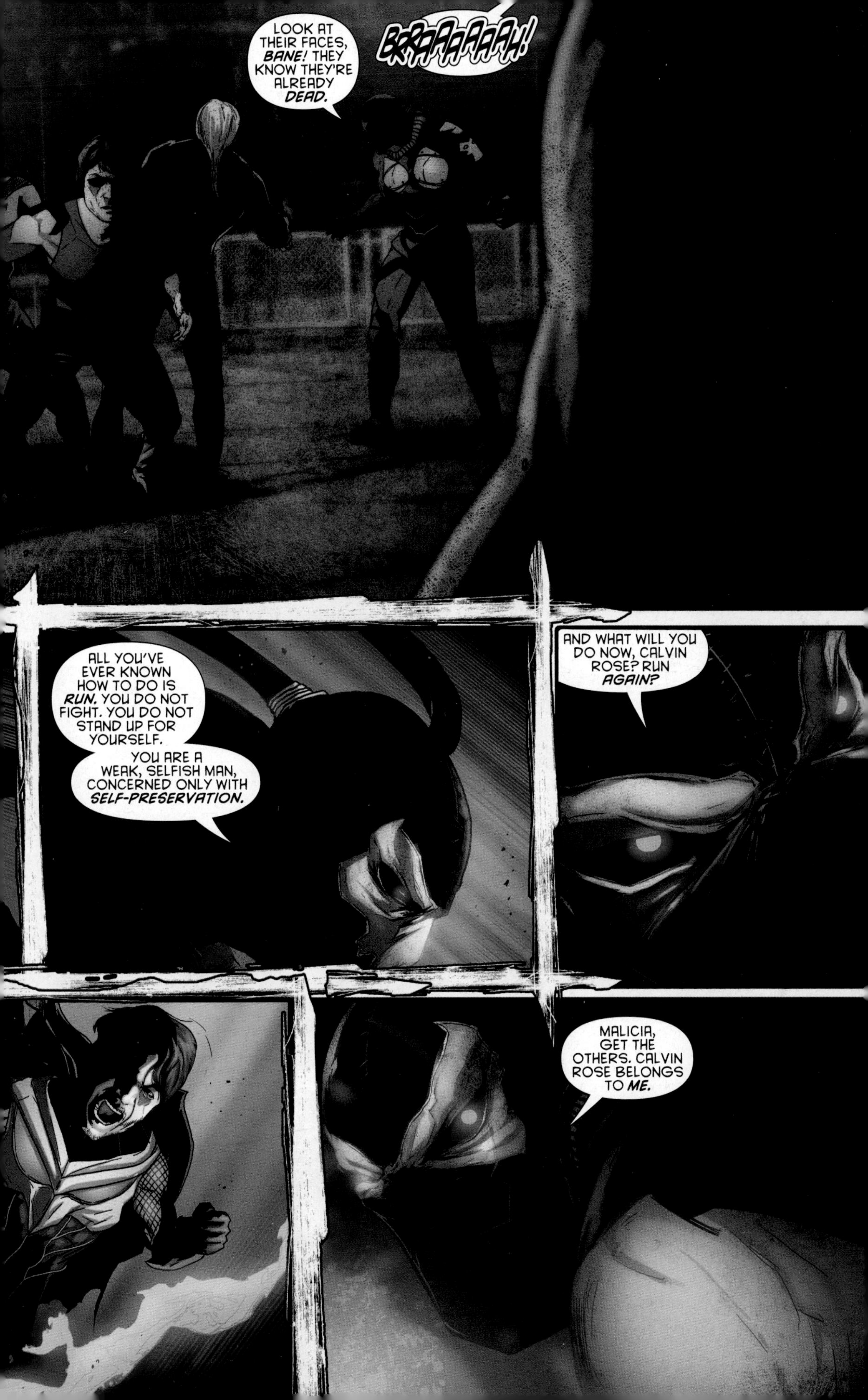
LOOK AT THEIR FACES, BANE! THEY KNOW THEY'RE ALREADY DEAD.
BRRAAAAAAAH!
ALL YOU'VE EVER KNOWN HOW TO DO IS RUN. YOU DO NOT FIGHT. YOU DO NOT STAND UP FOR YOURSELF.
YOU ARE A WEAK, SELFISH MAN, CONCERNED ONLY WITH SELF-PRESERVATION.
AND WHAT WILL YOU DO NOW, CALVIN ROSE? RUN AGAIN?
MALICIA, GET THE OTHERS. CALVIN ROSE BELONGS TO ME.

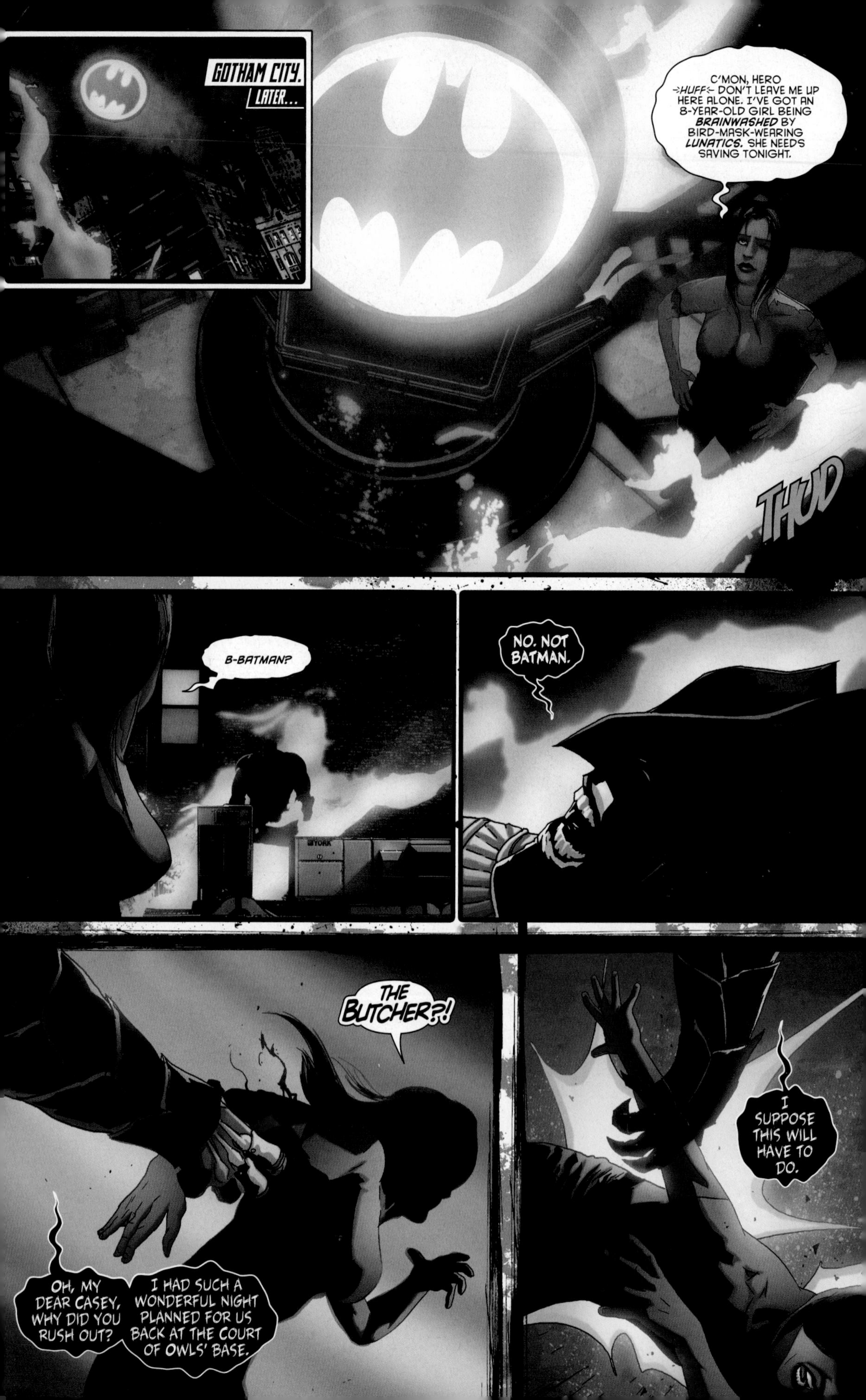
GOTHAM CITY.
LATER...
C'MON, HERO =HUFF= DON'T LEAVE ME UP HERE ALONE. I'VE GOT AN 8-YEAR-OLD GIRL BEING BRAINWASHED BY BIRD-MASK-WEARING LUNATICS. SHE NEEDS SAVING TONIGHT.
THUD
B-BATMAN?
YORK
NO. NOT BATMAN.
THE BUTCHER?!
OH, MY DEAR CASEY, WHY DID YOU RUSH OUT?
I HAD SUCH A WONDERFUL NIGHT PLANNED FOR US BACK AT THE COURT OF OWLS' BASE.
I SUPPOSE THIS WILL HAVE TO DO.

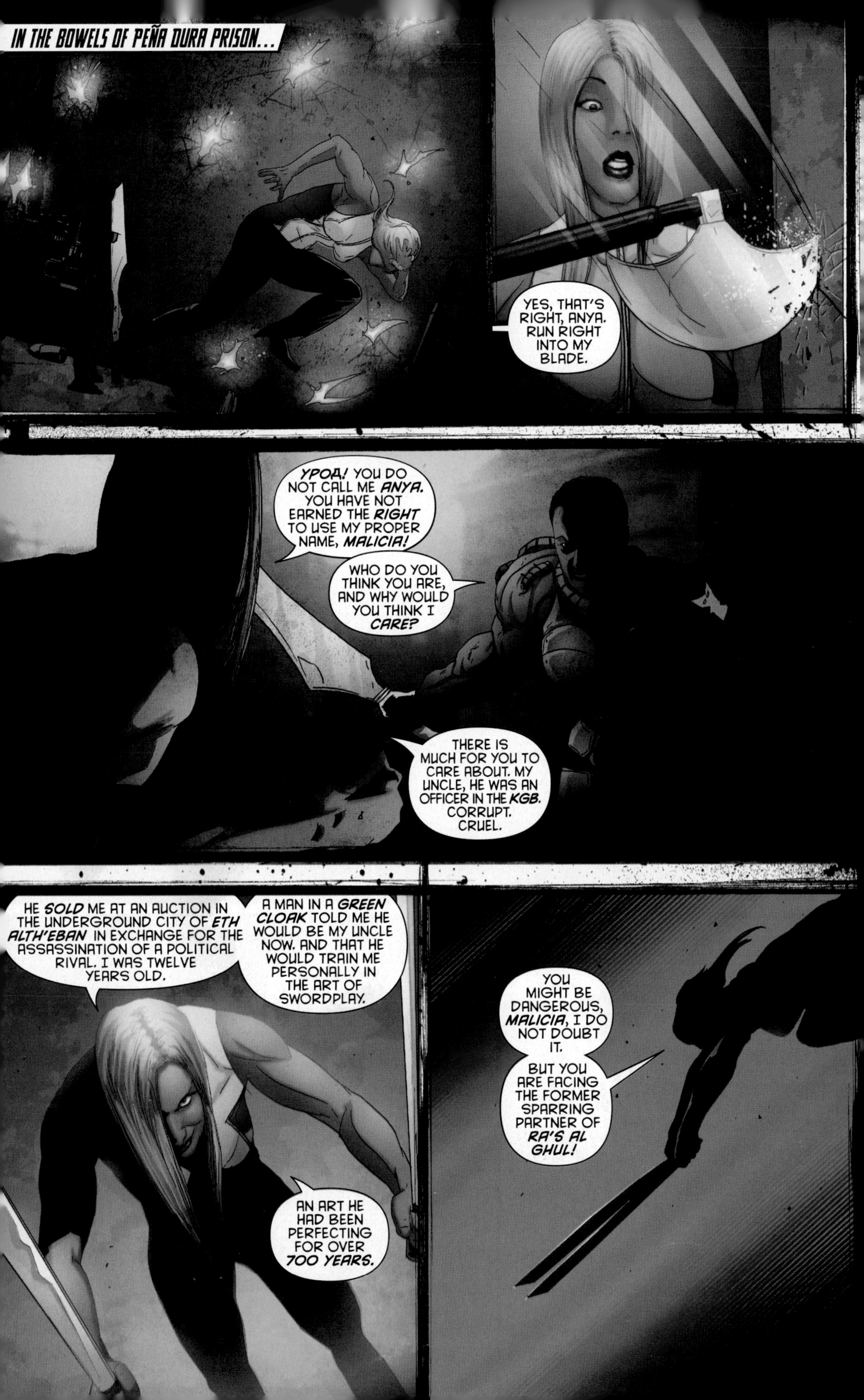
IN THE BOWELS OF PEÑA DURA PRISON...
YES, THAT'S RIGHT, ANYA. RUN RIGHT INTO MY BLADE.
УРОД! YOU DO NOT CALL ME ANYA. YOU HAVE NOT EARNED THE RIGHT TO USE MY PROPER NAME, MALICIA!
WHO DO YOU THINK YOU ARE, AND WHY WOULD YOU THINK I CARE?
THERE IS MUCH FOR YOU TO CARE ABOUT. MY UNCLE, HE WAS AN OFFICER IN THE KGB. CORRUPT. CRUEL.
HE SOLD ME AT AN AUCTION IN THE UNDERGROUND CITY OF ETH ALTH'EBAN IN EXCHANGE FOR THE ASSASSINATION OF A POLITICAL RIVAL. I WAS TWELVE YEARS OLD.
A MAN IN A GREEN CLOAK TOLD ME HE WOULD BE MY UNCLE NOW. AND THAT HE WOULD TRAIN ME PERSONALLY IN THE ART OF SWORDPLAY.
AN ART HE HAD BEEN PERFECTING FOR OVER 700 YEARS.
YOU MIGHT BE DANGEROUS, MALICIA, I DO NOT DOUBT IT.
BUT YOU ARE FACING THE FORMER SPARRING PARTNER OF RA'S AL GHUL!

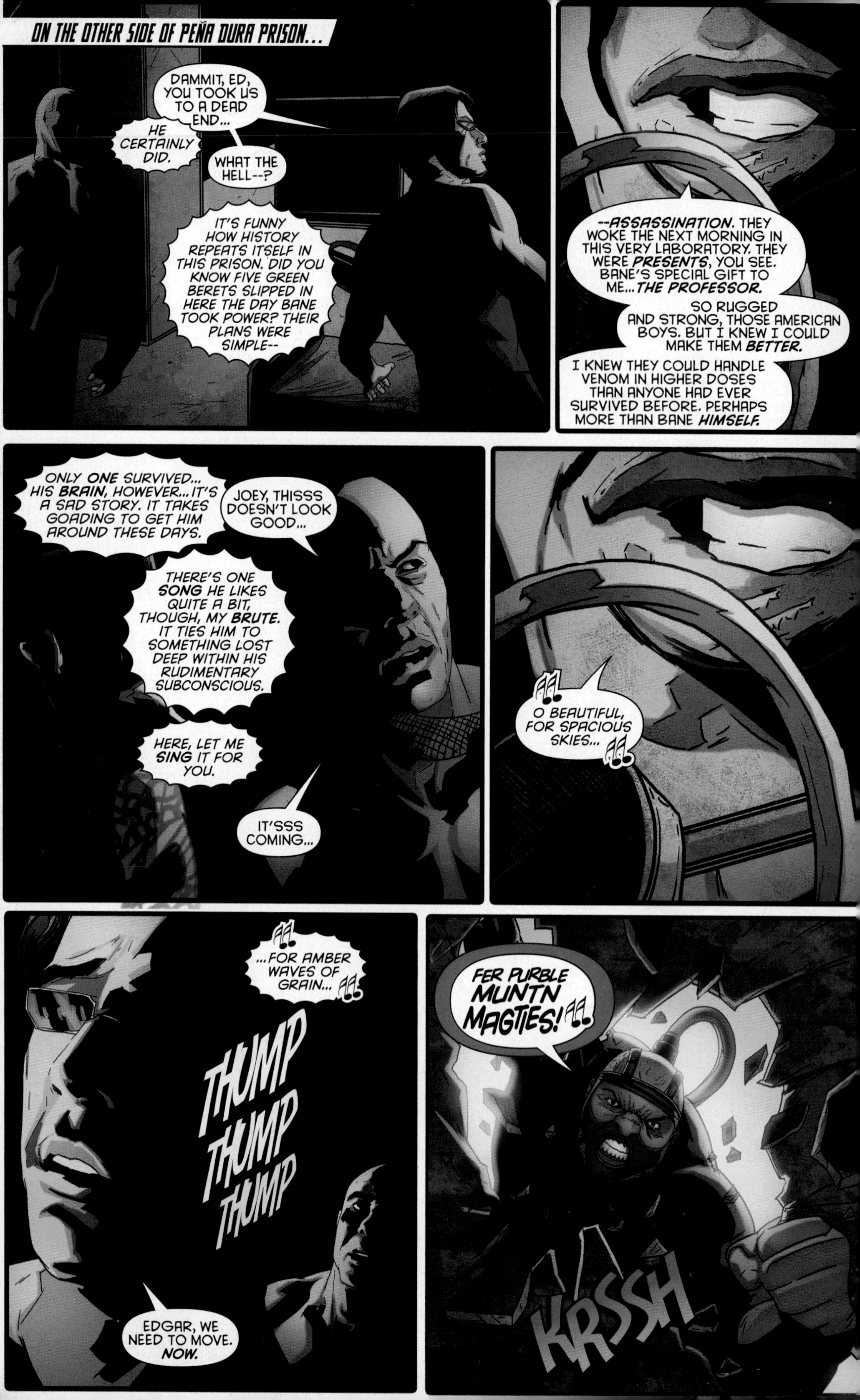
ON THE OTHER SIDE OF PEÑA DURA PRISON...
DAMMIT, ED, YOU TOOK US TO A DEAD END...
HE CERTAINLY DID.
WHAT THE HELL--?
IT'S FUNNY HOW HISTORY REPEATS ITSELF IN THIS PRISON. DID YOU KNOW FIVE GREEN BERETS SLIPPED IN HERE THE DAY BANE TOOK POWER? THEIR PLANS WERE SIMPLE--
--ASSASSINATION. THEY WOKE THE NEXT MORNING IN THIS VERY LABORATORY. THEY WERE PRESENTS, YOU SEE. BANE'S SPECIAL GIFT TO ME...THE PROFESSOR.
SO RUGGED AND STRONG, THOSE AMERICAN BOYS. BUT I KNEW I COULD MAKE THEM BETTER.
I KNEW THEY COULD HANDLE VENOM IN HIGHER DOSES THAN ANYONE HAD EVER SURVIVED BEFORE. PERHAPS MORE THAN BANE HIMSELF.
ONLY ONE SURVIVED... HIS BRAIN, HOWEVER... IT'S A SAD STORY. IT TAKES GOADING TO GET HIM AROUND THESE DAYS.
JOEY, THISSS DOESN'T LOOK GOOD...
THERE'S ONE SONG HE LIKES QUITE A BIT, THOUGH, MY BRUTE. IT TIES HIM TO SOMETHING LOST DEEP WITHIN HIS RUDIMENTARY SUBCONSCIOUS.
HERE, LET ME SING IT FOR YOU.
IT'SSS COMING...
O BEAUTIFUL, FOR SPACIOUS SKIES...
...FOR AMBER WAVES OF GRAIN...
THUMP THUMP THUMP
EDGAR, WE NEED TO MOVE. NOW.
FER PURBLE MUNTN MAGTIES!
KRSSH

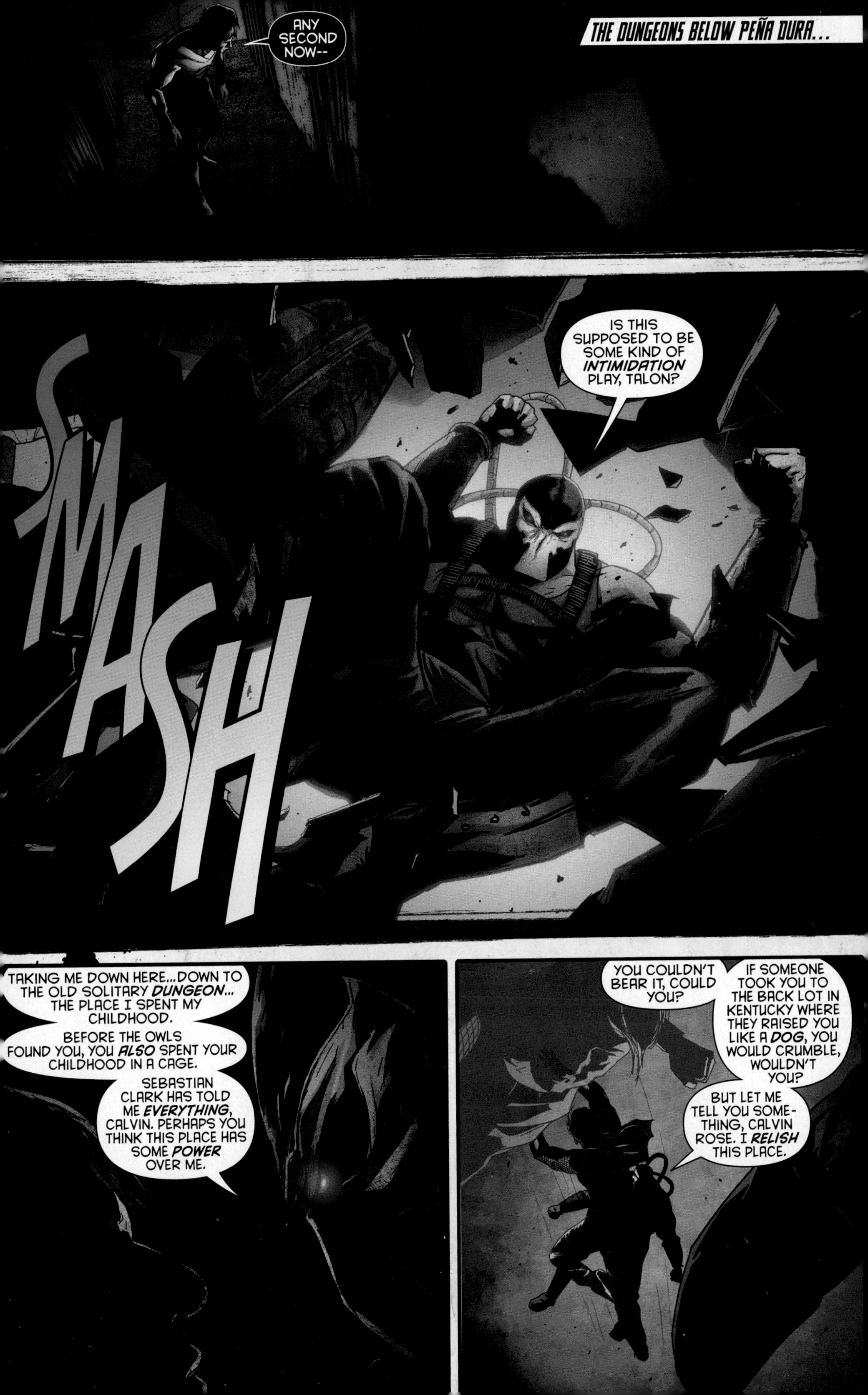
THE DUNGEONS BELOW PEÑA DURA...
ANY SECOND NOW--
SMASH
IS THIS SUPPOSED TO BE SOME KIND OF INTIMIDATION PLAY, TALON?
TAKING ME DOWN HERE...DOWN TO THE OLD SOLITARY DUNGEON... THE PLACE I SPENT MY CHILDHOOD.
BEFORE THE OWLS FOUND YOU, YOU ALSO SPENT YOUR CHILDHOOD IN A CAGE.
SEBASTIAN CLARK HAS TOLD ME EVERYTHING, CALVIN. PERHAPS YOU THINK THIS PLACE HAS SOME POWER OVER ME.
YOU COULDN'T BEAR IT, COULD YOU?
IF SOMEONE TOOK YOU TO THE BACK LOT IN KENTUCKY WHERE THEY RAISED YOU LIKE A DOG, YOU WOULD CRUMBLE, WOULDN'T YOU?
BUT LET ME TELL YOU SOME-THING, CALVIN ROSE. I RELISH THIS PLACE.

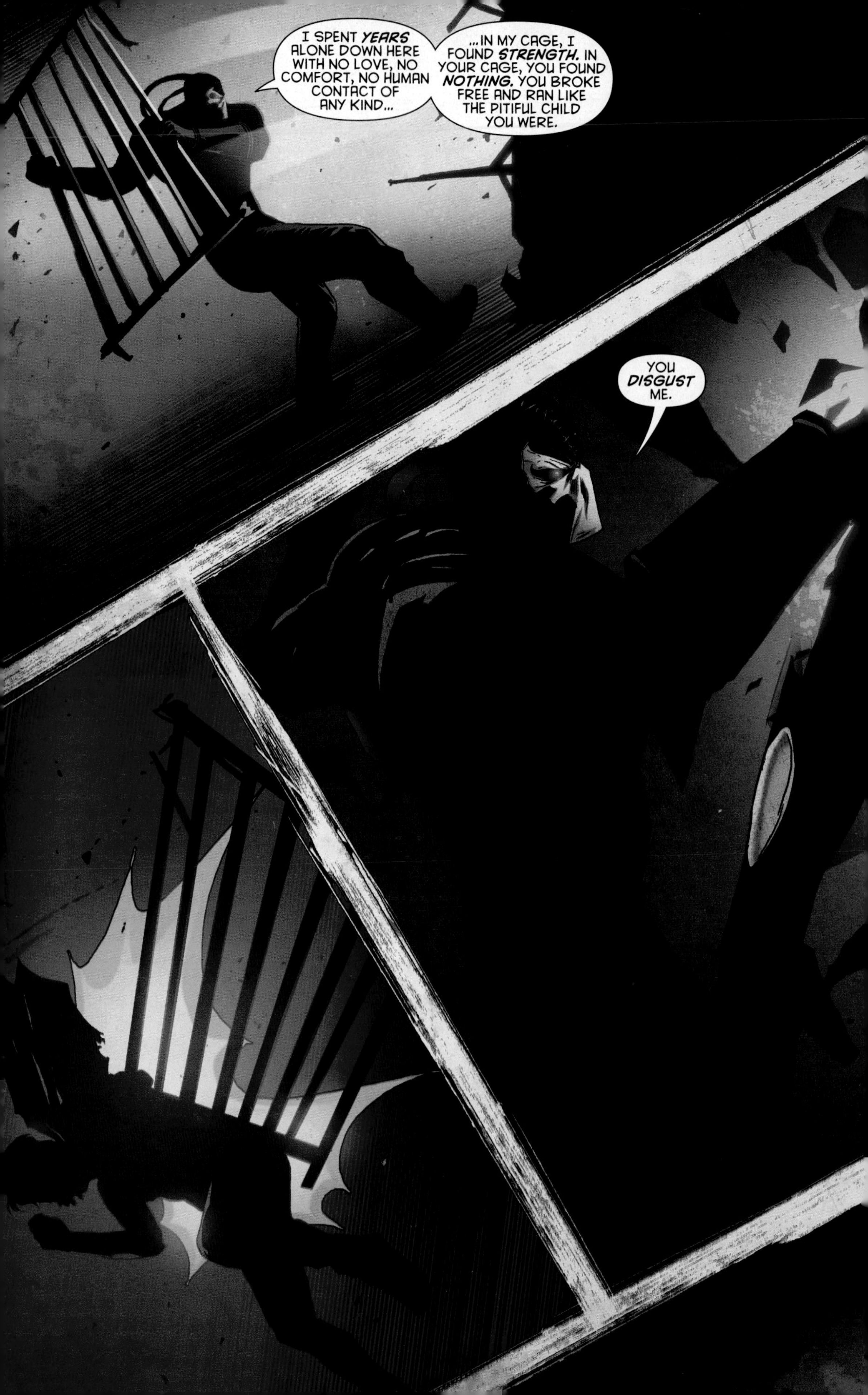
I SPENT YEARS ALONE DOWN HERE WITH NO LOVE, NO COMFORT, NO HUMAN CONTACT OF ANY KIND...
...IN MY CAGE, I FOUND STRENGTH. IN YOUR CAGE, YOU FOUND NOTHING. YOU BROKE FREE AND RAN LIKE THE PITIFUL CHILD YOU WERE.
YOU DISGUST ME.

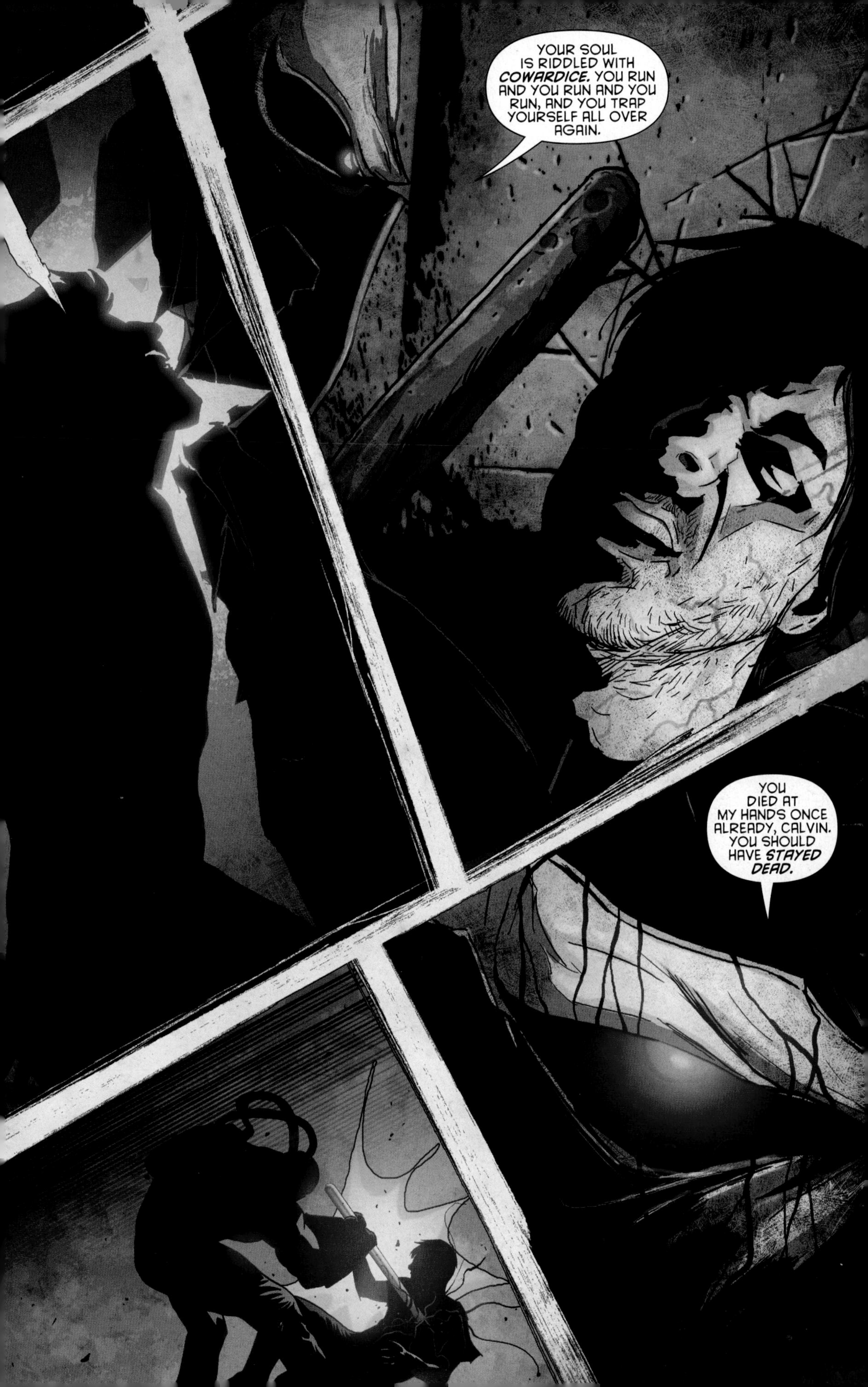
YOUR SOUL IS RIDDLED WITH COWARDICE. YOU RUN AND YOU RUN AND YOU RUN, AND YOU TRAP YOURSELF ALL OVER AGAIN.
YOU DIED AT MY HANDS ONCE ALREADY, CALVIN. YOU SHOULD HAVE STAYED DEAD.

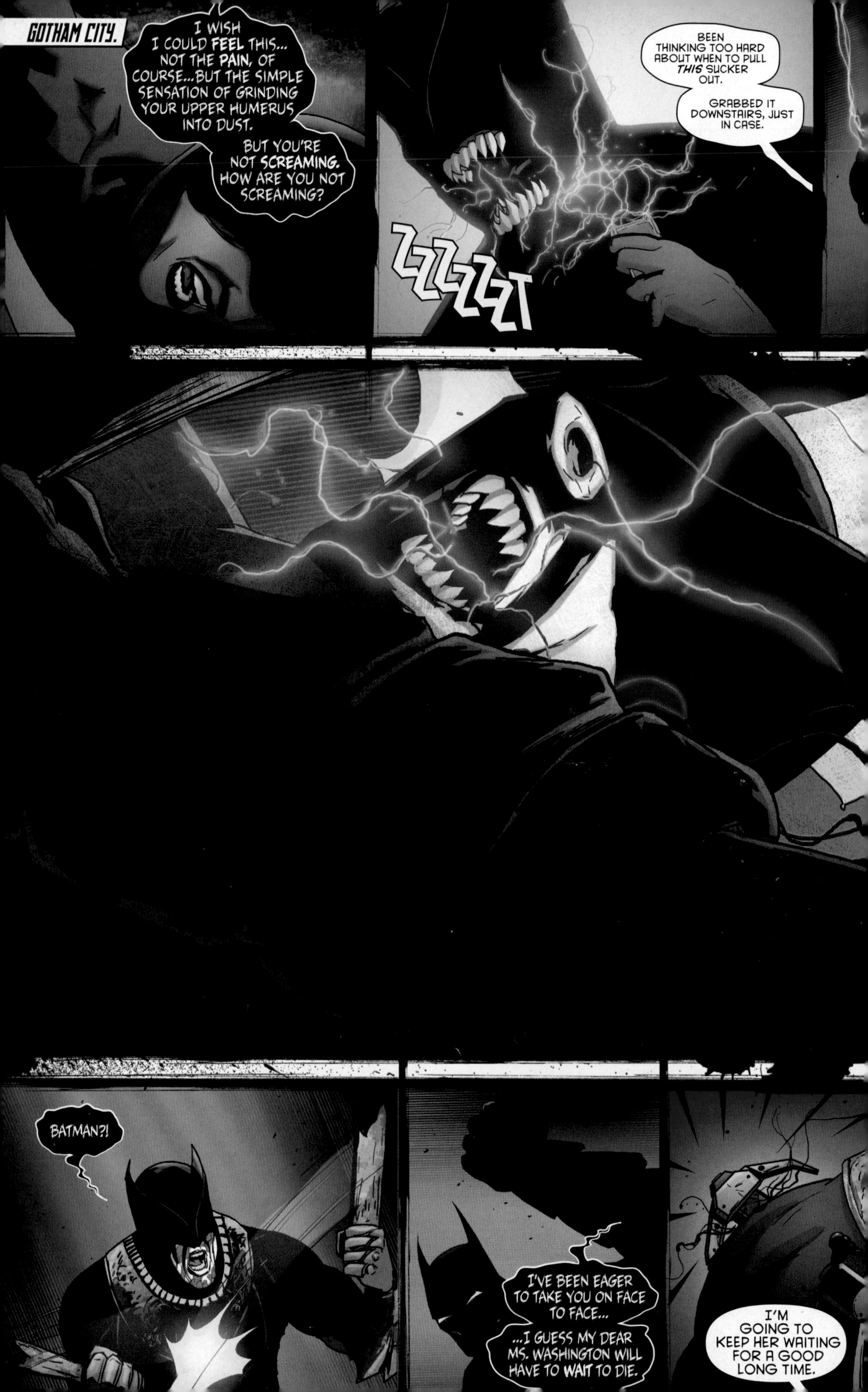
GOTHAM CITY.
I WISH I COULD FEEL THIS... NOT THE PAIN, OF COURSE...BUT THE SIMPLE SENSATION OF GRINDING YOUR UPPER HUMERUS INTO DUST.
BUT YOU'RE NOT SCREAMING. HOW ARE YOU NOT SCREAMING?
BEEN THINKING TOO HARD ABOUT WHEN TO PULL THIS SUCKER OUT.
GRABBED IT DOWNSTAIRS, JUST IN CASE.
ZZZZZZT
BATMAN?!
I'VE BEEN EAGER TO TAKE YOU ON FACE TO FACE...
...I GUESS MY DEAR MS. WASHINGTON WILL HAVE TO WAIT TO DIE.
I'M GOING TO KEEP HER WAITING FOR A GOOD LONG TIME.

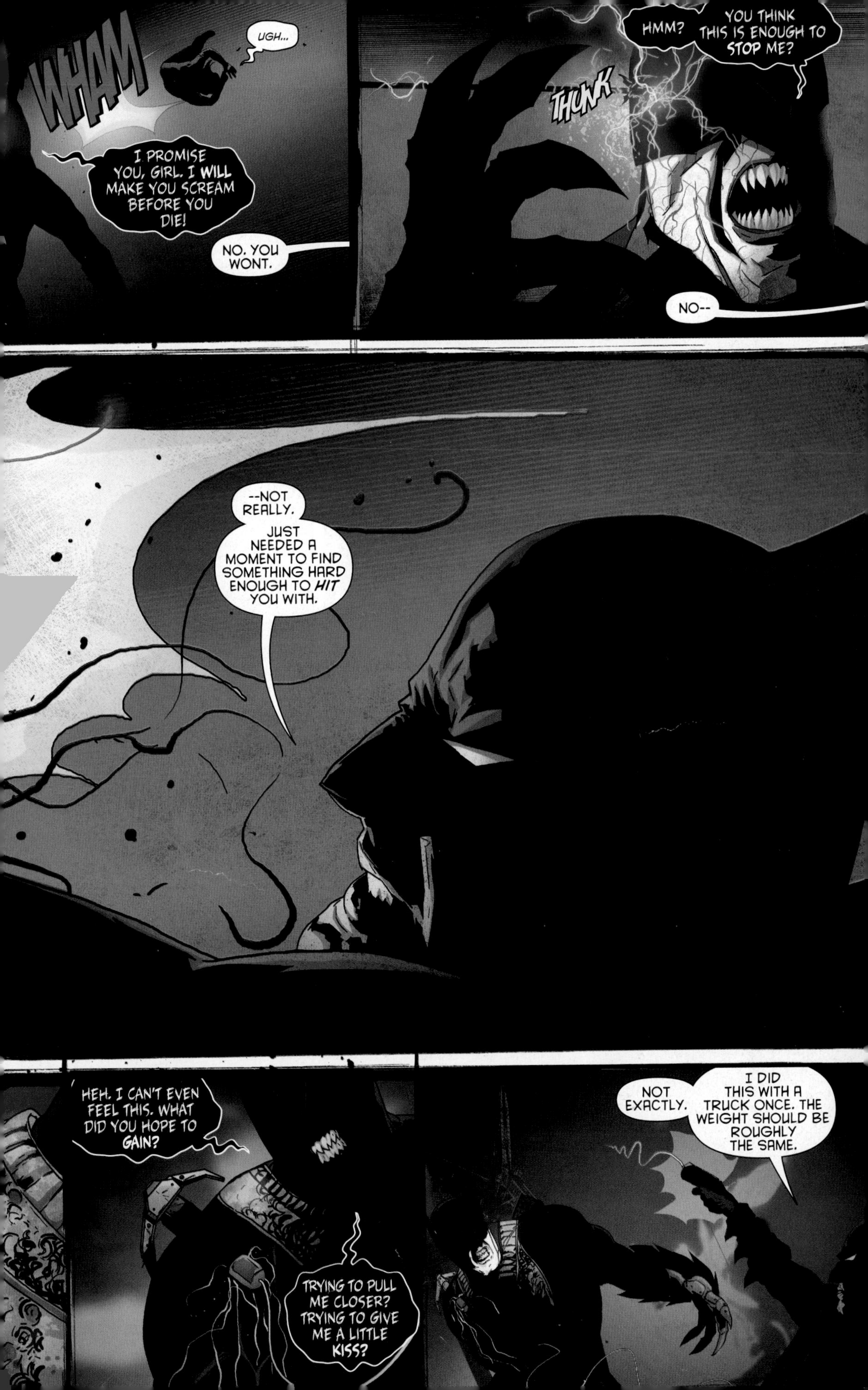
WHAM
UGH...
I PROMISE YOU, GIRL. I WILL MAKE YOU SCREAM BEFORE YOU DIE!
NO. YOU WONT.
THUNK
HMM?
YOU THINK THIS IS ENOUGH TO STOP ME?
NO--
--NOT REALLY.
JUST NEEDED A MOMENT TO FIND SOMETHING HARD ENOUGH TO HIT YOU WITH.
HEH. I CAN'T EVEN FEEL THIS. WHAT DID YOU HOPE TO GAIN?
TRYING TO PULL ME CLOSER? TRYING TO GIVE ME A LITTLE KISS?
NOT EXACTLY.
I DID THIS WITH A TRUCK ONCE. THE WEIGHT SHOULD BE ROUGHLY THE SAME.

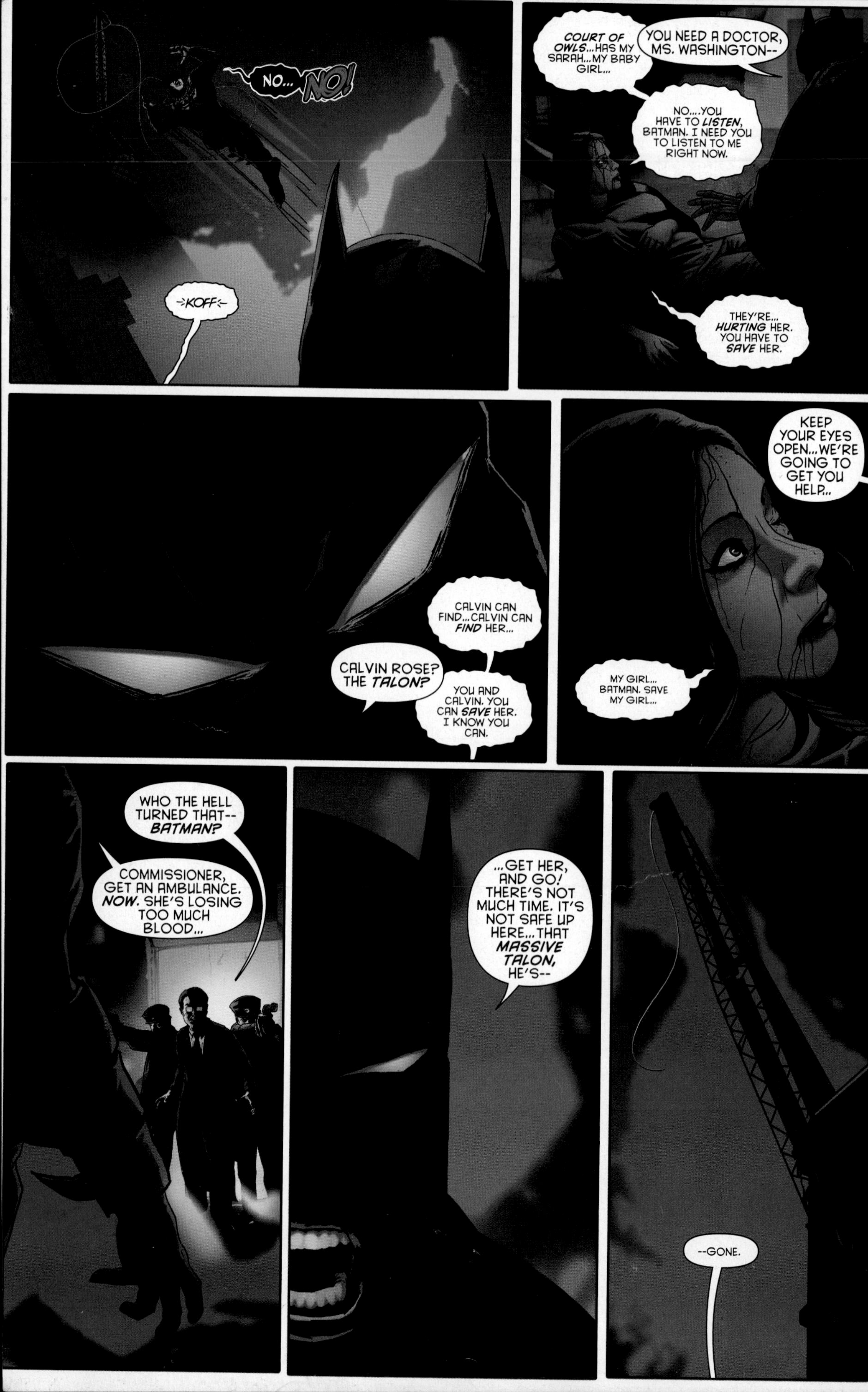

NO... NO!
-KOFF-
COURT OF OWLS... HAS MY SARAH... MY BABY GIRL...
YOU NEED A DOCTOR, MS. WASHINGTON--
NO.... YOU HAVE TO LISTEN, BATMAN. I NEED YOU TO LISTEN TO ME RIGHT NOW.
THEY'RE... HURTING HER. YOU HAVE TO SAVE HER.
CALVIN CAN FIND... CALVIN CAN FIND HER...
CALVIN ROSE? THE TALON?
YOU AND CALVIN. YOU CAN SAVE HER. I KNOW YOU CAN.
KEEP YOUR EYES OPEN... WE'RE GOING TO GET YOU HELP...
MY GIRL... BATMAN. SAVE MY GIRL...
WHO THE HELL TURNED THAT-- BATMAN?
COMMISSIONER, GET AN AMBULANCE. NOW. SHE'S LOSING TOO MUCH BLOOD...
...GET HER, AND GO! THERE'S NOT MUCH TIME. IT'S NOT SAFE UP HERE... THAT MASSIVE TALON, HE'S--
--GONE.

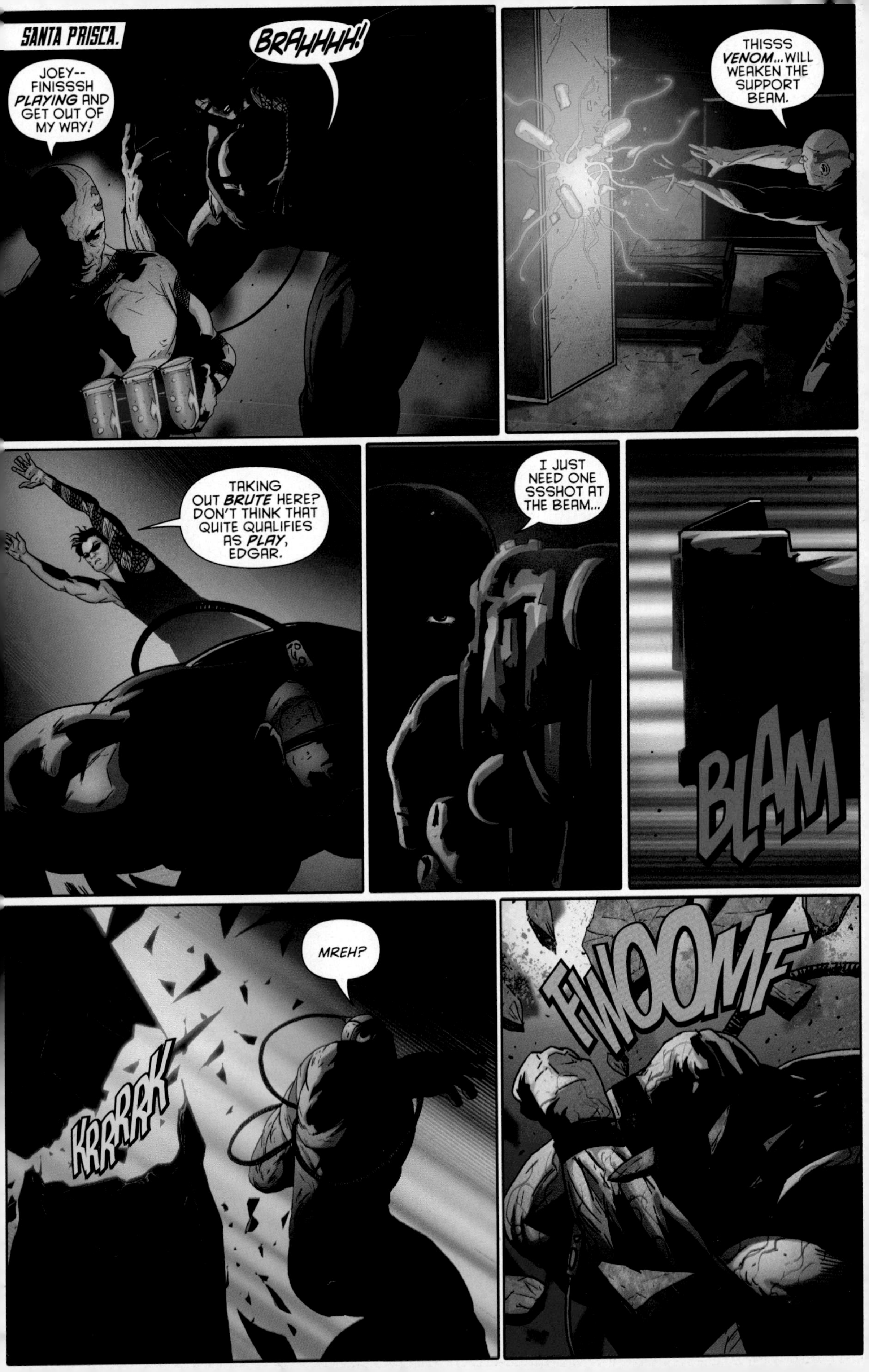
SANTA PRISCA.
BRAHHHH!
JOEY-- FINISSSH PLAYING AND GET OUT OF MY WAY!
THISSS VENOM... WILL WEAKEN THE SUPPORT BEAM.
TAKING OUT BRUTE HERE? DON'T THINK THAT QUITE QUALIFIES AS PLAY, EDGAR.
I JUST NEED ONE SSSHOT AT THE BEAM...
BLAM
MREH?
KRRRRK
FWOOMF

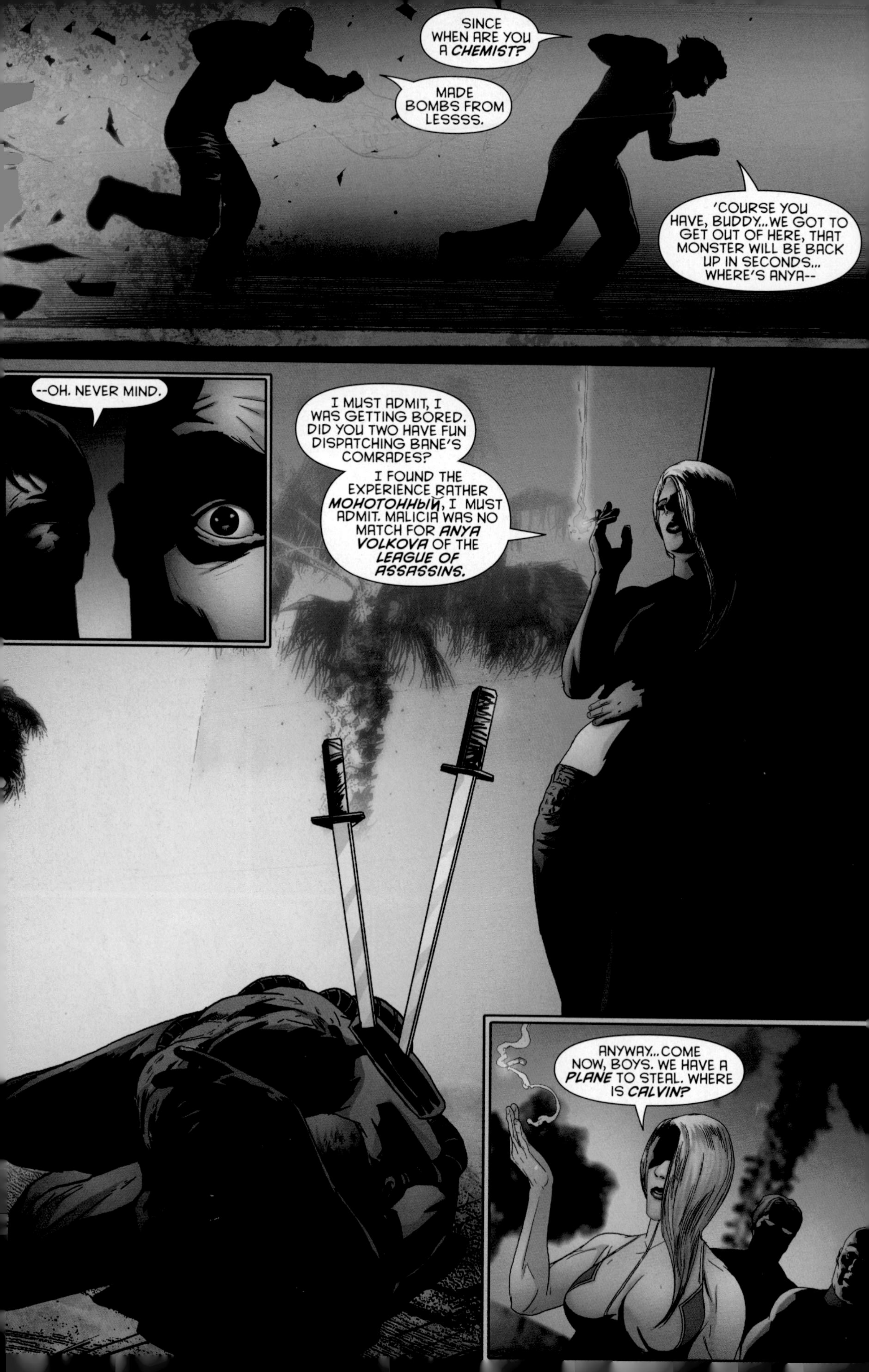
SINCE WHEN ARE YOU A CHEMIST?
MADE BOMBS FROM LESSSS.
'COURSE YOU HAVE, BUDDY...WE GOT TO GET OUT OF HERE, THAT MONSTER WILL BE BACK UP IN SECONDS... WHERE'S ANYA--
--OH. NEVER MIND.
I MUST ADMIT, I WAS GETTING BORED. DID YOU TWO HAVE FUN DISPATCHING BANE'S COMRADES?
I FOUND THE EXPERIENCE RATHER МОНОТОННЫЙ, I MUST ADMIT. MALICIA WAS NO MATCH FOR ANYA VOLKOVA OF THE LEAGUE OF ASSASSINS.
ANYWAY...COME NOW, BOYS. WE HAVE A PLANE TO STEAL. WHERE IS CALVIN?

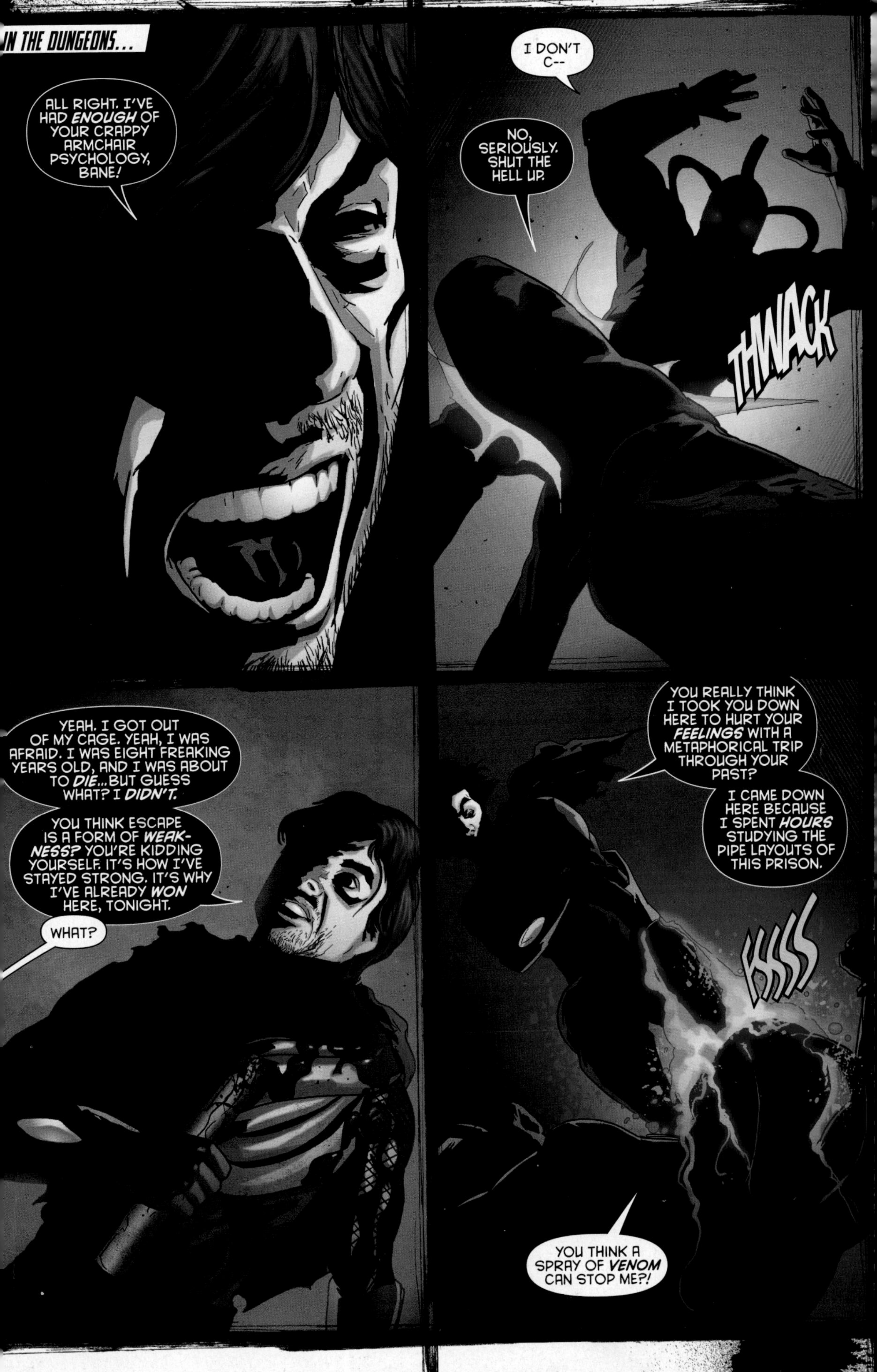
IN THE DUNGEONS...
ALL RIGHT. I'VE HAD ENOUGH OF YOUR CRAPPY ARMCHAIR PSYCHOLOGY, BANE!
I DON'T C--
NO, SERIOUSLY. SHUT THE HELL UP.
THWACK
YEAH. I GOT OUT OF MY CAGE. YEAH, I WAS AFRAID. I WAS EIGHT FREAKING YEARS OLD, AND I WAS ABOUT TO DIE...BUT GUESS WHAT? I DIDN'T.
YOU THINK ESCAPE IS A FORM OF WEAK-NESS? YOU'RE KIDDING YOURSELF. IT'S HOW I'VE STAYED STRONG. IT'S WHY I'VE ALREADY WON HERE, TONIGHT.
WHAT?
YOU REALLY THINK I TOOK YOU DOWN HERE TO HURT YOUR FEELINGS WITH A METAPHORICAL TRIP THROUGH YOUR PAST?
I CAME DOWN HERE BECAUSE I SPENT HOURS STUDYING THE PIPE LAYOUTS OF THIS PRISON.
YOU THINK A SPRAY OF VENOM CAN STOP ME?!

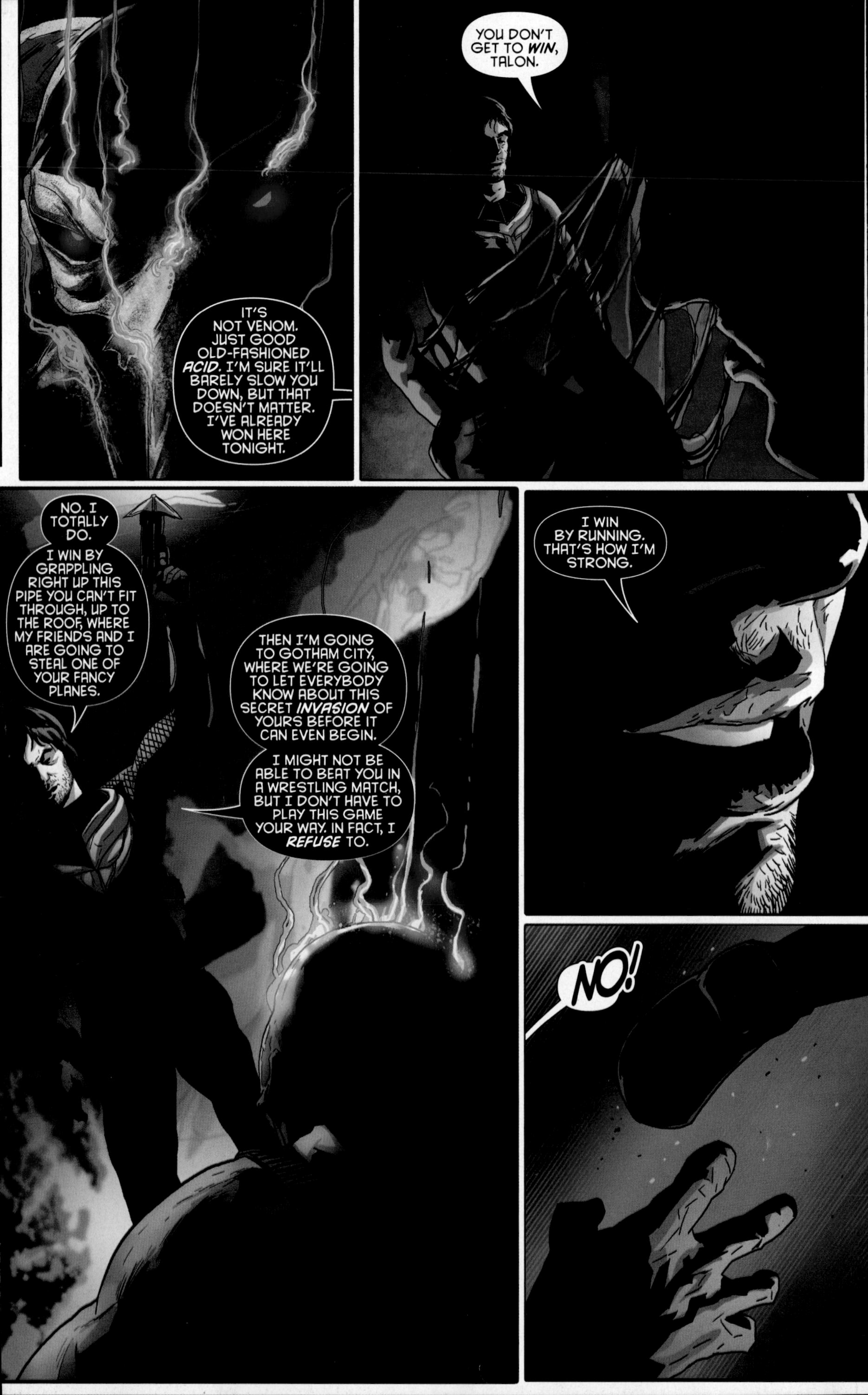
IT'S NOT VENOM. JUST GOOD OLD-FASHIONED ACID. I'M SURE IT'LL BARELY SLOW YOU DOWN, BUT THAT DOESN'T MATTER. I'VE ALREADY WON HERE TONIGHT.
YOU DON'T GET TO WIN, TALON.
NO. I TOTALLY DO.
I WIN BY GRAPPLING RIGHT UP THIS PIPE YOU CAN'T FIT THROUGH, UP TO THE ROOF, WHERE MY FRIENDS AND I ARE GOING TO STEAL ONE OF YOUR FANCY PLANES.
THEN I'M GOING TO GOTHAM CITY, WHERE WE'RE GOING TO LET EVERYBODY KNOW ABOUT THIS SECRET INVASION OF YOURS BEFORE IT CAN EVEN BEGIN.
I MIGHT NOT BE ABLE TO BEAT YOU IN A WRESTLING MATCH, BUT I DON'T HAVE TO PLAY THIS GAME YOUR WAY. IN FACT, I REFUSE TO.
I WIN BY RUNNING. THAT'S HOW I'M STRONG.
NO!

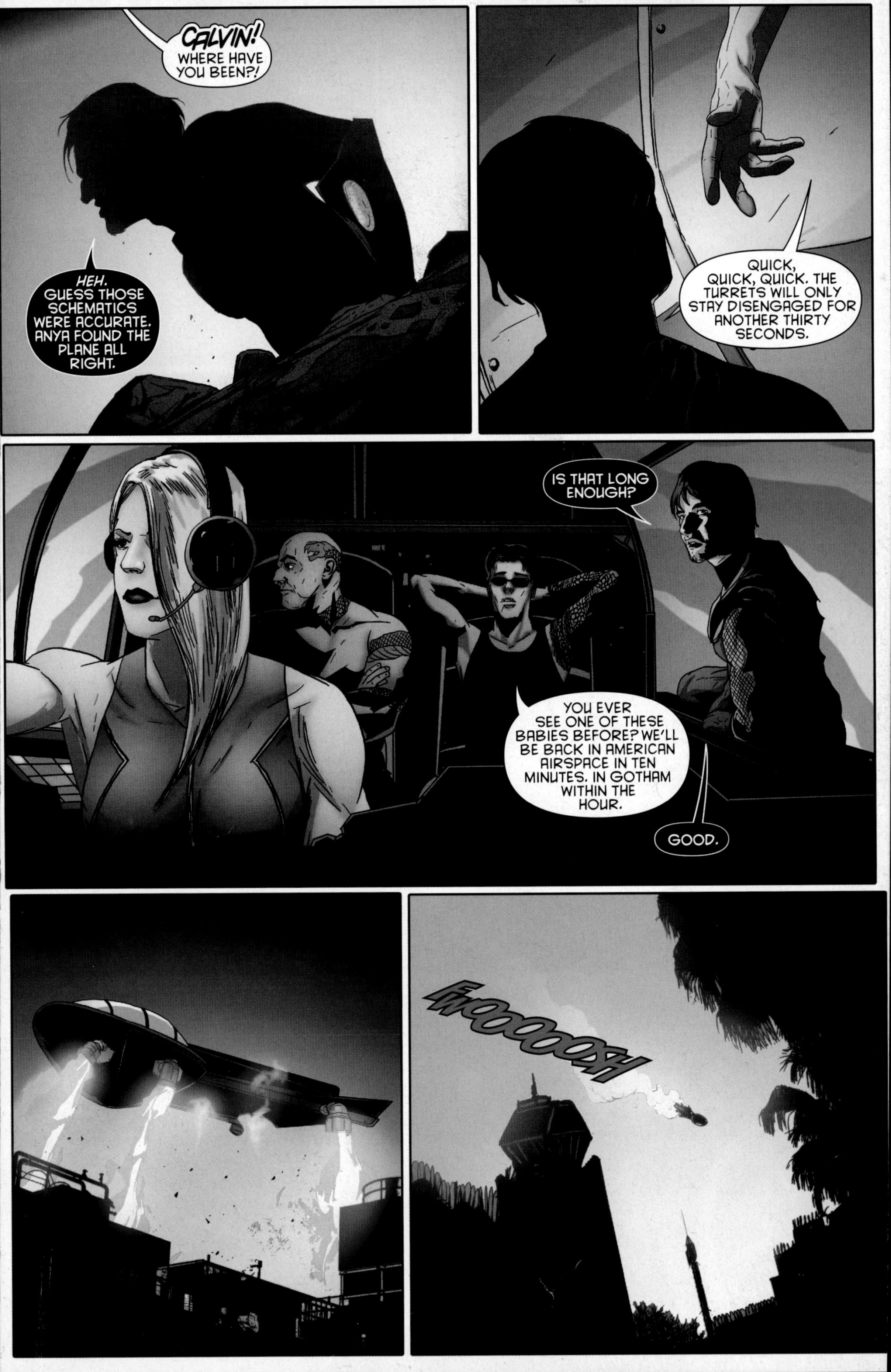
CALVIN! WHERE HAVE YOU BEEN?!
HEH. GUESS THOSE SCHEMATICS WERE ACCURATE. ANYA FOUND THE PLANE ALL RIGHT.
QUICK, QUICK, QUICK. THE TURRETS WILL ONLY STAY DISENGAGED FOR ANOTHER THIRTY SECONDS.
IS THAT LONG ENOUGH?
YOU EVER SEE ONE OF THESE BABIES BEFORE? WE'LL BE BACK IN AMERICAN AIRSPACE IN TEN MINUTES. IN GOTHAM WITHIN THE HOUR.
GOOD.
FWOOOOOSH

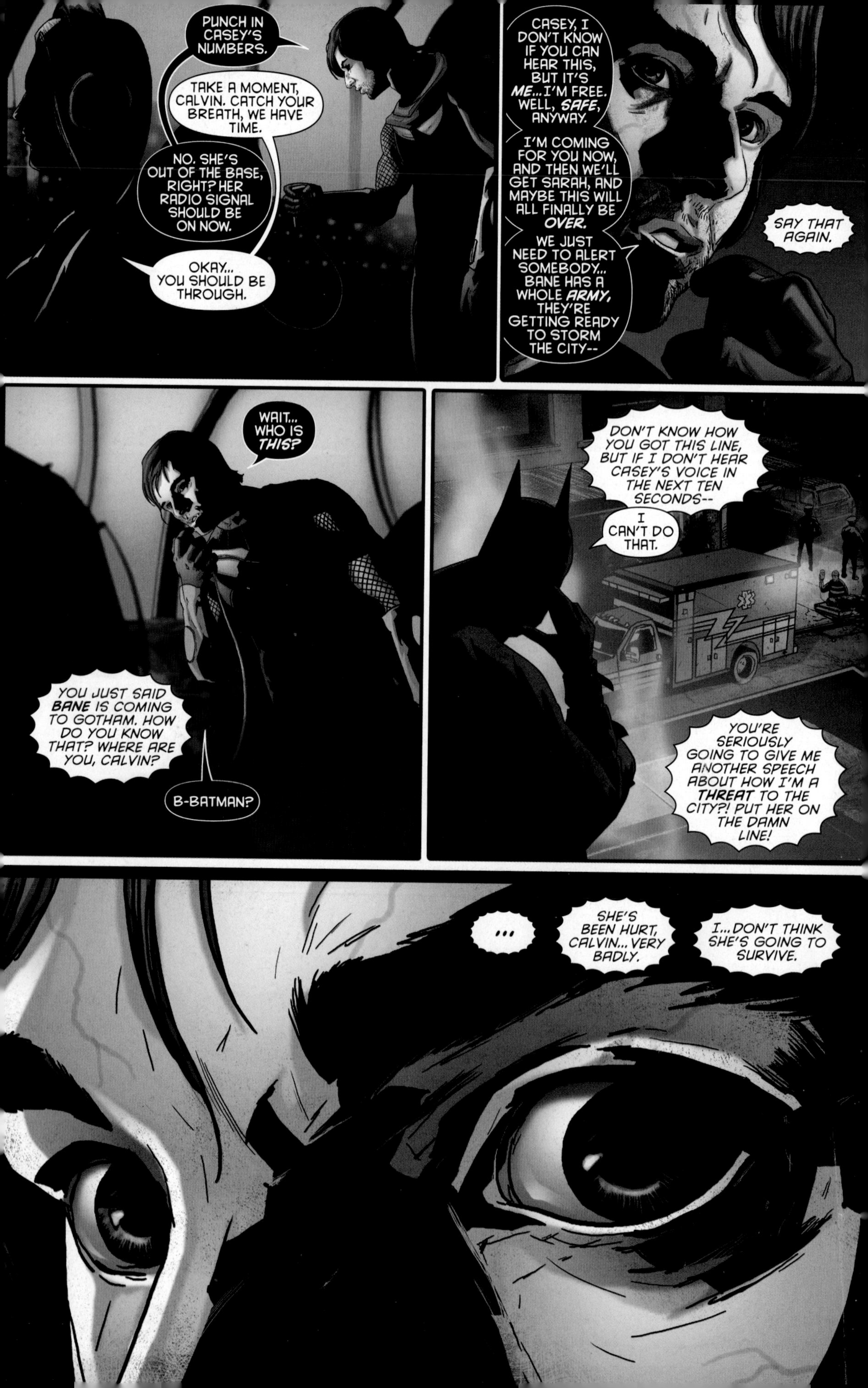
PUNCH IN CASEY'S NUMBERS.
TAKE A MOMENT, CALVIN. CATCH YOUR BREATH, WE HAVE TIME.
NO. SHE'S OUT OF THE BASE, RIGHT? HER RADIO SIGNAL SHOULD BE ON NOW.
OKAY... YOU SHOULD BE THROUGH.
CASEY, I DON'T KNOW IF YOU CAN HEAR THIS, BUT IT'S *ME*...I'M FREE. WELL, *SAFE*, ANYWAY.
I'M COMING FOR YOU NOW, AND THEN WE'LL GET SARAH, AND MAYBE THIS WILL ALL FINALLY BE *OVER*.
WE JUST NEED TO ALERT SOMEBODY... BANE HAS A WHOLE *ARMY*, THEY'RE GETTING READY TO STORM THE CITY--
SAY THAT AGAIN.
WAIT... WHO IS *THIS?*
YOU JUST SAID *BANE* IS COMING TO GOTHAM. HOW DO YOU KNOW THAT? WHERE ARE YOU, CALVIN?
B-BATMAN?
DON'T KNOW HOW YOU GOT THIS LINE, BUT IF I DON'T HEAR CASEY'S VOICE IN THE NEXT TEN SECONDS--
I CAN'T DO THAT.
YOU'RE SERIOUSLY GOING TO GIVE ME ANOTHER SPEECH ABOUT HOW I'M A *THREAT* TO THE CITY?! PUT HER ON THE DAMN LINE!
...
SHE'S BEEN HURT, CALVIN... VERY BADLY.
I...DON'T THINK SHE'S GOING TO SURVIVE.

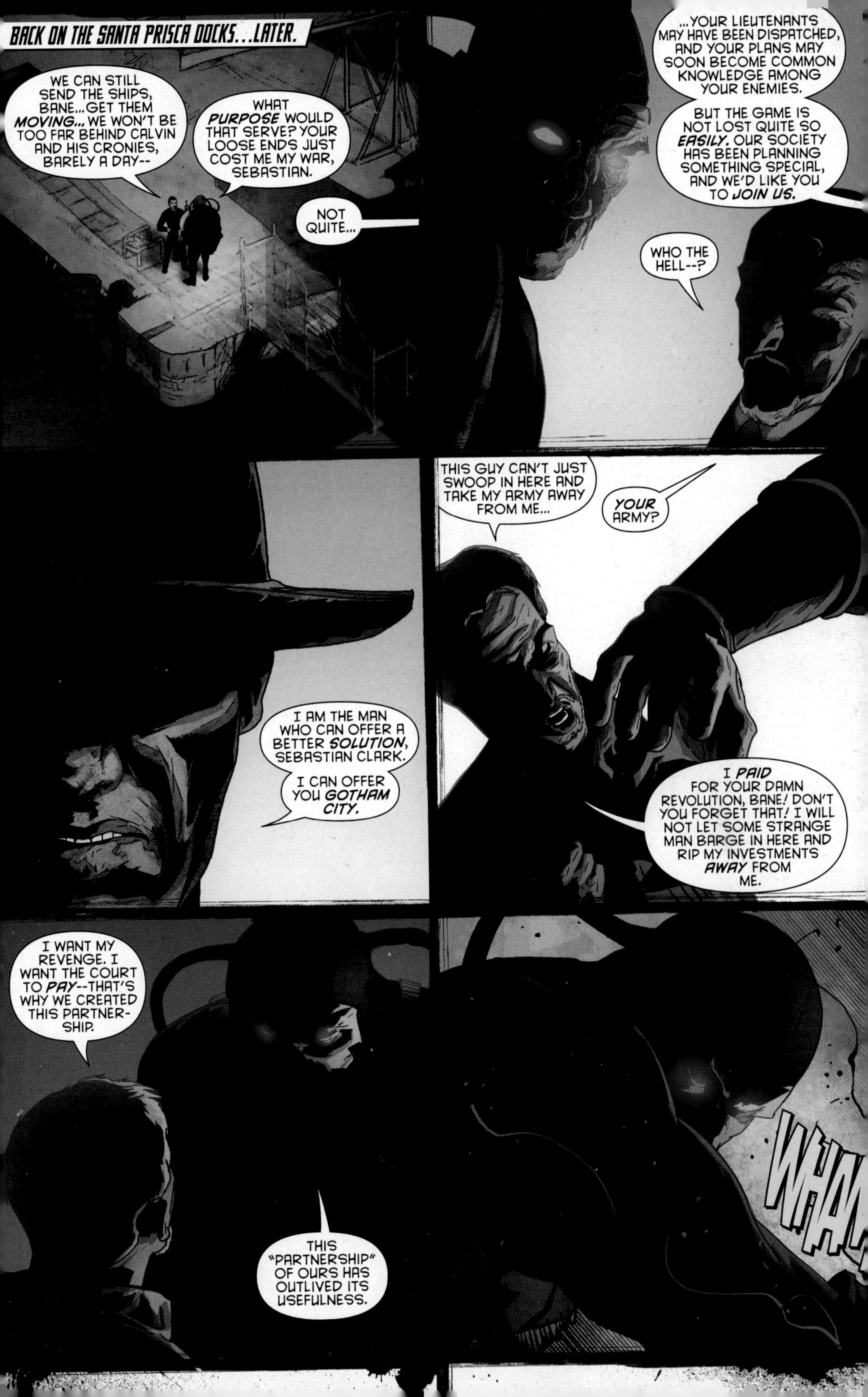
BACK ON THE SANTA PRISCA DOCKS...LATER.
WE CAN STILL SEND THE SHIPS, BANE...GET THEM MOVING... WE WON'T BE TOO FAR BEHIND CALVIN AND HIS CRONIES, BARELY A DAY--
WHAT PURPOSE WOULD THAT SERVE? YOUR LOOSE ENDS JUST COST ME MY WAR, SEBASTIAN.
NOT QUITE...
...YOUR LIEUTENANTS MAY HAVE BEEN DISPATCHED, AND YOUR PLANS MAY SOON BECOME COMMON KNOWLEDGE AMONG YOUR ENEMIES.
BUT THE GAME IS NOT LOST QUITE SO EASILY. OUR SOCIETY HAS BEEN PLANNING SOMETHING SPECIAL, AND WE'D LIKE YOU TO JOIN US.
WHO THE HELL--?
I AM THE MAN WHO CAN OFFER A BETTER SOLUTION, SEBASTIAN CLARK.
I CAN OFFER YOU GOTHAM CITY.
THIS GUY CAN'T JUST SWOOP IN HERE AND TAKE MY ARMY AWAY FROM ME...
YOUR ARMY?
I PAID FOR YOUR DAMN REVOLUTION, BANE! DON'T YOU FORGET THAT! I WILL NOT LET SOME STRANGE MAN BARGE IN HERE AND RIP MY INVESTMENTS AWAY FROM ME.
I WANT MY REVENGE. I WANT THE COURT TO PAY--THAT'S WHY WE CREATED THIS PARTNERSHIP.
THIS "PARTNERSHIP" OF OURS HAS OUTLIVED ITS USEFULNESS.
WHA

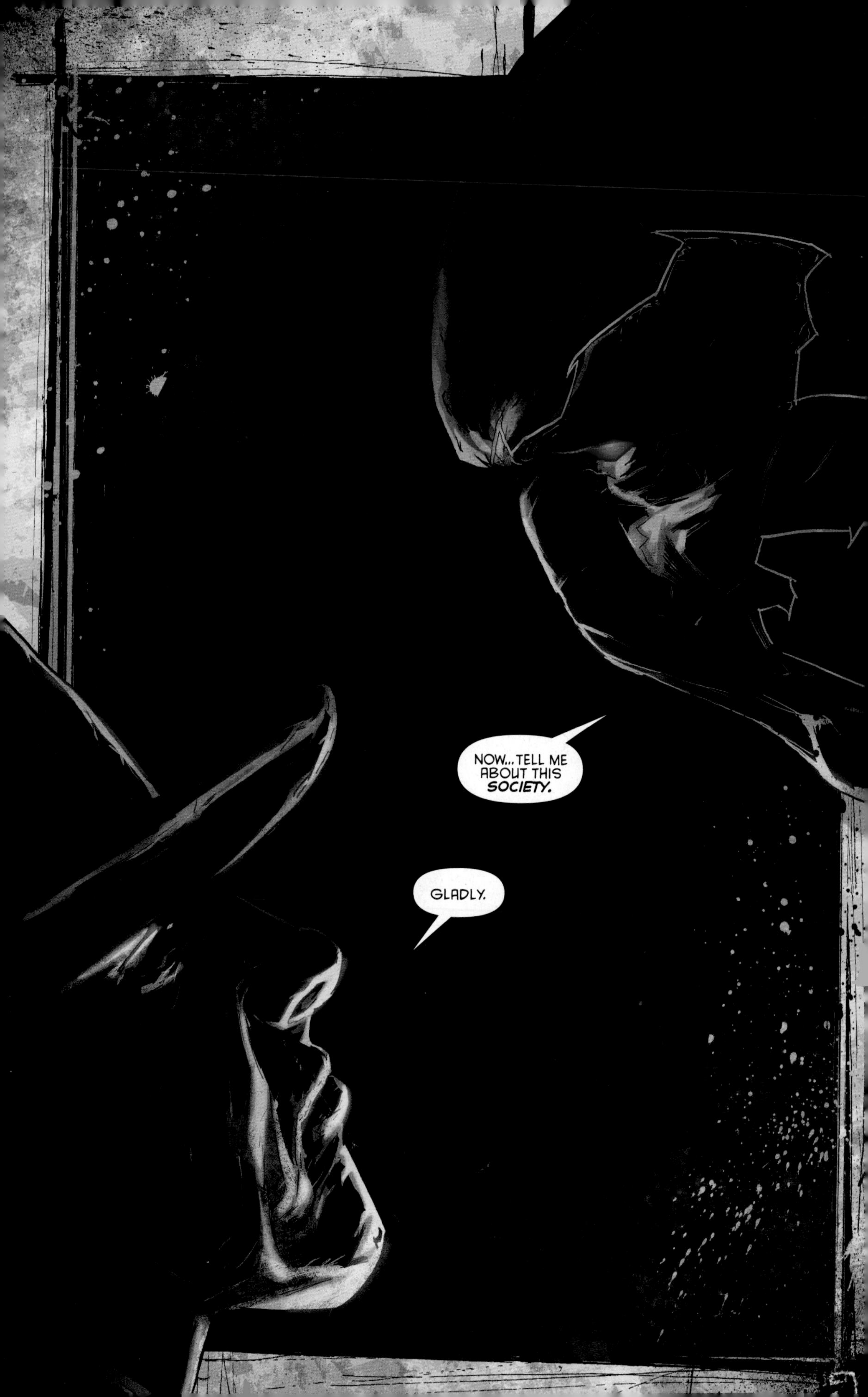
NOW... TELL ME ABOUT THIS *SOCIETY.*
GLADLY.

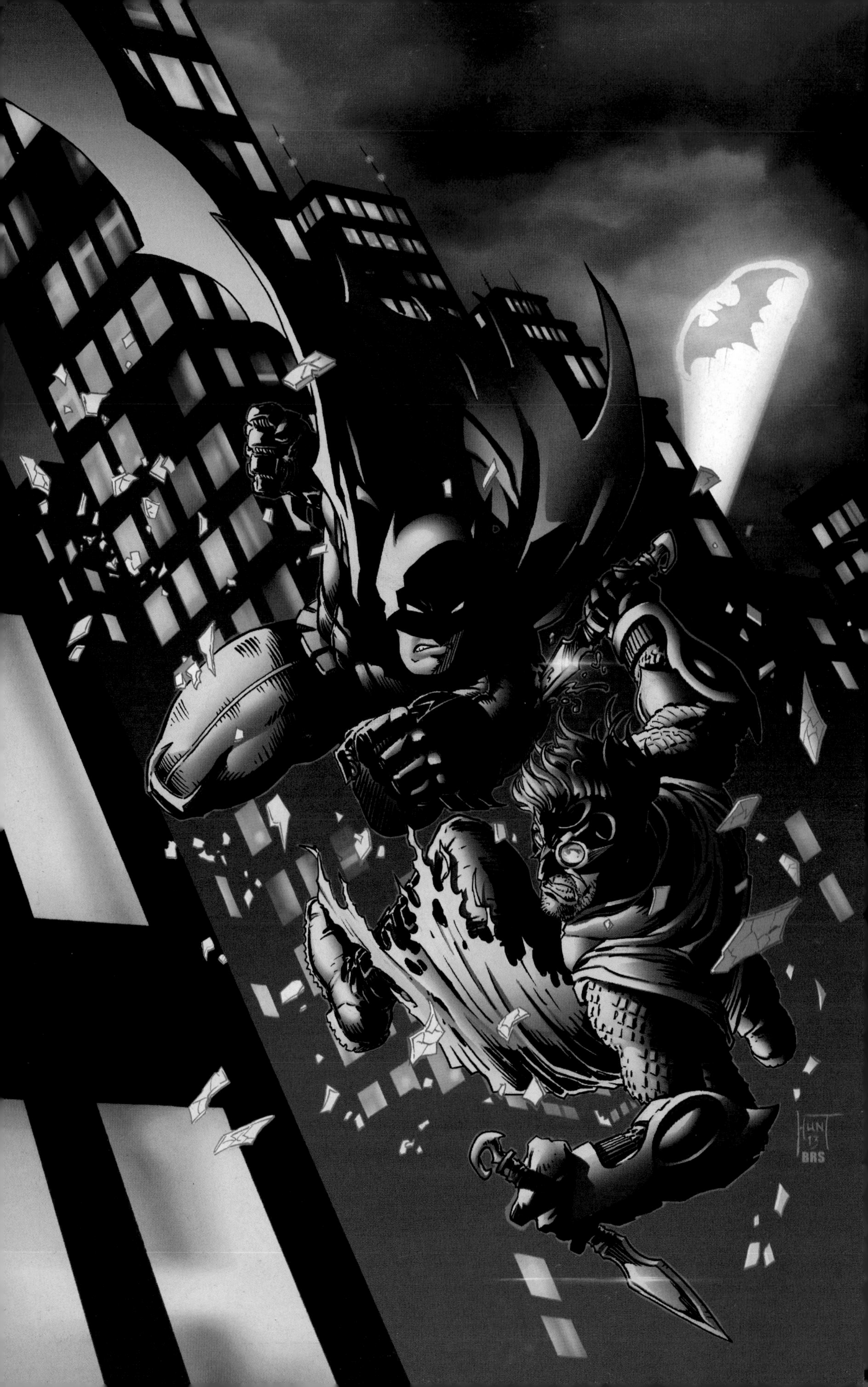

SMITH

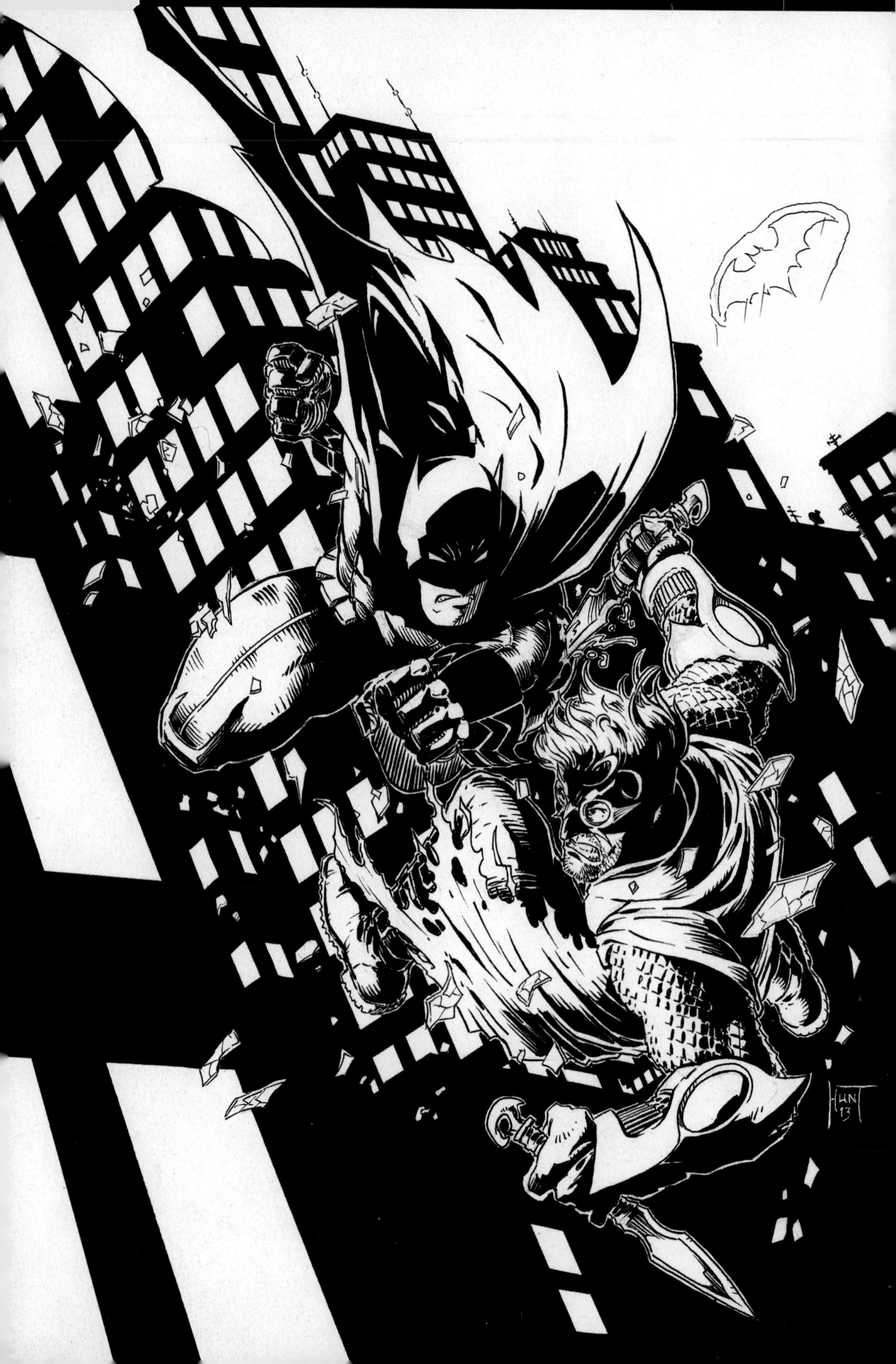

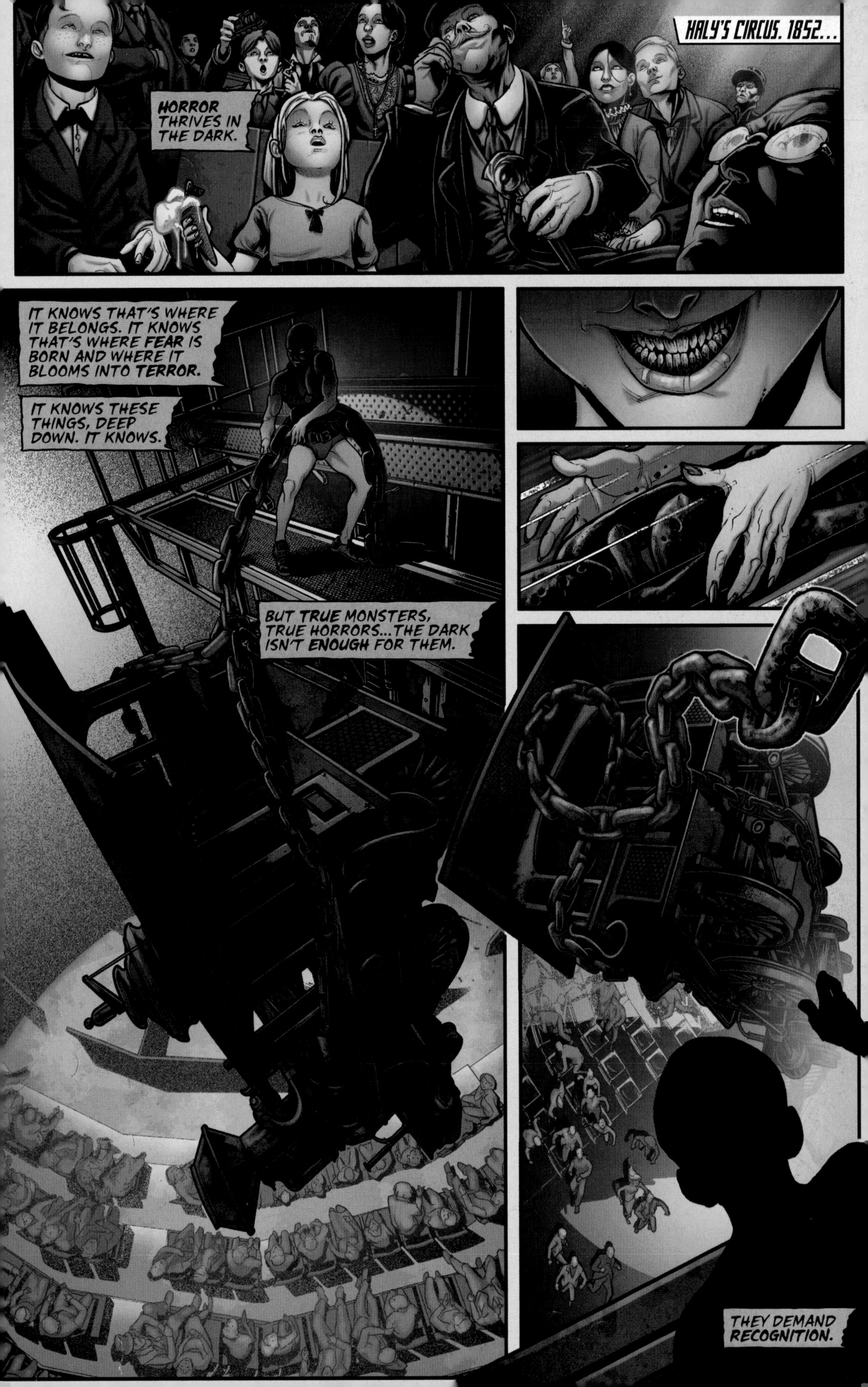
HALY'S CIRCUS. 1852...
HORROR THRIVES IN THE DARK.
IT KNOWS THAT'S WHERE IT BELONGS. IT KNOWS THAT'S WHERE FEAR IS BORN AND WHERE IT BLOOMS INTO TERROR.
IT KNOWS THESE THINGS, DEEP DOWN. IT KNOWS.
BUT TRUE MONSTERS, TRUE HORRORS...THE DARK ISN'T ENOUGH FOR THEM.
THEY DEMAND RECOGNITION.

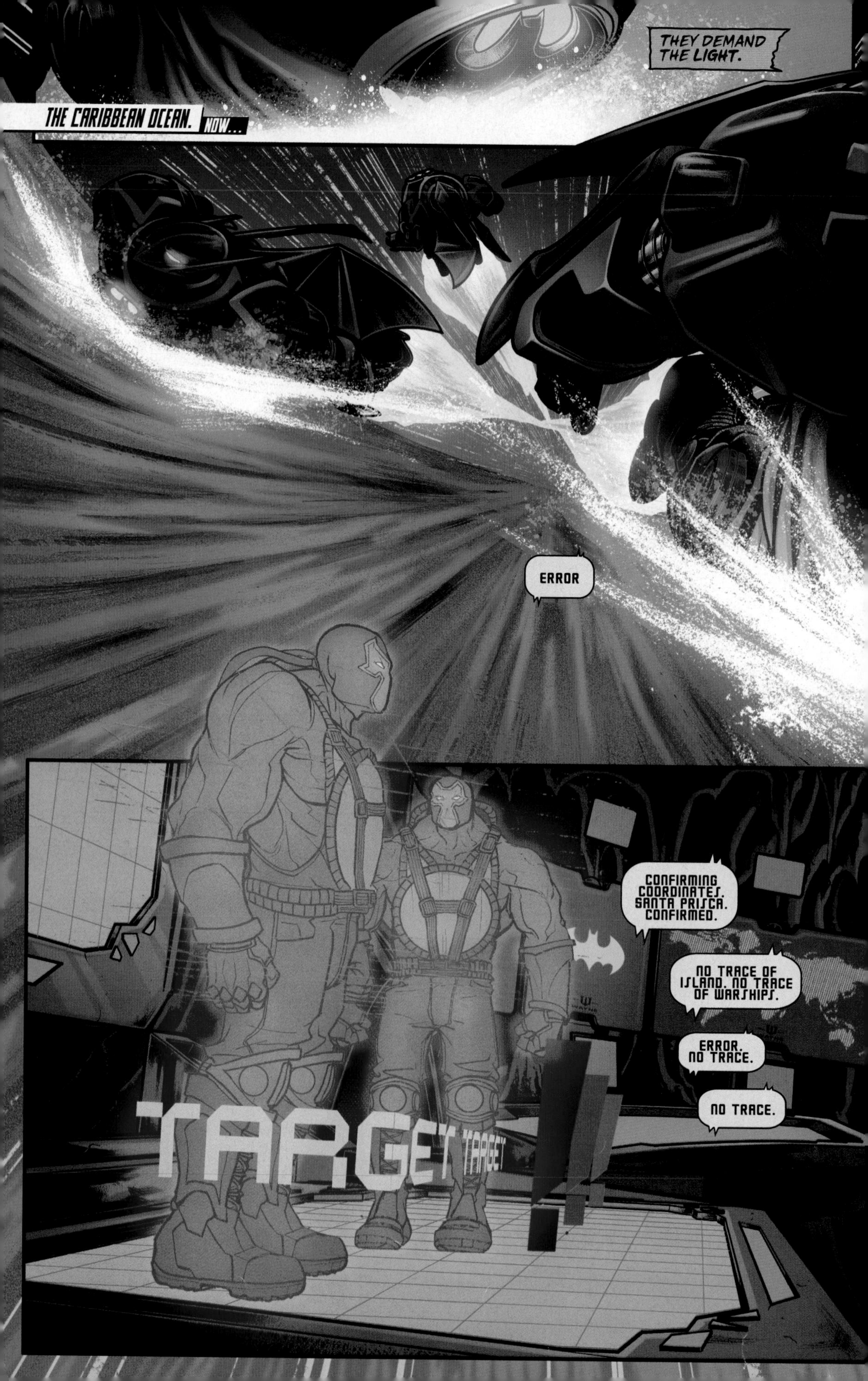
THEY DEMAND THE LIGHT.
THE CARIBBEAN OCEAN. NOW...
ERROR
CONFIRMING COORDINATES. SANTA PRISCA. CONFIRMED.
NO TRACE OF ISLAND. NO TRACE OF WARSHIPS.
ERROR. NO TRACE.
NO TRACE.
TARGET TARGET

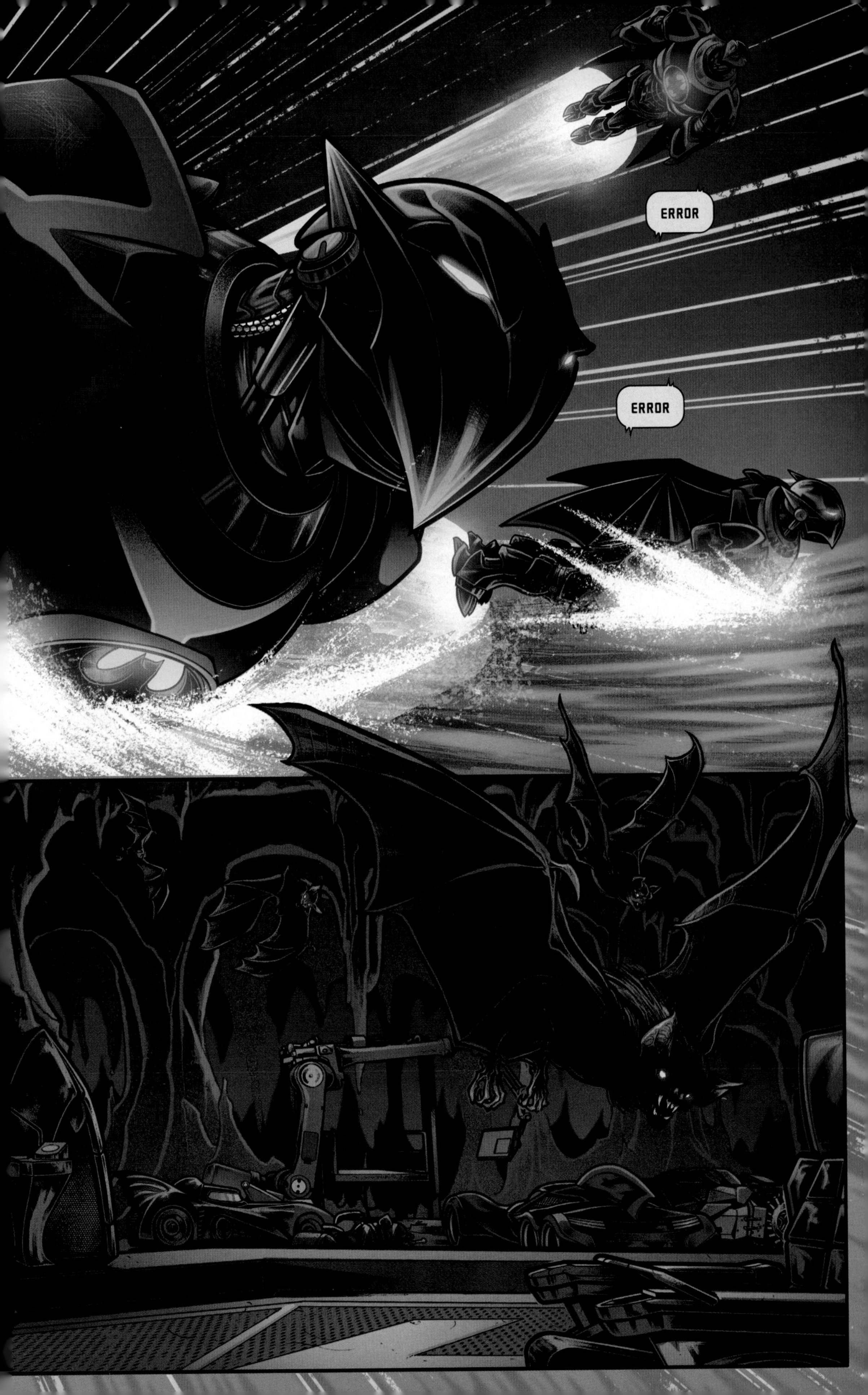
ERROR
ERROR

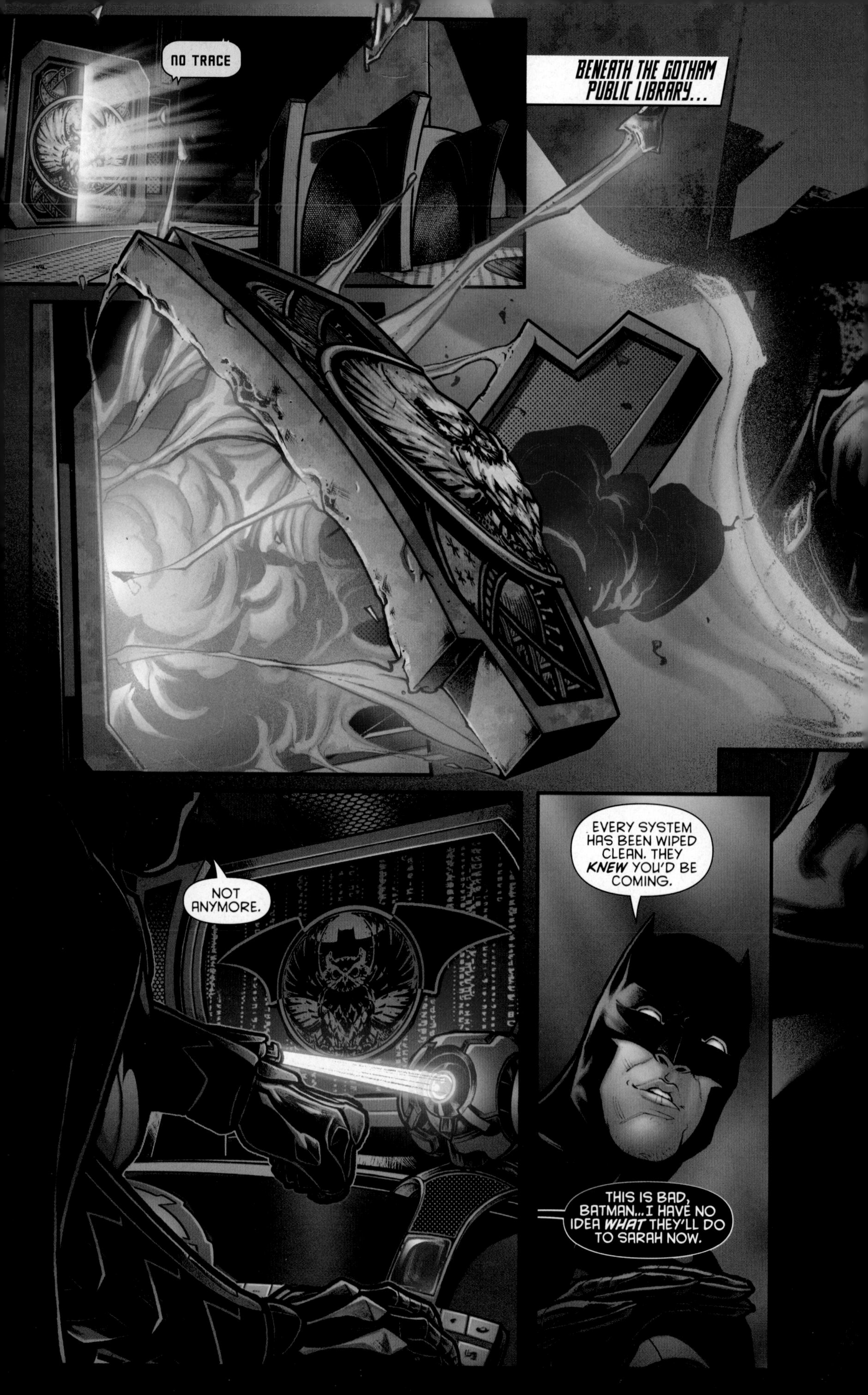
NO TRACE
BENEATH THE GOTHAM PUBLIC LIBRARY...
NOT ANYMORE.
EVERY SYSTEM HAS BEEN WIPED CLEAN. THEY KNEW YOU'D BE COMING.
THIS IS BAD, BATMAN... I HAVE NO IDEA WHAT THEY'LL DO TO SARAH NOW.

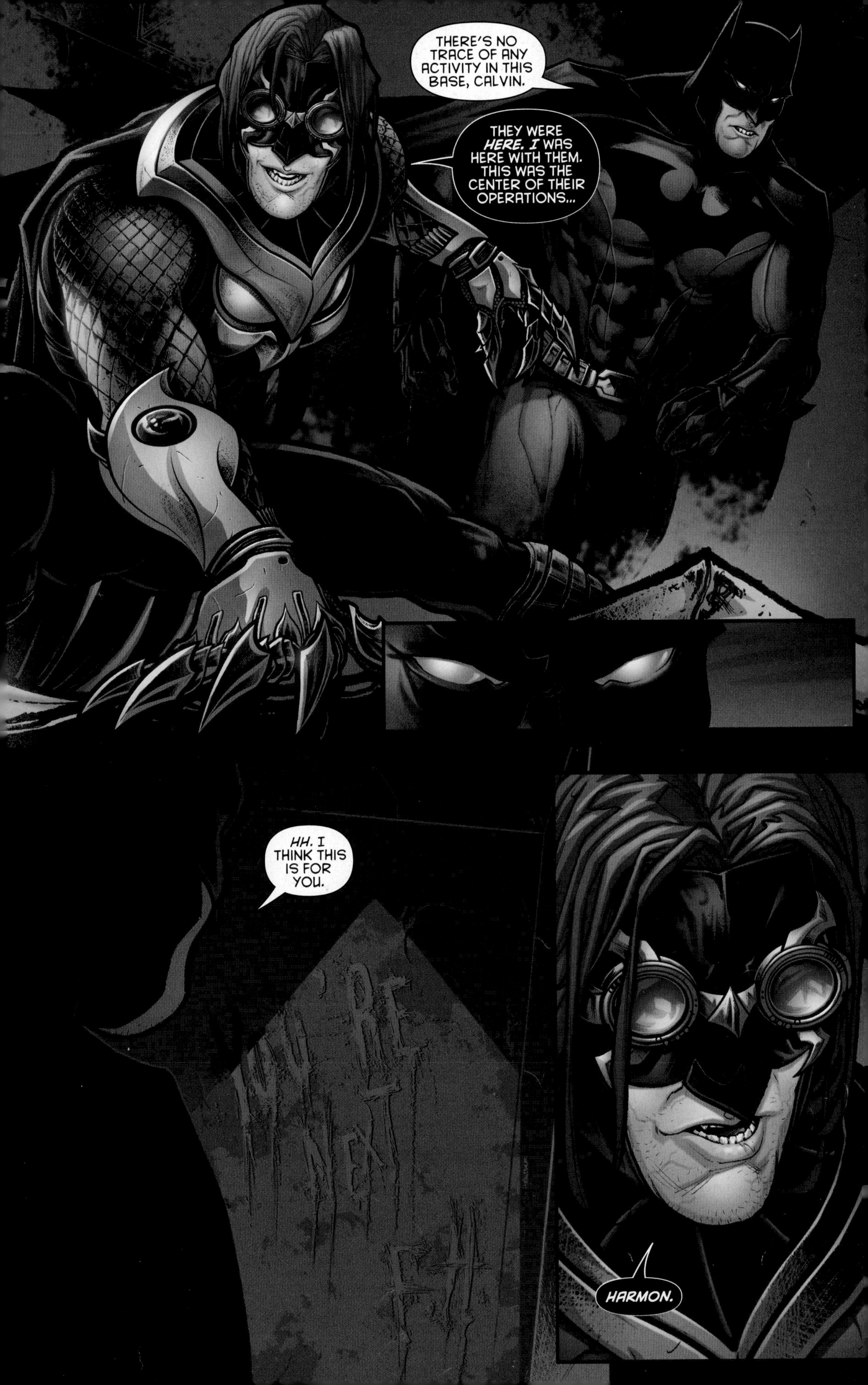
THERE'S NO TRACE OF ANY ACTIVITY IN THIS BASE, CALVIN.
THEY WERE *HERE. I* WAS HERE WITH THEM. THIS WAS THE CENTER OF THEIR OPERATIONS...
HH. I THINK THIS IS FOR YOU.
HARMON.

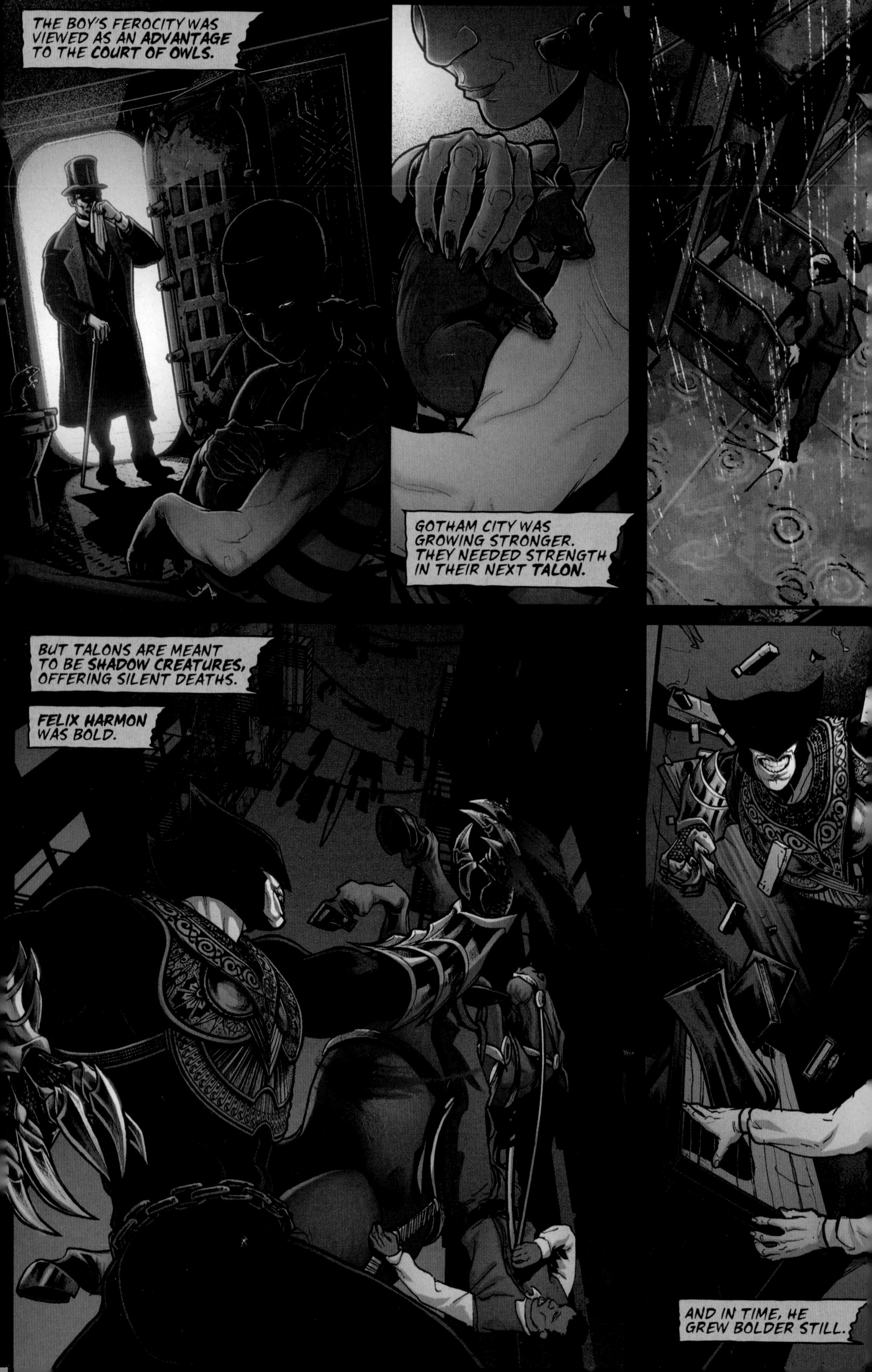
THE BOY'S FEROCITY WAS VIEWED AS AN ADVANTAGE TO THE COURT OF OWLS.
GOTHAM CITY WAS GROWING STRONGER. THEY NEEDED STRENGTH IN THEIR NEXT TALON.
BUT TALONS ARE MEANT TO BE SHADOW CREATURES, OFFERING SILENT DEATHS.
FELIX HARMON WAS BOLD.
AND IN TIME, HE GREW BOLDER STILL.

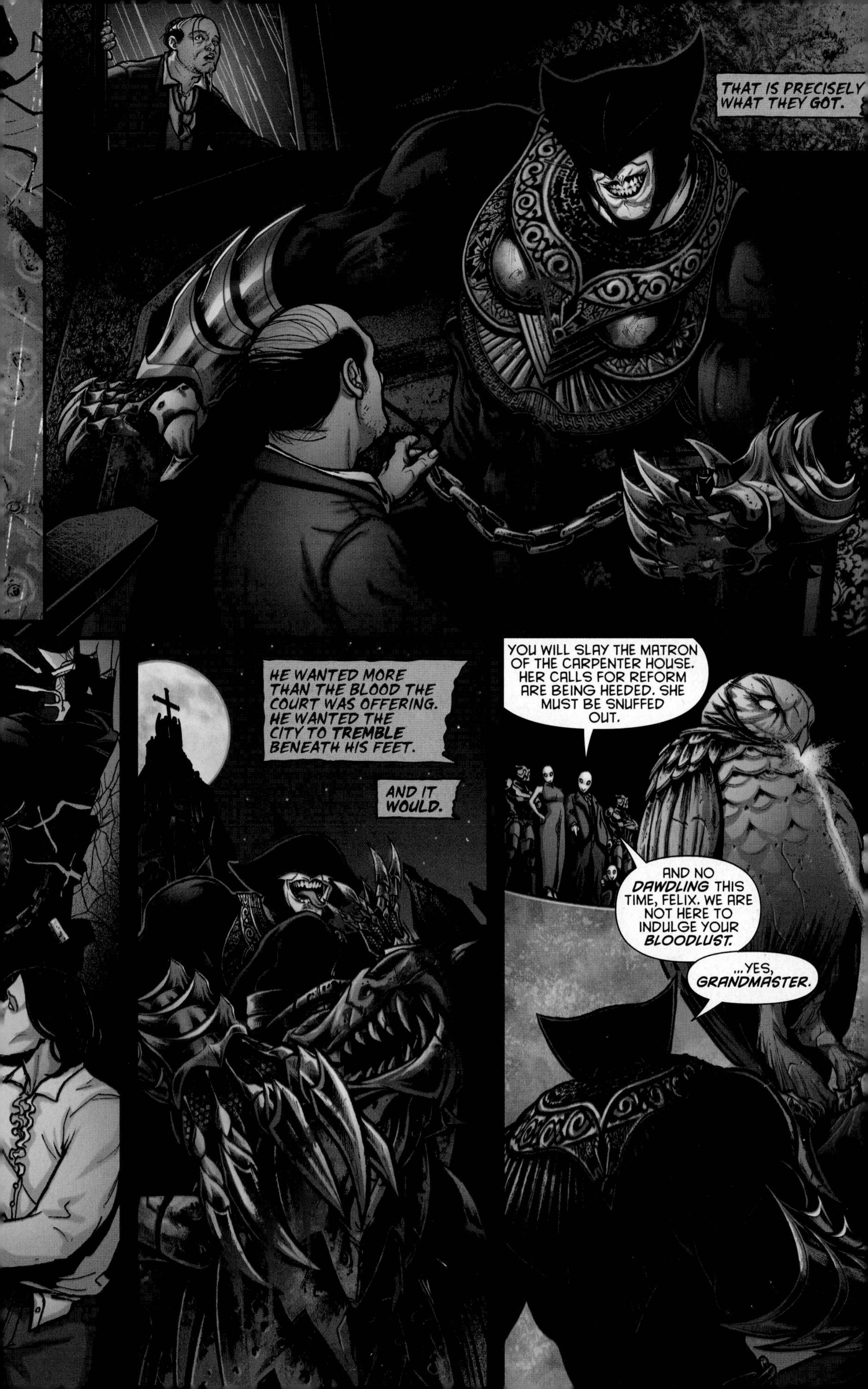
THAT IS PRECISELY WHAT THEY GOT.
HE WANTED MORE THAN THE BLOOD THE COURT WAS OFFERING. HE WANTED THE CITY TO TREMBLE BENEATH HIS FEET.
AND IT WOULD.
YOU WILL SLAY THE MATRON OF THE CARPENTER HOUSE. HER CALLS FOR REFORM ARE BEING HEEDED. SHE MUST BE SNUFFED OUT.
AND NO DAWDLING THIS TIME, FELIX. WE ARE NOT HERE TO INDULGE YOUR BLOODLUST.
...YES, GRANDMASTER.

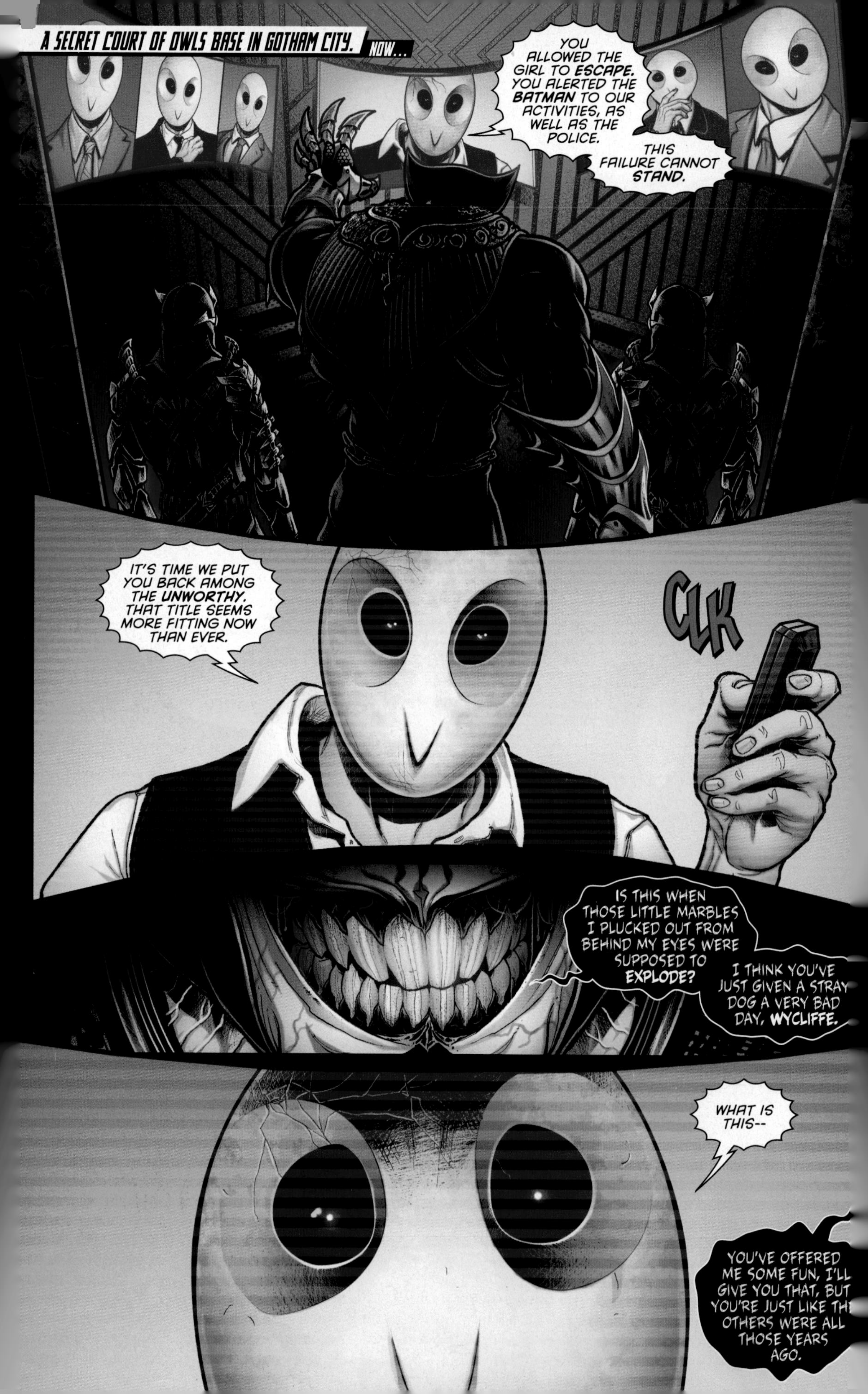
A SECRET COURT OF OWLS BASE IN GOTHAM CITY.
NOW...
YOU ALLOWED THE GIRL TO ESCAPE. YOU ALERTED THE BATMAN TO OUR ACTIVITIES, AS WELL AS THE POLICE.
THIS FAILURE CANNOT STAND.
IT'S TIME WE PUT YOU BACK AMONG THE UNWORTHY. THAT TITLE SEEMS MORE FITTING NOW THAN EVER.
CLK
IS THIS WHEN THOSE LITTLE MARBLES I PLUCKED OUT FROM BEHIND MY EYES WERE SUPPOSED TO EXPLODE?
I THINK YOU'VE JUST GIVEN A STRAY DOG A VERY BAD DAY, WYCLIFFE.
WHAT IS THIS--
YOU'VE OFFERED ME SOME FUN, I'LL GIVE YOU THAT, BUT YOU'RE JUST LIKE THE OTHERS WERE ALL THOSE YEARS AGO.

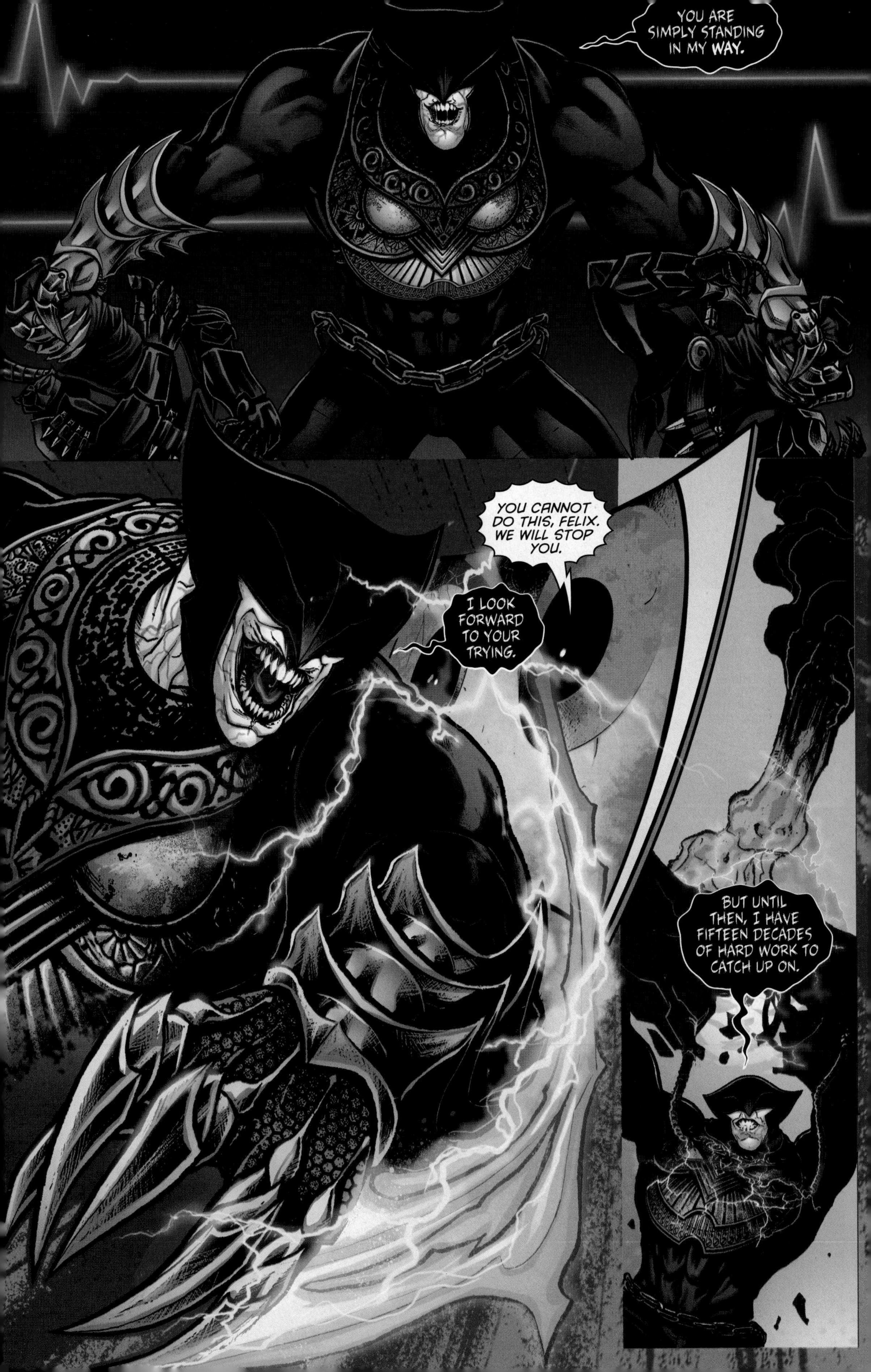

YOU ARE SIMPLY STANDING IN MY WAY.
YOU CANNOT DO THIS, FELIX. WE WILL STOP YOU.
I LOOK FORWARD TO YOUR TRYING.
BUT UNTIL THEN, I HAVE FIFTEEN DECADES OF HARD WORK TO CATCH UP ON.

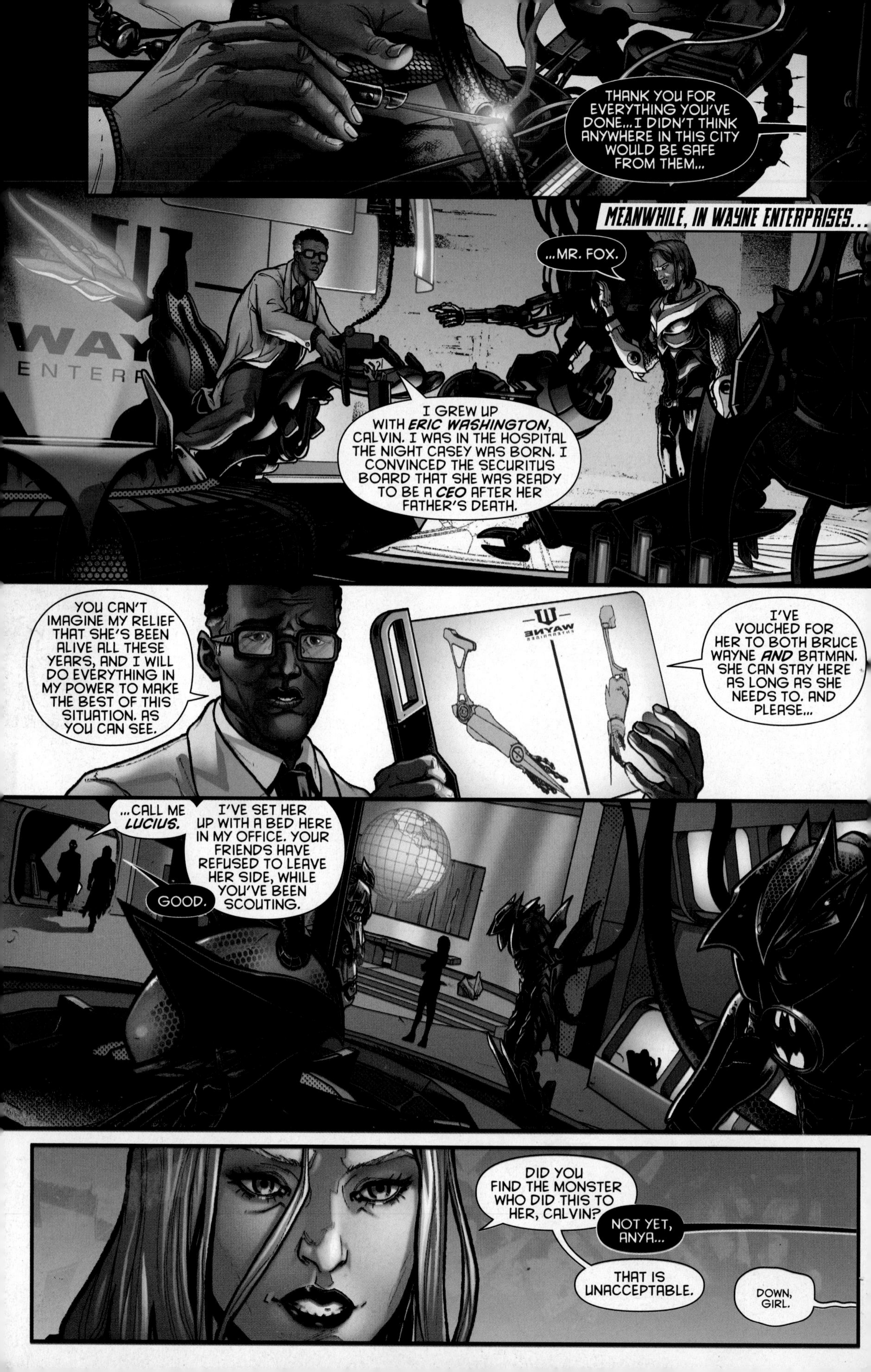
THANK YOU FOR EVERYTHING YOU'VE DONE...I DIDN'T THINK ANYWHERE IN THIS CITY WOULD BE SAFE FROM THEM...
MEANWHILE, IN WAYNE ENTERPRISES...
...MR. FOX.
I GREW UP WITH ERIC WASHINGTON, CALVIN. I WAS IN THE HOSPITAL THE NIGHT CASEY WAS BORN. I CONVINCED THE SECURITUS BOARD THAT SHE WAS READY TO BE A CEO AFTER HER FATHER'S DEATH.
YOU CAN'T IMAGINE MY RELIEF THAT SHE'S BEEN ALIVE ALL THESE YEARS, AND I WILL DO EVERYTHING IN MY POWER TO MAKE THE BEST OF THIS SITUATION. AS YOU CAN SEE.
I'VE VOUCHED FOR HER TO BOTH BRUCE WAYNE AND BATMAN. SHE CAN STAY HERE AS LONG AS SHE NEEDS TO. AND PLEASE...
...CALL ME LUCIUS.
I'VE SET HER UP WITH A BED HERE IN MY OFFICE. YOUR FRIENDS HAVE REFUSED TO LEAVE HER SIDE, WHILE YOU'VE BEEN SCOUTING.
GOOD.
DID YOU FIND THE MONSTER WHO DID THIS TO HER, CALVIN?
NOT YET, ANYA...
THAT IS UNACCEPTABLE.
DOWN, GIRL.

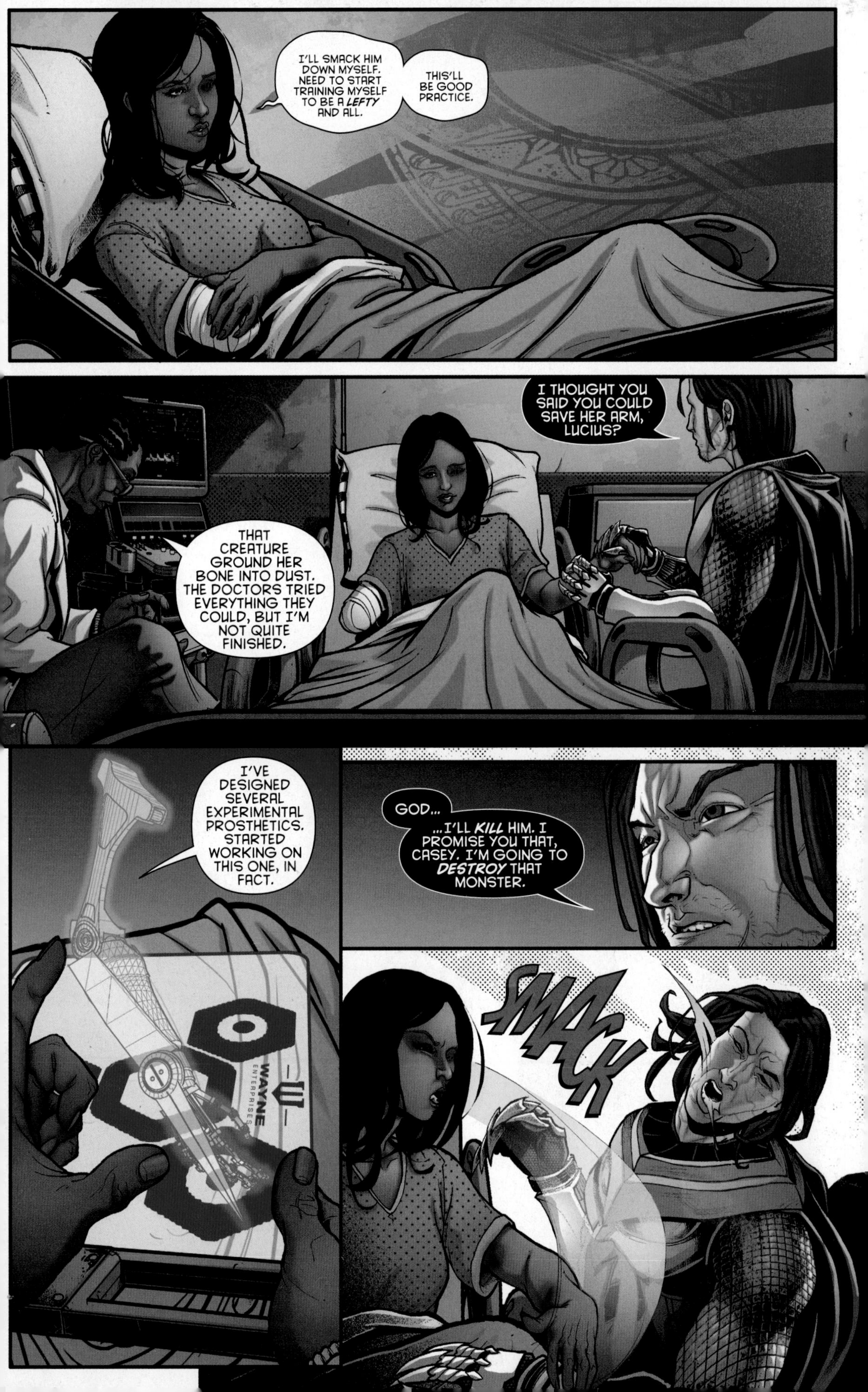
I'LL SMACK HIM DOWN MYSELF. NEED TO START TRAINING MYSELF TO BE A *LEFTY* AND ALL.
THIS'LL BE GOOD PRACTICE.
I THOUGHT YOU SAID YOU COULD SAVE HER ARM, LUCIUS?
THAT CREATURE GROUND HER BONE INTO DUST. THE DOCTORS TRIED EVERYTHING THEY COULD, BUT I'M NOT QUITE FINISHED.
I'VE DESIGNED SEVERAL EXPERIMENTAL PROSTHETICS. STARTED WORKING ON THIS ONE, IN FACT.
WAYNE ENTERPRISES
GOD...
...I'LL *KILL* HIM. I PROMISE YOU THAT, CASEY. I'M GOING TO *DESTROY* THAT MONSTER.
SMACK

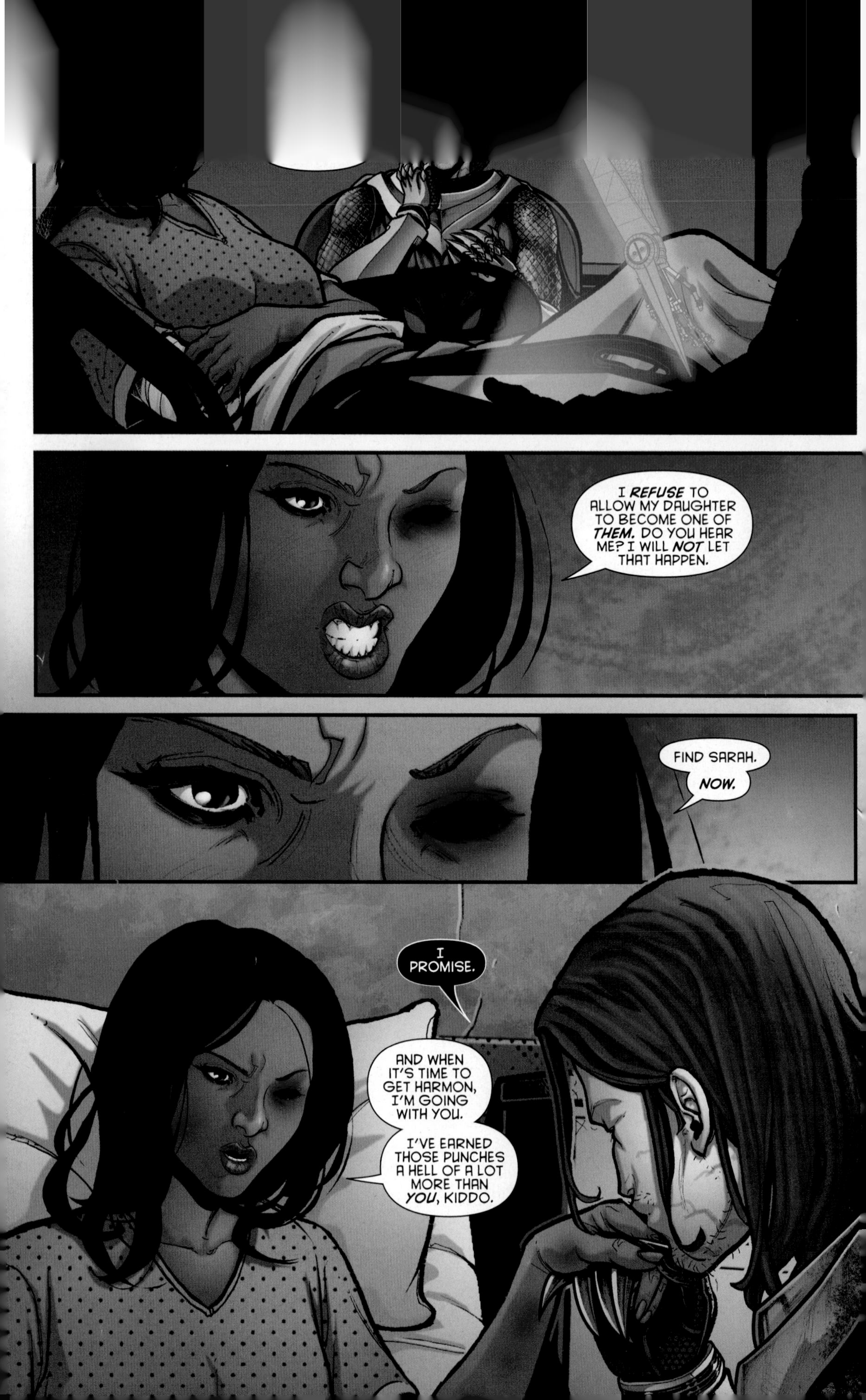
I REFUSE TO ALLOW MY DAUGHTER TO BECOME ONE OF THEM. DO YOU HEAR ME? I WILL NOT LET THAT HAPPEN.
FIND SARAH. NOW.
I PROMISE.
AND WHEN IT'S TIME TO GET HARMON, I'M GOING WITH YOU.
I'VE EARNED THOSE PUNCHES A HELL OF A LOT MORE THAN YOU, KIDDO.

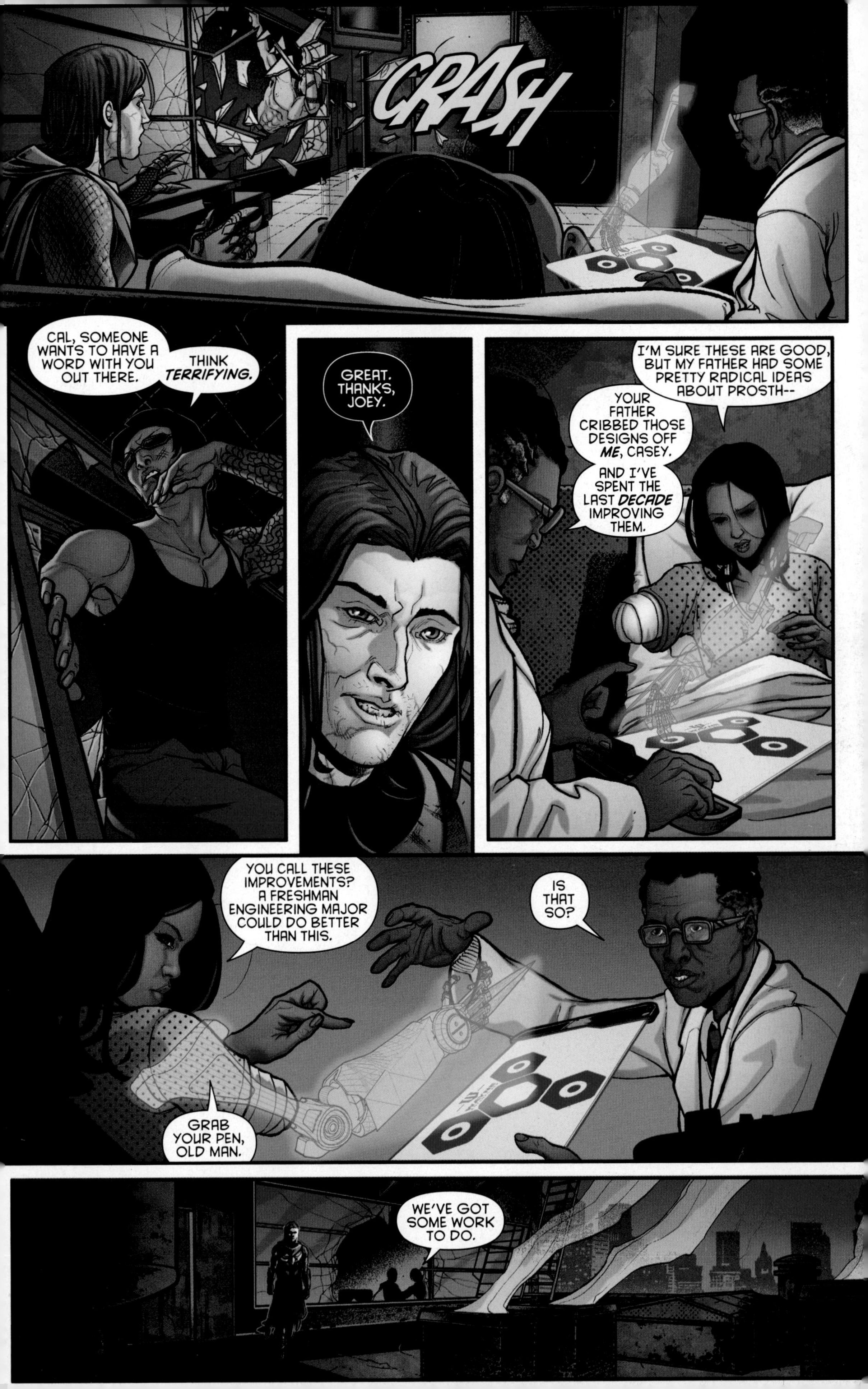
CRASH
CAL, SOMEONE WANTS TO HAVE A WORD WITH YOU OUT THERE.
THINK TERRIFYING.
GREAT. THANKS, JOEY.
I'M SURE THESE ARE GOOD, BUT MY FATHER HAD SOME PRETTY RADICAL IDEAS ABOUT PROSTH--
YOUR FATHER CRIBBED THOSE DESIGNS OFF ME, CASEY.
AND I'VE SPENT THE LAST DECADE IMPROVING THEM.
YOU CALL THESE IMPROVEMENTS? A FRESHMAN ENGINEERING MAJOR COULD DO BETTER THAN THIS.
IS THAT SO?
GRAB YOUR PEN, OLD MAN.
WE'VE GOT SOME WORK TO DO.

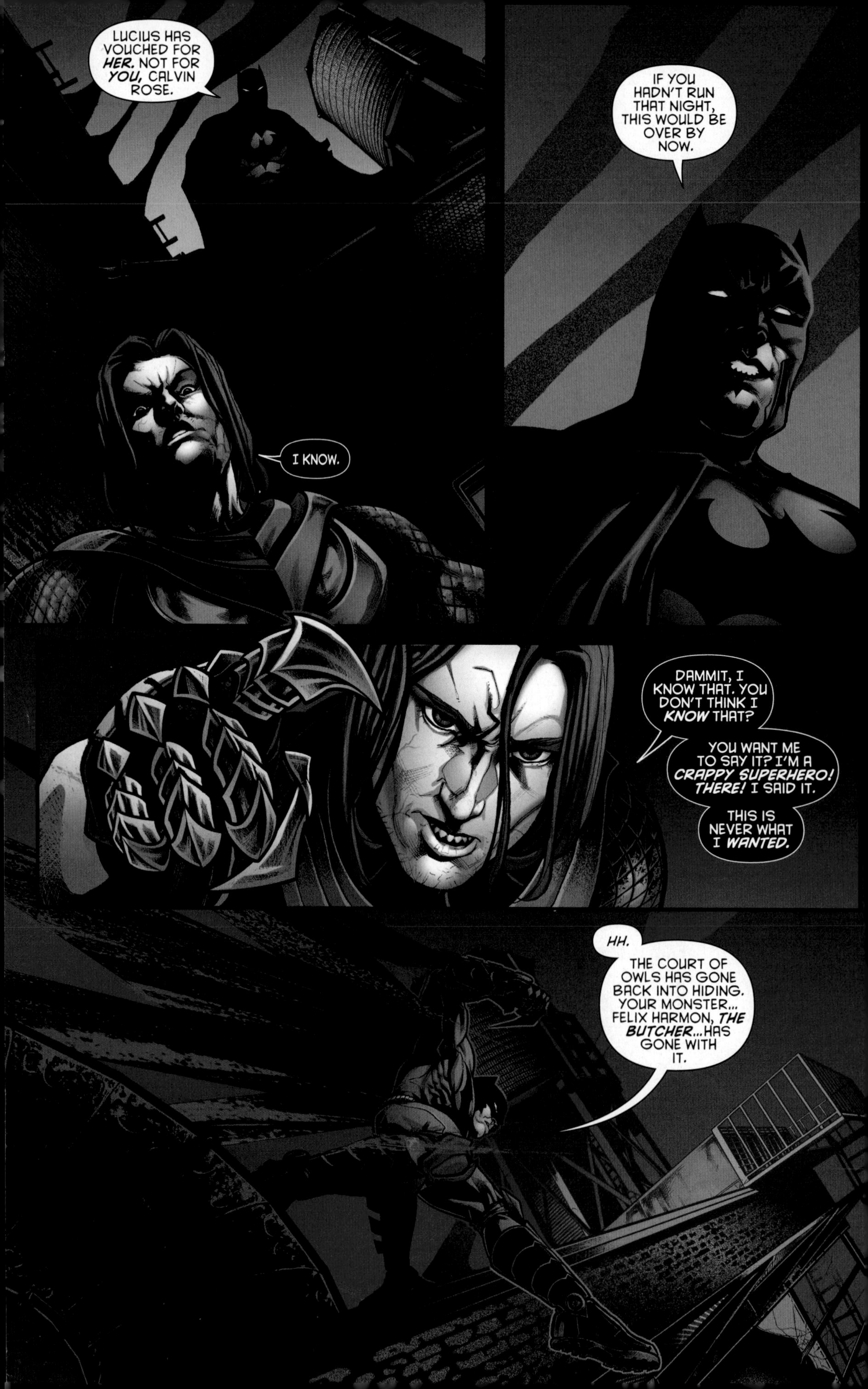
LUCIUS HAS VOUCHED FOR HER. NOT FOR YOU, CALVIN ROSE.
IF YOU HADN'T RUN THAT NIGHT, THIS WOULD BE OVER BY NOW.
I KNOW.
DAMMIT, I KNOW THAT. YOU DON'T THINK I KNOW THAT?
YOU WANT ME TO SAY IT? I'M A CRAPPY SUPERHERO! THERE! I SAID IT.
THIS IS NEVER WHAT I WANTED.
HH.
THE COURT OF OWLS HAS GONE BACK INTO HIDING. YOUR MONSTER... FELIX HARMON, THE BUTCHER...HAS GONE WITH IT.

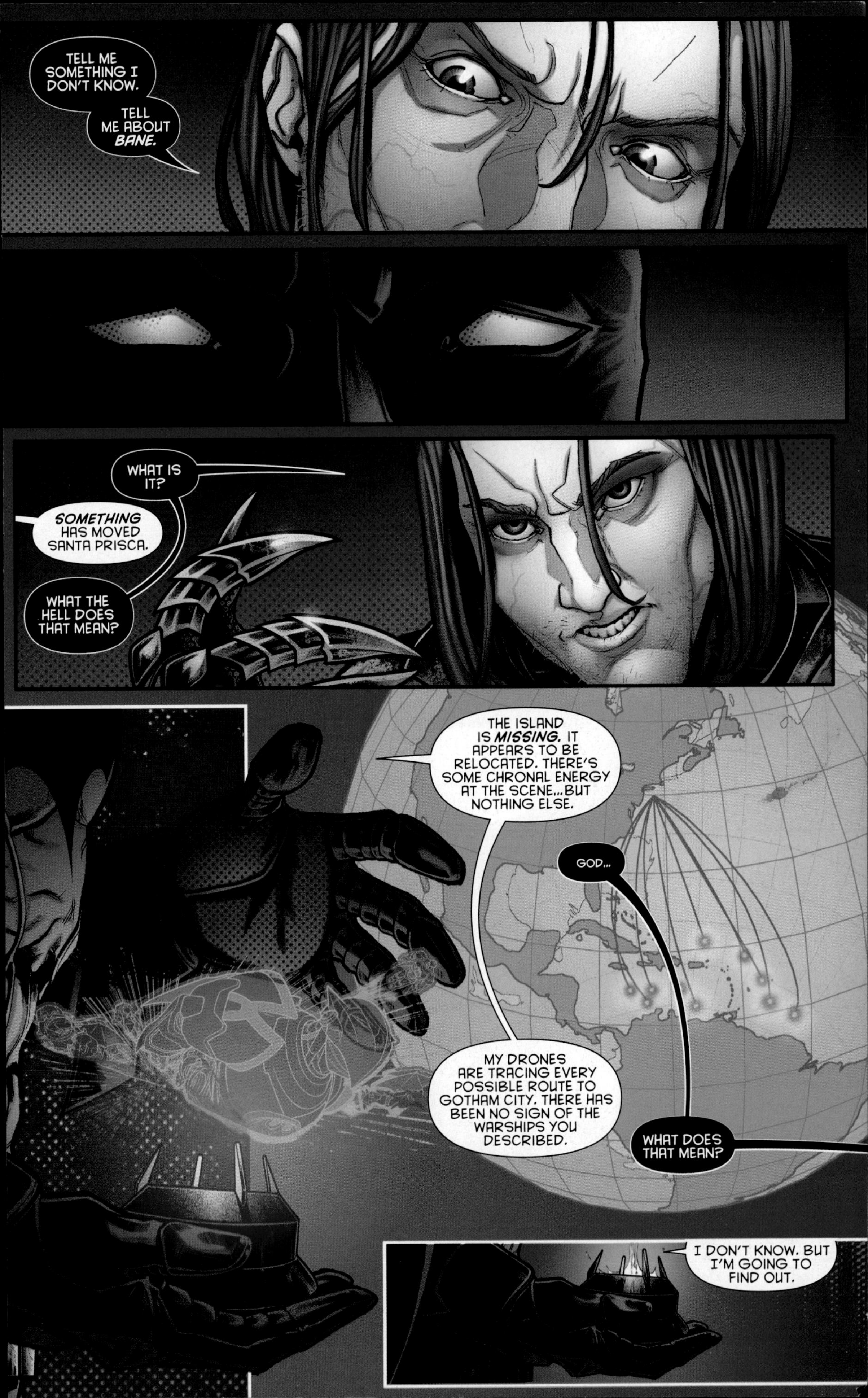
TELL ME SOMETHING I DON'T KNOW.
TELL ME ABOUT *BANE.*
WHAT IS IT?
SOMETHING HAS MOVED SANTA PRISCA.
WHAT THE HELL DOES THAT MEAN?
THE ISLAND IS *MISSING.* IT APPEARS TO BE RELOCATED. THERE'S SOME CHRONAL ENERGY AT THE SCENE...BUT NOTHING ELSE.
GOD...
MY DRONES ARE TRACING EVERY POSSIBLE ROUTE TO GOTHAM CITY. THERE HAS BEEN NO SIGN OF THE WARSHIPS YOU DESCRIBED.
WHAT DOES THAT MEAN?
I DON'T KNOW. BUT I'M GOING TO FIND OUT.

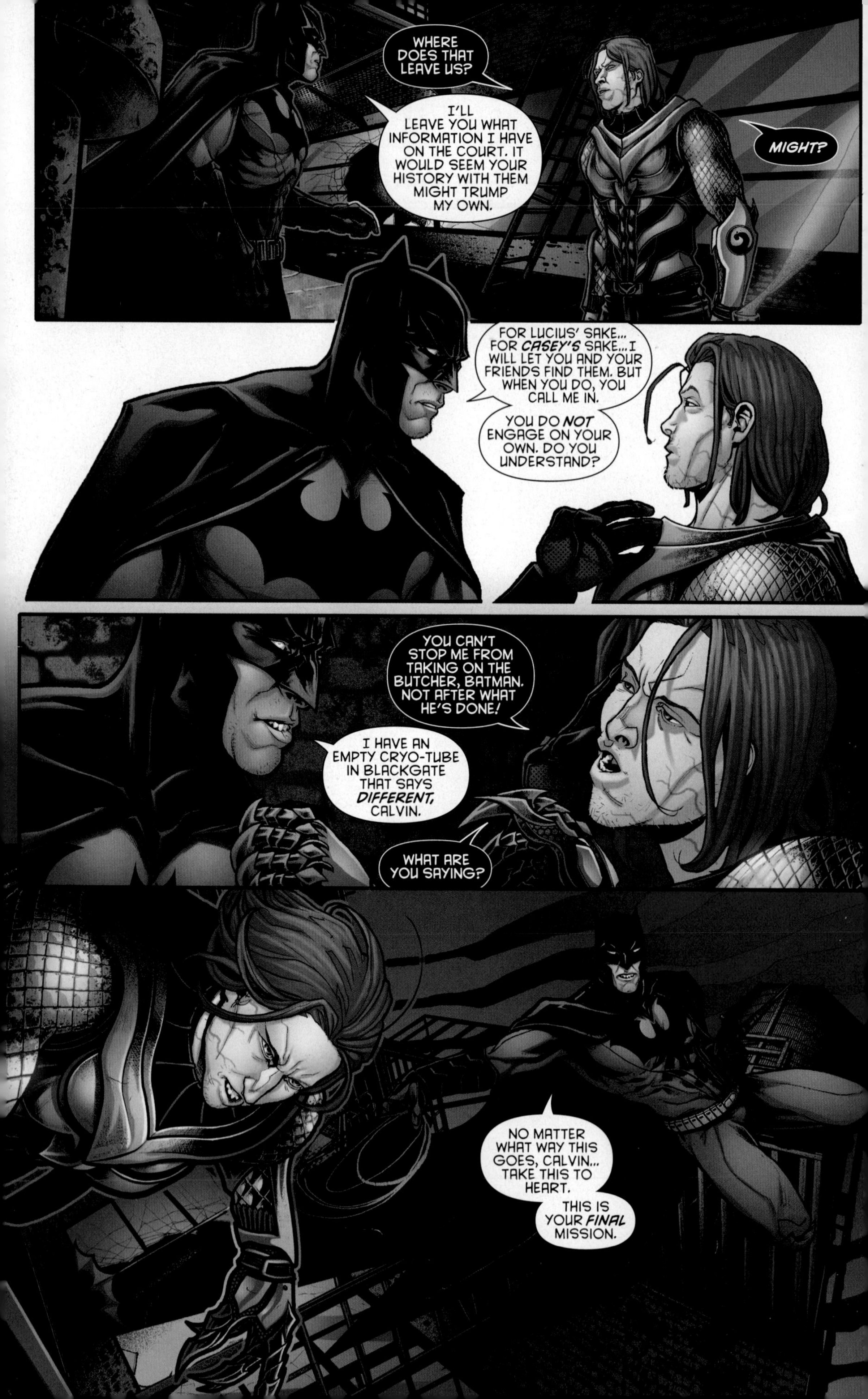
WHERE DOES THAT LEAVE US?
I'LL LEAVE YOU WHAT INFORMATION I HAVE ON THE COURT. IT WOULD SEEM YOUR HISTORY WITH THEM MIGHT TRUMP MY OWN.
MIGHT?
FOR LUCIUS' SAKE... FOR CASEY'S SAKE... I WILL LET YOU AND YOUR FRIENDS FIND THEM. BUT WHEN YOU DO, YOU CALL ME IN.
YOU DO NOT ENGAGE ON YOUR OWN. DO YOU UNDERSTAND?
YOU CAN'T STOP ME FROM TAKING ON THE BUTCHER, BATMAN. NOT AFTER WHAT HE'S DONE!
I HAVE AN EMPTY CRYO-TUBE IN BLACKGATE THAT SAYS DIFFERENT, CALVIN.
WHAT ARE YOU SAYING?
NO MATTER WHAT WAY THIS GOES, CALVIN... TAKE THIS TO HEART.
THIS IS YOUR FINAL MISSION.

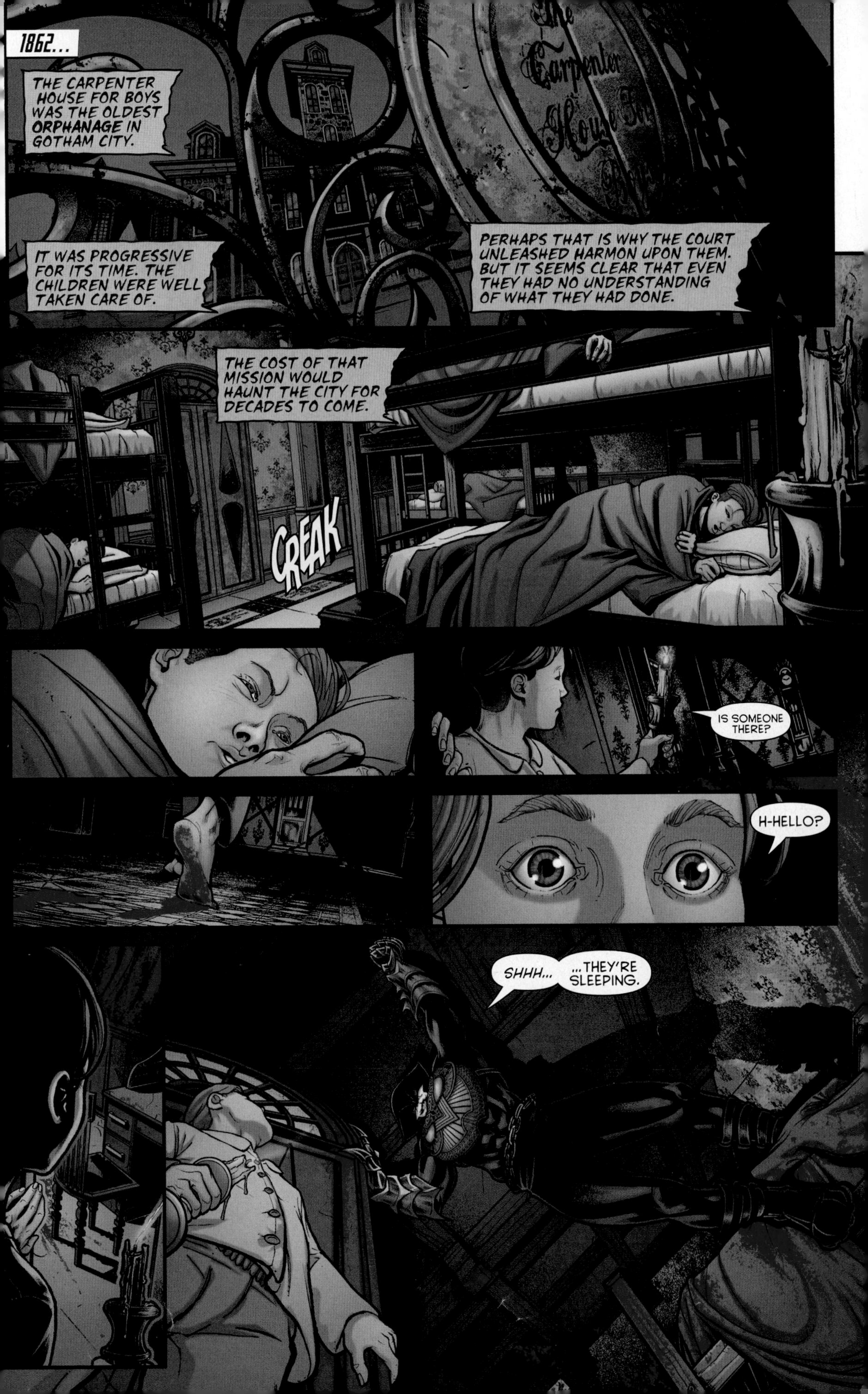
1862...
THE CARPENTER HOUSE FOR BOYS WAS THE OLDEST ORPHANAGE IN GOTHAM CITY.
IT WAS PROGRESSIVE FOR ITS TIME. THE CHILDREN WERE WELL TAKEN CARE OF.
PERHAPS THAT IS WHY THE COURT UNLEASHED HARMON UPON THEM. BUT IT SEEMS CLEAR THAT EVEN THEY HAD NO UNDERSTANDING OF WHAT THEY HAD DONE.
THE COST OF THAT MISSION WOULD HAUNT THE CITY FOR DECADES TO COME.
CREAK
IS SOMEONE THERE?
H-HELLO?
SHHH...
...THEY'RE SLEEPING.

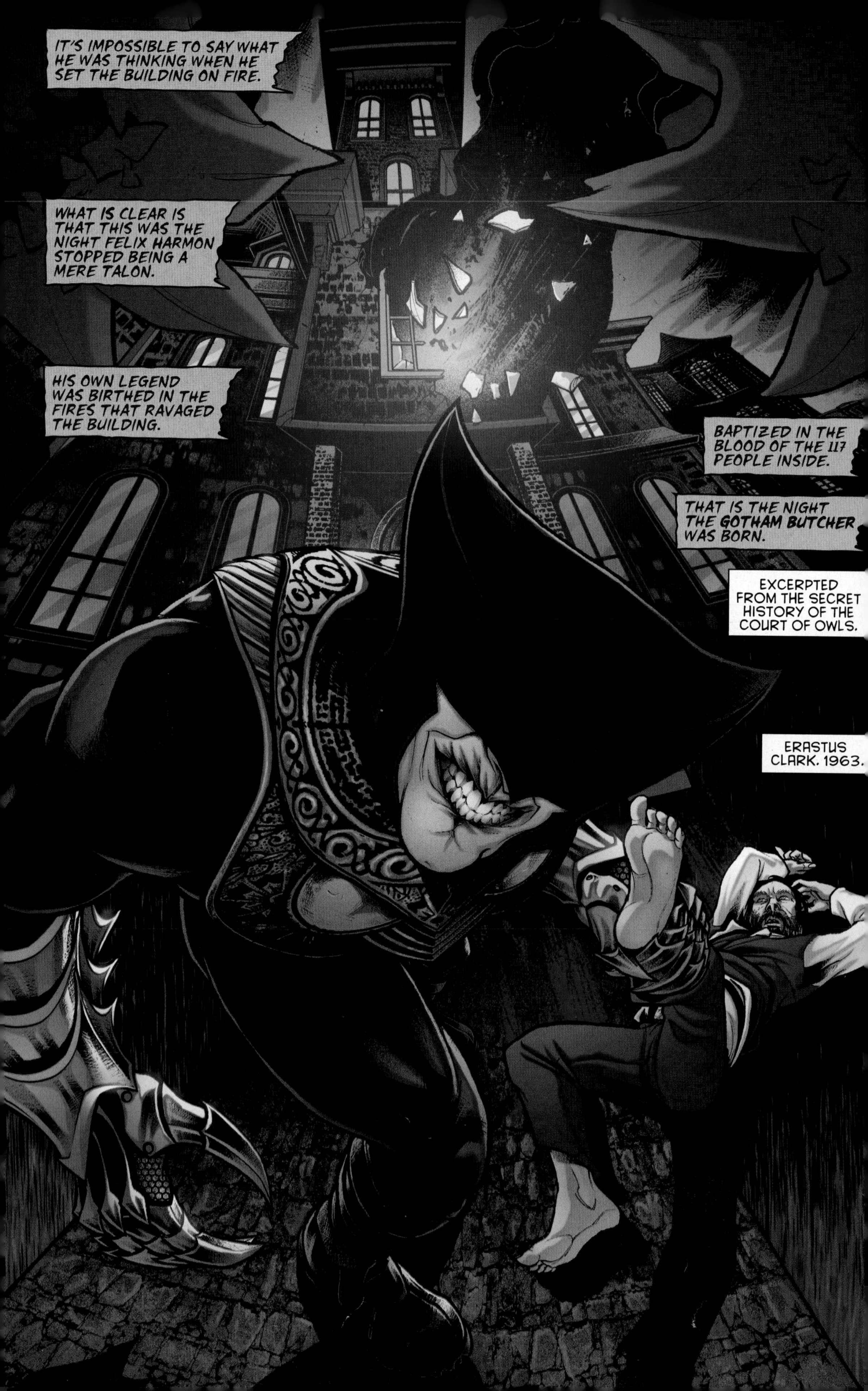
IT'S IMPOSSIBLE TO SAY WHAT HE WAS THINKING WHEN HE SET THE BUILDING ON FIRE.
WHAT IS CLEAR IS THAT THIS WAS THE NIGHT FELIX HARMON STOPPED BEING A MERE TALON.
HIS OWN LEGEND WAS BIRTHED IN THE FIRES THAT RAVAGED THE BUILDING.
BAPTIZED IN THE BLOOD OF THE 117 PEOPLE INSIDE.
THAT IS THE NIGHT THE **GOTHAM BUTCHER** WAS BORN.
EXCERPTED FROM THE SECRET HISTORY OF THE COURT OF OWLS.
ERASTUS CLARK. 1963.

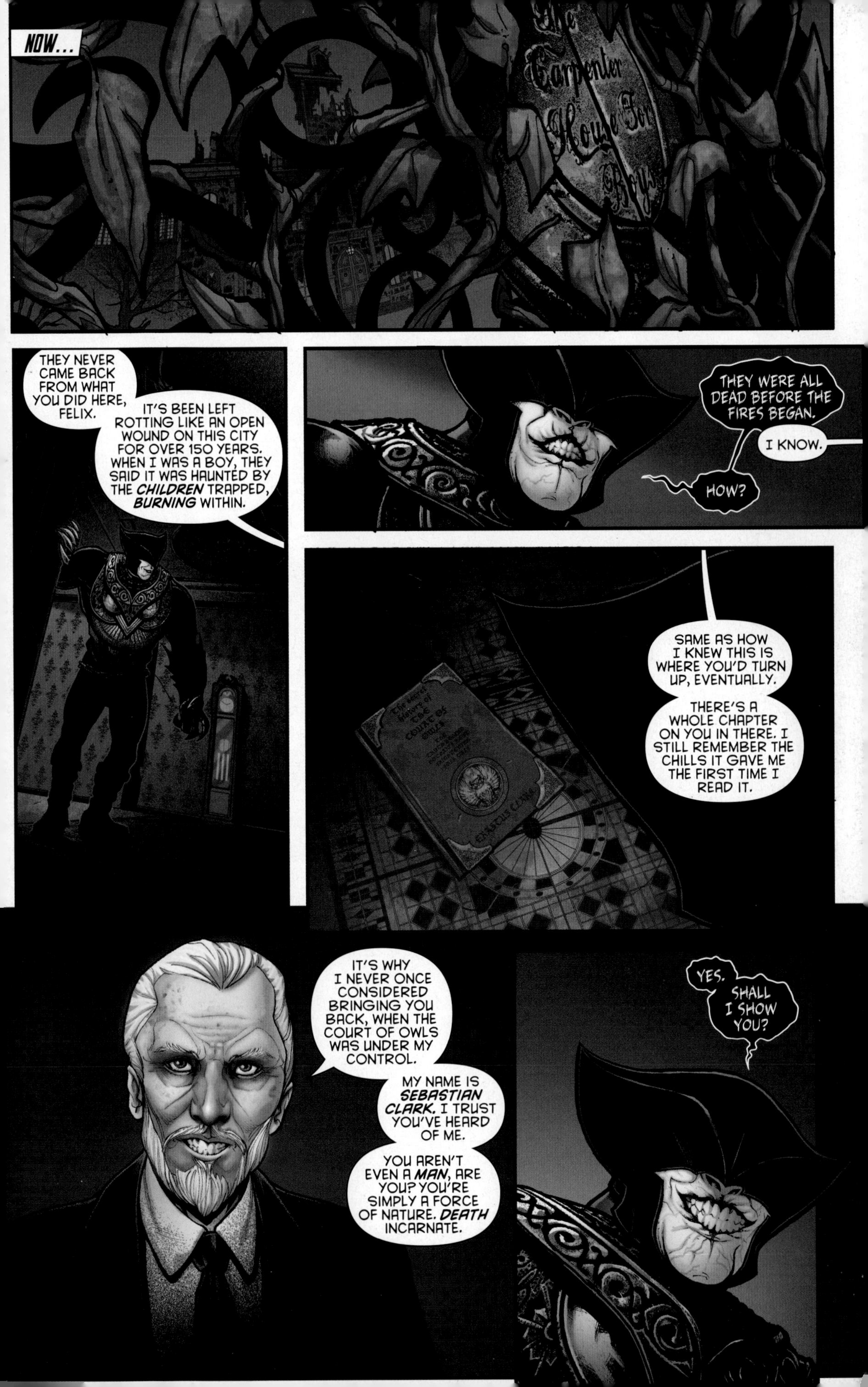
NOW...
The Carpenter House For Boys
THEY NEVER CAME BACK FROM WHAT YOU DID HERE, FELIX.
IT'S BEEN LEFT ROTTING LIKE AN OPEN WOUND ON THIS CITY FOR OVER 150 YEARS. WHEN I WAS A BOY, THEY SAID IT WAS HAUNTED BY THE CHILDREN TRAPPED, BURNING WITHIN.
THEY WERE ALL DEAD BEFORE THE FIRES BEGAN.
I KNOW.
HOW?
SAME AS HOW I KNEW THIS IS WHERE YOU'D TURN UP, EVENTUALLY.
THERE'S A WHOLE CHAPTER ON YOU IN THERE. I STILL REMEMBER THE CHILLS IT GAVE ME THE FIRST TIME I READ IT.
IT'S WHY I NEVER ONCE CONSIDERED BRINGING YOU BACK, WHEN THE COURT OF OWLS WAS UNDER MY CONTROL.
MY NAME IS SEBASTIAN CLARK. I TRUST YOU'VE HEARD OF ME.
YOU AREN'T EVEN A MAN, ARE YOU? YOU'RE SIMPLY A FORCE OF NATURE. DEATH INCARNATE.
YES.
SHALL I SHOW YOU?

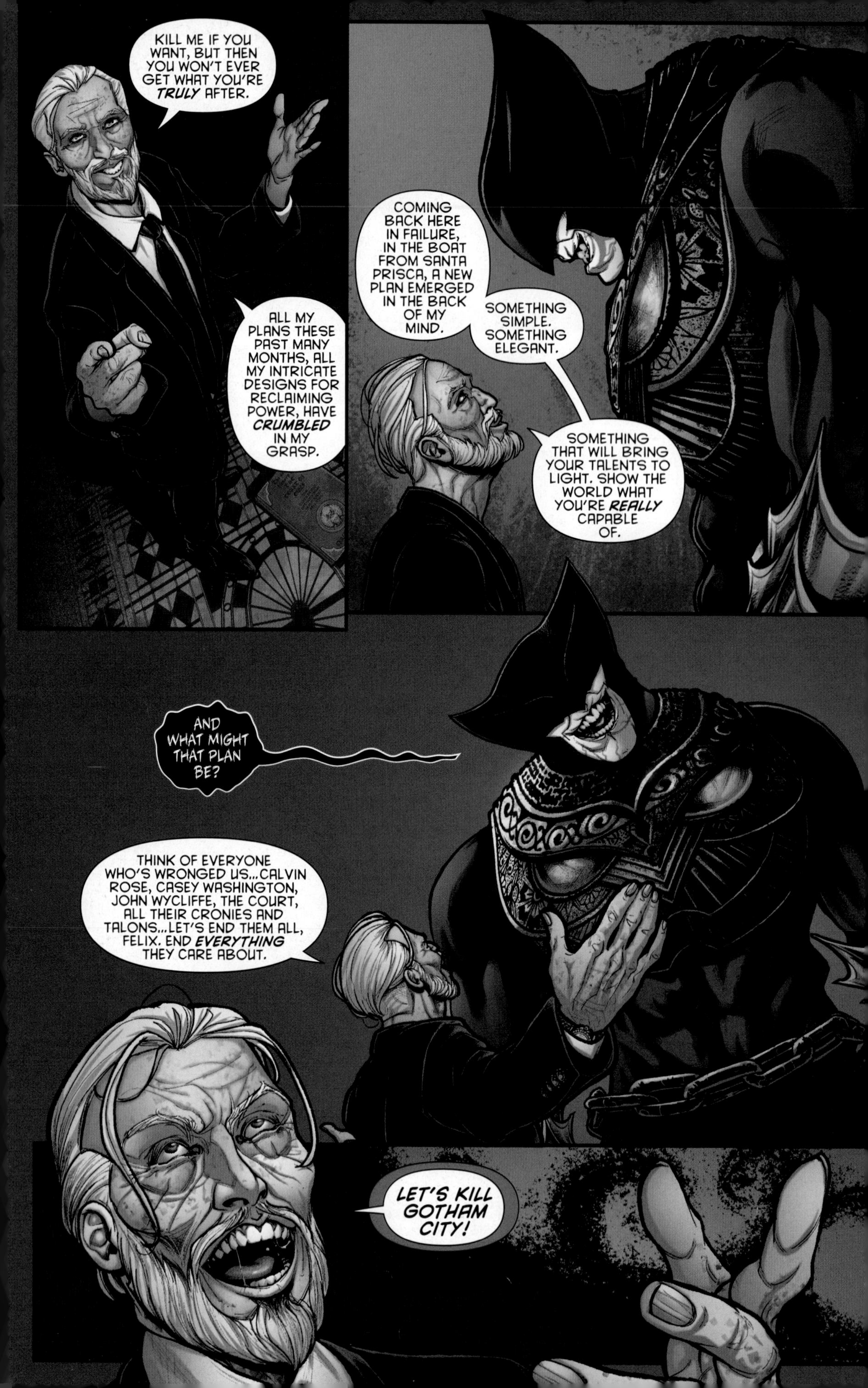
KILL ME IF YOU WANT, BUT THEN YOU WON'T EVER GET WHAT YOU'RE TRULY AFTER.
ALL MY PLANS THESE PAST MANY MONTHS, ALL MY INTRICATE DESIGNS FOR RECLAIMING POWER, HAVE CRUMBLED IN MY GRASP.
COMING BACK HERE IN FAILURE, IN THE BOAT FROM SANTA PRISCA, A NEW PLAN EMERGED IN THE BACK OF MY MIND.
SOMETHING SIMPLE. SOMETHING ELEGANT.
SOMETHING THAT WILL BRING YOUR TALENTS TO LIGHT. SHOW THE WORLD WHAT YOU'RE REALLY CAPABLE OF.
AND WHAT MIGHT THAT PLAN BE?
THINK OF EVERYONE WHO'S WRONGED US...CALVIN ROSE, CASEY WASHINGTON, JOHN WYCLIFFE, THE COURT, ALL THEIR CRONIES AND TALONS...LET'S END THEM ALL, FELIX. END EVERYTHING THEY CARE ABOUT.
LET'S KILL GOTHAM CITY!

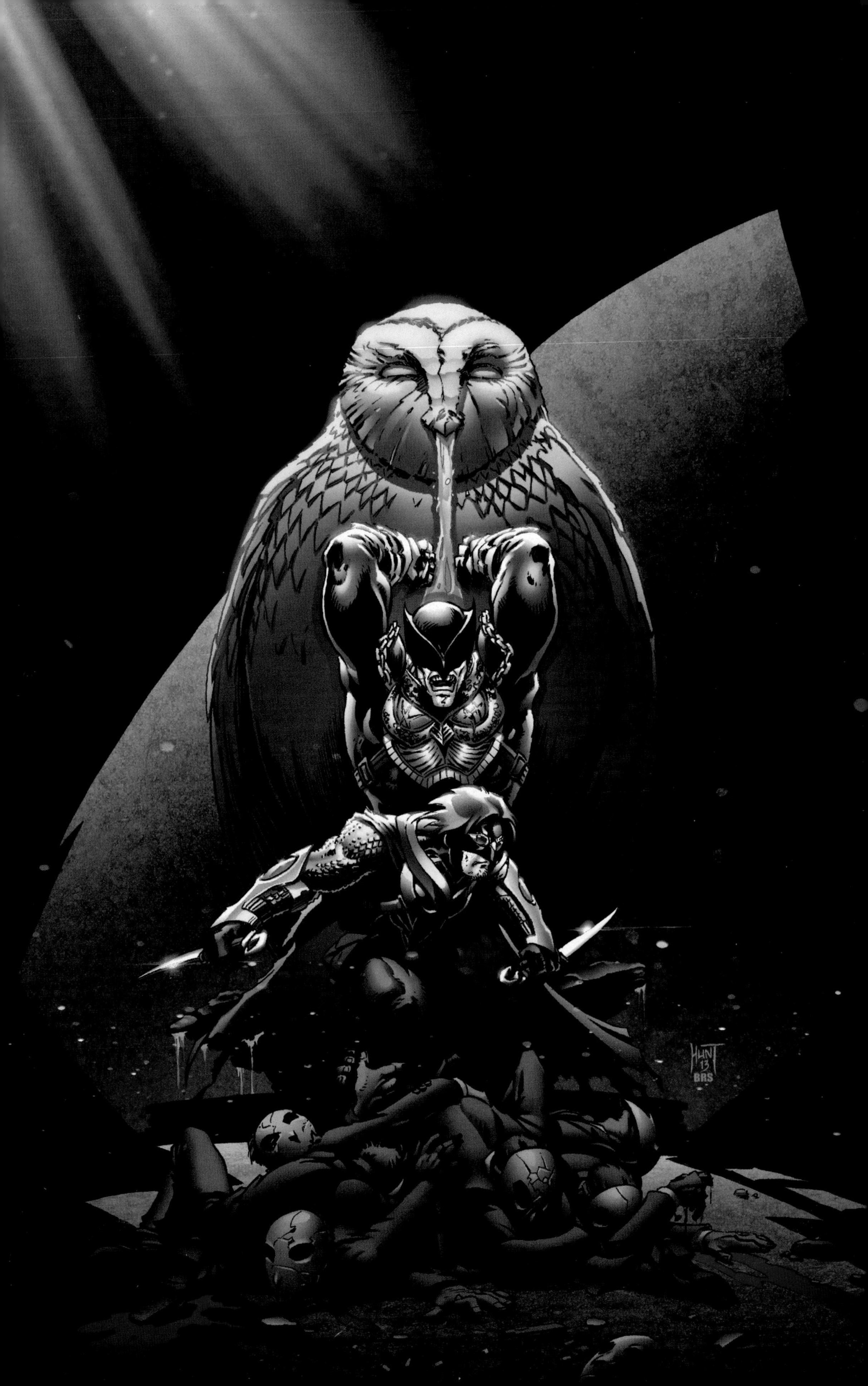
HUNT
13
BRS

OWLFALL

JAMES TYNION IV writer **EMANUEL SIMEONI** artist cover art by **KEN HUNT & BRETT SMITH**

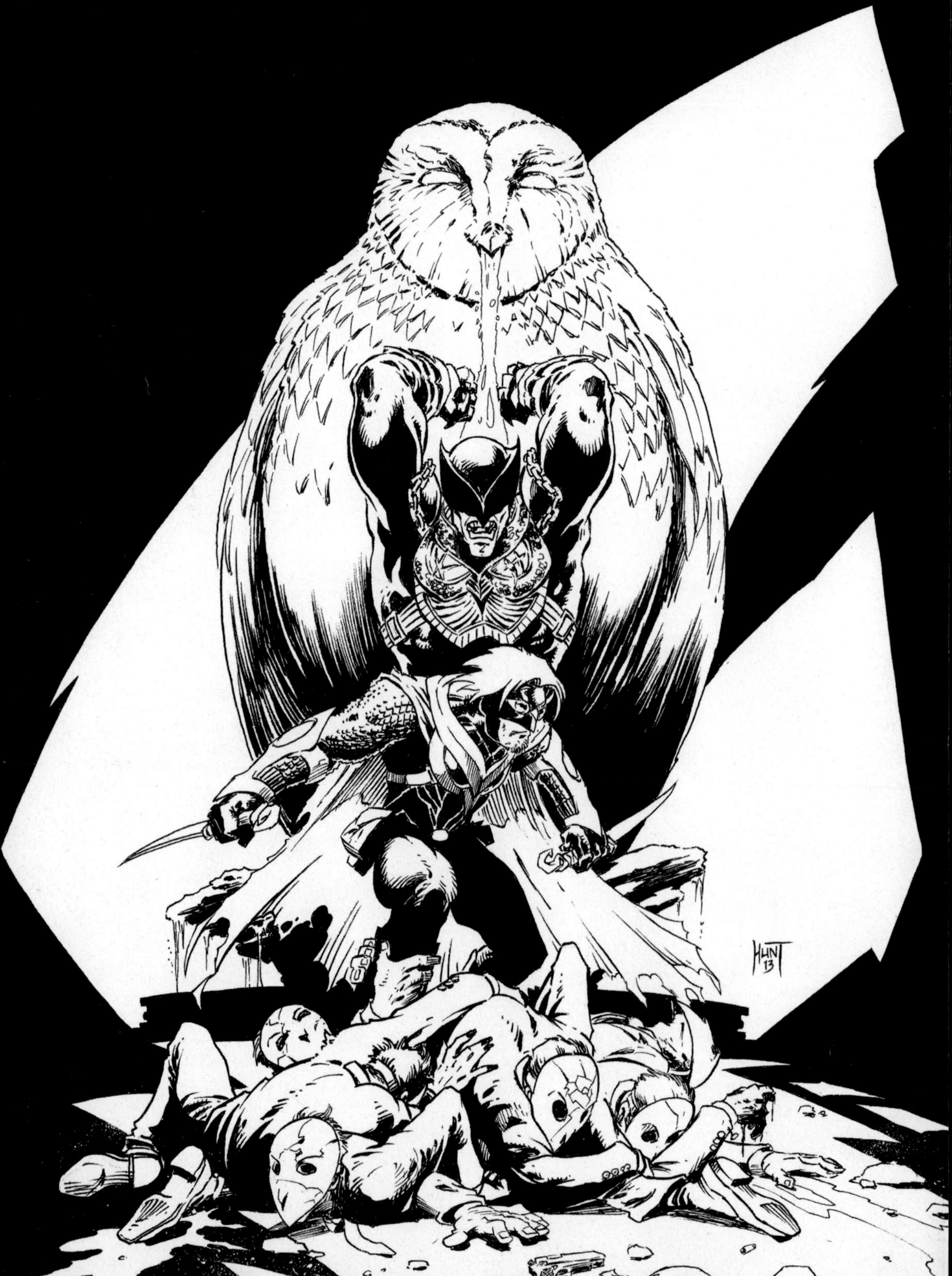
HUNT
13

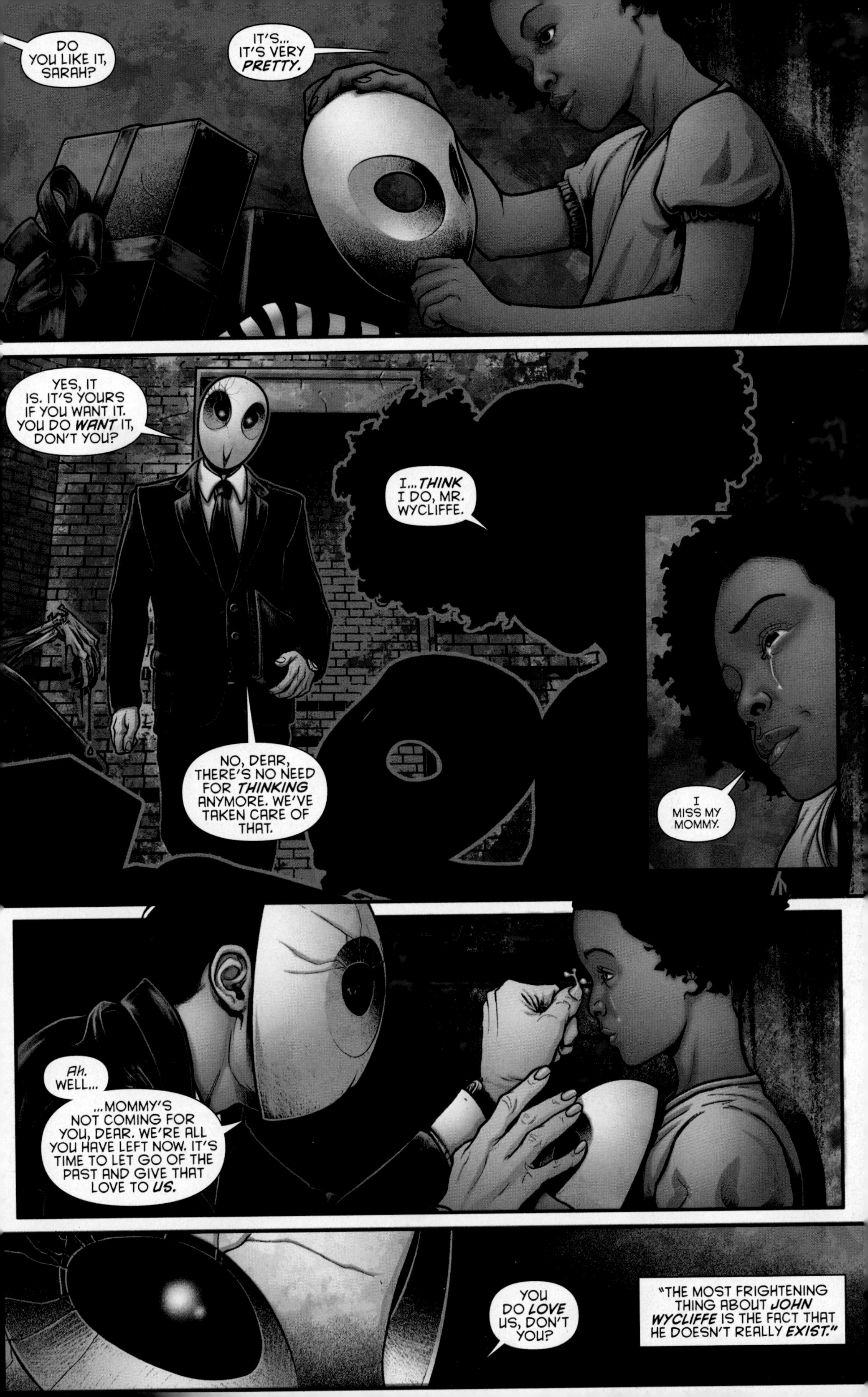
DO YOU LIKE IT, SARAH?
IT'S... IT'S VERY *PRETTY.*
YES, IT IS. IT'S YOURS IF YOU WANT IT. YOU DO *WANT* IT, DON'T YOU?
I...*THINK* I DO, MR. WYCLIFFE.
NO, DEAR, THERE'S NO NEED FOR *THINKING* ANYMORE. WE'VE TAKEN CARE OF THAT.
I MISS MY MOMMY.
AH. WELL...
...MOMMY'S NOT COMING FOR YOU, DEAR. WE'RE ALL YOU HAVE LEFT NOW. IT'S TIME TO LET GO OF THE PAST AND GIVE THAT LOVE TO *US.*
YOU DO *LOVE* US, DON'T YOU?
"THE MOST FRIGHTENING THING ABOUT *JOHN WYCLIFFE* IS THE FACT THAT HE DOESN'T REALLY *EXIST.*"

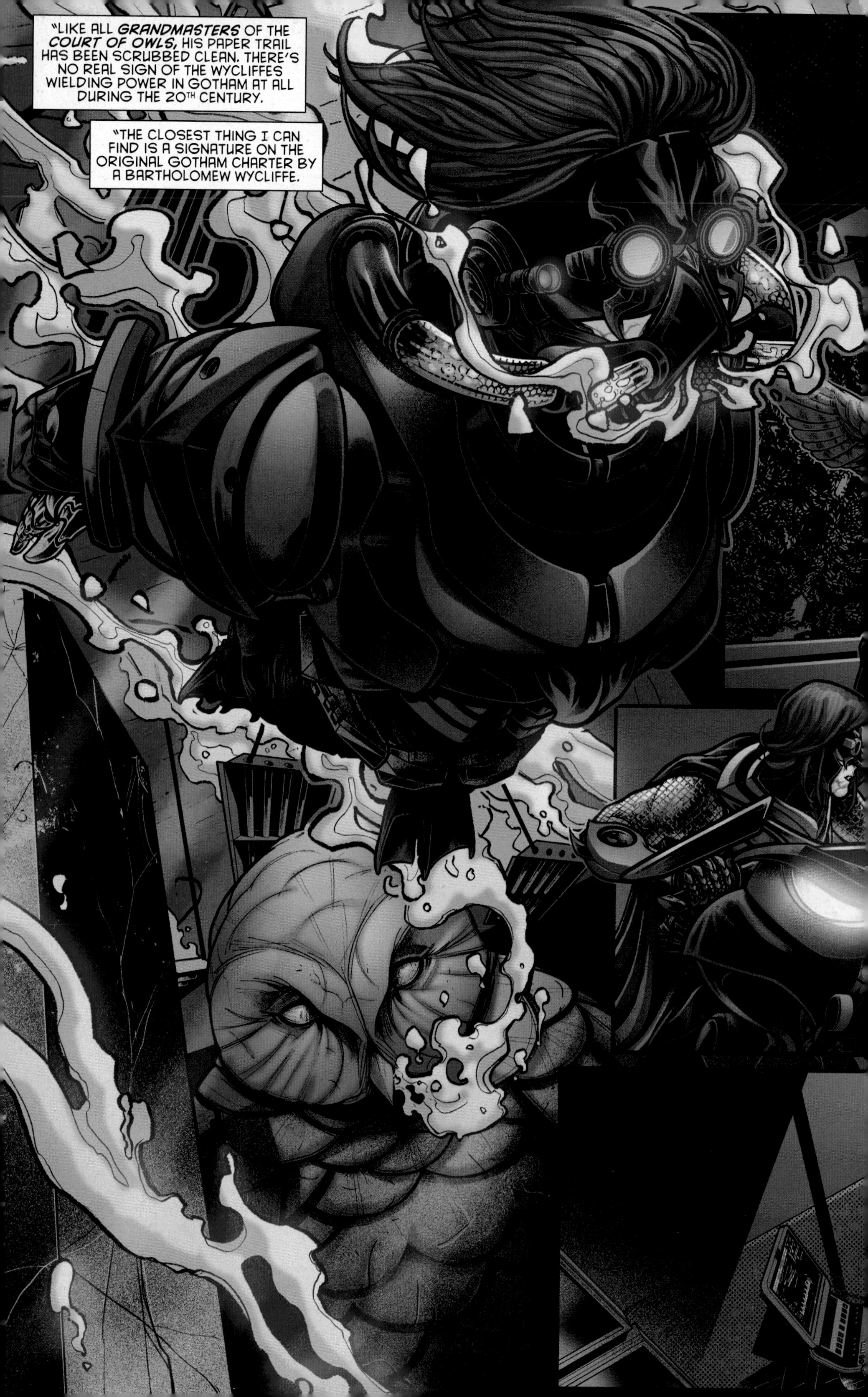
"LIKE ALL GRANDMASTERS OF THE COURT OF OWLS, HIS PAPER TRAIL HAS BEEN SCRUBBED CLEAN. THERE'S NO REAL SIGN OF THE WYCLIFFES WIELDING POWER IN GOTHAM AT ALL DURING THE 20TH CENTURY.
"THE CLOSEST THING I CAN FIND IS A SIGNATURE ON THE ORIGINAL GOTHAM CHARTER BY A BARTHOLOMEW WYCLIFFE.

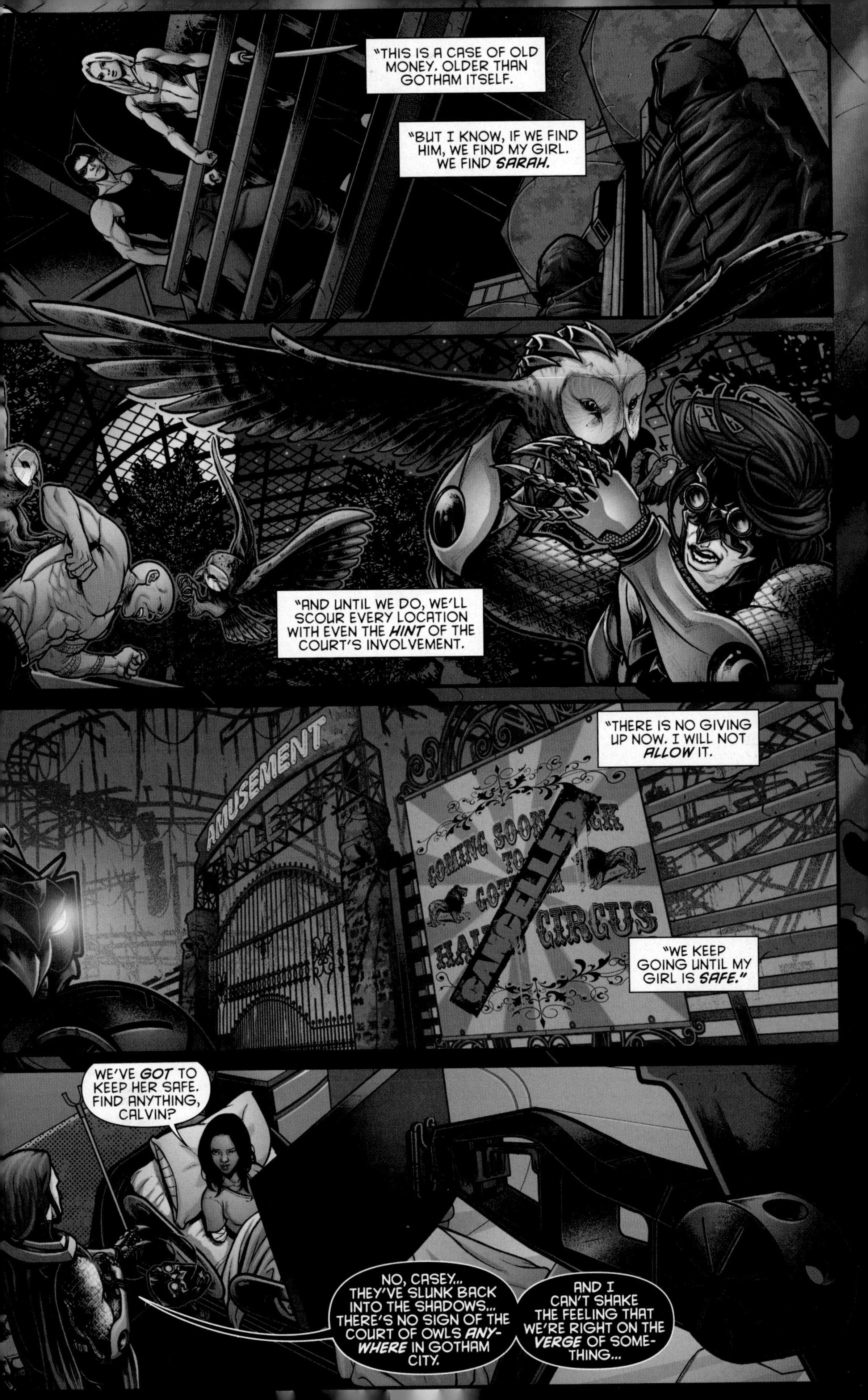
"THIS IS A CASE OF OLD MONEY. OLDER THAN GOTHAM ITSELF.
"BUT I KNOW, IF WE FIND HIM, WE FIND MY GIRL. WE FIND *SARAH.*
"AND UNTIL WE DO, WE'LL SCOUR EVERY LOCATION WITH EVEN THE *HINT* OF THE COURT'S INVOLVEMENT.
"THERE IS NO GIVING UP NOW. I WILL NOT *ALLOW* IT.
AMUSEMENT MILE
COMING SOON
CANCELLED
CIRCUS
"WE KEEP GOING UNTIL MY GIRL IS *SAFE."*
WE'VE *GOT* TO KEEP HER SAFE. FIND ANYTHING, CALVIN?
NO, CASEY... THEY'VE SLUNK BACK INTO THE SHADOWS... THERE'S NO SIGN OF THE COURT OF OWLS *ANY-WHERE* IN GOTHAM CITY.
AND I CAN'T SHAKE THE FEELING THAT WE'RE RIGHT ON THE *VERGE* OF SOME-THING...

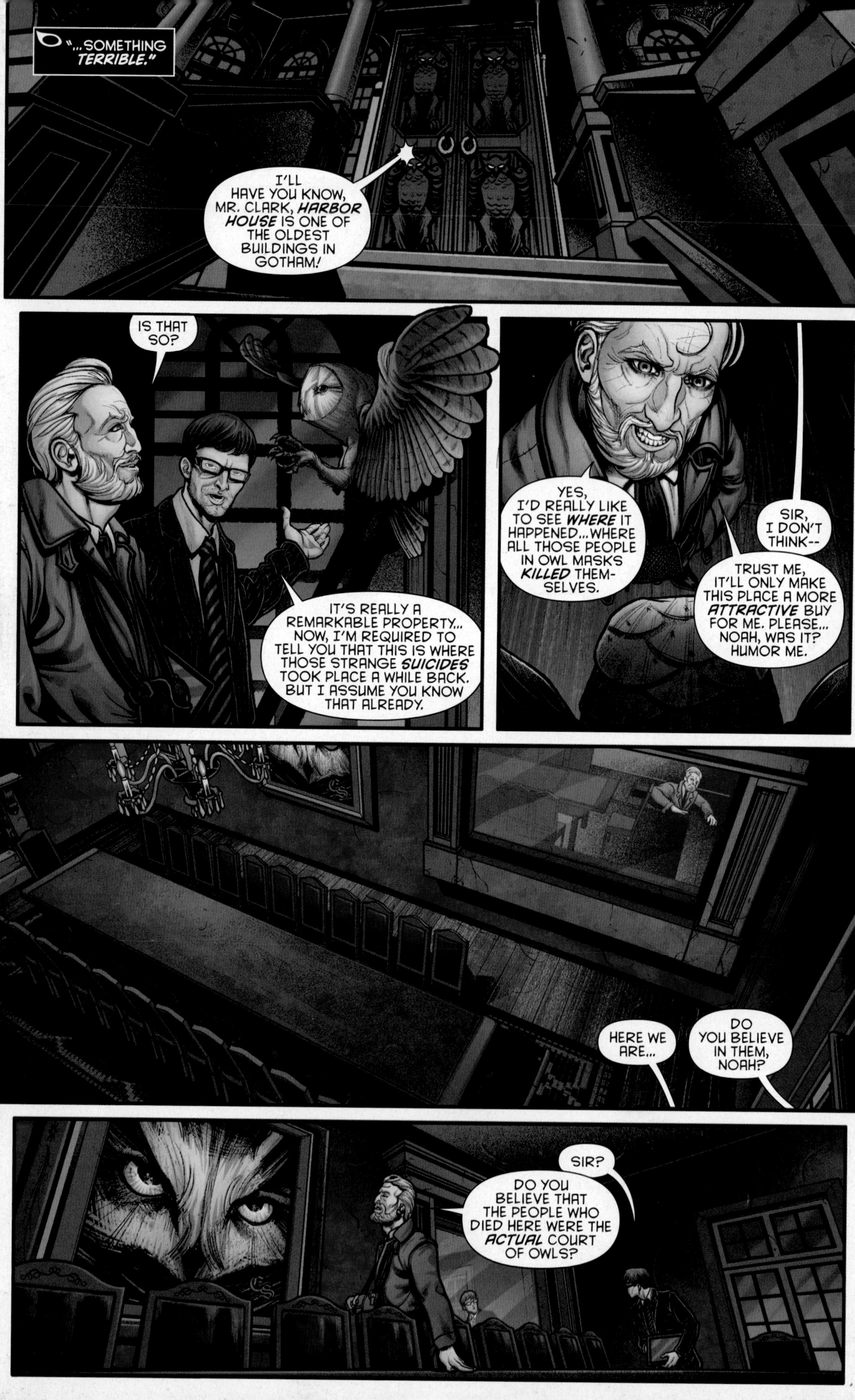
"...SOMETHING TERRIBLE."
I'LL HAVE YOU KNOW, MR. CLARK, HARBOR HOUSE IS ONE OF THE OLDEST BUILDINGS IN GOTHAM!
IS THAT SO?
IT'S REALLY A REMARKABLE PROPERTY... NOW, I'M REQUIRED TO TELL YOU THAT THIS IS WHERE THOSE STRANGE SUICIDES TOOK PLACE A WHILE BACK. BUT I ASSUME YOU KNOW THAT ALREADY.
YES, I'D REALLY LIKE TO SEE WHERE IT HAPPENED...WHERE ALL THOSE PEOPLE IN OWL MASKS KILLED THEMSELVES.
SIR, I DON'T THINK--
TRUST ME, IT'LL ONLY MAKE THIS PLACE A MORE ATTRACTIVE BUY FOR ME. PLEASE... NOAH, WAS IT? HUMOR ME.
HERE WE ARE...
DO YOU BELIEVE IN THEM, NOAH?
SIR?
DO YOU BELIEVE THAT THE PEOPLE WHO DIED HERE WERE THE ACTUAL COURT OF OWLS?

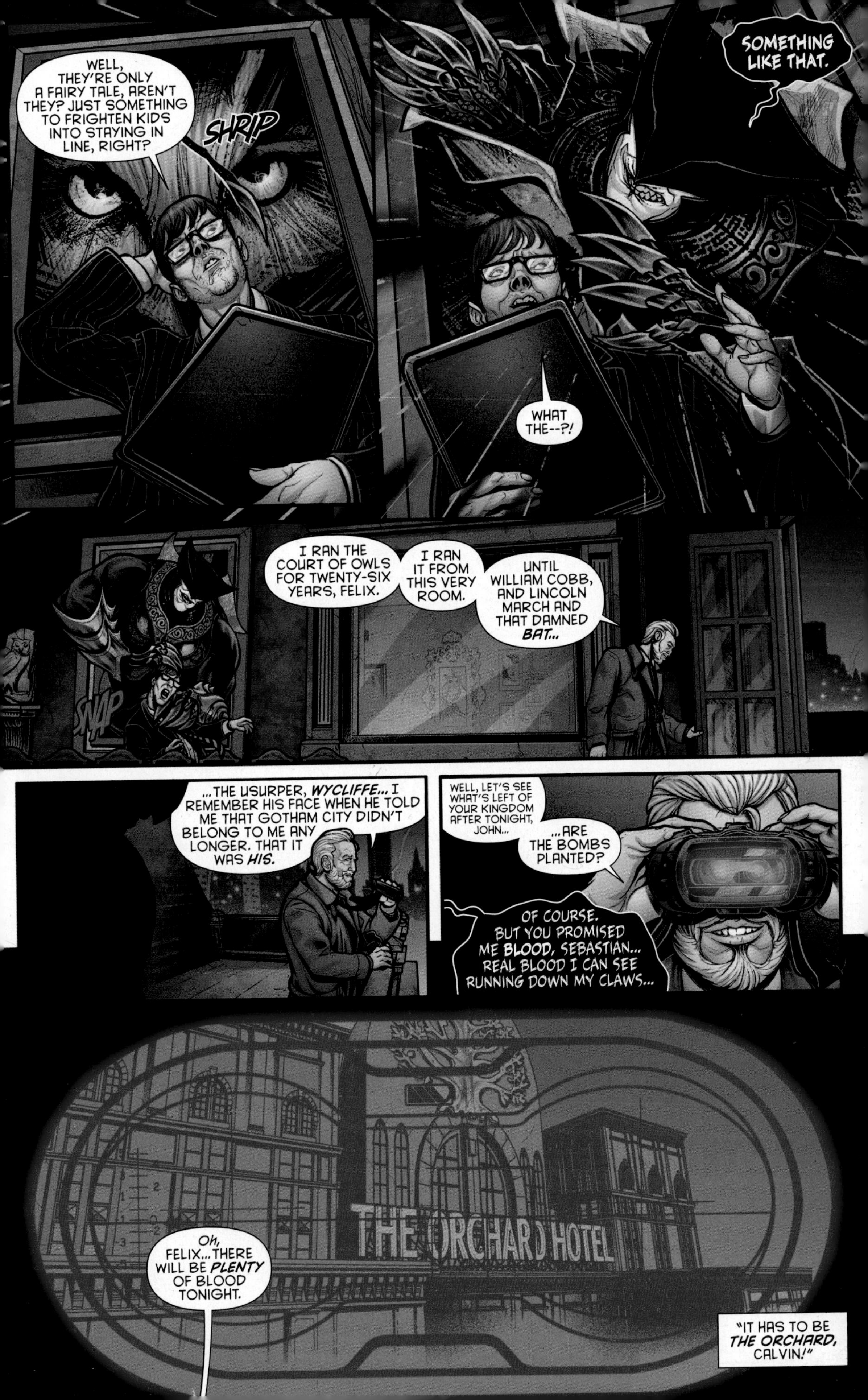
WELL, THEY'RE ONLY A FAIRY TALE, AREN'T THEY? JUST SOMETHING TO FRIGHTEN KIDS INTO STAYING IN LINE, RIGHT?
SHRIP
SOMETHING LIKE THAT.
WHAT THE--?!
I RAN THE COURT OF OWLS FOR TWENTY-SIX YEARS, FELIX.
I RAN IT FROM THIS VERY ROOM.
UNTIL WILLIAM COBB, AND LINCOLN MARCH AND THAT DAMNED BAT...
SNAP
...THE USURPER, WYCLIFFE... I REMEMBER HIS FACE WHEN HE TOLD ME THAT GOTHAM CITY DIDN'T BELONG TO ME ANY LONGER. THAT IT WAS HIS.
WELL, LET'S SEE WHAT'S LEFT OF YOUR KINGDOM AFTER TONIGHT, JOHN...
...ARE THE BOMBS PLANTED?
OF COURSE. BUT YOU PROMISED ME BLOOD, SEBASTIAN... REAL BLOOD I CAN SEE RUNNING DOWN MY CLAWS...
THE ORCHARD HOTEL
Oh, FELIX... THERE WILL BE PLENTY OF BLOOD TONIGHT.
"IT HAS TO BE THE ORCHARD, CALVIN!"

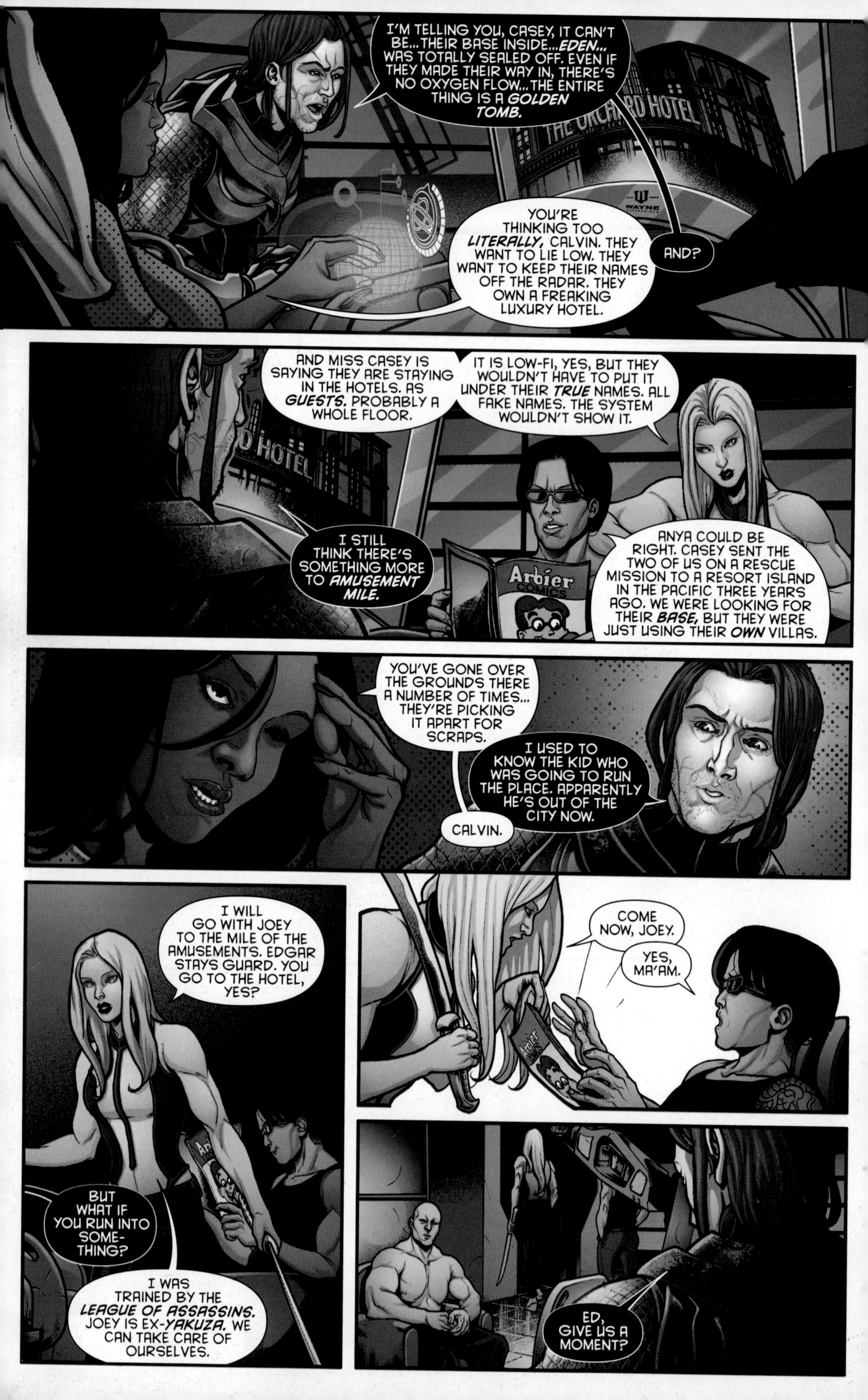

I'M TELLING YOU, CASEY, IT CAN'T BE...THEIR BASE INSIDE...EDEN... WAS TOTALLY SEALED OFF. EVEN IF THEY MADE THEIR WAY IN, THERE'S NO OXYGEN FLOW...THE ENTIRE THING IS A GOLDEN TOMB.
YOU'RE THINKING TOO LITERALLY, CALVIN. THEY WANT TO LIE LOW. THEY WANT TO KEEP THEIR NAMES OFF THE RADAR. THEY OWN A FREAKING LUXURY HOTEL.
AND?
AND MISS CASEY IS SAYING THEY ARE STAYING IN THE HOTELS. AS GUESTS. PROBABLY A WHOLE FLOOR.
IT IS LOW-FI, YES, BUT THEY WOULDN'T HAVE TO PUT IT UNDER THEIR TRUE NAMES. ALL FAKE NAMES. THE SYSTEM WOULDN'T SHOW IT.
I STILL THINK THERE'S SOMETHING MORE TO AMUSEMENT MILE.
ANYA COULD BE RIGHT. CASEY SENT THE TWO OF US ON A RESCUE MISSION TO A RESORT ISLAND IN THE PACIFIC THREE YEARS AGO. WE WERE LOOKING FOR THEIR BASE, BUT THEY WERE JUST USING THEIR OWN VILLAS.
YOU'VE GONE OVER THE GROUNDS THERE A NUMBER OF TIMES... THEY'RE PICKING IT APART FOR SCRAPS.
I USED TO KNOW THE KID WHO WAS GOING TO RUN THE PLACE. APPARENTLY HE'S OUT OF THE CITY NOW.
CALVIN.
I WILL GO WITH JOEY TO THE MILE OF THE AMUSEMENTS. EDGAR STAYS GUARD. YOU GO TO THE HOTEL, YES?
BUT WHAT IF YOU RUN INTO SOME-THING?
I WAS TRAINED BY THE LEAGUE OF ASSASSINS. JOEY IS EX-YAKUZA. WE CAN TAKE CARE OF OURSELVES.
COME NOW, JOEY.
YES, MA'AM.
ED, GIVE US A MOMENT?

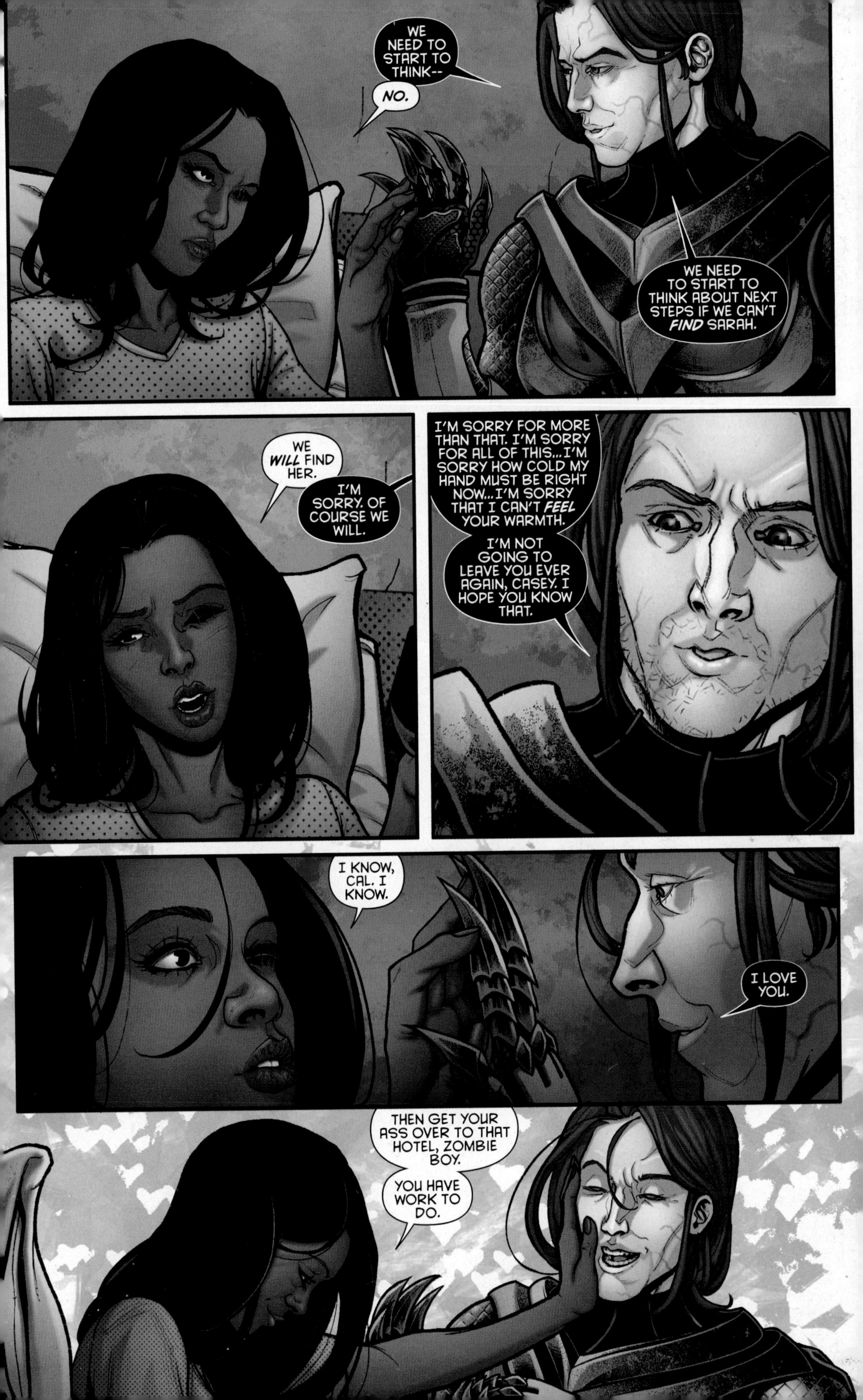
WE NEED TO START TO THINK--
NO.
WE NEED TO START TO THINK ABOUT NEXT STEPS IF WE CAN'T *FIND* SARAH.
WE *WILL* FIND HER.
I'M SORRY. OF COURSE WE WILL.
I'M SORRY FOR MORE THAN THAT. I'M SORRY FOR ALL OF THIS...I'M SORRY HOW COLD MY HAND MUST BE RIGHT NOW...I'M SORRY THAT I CAN'T *FEEL* YOUR WARMTH.
I'M NOT GOING TO LEAVE YOU EVER AGAIN, CASEY. I HOPE YOU KNOW THAT.
I KNOW, CAL. I KNOW.
I LOVE YOU.
THEN GET YOUR ASS OVER TO THAT HOTEL, ZOMBIE BOY.
YOU HAVE WORK TO DO.

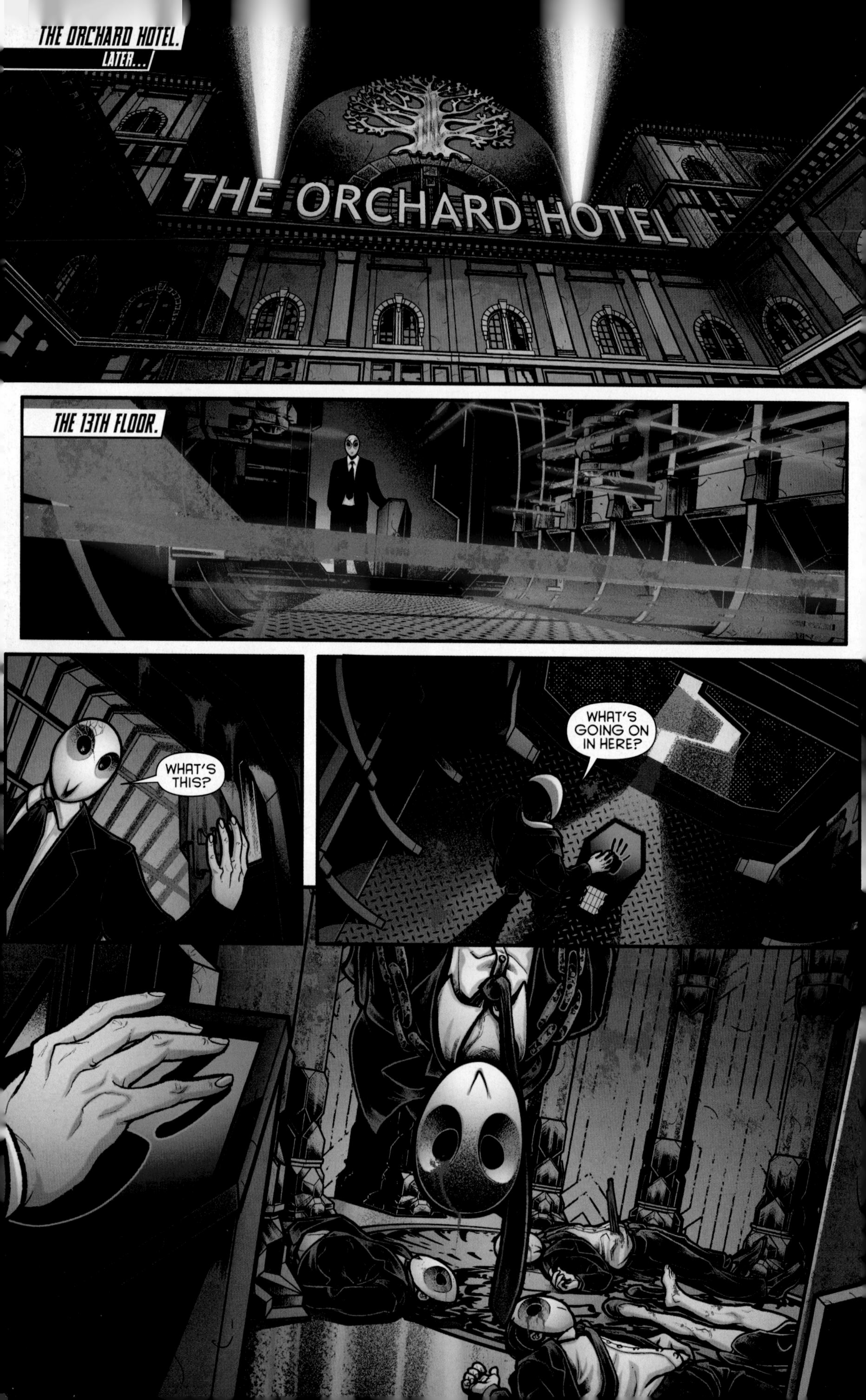
THE ORCHARD HOTEL.
LATER...
THE ORCHARD HOTEL
THE 13TH FLOOR.
WHAT'S THIS?
WHAT'S GOING ON IN HERE?

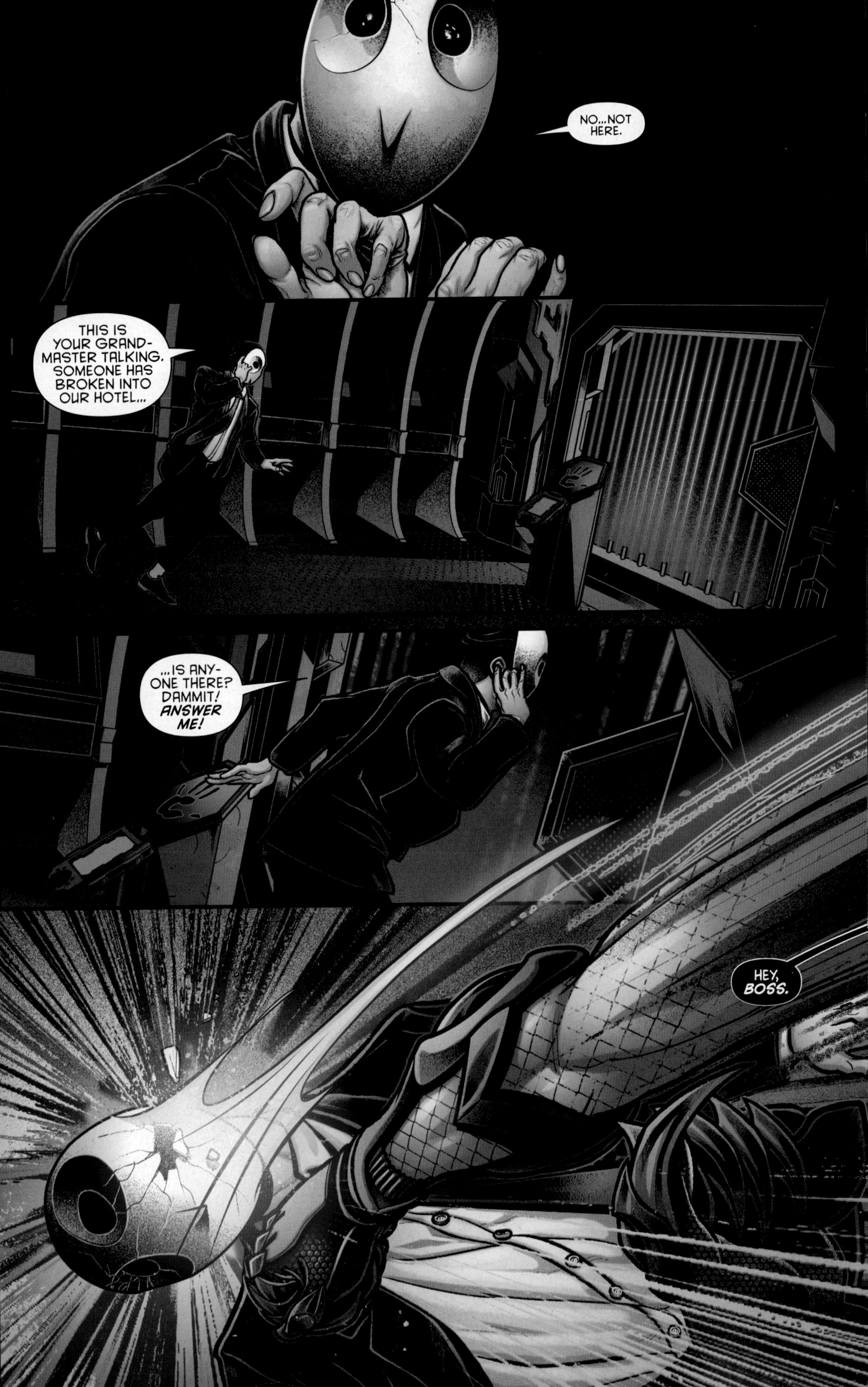
NO...NOT HERE.
THIS IS YOUR GRAND-MASTER TALKING. SOMEONE HAS BROKEN INTO OUR HOTEL...
...IS ANY-ONE THERE? DAMMIT! ANSWER ME!
HEY, BOSS.

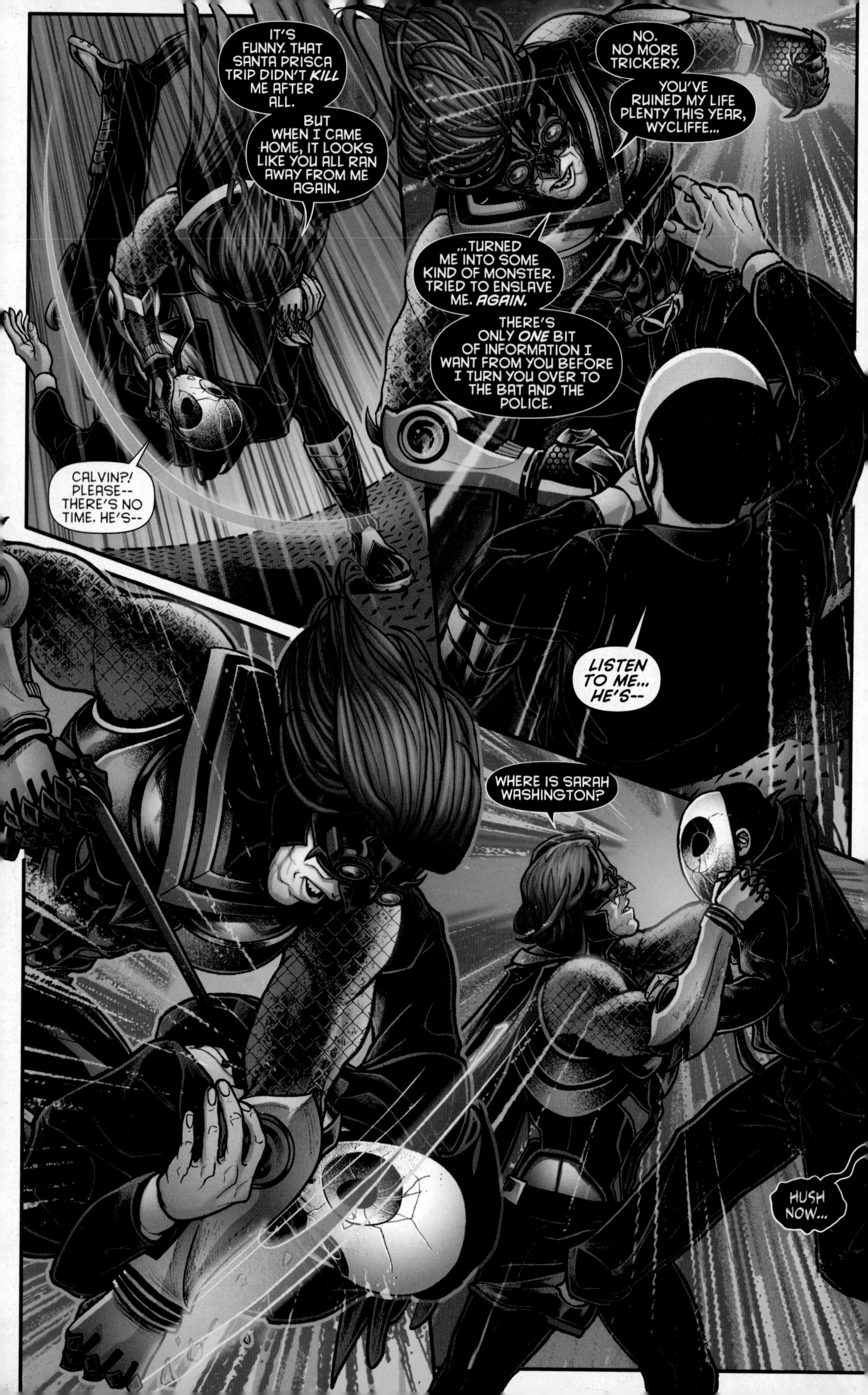
IT'S FUNNY. THAT SANTA PRISCA TRIP DIDN'T KILL ME AFTER ALL.
BUT WHEN I CAME HOME, IT LOOKS LIKE YOU ALL RAN AWAY FROM ME AGAIN.
NO. NO MORE TRICKERY.
YOU'VE RUINED MY LIFE PLENTY THIS YEAR, WYCLIFFE...
...TURNED ME INTO SOME KIND OF MONSTER. TRIED TO ENSLAVE ME. AGAIN.
THERE'S ONLY ONE BIT OF INFORMATION I WANT FROM YOU BEFORE I TURN YOU OVER TO THE BAT AND THE POLICE.
CALVIN?! PLEASE-- THERE'S NO TIME. HE'S--
LISTEN TO ME... HE'S--
WHERE IS SARAH WASHINGTON?
HUSH NOW...

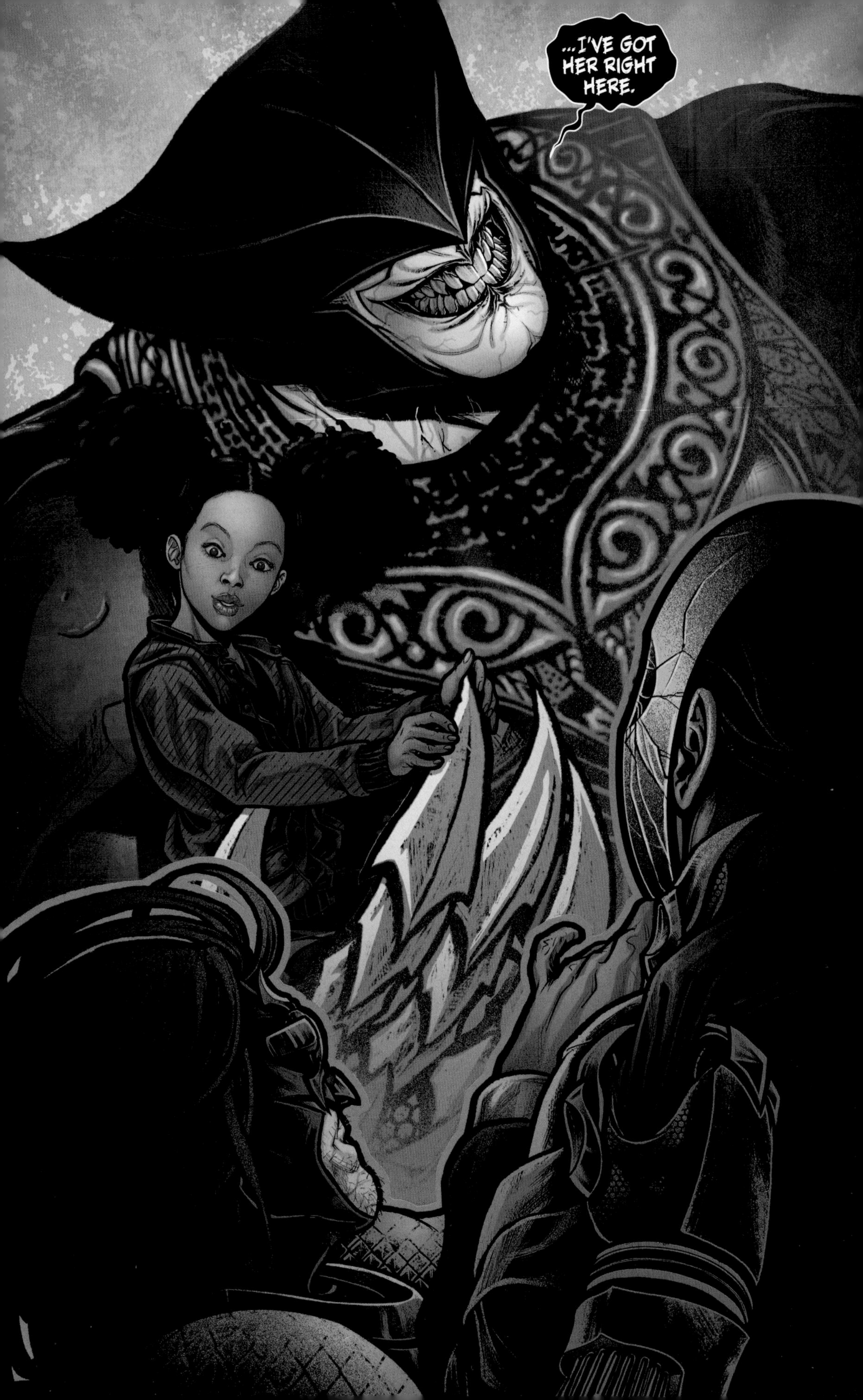
...I'VE GOT HER RIGHT HERE.

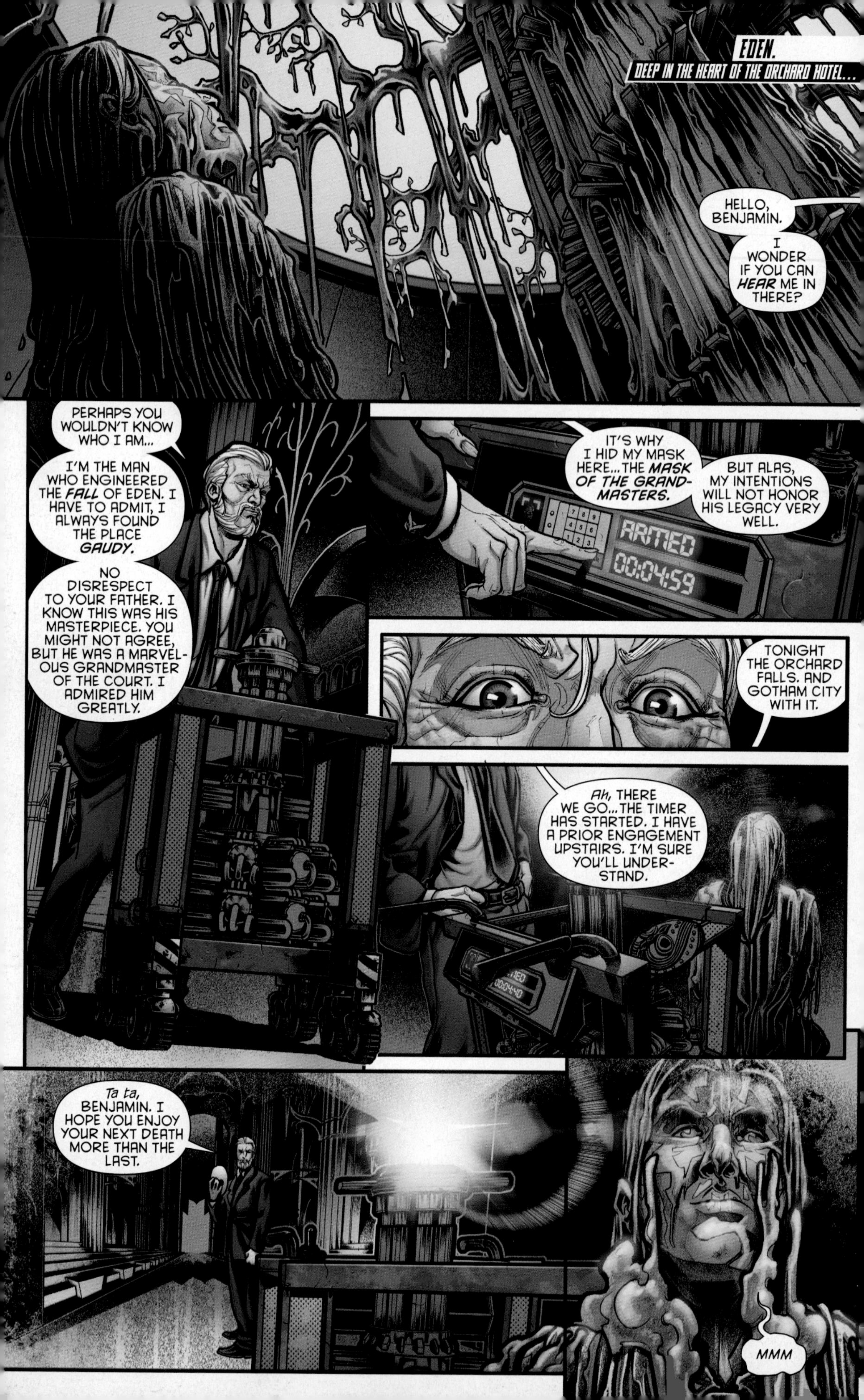
EDEN.
DEEP IN THE HEART OF THE ORCHARD HOTEL...
HELLO, BENJAMIN.
I WONDER IF YOU CAN HEAR ME IN THERE?
PERHAPS YOU WOULDN'T KNOW WHO I AM...
I'M THE MAN WHO ENGINEERED THE FALL OF EDEN. I HAVE TO ADMIT, I ALWAYS FOUND THE PLACE GAUDY.
NO DISRESPECT TO YOUR FATHER. I KNOW THIS WAS HIS MASTERPIECE. YOU MIGHT NOT AGREE, BUT HE WAS A MARVEL-OUS GRANDMASTER OF THE COURT. I ADMIRED HIM GREATLY.
IT'S WHY I HID MY MASK HERE...THE MASK OF THE GRAND-MASTERS.
BUT ALAS, MY INTENTIONS WILL NOT HONOR HIS LEGACY VERY WELL.
ARMED
00:04:59
TONIGHT THE ORCHARD FALLS. AND GOTHAM CITY WITH IT.
Ah, THERE WE GO...THE TIMER HAS STARTED. I HAVE A PRIOR ENGAGEMENT UPSTAIRS. I'M SURE YOU'LL UNDER-STAND.
Ta ta, BENJAMIN. I HOPE YOU ENJOY YOUR NEXT DEATH MORE THAN THE LAST.
MMM

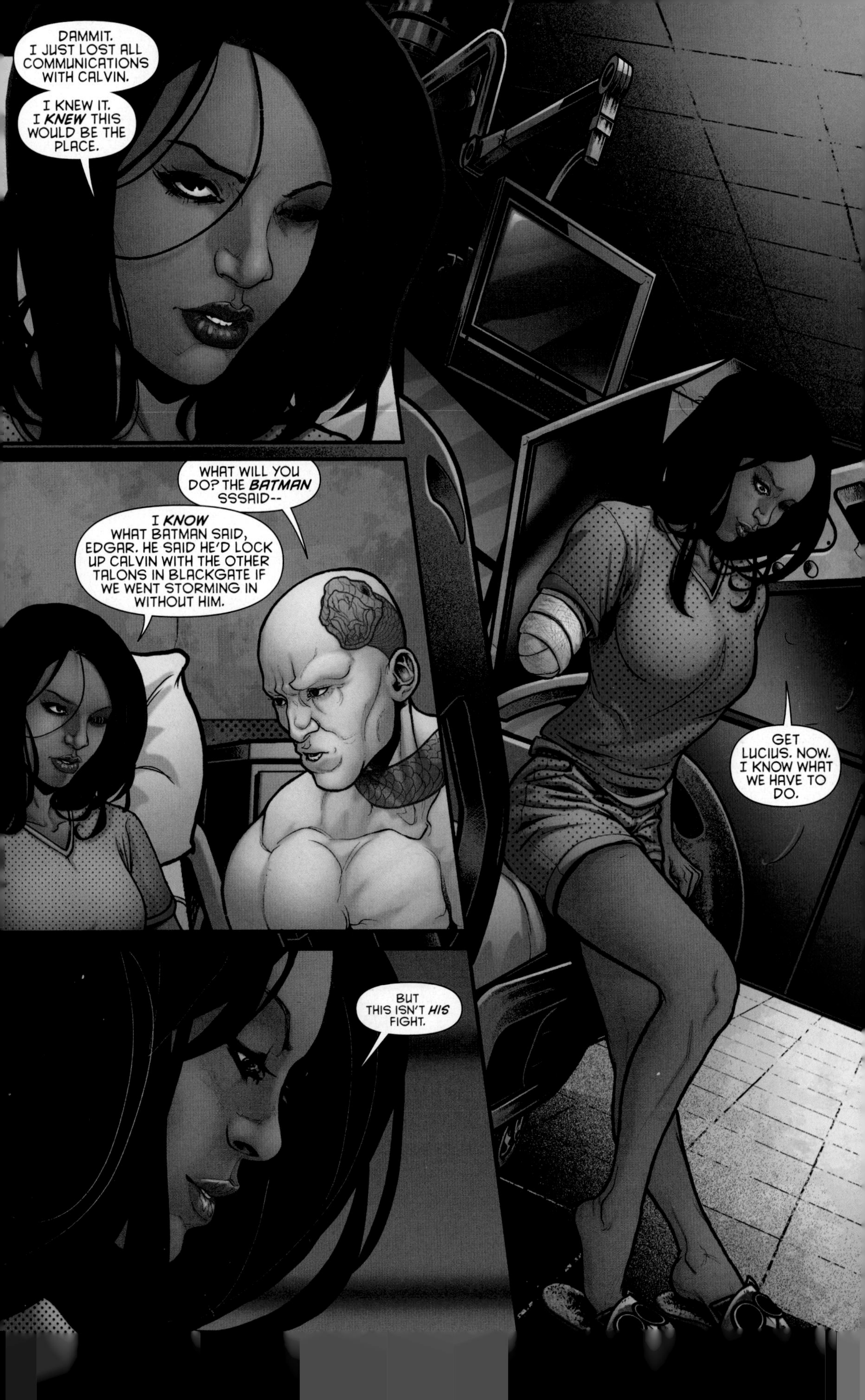
DAMMIT. I JUST LOST ALL COMMUNICATIONS WITH CALVIN.
I KNEW IT. I KNEW THIS WOULD BE THE PLACE.
WHAT WILL YOU DO? THE BATMAN SSSAID--
I KNOW WHAT BATMAN SAID, EDGAR. HE SAID HE'D LOCK UP CALVIN WITH THE OTHER TALONS IN BLACKGATE IF WE WENT STORMING IN WITHOUT HIM.
BUT THIS ISN'T HIS FIGHT.
GET LUCIUS. NOW. I KNOW WHAT WE HAVE TO DO.

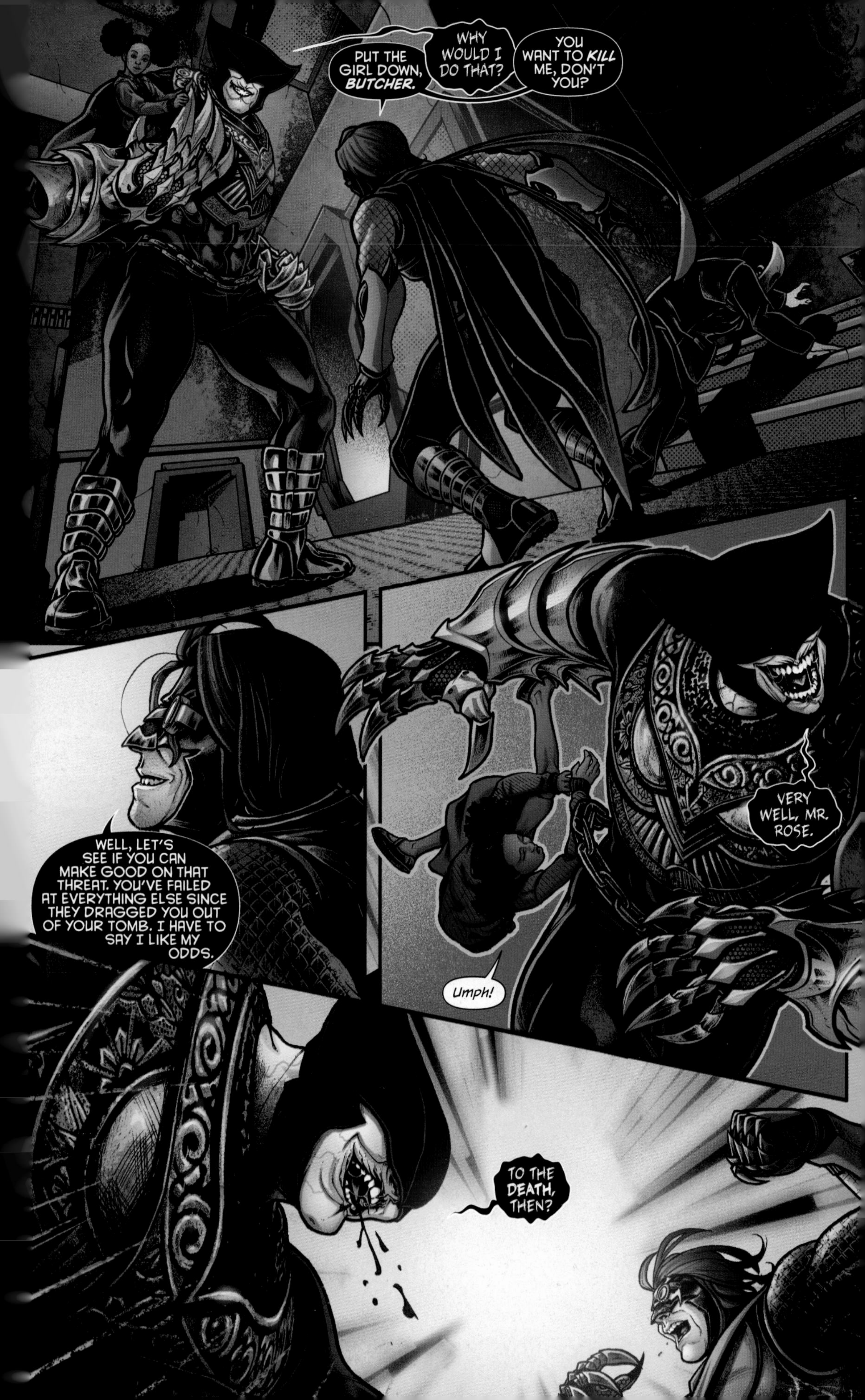
PUT THE GIRL DOWN, BUTCHER.
WHY WOULD I DO THAT?
YOU WANT TO KILL ME, DON'T YOU?
WELL, LET'S SEE IF YOU CAN MAKE GOOD ON THAT THREAT. YOU'VE FAILED AT EVERYTHING ELSE SINCE THEY DRAGGED YOU OUT OF YOUR TOMB. I HAVE TO SAY I LIKE MY ODDS.
VERY WELL, MR. ROSE.
Umph!
TO THE DEATH, THEN?

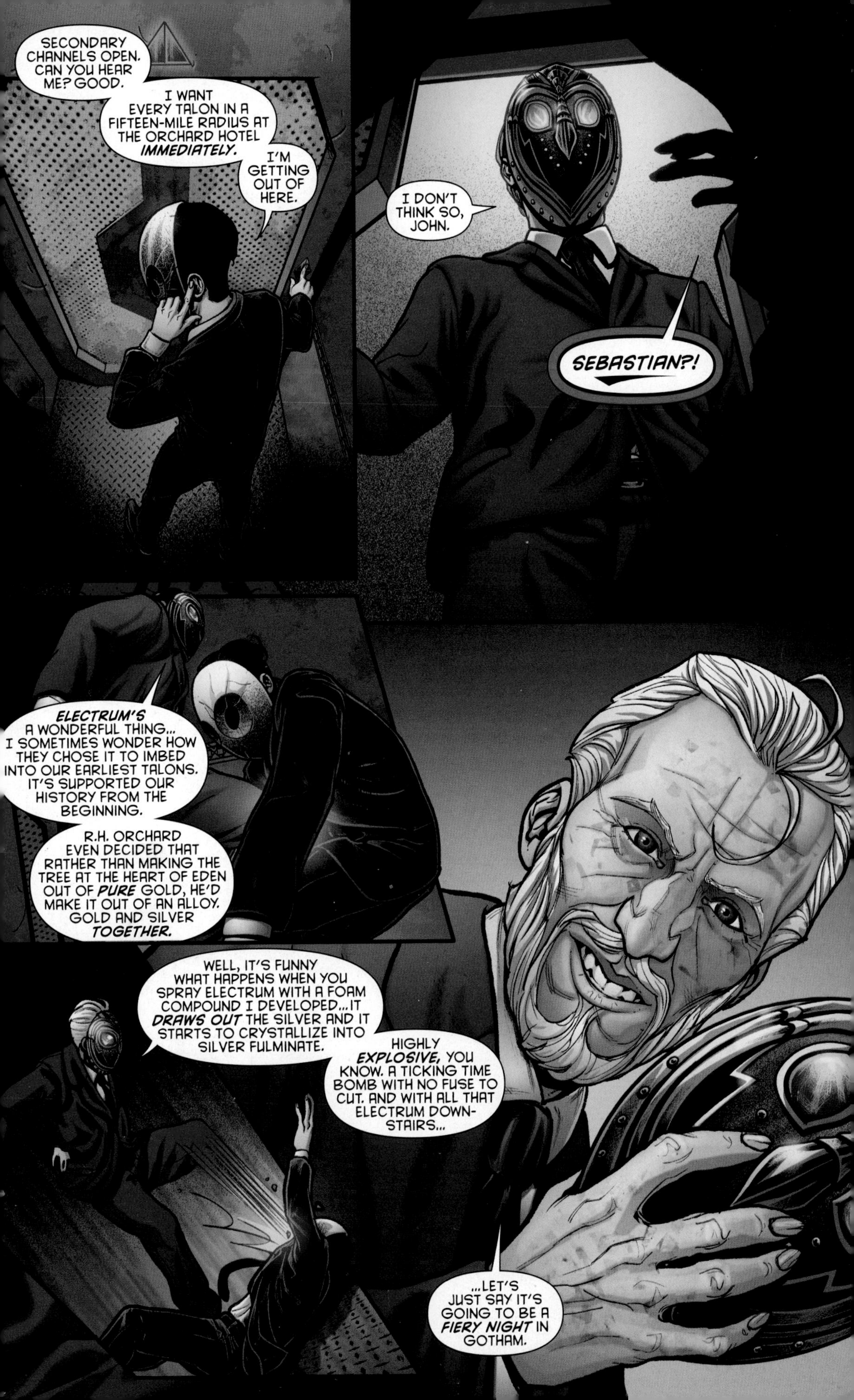
SECONDARY CHANNELS OPEN. CAN YOU HEAR ME? GOOD.
I WANT EVERY TALON IN A FIFTEEN-MILE RADIUS AT THE ORCHARD HOTEL *IMMEDIATELY.*
I'M GETTING OUT OF HERE.
I DON'T THINK SO, JOHN.
SEBASTIAN?!
ELECTRUM'S A WONDERFUL THING... I SOMETIMES WONDER HOW THEY CHOSE IT TO IMBED INTO OUR EARLIEST TALONS. IT'S SUPPORTED OUR HISTORY FROM THE BEGINNING.
R.H. ORCHARD EVEN DECIDED THAT RATHER THAN MAKING THE TREE AT THE HEART OF EDEN OUT OF *PURE* GOLD, HE'D MAKE IT OUT OF AN ALLOY. GOLD AND SILVER *TOGETHER.*
WELL, IT'S FUNNY WHAT HAPPENS WHEN YOU SPRAY ELECTRUM WITH A FOAM COMPOUND I DEVELOPED...IT *DRAWS OUT* THE SILVER AND IT STARTS TO CRYSTALLIZE INTO SILVER FULMINATE.
HIGHLY *EXPLOSIVE,* YOU KNOW. A TICKING TIME BOMB WITH NO FUSE TO CUT. AND WITH ALL THAT ELECTRUM DOWN-STAIRS...
...LET'S JUST SAY IT'S GOING TO BE A *FIERY NIGHT* IN GOTHAM.

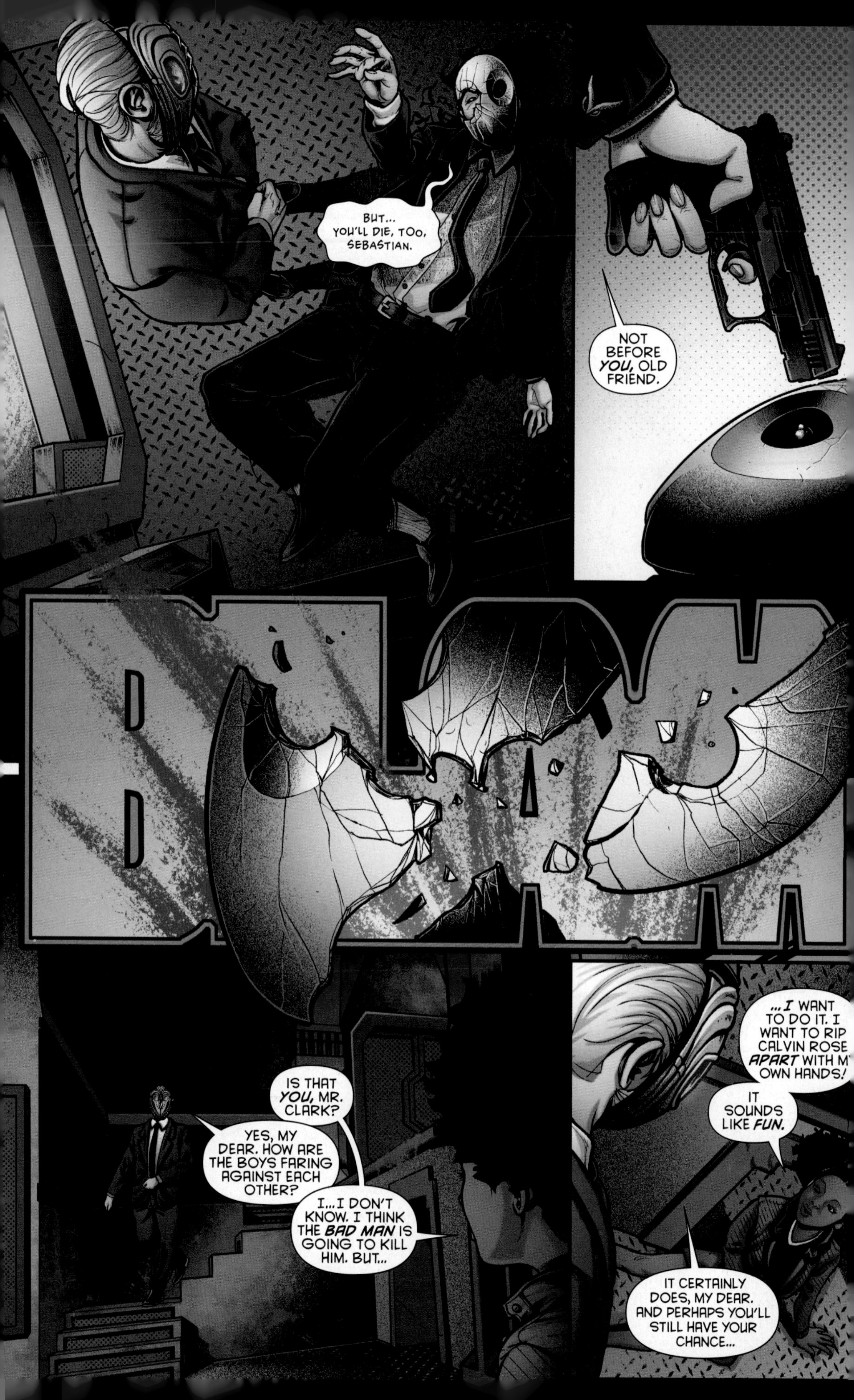
BUT... YOU'LL DIE, TOO, SEBASTIAN.
NOT BEFORE YOU, OLD FRIEND.
BLAM
IS THAT YOU, MR. CLARK?
YES, MY DEAR. HOW ARE THE BOYS FARING AGAINST EACH OTHER?
I...I DON'T KNOW. I THINK THE BAD MAN IS GOING TO KILL HIM. BUT...
...I WANT TO DO IT. I WANT TO RIP CALVIN ROSE APART WITH MY OWN HANDS!
IT SOUNDS LIKE FUN.
IT CERTAINLY DOES, MY DEAR. AND PERHAPS YOU'LL STILL HAVE YOUR CHANCE...

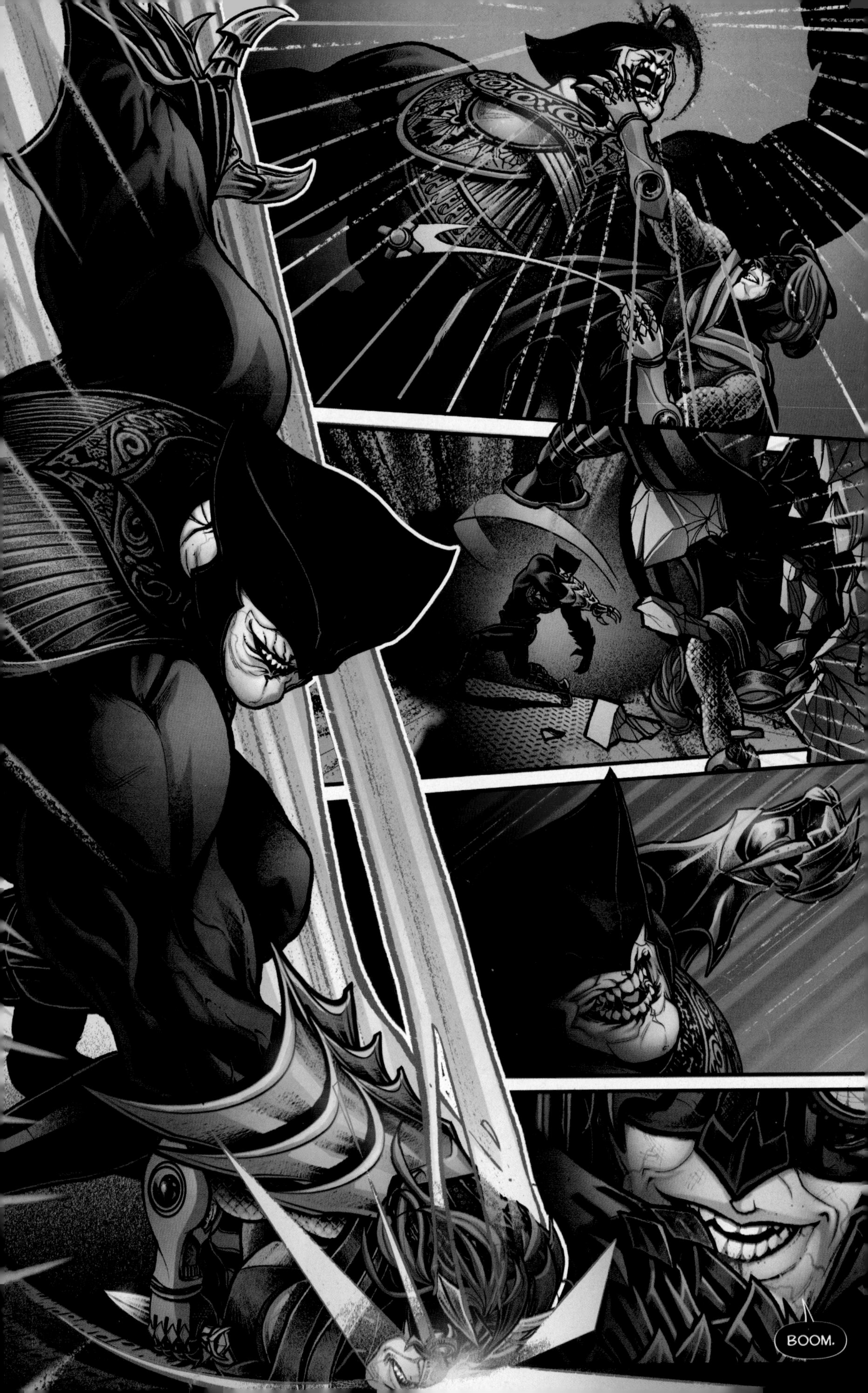
BOOM.

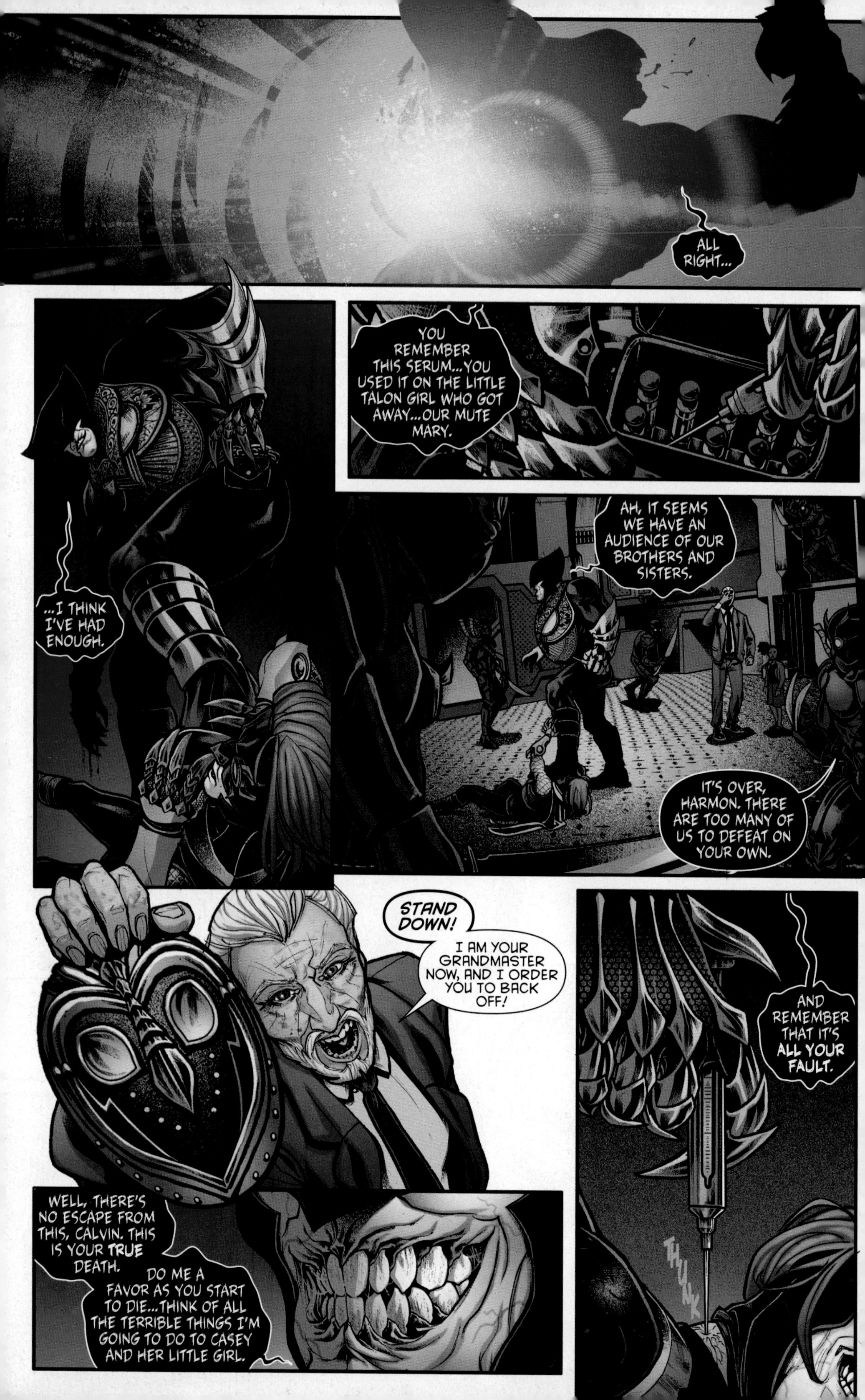

ALL RIGHT...
YOU REMEMBER THIS SERUM...YOU USED IT ON THE LITTLE TALON GIRL WHO GOT AWAY...OUR MUTE MARY.
...I THINK I'VE HAD ENOUGH.
AH, IT SEEMS WE HAVE AN AUDIENCE OF OUR BROTHERS AND SISTERS.
IT'S OVER, HARMON. THERE ARE TOO MANY OF US TO DEFEAT ON YOUR OWN.
STAND DOWN!
I AM YOUR GRANDMASTER NOW, AND I ORDER YOU TO BACK OFF!
WELL, THERE'S NO ESCAPE FROM THIS, CALVIN. THIS IS YOUR **TRUE** DEATH.
DO ME A FAVOR AS YOU START TO DIE...THINK OF ALL THE TERRIBLE THINGS I'M GOING TO DO TO CASEY AND HER LITTLE GIRL.
AND REMEMBER THAT IT'S **ALL YOUR FAULT.**
THUNK

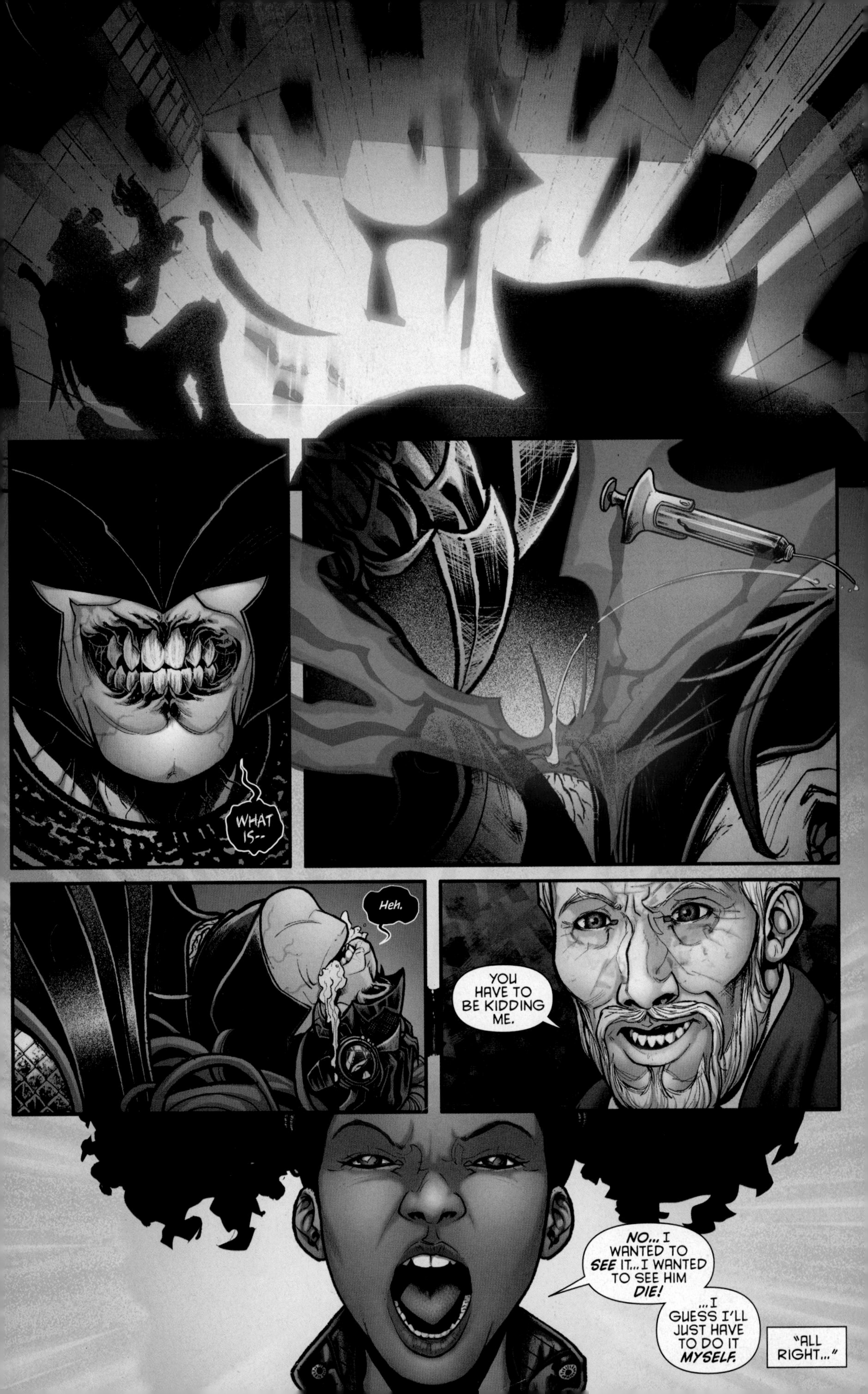
WHAT IS--
Heh.
YOU HAVE TO BE KIDDING ME.
NO... I WANTED TO SEE IT... I WANTED TO SEE HIM DIE!
...I GUESS I'LL JUST HAVE TO DO IT MYSELF.
"ALL RIGHT..."

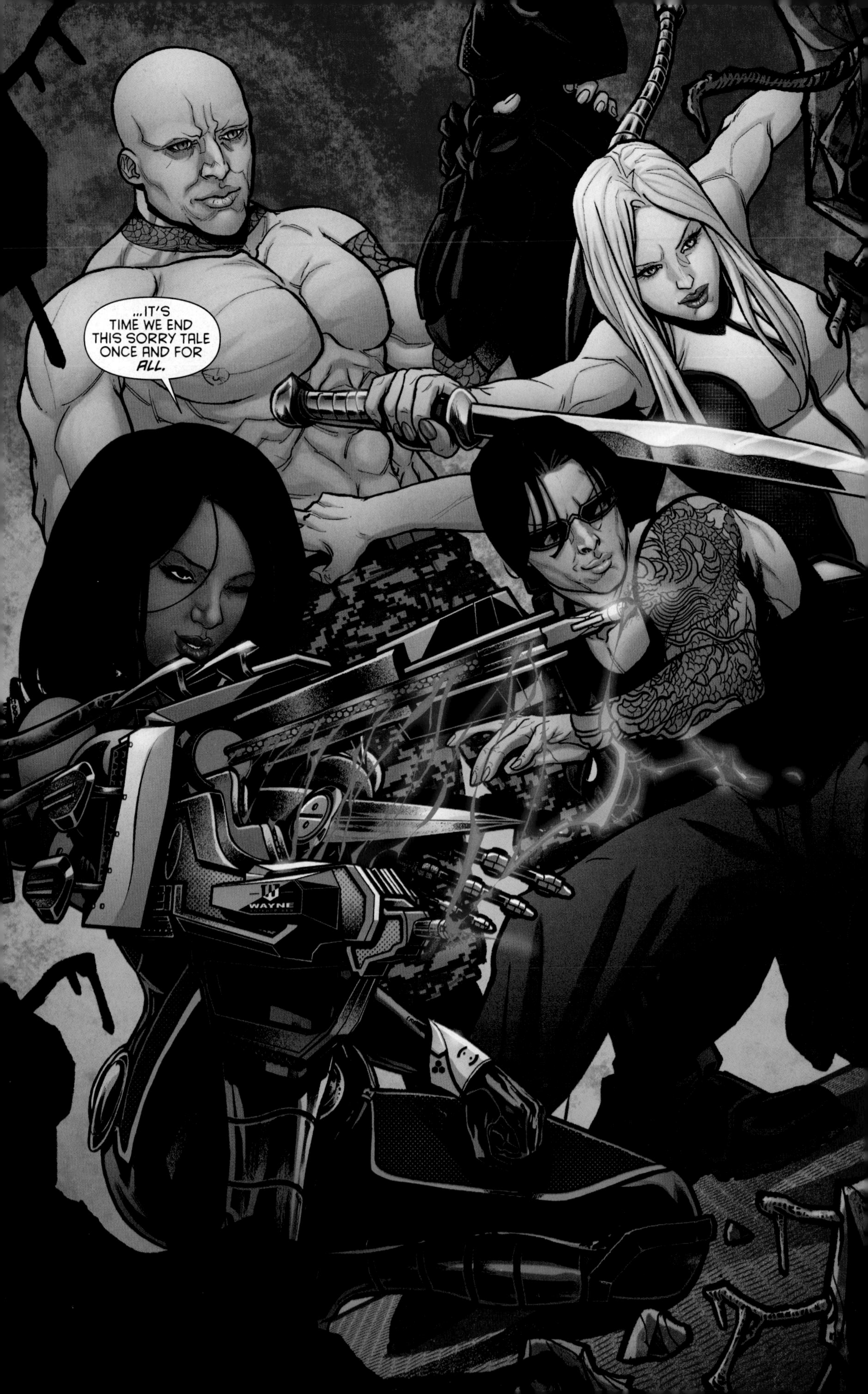
...IT'S TIME WE END THIS SORRY TALE ONCE AND FOR ALL.
WAYNE

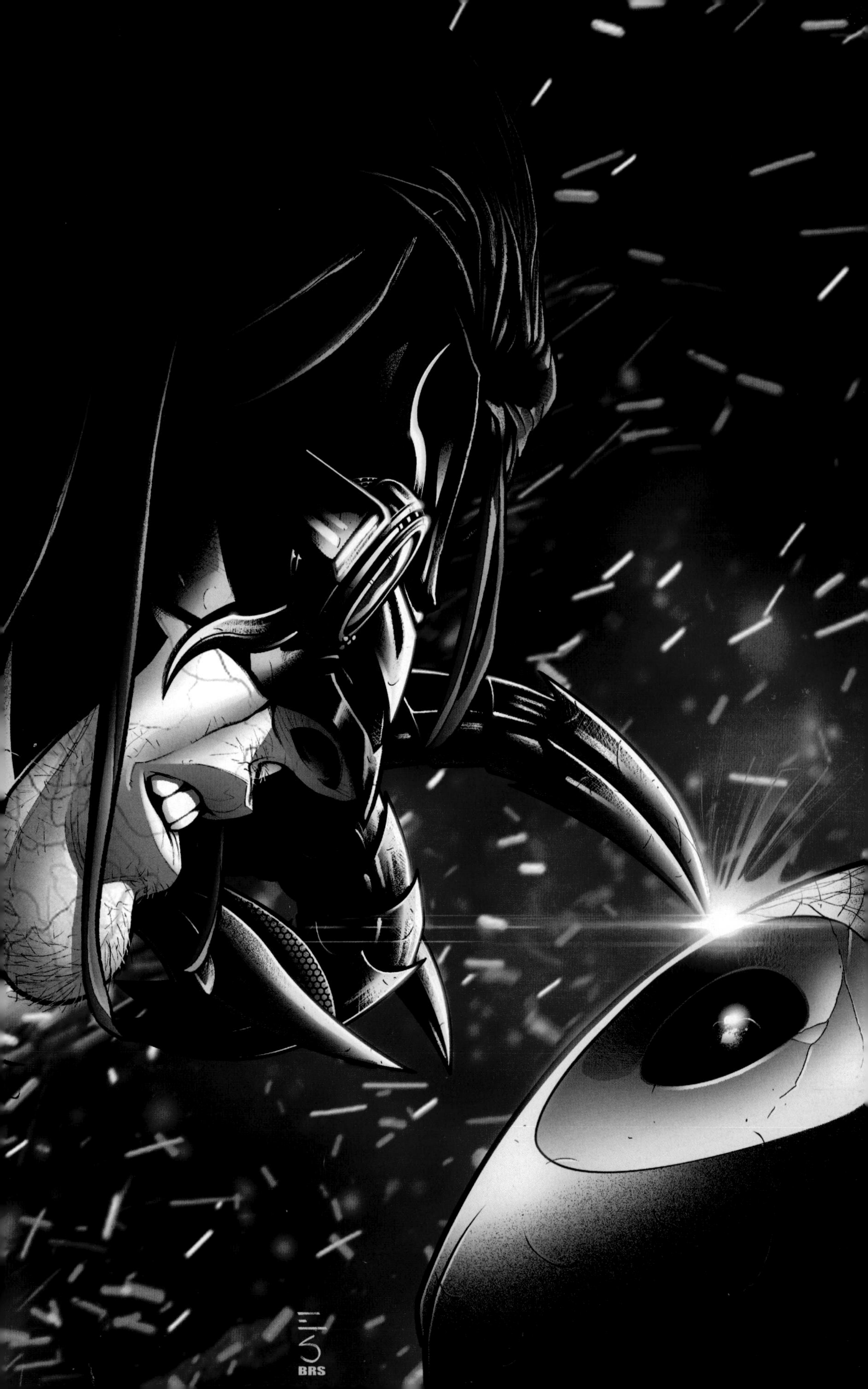
BRS

ETT SMITH

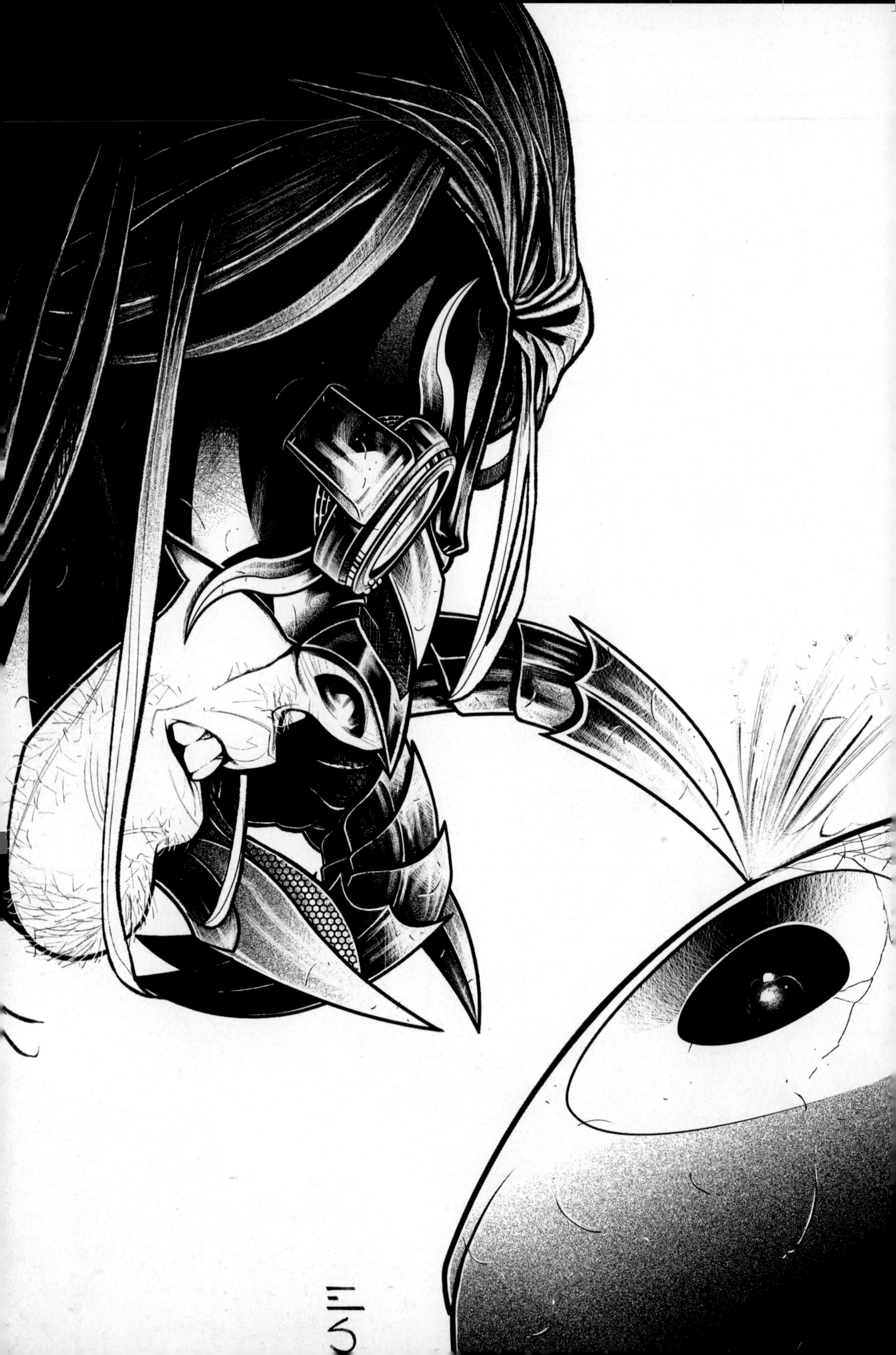

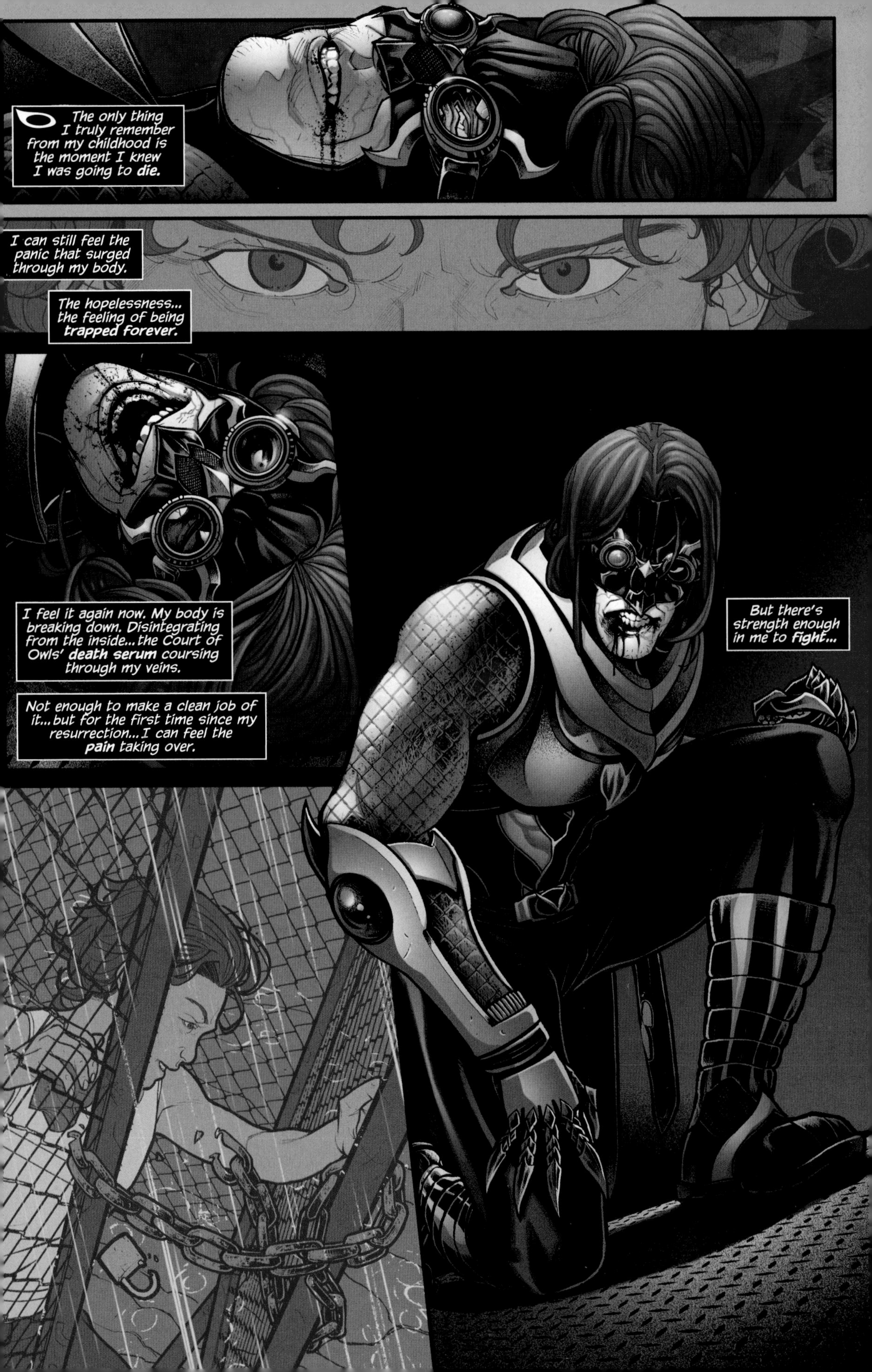
The only thing I truly remember from my childhood is the moment I knew I was going to **die.**
I can still feel the panic that surged through my body.
The hopelessness... the feeling of being **trapped forever.**
I feel it again now. My body is breaking down. Disintegrating from the inside...the Court of Owls' **death serum** coursing through my veins.
Not enough to make a clean job of it...but for the first time since my resurrection...I can feel the **pain** taking over.
But there's strength enough in me to **fight...**

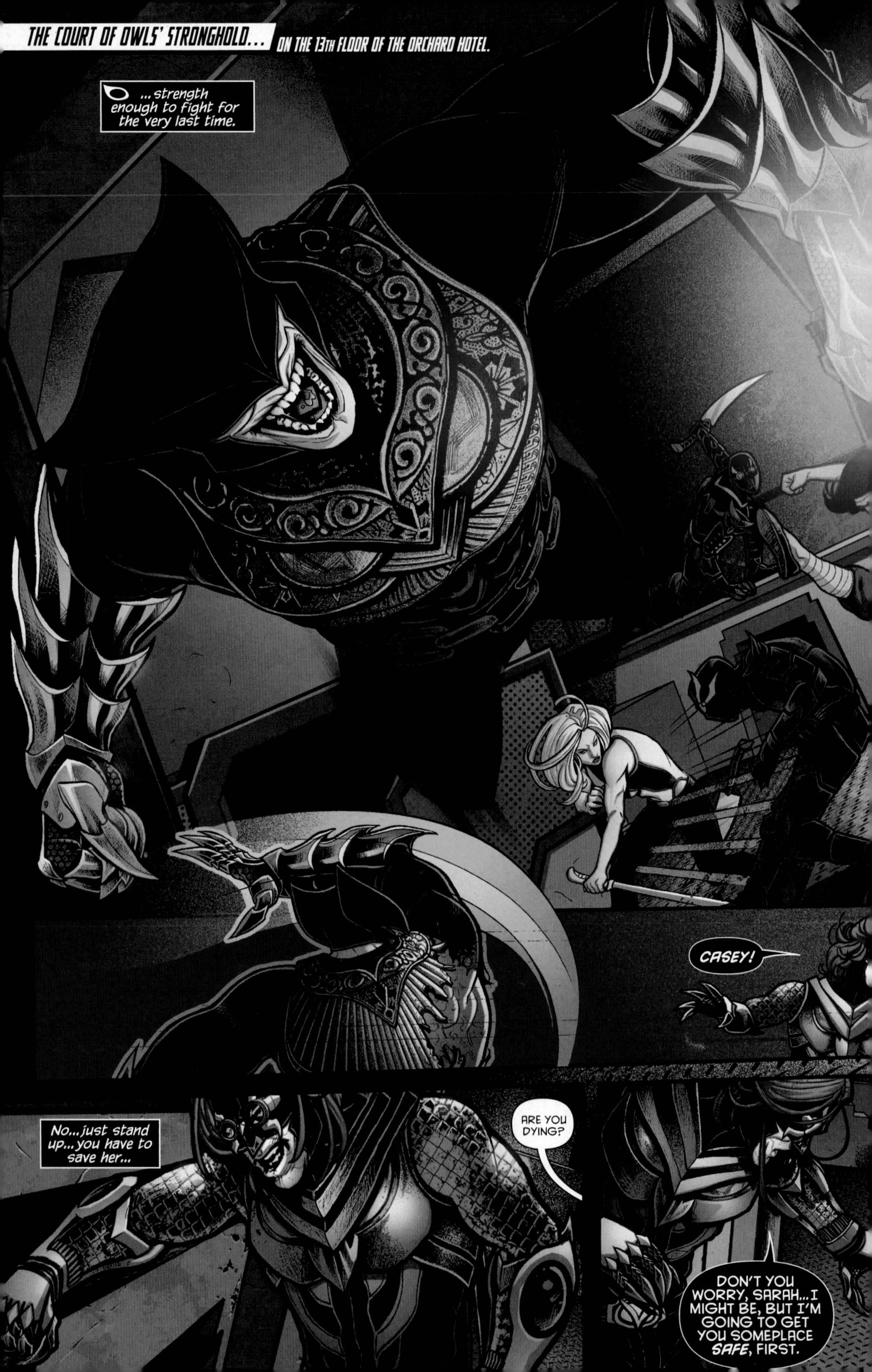
THE COURT OF OWLS' STRONGHOLD...
ON THE 13TH FLOOR OF THE ORCHARD HOTEL.
...strength enough to fight for the very last time.
CASEY!
No...just stand up...you have to save her...
ARE YOU DYING?
DON'T YOU WORRY, SARAH...I MIGHT BE, BUT I'M GOING TO GET YOU SOMEPLACE SAFE, FIRST.

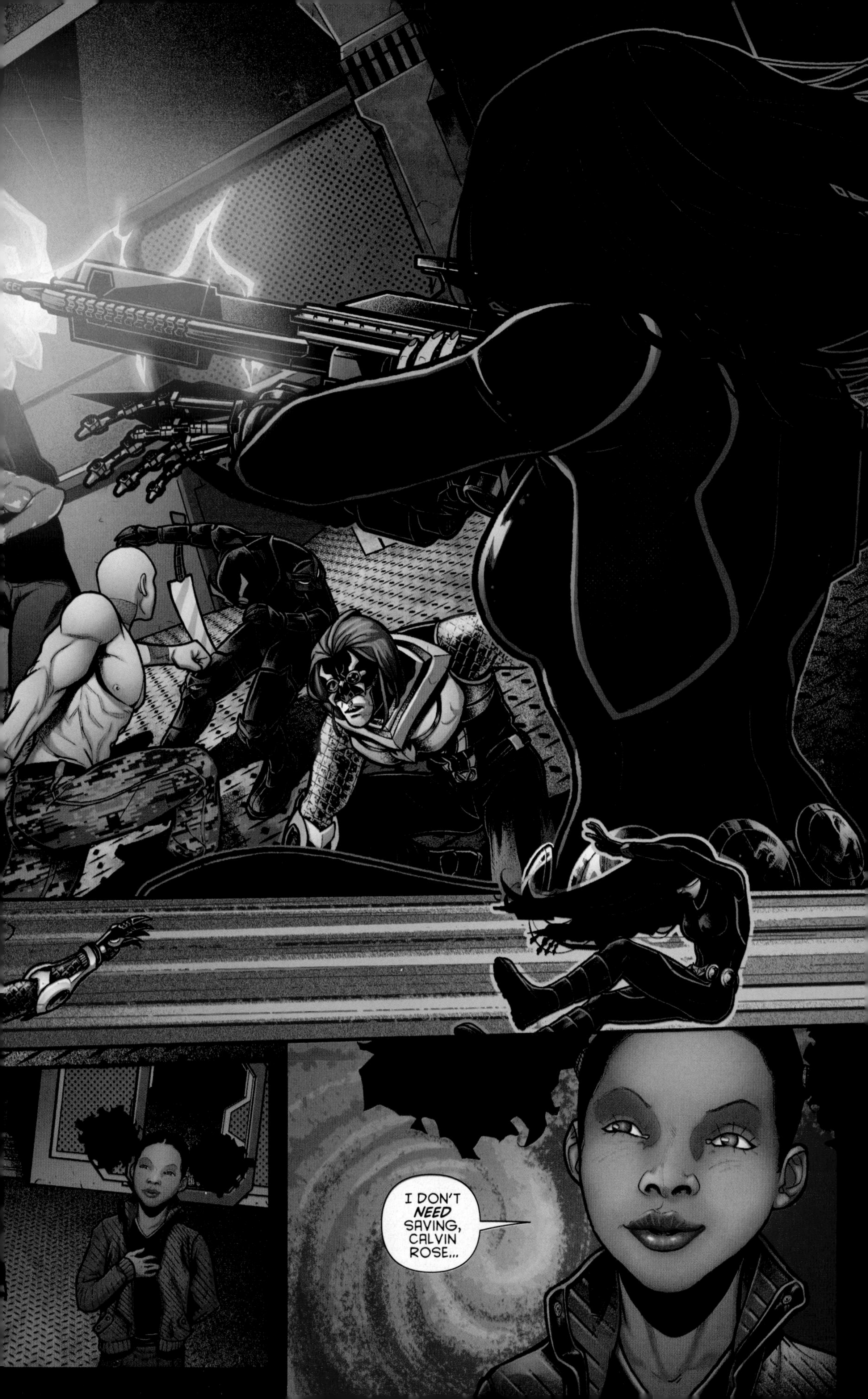
I DON'T *NEED* SAVING, CALVIN ROSE...

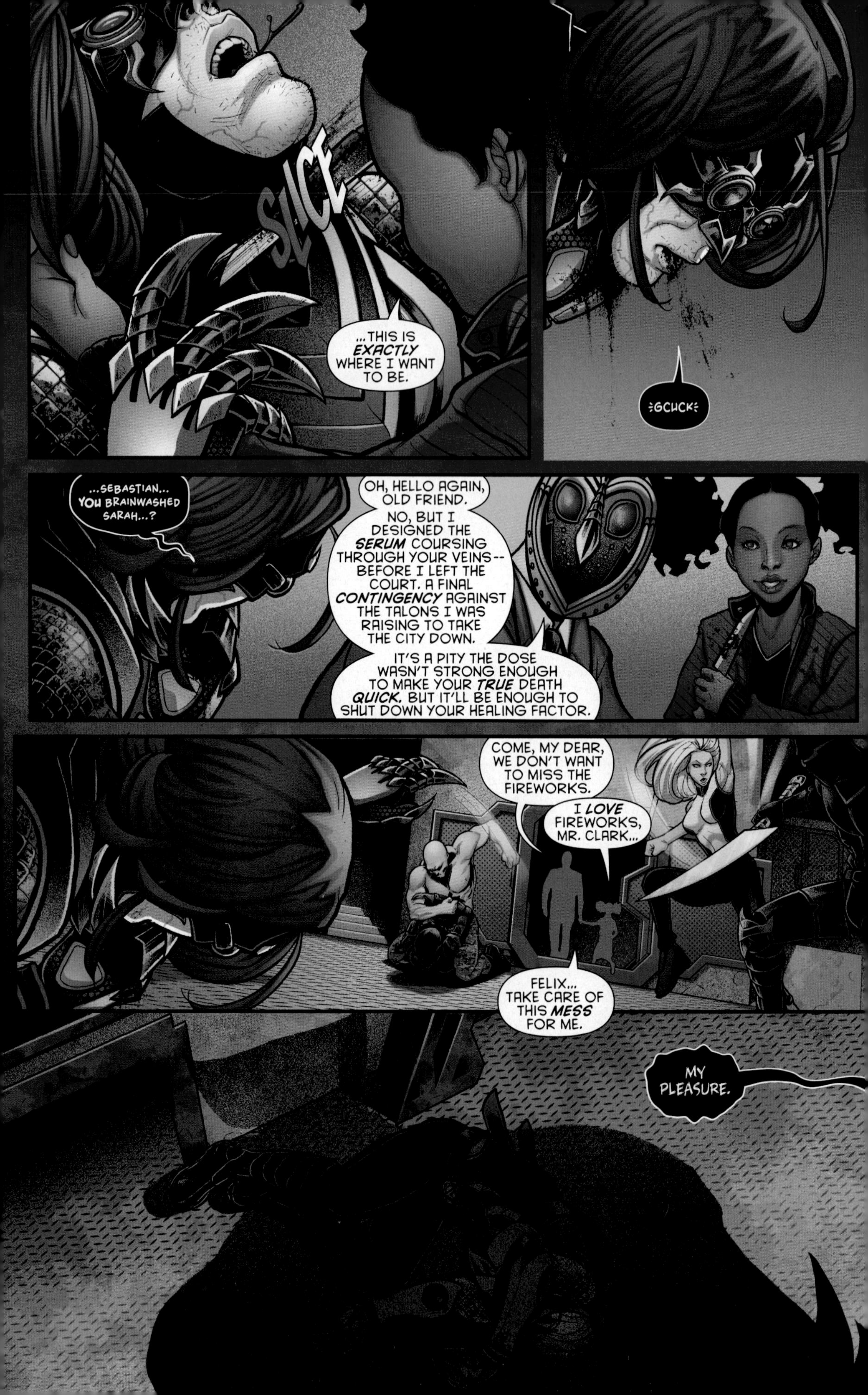
SLICE
...THIS IS EXACTLY WHERE I WANT TO BE.
GCHCK
...SEBASTIAN... YOU BRAINWASHED SARAH...?
OH, HELLO AGAIN, OLD FRIEND.
NO, BUT I DESIGNED THE SERUM COURSING THROUGH YOUR VEINS-- BEFORE I LEFT THE COURT. A FINAL CONTINGENCY AGAINST THE TALONS I WAS RAISING TO TAKE THE CITY DOWN.
IT'S A PITY THE DOSE WASN'T STRONG ENOUGH TO MAKE YOUR TRUE DEATH QUICK. BUT IT'LL BE ENOUGH TO SHUT DOWN YOUR HEALING FACTOR.
COME, MY DEAR, WE DON'T WANT TO MISS THE FIREWORKS.
I LOVE FIREWORKS, MR. CLARK...
FELIX... TAKE CARE OF THIS MESS FOR ME.
MY PLEASURE.

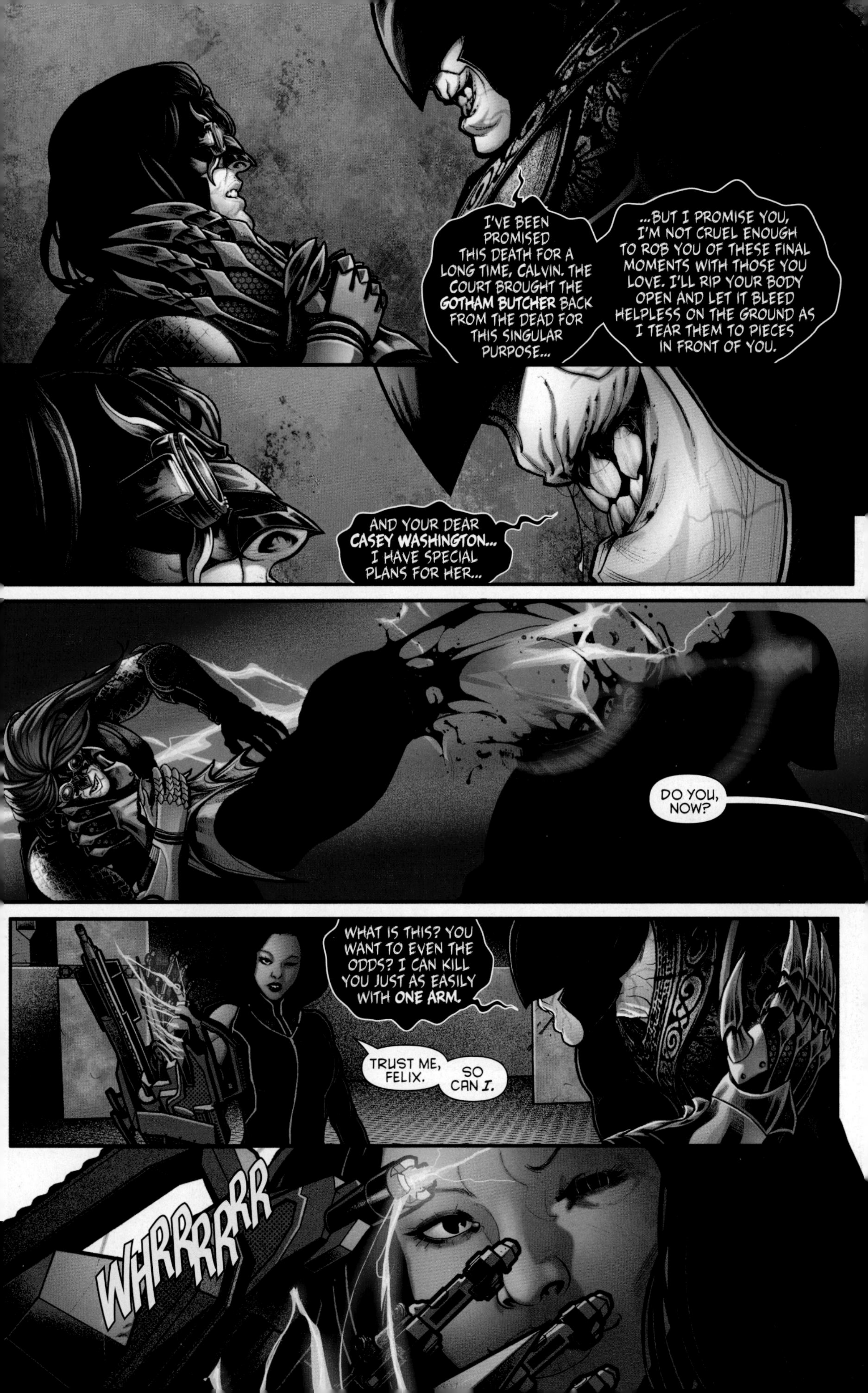
I'VE BEEN PROMISED THIS DEATH FOR A LONG TIME, CALVIN. THE COURT BROUGHT THE GOTHAM BUTCHER BACK FROM THE DEAD FOR THIS SINGULAR PURPOSE...
...BUT I PROMISE YOU, I'M NOT CRUEL ENOUGH TO ROB YOU OF THESE FINAL MOMENTS WITH THOSE YOU LOVE. I'LL RIP YOUR BODY OPEN AND LET IT BLEED HELPLESS ON THE GROUND AS I TEAR THEM TO PIECES IN FRONT OF YOU.
AND YOUR DEAR CASEY WASHINGTON... I HAVE SPECIAL PLANS FOR HER...
DO YOU, NOW?
WHAT IS THIS? YOU WANT TO EVEN THE ODDS? I CAN KILL YOU JUST AS EASILY WITH ONE ARM.
TRUST ME, FELIX.
SO CAN I.
WHRRRRRR

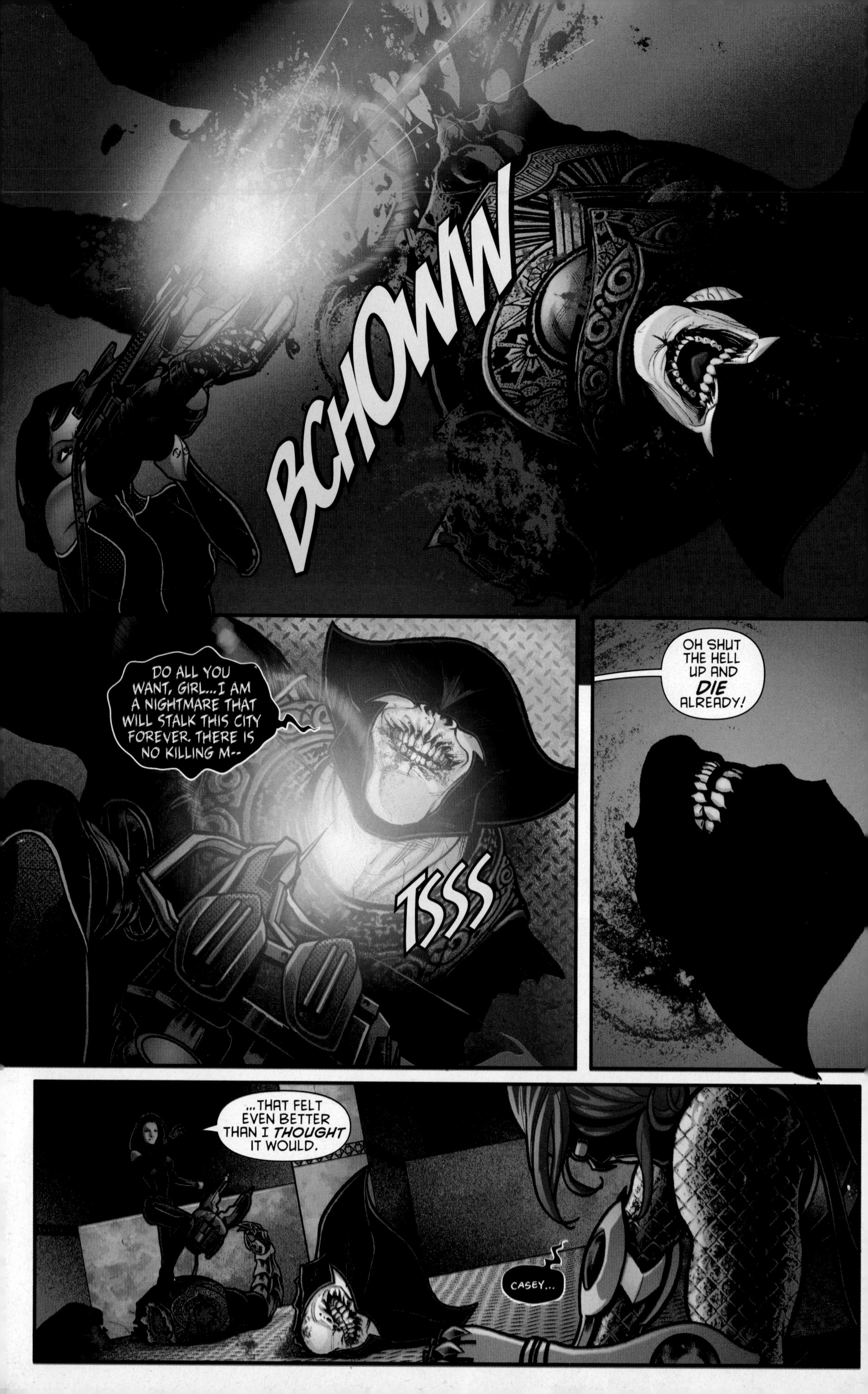
BCHOWW
DO ALL YOU WANT, GIRL...I AM A NIGHTMARE THAT WILL STALK THIS CITY FOREVER. THERE IS NO KILLING M--
TSSS
OH SHUT THE HELL UP AND *DIE* ALREADY!
...THAT FELT EVEN BETTER THAN I *THOUGHT* IT WOULD.
CASEY...

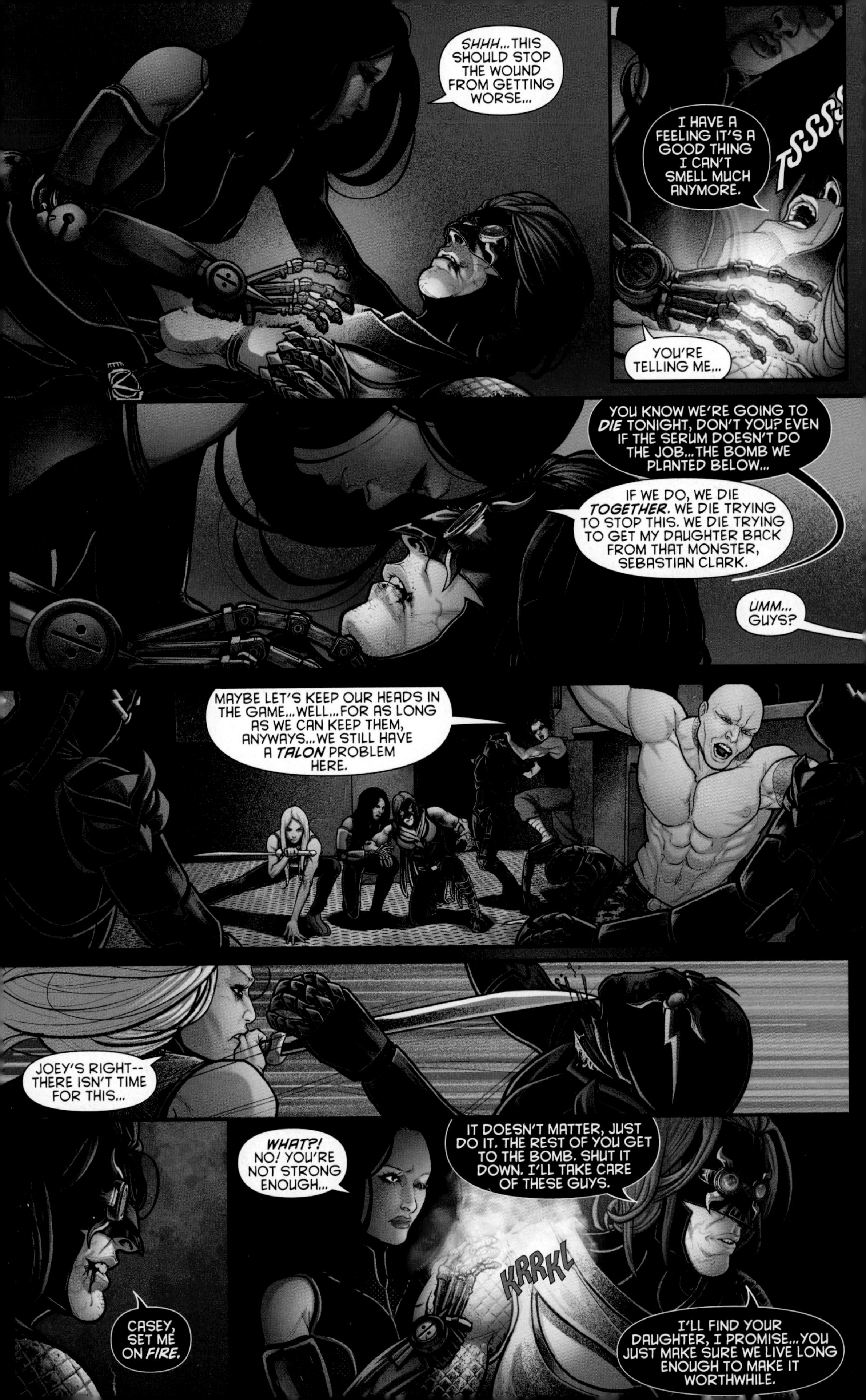
SHHH... THIS SHOULD STOP THE WOUND FROM GETTING WORSE...
I HAVE A FEELING IT'S A GOOD THING I CAN'T SMELL MUCH ANYMORE.
TSSSS
YOU'RE TELLING ME...
YOU KNOW WE'RE GOING TO DIE TONIGHT, DON'T YOU? EVEN IF THE SERUM DOESN'T DO THE JOB...THE BOMB WE PLANTED BELOW...
IF WE DO, WE DIE TOGETHER. WE DIE TRYING TO STOP THIS. WE DIE TRYING TO GET MY DAUGHTER BACK FROM THAT MONSTER, SEBASTIAN CLARK.
UMM... GUYS?
MAYBE LET'S KEEP OUR HEADS IN THE GAME...WELL...FOR AS LONG AS WE CAN KEEP THEM, ANYWAYS...WE STILL HAVE A TALON PROBLEM HERE.
JOEY'S RIGHT-- THERE ISN'T TIME FOR THIS...
CASEY, SET ME ON FIRE.
WHAT?! NO! YOU'RE NOT STRONG ENOUGH...
IT DOESN'T MATTER, JUST DO IT. THE REST OF YOU GET TO THE BOMB. SHUT IT DOWN. I'LL TAKE CARE OF THESE GUYS.
KRRKL
I'LL FIND YOUR DAUGHTER, I PROMISE...YOU JUST MAKE SURE WE LIVE LONG ENOUGH TO MAKE IT WORTHWHILE.

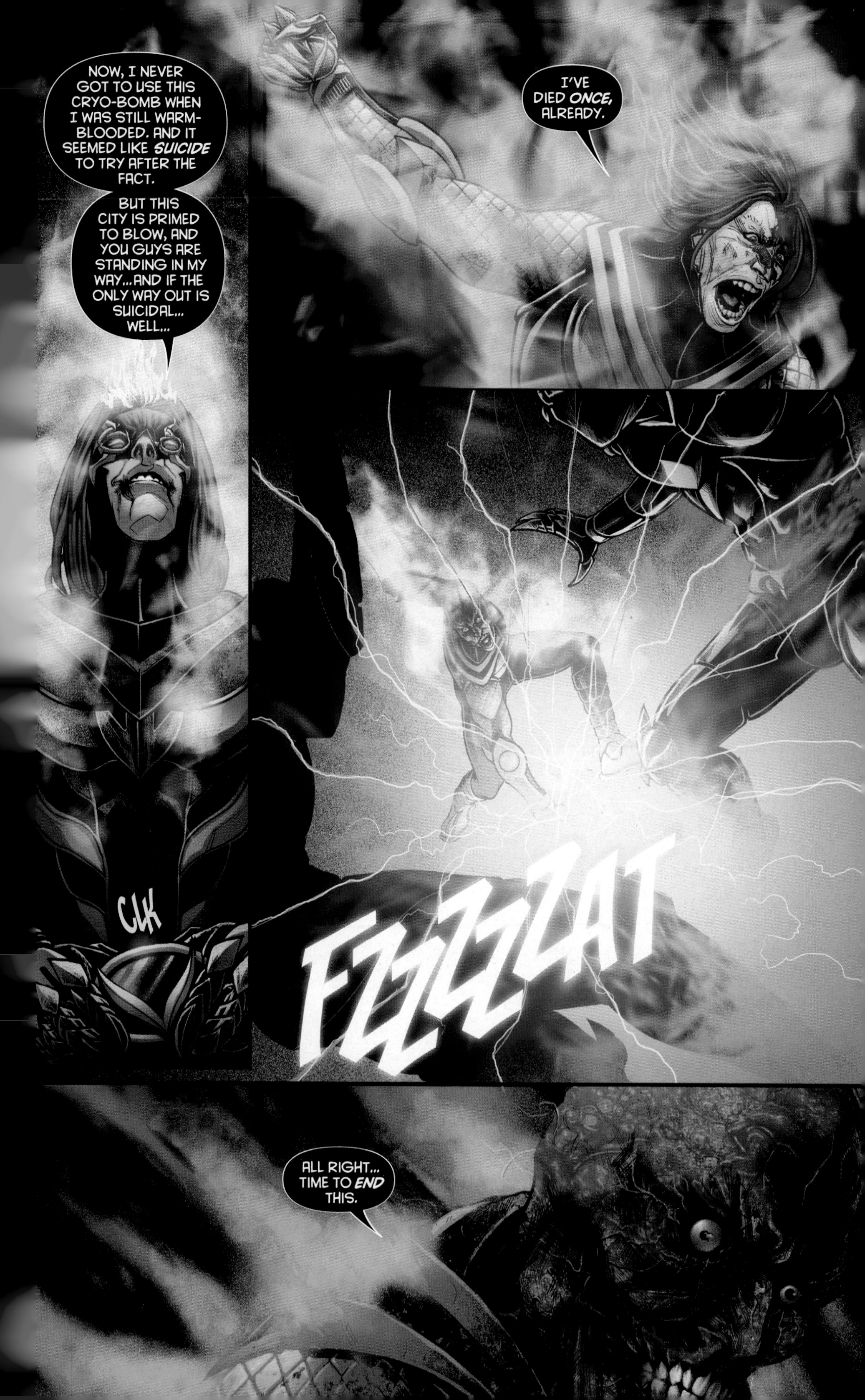
NOW, I NEVER GOT TO USE THIS CRYO-BOMB WHEN I WAS STILL WARM-BLOODED. AND IT SEEMED LIKE *SUICIDE* TO TRY AFTER THE FACT.
BUT THIS CITY IS PRIMED TO BLOW, AND YOU GUYS ARE STANDING IN MY WAY...AND IF THE ONLY WAY OUT IS SUICIDAL... WELL...
I'VE DIED *ONCE,* ALREADY.
CLK
FZZZZZAT
ALL RIGHT... TIME TO *END* THIS.

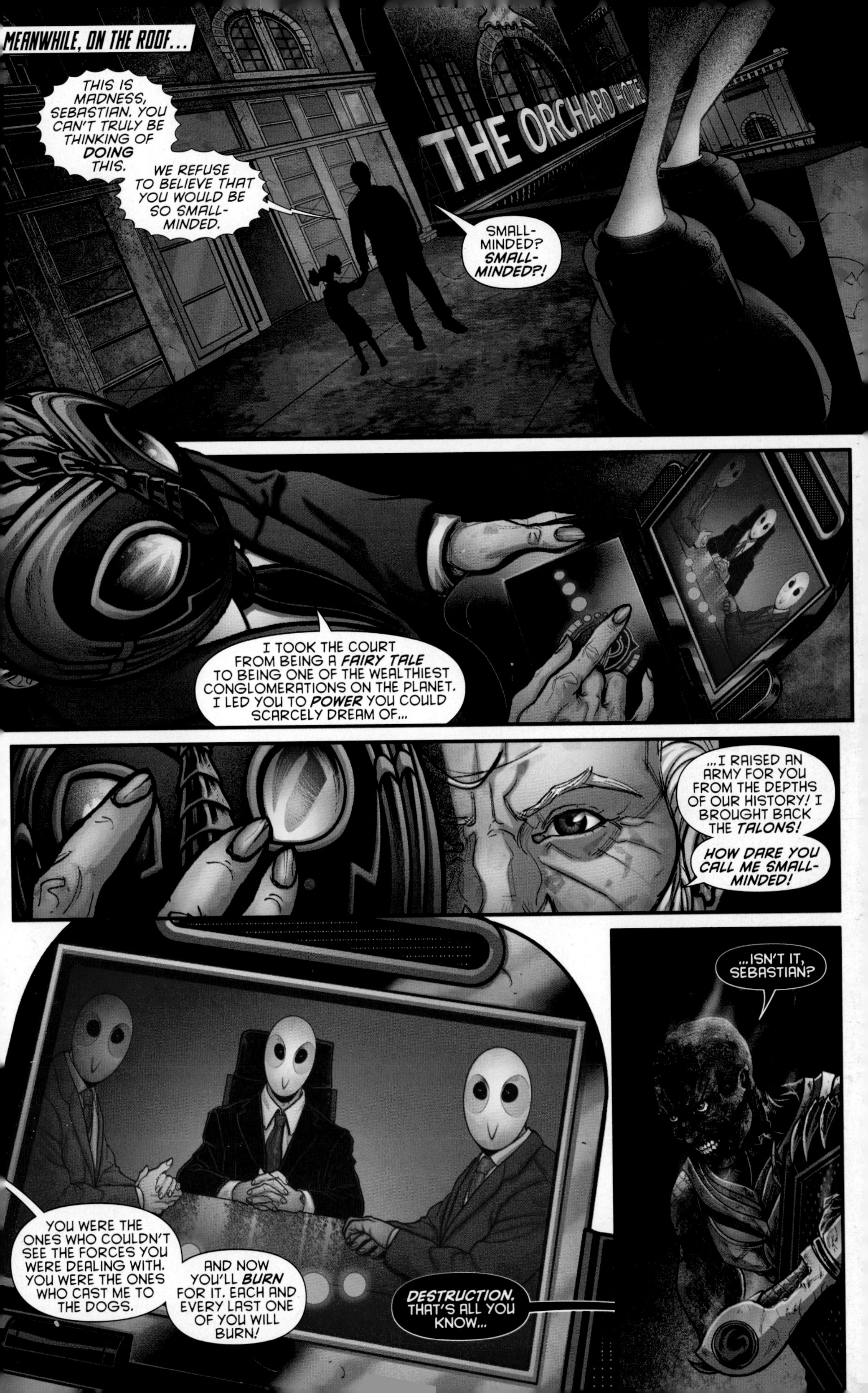
MEANWHILE, ON THE ROOF...
THIS IS MADNESS, SEBASTIAN. YOU CAN'T TRULY BE THINKING OF DOING THIS.
WE REFUSE TO BELIEVE THAT YOU WOULD BE SO SMALL-MINDED.
SMALL-MINDED? SMALL-MINDED?!
THE ORCHARD HOTEL
I TOOK THE COURT FROM BEING A FAIRY TALE TO BEING ONE OF THE WEALTHIEST CONGLOMERATIONS ON THE PLANET. I LED YOU TO POWER YOU COULD SCARCELY DREAM OF...
...I RAISED AN ARMY FOR YOU FROM THE DEPTHS OF OUR HISTORY! I BROUGHT BACK THE TALONS!
HOW DARE YOU CALL ME SMALL-MINDED!
YOU WERE THE ONES WHO COULDN'T SEE THE FORCES YOU WERE DEALING WITH. YOU WERE THE ONES WHO CAST ME TO THE DOGS.
AND NOW YOU'LL BURN FOR IT. EACH AND EVERY LAST ONE OF YOU WILL BURN!
DESTRUCTION. THAT'S ALL YOU KNOW...
...ISN'T IT, SEBASTIAN?

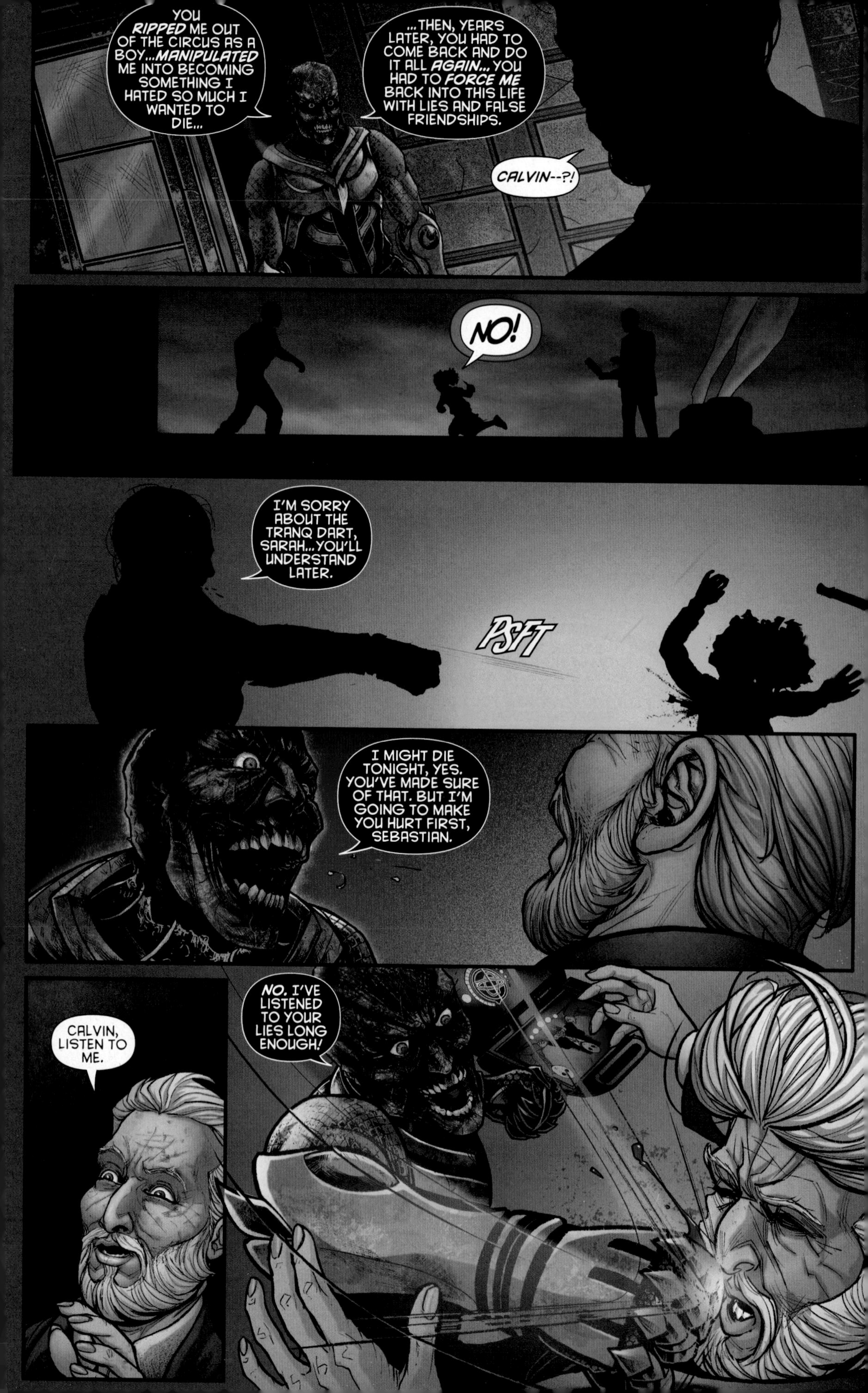
YOU RIPPED ME OUT OF THE CIRCUS AS A BOY...MANIPULATED ME INTO BECOMING SOMETHING I HATED SO MUCH I WANTED TO DIE...
...THEN, YEARS LATER, YOU HAD TO COME BACK AND DO IT ALL AGAIN... YOU HAD TO FORCE ME BACK INTO THIS LIFE WITH LIES AND FALSE FRIENDSHIPS.
CALVIN--?!
NO!
I'M SORRY ABOUT THE TRANQ DART, SARAH...YOU'LL UNDERSTAND LATER.
PSFT
I MIGHT DIE TONIGHT, YES. YOU'VE MADE SURE OF THAT. BUT I'M GOING TO MAKE YOU HURT FIRST, SEBASTIAN.
CALVIN, LISTEN TO ME.
NO. I'VE LISTENED TO YOUR LIES LONG ENOUGH!

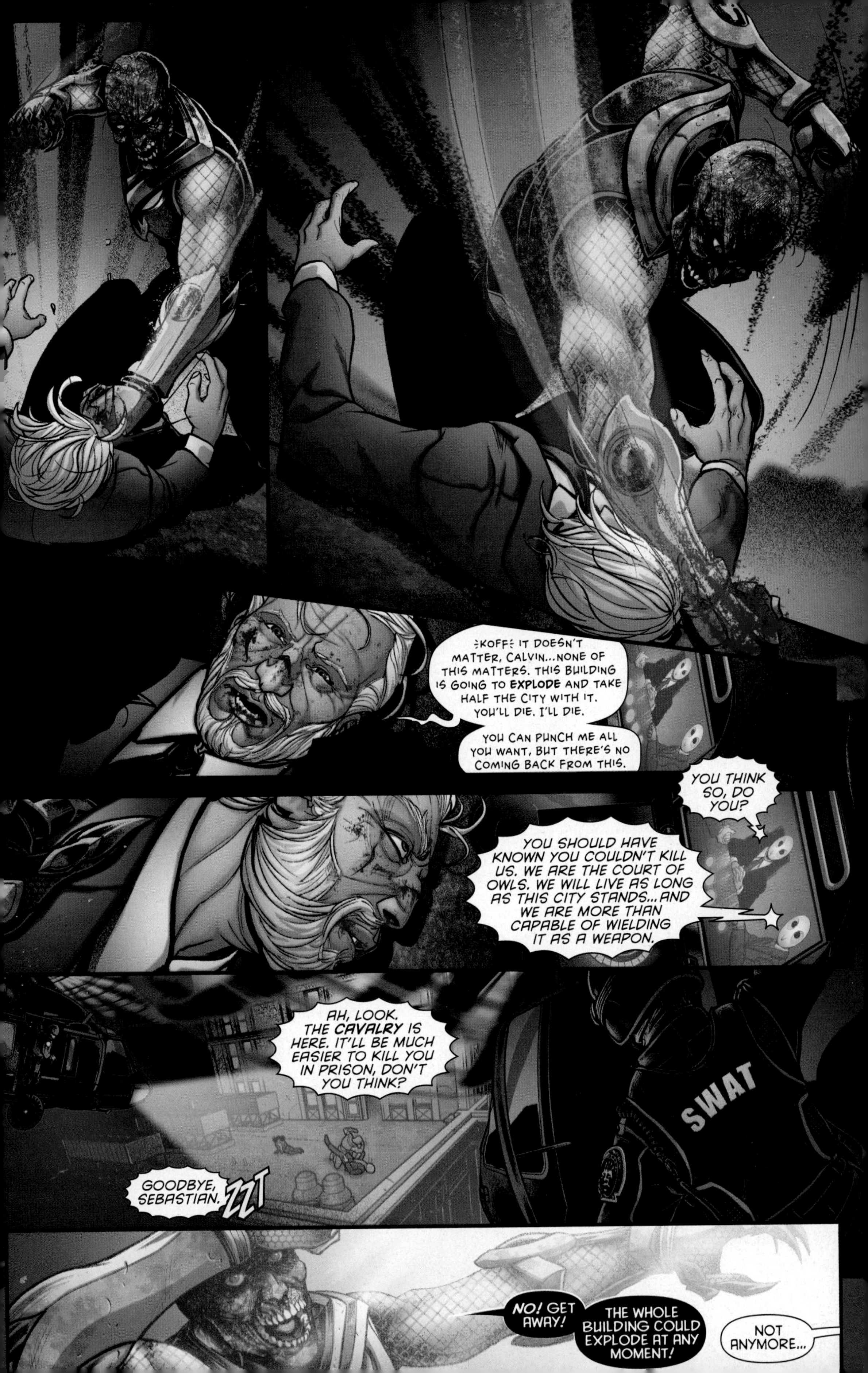

⫶KOFF⫶ IT DOESN'T MATTER, CALVIN...NONE OF THIS MATTERS. THIS BUILDING IS GOING TO EXPLODE AND TAKE HALF THE CITY WITH IT. YOU'LL DIE. I'LL DIE.
YOU CAN PUNCH ME ALL YOU WANT, BUT THERE'S NO COMING BACK FROM THIS.
YOU THINK SO, DO YOU?
YOU SHOULD HAVE KNOWN YOU COULDN'T KILL US. WE ARE THE COURT OF OWLS. WE WILL LIVE AS LONG AS THIS CITY STANDS...AND WE ARE MORE THAN CAPABLE OF WIELDING IT AS A WEAPON.
AH, LOOK. THE CAVALRY IS HERE. IT'LL BE MUCH EASIER TO KILL YOU IN PRISON, DON'T YOU THINK?
SWAT
GOODBYE, SEBASTIAN.
ZZT
NO! GET AWAY!
THE WHOLE BUILDING COULD EXPLODE AT ANY MOMENT!
NOT ANYMORE...

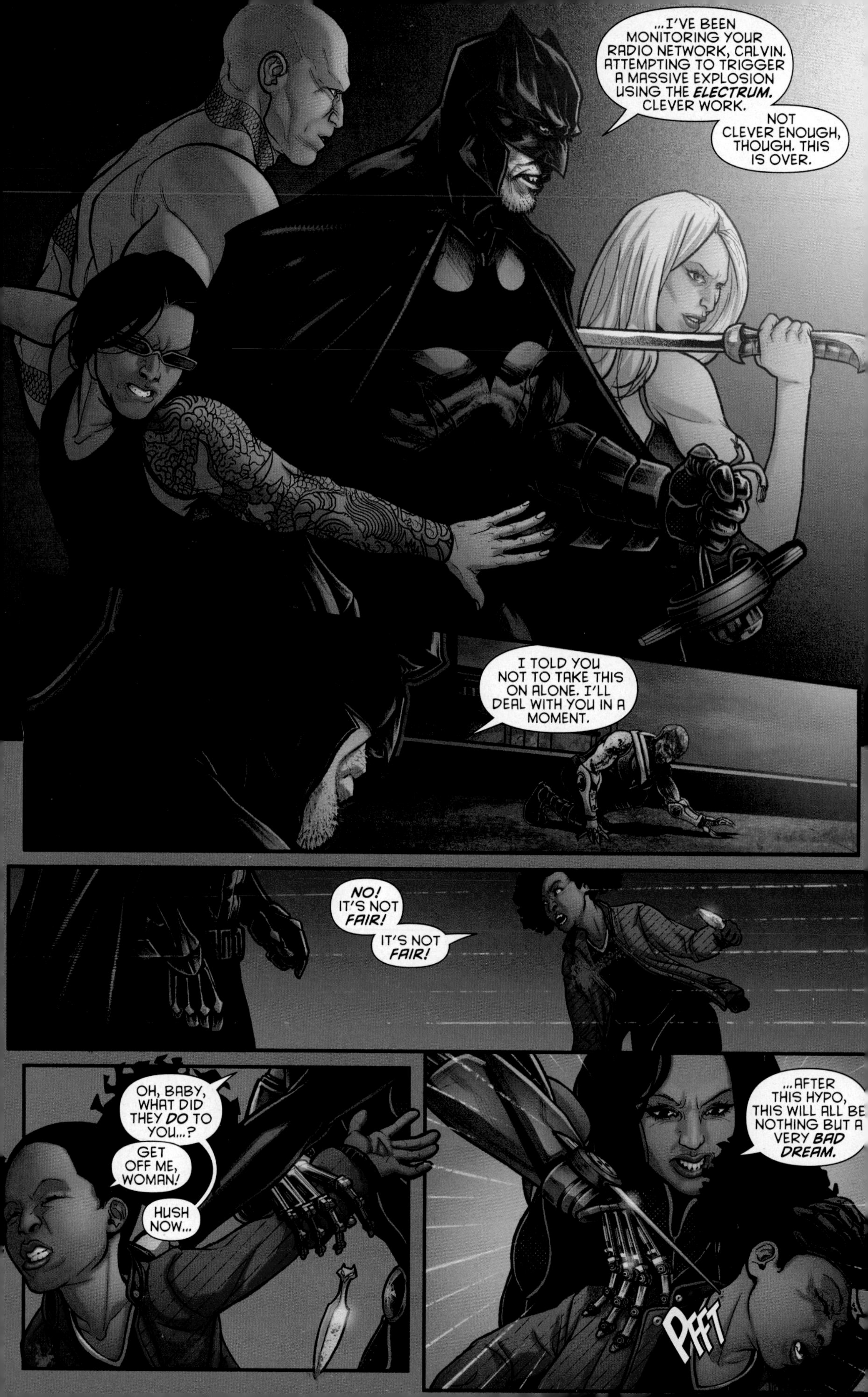
...I'VE BEEN MONITORING YOUR RADIO NETWORK, CALVIN. ATTEMPTING TO TRIGGER A MASSIVE EXPLOSION USING THE ELECTRUM. CLEVER WORK.
NOT CLEVER ENOUGH, THOUGH. THIS IS OVER.
I TOLD YOU NOT TO TAKE THIS ON ALONE. I'LL DEAL WITH YOU IN A MOMENT.
NO! IT'S NOT FAIR!
IT'S NOT FAIR!
OH, BABY, WHAT DID THEY DO TO YOU...?
GET OFF ME, WOMAN!
HUSH NOW...
...AFTER THIS HYPO, THIS WILL ALL BE NOTHING BUT A VERY BAD DREAM.
PFFT

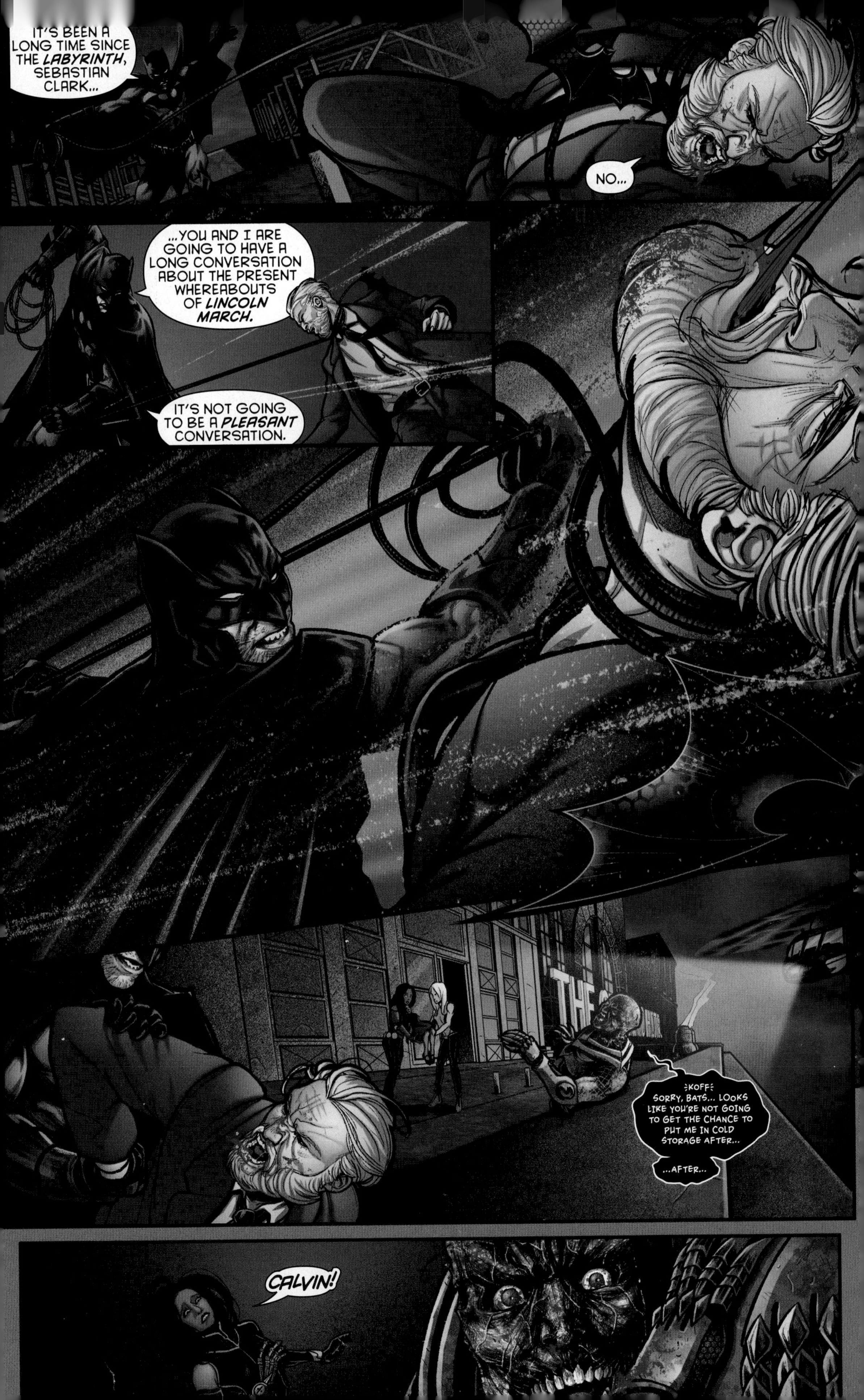
IT'S BEEN A LONG TIME SINCE THE LABYRINTH, SEBASTIAN CLARK...
NO...
...YOU AND I ARE GOING TO HAVE A LONG CONVERSATION ABOUT THE PRESENT WHEREABOUTS OF LINCOLN MARCH.
IT'S NOT GOING TO BE A PLEASANT CONVERSATION.
THE
KOFF
SORRY, BATS... LOOKS LIKE YOU'RE NOT GOING TO GET THE CHANCE TO PUT ME IN COLD STORAGE AFTER...
...AFTER...
CALVIN!

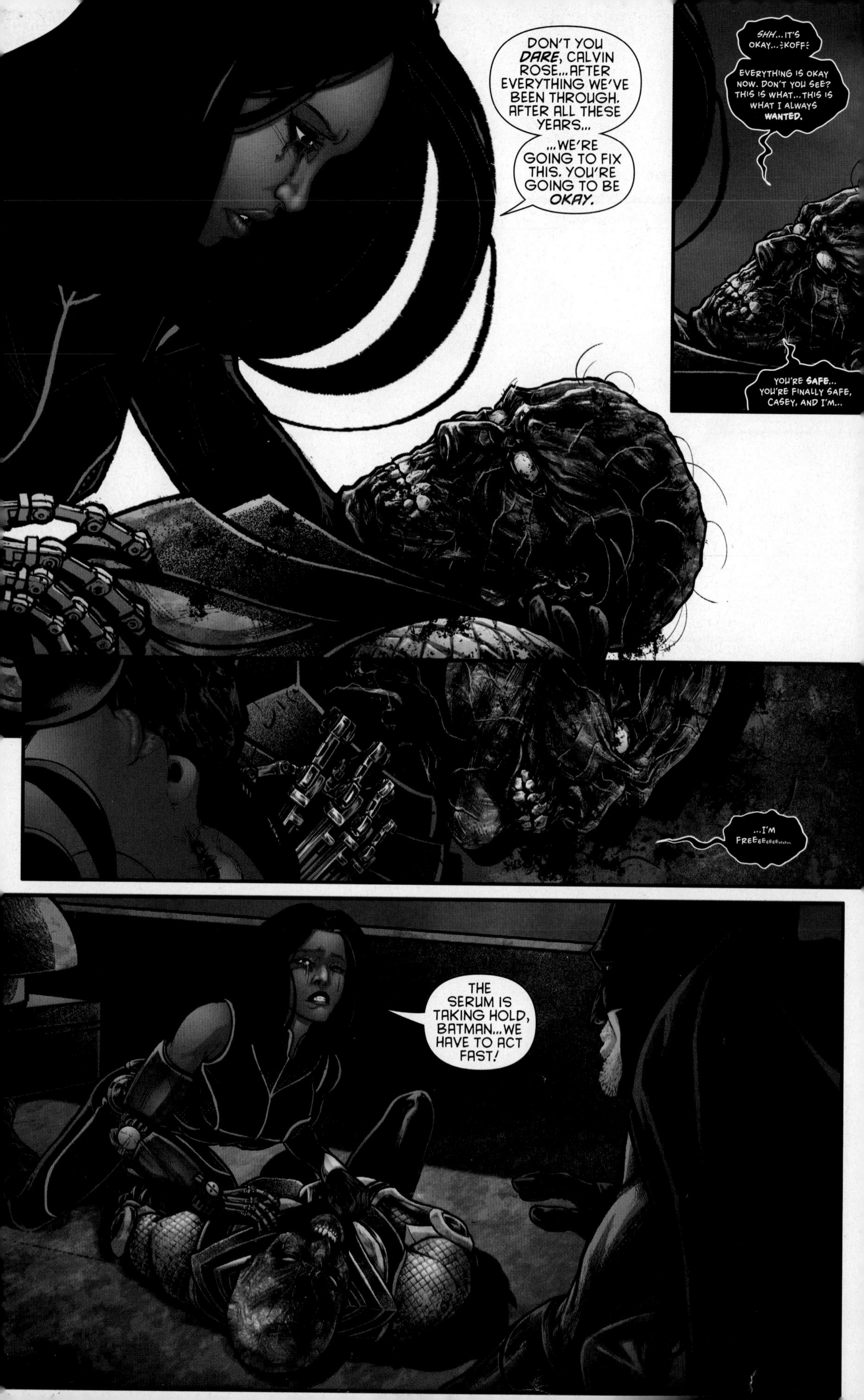
DON'T YOU DARE, CALVIN ROSE...AFTER EVERYTHING WE'VE BEEN THROUGH. AFTER ALL THESE YEARS...
...WE'RE GOING TO FIX THIS. YOU'RE GOING TO BE OKAY.
SHH... IT'S OKAY... KOFF
EVERYTHING IS OKAY NOW. DON'T YOU SEE? THIS IS WHAT...THIS IS WHAT I ALWAYS WANTED.
YOU'RE SAFE... YOU'RE FINALLY SAFE, CASEY, AND I'M...
...I'M FREEeeeeeee...
THE SERUM IS TAKING HOLD, BATMAN...WE HAVE TO ACT FAST!

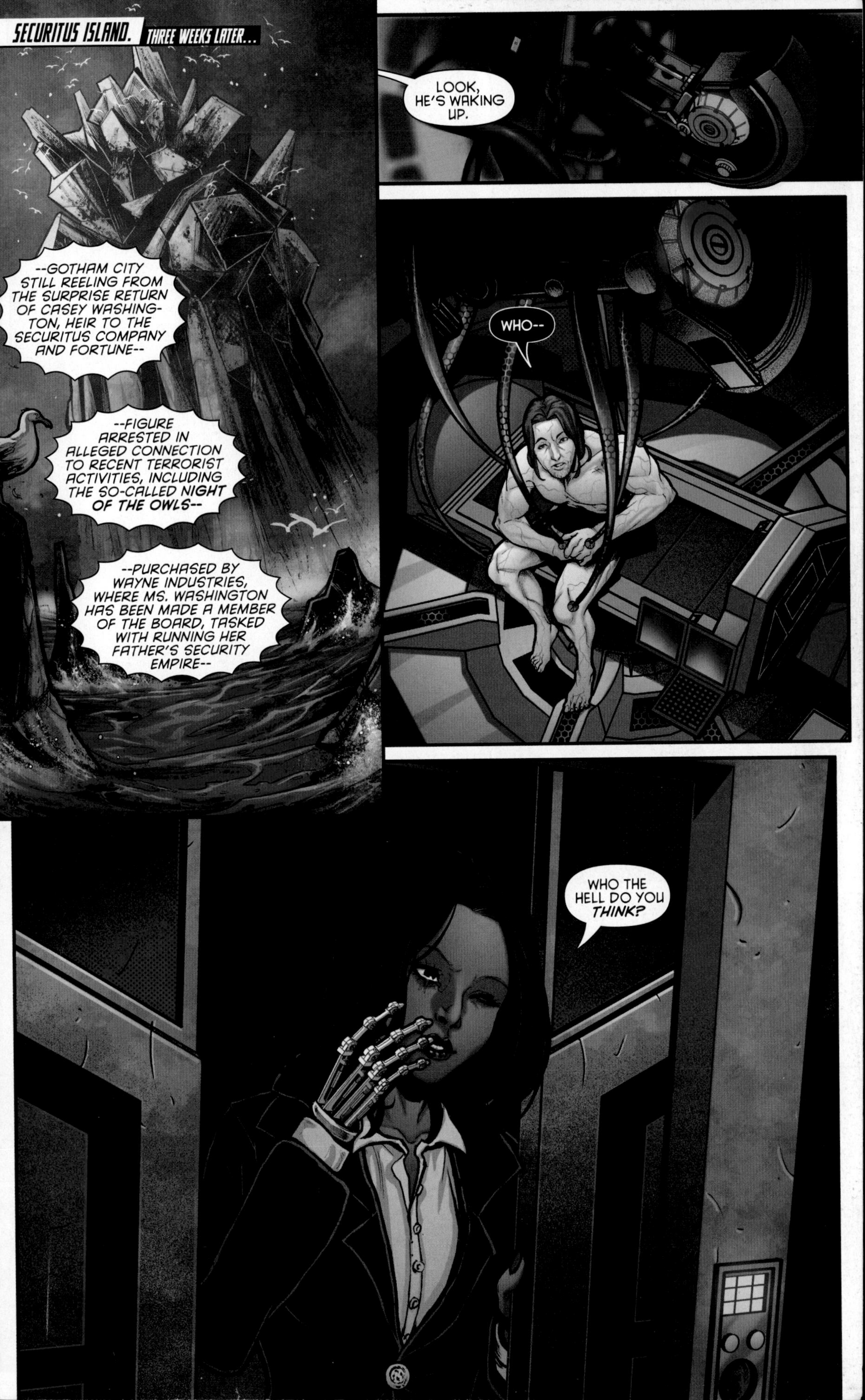
SECURITUS ISLAND. THREE WEEKS LATER...
--GOTHAM CITY STILL REELING FROM THE SURPRISE RETURN OF CASEY WASHING-TON, HEIR TO THE SECURITUS COMPANY AND FORTUNE--
--FIGURE ARRESTED IN ALLEGED CONNECTION TO RECENT TERRORIST ACTIVITIES, INCLUDING THE SO-CALLED NIGHT OF THE OWLS--
--PURCHASED BY WAYNE INDUSTRIES, WHERE MS. WASHINGTON HAS BEEN MADE A MEMBER OF THE BOARD, TASKED WITH RUNNING HER FATHER'S SECURITY EMPIRE--
LOOK, HE'S WAKING UP.
WHO--
WHO THE HELL DO YOU THINK?

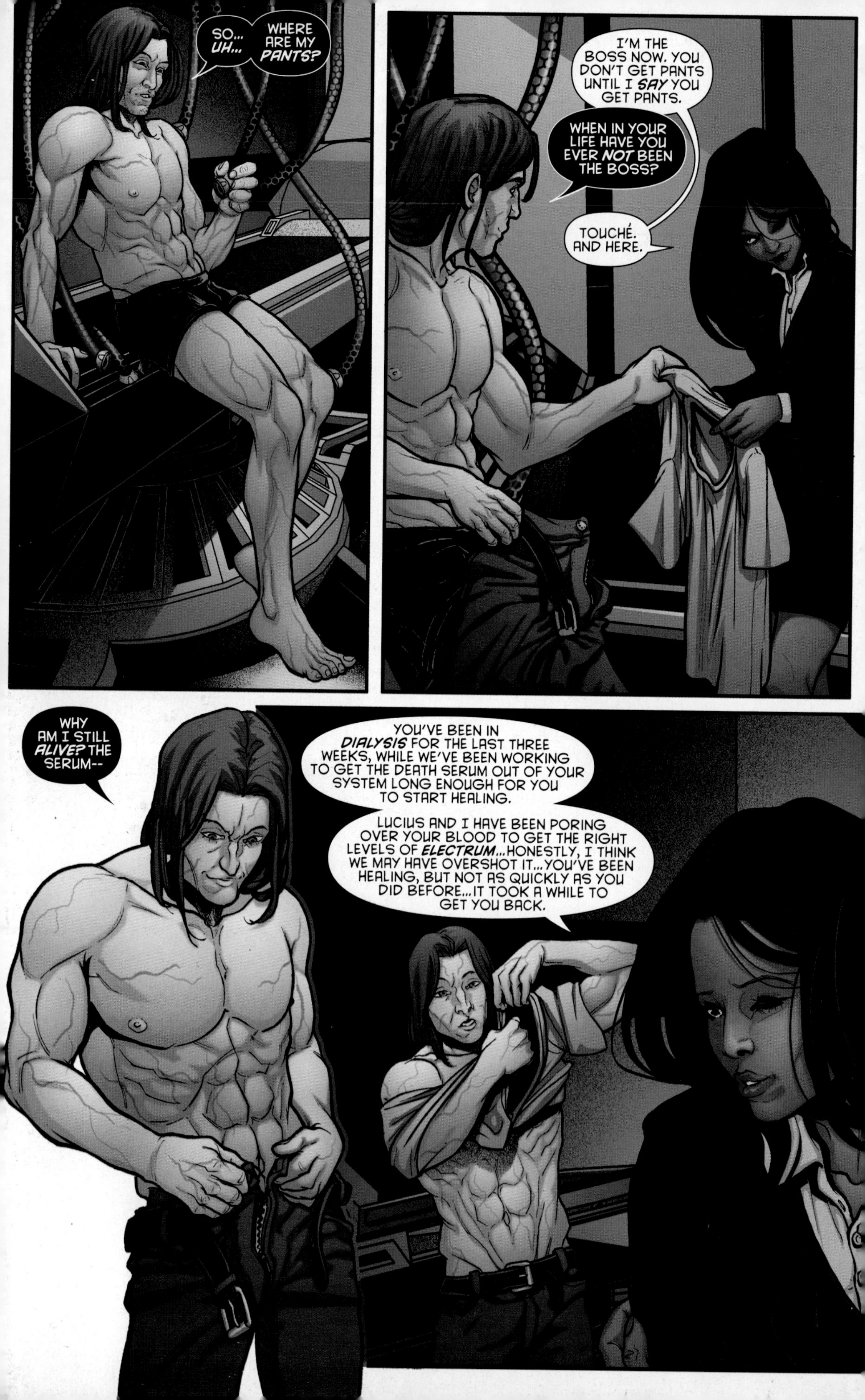
SO... UH...
WHERE ARE MY PANTS?
I'M THE BOSS NOW. YOU DON'T GET PANTS UNTIL I SAY YOU GET PANTS.
WHEN IN YOUR LIFE HAVE YOU EVER NOT BEEN THE BOSS?
TOUCHÉ. AND HERE.
WHY AM I STILL ALIVE? THE SERUM--
YOU'VE BEEN IN DIALYSIS FOR THE LAST THREE WEEKS, WHILE WE'VE BEEN WORKING TO GET THE DEATH SERUM OUT OF YOUR SYSTEM LONG ENOUGH FOR YOU TO START HEALING.
LUCIUS AND I HAVE BEEN PORING OVER YOUR BLOOD TO GET THE RIGHT LEVELS OF ELECTRUM...HONESTLY, I THINK WE MAY HAVE OVERSHOT IT...YOU'VE BEEN HEALING, BUT NOT AS QUICKLY AS YOU DID BEFORE...IT TOOK A WHILE TO GET YOU BACK.

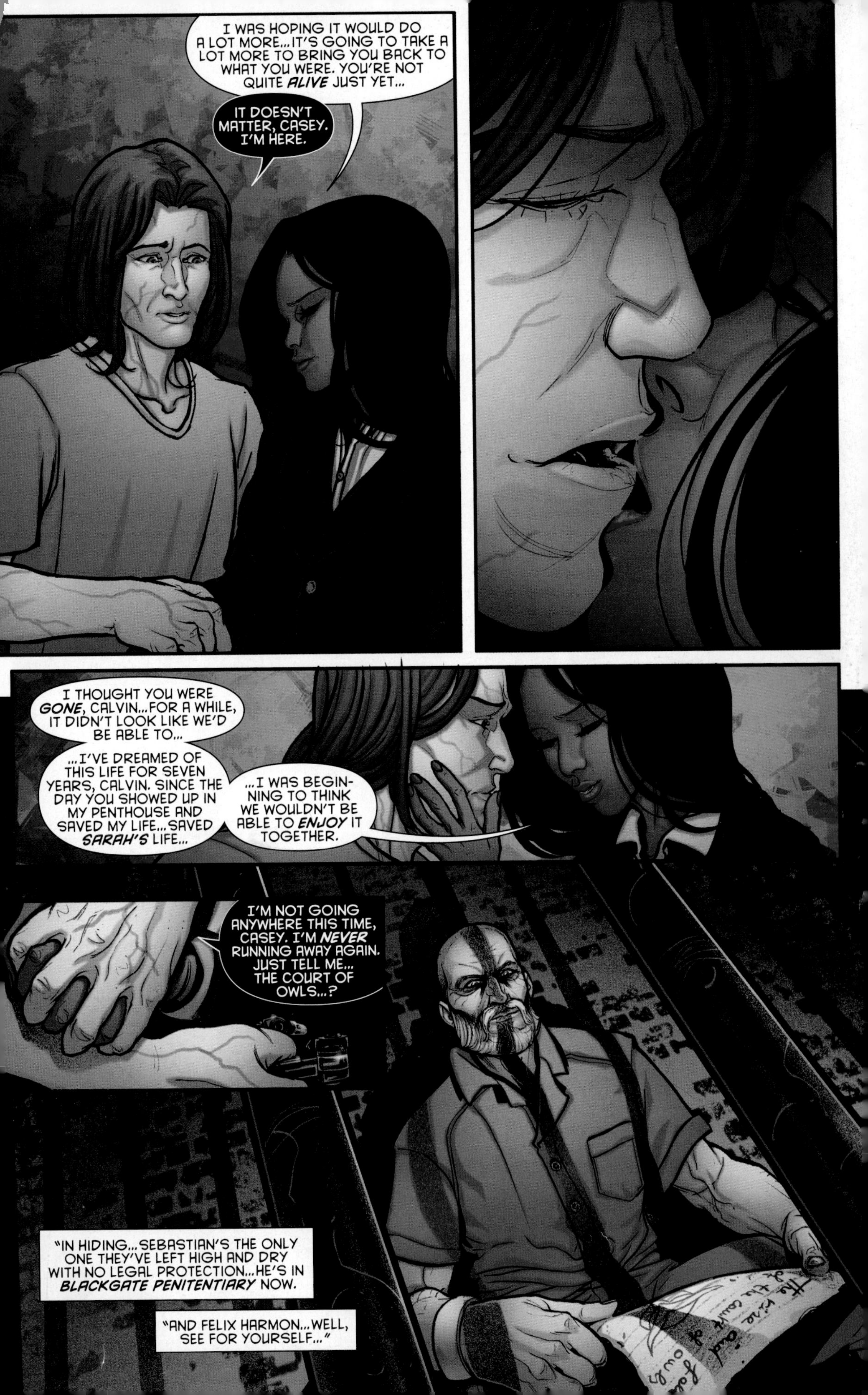

I WAS HOPING IT WOULD DO A LOT MORE...IT'S GOING TO TAKE A LOT MORE TO BRING YOU BACK TO WHAT YOU WERE. YOU'RE NOT QUITE *ALIVE* JUST YET...
IT DOESN'T MATTER, CASEY. I'M HERE.
I THOUGHT YOU WERE *GONE*, CALVIN...FOR A WHILE, IT DIDN'T LOOK LIKE WE'D BE ABLE TO...
...I'VE DREAMED OF THIS LIFE FOR SEVEN YEARS, CALVIN. SINCE THE DAY YOU SHOWED UP IN MY PENTHOUSE AND SAVED MY LIFE...SAVED *SARAH'S* LIFE...
...I WAS BEGINNING TO THINK WE WOULDN'T BE ABLE TO *ENJOY* IT TOGETHER.
I'M NOT GOING ANYWHERE THIS TIME, CASEY. I'M *NEVER* RUNNING AWAY AGAIN. JUST TELL ME... THE COURT OF OWLS...?
"IN HIDING...SEBASTIAN'S THE ONLY ONE THEY'VE LEFT HIGH AND DRY WITH NO LEGAL PROTECTION...HE'S IN *BLACKGATE PENITENTIARY* NOW.
"AND FELIX HARMON...WELL, SEE FOR YOURSELF..."

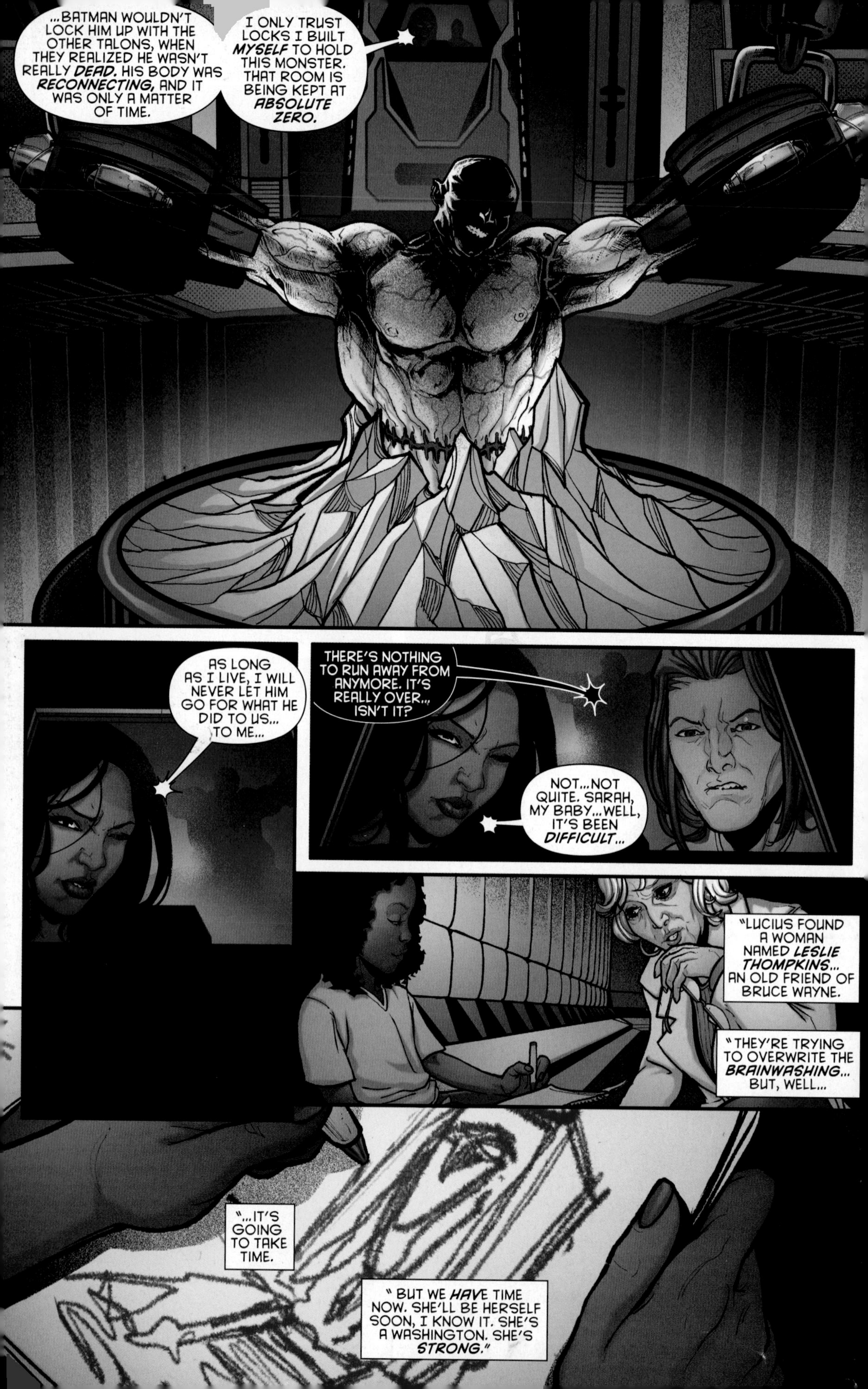
...BATMAN WOULDN'T LOCK HIM UP WITH THE OTHER TALONS, WHEN THEY REALIZED HE WASN'T REALLY *DEAD*. HIS BODY WAS *RECONNECTING*, AND IT WAS ONLY A MATTER OF TIME.
I ONLY TRUST LOCKS I BUILT *MYSELF* TO HOLD THIS MONSTER. THAT ROOM IS BEING KEPT AT *ABSOLUTE ZERO*.
AS LONG AS I LIVE, I WILL NEVER LET HIM GO FOR WHAT HE DID TO US... TO ME...
THERE'S NOTHING TO RUN AWAY FROM ANYMORE. IT'S REALLY OVER..., ISN'T IT?
NOT...NOT QUITE. SARAH, MY BABY...WELL, IT'S BEEN *DIFFICULT*...
"LUCIUS FOUND A WOMAN NAMED *LESLIE THOMPKINS*... AN OLD FRIEND OF BRUCE WAYNE.
"THEY'RE TRYING TO OVERWRITE THE *BRAINWASHING*... BUT, WELL...
"...IT'S GOING TO TAKE TIME.
"BUT WE *HAVE* TIME NOW. SHE'LL BE HERSELF SOON, I KNOW IT. SHE'S A WASHINGTON. SHE'S *STRONG*."

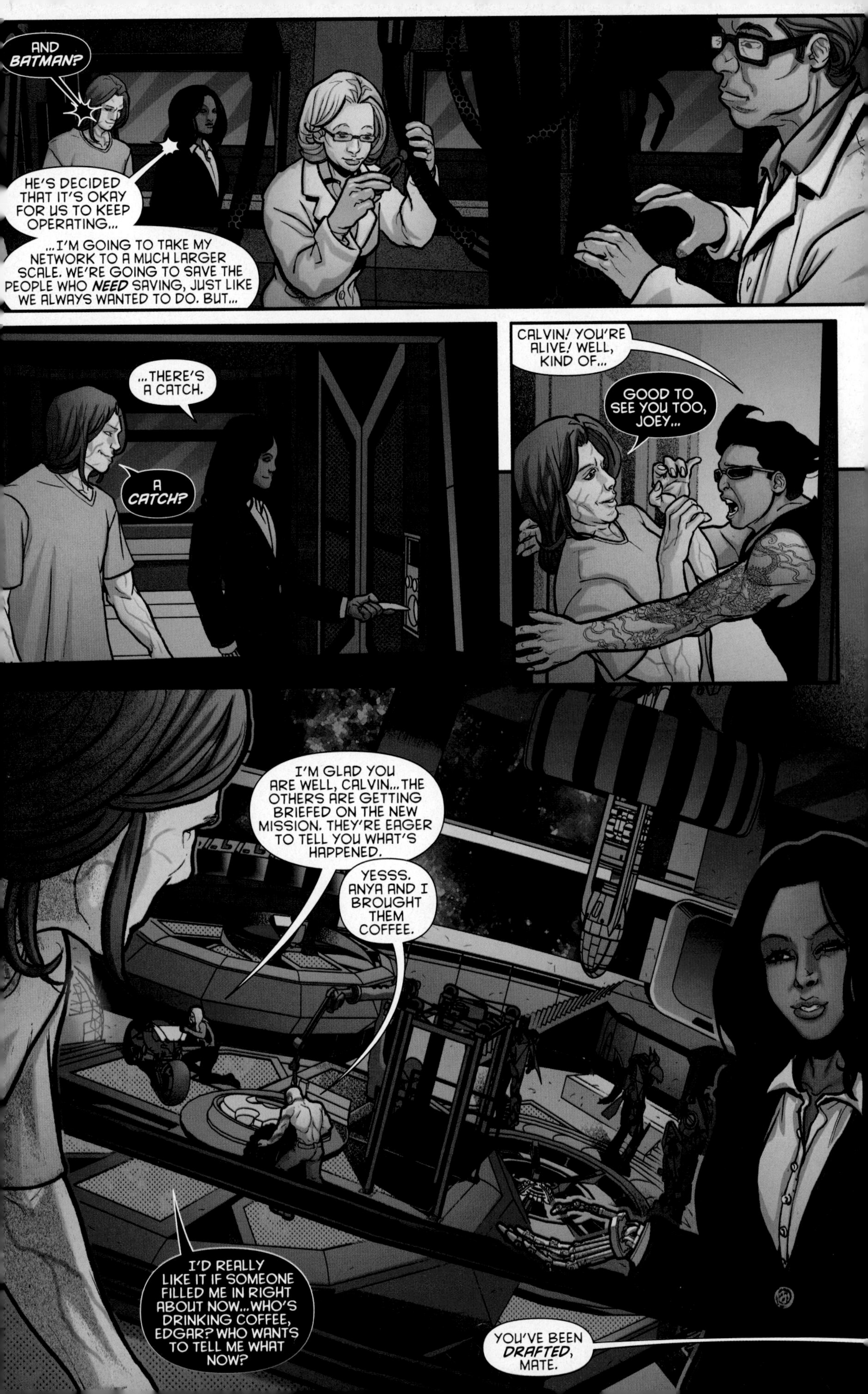
AND BATMAN?
HE'S DECIDED THAT IT'S OKAY FOR US TO KEEP OPERATING...
...I'M GOING TO TAKE MY NETWORK TO A MUCH LARGER SCALE. WE'RE GOING TO SAVE THE PEOPLE WHO NEED SAVING, JUST LIKE WE ALWAYS WANTED TO DO. BUT...
...THERE'S A CATCH.
A CATCH?
CALVIN! YOU'RE ALIVE! WELL, KIND OF...
GOOD TO SEE YOU TOO, JOEY...
I'M GLAD YOU ARE WELL, CALVIN... THE OTHERS ARE GETTING BRIEFED ON THE NEW MISSION. THEY'RE EAGER TO TELL YOU WHAT'S HAPPENED.
YESSS. ANYA AND I BROUGHT THEM COFFEE.
I'D REALLY LIKE IT IF SOMEONE FILLED ME IN RIGHT ABOUT NOW... WHO'S DRINKING COFFEE, EDGAR? WHO WANTS TO TELL ME WHAT NOW?
YOU'VE BEEN DRAFTED, MATE.

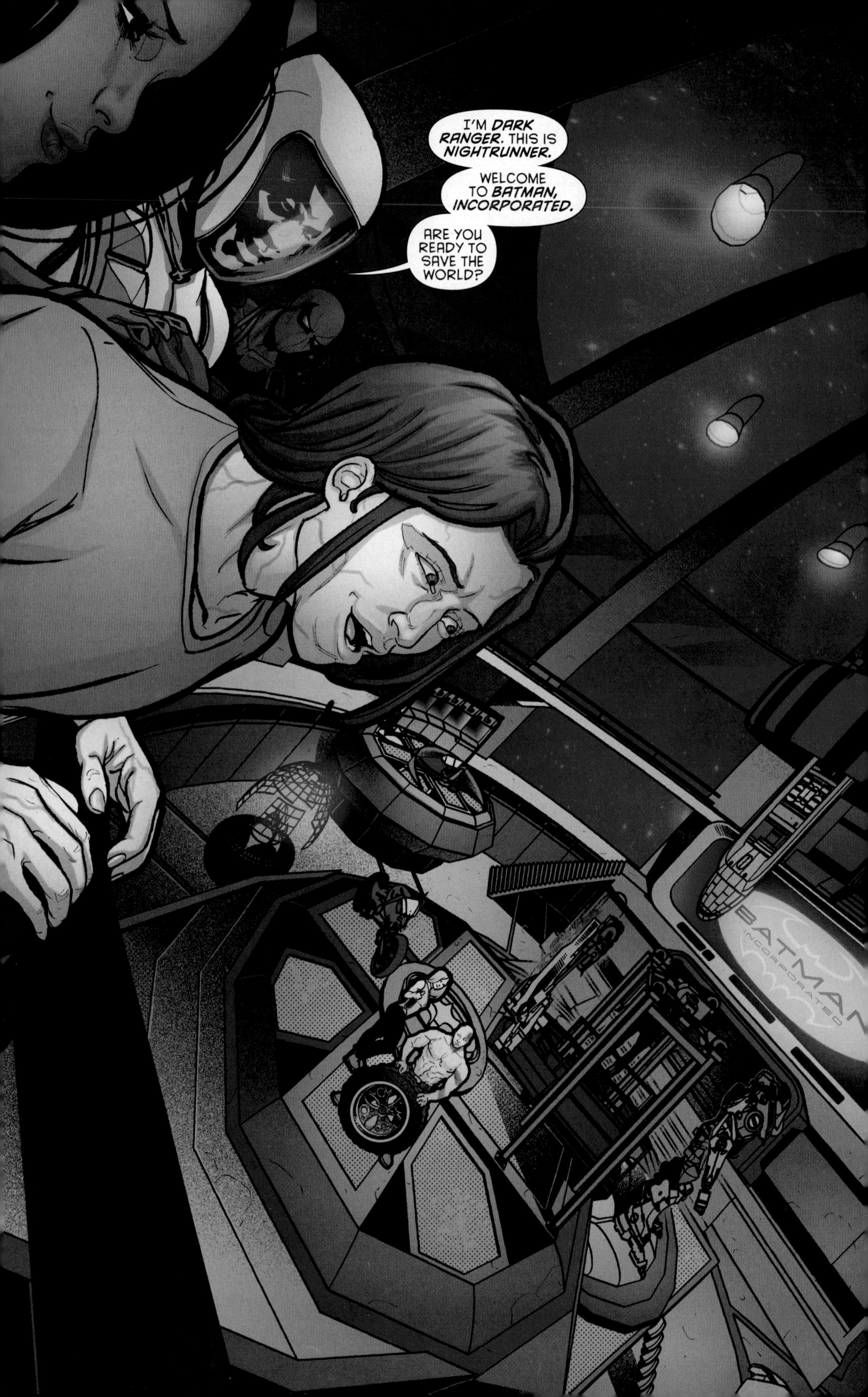
I'M DARK RANGER. THIS IS NIGHTRUNNER.
WELCOME TO BATMAN, INCORPORATED.
ARE YOU READY TO SAVE THE WORLD?
BATMAN INCORPORATED

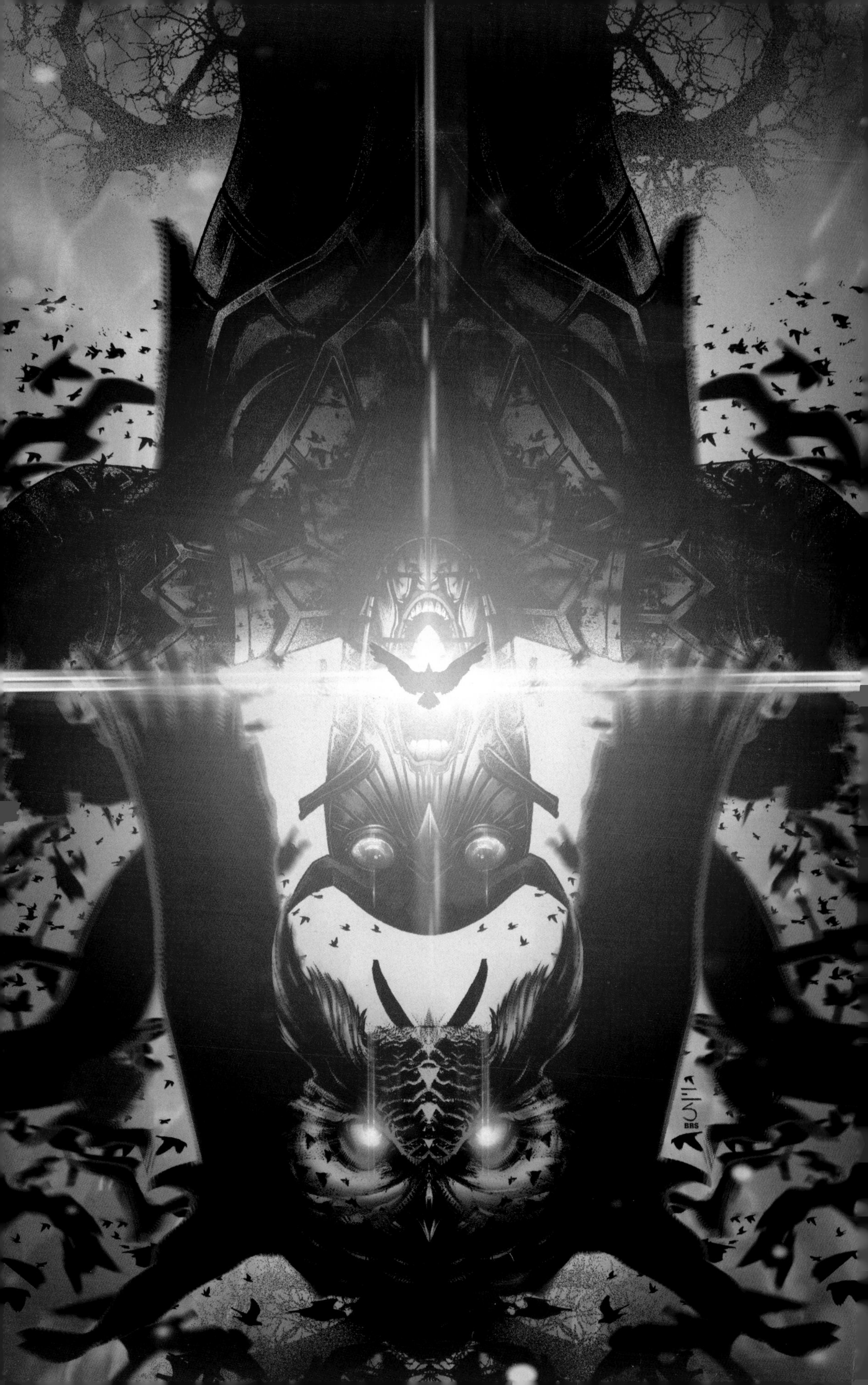

MARGUERITE BENNETT writer JORGE LUCAS artist cover art by EMANUEL SIMEONI & BRETT SMITH

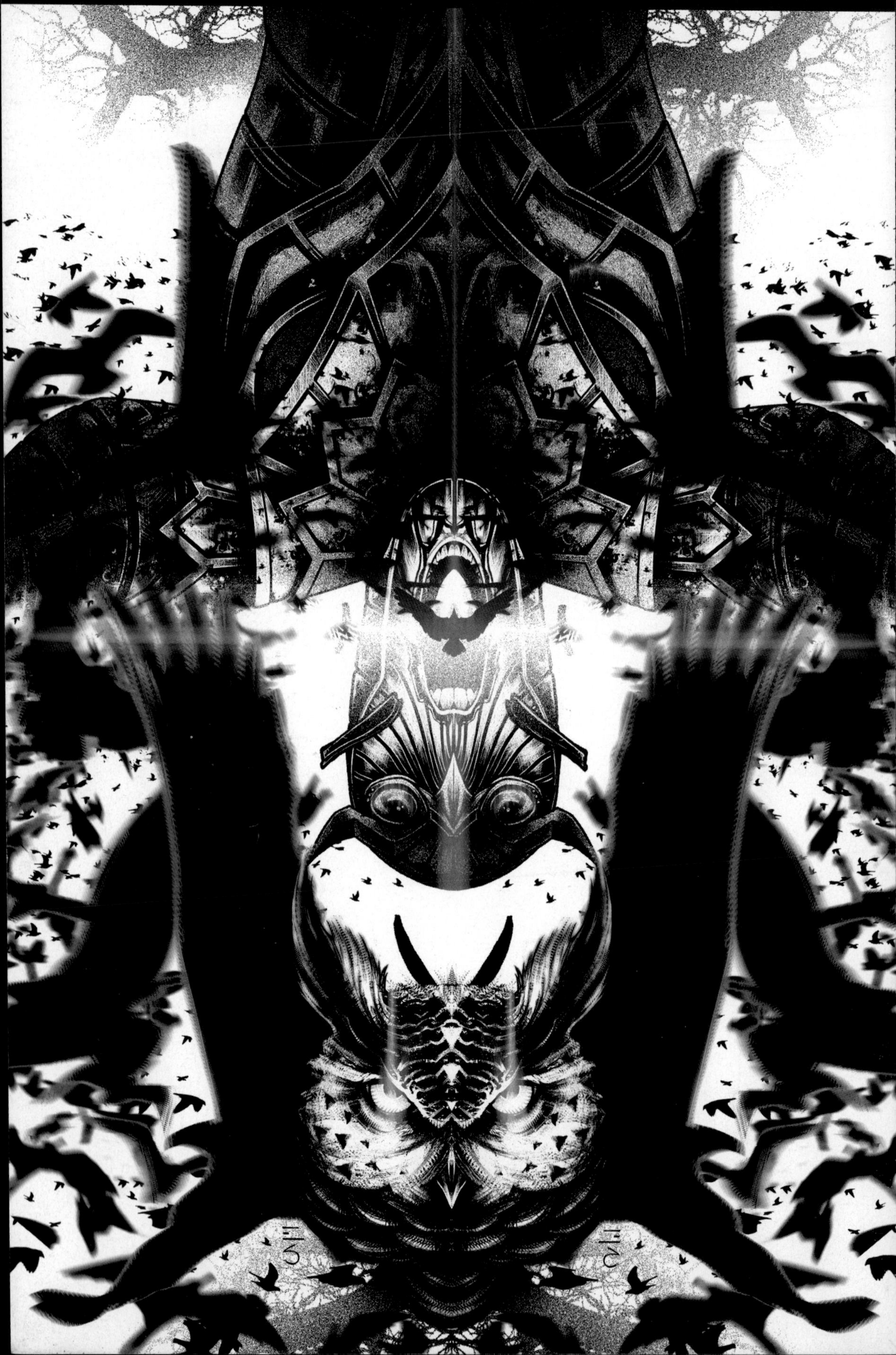

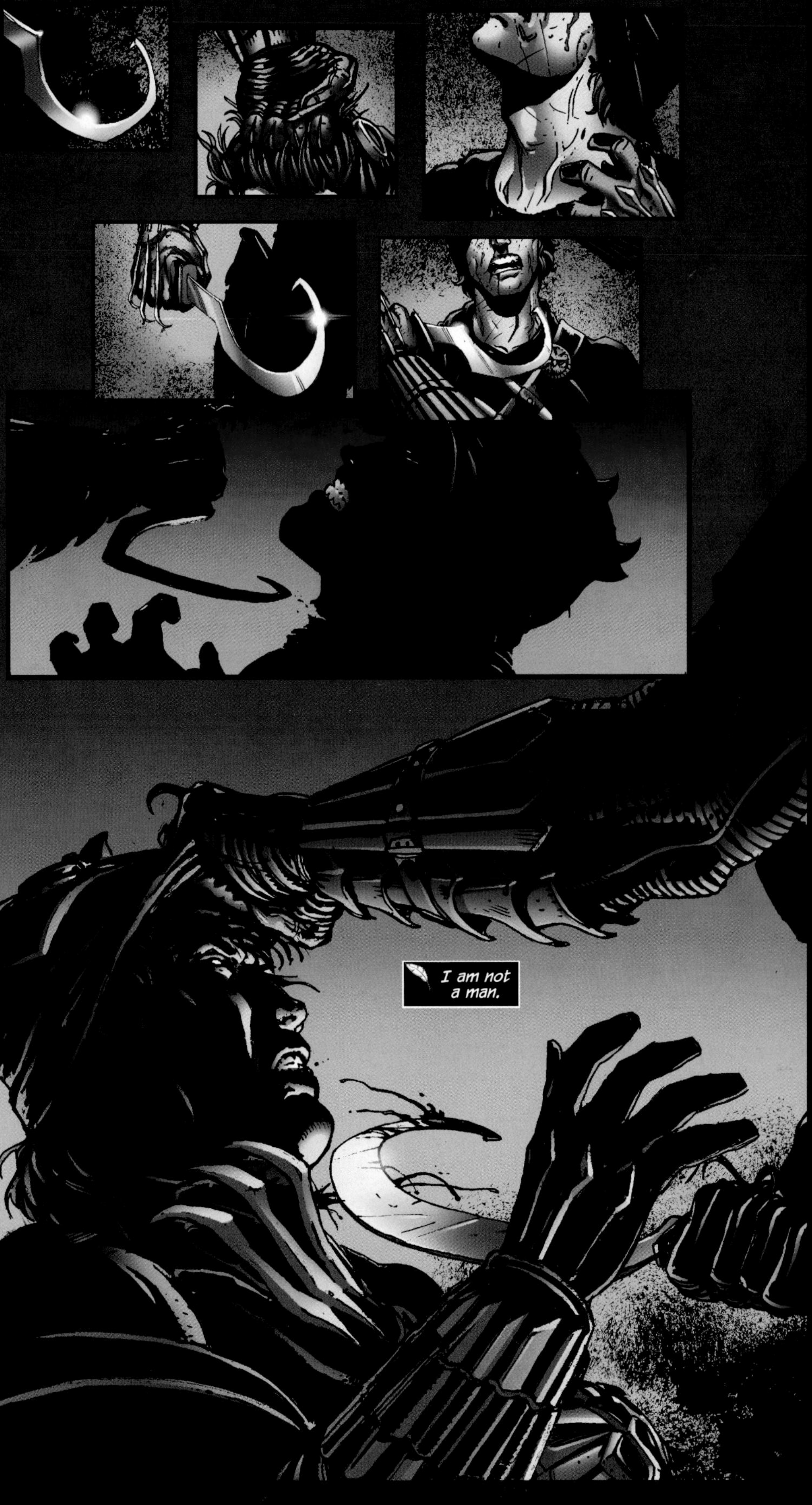
I am not a man.

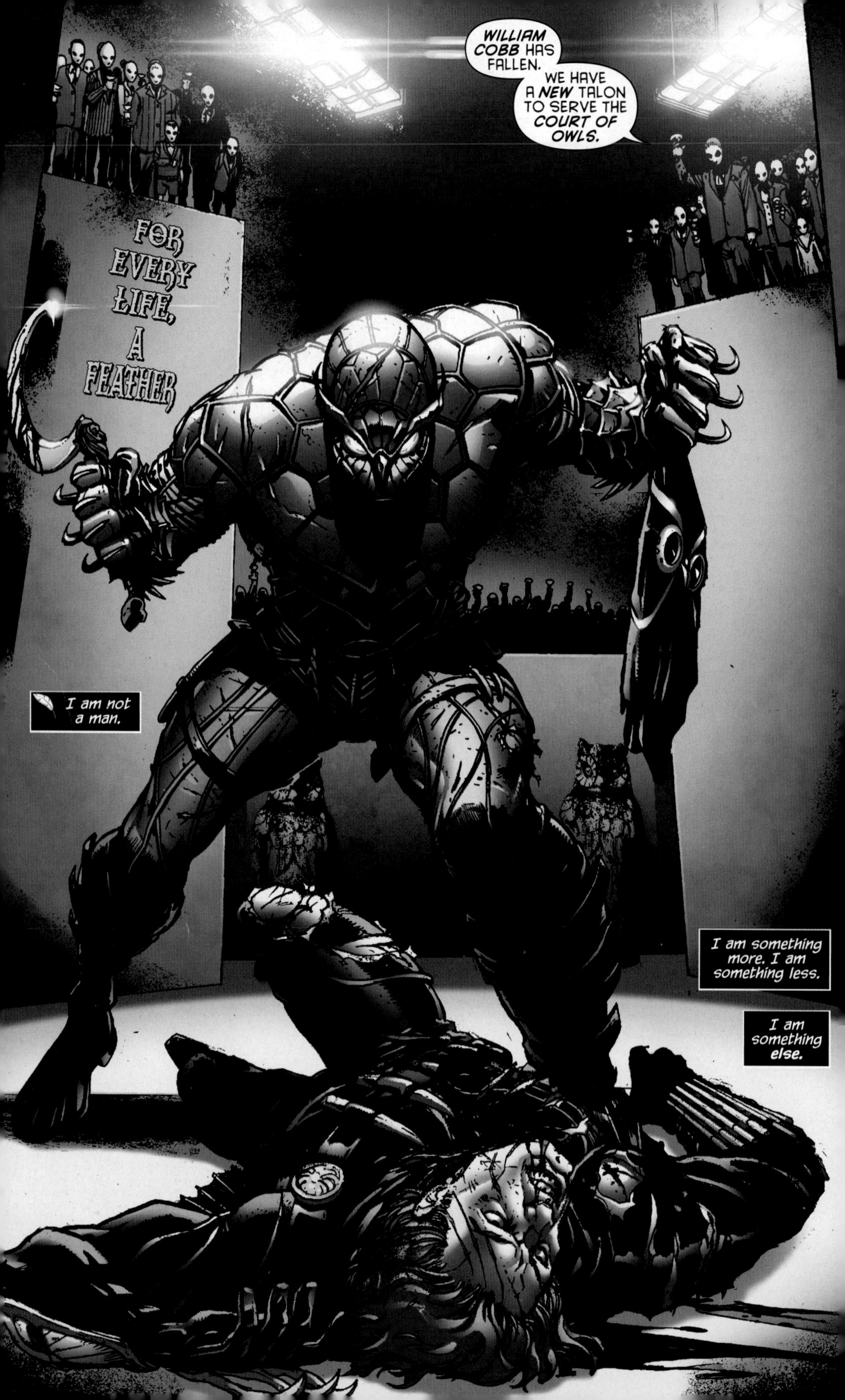
WILLIAM COBB HAS FALLEN.
WE HAVE A NEW TALON TO SERVE THE COURT OF OWLS.
FOR EVERY LIFE, A FEATHER
I am not a man.
I am something more. I am something less.
I am something else.

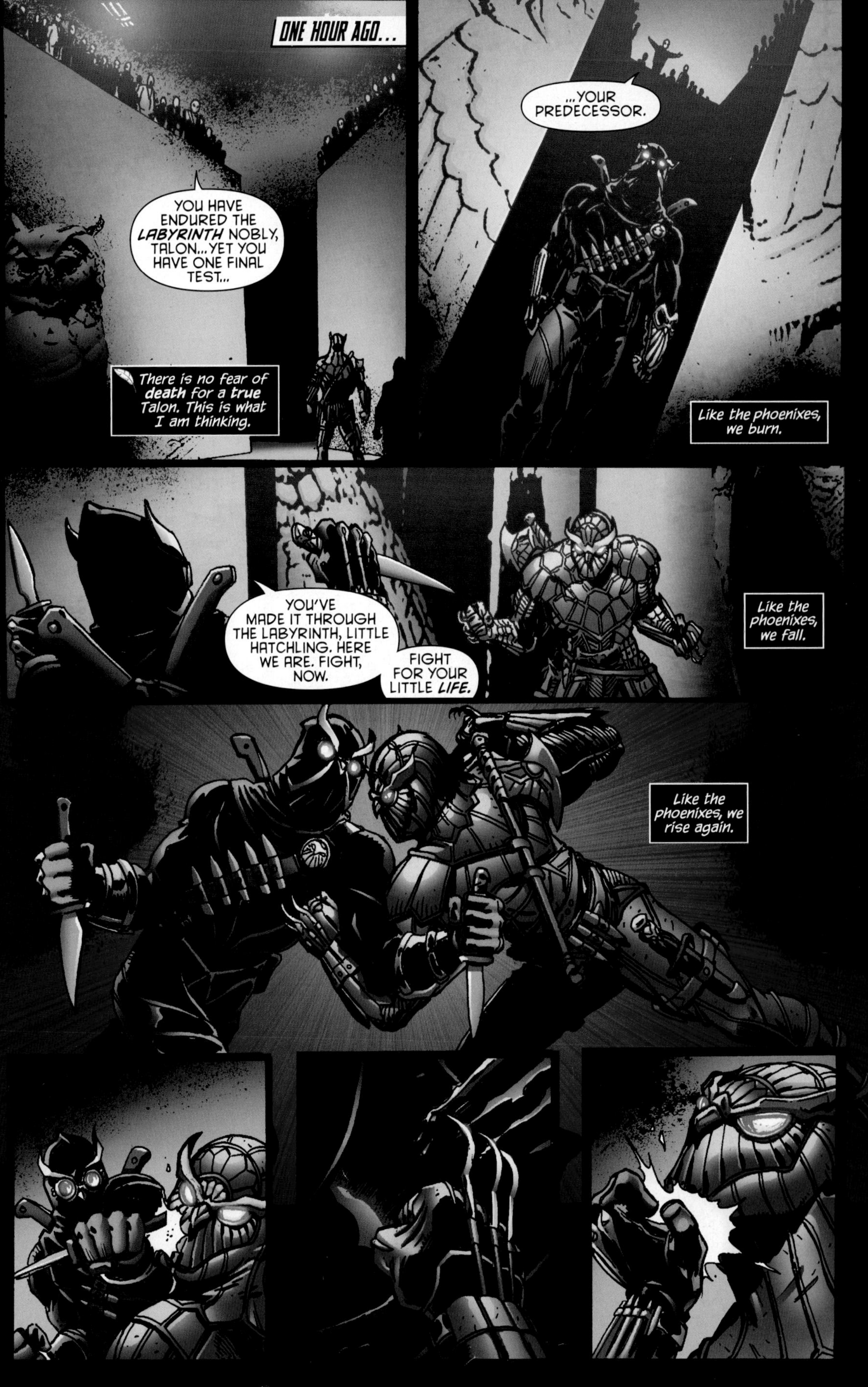
ONE HOUR AGO...
YOU HAVE ENDURED THE LABYRINTH NOBLY, TALON...YET YOU HAVE ONE FINAL TEST...
There is no fear of death for a true Talon. This is what I am thinking.
...YOUR PREDECESSOR.
Like the phoenixes, we burn.
YOU'VE MADE IT THROUGH THE LABYRINTH, LITTLE HATCHLING. HERE WE ARE. FIGHT, NOW.
FIGHT FOR YOUR LITTLE LIFE.
Like the phoenixes, we fall.
Like the phoenixes, we rise again.

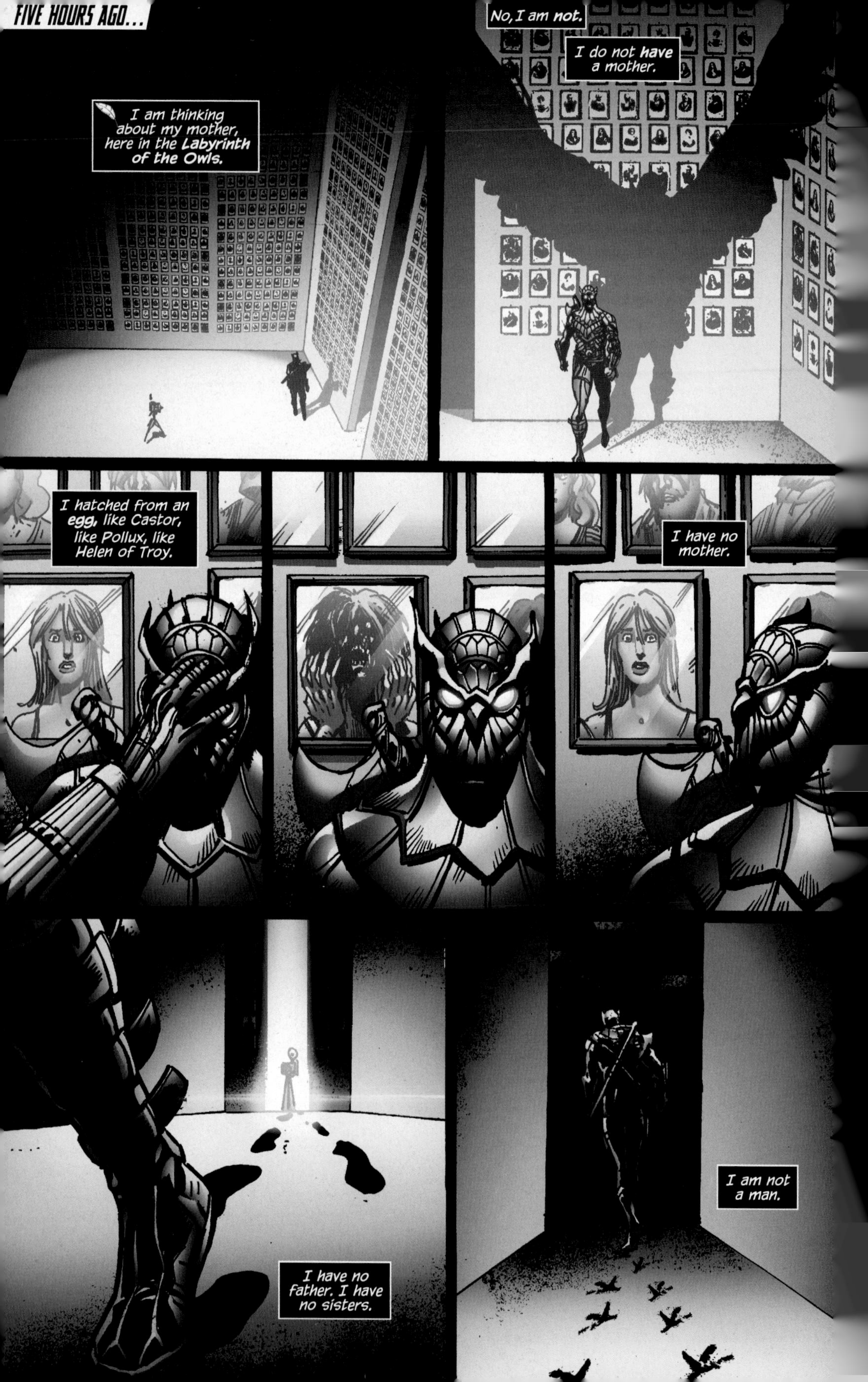
FIVE HOURS AGO...
I am thinking about my mother, here in the Labyrinth of the Owls.
No, I am not.
I do not have a mother.
I hatched from an egg, like Castor, like Pollux, like Helen of Troy.
I have no mother.
I have no father. I have no sisters.
I am not a man.

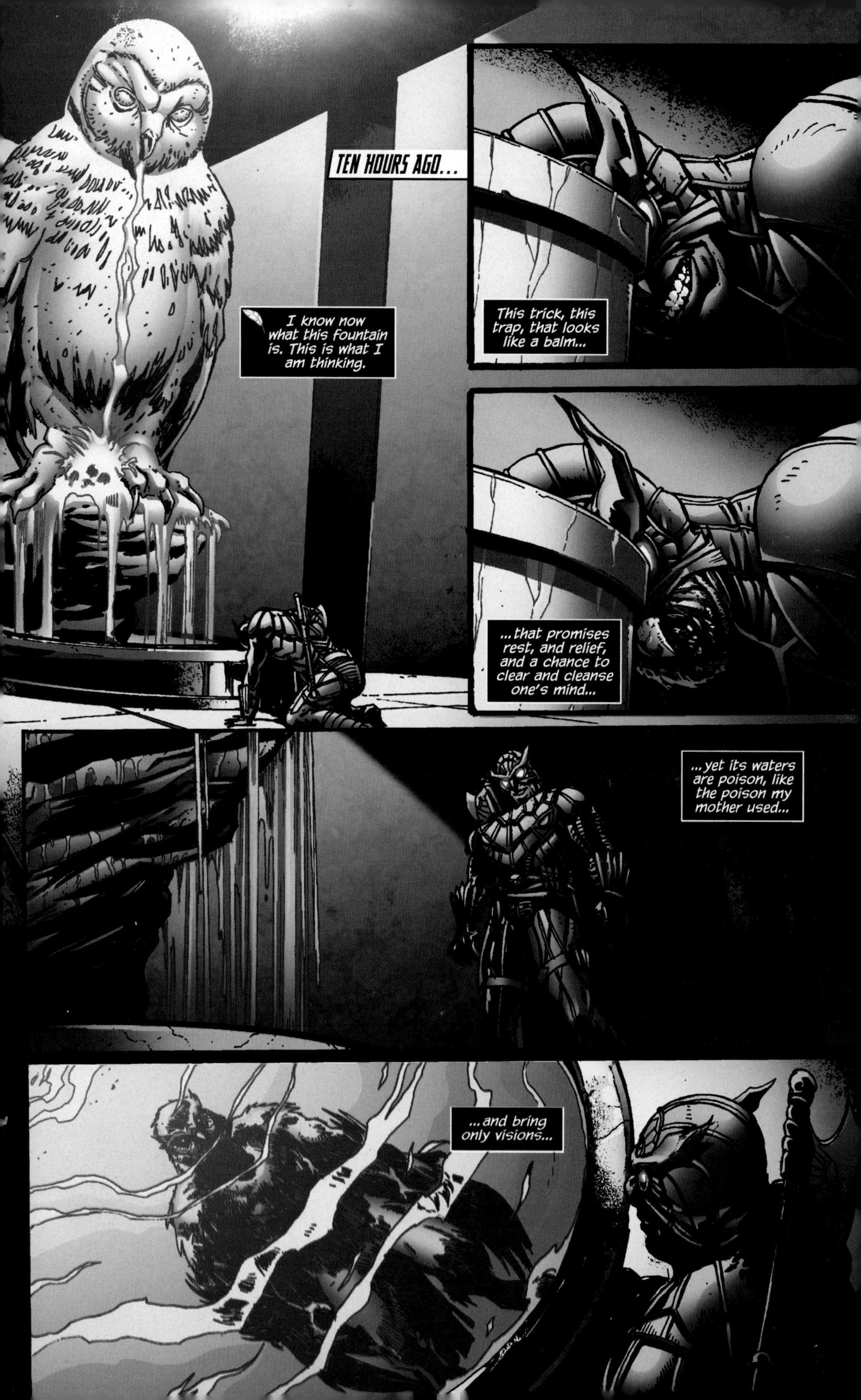
TEN HOURS AGO...
I know now what this fountain is. This is what I am thinking.
This trick, this trap, that looks like a balm...
...that promises rest, and relief, and a chance to clear and cleanse one's mind...
...yet its waters are poison, like the poison my mother used...
...and bring only visions...

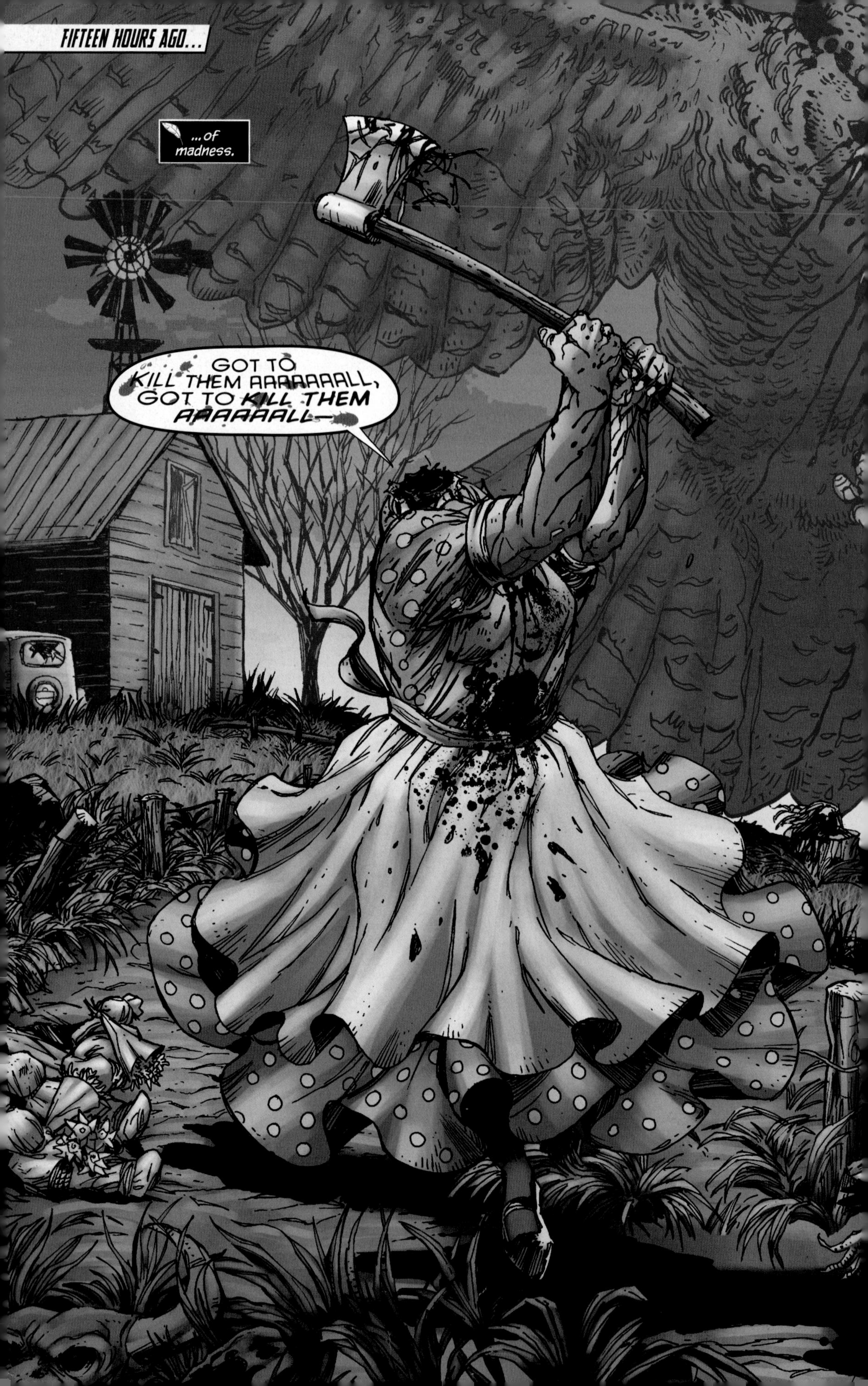
FIFTEEN HOURS AGO...
...of madness.
GOT TO KILL THEM AAAAAAAALL, GOT TO KILL THEM AAAAAALL—

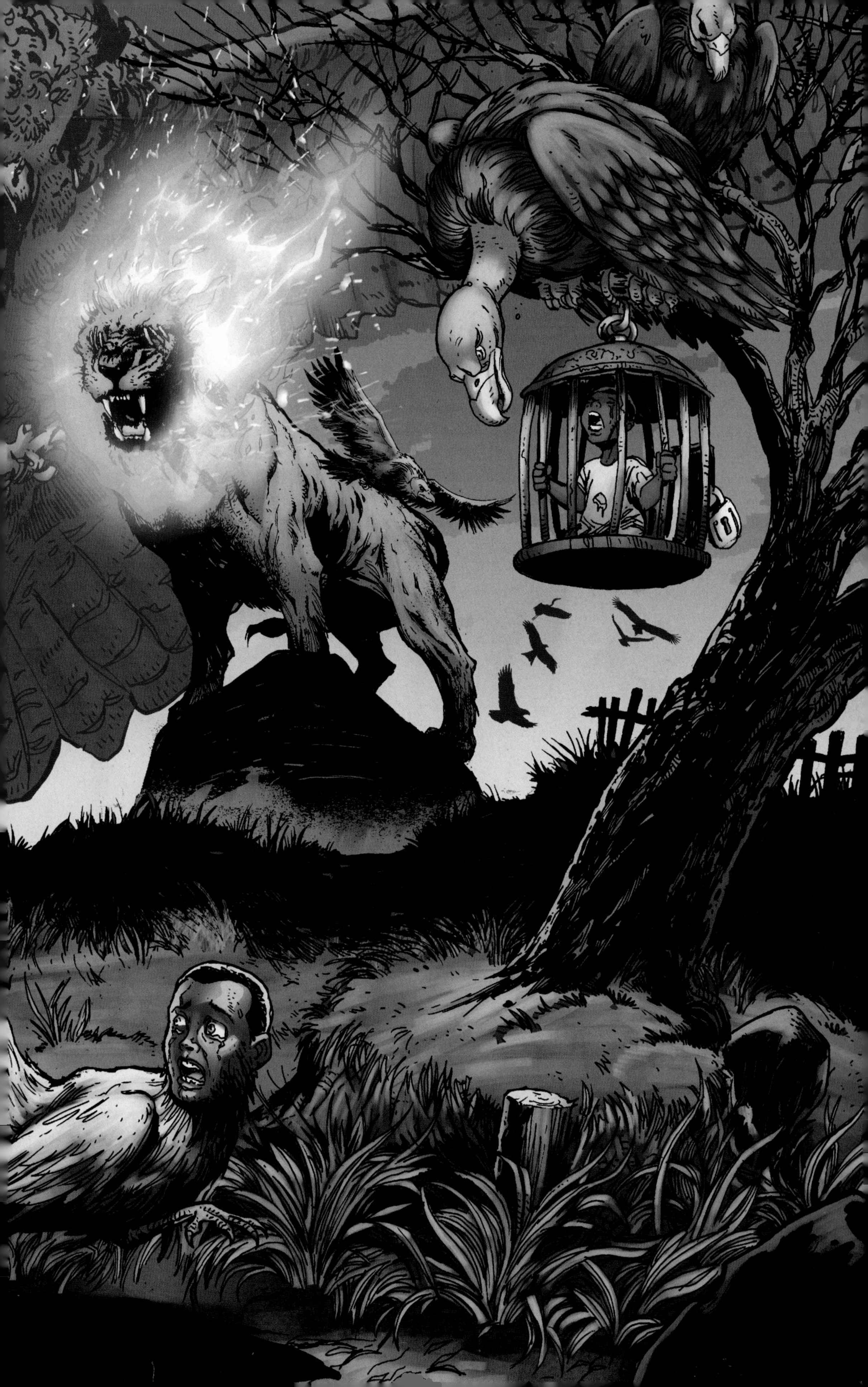

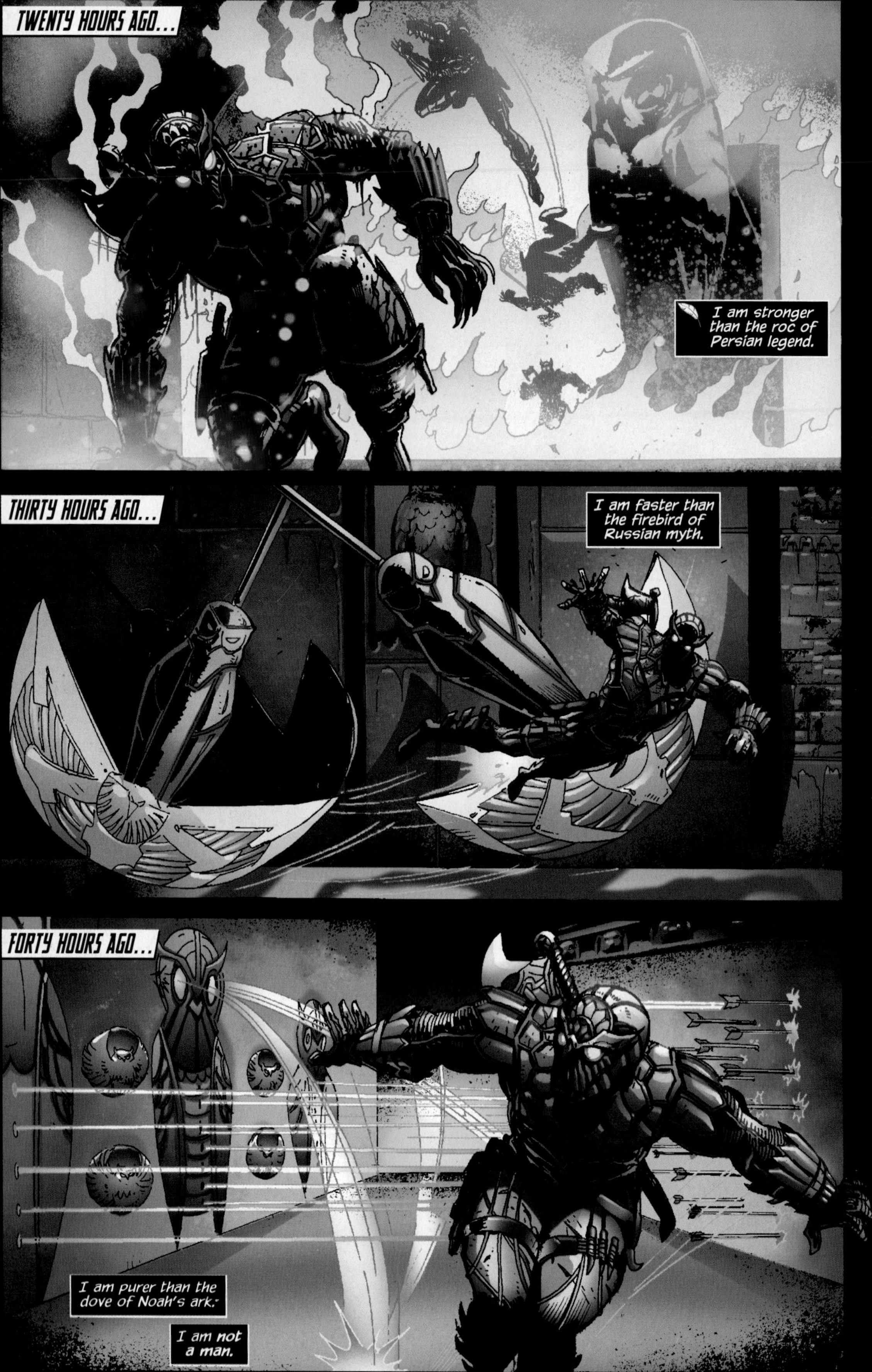
TWENTY HOURS AGO...
I am stronger than the roc of Persian legend.
THIRTY HOURS AGO...
I am faster than the firebird of Russian myth.
FORTY HOURS AGO...
I am purer than the dove of Noah's ark.
I am not a man.

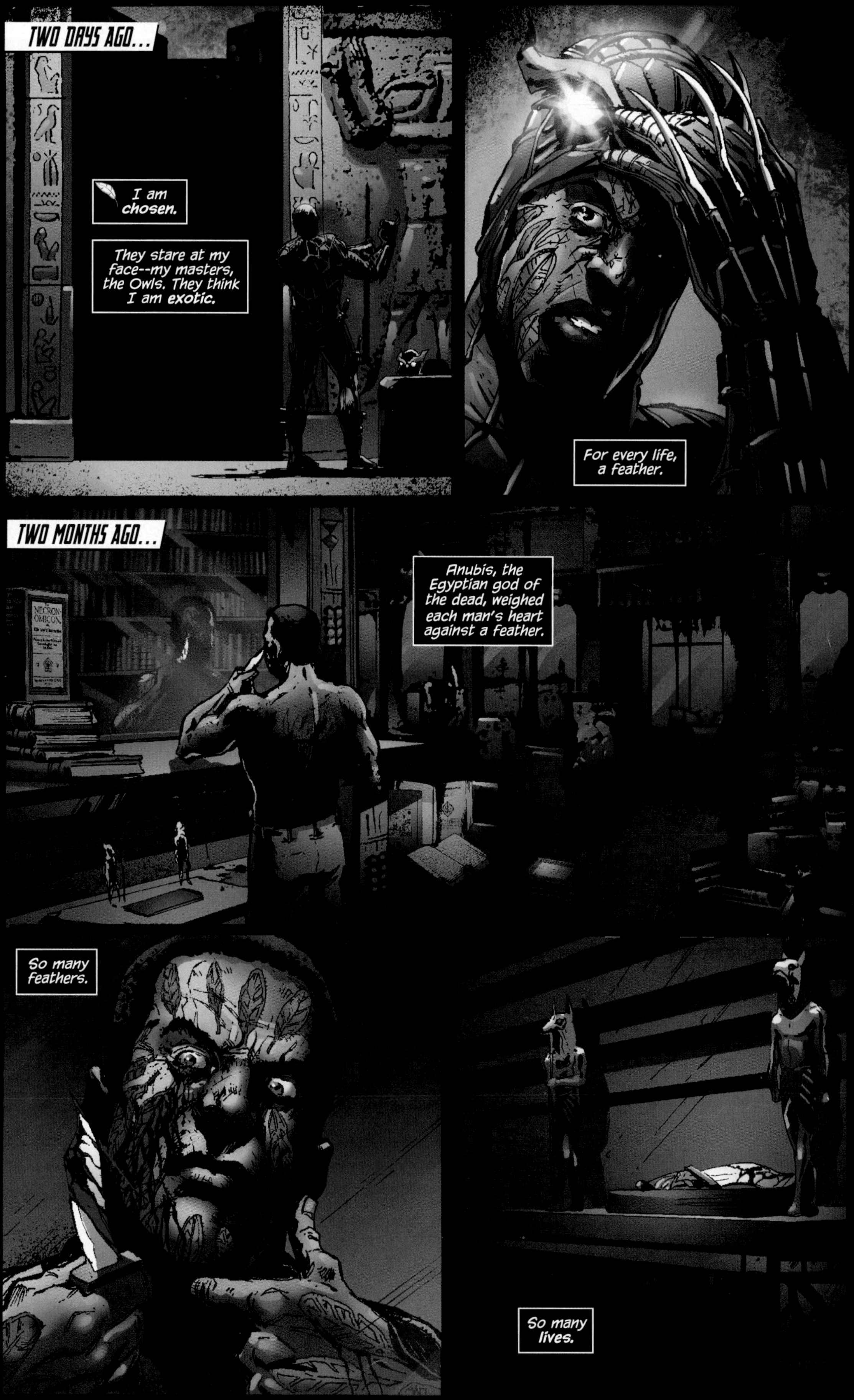
TWO DAYS AGO...
I am chosen.
They stare at my face--my masters, the Owls. They think I am exotic.
For every life, a feather.
TWO MONTHS AGO...
Anubis, the Egyptian god of the dead, weighed each man's heart against a feather.
So many feathers.
So many lives.

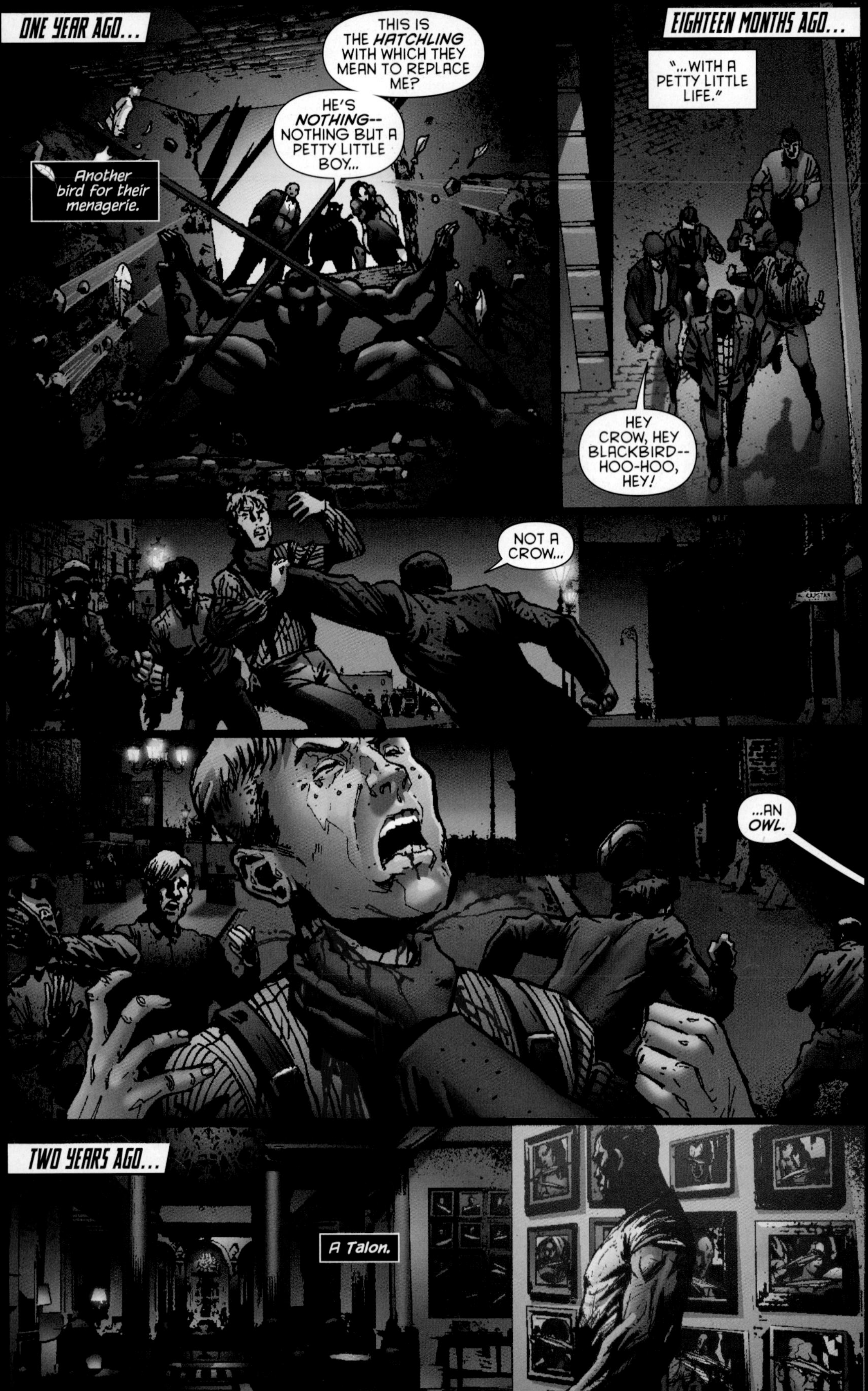
ONE YEAR AGO...
THIS IS THE HATCHLING WITH WHICH THEY MEAN TO REPLACE ME?
HE'S NOTHING-- NOTHING BUT A PETTY LITTLE BOY...
Another bird for their menagerie.
EIGHTEEN MONTHS AGO...
"...WITH A PETTY LITTLE LIFE."
HEY CROW, HEY BLACKBIRD-- HOO-HOO, HEY!
NOT A CROW...
...AN OWL.
TWO YEARS AGO...
A Talon.

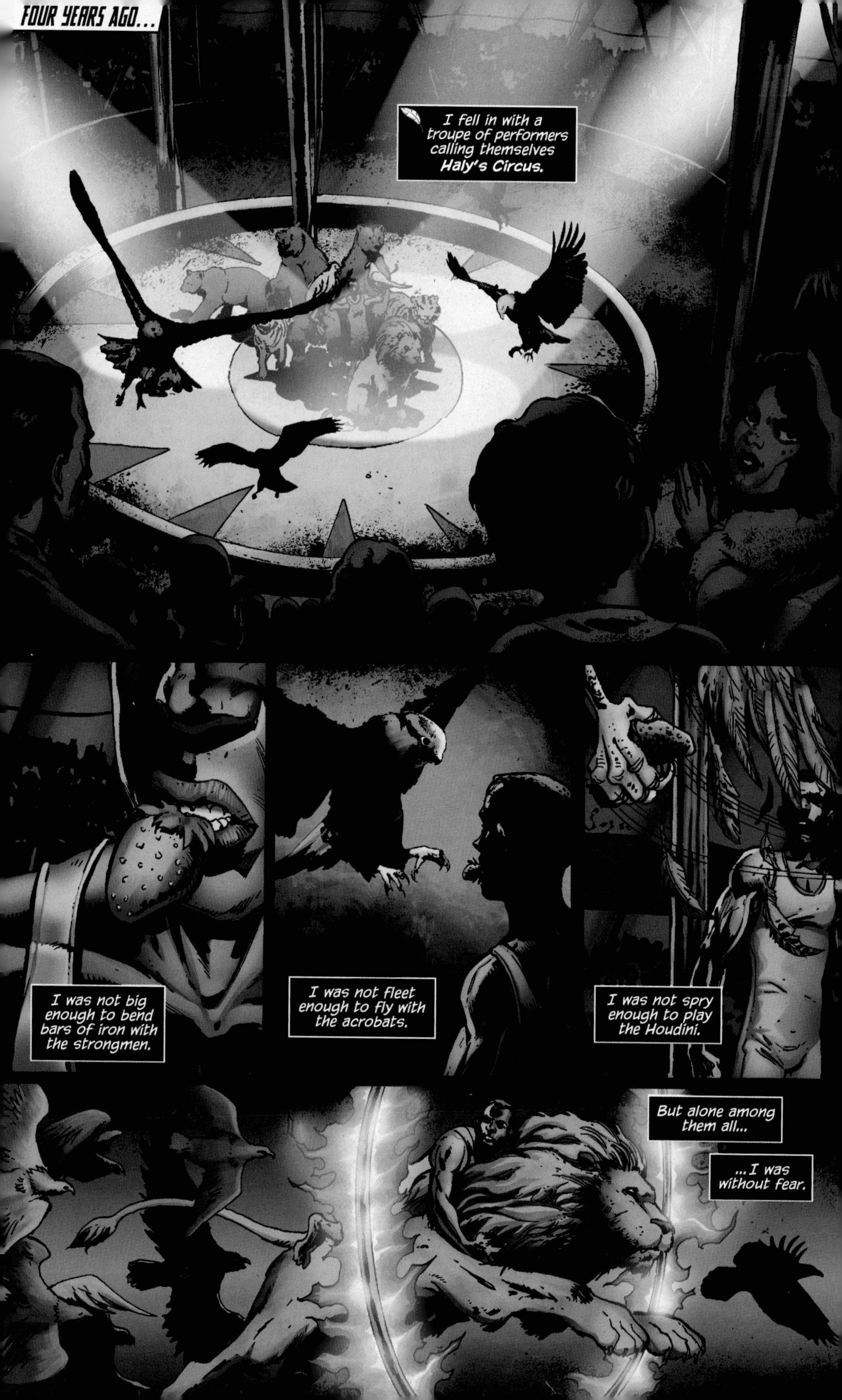
FOUR YEARS AGO...
I fell in with a troupe of performers calling themselves Haly's Circus.
I was not big enough to bend bars of iron with the strongmen.
I was not fleet enough to fly with the acrobats.
I was not spry enough to play the Houdini.
But alone among them all...
...I was without fear.

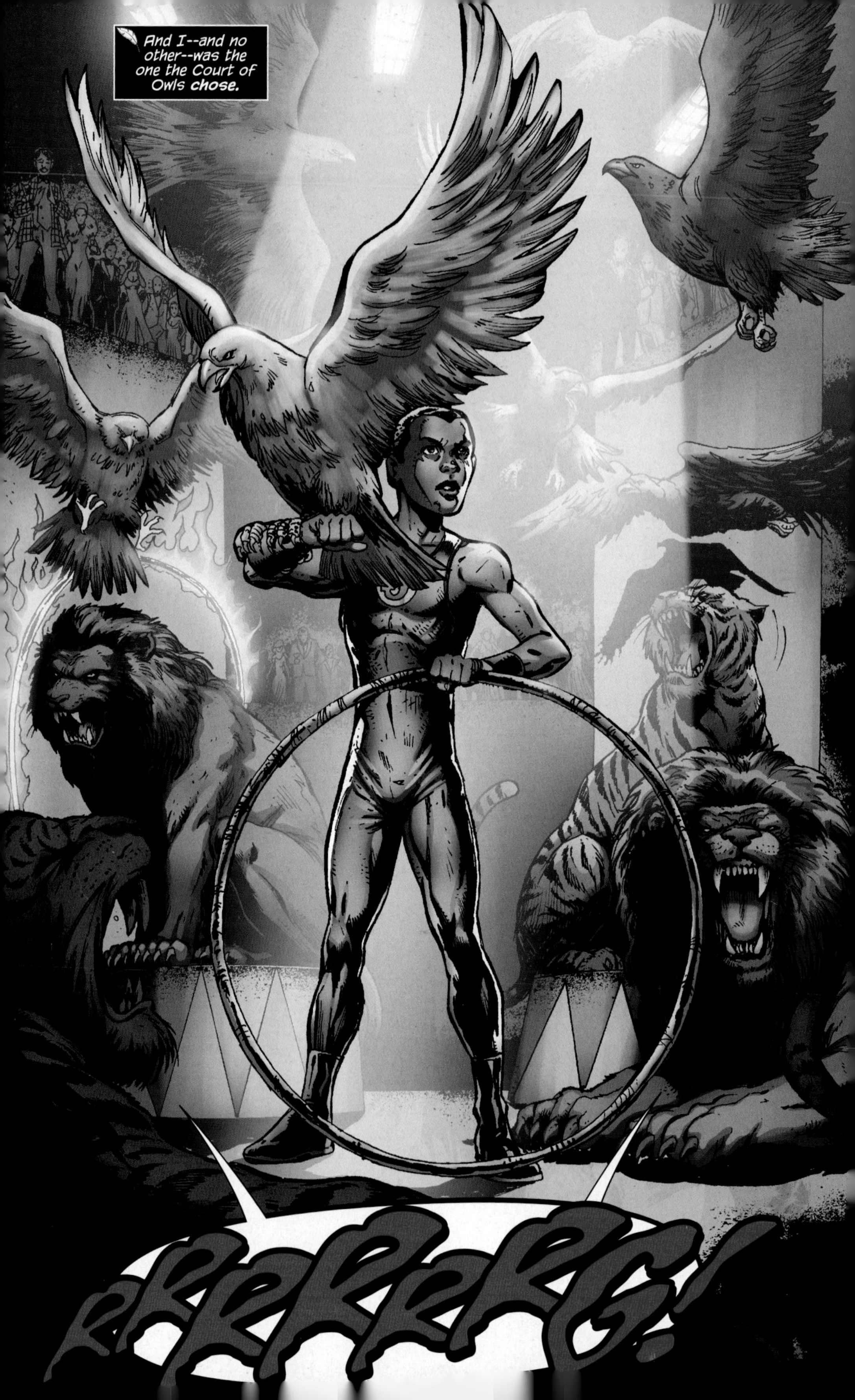
And I--and no other--was the one the Court of Owls chose.
RRRRRRG!

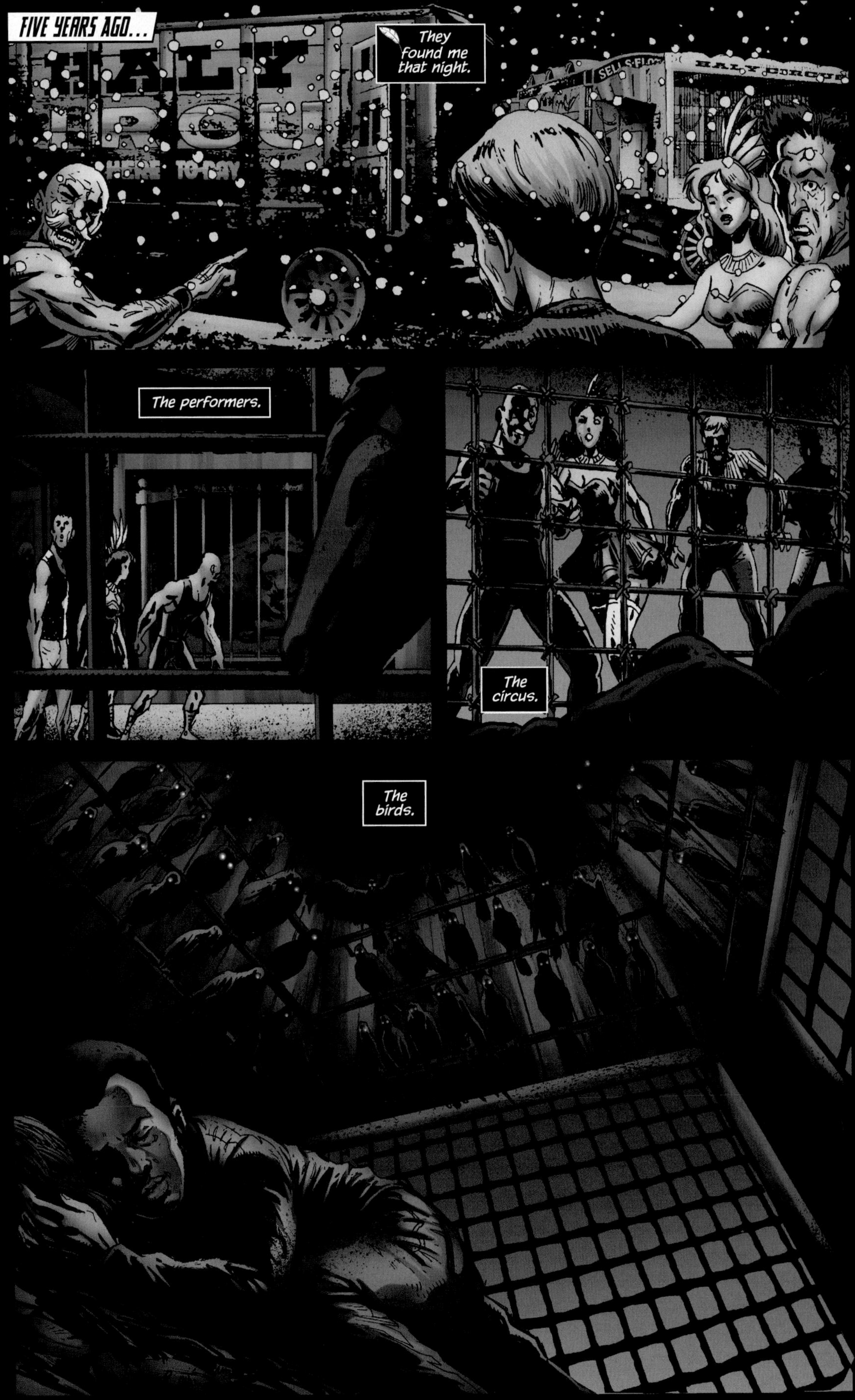
FIVE YEARS AGO...
HALY
HERE TO-DAY
They found me that night.
The performers.
The circus.
The birds.

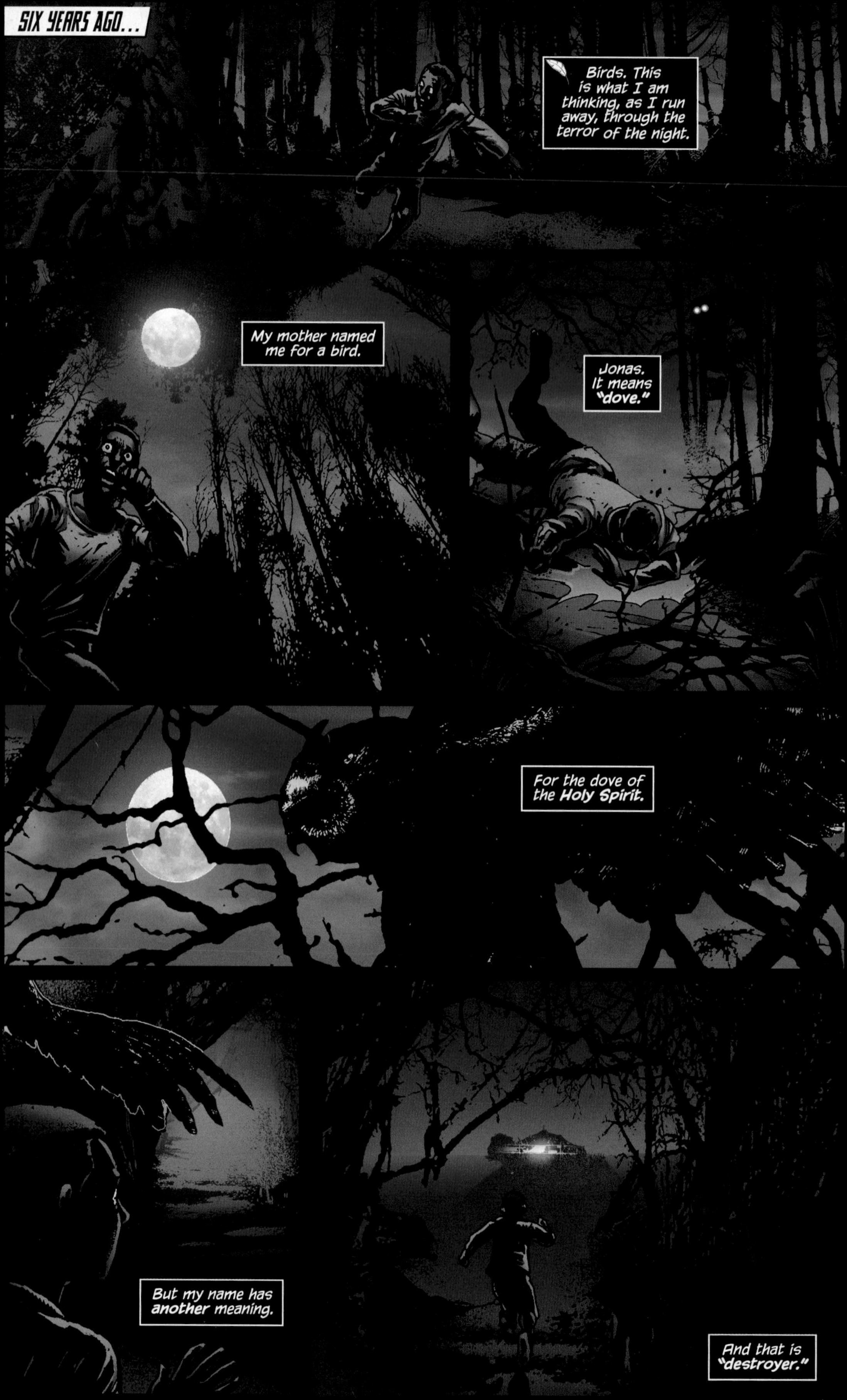
SIX YEARS AGO...
Birds. This is what I am thinking, as I run away, through the terror of the night.
My mother named me for a bird.
Jonas. It means "dove."
For the dove of the Holy Spirit.
But my name has another meaning.
And that is "destroyer."

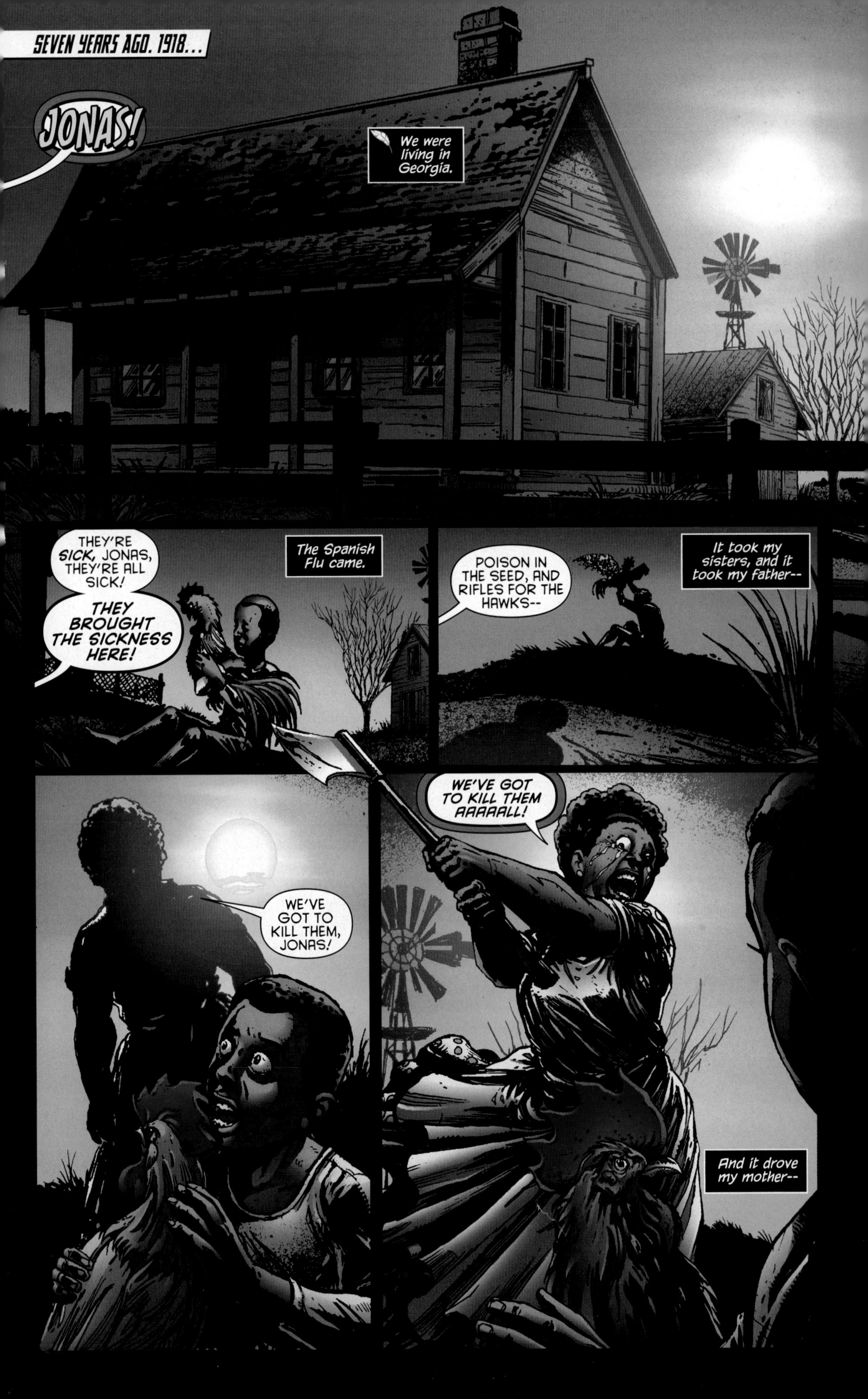
SEVEN YEARS AGO. 1918...
JONAS!
We were living in Georgia.
THEY'RE SICK, JONAS, THEY'RE ALL SICK!
THEY BROUGHT THE SICKNESS HERE!
The Spanish Flu came.
POISON IN THE SEED, AND RIFLES FOR THE HAWKS--
It took my sisters, and it took my father--
WE'VE GOT TO KILL THEM, JONAS!
WE'VE GOT TO KILL THEM AAAAALL!
And it drove my mother--

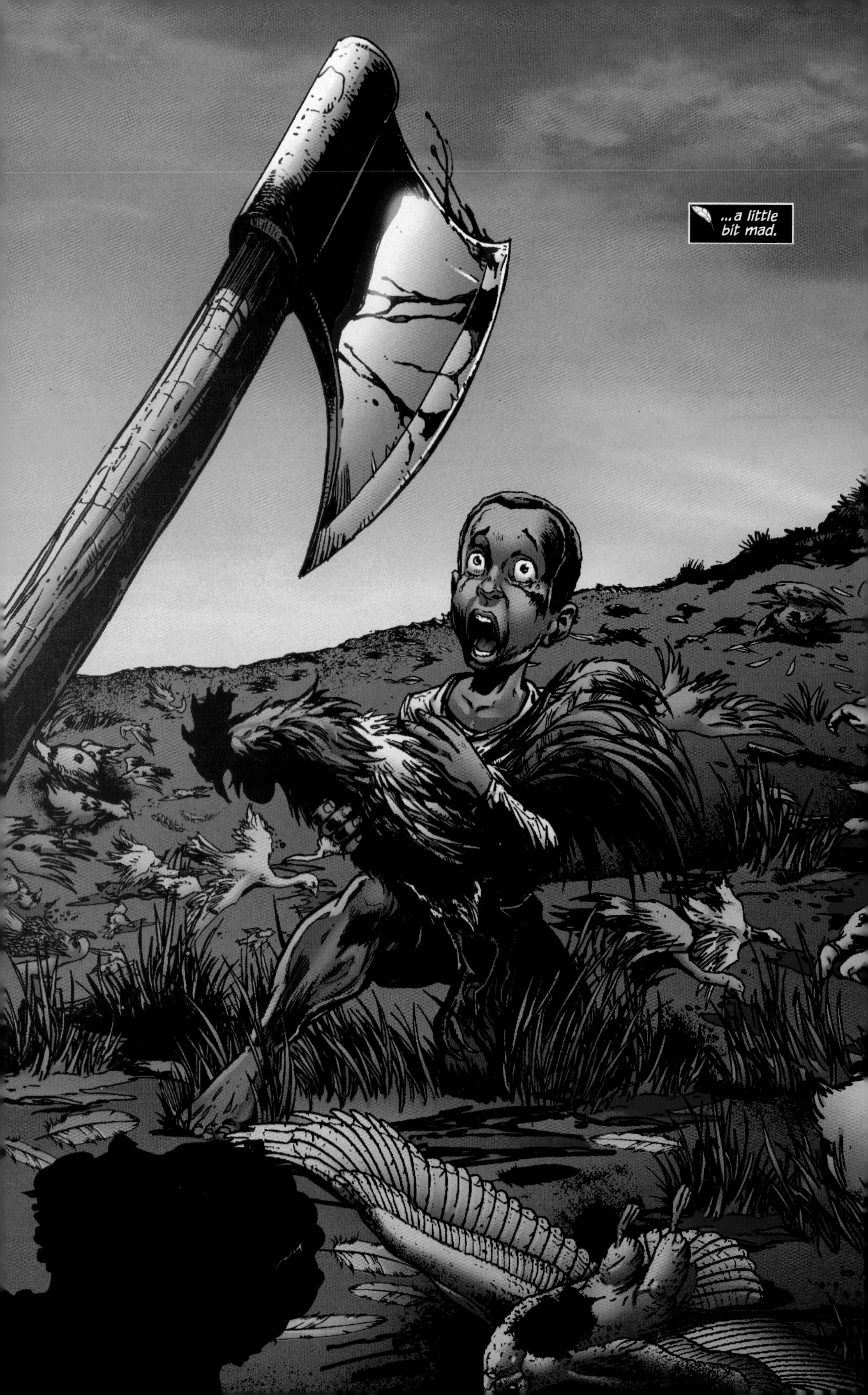
...a little bit mad.

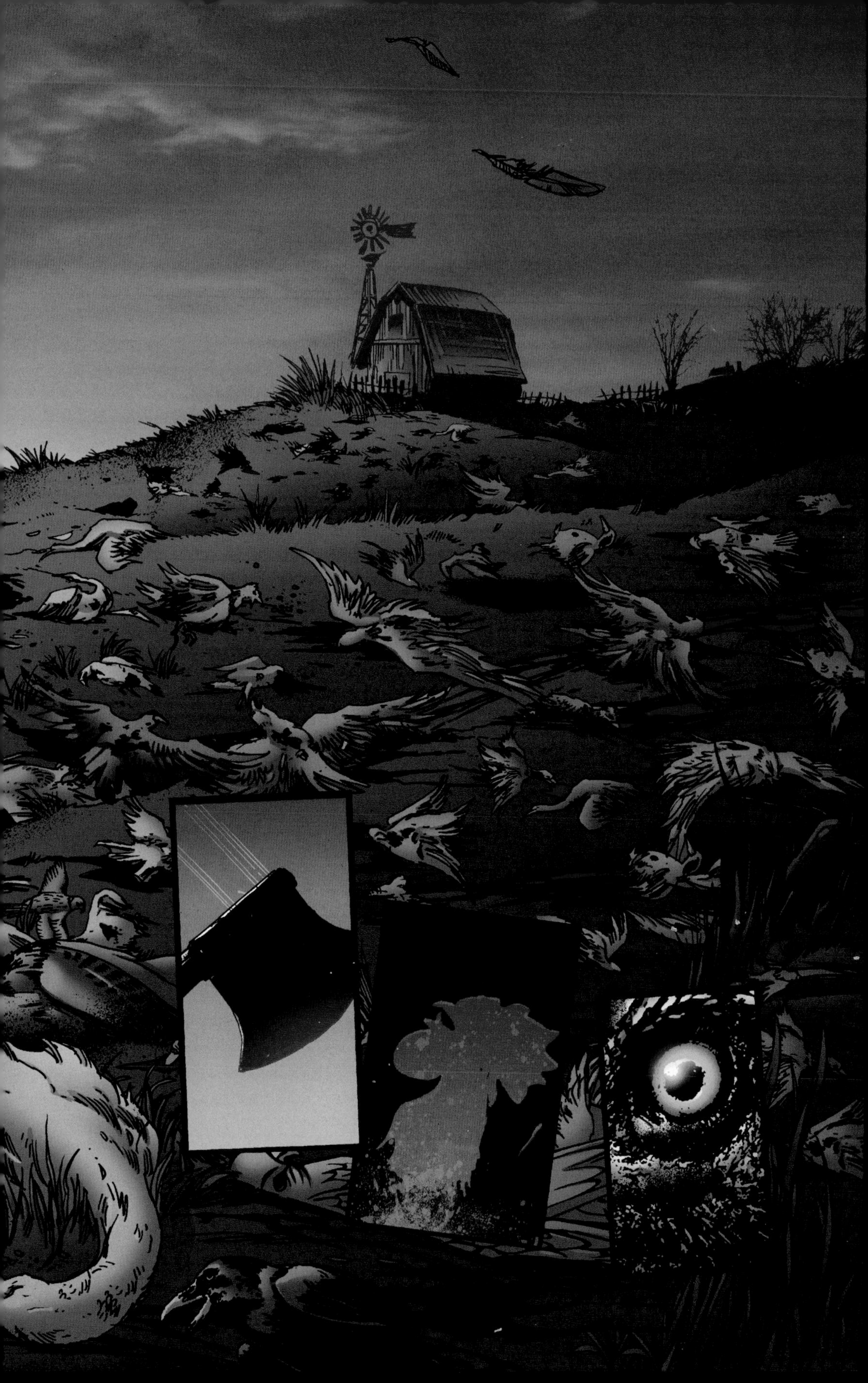

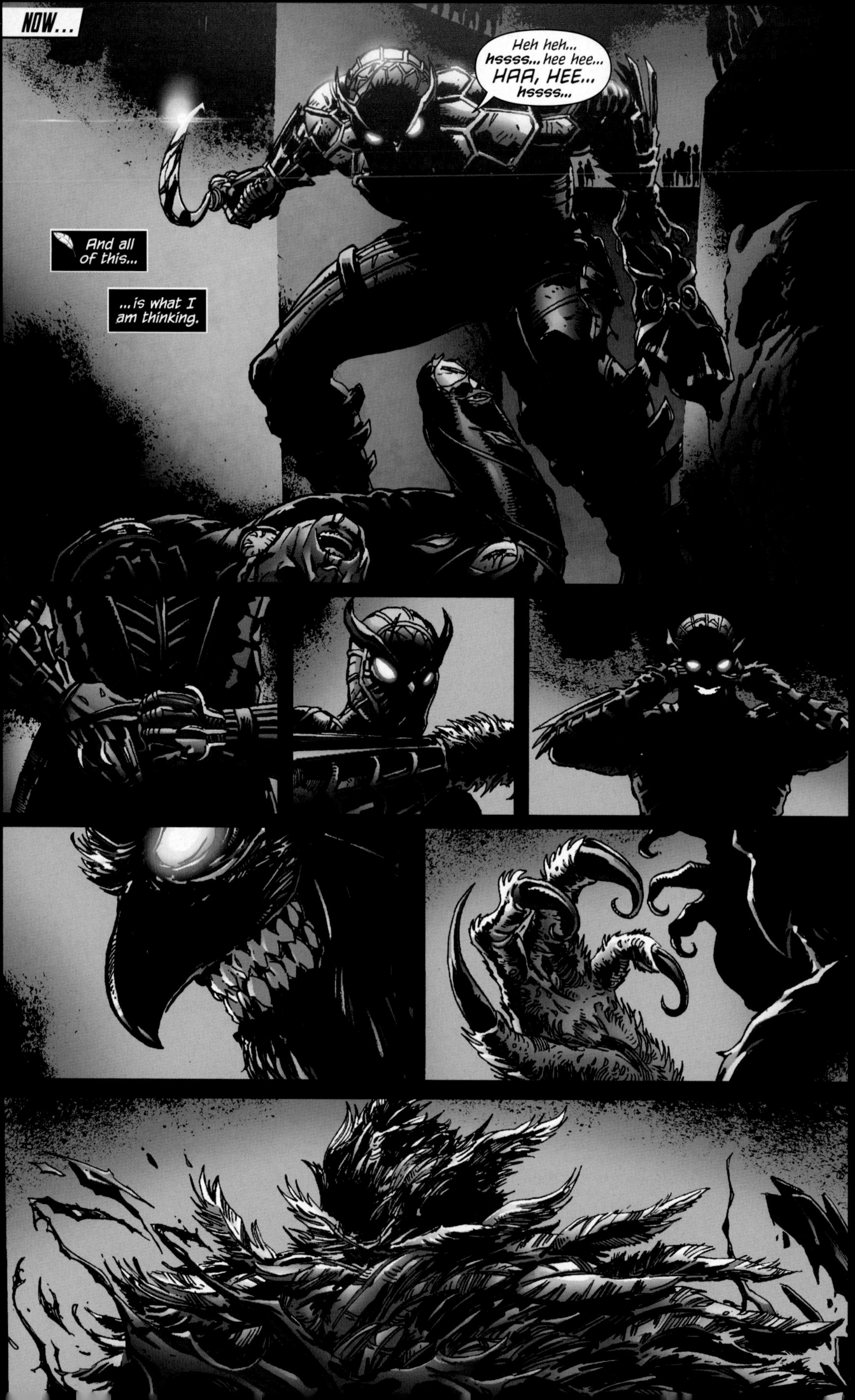
NOW...
Heh heh... hssss... hee hee... HAA, HEE... hssss...
And all of this...
...is what I am thinking.

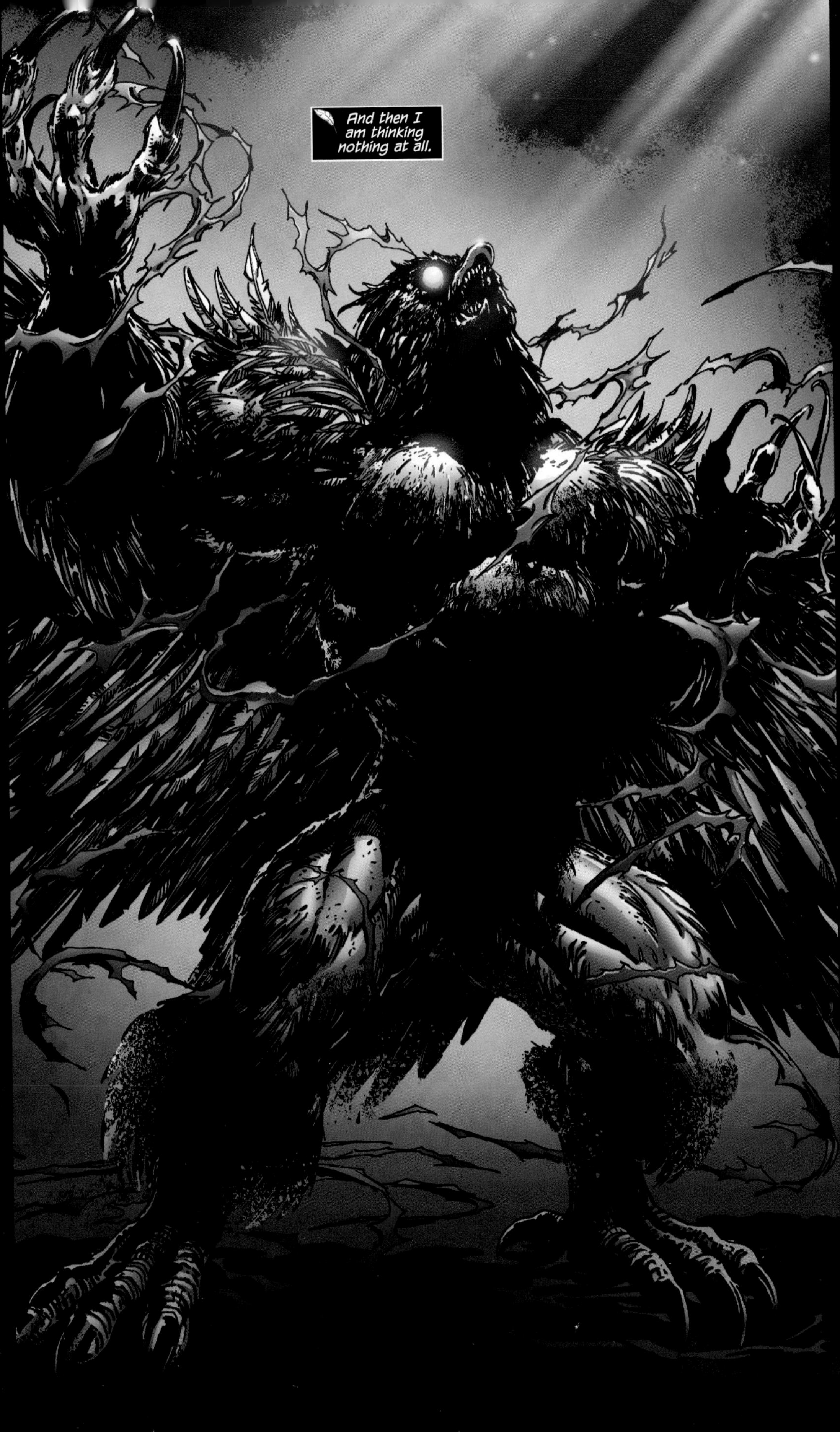
And then I am thinking nothing at all.

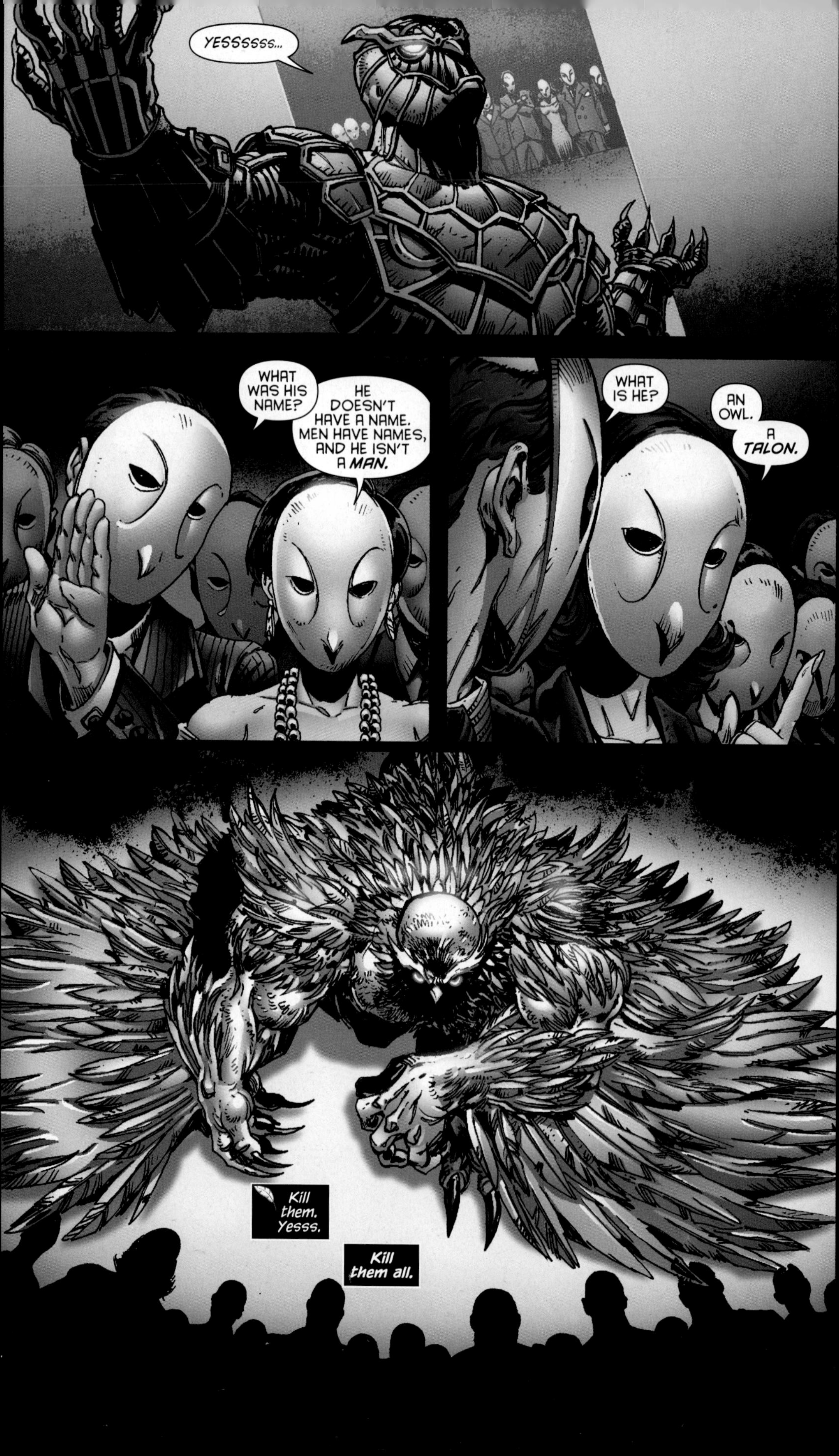

YESSSSSS...
WHAT WAS HIS NAME?
HE DOESN'T HAVE A NAME. MEN HAVE NAMES, AND HE ISN'T A *MAN.*
WHAT IS HE?
AN OWL.
A *TALON.*
Kill them. Yesss.
Kill them all.

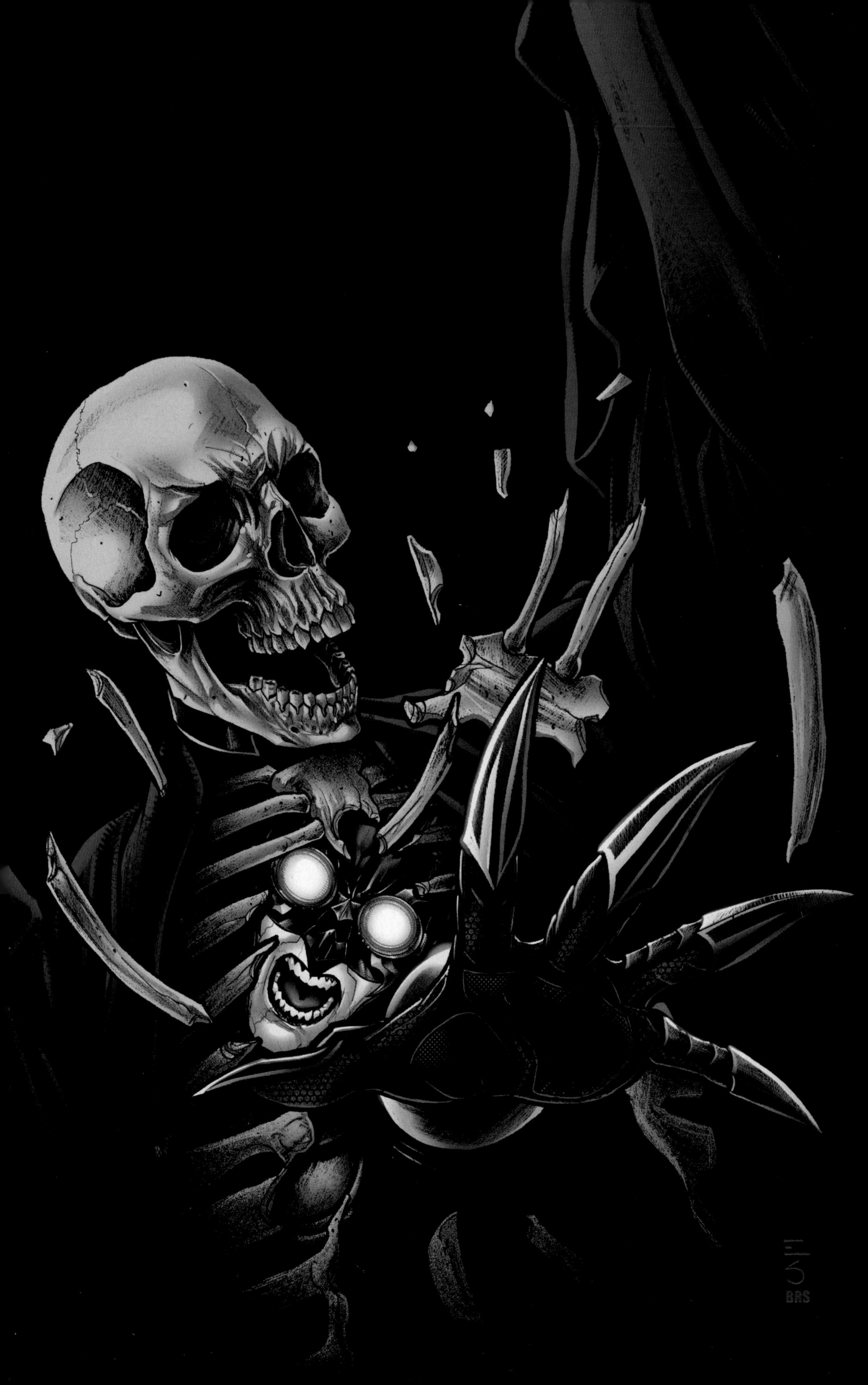
BRS

DEADMAN'S PARTY: PART 1

TIM SEELEY writer JORGE LUCAS artist cover art by EMANUEL SIMEONI & BRETT SMITH

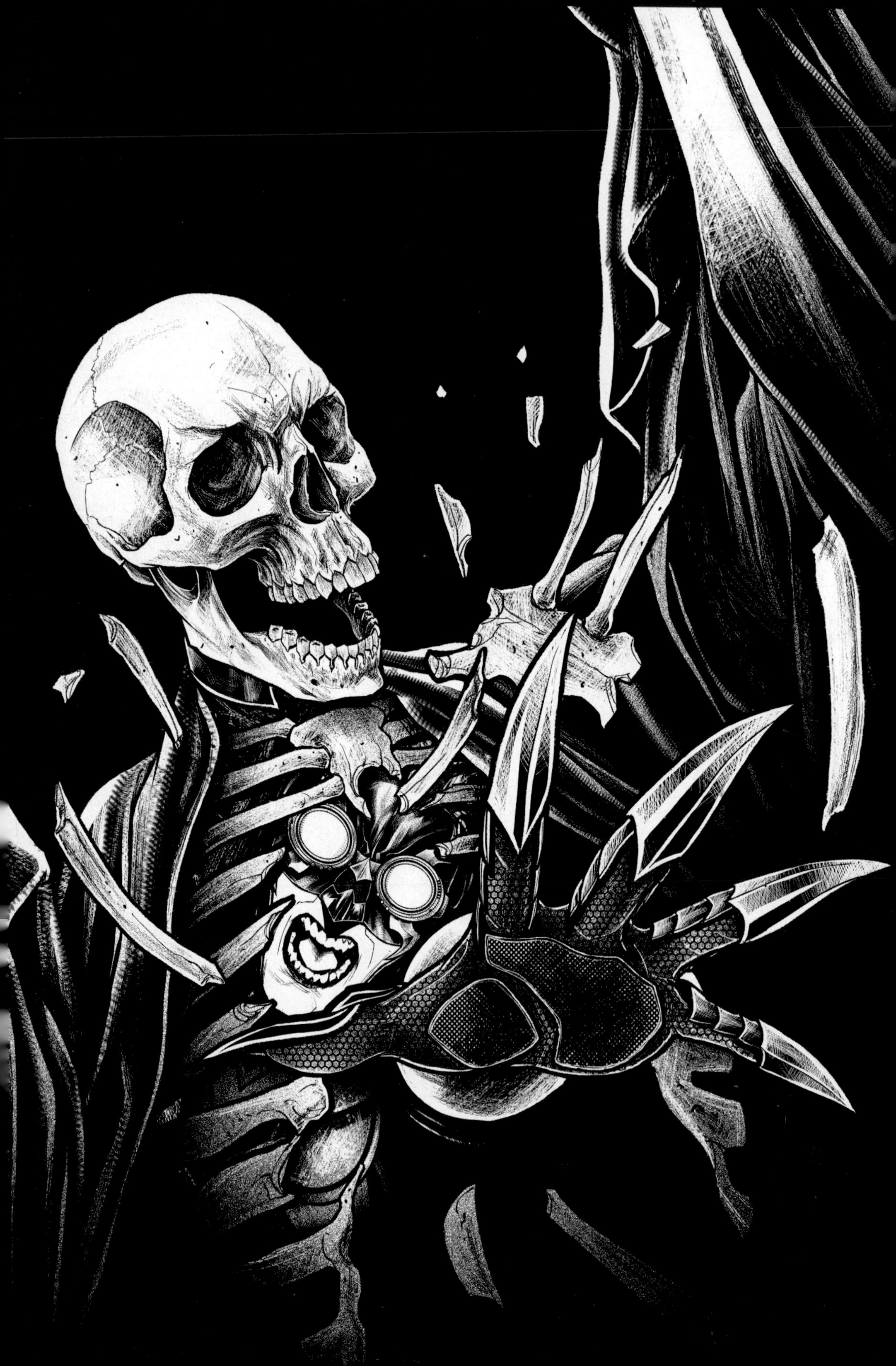

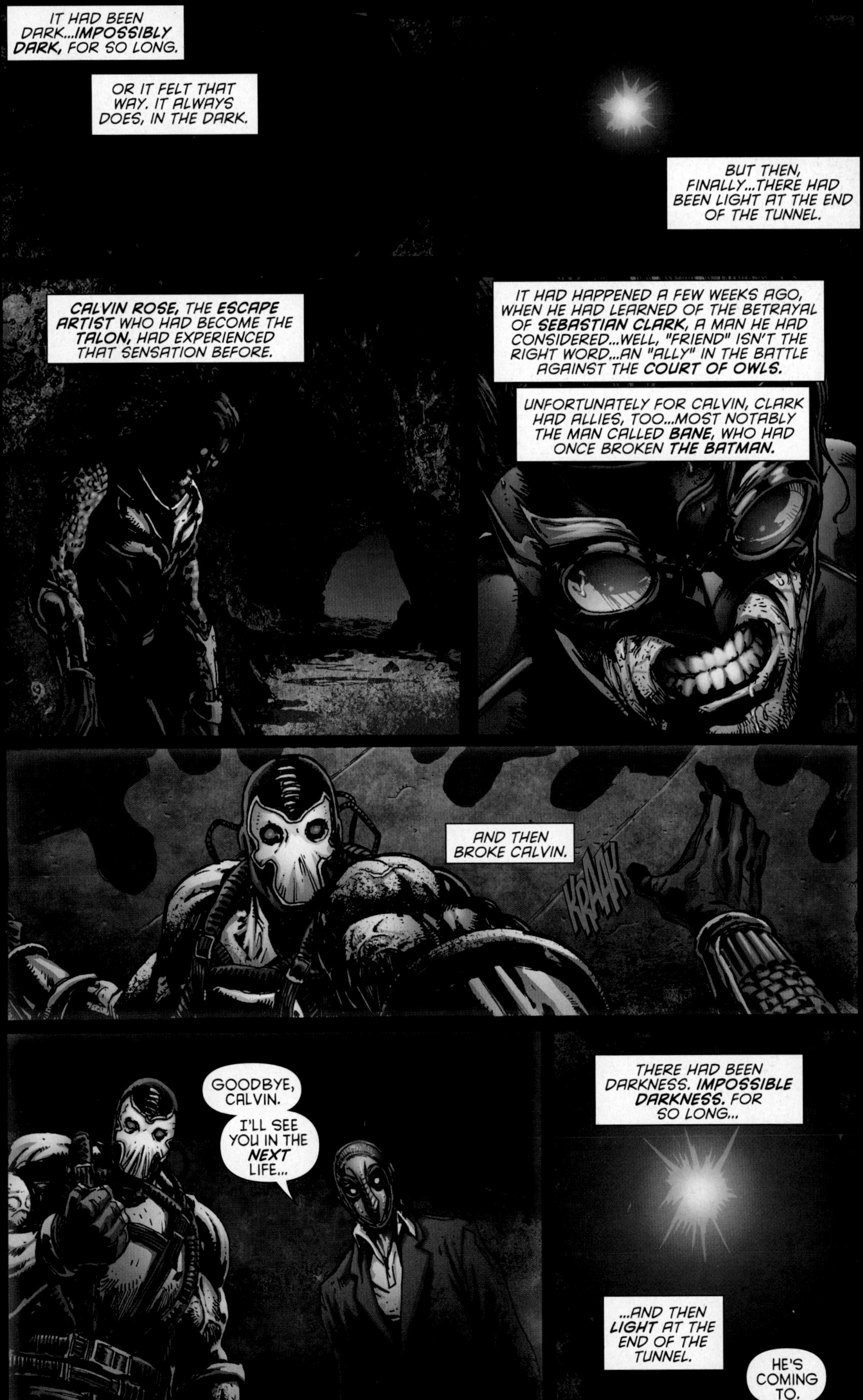

IT HAD BEEN DARK...IMPOSSIBLY DARK, FOR SO LONG.
OR IT FELT THAT WAY. IT ALWAYS DOES, IN THE DARK.
BUT THEN, FINALLY...THERE HAD BEEN LIGHT AT THE END OF THE TUNNEL.
CALVIN ROSE, THE ESCAPE ARTIST WHO HAD BECOME THE TALON, HAD EXPERIENCED THAT SENSATION BEFORE.
IT HAD HAPPENED A FEW WEEKS AGO, WHEN HE HAD LEARNED OF THE BETRAYAL OF SEBASTIAN CLARK, A MAN HE HAD CONSIDERED...WELL, "FRIEND" ISN'T THE RIGHT WORD...AN "ALLY" IN THE BATTLE AGAINST THE COURT OF OWLS.
UNFORTUNATELY FOR CALVIN, CLARK HAD ALLIES, TOO...MOST NOTABLY THE MAN CALLED BANE, WHO HAD ONCE BROKEN THE BATMAN.
AND THEN BROKE CALVIN.
KRAAK
GOODBYE, CALVIN.
I'LL SEE YOU IN THE NEXT LIFE...
THERE HAD BEEN DARKNESS. IMPOSSIBLE DARKNESS. FOR SO LONG...
...AND THEN LIGHT AT THE END OF THE TUNNEL.
HE'S COMING TO.

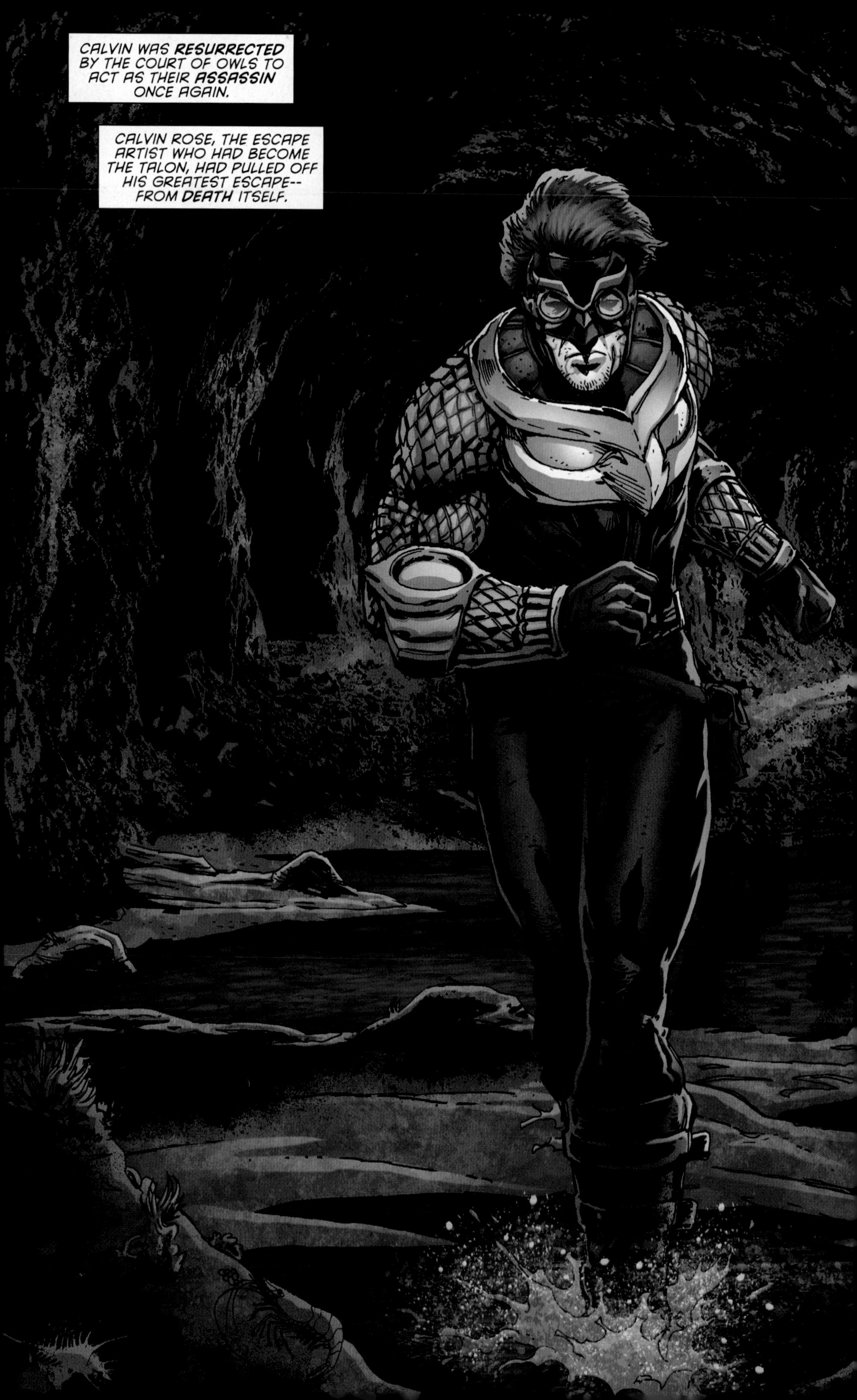
CALVIN WAS RESURRECTED BY THE COURT OF OWLS TO ACT AS THEIR ASSASSIN ONCE AGAIN.
CALVIN ROSE, THE ESCAPE ARTIST WHO HAD BECOME THE TALON, HAD PULLED OFF HIS GREATEST ESCAPE-- FROM DEATH ITSELF.

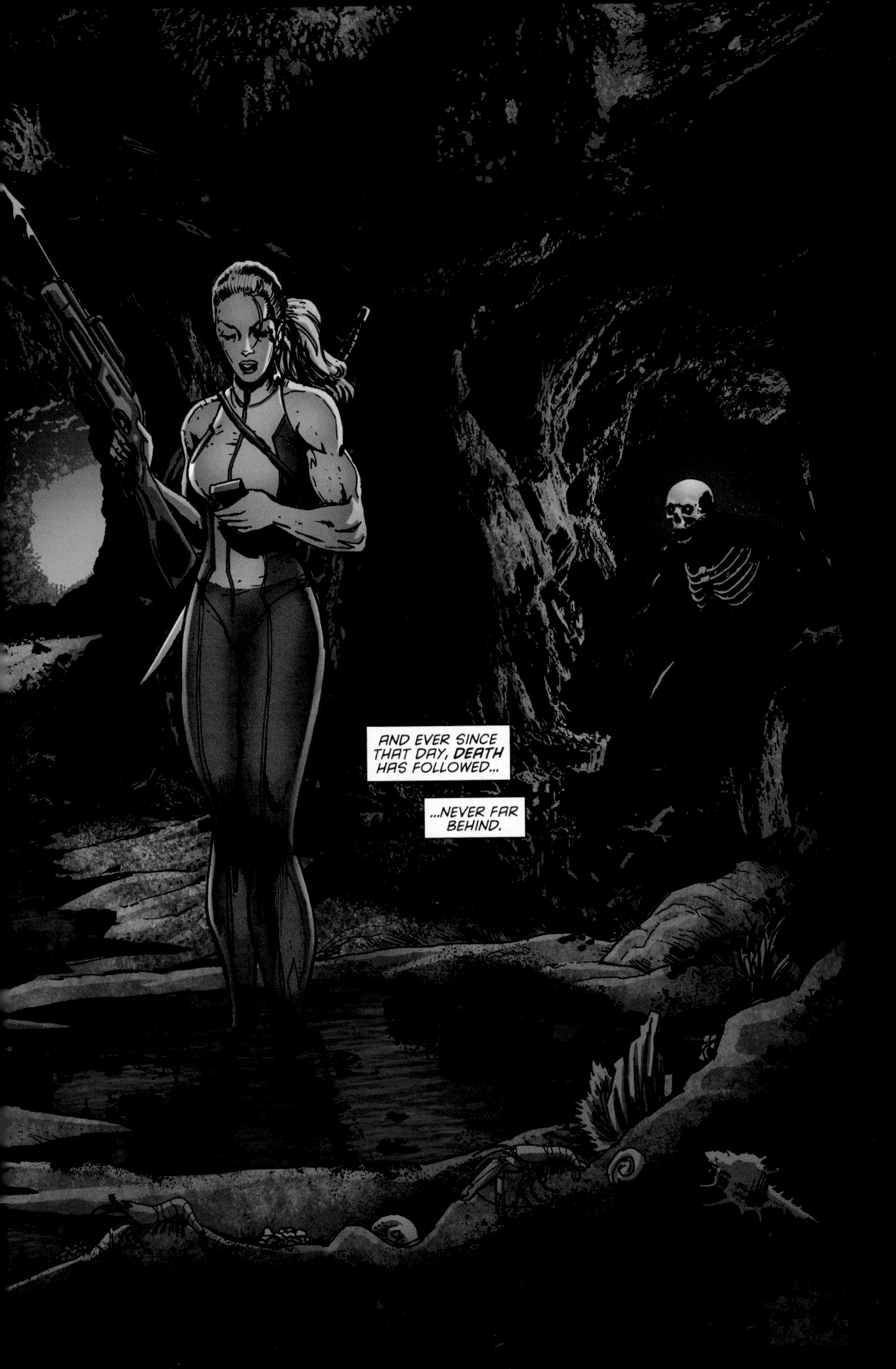
AND EVER SINCE THAT DAY, **DEATH** HAS FOLLOWED...
...NEVER FAR BEHIND.

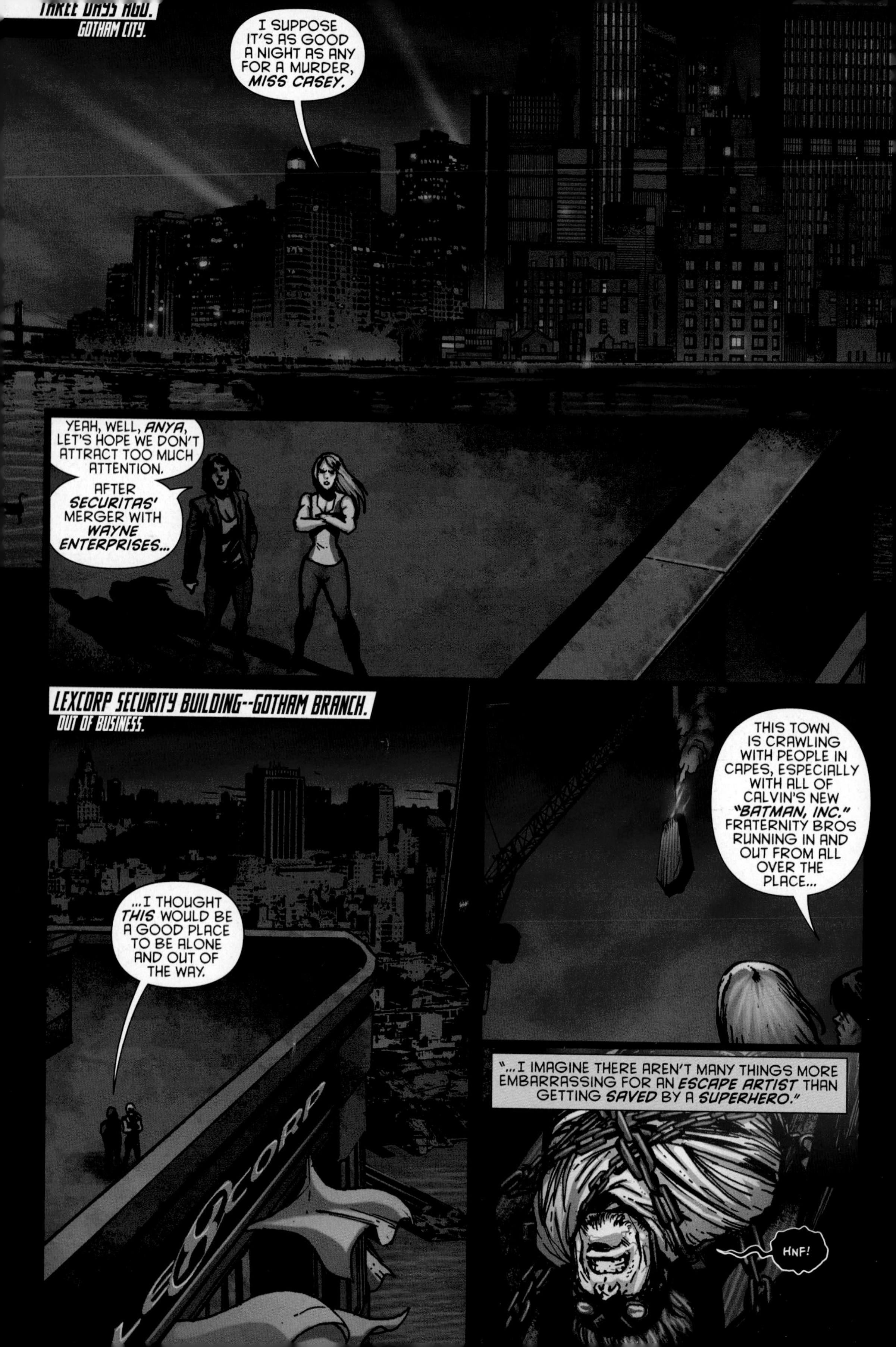
THREE DAYS AGO.
GOTHAM CITY.
I SUPPOSE IT'S AS GOOD A NIGHT AS ANY FOR A MURDER, MISS CASEY.
YEAH, WELL, ANYA, LET'S HOPE WE DON'T ATTRACT TOO MUCH ATTENTION.
AFTER SECURITAS' MERGER WITH WAYNE ENTERPRISES...
LEXCORP SECURITY BUILDING--GOTHAM BRANCH.
OUT OF BUSINESS.
...I THOUGHT THIS WOULD BE A GOOD PLACE TO BE ALONE AND OUT OF THE WAY.
THIS TOWN IS CRAWLING WITH PEOPLE IN CAPES, ESPECIALLY WITH ALL OF CALVIN'S NEW "BATMAN, INC." FRATERNITY BROS RUNNING IN AND OUT FROM ALL OVER THE PLACE...
"...I IMAGINE THERE AREN'T MANY THINGS MORE EMBARRASSING FOR AN ESCAPE ARTIST THAN GETTING SAVED BY A SUPERHERO."
HNF!

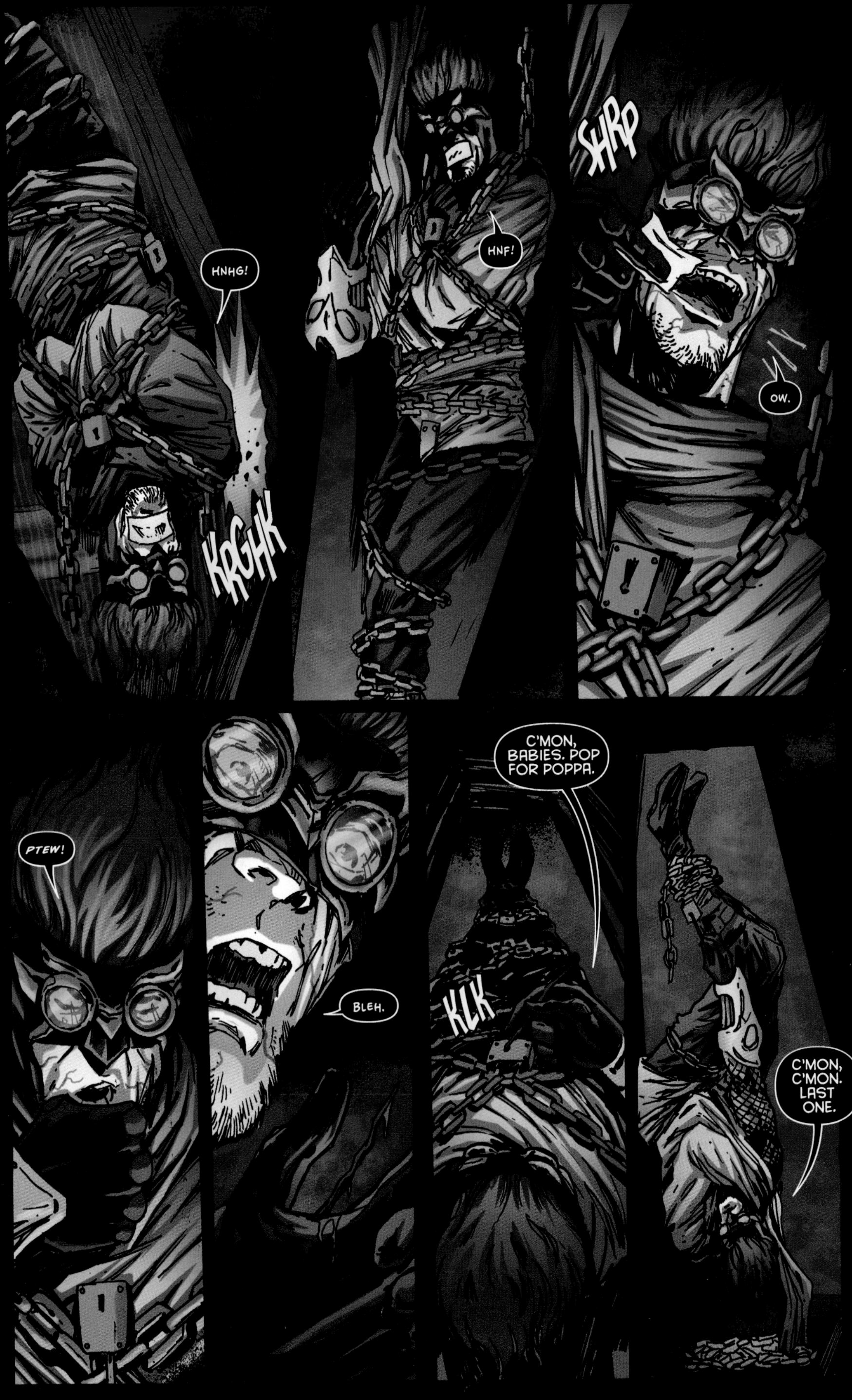
HNHG!
KRGHK
HNF!
SHRP
OW.
PTEW!
BLEH.
C'MON, BABIES. POP FOR POPPA.
KLK
C'MON, C'MON. LAST ONE.

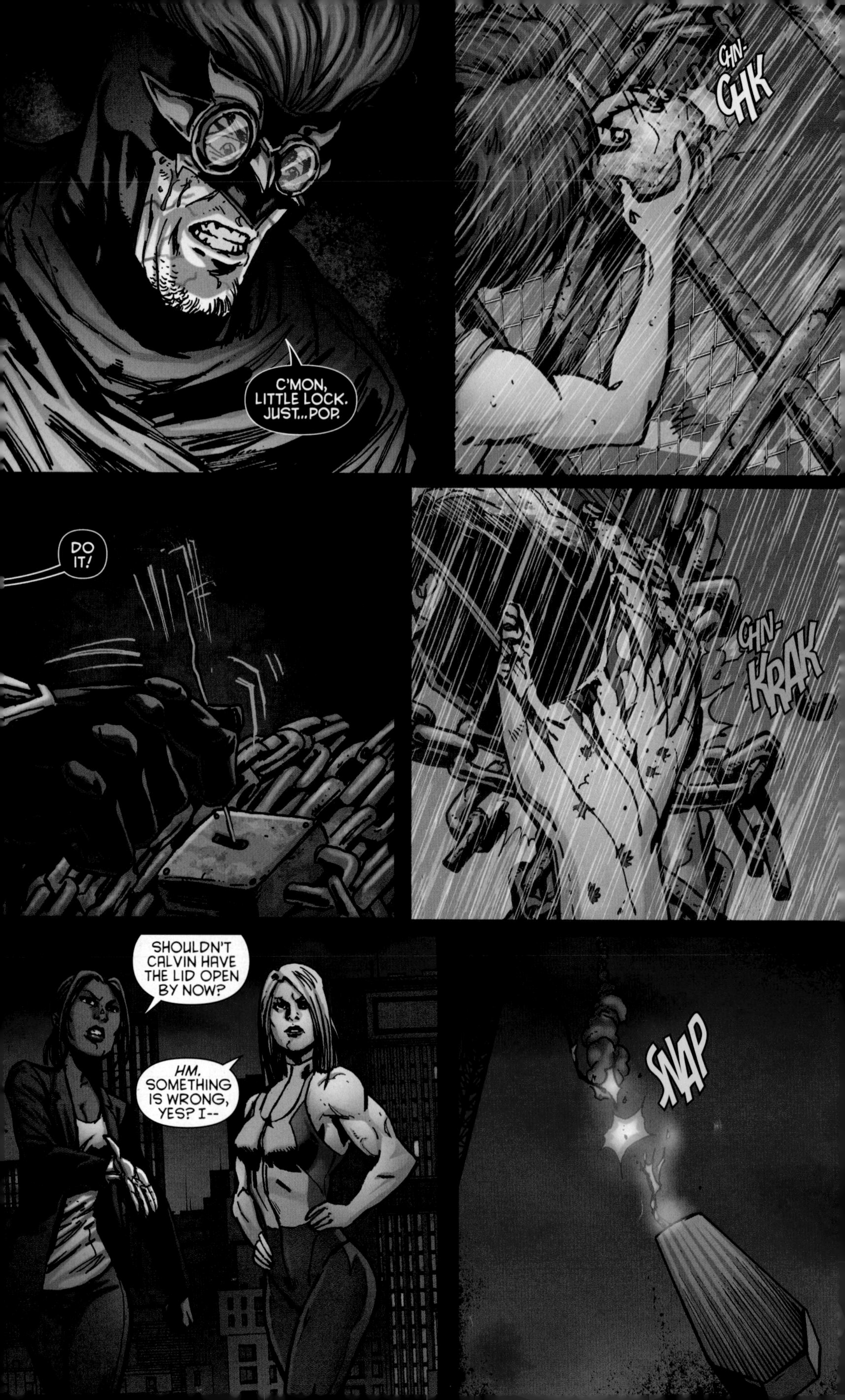

C'MON, LITTLE LOCK. JUST...POP.
CHN-CHK
DO IT!
CHN-KRAK
SHOULDN'T CALVIN HAVE THE LID OPEN BY NOW?
HM. SOMETHING IS WRONG, YES? I--
SNAP

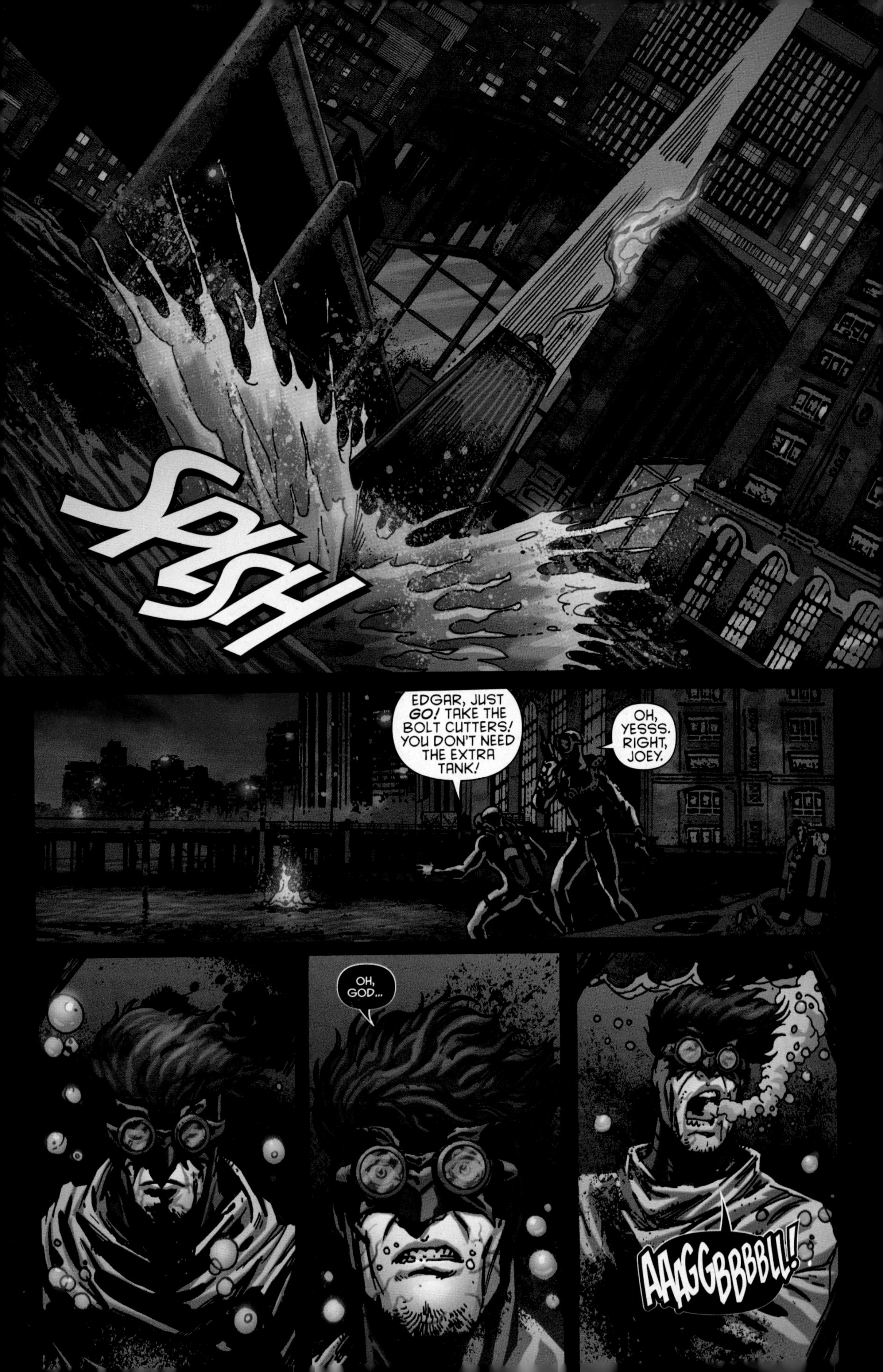
SPLSH
EDGAR, JUST GO! TAKE THE BOLT CUTTERS! YOU DON'T NEED THE EXTRA TANK!
OH, YESSS. RIGHT, JOEY.
OH, GOD...
AAAGGBBBBLL!

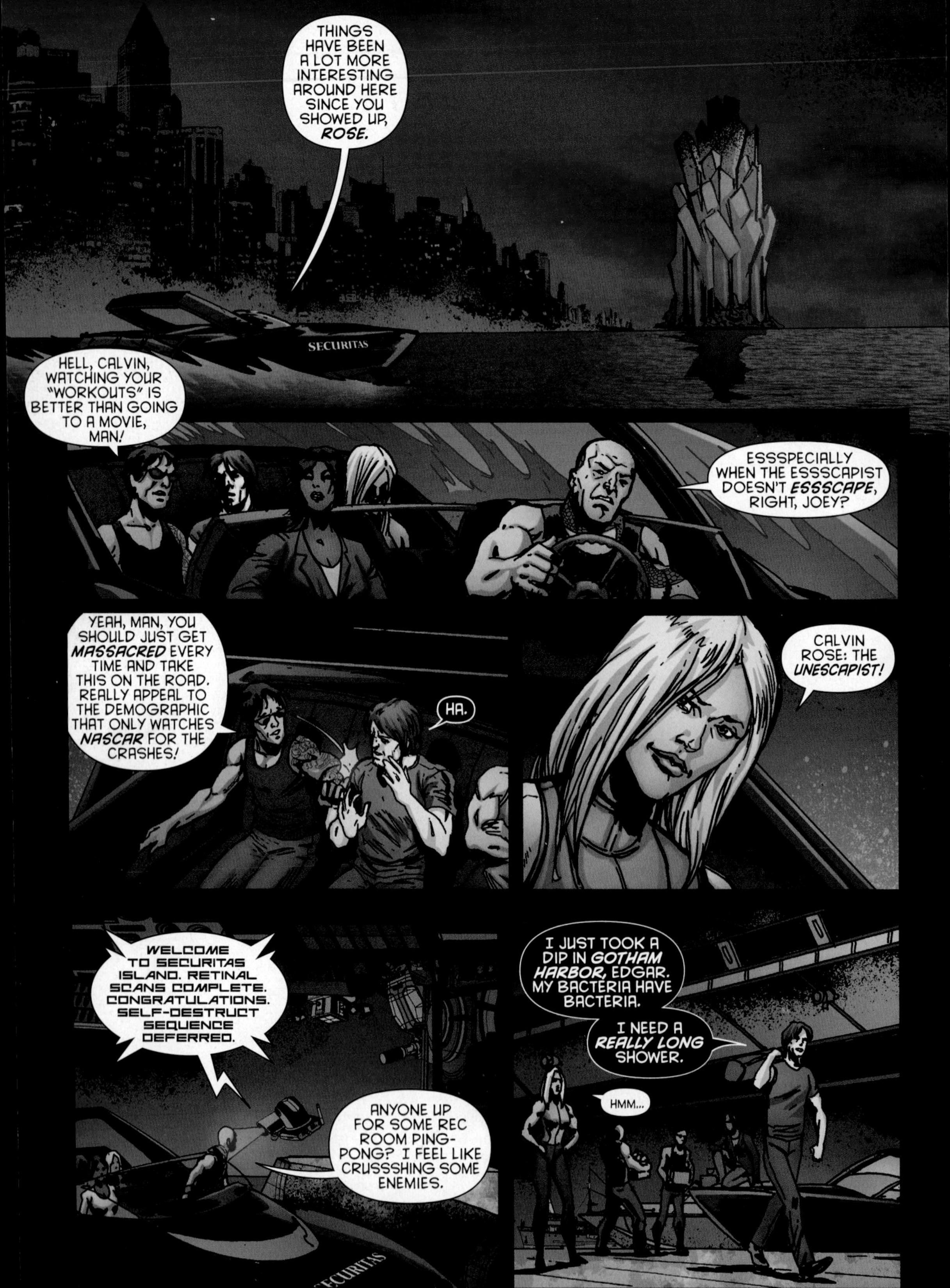
THINGS HAVE BEEN A LOT MORE INTERESTING AROUND HERE SINCE YOU SHOWED UP, ROSE.
SECURITAS
HELL, CALVIN, WATCHING YOUR "WORKOUTS" IS BETTER THAN GOING TO A MOVIE, MAN!
ESSSPECIALLY WHEN THE ESSSCAPIST DOESN'T ESSSCAPE, RIGHT, JOEY?
YEAH, MAN, YOU SHOULD JUST GET MASSACRED EVERY TIME AND TAKE THIS ON THE ROAD. REALLY APPEAL TO THE DEMOGRAPHIC THAT ONLY WATCHES NASCAR FOR THE CRASHES!
HA.
CALVIN ROSE: THE UNESCAPIST!
WELCOME TO SECURITAS ISLAND. RETINAL SCANS COMPLETE. CONGRATULATIONS. SELF-DESTRUCT SEQUENCE DEFERRED.
ANYONE UP FOR SOME REC ROOM PING-PONG? I FEEL LIKE CRUSSSHING SOME ENEMIES.
I JUST TOOK A DIP IN GOTHAM HARBOR, EDGAR. MY BACTERIA HAVE BACTERIA.
I NEED A REALLY LONG SHOWER.
HMM...

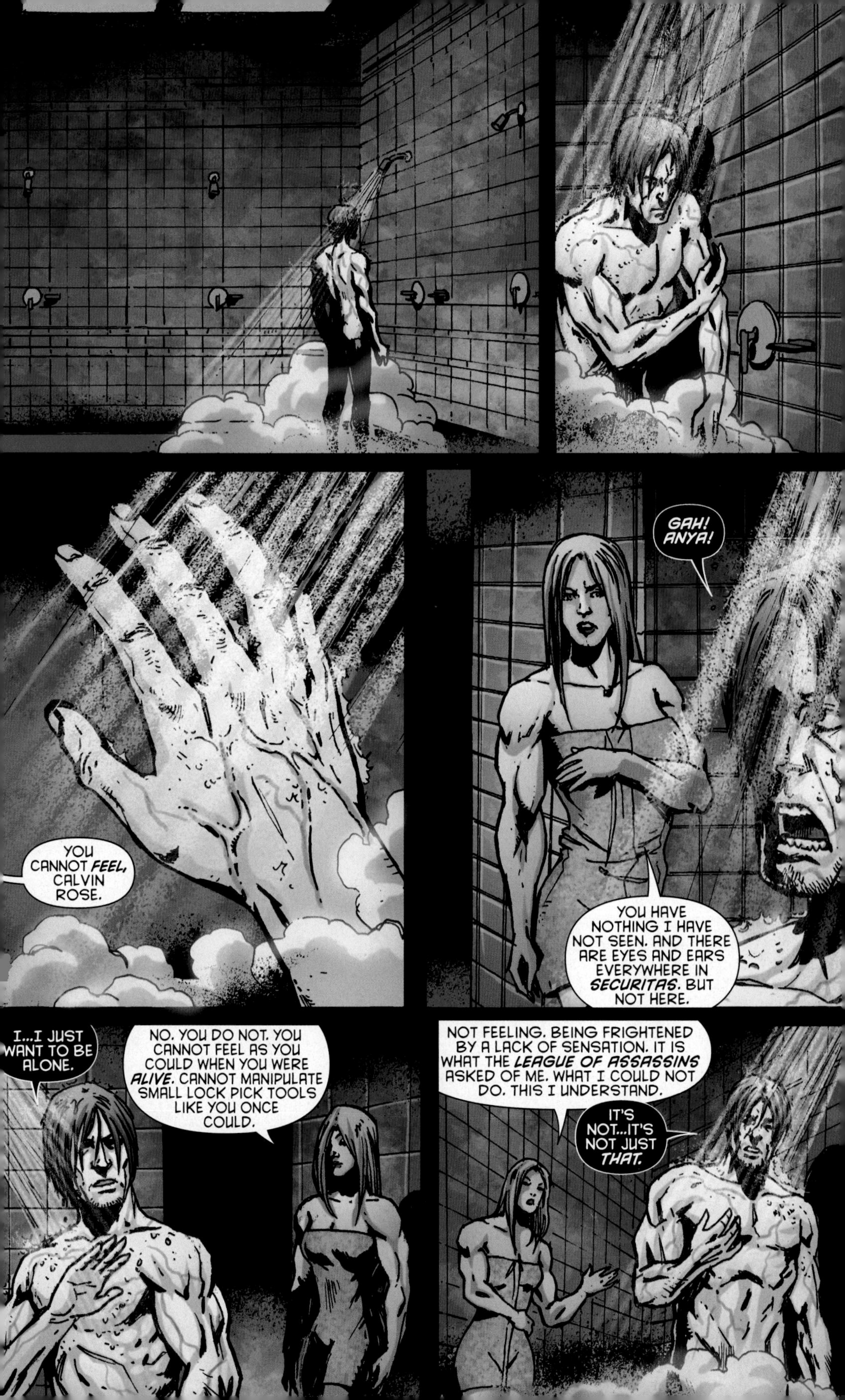
GAH! ANYA!
YOU CANNOT FEEL, CALVIN ROSE.
YOU HAVE NOTHING I HAVE NOT SEEN. AND THERE ARE EYES AND EARS EVERYWHERE IN SECURITAS. BUT NOT HERE.
I...I JUST WANT TO BE ALONE.
NO. YOU DO NOT. YOU CANNOT FEEL AS YOU COULD WHEN YOU WERE ALIVE. CANNOT MANIPULATE SMALL LOCK PICK TOOLS LIKE YOU ONCE COULD.
NOT FEELING. BEING FRIGHTENED BY A LACK OF SENSATION. IT IS WHAT THE LEAGUE OF ASSASSINS ASKED OF ME. WHAT I COULD NOT DO. THIS I UNDERSTAND.
IT'S NOT...IT'S NOT JUST THAT.

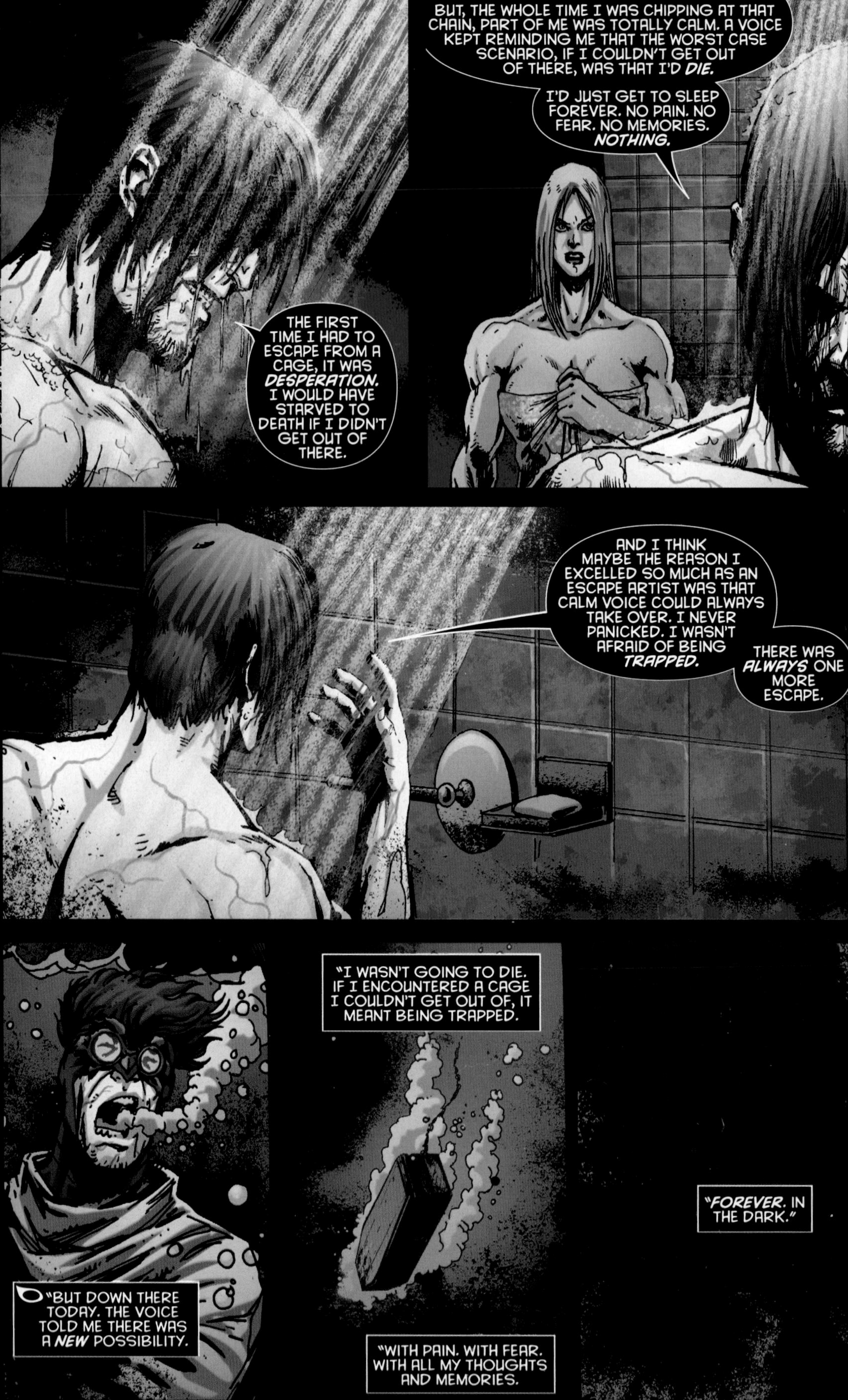
THE FIRST TIME I HAD TO ESCAPE FROM A CAGE, IT WAS DESPERATION. I WOULD HAVE STARVED TO DEATH IF I DIDN'T GET OUT OF THERE.
BUT, THE WHOLE TIME I WAS CHIPPING AT THAT CHAIN, PART OF ME WAS TOTALLY CALM. A VOICE KEPT REMINDING ME THAT THE WORST CASE SCENARIO, IF I COULDN'T GET OUT OF THERE, WAS THAT I'D DIE.
I'D JUST GET TO SLEEP FOREVER. NO PAIN. NO FEAR. NO MEMORIES. NOTHING.
AND I THINK MAYBE THE REASON I EXCELLED SO MUCH AS AN ESCAPE ARTIST WAS THAT CALM VOICE COULD ALWAYS TAKE OVER. I NEVER PANICKED. I WASN'T AFRAID OF BEING TRAPPED.
THERE WAS ALWAYS ONE MORE ESCAPE.
"BUT DOWN THERE TODAY. THE VOICE TOLD ME THERE WAS A NEW POSSIBILITY.
"I WASN'T GOING TO DIE. IF I ENCOUNTERED A CAGE I COULDN'T GET OUT OF, IT MEANT BEING TRAPPED.
"WITH PAIN. WITH FEAR. WITH ALL MY THOUGHTS AND MEMORIES.
"FOREVER. IN THE DARK."

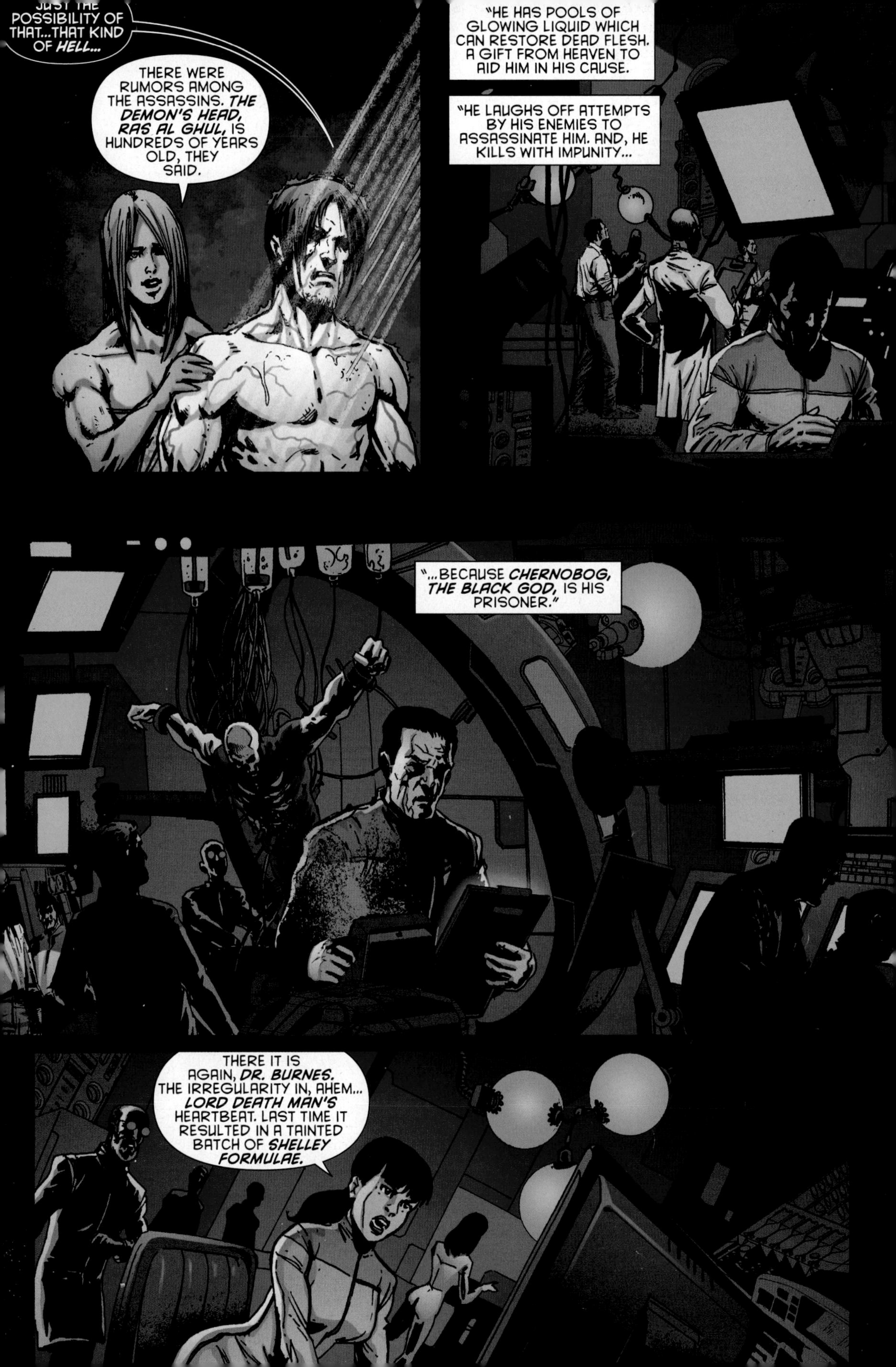
JUST THE POSSIBILITY OF THAT...THAT KIND OF HELL...
THERE WERE RUMORS AMONG THE ASSASSINS. THE DEMON'S HEAD, RAS AL GHUL, IS HUNDREDS OF YEARS OLD, THEY SAID.
"HE HAS POOLS OF GLOWING LIQUID WHICH CAN RESTORE DEAD FLESH. A GIFT FROM HEAVEN TO AID HIM IN HIS CAUSE.
"HE LAUGHS OFF ATTEMPTS BY HIS ENEMIES TO ASSASSINATE HIM. AND, HE KILLS WITH IMPUNITY...
"...BECAUSE CHERNOBOG, THE BLACK GOD, IS HIS PRISONER."
THERE IT IS AGAIN, DR. BURNES. THE IRREGULARITY IN, AHEM... LORD DEATH MAN'S HEARTBEAT. LAST TIME IT RESULTED IN A TAINTED BATCH OF SHELLEY FORMULAE.

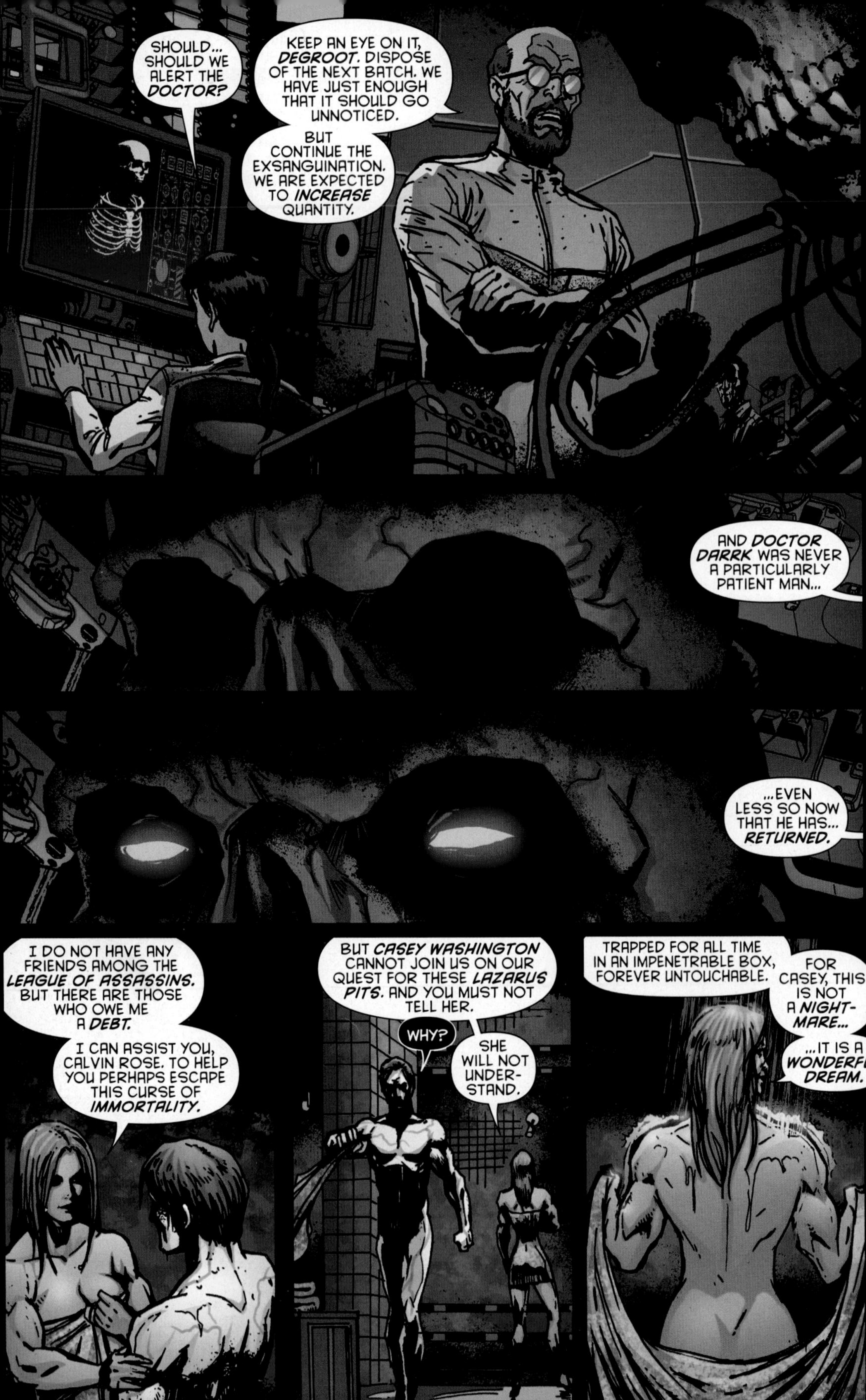

SHOULD... SHOULD WE ALERT THE DOCTOR?
KEEP AN EYE ON IT, DEGROOT. DISPOSE OF THE NEXT BATCH. WE HAVE JUST ENOUGH THAT IT SHOULD GO UNNOTICED.
BUT CONTINUE THE EXSANGUINATION. WE ARE EXPECTED TO INCREASE QUANTITY.
AND DOCTOR DARRK WAS NEVER A PARTICULARLY PATIENT MAN...
...EVEN LESS SO NOW THAT HE HAS... RETURNED.
I DO NOT HAVE ANY FRIENDS AMONG THE LEAGUE OF ASSASSINS. BUT THERE ARE THOSE WHO OWE ME A DEBT.
I CAN ASSIST YOU, CALVIN ROSE. TO HELP YOU PERHAPS ESCAPE THIS CURSE OF IMMORTALITY.
BUT CASEY WASHINGTON CANNOT JOIN US ON OUR QUEST FOR THESE LAZARUS PITS. AND YOU MUST NOT TELL HER.
WHY?
SHE WILL NOT UNDER-STAND.
TRAPPED FOR ALL TIME IN AN IMPENETRABLE BOX, FOREVER UNTOUCHABLE.
FOR CASEY, THIS IS NOT A NIGHT-MARE...
...IT IS A WONDERFUL DREAM.

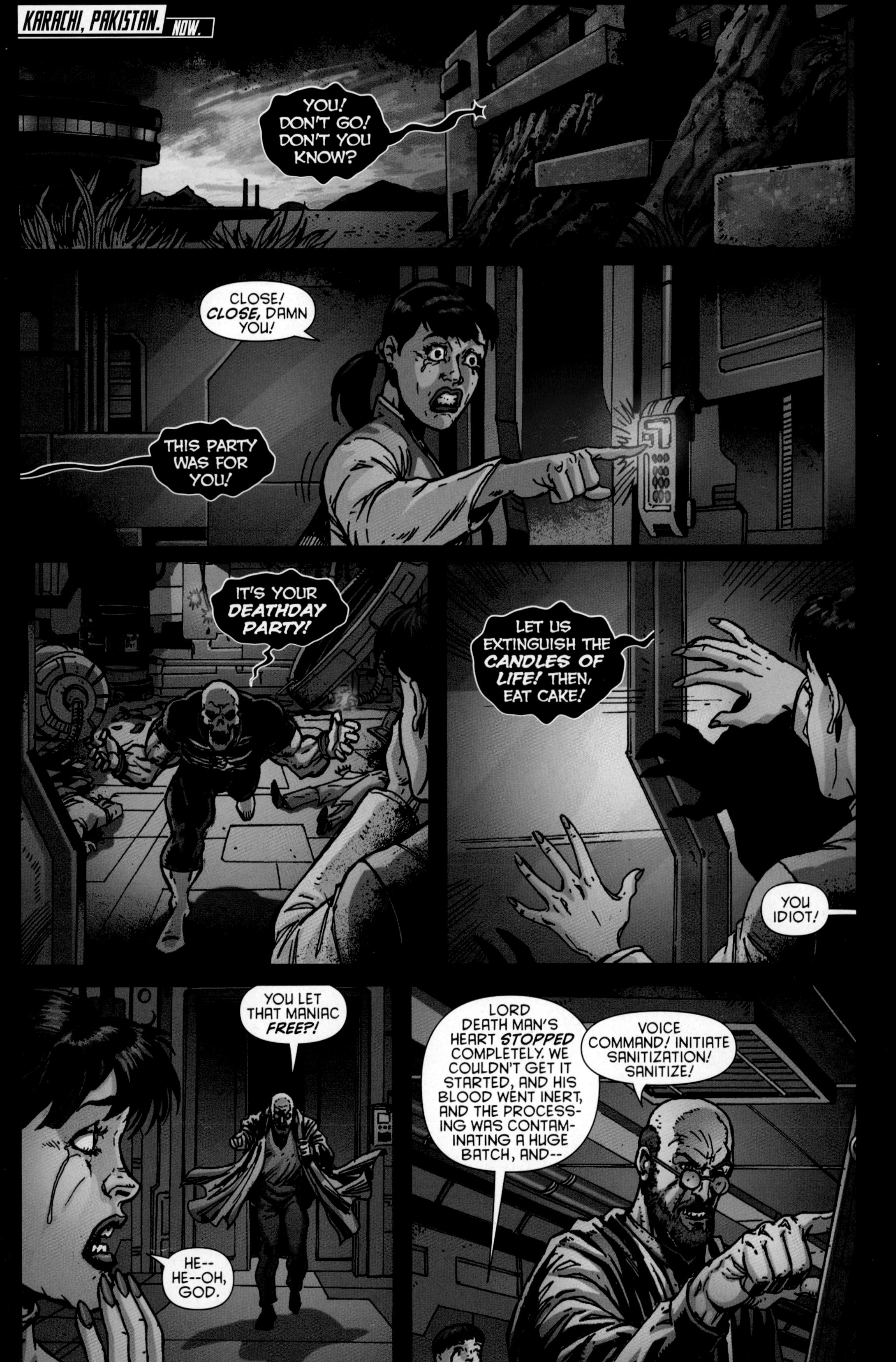
KARACHI, PAKISTAN. NOW.
YOU! DON'T GO! DON'T YOU KNOW?
CLOSE! CLOSE, DAMN YOU!
THIS PARTY WAS FOR YOU!
IT'S YOUR DEATHDAY PARTY!
LET US EXTINGUISH THE CANDLES OF LIFE! THEN, EAT CAKE!
YOU IDIOT!
YOU LET THAT MANIAC FREE?!
HE-- HE--OH, GOD.
LORD DEATH MAN'S HEART STOPPED COMPLETELY. WE COULDN'T GET IT STARTED, AND HIS BLOOD WENT INERT, AND THE PROCESSING WAS CONTAMINATING A HUGE BATCH, AND--
VOICE COMMAND! INITIATE SANITIZATION! SANITIZE!

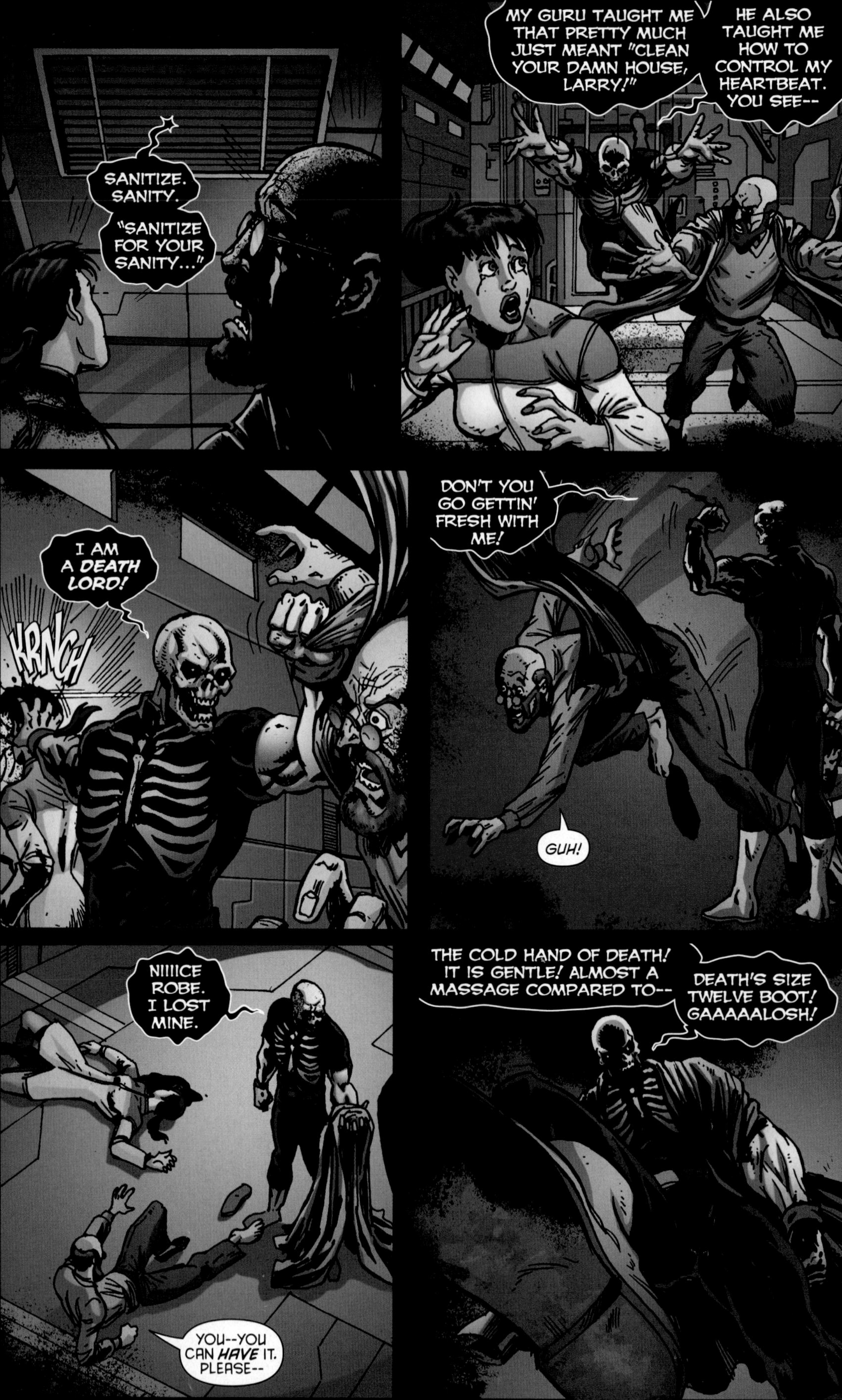
SANITIZE. SANITY.
"SANITIZE FOR YOUR SANITY..."
MY GURU TAUGHT ME THAT PRETTY MUCH JUST MEANT "CLEAN YOUR DAMN HOUSE, LARRY!"
HE ALSO TAUGHT ME HOW TO CONTROL MY HEARTBEAT. YOU SEE--
I AM A *DEATH LORD!*
KRNCH
DON'T YOU GO GETTIN' FRESH WITH ME!
GUH!
NIIIICE ROBE. I LOST MINE.
YOU--YOU CAN *HAVE* IT. PLEASE--
THE COLD HAND OF DEATH! IT IS GENTLE! ALMOST A MASSAGE COMPARED TO--
DEATH'S SIZE TWELVE BOOT! GAAAAALOSH!

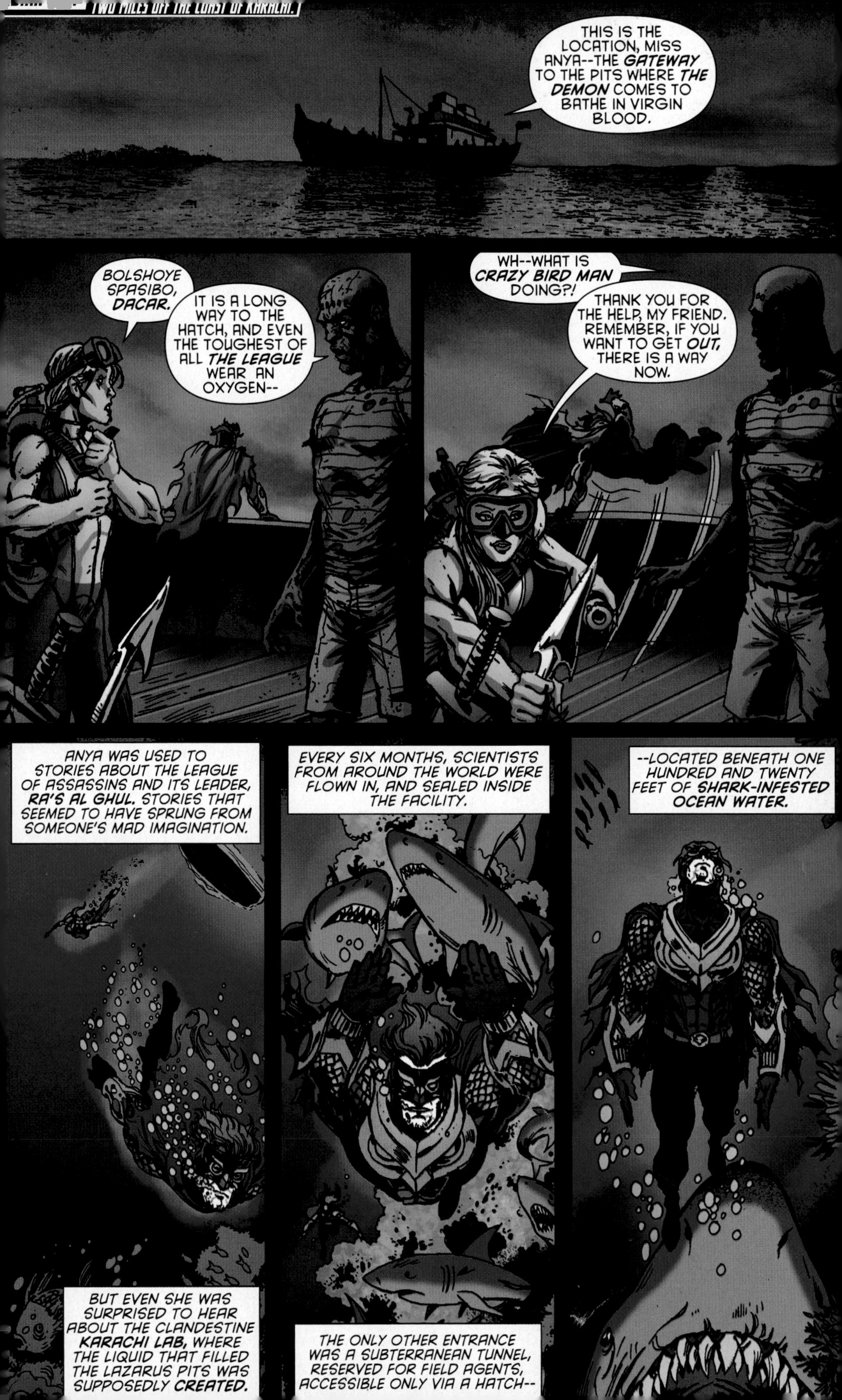
TWO MILES OFF THE COAST OF KARACHI.
THIS IS THE LOCATION, MISS ANYA--THE GATEWAY TO THE PITS WHERE THE DEMON COMES TO BATHE IN VIRGIN BLOOD.
BOLSHOYE SPASIBO, DACAR.
IT IS A LONG WAY TO THE HATCH, AND EVEN THE TOUGHEST OF ALL THE LEAGUE WEAR AN OXYGEN--
WH--WHAT IS CRAZY BIRD MAN DOING?!
THANK YOU FOR THE HELP, MY FRIEND. REMEMBER, IF YOU WANT TO GET OUT, THERE IS A WAY NOW.
ANYA WAS USED TO STORIES ABOUT THE LEAGUE OF ASSASSINS AND ITS LEADER, RA'S AL GHUL. STORIES THAT SEEMED TO HAVE SPRUNG FROM SOMEONE'S MAD IMAGINATION.
BUT EVEN SHE WAS SURPRISED TO HEAR ABOUT THE CLANDESTINE KARACHI LAB, WHERE THE LIQUID THAT FILLED THE LAZARUS PITS WAS SUPPOSEDLY CREATED.
EVERY SIX MONTHS, SCIENTISTS FROM AROUND THE WORLD WERE FLOWN IN, AND SEALED INSIDE THE FACILITY.
THE ONLY OTHER ENTRANCE WAS A SUBTERRANEAN TUNNEL, RESERVED FOR FIELD AGENTS, ACCESSIBLE ONLY VIA A HATCH--
--LOCATED BENEATH ONE HUNDRED AND TWENTY FEET OF SHARK-INFESTED OCEAN WATER.

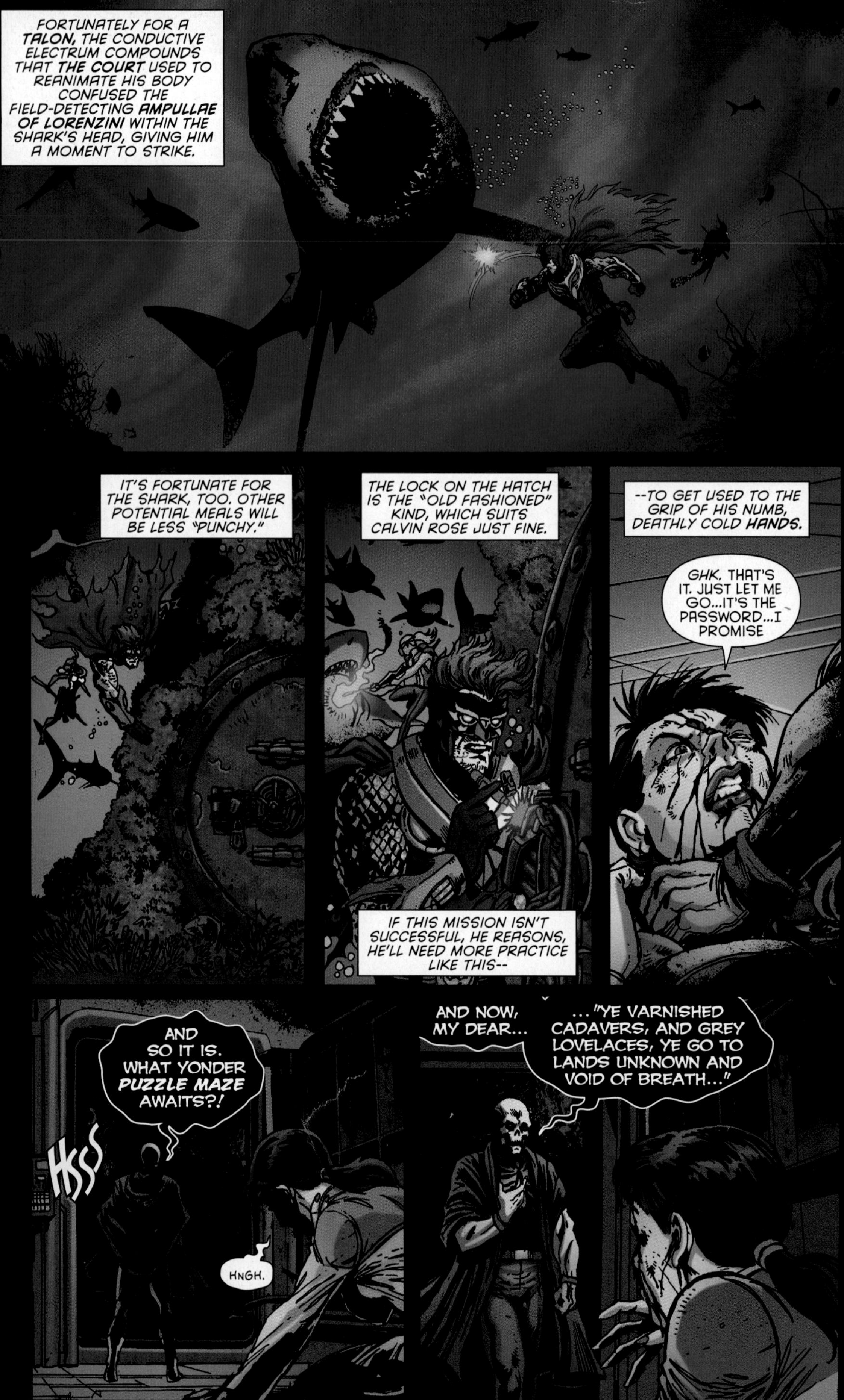
FORTUNATELY FOR A TALON, THE CONDUCTIVE ELECTRUM COMPOUNDS THAT THE COURT USED TO REANIMATE HIS BODY CONFUSED THE FIELD-DETECTING AMPULLAE OF LORENZINI WITHIN THE SHARK'S HEAD, GIVING HIM A MOMENT TO STRIKE.
IT'S FORTUNATE FOR THE SHARK, TOO. OTHER POTENTIAL MEALS WILL BE LESS "PUNCHY."
THE LOCK ON THE HATCH IS THE "OLD FASHIONED" KIND, WHICH SUITS CALVIN ROSE JUST FINE.
IF THIS MISSION ISN'T SUCCESSFUL, HE REASONS, HE'LL NEED MORE PRACTICE LIKE THIS--
--TO GET USED TO THE GRIP OF HIS NUMB, DEATHLY COLD HANDS.
GHK. THAT'S IT. JUST LET ME GO...IT'S THE PASSWORD...I PROMISE
HSSS
AND SO IT IS. WHAT YONDER PUZZLE MAZE AWAITS?!
HNGH.
AND NOW, MY DEAR...
..."YE VARNISHED CADAVERS, AND GREY LOVELACES, YE GO TO LANDS UNKNOWN AND VOID OF BREATH..."

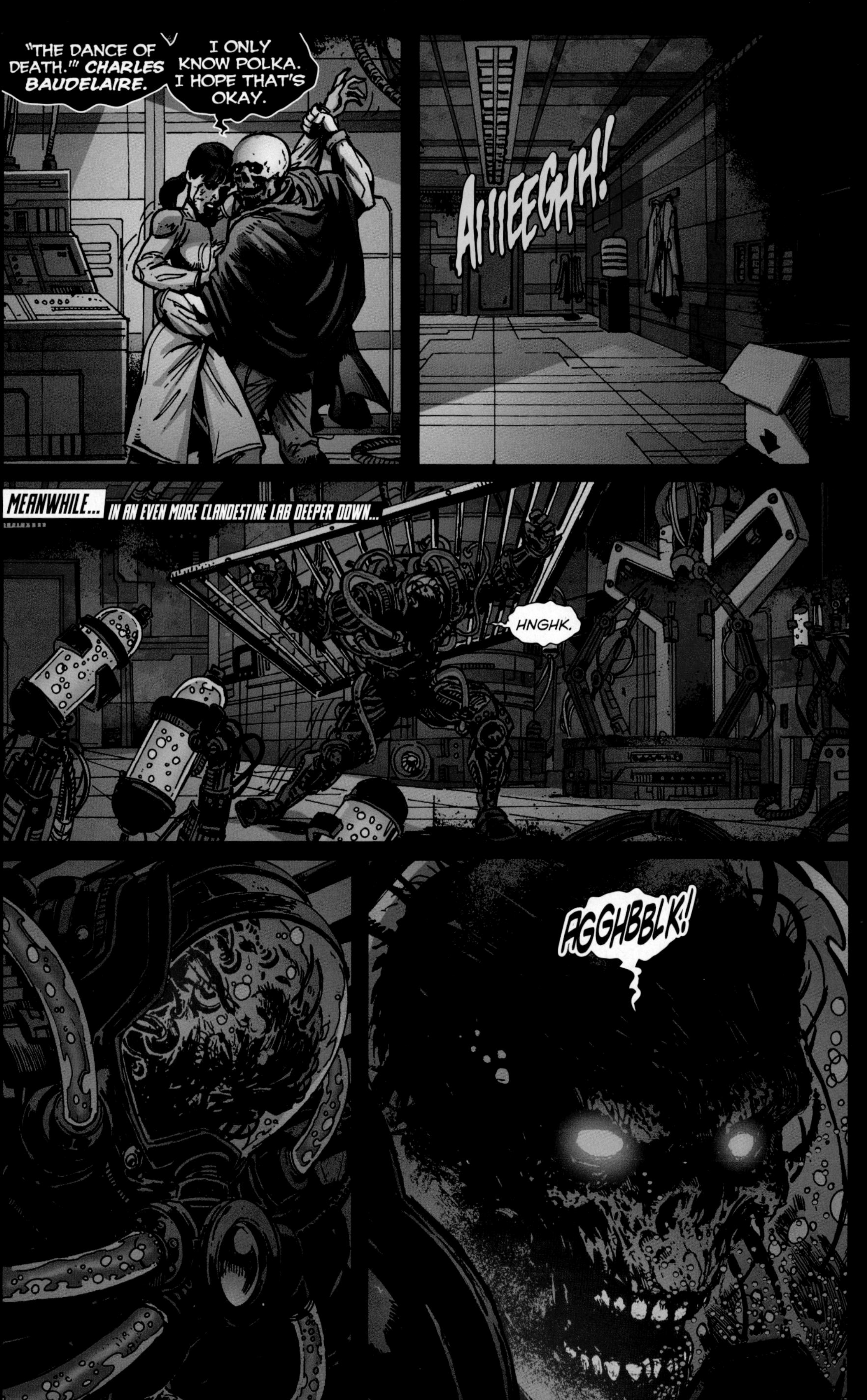
"THE DANCE OF DEATH."' CHARLES BAUDELAIRE.
I ONLY KNOW POLKA. I HOPE THAT'S OKAY.
AIIIEEGHH!
MEANWHILE... IN AN EVEN MORE CLANDESTINE LAB DEEPER DOWN...
HNGHK.
AGGHBBLK!

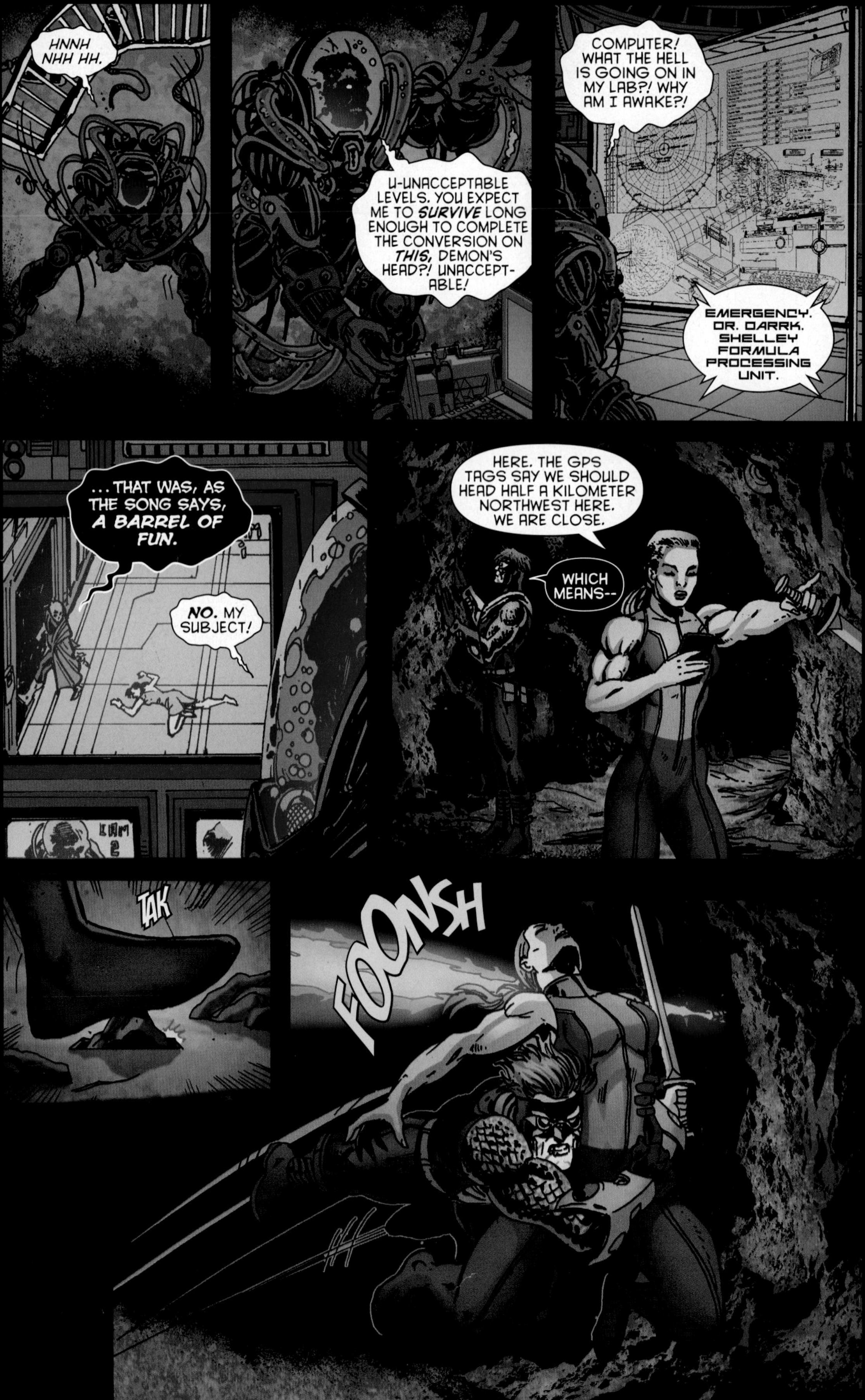
HNNH NHH HH.
U-UNACCEPTABLE LEVELS. YOU EXPECT ME TO SURVIVE LONG ENOUGH TO COMPLETE THE CONVERSION ON THIS, DEMON'S HEAD?! UNACCEPT-ABLE!
COMPUTER! WHAT THE HELL IS GOING ON IN MY LAB?! WHY AM I AWAKE?!
EMERGENCY. DR. DARRK. SHELLEY FORMULA PROCESSING UNIT.
...THAT WAS, AS THE SONG SAYS, A BARREL OF FUN.
NO. MY SUBJECT!
HERE. THE GPS TAGS SAY WE SHOULD HEAD HALF A KILOMETER NORTHWEST HERE. WE ARE CLOSE.
WHICH MEANS--
TAK
FOONSH

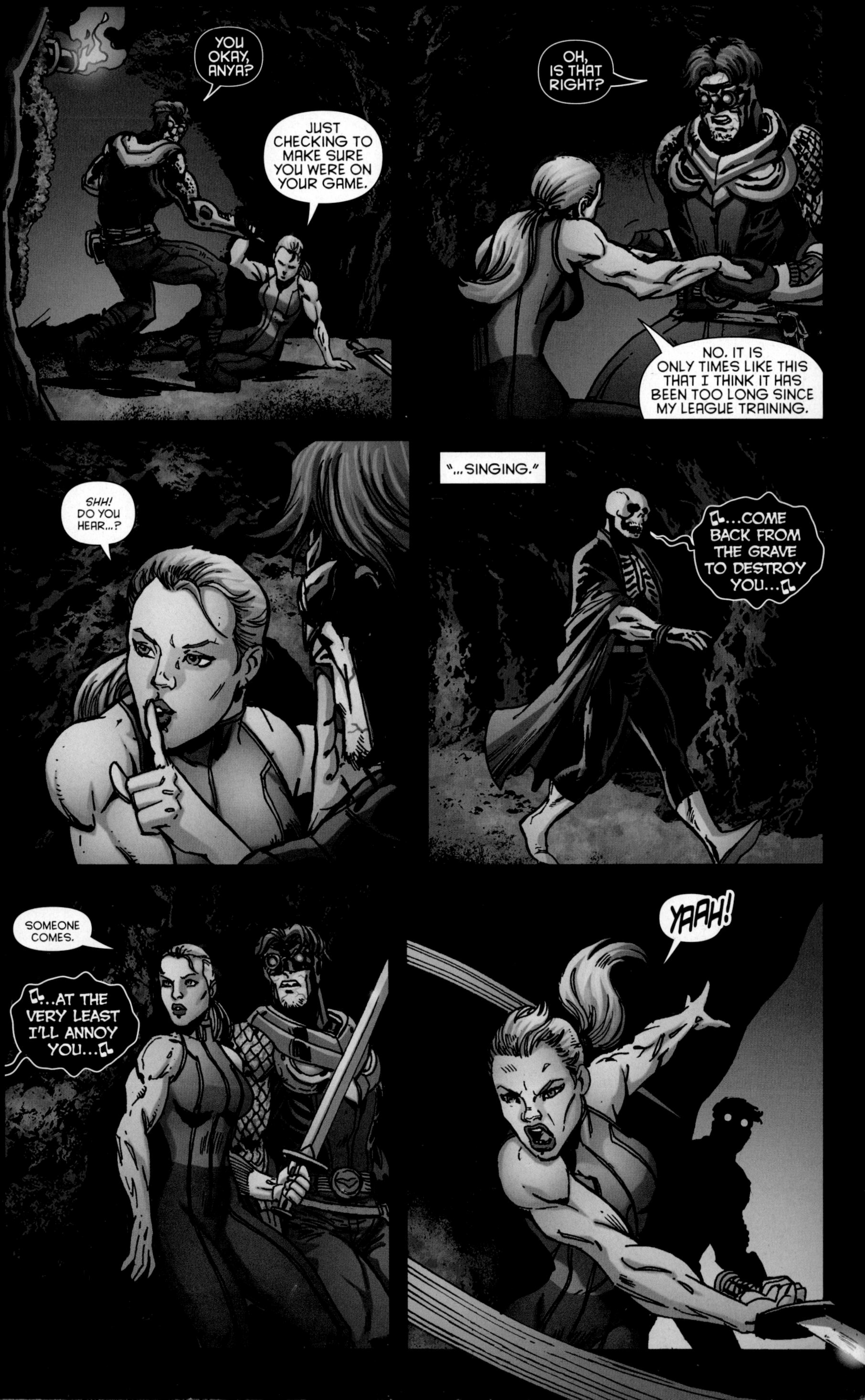
YOU OKAY, ANYA?
JUST CHECKING TO MAKE SURE YOU WERE ON YOUR GAME.
OH, IS THAT RIGHT?
NO. IT IS ONLY TIMES LIKE THIS THAT I THINK IT HAS BEEN TOO LONG SINCE MY LEAGUE TRAINING.
SHH! DO YOU HEAR...?
"...SINGING."
♫...COME BACK FROM THE GRAVE TO DESTROY YOU...♫
SOMEONE COMES.
♫..AT THE VERY LEAST I'LL ANNOY YOU...♫
YAAH!

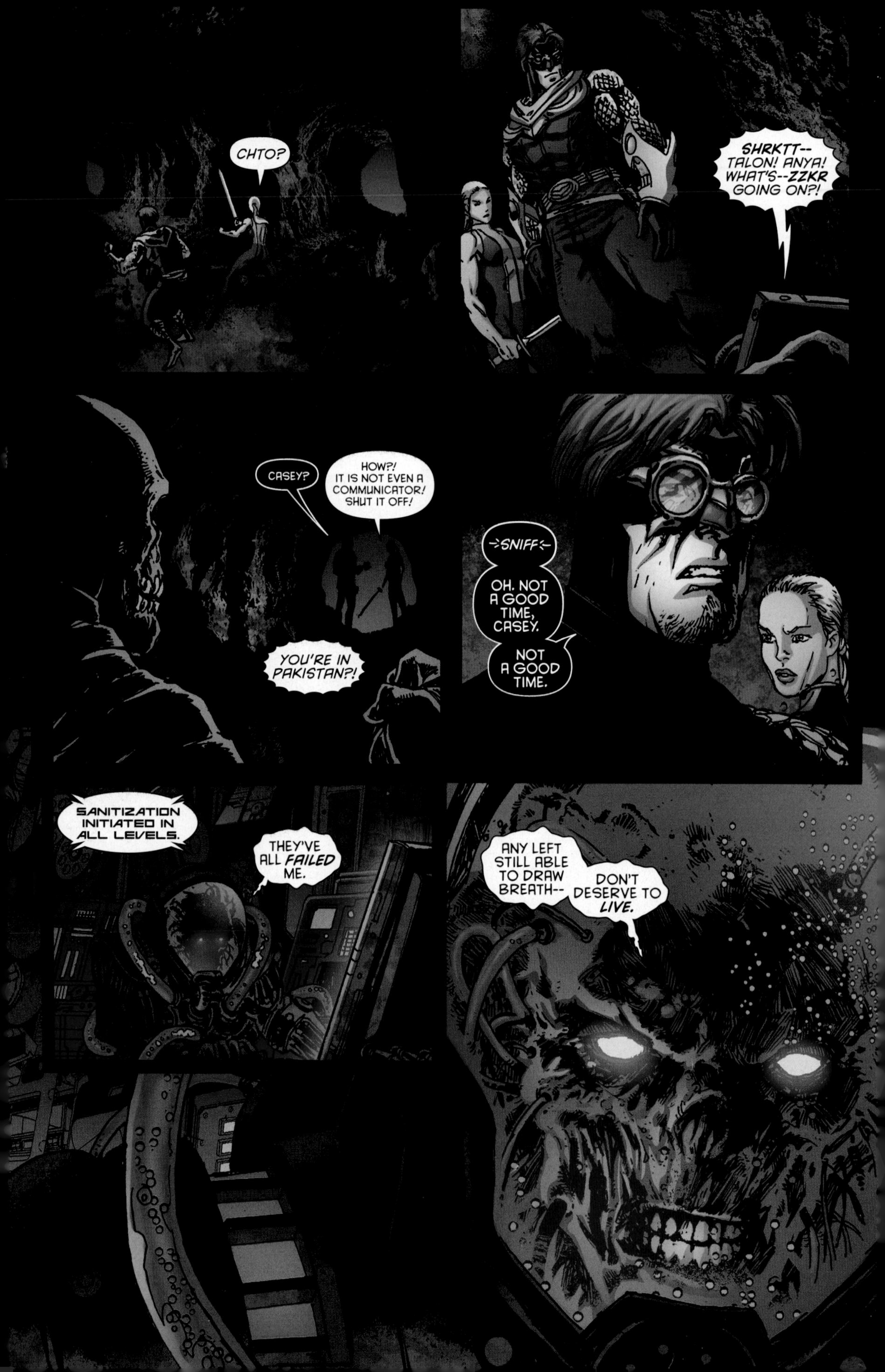
CHTO?
SHRKTT-- TALON! ANYA! WHAT'S--ZZKR GOING ON?!
CASEY?
HOW?! IT IS NOT EVEN A COMMUNICATOR! SHUT IT OFF!
YOU'RE IN PAKISTAN?!
SNIFF
OH. NOT A GOOD TIME, CASEY.
NOT A GOOD TIME.
SANITIZATION INITIATED IN ALL LEVELS.
THEY'VE ALL FAILED ME.
ANY LEFT STILL ABLE TO DRAW BREATH--
DON'T DESERVE TO LIVE.

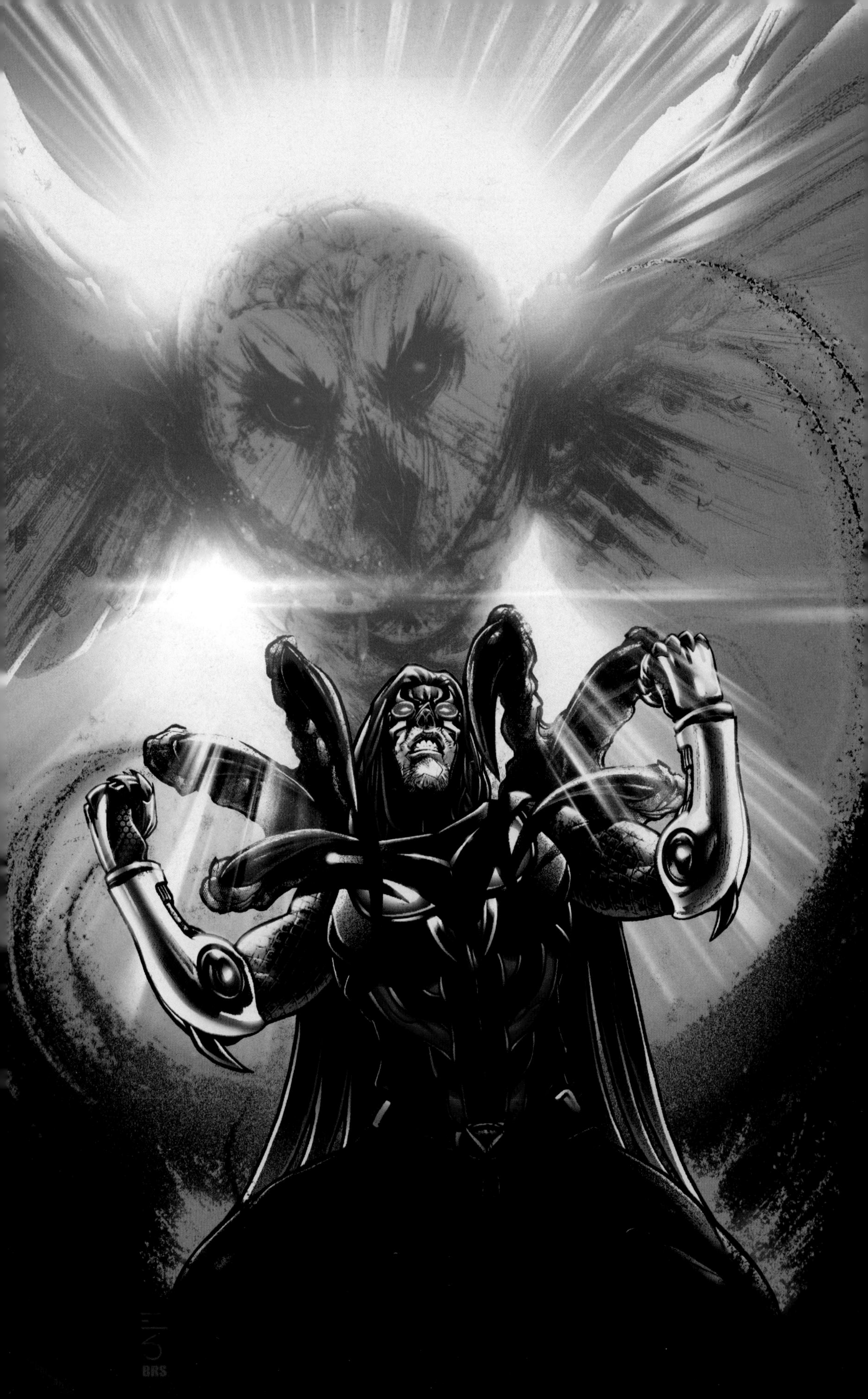
BRS

DEADMAN'S PARTY: PART 2

TIM SEELEY writer **JORGE LUCAS** artist cover art by **EMANUEL SIMEONI & BRETT SMITH**

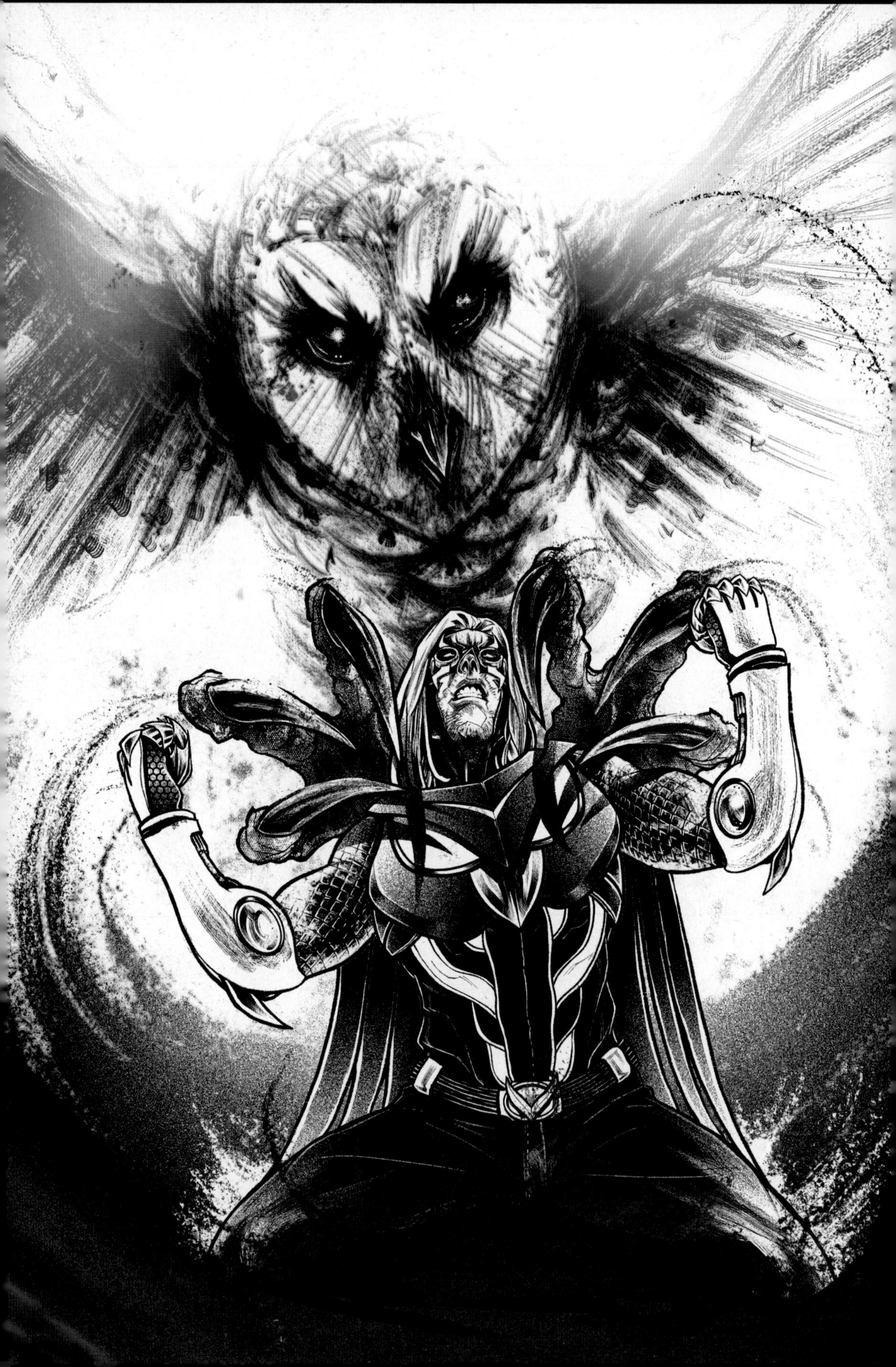

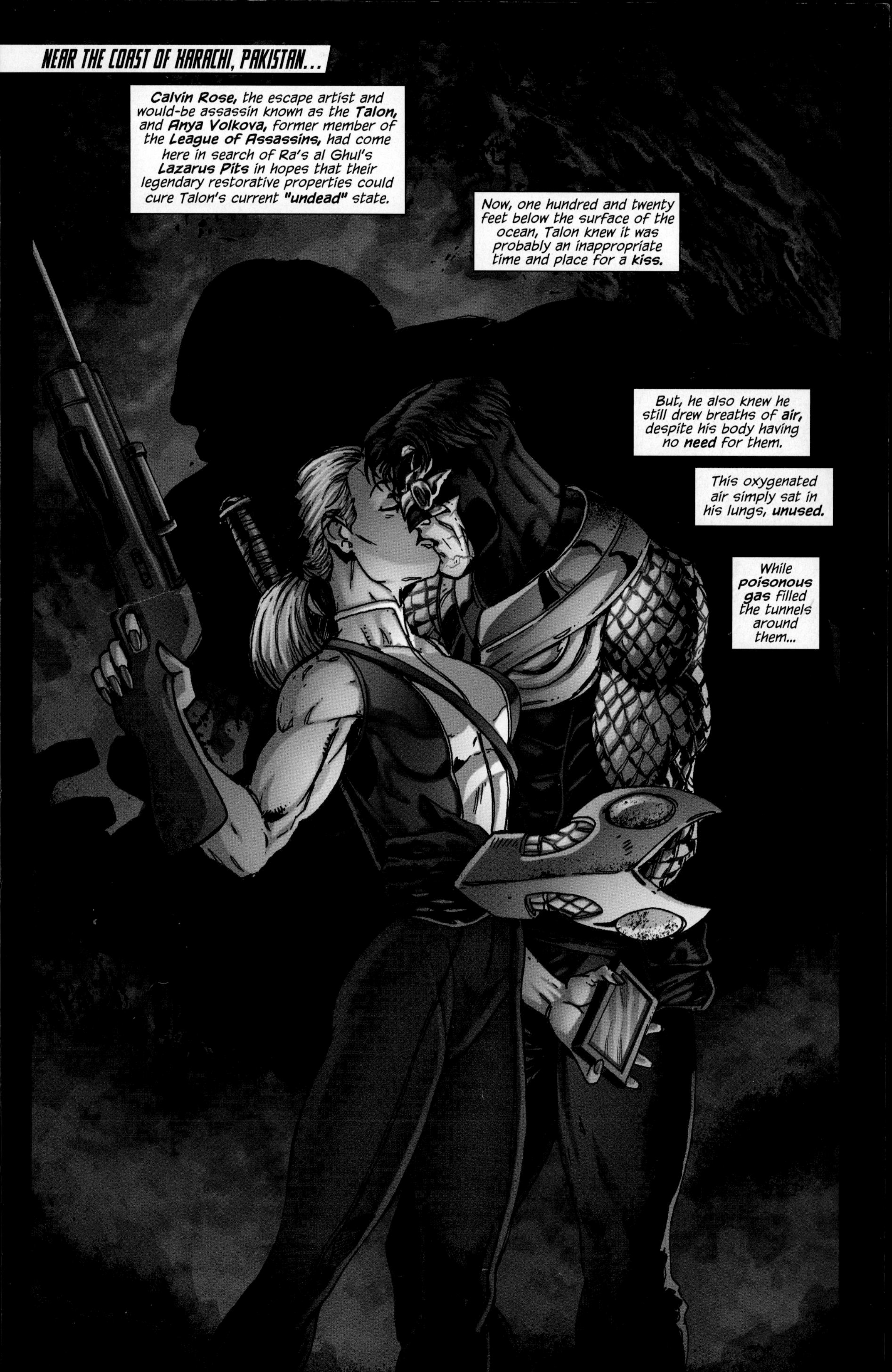
NEAR THE COAST OF KARACHI, PAKISTAN...
Calvin Rose, the escape artist and would-be assassin known as the Talon, and Anya Volkova, former member of the League of Assassins, had come here in search of Ra's al Ghul's Lazarus Pits in hopes that their legendary restorative properties could cure Talon's current "undead" state.
Now, one hundred and twenty feet below the surface of the ocean, Talon knew it was probably an inappropriate time and place for a kiss.
But, he also knew he still drew breaths of air, despite his body having no need for them.
This oxygenated air simply sat in his lungs, unused.
While poisonous gas filled the tunnels around them...

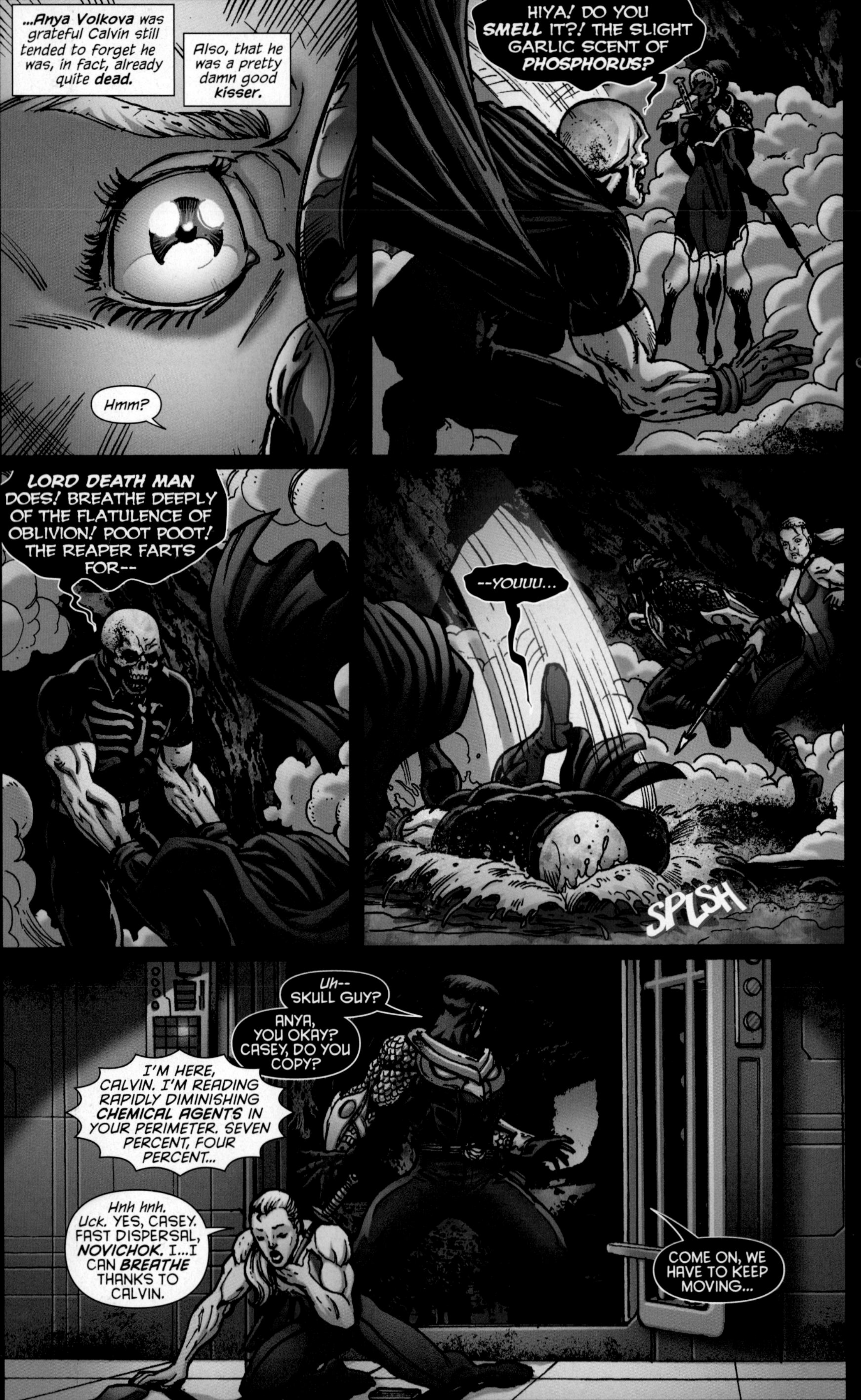

...Anya Volkova was grateful Calvin still tended to forget he was, in fact, already quite dead.
Also, that he was a pretty damn good kisser.
Hmm?
HIYA! DO YOU SMELL IT?! THE SLIGHT GARLIC SCENT OF PHOSPHORUS?
LORD DEATH MAN DOES! BREATHE DEEPLY OF THE FLATULENCE OF OBLIVION! POOT POOT! THE REAPER FARTS FOR--
--YOUUU...
SPLSH
Uh-- SKULL GUY?
ANYA, YOU OKAY? CASEY, DO YOU COPY?
I'M HERE, CALVIN. I'M READING RAPIDLY DIMINISHING CHEMICAL AGENTS IN YOUR PERIMETER. SEVEN PERCENT, FOUR PERCENT...
Hnh hnh. Uck. YES, CASEY. FAST DISPERSAL, NOVICHOK. I...I CAN BREATHE THANKS TO CALVIN.
COME ON, WE HAVE TO KEEP MOVING...

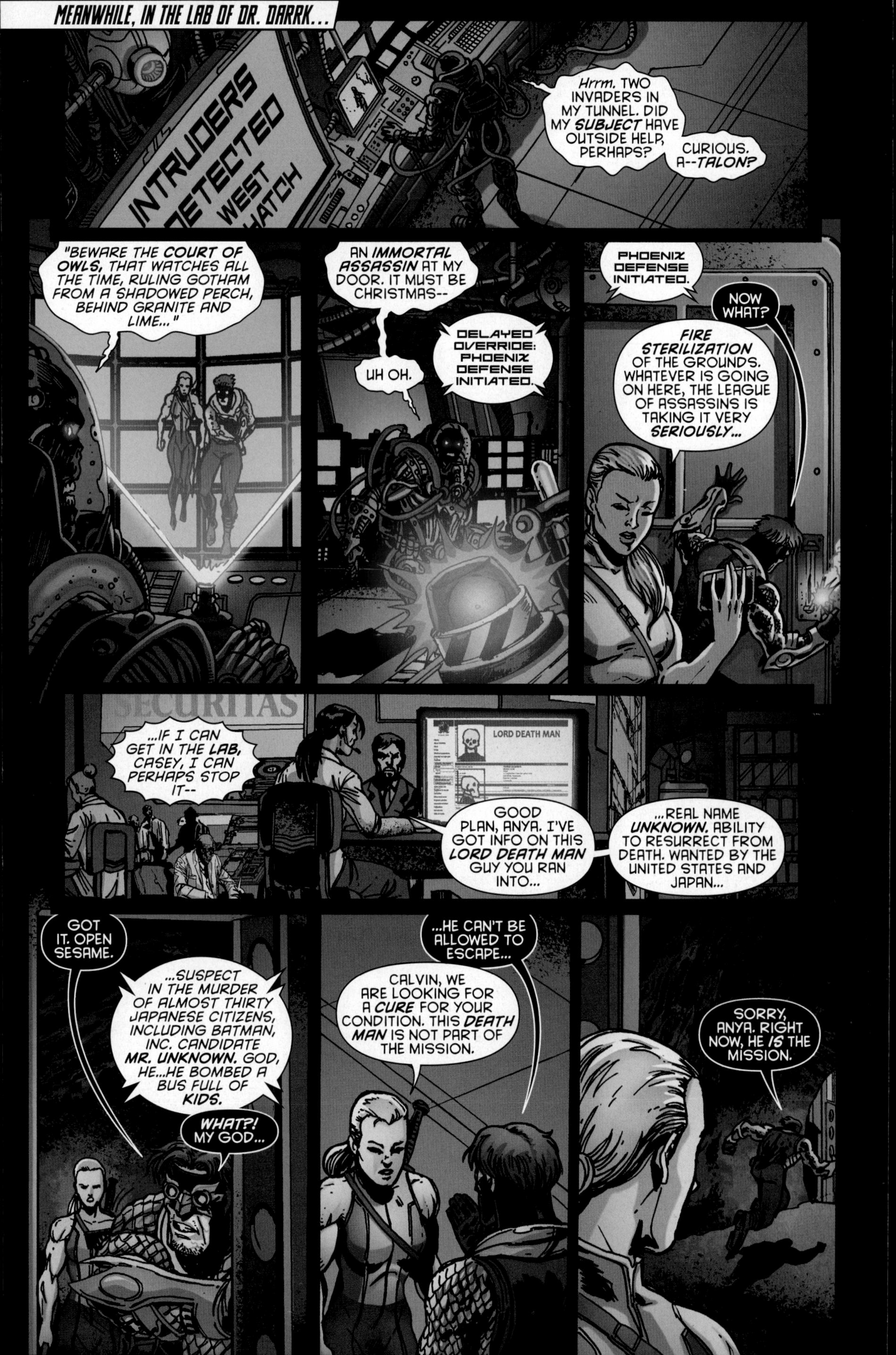
MEANWHILE, IN THE LAB OF DR. DARRK...
INTRUDERS DETECTED WEST HATCH
Hrrm. TWO INVADERS IN MY TUNNEL. DID MY SUBJECT HAVE OUTSIDE HELP, PERHAPS?
CURIOUS. A--TALON?
"BEWARE THE COURT OF OWLS, THAT WATCHES ALL THE TIME, RULING GOTHAM FROM A SHADOWED PERCH, BEHIND GRANITE AND LIME..."
AN IMMORTAL ASSASSIN AT MY DOOR. IT MUST BE CHRISTMAS--
UH OH.
DELAYED OVERRIDE: PHOENIX DEFENSE INITIATED.
PHOENIX DEFENSE INITIATED.
NOW WHAT?
FIRE STERILIZATION OF THE GROUNDS. WHATEVER IS GOING ON HERE, THE LEAGUE OF ASSASSINS IS TAKING IT VERY SERIOUSLY...
SECURITAS
...IF I CAN GET IN THE LAB, CASEY, I CAN PERHAPS STOP IT--
LORD DEATH MAN
GOOD PLAN, ANYA. I'VE GOT INFO ON THIS LORD DEATH MAN GUY YOU RAN INTO...
...REAL NAME UNKNOWN. ABILITY TO RESURRECT FROM DEATH. WANTED BY THE UNITED STATES AND JAPAN...
GOT IT. OPEN SESAME.
...SUSPECT IN THE MURDER OF ALMOST THIRTY JAPANESE CITIZENS, INCLUDING BATMAN, INC. CANDIDATE MR. UNKNOWN. GOD, HE...HE BOMBED A BUS FULL OF KIDS.
WHAT?! MY GOD...
...HE CAN'T BE ALLOWED TO ESCAPE...
CALVIN, WE ARE LOOKING FOR A CURE FOR YOUR CONDITION. THIS DEATH MAN IS NOT PART OF THE MISSION.
SORRY, ANYA. RIGHT NOW, HE IS THE MISSION.

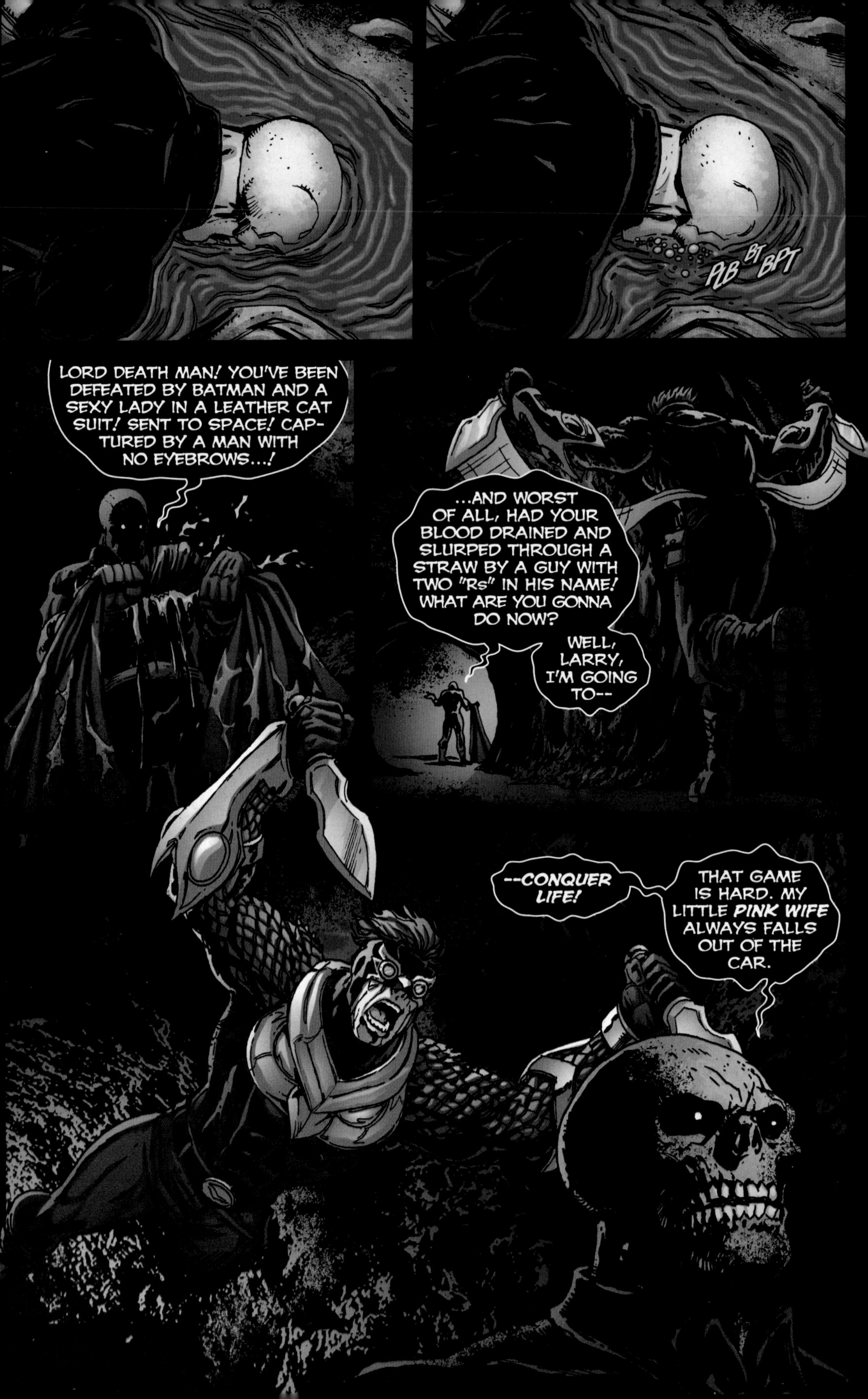
PLB BT BPT
LORD DEATH MAN! YOU'VE BEEN DEFEATED BY BATMAN AND A SEXY LADY IN A LEATHER CAT SUIT! SENT TO SPACE! CAPTURED BY A MAN WITH NO EYEBROWS...!
...AND WORST OF ALL, HAD YOUR BLOOD DRAINED AND SLURPED THROUGH A STRAW BY A GUY WITH TWO "Rs" IN HIS NAME! WHAT ARE YOU GONNA DO NOW?
WELL, LARRY, I'M GOING TO--
--CONQUER LIFE!
THAT GAME IS HARD. MY LITTLE PINK WIFE ALWAYS FALLS OUT OF THE CAR.

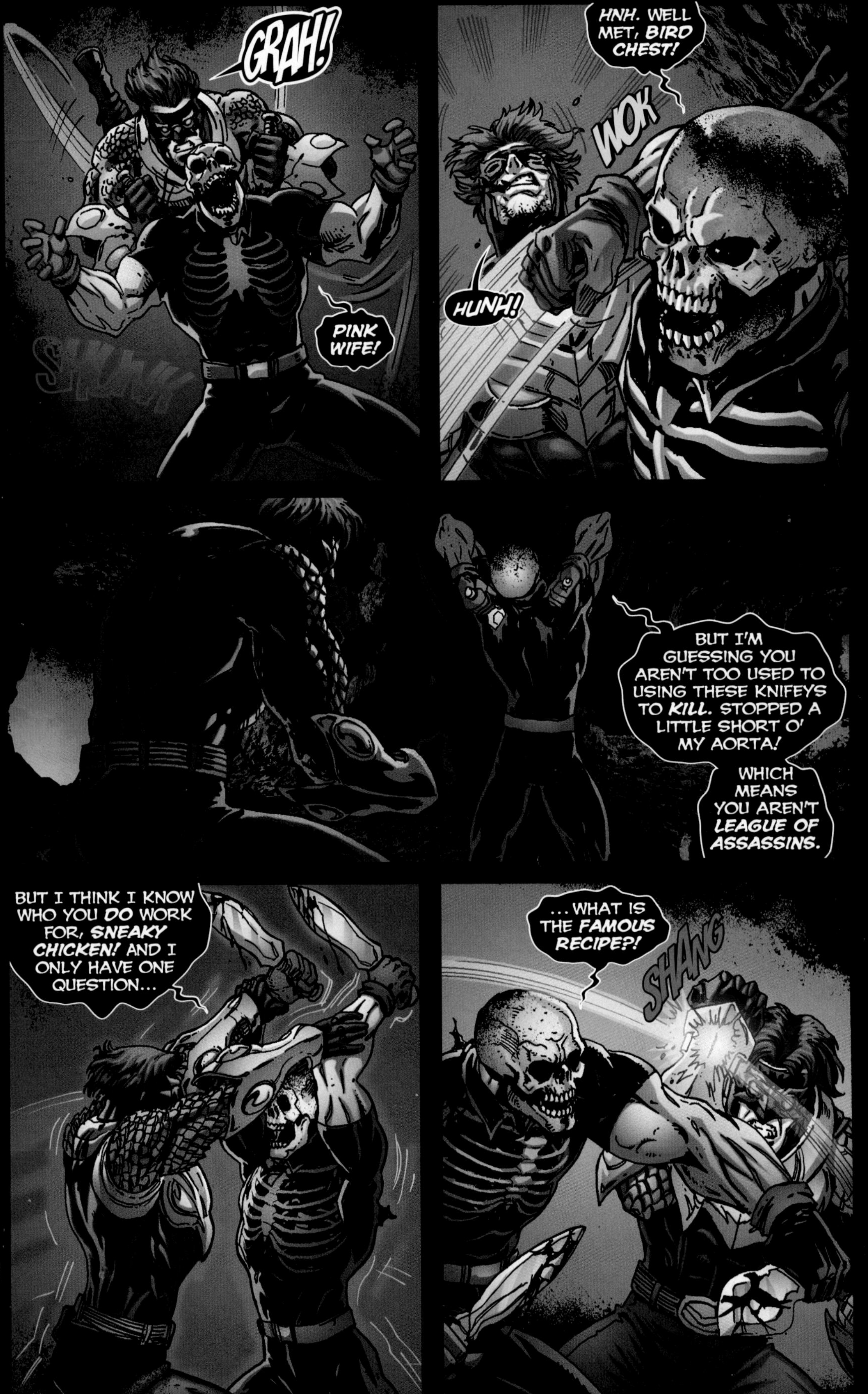
GRAH!
PINK WIFE!
SHUNK
HNH. WELL MET, BIRD CHEST!
WOK
HUNH!
BUT I'M GUESSING YOU AREN'T TOO USED TO USING THESE KNIFEYS TO KILL. STOPPED A LITTLE SHORT O' MY AORTA!
WHICH MEANS YOU AREN'T LEAGUE OF ASSASSINS.
BUT I THINK I KNOW WHO YOU DO WORK FOR, SNEAKY CHICKEN! AND I ONLY HAVE ONE QUESTION...
...WHAT IS THE FAMOUS RECIPE?!
SHANG

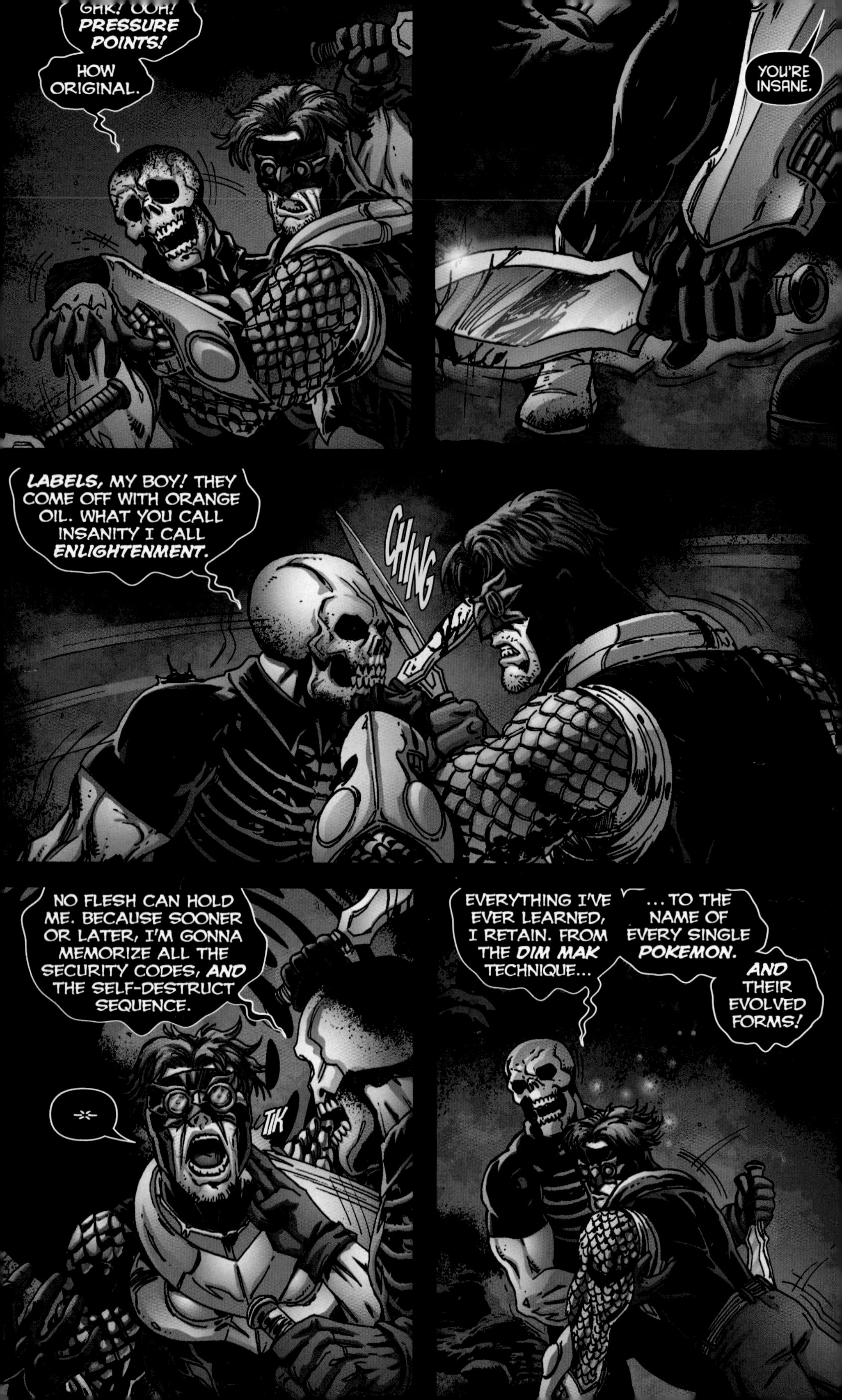
GHK! OOH! PRESSURE POINTS!
HOW ORIGINAL.
YOU'RE INSANE.
LABELS, MY BOY! THEY COME OFF WITH ORANGE OIL. WHAT YOU CALL INSANITY I CALL ENLIGHTENMENT.
CHING
NO FLESH CAN HOLD ME. BECAUSE SOONER OR LATER, I'M GONNA MEMORIZE ALL THE SECURITY CODES, AND THE SELF-DESTRUCT SEQUENCE.
TIK
EVERYTHING I'VE EVER LEARNED, I RETAIN. FROM THE DIM MAK TECHNIQUE...
...TO THE NAME OF EVERY SINGLE POKEMON.
AND THEIR EVOLVED FORMS!

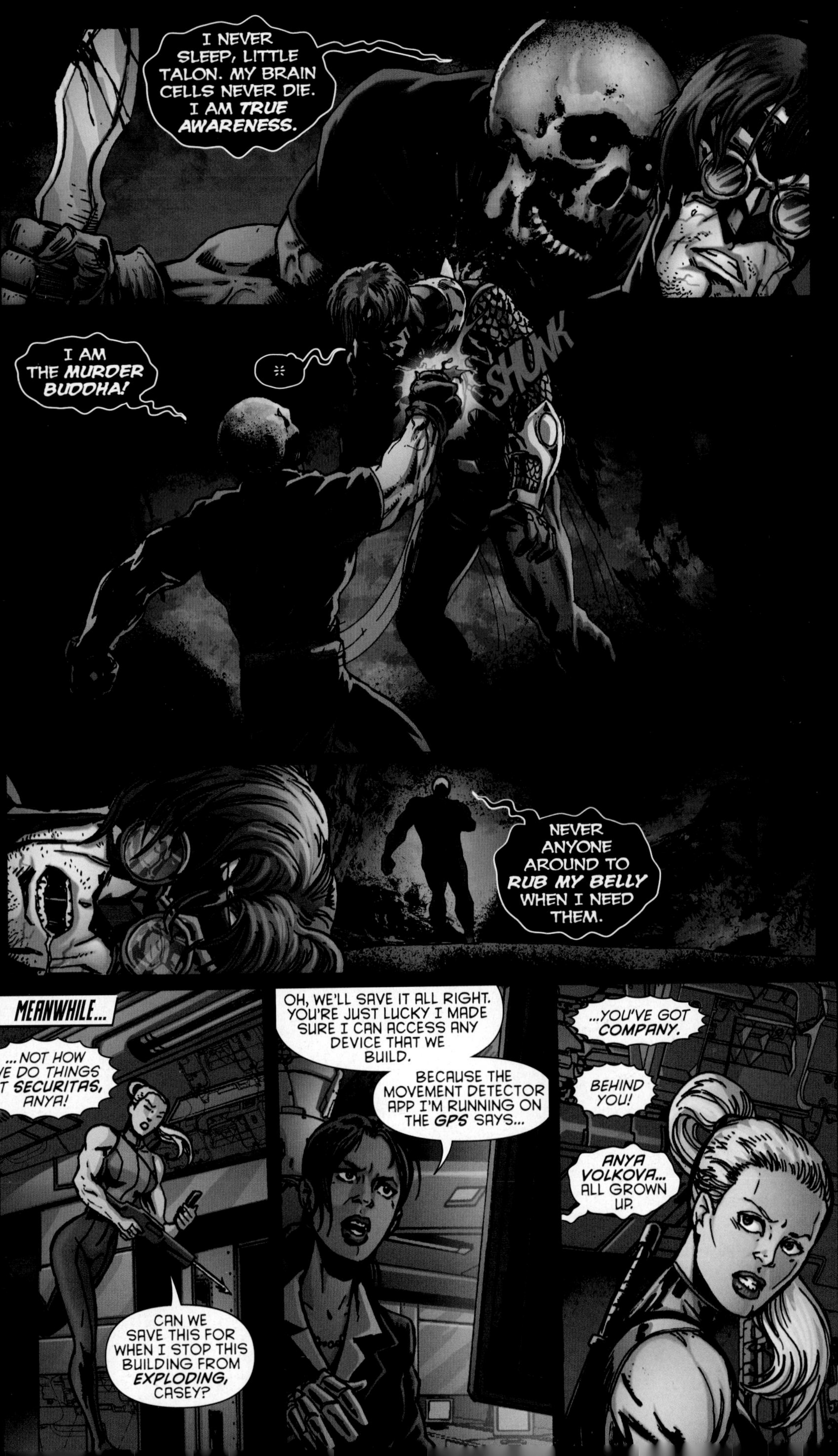

I NEVER SLEEP, LITTLE TALON. MY BRAIN CELLS NEVER DIE. I AM TRUE AWARENESS.
I AM THE MURDER BUDDHA!
SHUNK
NEVER ANYONE AROUND TO RUB MY BELLY WHEN I NEED THEM.
MEANWHILE...
...NOT HOW WE DO THINGS AT SECURITAS, ANYA!
CAN WE SAVE THIS FOR WHEN I STOP THIS BUILDING FROM EXPLODING, CASEY?
OH, WE'LL SAVE IT ALL RIGHT. YOU'RE JUST LUCKY I MADE SURE I CAN ACCESS ANY DEVICE THAT WE BUILD.
BECAUSE THE MOVEMENT DETECTOR APP I'M RUNNING ON THE GPS SAYS...
...YOU'VE GOT COMPANY.
BEHIND YOU!
ANYA VOLKOVA... ALL GROWN UP.

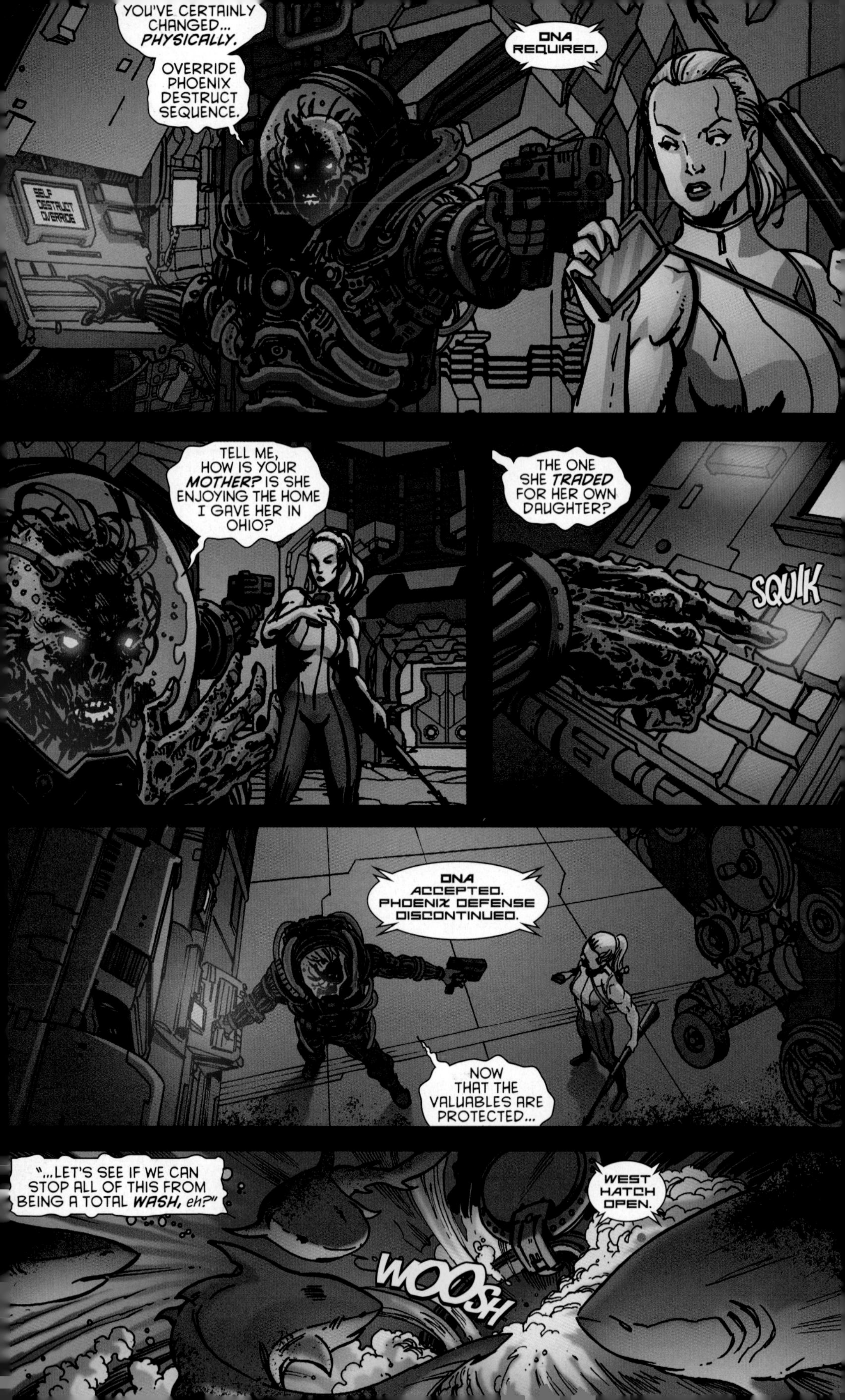

YOU'VE CERTAINLY CHANGED... *PHYSICALLY.*
OVERRIDE PHOENIX DESTRUCT SEQUENCE.
SELF DESTRUCT OVERRIDE
DNA REQUIRED.
TELL ME, HOW IS YOUR *MOTHER?* IS SHE ENJOYING THE HOME I GAVE HER IN OHIO?
THE ONE SHE *TRADED* FOR HER OWN DAUGHTER?
SQUIK
DNA ACCEPTED. PHOENIX DEFENSE DISCONTINUED.
NOW THAT THE VALUABLES ARE PROTECTED...
"...LET'S SEE IF WE CAN STOP ALL OF THIS FROM BEING A TOTAL *WASH,* eh?"
WEST HATCH OPEN.
WOOSH

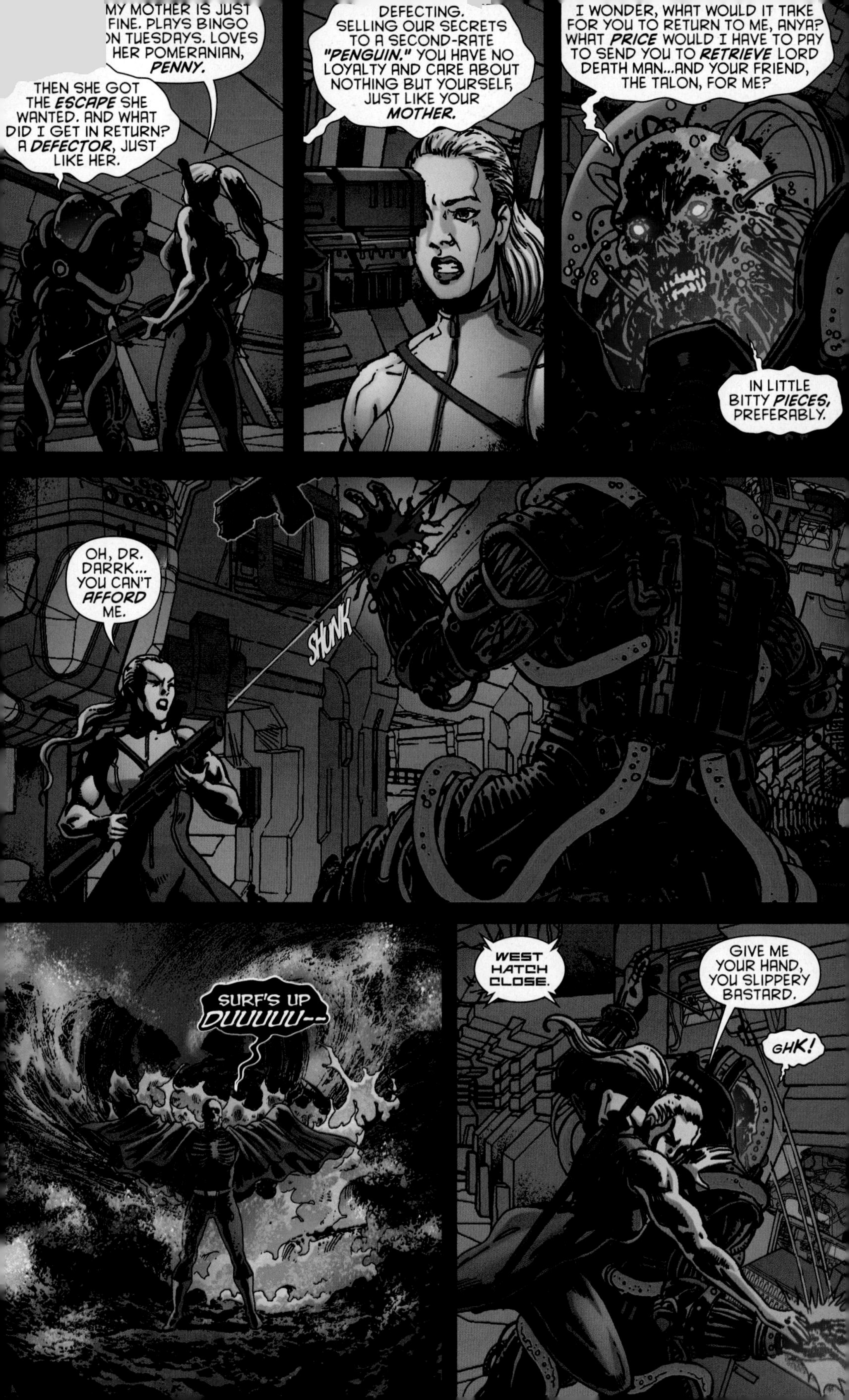

MY MOTHER IS JUST FINE. PLAYS BINGO ON TUESDAYS. LOVES HER POMERANIAN, PENNY.
THEN SHE GOT THE ESCAPE SHE WANTED. AND WHAT DID I GET IN RETURN? A DEFECTOR, JUST LIKE HER.
DEFECTING. SELLING OUR SECRETS TO A SECOND-RATE "PENGUIN." YOU HAVE NO LOYALTY AND CARE ABOUT NOTHING BUT YOURSELF, JUST LIKE YOUR MOTHER.
I WONDER, WHAT WOULD IT TAKE FOR YOU TO RETURN TO ME, ANYA? WHAT PRICE WOULD I HAVE TO PAY TO SEND YOU TO RETRIEVE LORD DEATH MAN...AND YOUR FRIEND, THE TALON, FOR ME?
IN LITTLE BITTY PIECES, PREFERABLY.
OH, DR. DARRK... YOU CAN'T AFFORD ME.
SHUNK
SURF'S UP DUUUUU--
WEST HATCH CLOSE.
GIVE ME YOUR HAND, YOU SLIPPERY BASTARD.
GHK!

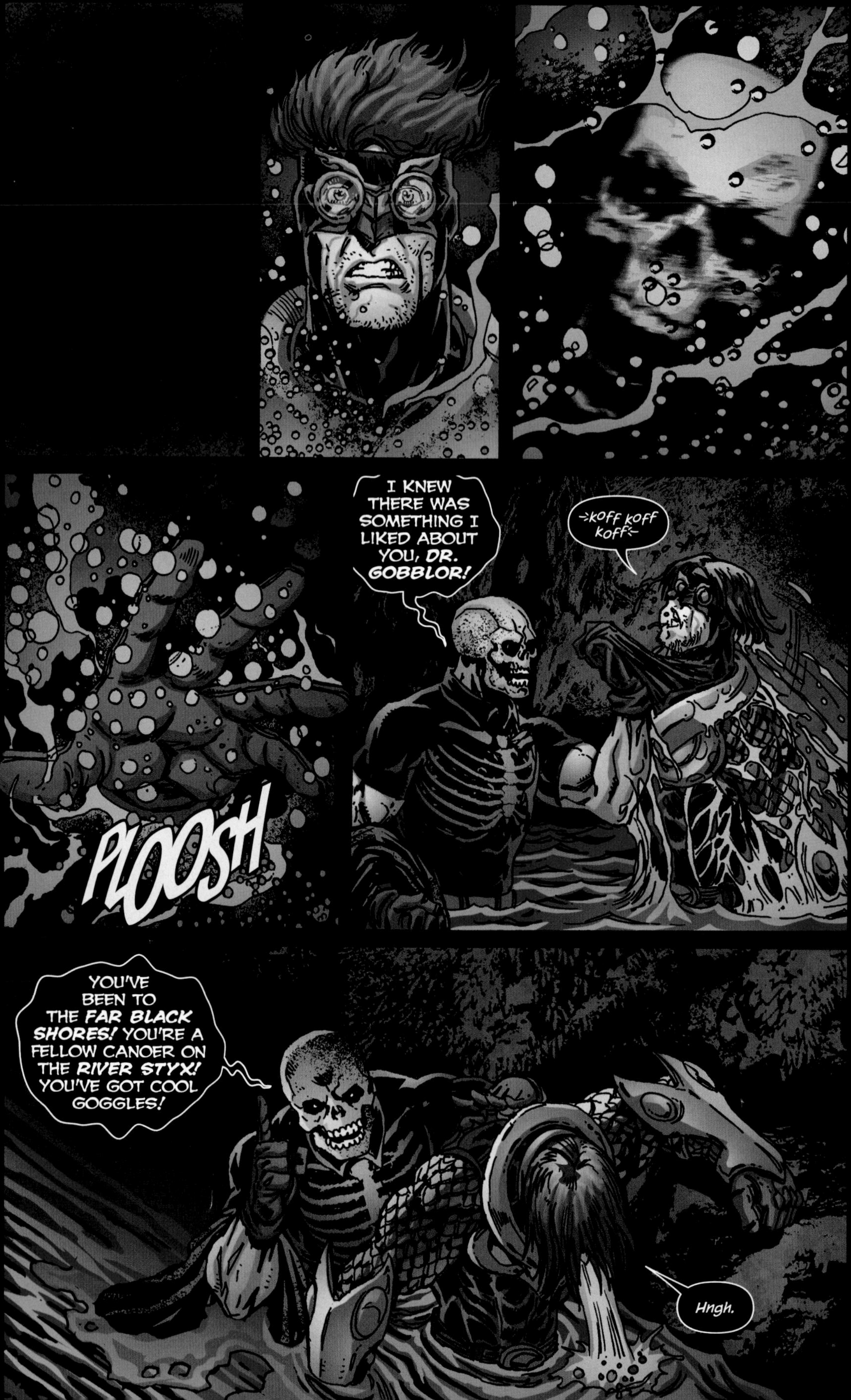
PLOOSH
I KNEW THERE WAS SOMETHING I LIKED ABOUT YOU, DR. GOBBLOR!
~KOFF KOFF KOFF~
YOU'VE BEEN TO THE FAR BLACK SHORES! YOU'RE A FELLOW CANOER ON THE RIVER STYX! YOU'VE GOT COOL GOGGLES!
Hngh.

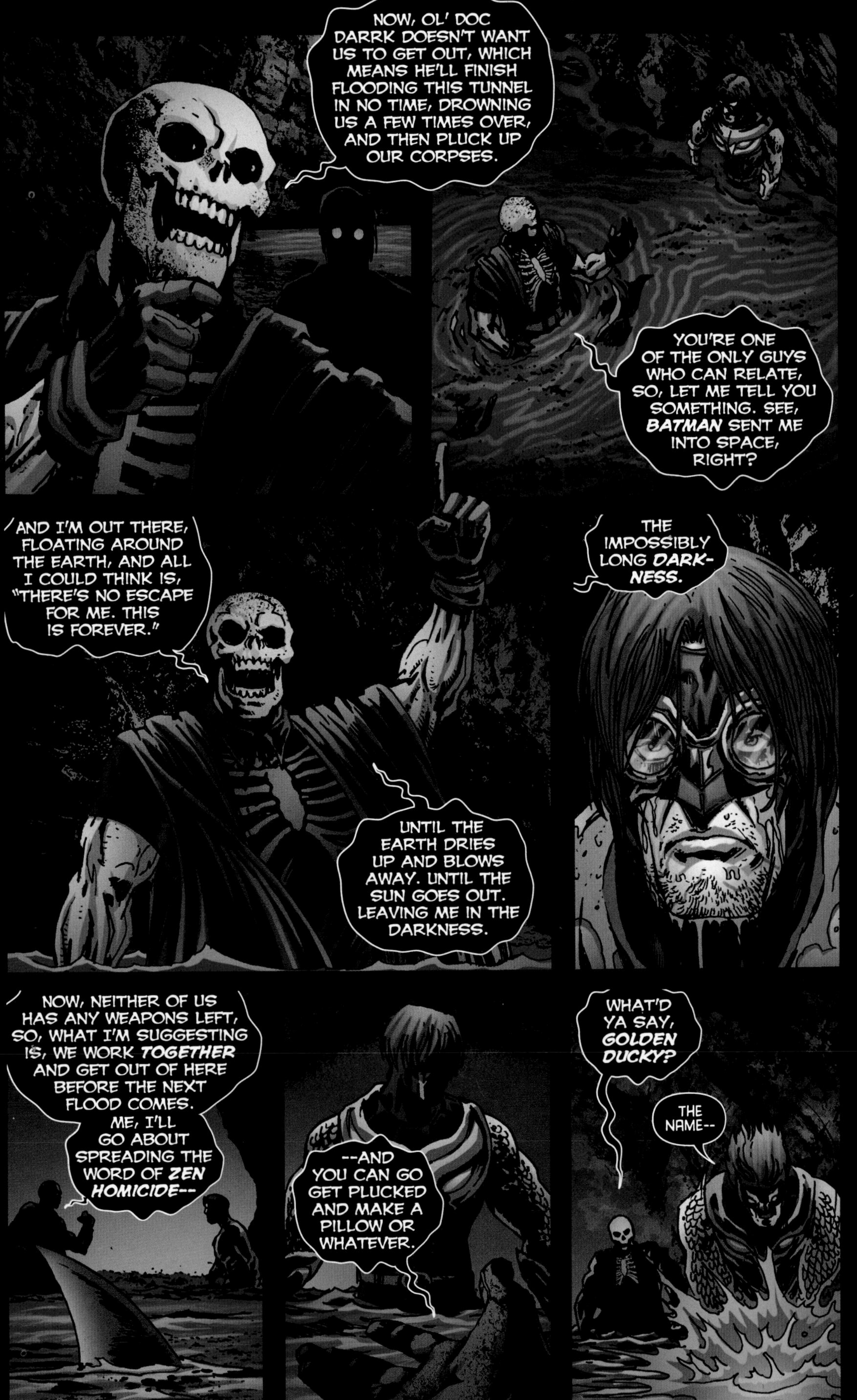
NOW, OL' DOC DARRK DOESN'T WANT US TO GET OUT, WHICH MEANS HE'LL FINISH FLOODING THIS TUNNEL IN NO TIME, DROWNING US A FEW TIMES OVER, AND THEN PLUCK UP OUR CORPSES.
YOU'RE ONE OF THE ONLY GUYS WHO CAN RELATE, SO, LET ME TELL YOU SOMETHING. SEE, BATMAN SENT ME INTO SPACE, RIGHT?
AND I'M OUT THERE, FLOATING AROUND THE EARTH, AND ALL I COULD THINK IS, "THERE'S NO ESCAPE FOR ME. THIS IS FOREVER."
UNTIL THE EARTH DRIES UP AND BLOWS AWAY. UNTIL THE SUN GOES OUT. LEAVING ME IN THE DARKNESS.
THE IMPOSSIBLY LONG DARKNESS.
NOW, NEITHER OF US HAS ANY WEAPONS LEFT, SO, WHAT I'M SUGGESTING IS, WE WORK TOGETHER AND GET OUT OF HERE BEFORE THE NEXT FLOOD COMES.
ME, I'LL GO ABOUT SPREADING THE WORD OF ZEN HOMICIDE--
--AND YOU CAN GO GET PLUCKED AND MAKE A PILLOW OR WHATEVER.
WHAT'D YA SAY, GOLDEN DUCKY?
THE NAME--

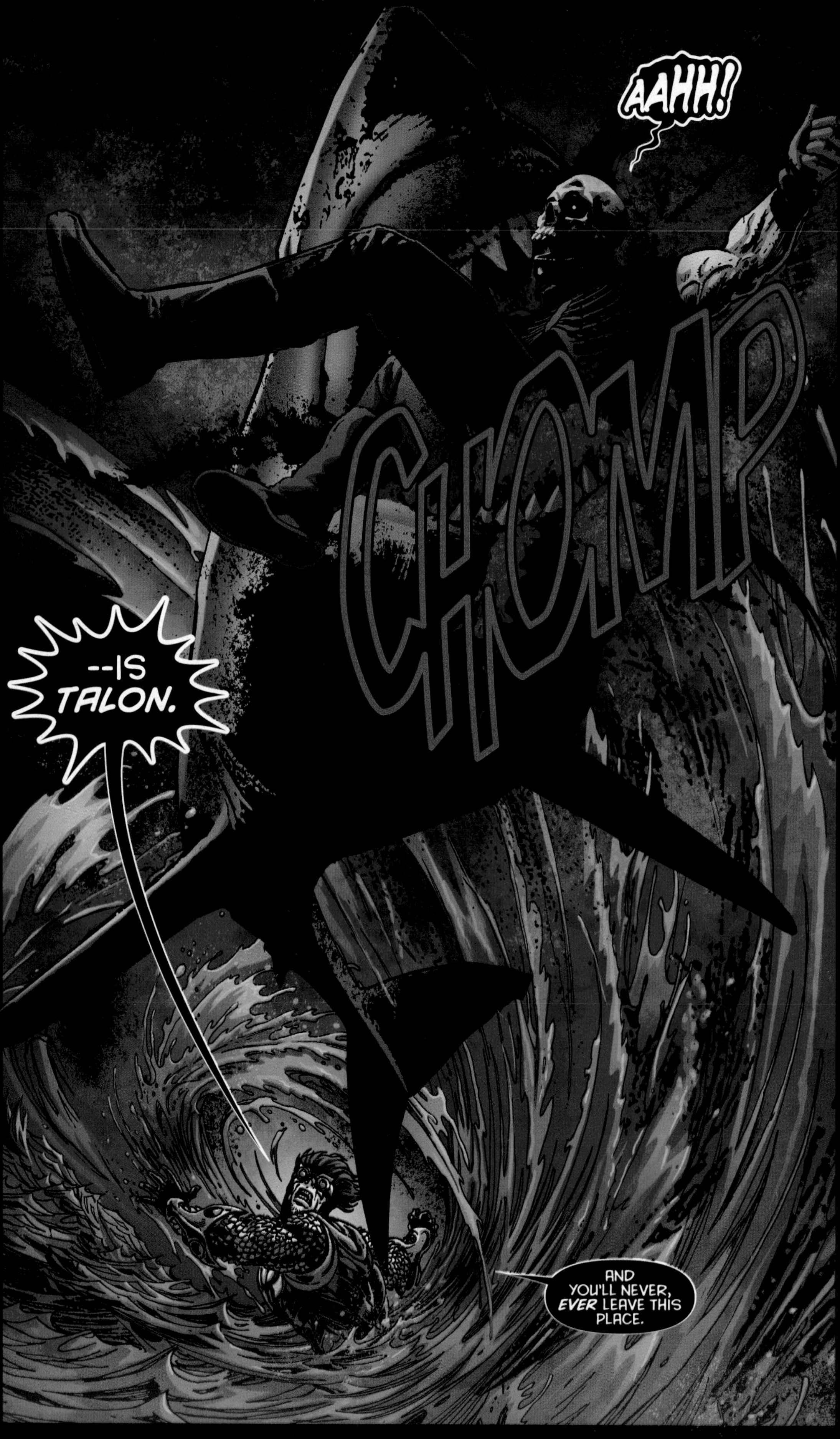

AAHH!
CHOMP
--IS TALON.
AND YOU'LL NEVER, EVER LEAVE THIS PLACE.

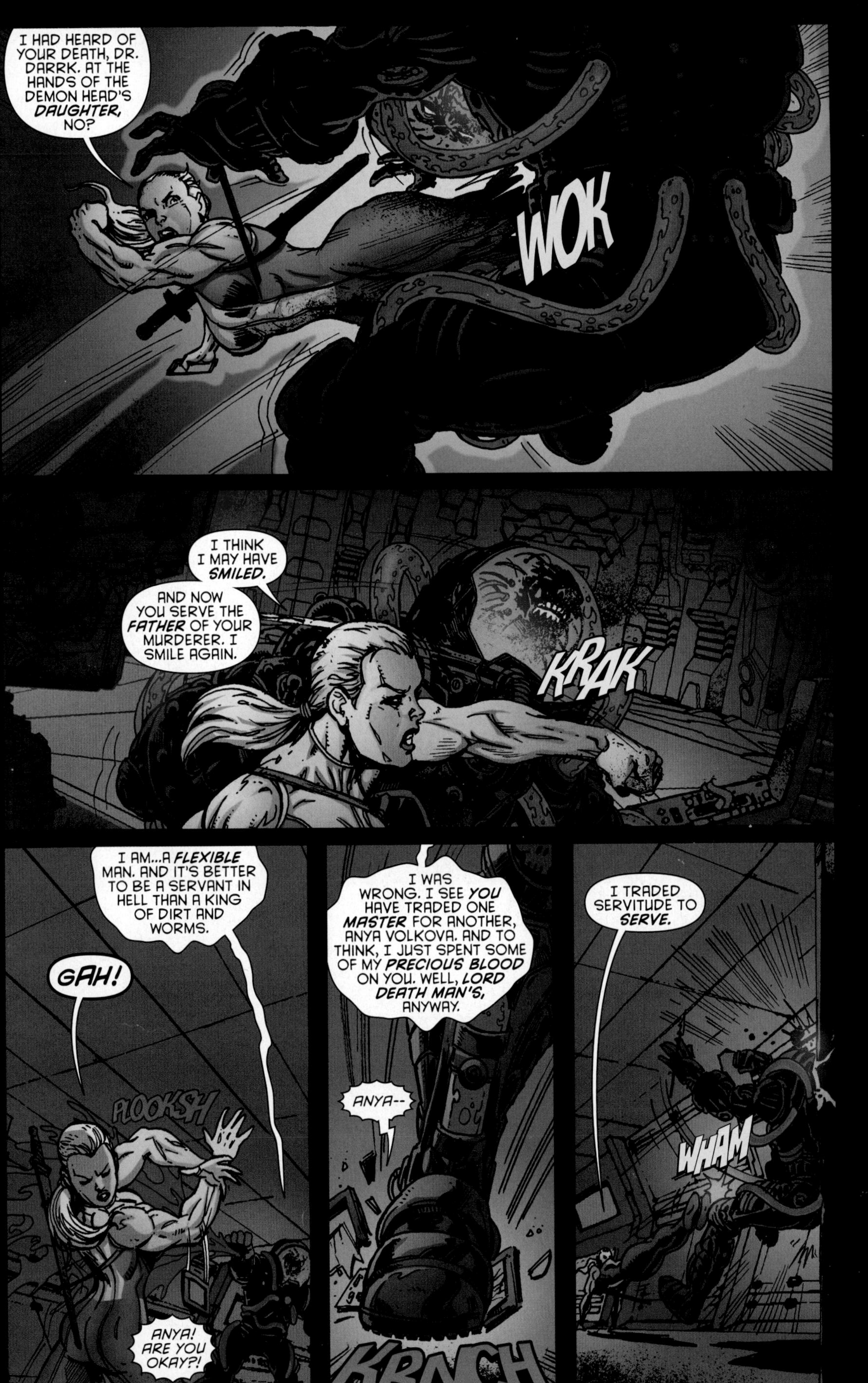
I HAD HEARD OF YOUR DEATH, DR. DARRK. AT THE HANDS OF THE DEMON HEAD'S DAUGHTER, NO?
WOK
I THINK I MAY HAVE SMILED.
AND NOW YOU SERVE THE FATHER OF YOUR MURDERER. I SMILE AGAIN.
KRAK
I AM...A FLEXIBLE MAN. AND IT'S BETTER TO BE A SERVANT IN HELL THAN A KING OF DIRT AND WORMS.
GAH!
PLOOKSH
ANYA! ARE YOU OKAY?!
I WAS WRONG. I SEE YOU HAVE TRADED ONE MASTER FOR ANOTHER, ANYA VOLKOVA. AND TO THINK, I JUST SPENT SOME OF MY PRECIOUS BLOOD ON YOU. WELL, LORD DEATH MAN'S, ANYWAY.
ANYA--
KRNCH
I TRADED SERVITUDE TO SERVE.
WHAM

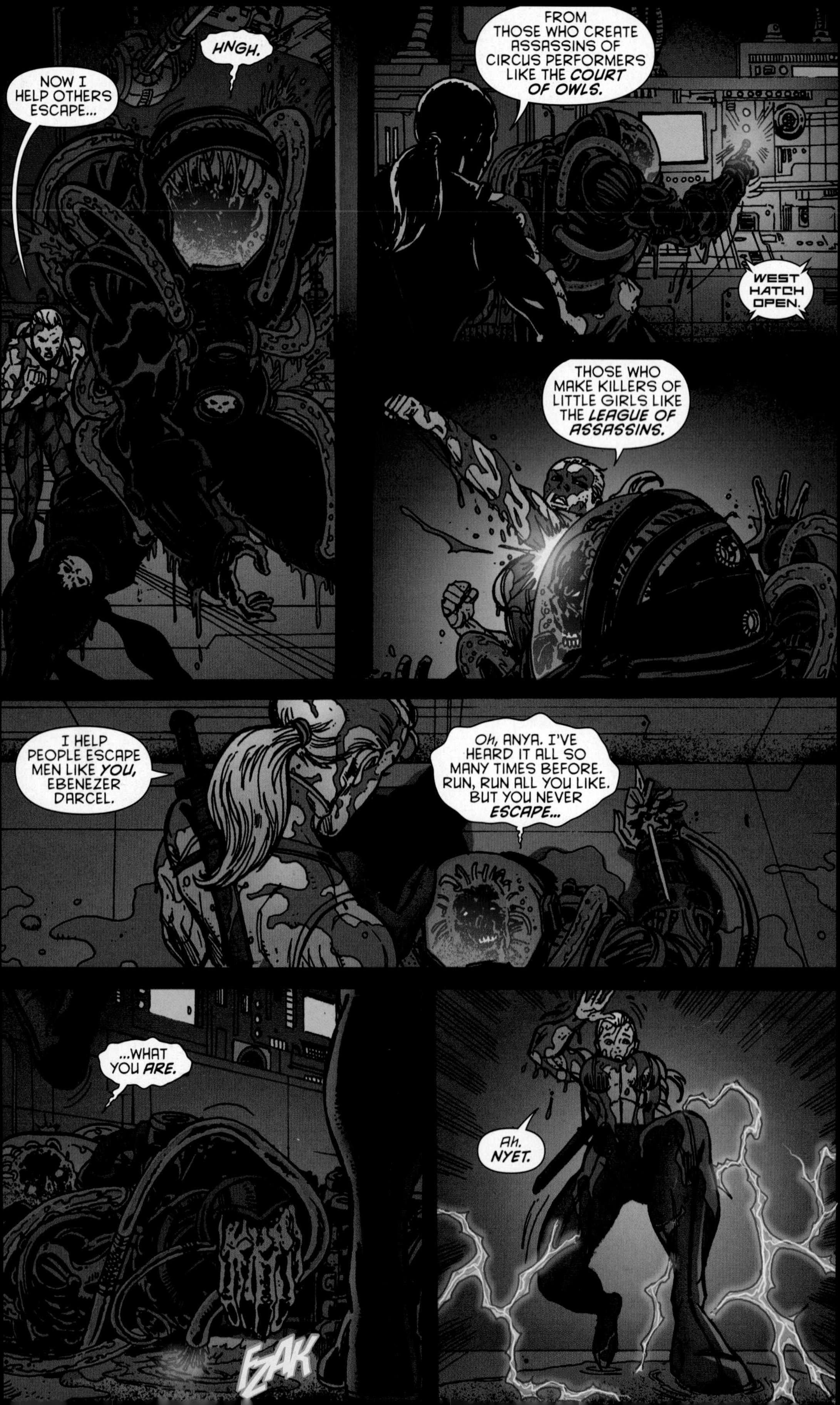
HNGH.
NOW I HELP OTHERS ESCAPE...
FROM THOSE WHO CREATE ASSASSINS OF CIRCUS PERFORMERS LIKE THE COURT OF OWLS.
WEST HATCH OPEN.
THOSE WHO MAKE KILLERS OF LITTLE GIRLS LIKE THE LEAGUE OF ASSASSINS.
I HELP PEOPLE ESCAPE MEN LIKE YOU, EBENEZER DARCEL.
Oh, ANYA. I'VE HEARD IT ALL SO MANY TIMES BEFORE. RUN, RUN ALL YOU LIKE. BUT YOU NEVER ESCAPE...
...WHAT YOU ARE.
FZAK
Ah. NYET.

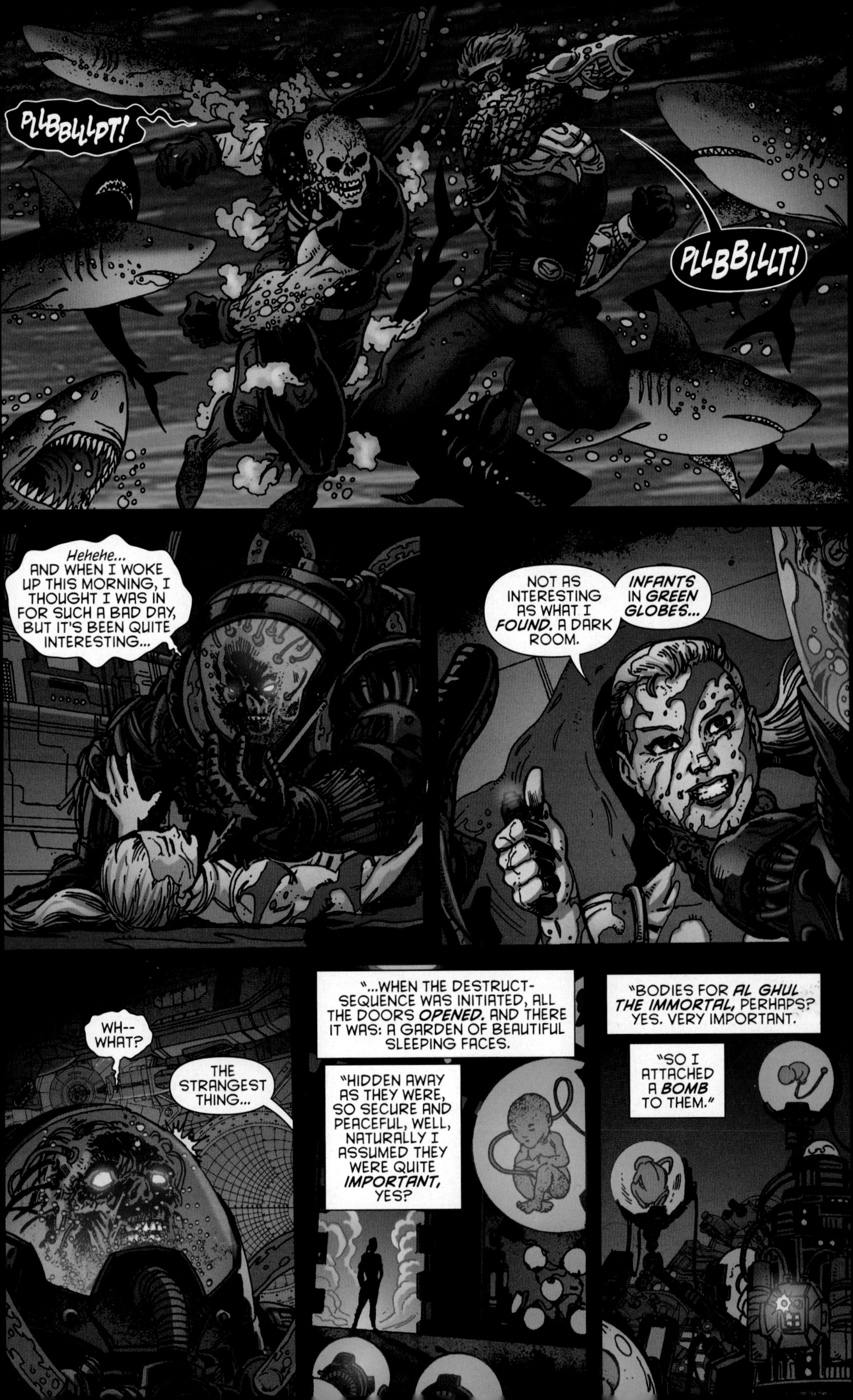
PLLBBLLPT!
PLLBBLLLT!
Hehehe... AND WHEN I WOKE UP THIS MORNING, I THOUGHT I WAS IN FOR SUCH A BAD DAY, BUT IT'S BEEN QUITE INTERESTING...
NOT AS INTERESTING AS WHAT I FOUND. A DARK ROOM.
INFANTS IN GREEN GLOBES...
WH-- WHAT?
THE STRANGEST THING...
"...WHEN THE DESTRUCT-SEQUENCE WAS INITIATED, ALL THE DOORS OPENED. AND THERE IT WAS: A GARDEN OF BEAUTIFUL SLEEPING FACES.
"HIDDEN AWAY AS THEY WERE, SO SECURE AND PEACEFUL, WELL, NATURALLY I ASSUMED THEY WERE QUITE IMPORTANT, YES?
"BODIES FOR AL GHUL THE IMMORTAL, PERHAPS? YES. VERY IMPORTANT.
"SO I ATTACHED A BOMB TO THEM."

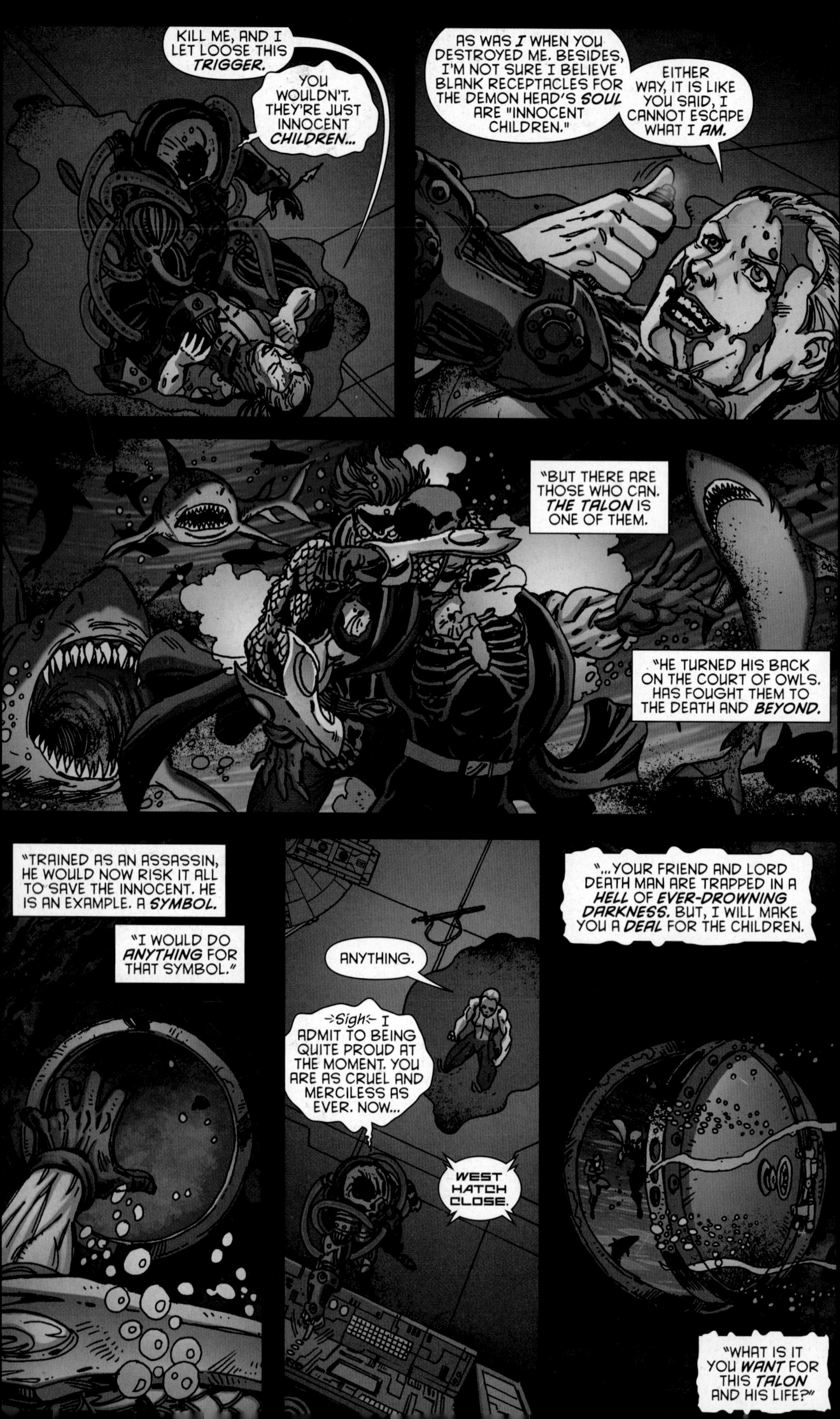

KILL ME, AND I LET LOOSE THIS *TRIGGER.*
YOU WOULDN'T. THEY'RE JUST INNOCENT *CHILDREN...*
AS WAS *I* WHEN YOU DESTROYED ME. BESIDES, I'M NOT SURE I BELIEVE BLANK RECEPTACLES FOR THE DEMON HEAD'S *SOUL* ARE "INNOCENT CHILDREN."
EITHER WAY, IT IS LIKE YOU SAID, I CANNOT ESCAPE WHAT I *AM.*
"BUT THERE ARE THOSE WHO CAN. *THE TALON* IS ONE OF THEM.
"HE TURNED HIS BACK ON THE COURT OF OWLS. HAS FOUGHT THEM TO THE DEATH AND *BEYOND.*
"TRAINED AS AN ASSASSIN, HE WOULD NOW RISK IT ALL TO SAVE THE INNOCENT. HE IS AN EXAMPLE. A *SYMBOL.*
"I WOULD DO *ANYTHING* FOR THAT SYMBOL."
ANYTHING.
Sigh I ADMIT TO BEING QUITE PROUD AT THE MOMENT. YOU ARE AS CRUEL AND MERCILESS AS EVER. NOW...
WEST HATCH CLOSE.
"...YOUR FRIEND AND LORD DEATH MAN ARE TRAPPED IN A *HELL* OF *EVER-DROWNING DARKNESS.* BUT, I WILL MAKE YOU A *DEAL* FOR THE CHILDREN.
"WHAT IS IT YOU *WANT* FOR THIS *TALON* AND HIS LIFE?"

LATER.
GOTHAM CITY...

LEXCORP SECURITY BUILDING--GOTHAM BRANCH.
OUT OF BUSINESS.

ANOTHER LOVELY NIGHT FOR A *MURDER.*

SHH, ANYA. SARAH'S HERE.

HGUK!

BURNING ROPE SUSPENDED COFFIN ESCAPE-- TAKE TWO.

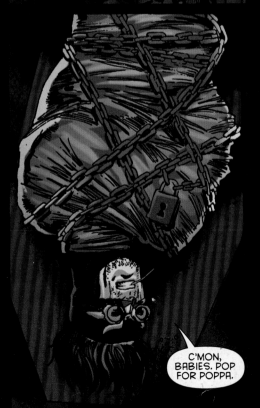

C'MON, BABIES. POP FOR POPPA.

TA-DA. THANK YOU, LADIES AND GENTLEMEN.

AND, JUST LIKE THAT, YOU'RE BACK TO *ESCAPING.*

I DO HAVE TO SAY, AT LEAST YOU'RE A PRETTIER *COLOR* THIS TIME AROUND.

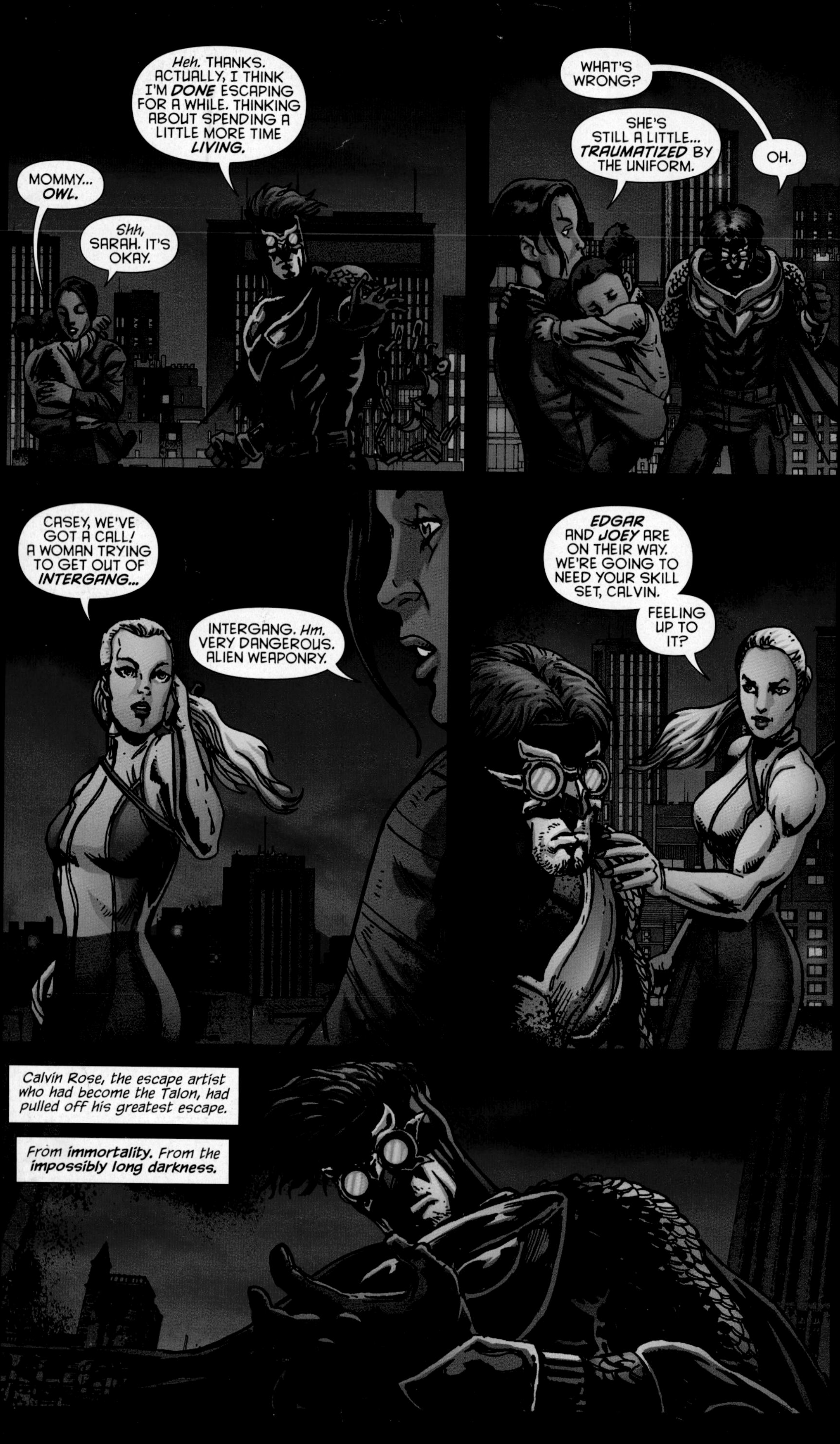

MOMMY... OWL.
Heh. THANKS. ACTUALLY, I THINK I'M DONE ESCAPING FOR A WHILE. THINKING ABOUT SPENDING A LITTLE MORE TIME LIVING.
Shh, SARAH. IT'S OKAY.
WHAT'S WRONG?
SHE'S STILL A LITTLE... TRAUMATIZED BY THE UNIFORM.
OH.
CASEY, WE'VE GOT A CALL! A WOMAN TRYING TO GET OUT OF INTERGANG...
INTERGANG. Hm. VERY DANGEROUS. ALIEN WEAPONRY.
EDGAR AND JOEY ARE ON THEIR WAY. WE'RE GOING TO NEED YOUR SKILL SET, CALVIN.
FEELING UP TO IT?
Calvin Rose, the escape artist who had become the Talon, had pulled off his greatest escape.
From immortality. From the impossibly long darkness.

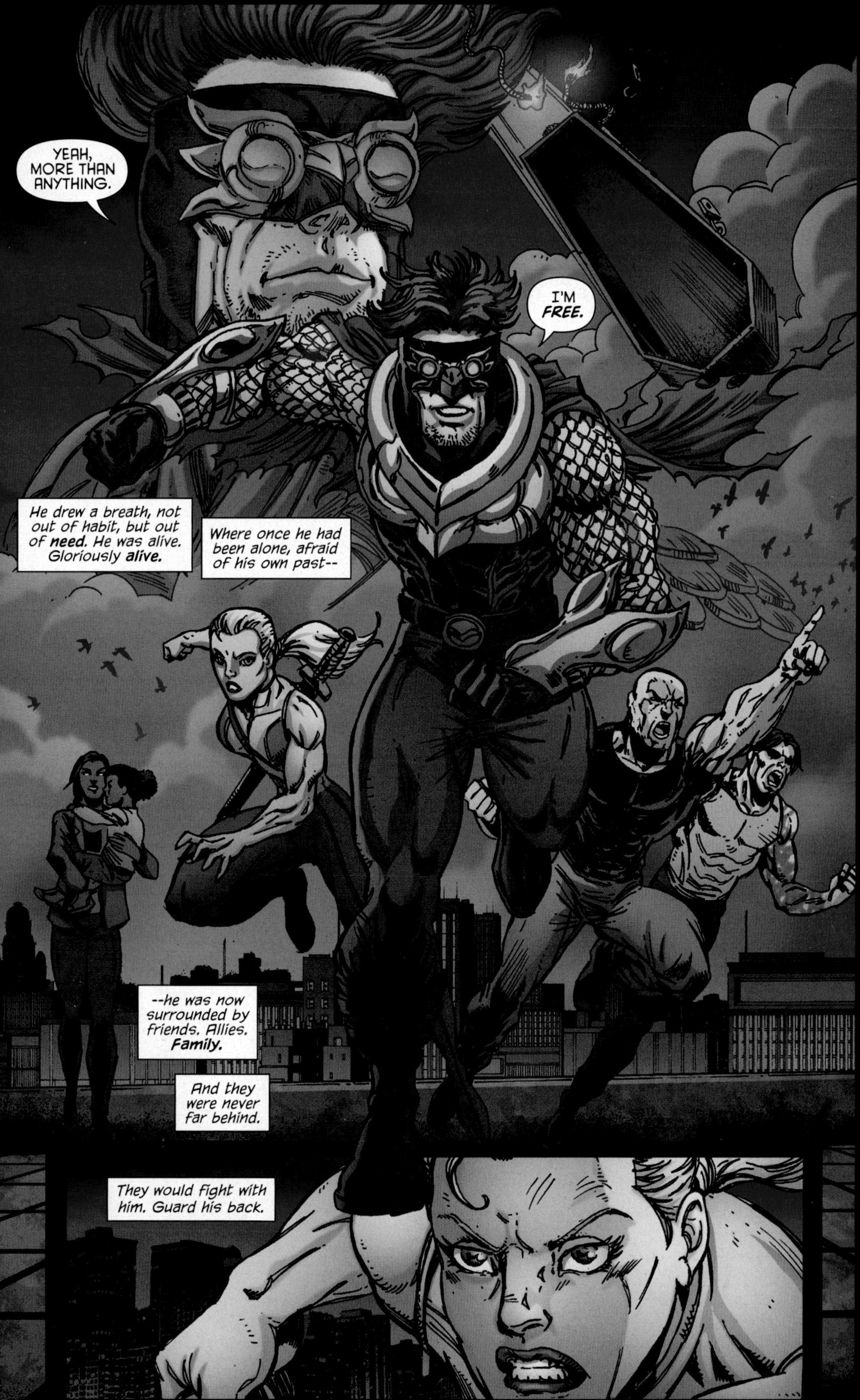
YEAH, MORE THAN ANYTHING.
I'M FREE.
He drew a breath, not out of habit, but out of need. He was alive. Gloriously alive.
Where once he had been alone, afraid of his own past--
--he was now surrounded by friends. Allies. Family.
And they were never far behind.
They would fight with him. Guard his back.

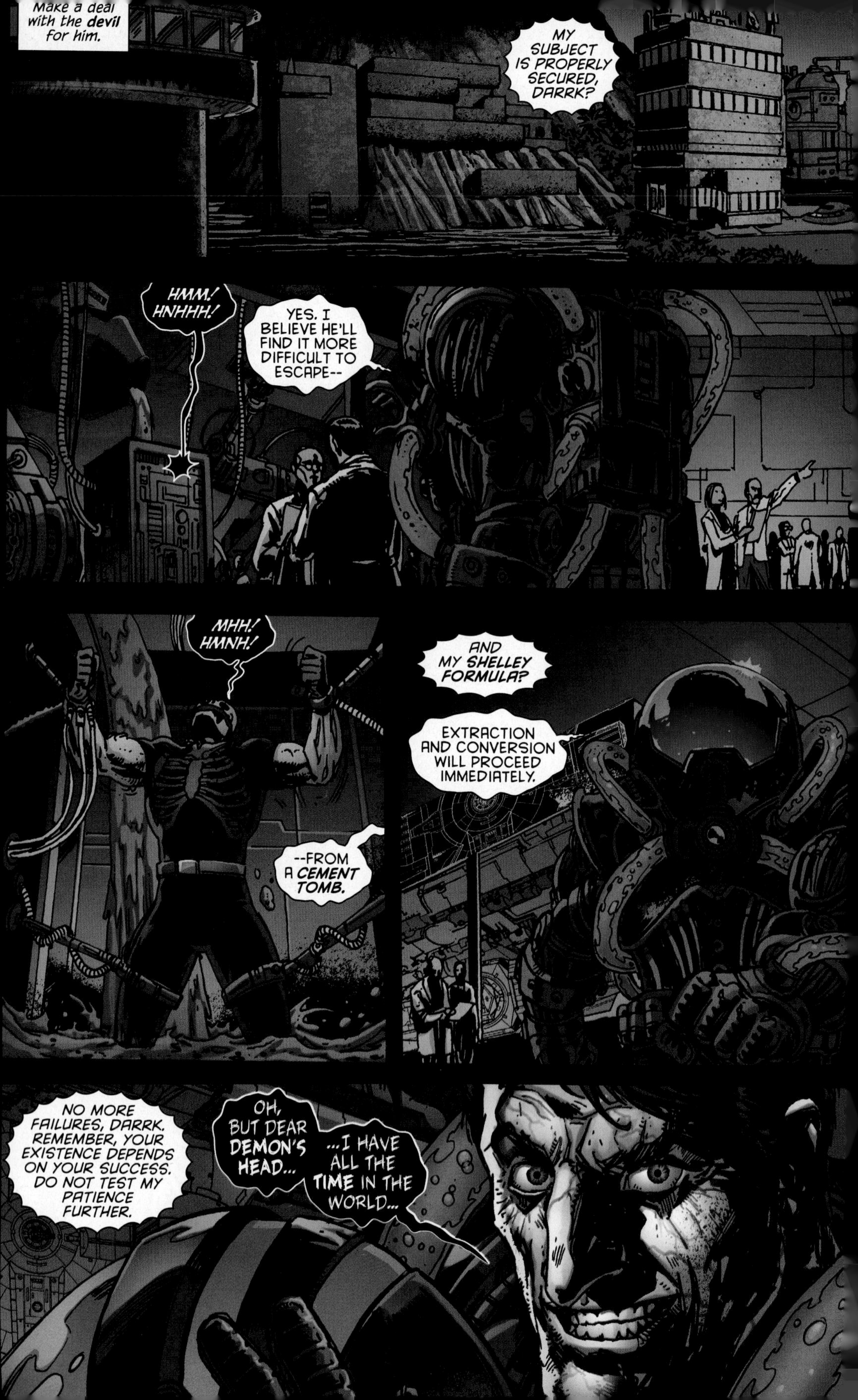

Make a deal with the devil for him.
MY SUBJECT IS PROPERLY SECURED, DARRK?
HMM! HNHHH!
YES. I BELIEVE HE'LL FIND IT MORE DIFFICULT TO ESCAPE--
MHH! HMNH!
--FROM A CEMENT TOMB.
AND MY SHELLEY FORMULA?
EXTRACTION AND CONVERSION WILL PROCEED IMMEDIATELY.
NO MORE FAILURES, DARRK. REMEMBER, YOUR EXISTENCE DEPENDS ON YOUR SUCCESS. DO NOT TEST MY PATIENCE FURTHER.
OH, BUT DEAR DEMON'S HEAD...
...I HAVE ALL THE TIME IN THE WORLD...

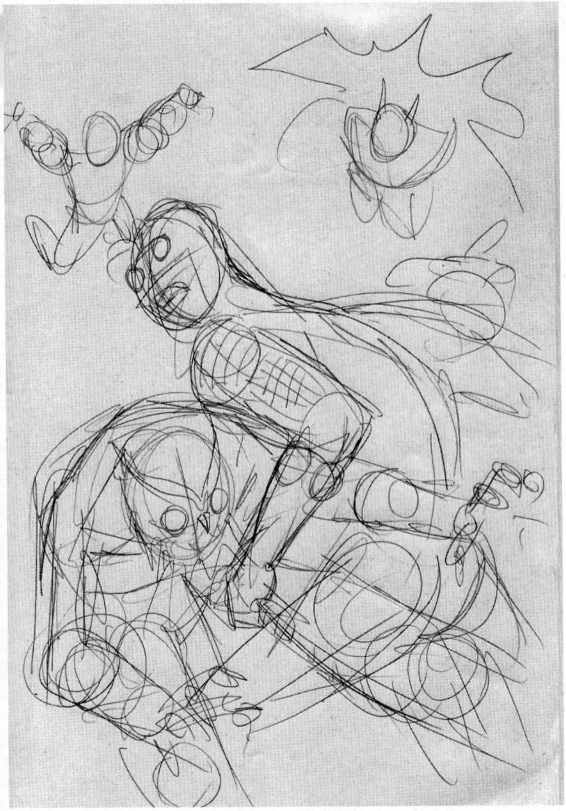
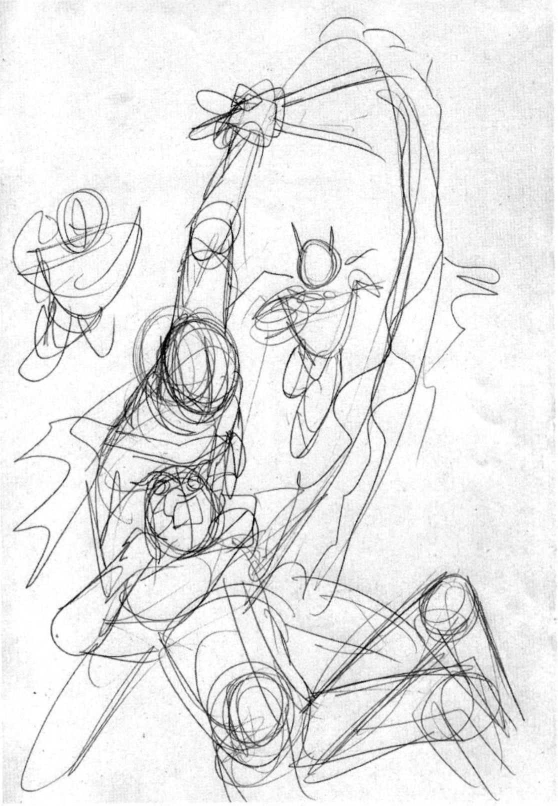
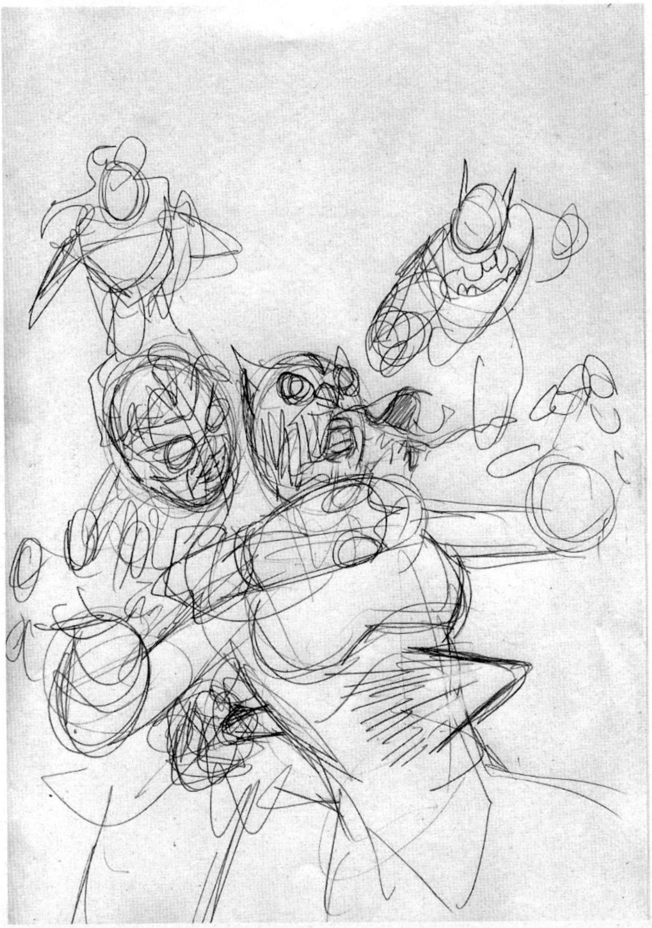

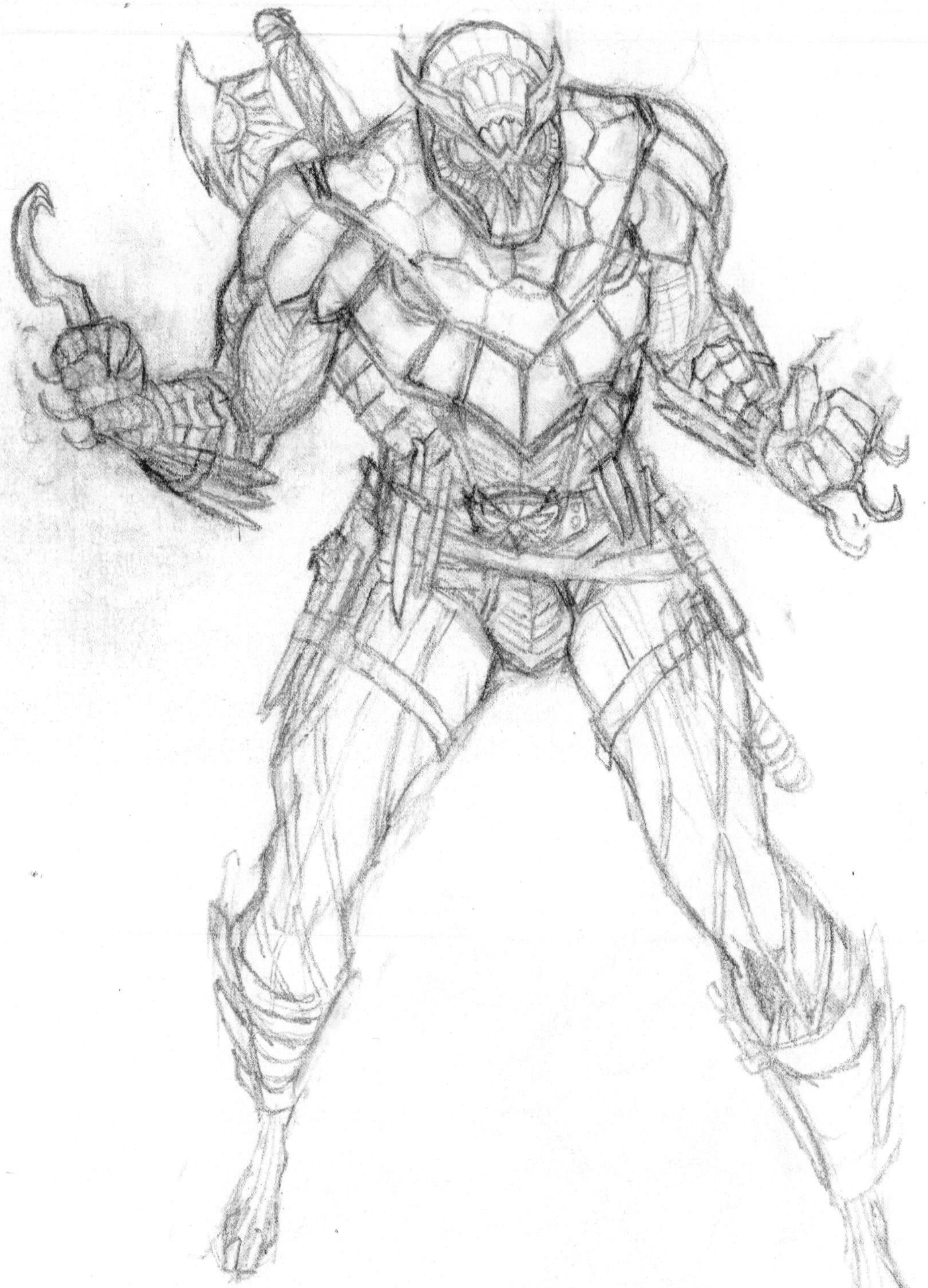

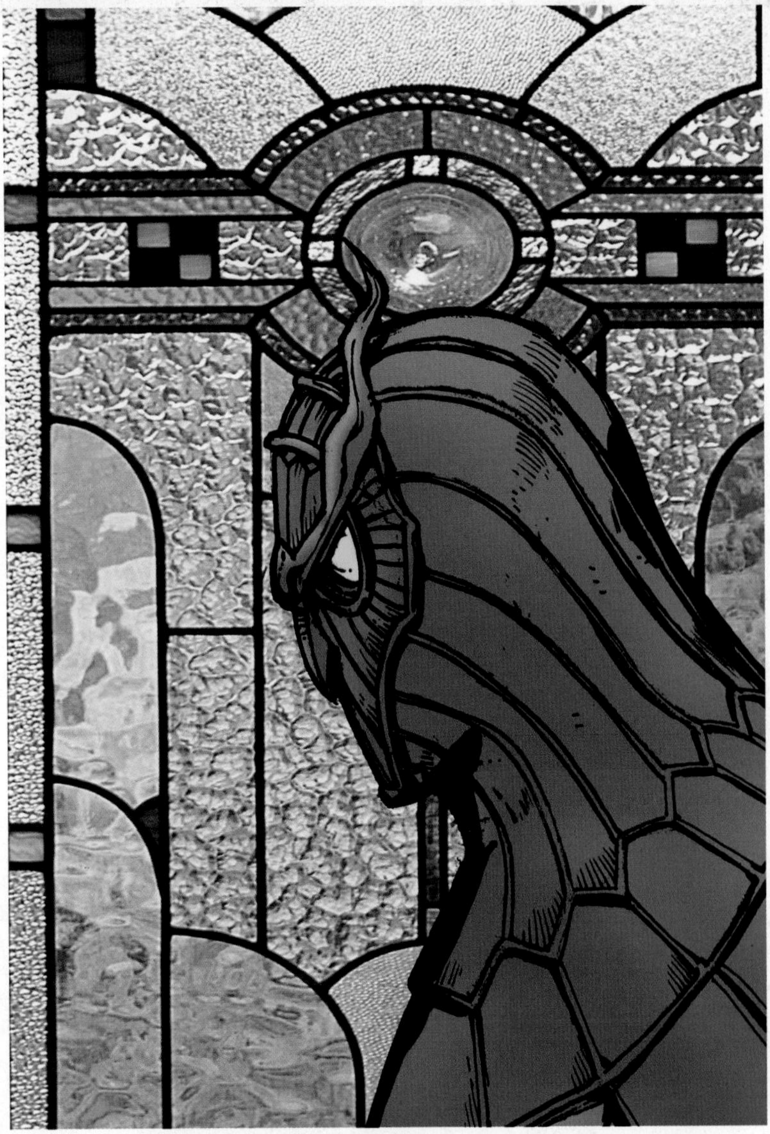

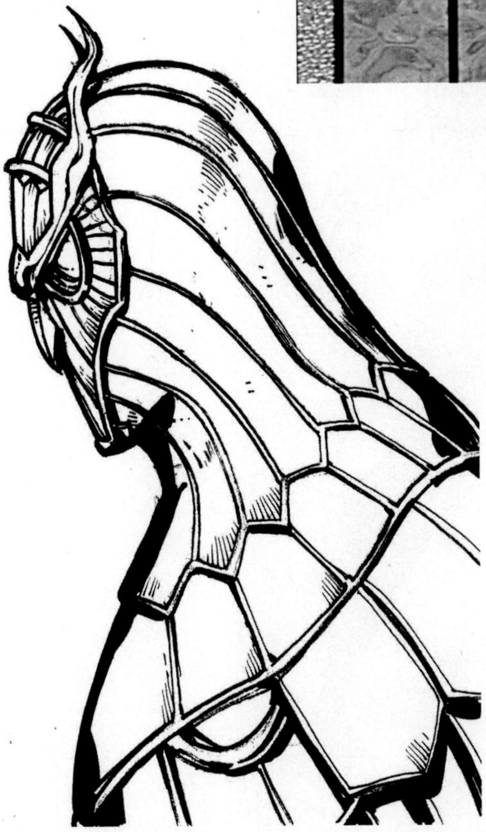

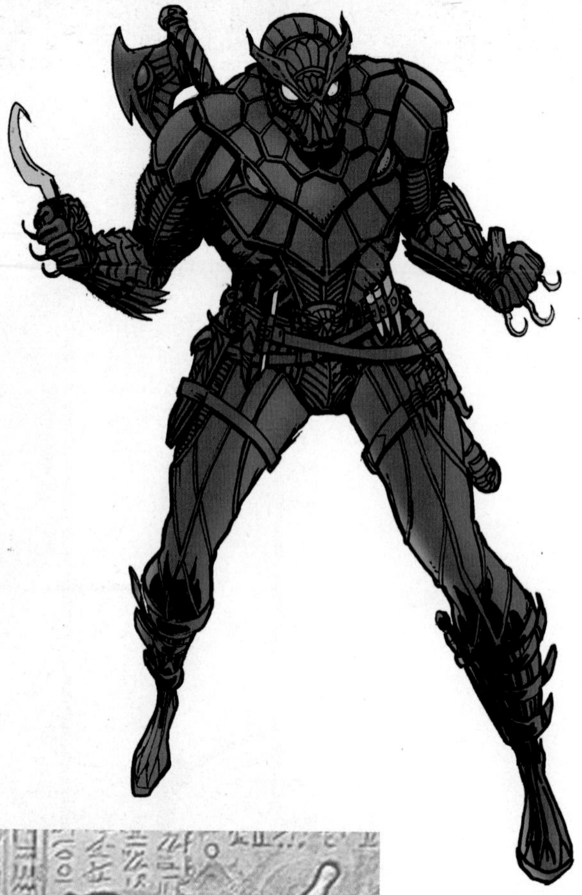

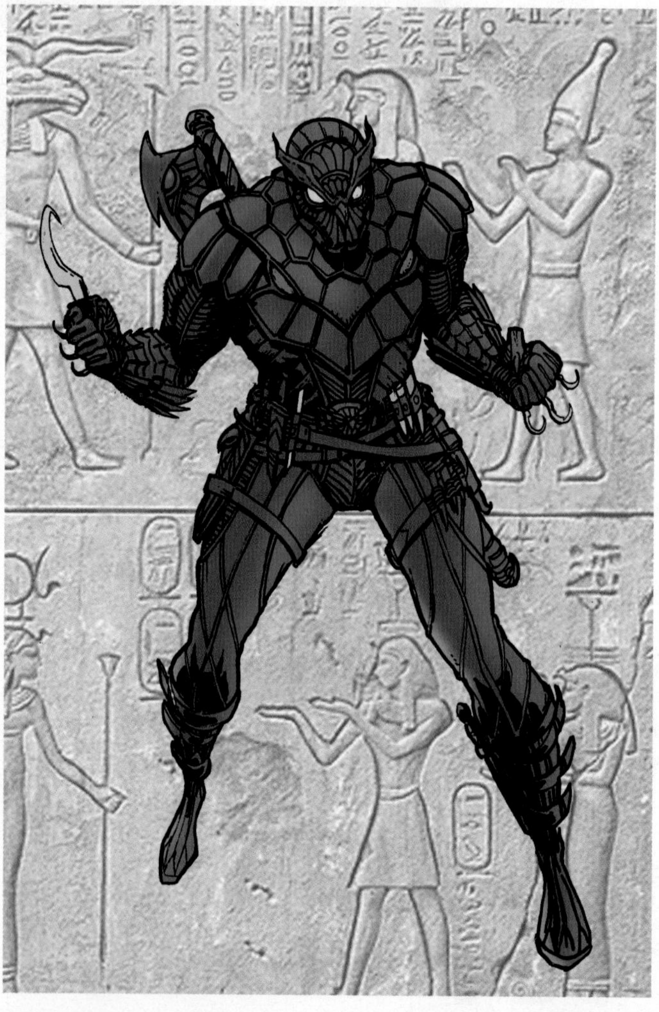

B
A
N
E

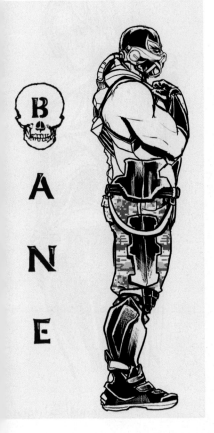

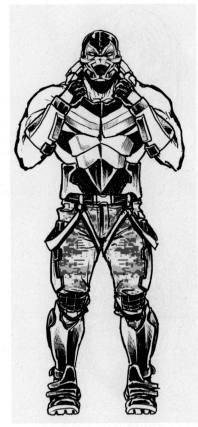

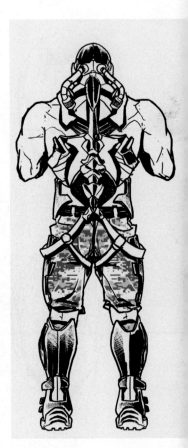

Calvin Rose

Emanuel Simeoni

START AT THE BEGINNING!

BATMAN VOLUME 1: THE COURT OF OWLS

BATMAN VOL. 2: THE CITY OF OWLS

with SCOTT SNYDER and GREG CAPULLO

BATMAN VOL. 3: DEATH OF THE FAMILY

with SCOTT SNYDER and GREG CAPULLO

BATMAN: NIGHT OF THE OWLS

with SCOTT SNYDER and GREG CAPULLO

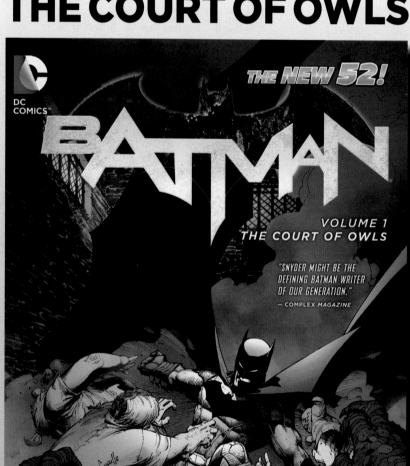

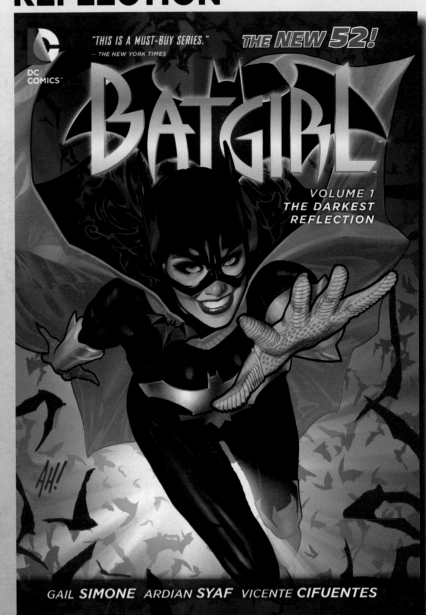

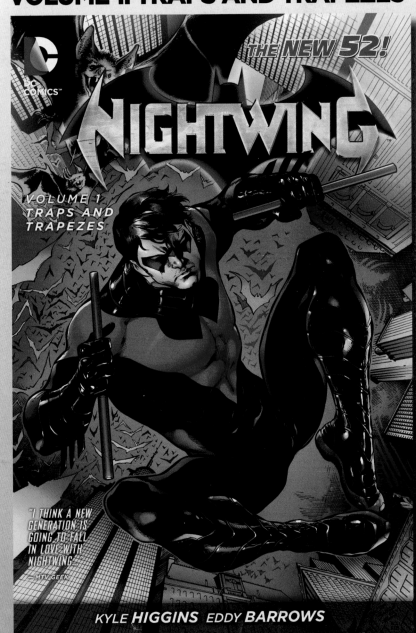

DC COMICS™

START AT THE BEGINNING!

SUICIDE SQUAD
VOLUME 1: KICKED IN THE TEETH

SUICIDE SQUAD VOL. 2: BASILISK RISING

SUICIDE SQUAD VOL. 3: DEATH IS FOR SUCKERS

DEATHSTROKE VOL. 1: LEGACY

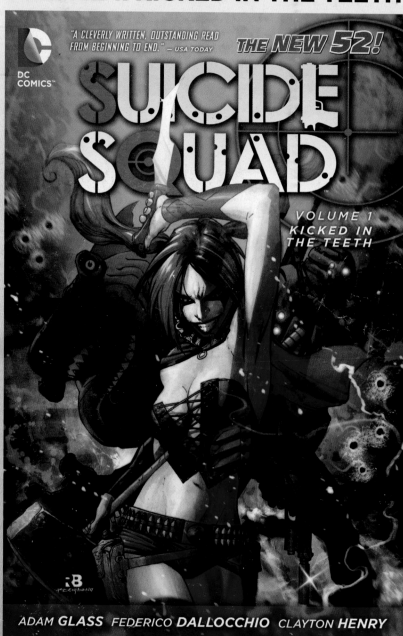

ADAM GLASS   FEDERICO DALLOCCHIO   CLAYTON HENRY